Writing Taiwan

ASIA-PACIFIC:
CULTURE,
POLITICS,
AND SOCIETY

EDITORS: REY CHOW,
H. D. HAROOTUNIAN,
AND MASAO MIYOSHI

Edited by David Der-wei Wang & Carlos Rojas

WRITING

A NEW LITERARY HISTORY

TAIWAN

DUKE UNIVERSITY PRESS • Durham & London 2007

© 2007 DUKE UNIVERSITY PRESS
ALL RIGHTS RESERVED

DESIGNED BY JENNIFER HILL
TYPESET IN SCALA BY TSENG
INFORMATION SYSTEMS, INC.

LIBRARY OF CONGRESS CATALOGING-
IN-PUBLICATION DATA AND REPUBLICATION
ACKNOWLEDGMENTS APPEAR ON THE LAST
PRINTED PAGE OF THIS BOOK.

DUKE UNIVERSITY PRESS GRATEFULLY
ACKNOWLEDGES THE SUPPORT OF THE
CHIANG CHING-KUO FOUNDATION, WHICH
PROVIDED FUNDS TOWARD THE
PRODUCTION OF THIS BOOK.

CONTENTS

PREFACE
David Der-wei Wang vii

INTRODUCTION
Carlos Rojas 1

PART ONE: THE LIMITS OF TAIWAN LITERATURE

1 Representing Taiwan: Shifting Geopolitical Frameworks
   Sung-sheng Yvonne Chang 17

2 Postmodern or Postcolonial? An Inquiry into Postwar Taiwanese Literary History
   Fangming Chen 26

3 On the Concept of Taiwan Literature
   Xiaobing Tang 51

PART TWO: CULTURAL POLITICS

4 The Importance of Being Perverse: China and Taiwan, 1931–1937
   Joyce C. H. Liu 93

5 "On Our Destitute Dinner Table": *Modern Poetry Quarterly* in the 1950s
   Michelle Yeh 113

6 The Literary Development of Zhong Lihe and Postcolonial Discourse in Taiwan
   Fenghuang Ying 140

7 Wang Wenxing's *Backed against the Sea*, Parts I and II: The Meaning of Modernism in Taiwan's Contemporary Literature
   Sung-sheng Yvonne Chang 156

PART THREE: HISTORY, TRUTH, AND TEXTUAL ARTIFICE

8 The Monster That Is History: Jiang Gui's *A Tale of Modern Monsters*
   David Der-wei Wang 181

9 Taiwanese Identity and the Crisis of Memory: Post-Chiang Mystery
   Yomi Braester 213

10 Doubled Configuration: Reading Su Weizhen's Theatricality
   Gang Gary Xu 233

11 Techniques behind Lies and the Artistry of Truth:
   Writing about the Writings of Zhang Dachun
   Kim-chu Ng 253

PART FOUR: SPECTRAL TOPOGRAPHIES AND CIRCUITS OF DESIRE

12. Travel in Early-Twentieth-Century Asia: On Wu Zhuoliu's "Nanking Journals" and His Notion of Taiwan's Alternative Modernity
    Ping-hui Liao   285

13. Mapping Identity in a Postcolonial City: Intertextuality and Cultural Hybridity in Zhu Tianxin's *Ancient Capital*
    Lingchei Letty Chen   301

14. Li Yongping and Spectral Cartography
    Carlos Rojas   324

15. History, Exchange, and the Object Voice: Reading Li Ang's *The Strange Garden* and *All Sticks Are Welcome in the Censer of Beigang*
    Chaoyang Liao   348

16. Reenchanting the Image in Global Culture: Reification and Nostalgia in Zhu Tianwen's Fiction
    Ban Wang   370

APPENDIX: Chinese Characters for Authors' Names and Titles of Works   389
CONTRIBUTORS   395
INDEX   397

PREFACE

David Der-wei Wang

Literature from Taiwan occupies one of the most contested zones in the mapping of modernity and modernization on Chinese culture. Two hundred miles southeast of mainland China, and sparsely populated before the sixteenth century, the island had traditionally been regarded as being located on the margins of Chinese politics and humanities. It would, nevertheless, serve as an unlikely pathway through which China entered a succession of global modernities. Between the sixteenth century and the late nineteenth, when China was undergoing a final dynastic cycle and settling into an increasingly confused stagnation, the island had already diverged onto a fateful path of its own. It was alternately inhabited or dominated by ruthless pirates, scheming exiles, venturesome settlers, and Ming loyalists followed by Qing pacifiers, to say nothing of Dutch and Spanish colonizers. In 1895, as a result of the Chinese defeat in the First Sino-Japanese War, Taiwan was ceded to Japan. Over the next five decades, the island became Japan's most treasured colony and a testing ground for Japanese cultural and political assimilation. In 1945, at the end of the Second Sino-Japanese War, Taiwan was returned to China; but then, reverting to its traditional role, Taiwan became the refuge of the Nationalist government after the Chinese Communists took over the mainland in 1949.

Thanks to these experiences, modern Taiwan literature is rich in conflicting legacies, impulses, and ideological forces. In many ways, it surpasses the mainland tradition when one pays attention to such matters as theoretical complexity and polemical intensity. Taiwan literature was first forced into its "modern" existence at the beginning of the twentieth century when Japan initiated its colonial regime. The next five decades were to see, in both writing and reading, strenuous conflict and compromise between colonial discourse and indigenous consciousness; between modern viewpoints achieved via Japanese mediation and revolutionary thoughts brought back from China; between fascination with the novelty of a colonizer's culture and loyalty to Chinese tradition. Taiwan was both "the Island of Beauty," or Formosa, as early foreign explorers saw it, and "the Orphan of Asia," as viewed by Wu Zhuoliu, the pioneer of post-1945 Taiwan literature. So Taiwan literature came to illuminate an entire array of modern issues, ranging from postcolonial critique to oppositional cultural politics, from hybrid modernity to the circulation of cross-cultural capital—issues that continue to concern us today.

The year 1949 was, nevertheless, the greatest watershed in Taiwan's literary and cultural experience of modernity. This island on the margins of China was suddenly thrust into the focus of Chinese political antagonism, and the "Orphan of Asia" found itself drafted into the vanguard of international anticommunism. The subsequent history of the twentieth century would only compound Taiwan's changeable but always precarious world position, and literature would again contribute to, or be conditioned by, ongoing geopolitics. There would be no escape from issues like the dislocation of nationhood or the bifurcation of native soil or from modern intellectual maladies like identity angst and cultural ambivalence. And, despite Nationalist hegemony, Taiwan literature of the 1950s was already nurturing a generation of alternative voices. When the modernist poetry movement was launched in 1956, a recalcitrant and innovative discourse was established, however falteringly, in defiance of the mandate to produce anti-Communist literature. This modernism would prevail throughout the 1960s, meanwhile giving rise to an equally powerful dialogic counterpart—Taiwanese nativism.

Critics from both the Left and the Right, then and now, denigrate the modernist literature of 1960s Taiwan as selfish indulgence in personal nihilism or existentialism—and, most unforgivably, as disengagement from the current crisis. Looking back, these charges very well summarize the merits of the movement. Remarkable in a time of stifling political oppression and ideological fanaticism, the modernist movement in Taiwan, together with the subsequent rise of nativism, should be hailed for what it was: an unexpected achievement, particularly because it filled the void in mainland literature resulting from incessant political turmoil and the suppression of all independent experimentation.

Taiwan literature underwent a no less remarkable metamorphosis during the 1970s and the 1980s. The death of Chiang Kai-shek in 1975 triggered a cluster of important cultural and political events, starting with the highly politicized debate between nativism and modernism, and culminating in the recognition by the United States of mainland China in 1979 and the government's crackdown on mass demonstrations for independence in the same year. Faced with the rise of the indigenous movement on the island and the reentry of China onto the stage of world politics, Taiwanese writers had to rethink their position by answering certain questions: How could they address their Chinese experience when another China had emerged to reclaim its cultural and literary authenticity? How could they inscribe a new literary subjectivity at both domestic and international levels, in opposition to the one sanctioned by the Nationalist discourse? How could they find a poetics, somehow beyond the existing one of nativism versus modernism, through which to represent these challenges?

These questions propelled Taiwanese literati to explore and write about Taiwan with a new range of tactics. Taboos were challenged and totems renegotiated. Issues arising from public and private spheres interplayed with unprecedented vigor. In the hands of writers such as Wang Wenxing and Li Yongping, a new iconoclasm was accomplished, in terms not only of conceptual radicalism but also of literal acts of graphic desecration. The search for, or disavowal of, the "authenticity" of the Chinese language proved to be a catalyst igniting further contestation. Nationalist myth could be deciphered as mere magical realism; Taiwan's colonial experience could induce self-mocking laughter. Gender, ethnic identity, sexuality, nationalism, environmentalism, diaspora, and expatriatism, among all too many isms, briefly engaged writers and readers, so compellingly that, in many cases, when the spasm of writing and reading came to an end, decisive political action followed. Finally, the lifting after forty years of martial law in 1987, followed by the boom of the media market and increasingly active cultural and commercial exchange across the Taiwan Straits, presaged the advent of a fin de siècle ecology.

When beheld from the perspective of comparative world literature, modern Taiwan literature is one of a select few examples that have experienced so much volatility and produced such a cornucopia of literary innovations. It is ironic that, in the English-speaking world, so much has been written about the hegemonic disasters of mainland cultural history, yet so little about the multifarious sociopolitical, cultural, and literary dynamics of Taiwan. Geopolitics, of course, has been a factor in the eclipse of the Taiwanese literary experience. But perhaps it is more attributable to the fact that we English speakers have yet to think about modernism with a truly polyphonic and multi-topographic mind-set, one that is prepared to recognize forms of modernity that have no precedent in European experience. To talk about the opening up of Chinese literature in this, the new century, one must genuinely believe that Chinese writers have always been capable of complex and even contradictory thoughts, lifestyles, and textual representations and understand that the dissemination of words can no more be regulated by prescribed theories than the dissemination of power can be regulated by imposed boundaries.

This volume represents the first comprehensive survey in English of modern Taiwan literature since the end of the Second Sino-Japanese War. Its sixteen essays represent sixteen entryways into the complex network of this literature from 1945 to the present. Instead of formulating the issues and movements as a singular progressive line, the essays cross-reference one another in light of different government policies, communal tastes, and artistic trends. Together, they bring forward a complex chronology corresponding to a multifaceted Taiwanese cultural and political modernity. They collectively embrace four critical objectives: first, to critique the methodological frameworks that have constituted Taiwanese literary studies to date; second, to depict the enunciative endeavors, ranging from ideological treatises to avant-garde experiments, that have informed the discourse of Taiwanese cultural politics; third, to renegotiate time, temporality, and memory in the formation of the history of literary Taiwan; and, fourth, to observe the cartographic coordinates and spatial representations that have given form to the imaginary communities of Taiwan.

We hope that this volume will demonstrate that modern Taiwan literature has compounded volatile political and cultural circumstances into the generation of an actively circulating creative power. As a corollary, we believe that, if Chinese literature of the new century has renewed our sense of historicity, it has done so precisely through an innovative reconfiguration of history by means unanticipated among earlier writers and readers, not through a fulfillment of long-prophesied duties and achievements. *Writing Taiwan*, therefore, represents not merely a way to call attention to a Chinese literary terra incognita; writing Taiwan is a way of rewriting China.

INTRODUCTION

Carlos Rojas

Like many scholarly anthologies, this volume has its origins in a very specific point in time and space: an academic conference entitled "Writing Taiwan: Strategies of Representation" held at Columbia University in New York City from April 30 to May 2, 1998. Bringing together not only scholars of Taiwan literature but also prominent Taiwanese authors, including Zhang Dachun, Li Ang, and Ping Lu, this conference provided an occasion both to cast a retrospective glance back on the field of Taiwanese literary studies and to look forward to what future directions that field might take. At the same time, however, the spatiotemporal ground of the field of Taiwan literature itself was precisely one of the issues interrogated most energetically that weekend. What are the geographic and historical bounds of Taiwan literature? What are the cultural and political implications of any strategy that seeks to "write" those bounds? How might historical and geographic indeterminacies have left traces in the literary works themselves? Accordingly, the essays in this volume not only contain discussions of specific Taiwanese authors, works, and literary occasions from the 1930s to the present but also reflect in various ways on the question of what it means to use *Taiwan literature* as an analytic category in the first place.

The concept of *Taiwan literature* is itself grounded on something of a paradox. In an age in which literatures continue, by and large, to be defined, however awkwardly, by their national origin, the category Taiwan literature is located in an ambiguous epistemological hinterland. To begin with, it is grounded on a political fiction, but one that insistently and emphatically undercuts its own foundation. Furthermore, having spent half of the twentieth century as a Japanese colony and the other half in an umbilical, although highly self-conflicted, relation with the Chinese motherland, "Taiwan" effectively stands in the position of a (redoubled) colonial subject, mimicking the "imperial masters" in a way that defamiliarizes and challenges the ontological legitimacy of the category the nation-state itself. To put it another way, a recurrent concern throughout much of twentieth-century Taiwan literature is that of collective identity and cultural genealogy, as both individual authors and entire movements have alternately embraced and positioned themselves in opposition to China and Japan—with the result not only that "Taiwan" is in a supplemental, parasitic position with respect to its more hegemonic neighbors but, furthermore, that its own ambiguous status helps illuminate the constructedness of the naturalized category the nation-state that it mimics.

On the one hand, it is certainly true that, in the twentieth century, and particularly the latter half, Taiwan constituted a fairly autonomous literary community, in that many Taiwanese authors were directly or indirectly in communication with each other, while much "leftist" literature from the mainland (including the work of such canonical figures as Lu Xun and Mao Dun) was systematically proscribed. On the other hand, the diversity of the writers and the varieties of both textual form and subject matter that collectively make up the category Taiwan literature is enough to undermine all but the weakest claims to comparative homogeneity. A sense of this inherent diversity can be gained by considering the range of individual authors treated in this volume, a range that includes such figures as Yang Chichang, who studied Japanese literature in Tokyo in the early 1930s and did all his own poetic and fictional writing in Japanese; Li Yongping, who is an ethnic Chinese born in Malaysia and educated in Taiwan and the United States; and Liu Daren, who was born in mainland China and now holds a United Nations passport after having been effectively exiled from Taiwan in the 1970s on account of his political activism (see the essays by Joyce C. H. Liu, Carlos Rojas, and Yomi Braester, respectively). Despite the fact that Yang, Li, and Liu are all conventionally recognized as "Taiwanese" writers, there is no single necessary and sufficient condition that can serve to ground this common identity.

This volume seeks to explore and question not only the geographic bounds of Taiwan literature but also the chronological ones. Paralleling the fuzzy topographic boundaries of "Taiwan," the literary subject matter considered here is also poised uneasily under the chronological rubric of *modern* Taiwan literature. At its simplest, this designation simply draws attention to the empirical fact that all the authors and works date from the twentieth century. However, this chronological convenience occludes a deep-rooted schism within the concept of the modern itself. In the early-twentieth-century period, aesthetic modernism was introduced into China and Taiwan as an artistic and literary movement with a clear European genealogy. The embrace of the modern, therefore, came to involve a dual assertion of a break with the feudal fetters of traditional culture and a fascination with Western alterity. In the Taiwanese context, however, literary modernism also has a rather more specific significance as a movement that rose to visibility during the 1960s and is frequently contrasted with the cultural nostalgia of the nativist movement that followed it in the 1970s. At their extremes, modernism and nativism represent two very different attitudes toward how to yoke cultural-political concerns to aesthetic ones, and many of the essays in this volume draw on this terminological convenience even as they seek to critically interrogate the conventional understandings of these designations themselves (see, e.g., the essays by Fangming Chen, Sung-sheng Yvonne Chang, and Michelle Yeh).

Finally, the chronological indeterminacy of Taiwanese aesthetic modernism is further underscored by the ambiguous implications of its post-1960s legacy. Its original fascination with rarefied aesthetic concerns largely fell out of fashion during the 1970s and after, but modernism did not disappear from the map entirely, and several prominent writers, such as Wang Wenxing and Li Yongping (discussed in detail in the chapters by Chang and Rojas, respectively), continued to labor well into the late 1990s on vast literary projects that reflect no small degree of modernist influence. Read today, Wang's and Li's modernist works strike the reader as singularly anachronistic, as nostalgic returns to the forward-looking tendencies of an earlier era. This systematic untimeliness is particularly ironic in the case of the modernist movement since modernism had always (at least in theory) prided itself on its historical "timeliness," even as the movements in Taiwan were, in part, themselves explicitly or implicitly modeled on the precedent of a European modernism that had already largely run its course.

In short, one might say that this volume as a whole is premised on an attitude of what Gayatri Spivak has labeled, in another context, *strategic essentialism*. That is to say, the essays tactically resurrect a series of conceptual categories (that of Taiwan literature itself, but also the panoply of internal chronological and thematic categories into which Taiwan literature may be divided) for academic, social, or quasi-political purposes, even after the epistemological validity of those categories has been brought into question. Alternatively, we could paraphrase Xiaobing Tang when, in his essay, he suggests that we embrace the term Taiwan literature precisely because of its inherent semantic "ambiguity," which refuses to reduce the plurality of Taiwan literature to a specific set of necessary and sufficient conditions (geographic, linguistic, ethnic, or other).

This antifoundational approach to Taiwan literature is also reflected in the title of the volume as a whole: *Writing Taiwan*, which is an imperfect translation of the Chinese phrase (and title of the original conference) *Wenxue Taiwan*. The latter phrase is itself a precise syntactic inversion of the term conventionally used to designate Taiwan literature (or Taiwanese literature): *Taiwan wenxue*. In titling this book, we have used the inverse construction as a reminder that the category Taiwan literature is never a straightforward given but is continually being reconstituted through the act of *writing* itself. For us, literature is not a transparent window into a preexisting sociocultural space (e.g., "Taiwan"); rather, it functions as a multiangled prism through which that same sociocultural space is refracted and contested. Similarly, the act of scholarly inquiry is never limited to mining the depths of preexisting orders of knowledge but necessarily participates in the construction and shaping of those same epistemological categories. In short, the expression Writing Taiwan stands as a useful reminder that "Taiwan" itself, as a social/cultural/political entity, is not a self-evident, preexisting category but a discursive and political construct that is continually being constituted and contested through a multifaceted process of "writing," literary or otherwise. Our goal in this volume, therefore, is to use readings of a handful of prominent authors and literary phenomena to explore some of the issues involved in reading Taiwan literature and in "writing" Taiwan.

This volume is divided thematically into four interrelated parts. While the preceding considerations of the methodological and epistemological issues involved in the very act of writing about Taiwan literature color and inform all the essays, they are addressed most directly in the three essays in part 1. In part 2, the focus shifts from these sorts of meta-analytic issues to a consideration of the sociocultural grounds from which various specific traditions, genres, and literary movements sprang. The structure of the latter half of the volume then takes the provisional chronotope of modern Taiwan literature and breaks it down into its individual components of *chronos* and *topos*, or time and space. Specifically, part 3 turns to the twin themes of history and memory, together with the erasures and lacunae on which they are necessarily grounded. The essays in part 4 consider how the themes of geography, cartographic representation, and spatial/psychic circulation are developed and challenged in the works of a number of Taiwanese authors. Within these broad thematic groupings, each part draws on a broad range of perspectives and theoretical approaches as well as on material from a variety of historical periods.

Sung-sheng Yvonne Chang opens the volume with a short position paper reflecting on the analytic strategies implicit in the act of "writing Taiwan" itself. Echoing Edward Said's well-known postulate concerning the inherent impossibility of a purely "objective" pursuit of knowledge for its own sake, Chang presents a critical survey of the twentieth-century genealogy of the analytic category Taiwan literature and details how it has been perpetually intertwined with "other" sociopolitical considerations. Like Said, Chang concludes that a recognition of such imbrications of political and scholarly tendencies is not a justification for abandoning the object of scholarly inquiry altogether but a demand for more careful and self-critical awareness of the practical ramifications and implications of one's research.

Fangming Chen is one of the most prolific and influential Taiwan-based scholars working on the topic of Taiwan literature, and his essay engages more specifically with the question of historical periodization that has been so prevalent both in broad surveys of Taiwanese literary history and in more detailed engagements with specific authors or works. Chen critiques the widespread tendency in Taiwanese literary studies to force literary works into boilerplate analytic categories based on what are perceived to have been the general thematic and stylistic tendencies (e.g., nativism, modernism) of the decade in which they happened to have been composed. This periodizing critique intersects with another line of argument in Chen's essay, concerning the relevance of the label postmodernism to contemporary Taiwanese literary and cultural production. The engagement with the concept postmodernism is highly ironic here as it not only is a historical category par excellence but also implicitly brings into question the validity of the sorts of historical grand narratives on which such categories are premised. Chen, for his part, contends that the application of the concept postmodernism to contemporary Taiwan literature amounts to a form of epistemological imperialism because it effectively ignores the historical, social, and cultural specificities out of which that literature has arisen. He argues, in short, that the contemporary burgeoning of counterhegemonic literary trends is more properly viewed in the context of Taiwan's emergence from under the long shadow of colonialism, rather than as a mere reprise of the West's earlier brush with postmodernism.

In the following essay, Xiaobing Tang similarly presents a critical overview of recent discussions of Taiwan literature from the past several decades. Tang addresses many of the same scholars and critics as does Fangming Chen and even takes issue with the unacknowledged nativist subtext of some of Chen's own earlier writings on the subject (suggesting that Chen silently reduces the category Taiwan literature to include only the rather more narrow subsection of works that conform to his own nativist sociopolitical sympathies). Tang is reluctant to end his essay with an overarching summary that would function as a new objective orthodoxy in place of the earlier scholarly interventions that he has critiqued and, instead, settles for a rather more modest conclusion, which, appropriately enough, is also intimately concerned with the problem of translation. Specifically, he addresses the issue of the preferred English translation of the Chinese term *Taiwan wenxue*. Of the two syntactic possibilities, Taiwanese literature and Taiwan literature, Tang notes that the former contains the seeds of a range of potential specific readings (e.g., literature *in* the "Taiwanese" dialect, or *by* native "Taiwanese" writers, etc.), each of which problematically forecloses a range of other potential interpretations. Instead, Tang supports the latter translation, precisely because of the ambiguity implicit in its syntax.

Whereas the essays in part 1 seek to interrogate the textual and paratextual components of Taiwan literature as a literary, academic, and sociopolitical field, those in part 2 deploy a similar array of methodological paradigms to analyze several of the individual genres, movements, and groups that collectively constitute Taiwan literature. These essays seek to interrogate the assumed sacrosanctity of literary production by exploring its inevitable complicity with cultural and political concerns. Each takes as its primary subject a literary movement or cultural phenomenon—to a greater or lesser extent, the category modernism—rather than focusing exclusively on a single author or literary work. In particular, each of the four essays engages, to a greater or lesser extent, with the category modernism. More, perhaps, than any other aesthetic movement, modernism is characterized by a paradoxical combination of engagement with and detachment from the historical conditions under which it emerged. As its name suggests, it sees itself as being rooted in the modern, the present, the here and now, and is typically presented as being a reflection of but also a response to the profound social, technological, and aesthetic transformations to which the modern period has given rise. At the same time, however, modernism's historical self-identity is premised on a paradoxical perspective rooted in the future perfect, whereby the contemporary observer vicariously assumes the backward-looking perspective of imagined future observers.

In the first essay of this part, Joyce C. H. Liu considers the "perverse" writings of Yang Chichang, "the first Taiwanese modernist poet and novelist," and specifically attends to their position in relation to a cluster of modernist debates in Taiwan during the 1930s. The historical context of these debates is interesting because, while they anticipate the 1960s Taiwanese modernist movement by several decades, they nevertheless coincide with one of the more prominent modernist movements in mainland China: Shanghai new perceptionism. Liu posits that, when Yang Chichang's work is regarded in its wider historical context, its apparently decadent and perverse components can be viewed in terms of the psychoanalytic category the abject, itself a displaced expression of a counterhegemonic challenge to a "totalitarian discursive field."

In her essay, Michelle Yeh echoes Fangming Chen's earlier point regarding the inherent limitations of the stylistic categories into which conventional periodizations typically divide the heterogeneous terrain of Taiwan literature. Specifically, Yeh uses the 1950s journal *Modern Poetry Quarterly* as a prism through which to critically reexamine the relation between 1960s modernism and 1970s nativism. In so doing, she draws on Bourdieu's notions of the habitus and the cultural field and seeks to map out the precise ways in which the modernist cultural field was conditioned, thematically and institutionally, by the journal. In particular, she explores how, in the face of stark economic adversity, the poets associated with it adeptly manipulated complex flows of various forms of capital—not only conventional economic capital but also cultural and symbolic capital—in their quest for societal legitimacy. One of the more intriguing subtexts of Yeh's essay involves how the pages of the *Modern Poetry Quarterly* came, in effect, to function as a limited public sphere, wherein like-minded individuals were able to exchange thoughts on aesthetic, cultural, and social issues.

Like Michelle Yeh, Fenghuang Ying looks back to the 1950s for a new perspective on the later, and more visible, literary movements. Specifically, Ying examines how the posthumous literary legacy of the author Zhong Lihe, largely unappreciated during his own lifetime, became a potent touchstone against which a wide variety of subsequent writers attempted to define themselves. During the 1960s and 1970s, nativist critics found in Zhong's works a convenient foil for their own process of self-definition. Fenghuang Ying herself adroitly combines a consideration of Zhong's own writings with a parallel consideration of his status as a symbolic coin of exchange in subsequent literary debates. In this way, Ying effectively picks up Fangming Chen's critical reading of the historical and stylistic categories of modernism and nativism and extends that critique to a consideration of the sociocultural conditions out of which those sorts of stylistic identification arose.

In the final essay in the part, Yvonne Chang completes this round of modernist reflections by turning to the recent work of Wang Wenxing, who, in a postmodern era in which traditional modernism is arguably already largely passé, has continued to labor diligently on his twenty-two-year Joycean opus, *Backed against the Sea*, a two-part work notable as much for its prodigious literary ambition as for its apparent historical untimeliness. Rather than merely presenting a straightforward reading of the work, Chang uses the novel as a means by which to reconsider the sociocultural status of Taiwanese literary modernism itself. She begins with the premise that, despite the modernists' ostensible concerns with rarefied, aesthetic issues, a more complete consideration of the significance of the Taiwanese modernist movement must address the fact that its authors were "reacting against a politically instituted, conservative dominant culture." She proceeds to juxtapose a consideration of the sociopolitical underpinnings of Taiwanese literary modernism with a reading of how comparable sociocultural issues are played out within the fictional frame of the novel itself. Chang's approach is, therefore, grounded on the seemingly paradoxical strategy of delinking a consideration of modernism as a cultural and institutional category from an exclusive focus on the contents of modernist works themselves while conducting a close reading of the actual *content* of one of its most prominent works.

Part 3 turns to the issue of time itself and specifically to the themes of history and memory in Taiwan literature. Questions that the various essays seek to address include: How do history and personal memory figure in literature? How do literary works anticipate their own historicity? And what are the relations between historical amnesia and fictional artifice? Of particular interest here are the process of mediation between personal memory and historical memorialization as well as the epistemological aporias inherent in each. Andreas Huyssen has suggested that the recent fascination with memory and memorialization in European and American culture is intimately related to a widespread sociocultural anxiety posed by the threat of amnesia: "Whether it is a paradox or a dialectic, the spread of amnesia in our culture is matched by a relentless fascination with memory and the past."[1] In the Taiwanese context, we may postulate that the fascination with history and memory is being played out against not only the backdrop of what David Harvey describes as the "space-time conflation" inherent in postmodernism but also against stark political controls, during much of the twentieth century, over what forms those historical narratives would be permitted to take.[2]

The part opens with David Der-wei Wang's essay on the figure of history in Jiang Gui's novel *A Tale of Modern Monsters*, published in English translation under the title *The Whirlwind*. Wang begins by observing that the title of this mid-twentieth-century novel was inspired by that of a late Ming novel about bureaucratic corruption, then presents an etymological examination of the term for monster used, drawing attention to the fact that this word, *taowu*, also literally means "history." Like Eileen Chang's roughly contemporary *Red Earth*, *A Tale of Modern Monsters* is an anti-Communist work that proved disturbing precisely insofar as it exceeded, and challenged, the ideological boundaries within which it was originally intended to exist. Wang is particularly interested in how the novel underscores the odd paradox inherent in the orthodox, time-honored strategy of using the evils of the past to help improve the present. For Wang, Jiang's novel testifies to the degree to which this strategy of evoking historical monsters for the sake of exorcising them necessarily also achieves the opposite effect, breathing new life into the monster of history. That is to say, even as one seeks to dismember the monster of history and lay it to rest, one is always re-membering and reconstituting this historical monstrosity in the process of recalling it.

In the following chapter, Yomi Braester turns from the issue of history to that of personal memory and specifically considers how the genre of the postmodern mystery novel is developed by the writers Chen Yingzhen and Liu Daren. Braester argues that these two authors, both politically persecuted under the Chiang regime, use in their novels variations of a *Rashōmon* structure (one in which the reader is presented with various competing versions of the same incident, with no single interpretation being granted epistemological priority over the others). Unlike conventional mysteries, which gradually guide the reader along a path of discovery, these "post-Chiang" mysteries instead, Braester argues, foreground moments of silence and indeterminacy. More than any single criminal act, what they are ultimately bearing witness to is an entire system of "law" grounded in a long-imposed silence and a "chronic manipulation of memory that [have] maimed writers' capacity to bear witness."

Gang Gary Xu looks, in the following essay, at the trope of theatricality as it is developed on several different levels in the work of the contemporary female novelist Su Weizhen. He argues that Su not only employs explicit metaphors of theatricality in her writing but also uses her fiction to explore some of the deeper ontological issues occasioned by the notion of theatrical performance itself. For example, he examines how the doubled protagonist, Chenmian, in Su's novel *The Island of Silence* can be seen as a figure for the working out of the phenomenon of psychological splitting inherent in theatrical performance; alternatively, the doubling can also be read as a symptom of the personal trauma that she has undergone: "When the burden of the traumatic memory is no longer bearable, the psychopathic splitting or the multiple-personality disorder produces the second Chenmian."

In his influential exposition of speech act theory, J. R. Searle famously bracketed "parasitic" forms of performative utterances, such as those said by an actor on the stage, and outright lies on the grounds that they deliberately flaunt the felicity conditions on which conventional discourse is premised.[3] Xu's essay on Su Weizhen explores the epistemological and ontological implications of this domain of theatricality; Kim-chu Ng similarly grapples, in the following essay on Zhang Dachun, with the ontological and ethical implications of Zhang's reliance on mendacity in his prolific and eclectic fictional output. Ng argues that Zhang's narrative strategy and ontological premises ultimately fail to break out of the metatextual trap that his literary project sets for itself: it remains grounded at the level of mere language play and, consequently, fails to engage in a more substantive way with tangible social and ethical issues outside the text. Zhang, Ng concludes, ultimately remains imprisoned within what we might call his own apartment building of language — bringing together Ng's discussion of Fredric Jameson's notion of the prison-house of language and the title of Zhang's own short story "Guided Tour of an Apartment Complex."

The interest in temporality developed in part 3 is paralleled, in part 4, by an attention to tropes of spatiality. This part brings together essays on travel literature (Ping-hui Liao) and the metaphorics of spatial representation (Rojas, Chen) and essays attentive to the transnational flows of capital and commodities (Ban Wang and Chen) and the psychic flows of object relations (Chaoyang Liao). A recurrent theme in all the essays is how the spatial integrity of Taiwan as a body politic, as well as of the embodied subject, is repeatedly challenged by these sorts of fluidity while it is simultaneously subjected to an imaginary reinvestment at the level of psychic and political fantasy.

Taiwan's twentieth-century identity as a distinct geographic entity is inseparable from considerations of its relation to mainland China and Japan. Accordingly, it is appropriate that this final part on spatial imaginations begins with an essay by Ping-hui Liao presenting a close reading of a series of early-twentieth-century travel writings in which the Taiwanese author Wu Zhuoliu recalls his eighteen-month trip to mainland China, a series that is in intertextual dialogue with an influential tradition of Japanese travel writings. Liao suggests that these texts illustrate Wu's complex attitudes toward imagined identity, affinity, and rejection, played out against the triangulated national space of colonial Taiwan, Japan, and mainland China.

Lingchei Letty Chen picks up this twin theme of travel and geography as she considers the way in which metaphors of mapping are deployed in Zhu Tianxin's novel *Ancient Capital*. In particular, she describes how Zhu Tianxin occasionally invokes the figure of the female body as a cartographic representation of the island of Taiwan. Furthermore, just as Wu Zhuoliu's text is in dialogue with Akutagawa Ryunosuke's *Travels in China*, Zhu Tianxin's *Ancient Capital* is similarly in a dialogue with Kawabata Yasunari's novel about Kyoto, *The Old Capital*. More specifically, Chen unpacks a dense intertextual web in Zhu Tianxin's work wherein the representation of Taipei is, in effect, haunted by the spectral presence of the Japanese city of Kyoto.

Carlos Rojas picks up a similar cartographic fascination as an entry point into the fiction of another prominent contemporary writer, the Malaysia-born author Li Yongping. Rojas argues that Li uses the figure of a Taipei road map as a trope for Taiwan's chiasmatic maturational relation with the Chinese mainland. Underlying this textual fascination with cartographic boundaries, he suggests, is a salient anxiety about the cultural and epistemological status of geographic boundaries themselves.

In the following essay, Chaoyang Liao addresses the relation between object relations and voice in two of Li Ang's most recent works, *The Strange Garden* and *All Sticks Are Welcome in the Censer of Beigang*. Exploring the relation between the roles of the voice and the gaze, Liao examines the way in which these works comment on the significance of object relations and psychic circulation in a postmodern social space, suggesting that "the circularity of exchange" may serve as "a viable way to survive and transcend psychic and historical trauma." Specifically, he begins with a consideration of how two of the stories from Li's recent controversial collection *All Sticks* focus on the status of the voice and the gaze, respectively; he connects this with her early novel, *The Strange Garden*, which, he suggests, presents a "sphere of reciprocity where . . . gaze and voice engage in free exchange." Liao's piece combines an informed and nuanced discussion of psychoanalytic theory with a provocative exploration of how psychoanalysis can be brought to bear on the relation between the fictional text and the historico-political environment that both produced and, ultimately, contains it.

In the final essay, Ban Wang examines the ways in which Zhu Tianwen's works reflect the changing status of visual imagery within postmodern culture. This essay constitutes a convenient bookend to the collection because its stress on *global* flows of commodity and capital reiterates the anxiety about the specificity of "Taiwan" as a heuristic chronotope. Ban Wang essentially inverts Benjamin's well-known postulate about the loss of the "aura" in an age increasingly dominated by modern technologies of mechanical reproduction, arguing instead that the postmodern culture of virtual imagery has produced a space within which the aura can, in effect, be nostalgically reinvested with affect. This rereading of the postmodern reapparition of the Benjaminian aura can also be brought to bear on the concept of national and ethnic identity. It is conventional wisdom that transnational flows of capital, commodities, and cultures have the potential to challenge the integrity of autonomous nations and their respective societies and cultures, threatening to reduce everything to the lowest common cultural denominator. However, works such as Zhu Tianwen's point to how it might be possible to theorize the reconsolidation of local specificities. This reapparition of different forms of localized identity within a postmodern, and postnational, context invites us to critically reconsider the concept of national identity itself.

The contributors to this volume represent scholars based in Taiwan (Pinghui Liao, Chaoyang Liao, Joyce C. H. Liu, Fangming Chen, and Fenghuang Ying), scholars from Taiwan currently based in the United States (Sungsheng Yvonne Chang, David Der-wei Wang, Lingchei Letty Chen, and Michelle Yeh), mainlanders currently based in the United States (Ban Wang, Xiaobing Tang, Gang Gary Xu), and scholars of American, European, and Middle Eastern descent based in the United States (Yomi Braester and Carlos Rojas) as well as a Malaysian-Chinese critic currently based in Taiwan (Kim-chu Ng). Collectively, this diverse panoply of voices seeks to both contest and defamiliarize conventional assumptions about the nature of Taiwan literature even as it attempts to provide the basis for a new mapping of this variegated terrain. Although the various essays gathered here represent a heterogeneous array of perspectives and positions that would defy straightforward summary, one quality that they all share is that they resist the reading of Taiwan literature through the lens of preestablished conceptual templates, favoring instead a hermeneutical strategy comparable to what Michel de Certeau describes as "walking in the city," whereby "practitioners of the city" are literally walkers "whose bodies follow the thicks and thins of an urban 'text' they write without being able to read it. . . . The networks of these moving, intersecting writings compose a manifold story that has neither author nor spectator, shaped out of fragments of trajectories and alterations of spaces."[4] The present volume sets us on a similar walk through the urban forest of modern Taiwan literature, the bounds and configurations of which are produced and contested through the act of reading itself.

Another recurrent theme shared by many of the essays in this volume involves an inversion of the conventional category Taiwan literature, where the determining factor becomes not so much the ostensible "Taiwan-ness" of the fictional literature as the "literariness" of the political fiction of "Taiwan" itself. Furthermore, to the extent that the category Taiwan literature is based on a political fiction, it simultaneously gains additional cogency from the deep-rooted conviction in Chinese culture, dating back at least to the nineteenth century, that the fates of fiction and politics are themselves intimately intertwined. Reformist writers such as Liang Qichao and Lu Xun insisted that fiction was in a unique position to revive the fortunes of the ailing Chinese nation by speaking directly to the spirits of the masses. In the twentieth century, discussions of Taiwan fiction have similarly been closely bound up with considerations of the political fiction of "Taiwan" as a sociocultural category.

As Xiaobing Tang observes in his essay, any attempt to concretize the bounds of Taiwan literature will inevitably delimit that category in a politically significant manner. Should one look to the sociocultural background of the authors, the language or dialect in which the literature was written, the ideological subtext vis-à-vis Taiwanese culture and identity? Yvonne Chang points out that the act of delimiting the category Taiwan literature will necessarily involve a process of "bracketing," whereby certain authors and texts are set aside as inconvenient supplements to the overall model. For instance, a nativist approach to Taiwan literature will tend to bracket the contributions of mainland émigrés as being somehow not wholly "authentic." Rather than propose a fixed and bounded definition of Taiwan literature, therefore, we instead prefer to approach it as a "minor literature," as Deleuze and Guattari describe in another context the attempt to carve out a distinctive and oppositional literary field from within the confines of a more hegemonic linguistic space.[5]

To the extent that this deliberately eclectic volume has a unifying theme, it would probably be to suggest a return to, and a reconsideration of, Taiwan literature in light of a logic of doubled supplementarity. On the one hand, Taiwan literature (however this may be understood) has historically been seen as an awkward supplement to either Japanese or Chinese literature, and this liminal status has allowed it to be used as a foil against which to buttress the imagined integrity of those other national literatures. On the other hand, Taiwan literature's gradual emergence as an autonomous and recognizable category has, in turn, relied on a parallel strategy of bracketing an array of awkward supplements of its own: those works, authors, or genres that cannot be completely excluded but that also do not fit comfortably within the grand narrative that Taiwan literature (and its exponents) seeks to establish for itself.

NOTES

1 Andreas Huyssen, *Twilight Memories: Marking Time in a Culture of Amnesia* (New York: Routledge, 1995), 254.
2 David Harvey, *The Condition of Postmodernity: An Enquiry into the Origins of Cultural Change* (New York: Blackwell, 1989).
3 Searle is discussed in Jacques Derrida, *Limited Inc.* (Evanston: Northwestern University Press, 1988).
4 Michel de Certeau, *The Practice of Everyday Life* (Berkeley and Los Angeles: University of California Press, 1984), 93.
5 Gilles Deleuze and Félix Guattari, *Kafka: Toward a Minor Literature*, trans. Dana Polan (Minneapolis: University of Minnesota Press, 1986).

THE LIMITS OF
TAIWAN LITERATURE

WITH THE APRIL 17, 1895, signing of the Treaty of Shimonoseki at the end of the First Sino-Japanese War (1894–95), China's Qing dynasty ceded the island of Taiwan to Japan. Taiwan quickly became a key element in Japan's imperialist plans to develop an East Asian Co-Prosperity Sphere, and the Japanese consequently invested considerable resources in building up the island's physical infrastructure, strengthening its education system, and pursuing a process of assimilation. This process of colonization was ratcheted to a new level in 1937 during the Second Sino-Japanese War, whereupon Governor-General Hasegawa Kiyoshi instituted the *kōminka* policy, which sought to fashion Taiwan's residents into loyal (Japanese) imperial subjects by abolishing the Chinese-language sections of newspapers, substituting Japanese names for Chinese ones, and recruiting Taiwanese to serve in the Japanese military. Taiwan remained a Japanese colony until Japan's defeat at the end of World War II, when the Allies agreed in October 25, 1945, to return the island to China, now under the control of Chiang Kai-shek's Nationalist Party. While many of Taiwan's residents initially welcomed the departure of the Japanese, the repressive and autocratic Nationalist regime under Commander Chen Yi quickly chilled their enthusiasm for the new regime. In early 1947, a series of popular protests known as the February Twenty-eighth Incident briefly allowed native Taiwanese to regain political control of the island, but these efforts were quickly squashed by a military crackdown resulting in the executions of thousands of Taiwanese, including many of Taiwan's intellectual elite.

Following their defeat by the Communists in 1949, the Nationalists retreated to Taiwan, where they hoped to set up a temporary base while they waited for an opportunity to regain control over the Chinese mainland. Although originally conceived as a temporary political exigency, this situation quickly developed into an intractable status quo, both Beijing and Taipei insisting that theirs was the legitimate authority over a unified China (including the "province" of Taiwan). Initially, the international community

PART
ONE

generally sided with the Nationalists in Taiwan, maintaining diplomatic relations with the Republic of China (Taiwan) rather than with the People's Republic of China (mainland China), and allowing Taiwan to represent "China" in such international venues as the Olympics and the United Nations Security Council. In the 1970s, Taiwan experienced a series of diplomatic setbacks, beginning with the loss of its UN Security Council seat to China in 1971, followed by the termination of formal diplomatic relations with many of its former allies, including the United States. At the same time, however, it experienced a period of rapid economic growth during the 1970s and 1980s, fueled in particular by manufacturing and exports. Martial law was finally lifted in September 1987, thereby legalizing oppositional political parties, lifting implicit restrictions on cultural production, and facilitating a critical reexamination of Taiwan's history under the Japanese and the Nationalists.

The preceding historical narrative provides not only the context within which modern Taiwan literature has itself been written but also the framework for the primary analytic models for interpreting and making sense of it. For instance, Sung-sheng Yvonne Chang identifies in her essay three basic analytic models that characterized Taiwanese studies during the early postwar period (e.g., Taiwan as the "surrogate China," for foreign scholars unable, for political and practical reasons, to study and research in mainland China) and suggests that since the 1980s a number of more nuanced approaches have emerged, approaches that encourage, for instance, the inclusion of Japanese-language work from the pre-1949 period. In the following essay, Fangming Chen considers the way in which different analytic models might affect our understanding of the increasingly eclectic nature of Taiwan literature since the 1980s, as martial law was gradually loosened and finally lifted altogether in 1987. In particular, Chen is critical of the tendency to describe this literature as postmodern, arguing that this designation merely transplants Western categories onto Taiwan and that, instead, this literature is more accurately described as postcolonial, in reference to Taiwan's having spent most of the twentieth century under the colonial control of, first, the Japanese and, then, the Chinese Nationalists. It was also in the 1980s that a series of energetic debates emerged over the nature and limits of the discipline of Taiwanese literary studies itself. As Xiaobing Tang discusses in his essay, these debates were informed by parallel considerations of the nature of Taiwan, its relation with its own colonial history, and its position within a greater Chinese and East Asian cultural sphere.

1

Representing Taiwan:
Shifting Geopolitical Frameworks

Sung-sheng Yvonne Chang

What strikes me most about the title of the conference, "Writing Taiwan: Strategies of Representation," is the word *strategies*. Why strategies? It is true that the word can be interpreted in different ways: as interventionist theoretical lingo as well as the basis of the more conventional rhetorical strategies of literary representation (which is actually a focus of the conference's last panel). But, in a more fundamental sense, strategies are employed to achieve goals. And the participants here do appear to share a common goal: to reexamine and, ultimately, to advance the strategies of representing Taiwan to the outside world through literary scholarship and translations. Whether we consciously acknowledge it or not, there is an inevitable political subtext to all efforts at representing Taiwan today. On the one hand, the country is strenuously struggling to "expand its international living space" (to borrow a phrase used in another context by Thomas Gold).[1] On the other hand, greater penetration of global capitalism in the post–Cold War era has hiked the stakes of symbolic wars. As these factors have come increasingly to determine the condition of possibility for culturally representing Taiwan—whether through the publication of literary anthologies or various other ways of showcasing its creative products at film festivals, book fairs, and arts exhibits—strategies *are* important.

But let us refrain from critiquing such commercial activities of cultural brokerage from the moral high ground of either Marxist or liberal-humanist theories. Instead, I would like to urge that we keep in mind the political and economic subtexts of our own activities while examining the strategies of representing Taiwan at another—not necessarily higher but different—level: the academic level.

Whereas less oriented toward immediate, tangible goals, academe is certainly not a disinterested cultural space. After Said, who could be adamant enough to maintain that the acquisition of knowledge, and, for that matter, any type of intellectual activity, is inherently innocent? Not to mention the fact that political and economic interests everywhere have direct bearings on the institutional distribution of resources. Nonetheless, the processes, rather than the results, are more highly valued in scholarly researches, which in turn are governed by conceptual frameworks that scholars internalize via different channels in their personal lives and academic training. After a series of rapid shifts in theoretical paradigms in the last two decades, new critical models are now being applied to, and experimented with in, the study of Taiwanese literature, as the essays in the present volume undoubtedly testify. To fully appreciate the significance of this moment and the promise that it holds for the enhancement of the quality of our work, it is, perhaps, useful to take a brief retrospective look at the analytic models that have previously dominated research activities on Taiwan in the American academy.

Owing to the exceedingly institutionalized nature of scholarly fields in this country, there seem to be only a limited number of viable analytic models that prevail at any given time. In the early postwar years, the most prevalent model in Taiwanese studies was one that regarded Taiwan as "the other China." Conceived within the Cold War ideological frame, this approach clearly echoed such political conceptual pairs as "Red China versus Free China" and implied a perceived rivalry between two divergent paths along which the Third World countries pursued modernization: the capitalist, liberal-democratic and the socialist-Communist. Even today, such a binary mode of thinking remains popular among certain scholars. Lucien Pye, for example, faults China's political authorities for stigmatizing individuals in China's coastal regions, Taiwan, and Hong Kong who have successfully "modernized" themselves.[2] And the following argument from the late John King Fairbank similarly betrays a preoccupation with the liberal/radical ideological split in the aftermath of the May Fourth movement that culminated in the Communist/Nationalist war: after the Korean War, history has given the Nationalists a second chance; this allowed the Sino-liberals who went to Taiwan with the Nationalists to bring to fruition their gradualist reform program, aborted in 1949 when the majority of the Chinese people opted for the radical route of revolution.[3] Ultimately, such scholars have striven to answer such hypothetical historical questions as the following:

What would have happened to China without the Communist Revolution? The research value of Taiwan is, thus, seen as resting squarely on the fact that it has traveled "the road not taken"—that being from the point of view of socialist China, of course.

The second model treated Taiwan as a "surrogate China," an approach engendered by practical circumstances. Shut out by the Bamboo Curtain, an entire generation of Chinese anthropologists—including such eminent scholars as William Skinner and Arthur Wolf—have conducted their fieldwork in Taiwan as a substitute for "China proper."[4] Since the anthropologists focus on cultural markers that distinguish the Chinese people as a "we group" and cultural sediments take a long time to form, the civilizational temporal frame tends to be inclusive. Taiwan is the "part" from which one can presumably infer theoretical conclusions about the "whole," which is China.

The third model can be labeled the case study model, adopted mostly by social scientists. With their disciplines' predominantly modernist orientation, social scientists perceive Taiwan as one political entity on the rapidly transforming globe or simply as a geographic unit that has attracted the world's attention by virtue of its alleged "miracles" in recent decades. In this model, Taiwan's relation with China is neither asserted nor denied; its research value resides in its status either as a newly industrialized economy in East Asia or as a former Leninist state undergoing democratic transformation.[5]

If, in the case study model, the "China question" has been temporarily suspended, there is yet another, more problematic type of suspension in literary studies pertaining to Taiwan. This is a practice that I would like to label with a special term, *bracketing*. Bracketing refers to what a scholar does to evade or defer the proper treatment of certain crucial aspects of the research subject without adequate justification. Through bracketing, the scholar treats Taiwan nominally as "part of China" but, in fact, does not fully address the issue with historical contextualization, aside from acknowledging the legitimacy of this relation within its overall referential framework.[6] And this is what we have encountered in numerous topic-centered anthologies and collections of critical essays that juxtapose works on China and Taiwan under the category *Chinese* without addressing their crucial differences in the postwar era. Scholarship of this sort must not be dismissed as merely the product of unusual political circumstances. For bracketing takes place not only as a direct result of political constraints or ideological hang-ups but also as a habit, when scholars acquiesce to implicit institutional demands. While bracketing appears to be a psychological trait found in broader categories of intellectual life under authoritarian regimes, for the moment it suffices to say that this dubious practice is deeply entrenched in the entire structure of the scholarly institution. Rather than the individual's professional integrity, therefore, what interests me most is the kind of mechanisms that serve to ensure the popular acceptance and seeming normality of some distorted scholarly practices, such as the near-complete neglect of modern Taiwan literature written in Japanese during the martial law period. The high status habitually associated with questions concerning East-West literary relations qualifies as one such mechanism as it shapes people's scholarly agenda and diverts their attention, in a preemptive manner, from crucial aspects of modern Chinese/Taiwanese literary history.

In recent years, most of the once-dominant analytic models mentioned above have to varying degrees been rendered obsolete by new historical developments as well as new intellectual trends in academe. As the Cold War ended, Taiwan as "the other China" lost much of its research appeal. The world is now eagerly observing how postsocialist China handles its own capitalist experiment, and the renewed interest in the "alternative form of Chinese modernization" at least partially accounts for the sudden boom in studies of Shanghai and the city's treaty port past. In the meantime, as China progressively opens itself up, a substitute is no longer needed for empirical research. As the Taiwanese nationalists in the post–martial law period take to task the Nationalist government's Sinocentric cultural narrative, some anthropologists of the younger generation have also reverted to a revisionist approach to the Taiwan question. After all, treating Taiwan as a specimen of Chinese folk culture is predicated on the problematic assumption that divergent courses of modernization have not meaningfully affected cultural practices, including religious rituals, in an everyday sense. By contrast, the modernist approach of the social scientists fares better in the post–Cold War milieu. Yet, adhering to the concept of the modern nation-state as the primary point of reference, this approach tends to fall short of satisfactorily dealing with the phenomenon of globalization, which is undeniably exerting a significant impact on Chinese societies in the "Greater China" sphere, including Taiwan.

It would be an understatement to say that changes in studies of Taiwanese literature have also been dramatic. Within Taiwan itself, the lifting of martial law and the ascending nativist imperative have compelled scholars to stop bracketing the stigmatized prewar period of modern Taiwanese literary history, in which some of its best works were written in the Japanese language. Whereas even as late as the mid-1980s the term *Taiwan wenxue* [Taiwan literature]—used without qualification—was still regarded as a political liability, we are now witnessing concerted efforts at institutionalizing Taiwanese literary studies, with the Academia Sinica taking a valiant lead in the most recent years.[7] In the United States, the field has been given a boost by the participation of younger scholars whose point of origin is the People's Republic of China (PRC), who have brought with them fresh perspectives as well as ambitious intellectual agendas.[8] It is, therefore, not hard to imagine that, for everyone engaged in this exciting enterprise, the thorny, unresolved issue of referential frame—the temporal, spatial, and ethnic referential frames pertinent to literary historiography—has emerged as more urgent and more crucially relevant than ever.

Once the Japanese period is brought into the picture, the origin of modern Taiwan literature must be traced back to the mid-1920s. And it becomes evident that, since the May Fourth movement, none of the political and artistic trends on the Chinese mainland have affected literary developments in Taiwan in a direct, concurrent manner. With a seventy-odd-year history of its own, modern Taiwan literature inevitably fits awkwardly in the limited space of a single chapter, an appendix, or a few passing remarks inserted in books on modern Chinese literature. On the other hand, however, even if the aspired-to status of *national literature* were established for Taiwan literature, it still cannot be comprehended as an isolated phenomenon, without being situated in larger geopolitical referential frames. While such frames are, undoubtedly, multiple, in practice some are always privileged over others. For Taiwan-based literary scholars, many of the tacitly acknowledged, officially sanctioned referential frames have all of a sudden become problematic in the post–martial law period. In addition, the perceived relations between *self* and *other* have shifted violently and drastically from period to period in the tumultuous years of modern Taiwanese history. More specifically, the complex history of Taiwan has made several competing referential frames equally available to construct such perceptions. One can align with the Chinese in the PRC and take the West as the *other* on the basis of ethnic and civilizational histories. One can cling to the Cold War self-positioning as a member of the anti-Communist camp and regard the PRC as the *other*. Or one can try to restore ties with Japan, the former colonizer—ties that have been revamped through business partnerships in recent decades—by more openly acknowledging the positive legacy of a colonial modernity. These realities help explain why many literary scholars in Taiwan display such a vital concern with questions of history and identity, to the extent of bypassing immediately relevant questions regarding literature and aesthetics. This will probably remain the case in the field of Taiwanese literary studies in the foreseeable future.

One must, however, also take heed of the fact that highly institutionalized scholarly activities have their own brand of "politics of referential frames," the deployment of which inevitably compounds the issues of history and identity. In a broad sense, the struggle to effectively challenge referential frames that are taken for granted in dominant ideologies—patriarchal, Eurocentric, or heterosexual—lies at the heart of various recently popularized intellectual trends, trends that have significantly altered our visions of life, supplying us with a new intellectual agenda. At the top of that agenda is to treat the history of previously marginalized and repressed groups—be they ethnic minorities, women, or colonized people—as a legitimate frame of reference in scholarly research.

Scholars of Taiwan literature have ardently responded to such intellectual inspirations and adopted them as conceptual frameworks for their own inquiries with more or less critical discernment. New theoretical frameworks, such as those generated by postmodernist, postcolonialist, and feminist discourses, are, of course, never treated merely as conceptual tools. They provide the necessary symbolic capital that scholars need to empower themselves in the increasingly globalized academic field everywhere. Some scholars have apparently used them for the purpose of advancing an old—usually political—cause that has been a very high priority for them personally. Others have employed them as new means of evading the question of history and, thus, inadvertently regressed to the practice of bracketing. An interesting question, therefore, is how we ourselves envision the hierarchy of different historical referential frames and whether we can justify our own use of new theoretical frameworks with intellectual integrity.

Also worth mentioning is the fact that some emerging scholarly trends in the general field of Chinese studies seem to have a strong potential to further galvanize the politics of referential frames for Taiwanese literary studies and lead it in welcome directions. The discourse on "colonial/alternative modernity," for instance, distinguishes itself from postcolonialist theories that originated with scholars from former Western colonies and takes East Asian history of the last century and a half as its spatial and temporal referential frame.[9] This is likely to encourage inter-Asia comparative perspectives, rather than perpetuating the currently predominant approach to Taiwan literature that still privileges "China" in various ways. A comparison between Taiwan and South Korea, for example, with their shared experience of Japanese colonization and American-assisted postwar authoritarianism, could be extremely illuminating.

Or, as the globalization phenomenon challenges former concepts of boundaries, studies of worldwide trends and movements that involve ethnic Chinese in various groupings are already seeking to radically redefine "what China is."[10] There are scholars both within and outside Taiwan who have been toying with the provocative but still quite elusive concept postnational imagination.[11] It is certainly not the case that the institution of the modern nation has already been "posited" in any empirical sense; rather, the national imaginary has so frequently been carried beyond and across the geographic national boundaries that the question of national identity is rendered immensely more complex.

As a matter of fact, there exists an intricate link between the questions, What is China? and, What is Taiwan? in that both typically evoke ideologically constructed conceptual images. One highly intriguing phenomenon is that an important legacy of the postwar Nationalist regime's claim of Taiwan as "China"—legitimized by its United Nations seat until 1972—is its entitlement of Taiwanese residents as citizens of a nation-state. To treat their community as anything less than a nation is demeaning and psychologically unacceptable—not only to the militant Taiwanese nationalists but also to many others at a subconscious level. Opposing arguments over the entity's proper title ("Republic of China"? "Republic of Taiwan"?) are, thus, built on the same epistemic foundation.

Overall, such reconceptualizations promise to free scholars of Taiwan literature from the ideological hold of older referential frames, thus enabling us to move beyond the China/Taiwan deadlock in a narrowly politicized sense. But there is also danger: the possibility that a new and trendy intellectual agenda will lure us away from the foundational tasks of interpreting literary texts and analyzing literary culture produced by specific historical circumstances. The abysmal gaps in knowledge created in the underdeveloped field of Taiwanese literary studies by the long-standing practice of bracketing would, then, remain unfilled.

Undoubtedly, the specific academic field (as defined by Pierre Bourdieu) and institutional framework within which we situate ourselves and from which we derive our evaluative standards play determinative roles in shaping our scholarly discourses. It is, therefore, not surprising that scholars of Taiwan literature in the United States and those in Taiwan often have very different research objectives and methodological preferences. Moreover, locked into a rigid regional identity, scholars of Taiwan literature in the United States often complain that they are being ghettoized. In an age in which theories, not to mention scholars themselves, travel not only with round-trip tickets but also with memberships in frequent-flier programs, this situation is definitely undergoing dramatic changes. One unique feature of this conference is that we are all learning to speak to different, multiple audiences. This factor will, predictably, exert a substantial impact on our future research agendas. And what is even more encouraging is that, with its focus on the interpretation of literary texts, this conference simultaneously performs the function of reconsolidating a community that has literature as the primary content of its shared interest. At a time when the disciplinary identity of literary studies has become precarious in the American academy, we can be reassured of the validity of literature as a research category, with the emphatic reminder that it is necessarily embedded within larger frames of reference.

NOTES

1. Thomas Gold, keynote address to the Gateway Conference, University of Texas, Austin, April 1998.
2. See Lucien Pye, "How China's Nationalism Was Shanghaied," in Jonathan Unger, ed., *Chinese Nationalism* (Armonk: M. E. Sharpe, 1996), 86–112.
3. See John K. Fairbank, *The Great Chinese Revolution: 1800–1985* (New York: Harper and Row, 1986).
4. It may still be fresh in the memory of many of us that brochures for grants from the National Endowment for the Humanities, the American Council of Learned Societies, and the Social Science Research Council used to contain statements like the following: "Taiwan and Hong Kong are acceptable sites for research projects on China if the applicant is denied access to the mainland."

5 It is true that Thomas Gold's *State and Society in the Taiwan Miracle* (Armonk: M. E. Sharpe, 1986) still considers Taiwan's economic success an "alternative form of Chinese modernization" (xi). Yet, as the book explicitly contrasts Taiwan's political-economic performance with that of Latin American countries and, thus, situates it within a global context, the work serves as a good example of the case study approach. This approach has, apparently, gained popularity among scholars interested in contemporary Taiwan in recent years. In his "Cultural Policy on Postwar Taiwan" (in Stevan Harrell and Huang Chun-chieh, eds., *Cultural Change in Postwar Taiwan* [Boulder: Westview, 1994]), Edwin Winckler, e.g., accentuates the uniqueness of Taiwan by repeatedly referring to it as "a place like Taiwan."

6 I would offer my own *Modernism and the Nativist Resistance: Contemporary Chinese Fiction from Taiwan* (Durham: Duke University Press, 1993) as an example of this approach. Another interesting illustration of the practice of bracketing is found in "Postmodernism and China," ed. Arif Dirlik and Zhang Xudong, *boundary 2*, special issue, 24.3 (fall 1997). The editors' suggestion in their introduction that "Chinese postmodernism" is also postrevolutionary and postsocialist, apparently not applicable to "postmodernisms" found in other Chinese societies, undermines their seemingly well-intentioned efforts to include two essays on postmodern discourse and practice in Taiwan. They have taken special pains in announcing that the collection focuses for the most part on the People's Republic. Yet to do so without giving an adequate account of what falls outside this specified scope—the different historical context behind the two articles on Taiwan—fits well what I would designate as *bracketing*.

7 See Sung-sheng Y. Chang, "Beyond Cultural and National Identities: Current Re-Evaluations of the *Kominka* Literature from Taiwan's Japanese Period," *Journal of Modern Literature in Chinese* 1.1 (July 1997): 75–107.

8 Xiaobing Tang's "On the Concept of Taiwan Literature" (chapter 3 in this volume) serves as a good example: it attempts to examine the debate on Taiwanese literature with reference to the incomplete Chinese project of modernity as well as the varied and variable legacy of the May Fourth intellectual movement.

9 See, e.g., Tani E. Barlow, ed., *Formations of Colonial Modernity in East Asia* (Durham: Duke University Press, 1997).

10 Examples are studies of the Chinese diaspora and of "Chinese transnationalism." For the latter, see *Ungrounded Empire: The Cultural Politics of Modern Chinese Transnationalism*, ed. Ahwa Ong and Donald Nonini (New York: Routledge, 1997); and *Spaces of Their Own: Women's Public Sphere in Transnational China*, ed. Mayfair Yang (Minneapolis: University of Minnesota Press, 1999). See also the articles in "Modern Chinese Literary and Cultural Studies in the Age of Theory: Reimagining a Field," ed. Rey Chow, *boundary 2*, special issue, 25.3 (fall 1998).

11 See Arjun Appadurai, *Modernity at Large: Cultural Dimensions of Globalization* (Minneapolis: University of Minnesota Press, 1996).

2

Postmodern or Postcolonial? An Inquiry into Postwar Taiwanese Literary History

Fangming Chen

Literary history must always be considered in the context of the societal conditions that gave rise both to the literary works and to their authors. Accordingly, any explanation or evaluation of postwar Taiwanese literary history should also be placed within the context of Taiwan's historical development. It was not until the 1980s that discussions of Taiwanese literary history were finally able to receive relatively broad consideration. This is easily understandable, especially given that, after the lifting of martial law in 1987, Taiwanese society began to witness two phenomena: a rise in economic productivity and a comparable rise in cultural productivity. The content of Taiwan literature similarly enjoyed an expansion in both quality and quantity. At the same time, however, this period also gave rise to a sharp increase in discussions and polemics regarding the concept and characteristics of that literature.

The literary impulses hidden within society had already been subject to forty years of severe institutional repression, and, after the lifting of martial law, they flowed out with newfound vigor. The authoritarian rule, shaped by a single-value system, had previously demanded that literary workers bow to the ideological mold of institutional conformity. However, this does not imply that there did not exist any dissenting voices in Taiwanese society, just as a momentary lapse of attention does not necessarily entail a total loss of memory. After the lifting of martial law, all the subject matter previously classified as ideologically forbidden under the previous regime was freely used for literary creation. The large-scale appearance in Taiwan of nationalist literature, indigenous literature, "military-compound" [*juancun*] literature, feminist literature, gay literature, and ecological literature not only stood as testimony to the arrival of an intellectually pluralistic era but also pointed to an imminent, rich harvest of literary works.

With such a multifaceted literary scene, the question of the characteristics of Taiwan literature quickly became an important point of contention within academe. Many authors simultaneously and independently became openly critical of the existing authoritarian political regime. For instance, whereas an important goal of nationalist literature in Taiwan was the ultimate overthrow of the Han chauvinists who had held power for so long, a central theme in the newly emerging literature from Taiwan's indigenous peoples was a complete rejection of Han-chauvinist prejudices. Similarly, the appearance of military-compound literature was characterized by an increasing concern with the growing bias toward wealth and seniority. One of the primary tasks of feminist literature involved the unveiling and critique of the arrogance and brutality of male chauvinism, just as the critique of heterosexist prejudice was one of the important objectives of gay literature. In sum, the general direction of virtually all writers during this period, regardless of the specific literary form they were using, was characterized by a fundamental act of decentering. Precisely because it possessed these characteristics, Taiwan literature from the 1980s to the present has often been classified under the general rubric of postmodernism.

However, the concept of postmodern literature did not originate within Taiwanese society itself; it is purely an import from the West, specifically from the United States. The rise of postmodern literature in the West has its own specific historical conditions and socioeconomic foundations. Whether this precipitously borrowed concept is really appropriate as a description of the thought and position of Taiwanese writers must await more detailed study in the future. The purpose of this essay is merely to indicate that contemporary Taiwan literature developed out of specific sociohistorical conditions that are themselves intimately bound up with the entirety of Taiwan's colonial history. The character of Taiwan's recent history derives not only from the period of Japanese occupation but also from the political authoritarianism of the postwar period. If we wish to discuss the culturally pluralistic character of contemporary literature, it is necessary to locate that literature within this sociohistorical context.

From the perspective of Taiwan's colonial history, the literature created in the then-prevailing society should be considered colonial literature. If this view has any merit, then the current literary scene can only with difficulty be described as having postmodern characteristics. Instead, it would probably be more appropriate to use the term *postcolonial* to describe the flourishing Taiwan literature in the 1980s. The key issue here is whether Taiwan's postwar literary development constitutes the rise of its postmodern literature or, instead, represents the continued evolution of its postcolonial literature.

POSTWAR OR RECOLONIZED?

Taiwan literature can be seen as a typical product of a colonial society. During the entire course of its development, there was an unstable oppositional relation between the political center and the social periphery. The rulers located at the center would invariably seek to control the Taiwanese authors located at the margins. Similarly, Taiwanese writers would frequently draw on a variety of different literary genres to contest the authority of the ruling powers. This kind of historical progression could not help but make Taiwan literature an arena in which diverse political forces vied for power. Ever since the period of Japanese occupation, the authors standing in the position of the colonized have continuously struggled to define Taiwan literature while also attempting to articulate a periodizing explanation for Taiwanese literary history. Japanese scholars have adopted the notion of the "imperial gaze" while also relying on the discourse of the "extension of the interior" to explain Taiwan literature, designating it as a "literature of the outlying regions."[1] This description refers to those literary works produced by Japanese authors residing in Taiwan, but it significantly does not include those works produced by (ethnically Chinese) Taiwanese authors.

If, during the period of Japanese occupation, the works by native Taiwanese authors could not even be elevated to the level of "literature of the outlying regions," their marginal character can well be imagined. On the other hand, scholars from the People's Republic of China have tended to regard Taiwan literature from a centrist perspective and have used the description "a branch of Chinese literature" as the basis of their historical explanation.[2] Native Taiwanese authors, because of differences in historical perspective and political position, opened a polarizing war of words during the 1980s, leaving modern Taiwanese literary history with even more to be explained.[3] Within such a broad and complicated contestation of historical perspectives, the study of literary history becomes a risky endeavor. No matter how rich and multifaceted this controversy might be, it remains an incontrovertible fact that Taiwan literature is marked by a distinctly colonial character.

I once ventured the following formulation: "The popular literature of the 1920s, the leftist literature of the 1930s, the *kōminka* [imperialization] literature of the 1940s, the anti-Communist literature of the 1950s, the modernist literature of the 1960s, the nativist literature of the 1970s, and the recognition literature of the 1980s—each represents the literary style of its respective historical period."[4] This kind of historical periodization and labeling is actually only a rhetorical convenience. It can attend only to the main stylistic tendencies of each historical era and is, consequently, unable to take into account more marginal literary events. This approach not only entails dividing history into different periods but also postulates a figurative "rupture" between one period and the next, making it difficult to identify the characteristics that link successive periods together.[5] Simply dividing the historical spectrum into decades is clearly premised on an inherently arbitrary unit of temporal segmentation. Therefore, if we aspire to complete accuracy, we must bring literature into dialogue with political, economic, societal, and other relevant dimensions of the human experience; only then will it be possible to produce a truly representative explanation.

Even if we were to set aside the question of the precise durations of the various historical periods, we would still be left with the undeniable fact that, after 1945, Taiwan literature was characterized by anti-Communist, modernist, and nativist tendencies. Literary scholarship has accepted virtually unanimously the use of these various categories to demarcate the literary styles of their respective historical periods.[6] However, if we rely merely on these sorts of terms, it will be difficult to grapple effectively with the overarching continuity of Taiwan's literary history, and, instead, we will tend to see it as a process of sporadic and uneven development. Therefore, it is certainly worth attempting to establish a relatively stable historical perspective from which to summarize and evaluate the entire development of Taiwan literature.

During the period of Japanese occupation, Taiwan could be considered a colonial society. The kinds of new literary movements to which such societies gave birth cannot be equated with the literary movements of an ordinary society. A Han-chauvinist perspective will obviously overlook many of the complexities inherent in the actual content of that literature. Similarly, if one uses Han chauvinism to summarize the literature from the Japanese occupation to the postwar period, this would have the effect of painstakingly erasing from that tradition the true character of Taiwanese society.[7] Is it possible that, after the departure of the Japanese, the colonial quality of that tradition simply disappeared without a trace? Or that, after the arrival of the Nationalist government, the earlier colonial wounds were all suddenly healed? The most difficult period of Taiwanese literary history to understand is that between the end of the War of the Pacific (World War II) in 1945 and the February Twenty-eighth Incident of 1947 (the slaughter of thousands of Taiwanese by Chiang Kai-shek's Chinese troops and the beginning of martial law). Virtually all scholars have seen it as a moment of absolute rupture. It is as if the Taiwanese authors from the period of Japanese occupation had followed the Japanese warlords' surrender and abruptly declared that they were going to simply disappear and then, after the Nationalist government took control of Taiwan, immediately reappeared and made a new beginning. Nevertheless, realistically speaking, Taiwanese writers located at the interstices of these two eras would not necessarily have undergone any significant change at the level of ideology and spirit.

As is well-known, during the War of the Pacific Japan forcibly implemented the policy of imperialization, or kōminka, which took a devastating toll on the souls of Taiwanese authors. Even authors with very well-developed critical faculties, such as Yang Kui and Lü Heruo, ended up producing propagandistic works for the kōminka movement. When that powerful Japanese nationalism overrode Taiwanese society, the colonial authors simply lost their ability to resist.[8] Kōminka literature produced, within the perspective of Taiwanese literary history, a challenge to national self-recognition as well as perplexity at the level of ethnic identity. Therefore, these developments simply cannot be evaluated from the perspective of Chinese nationalism. Nevertheless, it must be asked whether the uncertainty and confusion experienced by Taiwanese writers after the end of the War of the Pacific can be neatly isolated from developments during the wartime period.

When the Nationalist government arrived in Taiwan in 1945, it forcefully brought Chinese nationalism. In order to suppress the traces of Japanese Pan-Asianism that remained in Taiwan, in 1946 the Nationalist government issued an official proclamation forbidding the use of Japanese, less than a decade after the Japanese warlords' inverse proclamation, in 1937, forbidding the use of Chinese. With the change in times came a change in the characteristics of the government. Those authors remaining in Taiwan had no alternative but to adapt to two different linguistic systems, and, furthermore, they also had to adapt to the different sets of nationalist ideologies lying behind each of those systems. The Nationalist government used military might to promote its Chinese nationalist ideology, replete with violence and intimidation. This fact is reflected not only in government structure, such as that constructed by the Taiwan Provincial Administrative Executive Office, but also in the discriminatory attitude toward indigenous Taiwanese that was implicit in the decrees regarding the use of the Chinese language issued by the government. The February Twenty-eighth Incident could be described as a tragedy resulting from cultural difference, and, as such, it clearly revealed the colonial quality of the Nationalist government. In Taiwan's colonial history (e.g., during the Dutch period in the seventeenth century), foreign rulers were extraordinary in their use of methods of extreme violence to suppress the initiatives of Taiwanese citizens.[9]

The introduction of Chinese nationalism into Taiwan can be seen as a fictional and even factional dissemination. In particular, the Nationalist government's raising of the Nationalist flag constituted a welcome to only those literary works favorable to its own position, while those authors who were critical of the political orthodoxy were vigorously excluded. For instance, the government rigorously suppressed the works of the May Fourth author Lu Xun and did not allow them to circulate in Taiwan at all.[10] This censorship testifies to the fact that the Nationalist government's "nationalism" was actually a divisive political ideal, based on considerations of what was advantageous to the "part," rather than what was actually best for the "whole" national populace itself. Taiwanese writers experienced no less suppression and humiliation under the Nationalists than under the Japanese kōminka regime. Apart from purely national distinctions between Japan and China, there is ultimately no significant difference between the legacy of Japanese warlordism and the language policy of and the cultural movements supported by the Chinese Nationalist government.

Therefore, from the perspective of literary history, the period following 1945 has been designated as postwar. This, however, merely points to a neutral and objective fact and cannot touch on the darkness of the inner world of the Taiwanese authors themselves. Moreover, it is even less able to address the predicament of the social environment in which these authors actually found themselves. The Japanese scholar Ozaki Hideki once remarked that literary development from 1937 to 1945 was characterized by "Taiwan literature [being in a] decisive battle."[11] If we can use the term *decisive battle* here, then why must it be used only to describe the military situation during this period, instead of embracing the inner pain and struggle of the Taiwanese authors themselves as well? Their spiritual decisive battle unfortunately lay in having to choose between resistance and submission to the powerful Nationalist government.[12] This sort of stark choice at the spiritual level did not end with the conclusion of the war. Instead, when Japanese Pan-Asianism was replaced by Chinese Nationalism as Taiwan's ruling regime, Taiwanese authors' intellectual confusion and the contradictions with which they were faced could not be encompassed by the simple term *postwar*. In reality, what they faced was a *recolonized era*.

Using the term *recolonized era* to replace *postwar era*, it becomes possible to characterize fairly accurately Taiwanese society after 1945. Not only does recolonized era allow us to relate back to the kōminka period following the War of the Pacific, but, at the same time, it also allows us to look forward to the post-1950 period during which anti-Communist literature reached its height. More specifically, past explanations have tended to use the historical fact of the Japanese surrender to mark a figurative turning point in Taiwanese literary history. As a result, authors who came of age during the war period, such as Lü Heruo, Zhang Wenhuan, and Long Yingzong, and the younger generation, including such figures as Wu Zhuoliu, Zhong Lihe, Zhong Zhaozheng, and Ye Shitao, have been effectively divided into two distinct groups.[13] Their dejection during the war, together with their disappearance during the period of Nationalist recovery, can, therefore, be seen as an extension of essentially the same sentiment. Yang Kui's execution, Zhang Wenhuan's imprisonment, Wu Xinrong's being placed under surveillance, Lü Heruo's involvement with a guerrilla group, Zhu Dianren's assassination—these examples are sufficient to demonstrate the peril of Taiwanese authors during the period of recolonization. In his commentary on Lü Heruo's and Zhu Dianren's literary careers, Zhang Henghao posed the following problem:

> They were both truthful recorders and thinkers with respect to the colonial period, even though they had never actually participated in the social resistance activities. But what seems really curious is that, when Japanese ruling power was replaced, in the postwar period, by Chen Yi's political control, Lü and Zhu both coincidentally made the same choice. At the point at which their respective liter-

ary careers were gradually blossoming, they both abruptly and without hesitation bid farewell to the creation of beautiful dreams and, instead, invested their creative energies in the current of social turmoil, loudly singing songs of liberation. This is truly a perplexing problem.[14]

The reason that Zhang felt confused by this situation was simply that he could not explain the ruling character of the Nationalist government. If we go a step further and compare the literary policies of the anti-Communist period and those of the kōminka period, then it becomes apparent that the ways in which politics intrudes into Taiwanese authors' work are, ultimately quite similar.

In view of this comparison, an earlier query of Zhang Henghao's can be easily answered. In January of the twenty-fifth year of the Zhaohe reign (i.e., 1940), the Pan-Taiwan Society of Artists was founded in order to accompany the *kōminka fenggong hui* [great and just society]. The second article of the constitution of the society read as follows: "This Society, in accordance with the national spirit, draws on the literary and artistic movements in order to join in a common effort to realize our collective goal of creating a new cultural system."[15] Precisely a decade later (May 1950), the Nationalist government, in order to promote the so-called anti-Communist literature and arts, similarly founded the Pan-Taiwan Society of Chinese Literature and Arts. Its constitution appears to have been written in the spirit of the kōminka movement: "In addition to uniting literary and artistic public figures from throughout the entire country, researching literary theory, launching new literary movements, and developing literary undertakings, [this society] is even more importantly concerned with advancing the cultural construction of the Three People's Principles[16] and completing the task of anti-Communist Russian resistance as well as that of restoring and rebuilding the nation."[17] The kōminka and the anti-Communist policies both encouraged Taiwanese authors to engage in the historic task of literarily dedicating themselves to their country. This task did not originate from within Taiwanese society itself; rather, it existed solely to consolidate a colonial regime imported from abroad.

Although the system of martial law was disguised by an anti-Communist facade, it was, nevertheless, undoubtedly merely another transformation of the preceding colonial system. If we can accept this premise, then Taiwan's colonial literature certainly did not end with the conclusion of the War of the

Pacific; rather, it traverses the 1945 juncture. In other words, colonial literature came into being in the 1920s, reached maturity during the 1930s, had a decisive engagement during the 1940s, then linked up with the anti-Communist era of the 1950s. Accordingly, it was not until the lifting of martial law that Taiwan was finally liberated from the colonial regime.

MODERNISM AND NATIVISM

If the neocolonial period is seen as having begun in 1945, then how can we explain the appearance of modernist literature in the 1960s and nativist literature in the 1970s? The rise of modernist literature in the 1960s has, in the past, been subjected to strenuous criticism on the grounds that its entry into Taiwan was merely a kind of "formal transplanting." However, why should this have happened in the first place? In discussing the literary history of the period, Ye Shitao used strong language to criticize this phenomenon: "Not only were they [the modernist authors] not yet able to accept the mainland literary tradition, but, furthermore, they did not understand Taiwan's three-hundred-year history of being colonized under foreign rule while at the same time also lacking an adequate understanding of the history of the new literary movement that developed during the period of Japanese occupation." Moreover, Ye specifically pointed to modernist literature's tendency to abandon reality:

> It has become a self-evident truth that these kinds of "rootless and parasitic" literary topics have become removed from the history and reality of Taiwan's public, while at the same time the tendency of the totally Westernized avant-garde literature is also completely incommensurate with Taiwan's literary history. Taiwan literature has its own long-standing tradition, leading back to the end of the Ming dynasty. There are common threads that can be pursued from classical Chinese to modern colloquial Chinese. It was only under the turmoil of the 1940s and 1950s that this tradition came to be severed.[18]

It is very clear that Ye Shitao is unable to find a historical ground from which to explain the uneven development of modernist literature. Apart from the broad generalizations of the literature's having lost its historical memory and broken away from Taiwanese reality, he completely fails to speak to the problem of the political atmosphere of the period. If it is considered from the perspective of the time of recolonization, the birth of modernist literature should not be surprising. Under the control of the colonial regime, writers, like other intellectuals, did not have any opportunity to come into contact with the past. In all colonized societies, "historical amnesia" is a ubiquitous cultural phenomenon. Bai Xianyong, the founder of *Modern Literature*, an important literary journal of the 1960s, provided an extremely accurate description: "These contemporary writers don't have any opportunity to read works from earlier periods. Since the works of Lu Xun, Mao Dun, and other leftist writers have all been censored, our contemporary writers cannot, therefore, benefit from the inheritance of previous eras and are, consequently, unable to find an object that they can imitate, copy, and contest."[19]

Is it not the common experience of colonial societies to be lacking in history, tradition, and memory? In spite of Bai Xianyong's having come to Taiwan from mainland China and, moreover, having been born into a ruling-class household, his experiences were, ultimately, no different from those of native-born Taiwanese authors. Under colonial rule, writers do not necessarily use orthodox means of resistance and criticism; rather, they use self-exile to express their spirit of resistance. Especially after their historical memory has completely disappeared, colonial writers do not have any spiritual stronghold to provide the ground for resistance, and their works necessarily project "rootlessness and exile."

This so-called state of self-exile is the authors' inability to come to terms with living under the political ideology and political system of Taiwan. Their only means of psychological release lay in borrowing inspiration from Western literature and using modernist creative techniques to express their inner anxiety, dejection, and hopelessness. As a result, the response to their problems definitely cannot be found outside Taiwan's repressive political regime. We must, therefore, doubt those approaches that offer only a partial exegesis of the modernist period. To take Lü Zhenghui's critique of Ye Shitao's historical view as an example, we can see that, to a large extent, it continued to diverge from the reality of Taiwan's colonial regime:

> The problem of Taiwan's Westernization is still much more complex than Ye Shitao imagined. The full-scale Westernization of the 1950s and 1960s must be viewed in the perspective of the post–World War II Cold War détente between the United States and the Soviet Union. China's division was, to a certain extent, comparable to the division of North and South Korea, North and South Vietnam,

and East and West Germany, insofar as they were all the products of the struggle between the United States and the Soviet Union. The unique development of Taiwan's culture during the 1950s and 1960s could be said to be a reflection of this "world" situation, and, similarly, Taiwan's nativist movement in the 1970s was also intimately related to America's political development in the Third World.[20]

Taiwan's anti-Communist policy was obviously intimately bound up with the postwar standoff between the two global superpowers as well as with Taiwan's status as a political satellite of the United States. However, this explanation would appear to absolve the Taiwanese colonial regime of all responsibility while at the same time completely erasing the subjectivity of the modernist authors. The constructive force of this environment is, perhaps, not something that Taiwan's rulers were able to control; however, the fact that the policies of the colonial regime were directly applied to the modernist writers themselves is something for which the rulers cannot escape responsibility. Therefore, authors wished to reflect as well as avoid not simply general resistance to the interference of the Americans and the Soviets but specifically the repressive culture that bound their flesh and spirit.

Up to this point, most Taiwanese discussions of modernist literature have adopted a negative and deprecatory attitude, influenced by the nativist debates of the 1970s. After the lifting of martial law, this attitude was gradually corrected, replaced by a more complete and balanced perspective.[21] Modernism in Western societies is primarily the product of the dual shock of capitalism and industrial civilization. The spiritual emptiness, isolation, and separation that accompany people's reification are all topics to which modernist authors have devoted a great deal of attention. Modernism in Taiwanese society has not followed a process of capitalist development; however, the political environment on the island has created an equivalent space, allowing modernism to drive straight in. The depression of Western intellectuals is the result of their facing the great machine of industrial civilization; the alienation of Taiwanese modernist authors is an effect of the power of the colonial regime. Peng Ruijin reached a similar conclusion: "During that period, when faced with that great ruling machine, when the individual did not receive any respect, and when humanity was subjected to severe condescension and distortion, an ideology stressing the liberation of the self remained very valuable and also had the courage to resist."[22] Peng's *great ruling machine* is simply another term for *hegemonic power*. Although modern literary works had not yet employed orthodox resistance, how could the search for interiority that characterized the entire period, together with the management of pure art, not be regarded as the best critical strategy against the ideological repression of the military regime?

If modernist literature can be seen as expressing a consciousness of self-exile, then the nativist literature that appeared in the 1970s can undoubtedly be seen as a spiritual return. *Release* and *return*—these two terms can be used to describe the two tendencies of colonial literature, orthodoxy and heterodoxy. In colonial societies, when the power of the rulers reaches its peak, writers invariably begin active self-exile. Whether that self-exile is internal or external, it is a gesture of silent protest. When the rulers' power starts to decline, writers are free finally to begin to "return home." For example, at the height of the anti-Communist period in the 1960s, foreign-born authors like Bai Xianyong and native authors like Chen Yingzhen both wrote many stories about people who had left home, mysteriously disappeared, or committed suicide. These sorts of works that take as their subject matter the destruction of human life could be said to reflect fairly directly their authors' state of psychological exile. The orthodox significance of modernist literary works in literary-historical terms should be approached from this angle.

During the early 1970s, the political premise that the Nationalist government "represents China" came under unprecedented attack in international circles, and, as a result, the colonial system in Taiwan, which had previously stood tall, also began to crumble. At this juncture, when the entire system of dominance was beginning to fall apart, Taiwanese authors began to use the political fissures to articulate their concern for the territory of Taiwan. Many of the literary characters that they created were based on models from their own immediate environments; this not only gave rise to the genre of nativist literature but also marked the height of a spirit of realism and of homecoming. Huafeng in the case of Wang Zhenhe, Yilan in the case of Huang Chunming, Jiling in the case of Wang Tuo, Lugang in the case of Li Ang, Yunlin in the case of Song Zelai, and Meinong in the case of Wu Jinfa: all of these native places became literary forces in the fashion for return that characterized the literary scene of the 1970s.

This is not to say that nativist literature must necessarily be restricted to direct representations of one's own native soil; neither does it constitute a denial of the continued development of modernist literature of the 1960s. The realist spirit that characterized nativist literature need not necessarily be firmly tied to the historical amnesia that was an explicit response to the prejudiced policies enforced during the period of martial law in Taiwan. The strategy of the colonizers is always to separate the people from their native soil, to exploit the indigenous resources while at the same time helping to prevent the colonized from achieving self-recognition. Therefore, nativist literature's rise was simply a matter of taking advantage of the instability of the colonial regime in order to regain attachment to the native soil and, thus, to retrieve lost memory. The reconstruction of historical memory is equivalent to the reconstruction of the emotional attachment between a people and their land; it is simply a matter of turning one's back on the strategies of the colonizers.

However, we must also remember that the critical spirit of 1970s realism was originally intended to uncover the biases inherent in the political-economic structure. As a result of the significant fetters placed on ideological investigation, the foundations of the system of colonial rule were not significantly challenged; instead, they became the scapegoat of 1960s modernist literature. From the modernist poetry debates of the early 1970s until the nativist literature debates that began in 1977, modernist literature and nativist literature represented two mutually opposed camps. Thus, literature was only obliquely critical of the political machine on which the Guomindang relied for survival, and, during the entire decade, that machine barely suffered at all.

The modernist poetry debates that surfaced between 1972 and 1973 originated in the Taiwanese poets' self-criticism of their loss of self-understanding. This is certainly not something that a writer strives to achieve; rather, it is the result of an oppressive political environment. However, these debates were directed not primarily at the unassailable regime of martial law but at the defenseless modernist poets themselves. One of the earliest critics of modernist poetry, Guan Jieming, had this to say: "Chinese poets truly mislearned their lessons from the Western authors; they will only be a danger to students and forever will only be copying, imitating, and parroting the words of others."[23] Elsewhere, he went on to criticize modernist poetry for being "an illustration of the simultaneous loss of identity and focus."[24] Guan appears to believe that modernist authors merely represent a reflection of Western aesthetic trends in Taiwan and, therefore, are merely passive objects of Westernization. Accordingly, he does not express any criticism of the repressive regime existing in Taiwan. When the official system prohibits all criticism, modernist artworks are borrowed to serve as scapegoats. Guan completely ignores the degree to which modernist literature has the potential to assume a positive significance. If modernist poetry constitutes concrete evidence of the simultaneous loss of both identity and focus, does this not testify to the success of the colonial regime's governance in Taiwan? When Guan speaks of "China" in his article, he is actually referring specifically to Taiwan. The fact that a writer with such a keen critical faculty should appear to confuse the identities of "China" and "Taiwan" stands as ample testimony to the degree to which historical amnesia afflicted Taiwan at the time.

The flame ignited by these debates over modernist poetry later spread to the debates over nativist literature. Begun in 1977, these constituted an ideological standoff between the writers and the political rulers. The attitude of "embracing the healthy earth" advocated by Taiwanese authors such as Wang Tuo was actually a reply by the subaltern to the ruling class. Wang wrote of his own works: "They all originate out of the unassailable love and respect felt for this land and its people."[25] His creative objective was clearly to restore the bond between the land and the people. By contrast, someone like Peng Ge, standing in the position of the rulers, used every conceivable means to mobilize grand narratives to defend the colonial system. In response to the arguments made by the nativist writers, he observed: "I hope that the small minority of detail-oriented people will be sincerely self-critical. I further hope that they will consider the predicament of the entire country, the difficulties of our 800-million-plus countrymen on the mainland, as well as the responsibility every intellectual should bear in this sort of era."[26] One of the ruling methods that the colonizers employ most effectively involves the use of grand narratives. The more grandiose the rhetoric, the easier it will be for the rulers' biases to be shielded from view, while the character and speech of the colonized become increasingly limited.

The nativist literature debates have been significant on a wide range of levels, and they have already been carefully examined by many scholars.[27] However, the most noteworthy of these commentaries is probably Wang Tuo's, one in which he uses the term *economic colonialism* to describe Taiwanese society during that period. Wang places particular emphasis on the fact that this term "refers specifically to a state of economic colonialism and not to political colonialism."[28] However, he is, perhaps, the first since 1945 to attempt to categorize the nature of Taiwanese society. He uses the phrase political colonialism to designate the model that has, he believes, no applicability to Taiwan and the phrase economic colonialism to refer specifically to Taiwan's relation to the United States. However, it is very clear that this kind of rhetoric already assumes that the Nationalist government can be seen as a proxy for economic colonialism. A ruling machine that relies on economic colonialism for its power is, undoubtedly, no more and no less than a form of political-colonial rule. If this kind of explanation is valid, then the nativist literature debates can, at some level, be seen as a thorough critique of the colonial system on the part of Taiwan's writers.

The ordering of Taiwan's literary heritage and the retrospective consideration of Taiwan's historical experience have both received only minimal attention. This testifies to the fact that Taiwan has only recently emerged from a deep historical amnesia. With the Kaohsiung Incident of 1979 (a clash between police and pro-democracy demonstrators), the last remnants of the nativist literature debate were temporarily brought to a close. However, this does not mean that the criticism of the colonial system also ended. The debates over unification that were first kindled at the beginning of 1980 actually followed closely on the unfinished discussions begun by the debates over nativist literature. It was only in the context of the Taiwanese literary perspective centering on Ye Shitao and Chen Yingzhen that Taiwanese authors for the first time began to use the phrase Taiwan literature in place of the more abstract Chinese literature.[29] This was part of a highly interesting literary polemic preceding the lifting of martial law. After a fiery baptism in the form of the heated debate, the term Taiwan literature finally settled down and assumed a fixed position.[30] The literary works produced by Taiwanese society had, in the end, to survive for forty years before they could attain a modicum of orthodox recognition. This, of course, is a highly ironic situation. The loss of cultural identity and self-recognition can be said to have seriously distorted Taiwanese literary history.

The debates over independence and unification from 1982 to 1984 represented one of the most penetrating critiques of the colonial system. The term Taiwan literature finally received wide acceptance, although that literature's form and content were still subject to a considerable degree of political and ideological constraint. Although the attempted recovery of historical memory had already begun in the 1970s, its effectiveness was, ultimately, very limited owing to the continuing control exercised by the oppressive military regime. Exploration of the internal contradictions existing within

Taiwanese society was still not possible. That had to wait until the lifting of martial law, whereupon the colonial structure of feudal Taiwanese society was finally opened up, and its multifaceted literature began to grow day by day.

POSTMODERN OR POSTCOLONIAL?

It is beyond dispute that Taiwan literature became much more eclectic and vital following the lifting of martial law, as testified to by literary trends including feminist and aboriginal literature as well as by the appearance of postmodern literature. This is easily understandable because the people's most fundamental desires and abilities had long been suppressed, but never completely destroyed. After these ideological fetters were finally removed, all sorts of previously hushed voices were finally able to speak. Furthermore, in a scenario reminiscent of postmodern Western societies, the development of a multiplicity of literatures went hand in hand with the growth of Taiwan's economic productivity. Therefore, a few literary critics explicitly designated this complex period a postmodern epoch.

The first person to announce that Taiwan had become a postmodern society was Luo Qing, who observed that the data concerning Taiwan's electronics sector, combined with the degree to which its service sector had already overtaken its manufacturing sector, was ample evidence that Taiwanese society "has formally entered that which is known as postmodern society. Moreover, from the perspective of its cultural development, Taiwan also clearly displays many postmodern characteristics."[31] Luo's pronouncement was immediately accepted by Meng Fan. In his own discussion of postmodernism, Meng extended this line of reasoning even further, arguing: "In the transitional period during which a postindustrial society had not fully formed, postmodern poetry could not yet achieve popularity in Taiwan's poetic circles."[32] The question of whether Taiwanese society had, in fact, witnessed the arrival of the postmodern period certainly remains very important.

Even if we temporarily put aside the issue of whether a Taiwanese postmodern or postindustrial society has formed and consider only the specific vicissitudes of the development of Taiwan's literary history, we may still ask whether post–martial law Taiwan literature may be designated postmodern in the first place. In the United States, the development of postmodernism followed on the heels of the decline of modernism, and the *post-* in postmodernism has two different connotations. On the one hand, it signals resistance to and rejection of modernism, most specifically during the 1960s. On the other hand, it designates an extension of modernism that developed in the 1970s and after.[33] Either way, the coining of the term *postmodernism* implies that that which preceded it was, in fact, a modern(ist) period. If we consider the development of Taiwan literature from this perspective, then, for postmodernism to have been successfully realized, there must have been a prior period of modernism. However, history indicates that, from the 1960s, Taiwan literature followed the trajectory of modernism to nativist realism to postmodernism. In other words, Western literary and intellectual trends follow a natural development, and, if we accept Luo Qing's explanation, then Taiwan literature has followed a pattern of discontinuous development. It is not that this form of discontinuous literary development cannot take place but that, in the context of the trends of Taiwan literature, it nevertheless appears quite abruptly. Luo Qing's designation of post-1980s Taiwanese society as postmodern has already been subjected to strong criticism. Chen Guangxing has stated that this view represents "the gradual eruption of a complication arising from the blind pursuit of the popular sign of postmodernity."[34] That is to say, he believes that Luo Qing's designation has no actual grounding in either the inner content of Taiwanese society or Taiwan's literary development.

If we wish to describe Taiwan's post-1980s literary phenomenon, we cannot ignore the entire developmental process that led to it. If the period of Japanese occupation can be termed colonial and the post-1945 period neocolonial, then the period following the lifting of martial law can be termed postcolonial. The *post-* refers not to the end of the colonial experience but to the fact that contact between the colonized and the colonial regime had already begun. With regard to the regime, colonial authors will invariably express active resistance (such as criticism) or passive resistance (e.g., in the form of self-exile or banishment). Therefore, this *post-* connotes a strong quality of resistance.

Using this sort of perspective to survey twentieth-century Taiwanese literary history, one reaches the clear conclusion that Taiwanese authors never abandoned their resistance to the dominance of the colonial power. During the maturational period of leftist literature in the 1930s, they actively criticized the encroachment of Japanese imperialism, and, during the period of kōminka literature during the 1940s, they adopted a spirit of passive exile. During the anti-Communist period of the 1950s and the modernist period of the 1960s, this spirit of exile developed even more. Finally, during the realist period of the 1970s and after, active critique once again rose to the surface. The uneasy relation of margin to center that Taiwanese authors adopted with respect to the rulers permeated the entire body of "new literature." Postmodernism stresses the theme of rejection of the center or of a "culture of resistance."[35] It can be said that this kind of spirit is richly embedded within Taiwanese literary works.

The character of postmodernism is quite similar to that of postcolonialism, and this is probably the primary reason that some Taiwanese scholars have confused the two concepts. Postmodernism is located within a discourse of deconstructing the narratives of centralized state power and of Euro-American logocentrism. Postcolonialism, by contrast, is located within a discourse of dissolving imperialist and colonial dichotomies of center and margin.[36] Both these systems of thought are concerned with critiquing the center as well as with advocating cultural plurality and affirming the existence and status of the other. Therefore, critics frequently conflate them. However, postmodernism developed out of high-capitalist Euro-America, while postcolonialism has its roots in the Third World. Even more noteworthy, the ultimate subject of postmodernism lies in the *deconstruction* of subjectivity, while postcolonialism aspires to the *reconstruction* of subjectivity. There are many contexts in which these two bodies of thought may mutually reinforce each other, but their respective spiritual contents must be carefully distinguished.

While Liao Xianhao was editing his 1996 *Bashi si nian duanpian xiaoshuo xuan* [A selection of short fiction from the year 1984], he openly pronounced that postmodern thought had already started to take root in Taiwan. He cited several short stories from 1995 as evidence that a "postmodern spirit" was already evident in every corner of society. His was an extremely broad understanding of the meaning of postmodernity:

> These various schools of thought that are grouped under the rubric of postmodernism all take "antienlightenment" as their basis, and, in their respective subjects, they each elaborate a "grand narrative." Examples of this tendency can be seen in feminism's grand narrative of a critique of patriarchy, gender discourse's critique of gender determination, postcolonialism's critique of colonialism, sub-

> alternity's critique of hegemonic discourses, information technologies critiquing traditional modes of information dissemination. . . .[37]

This kind of argument conveniently intersects with my position at several points. This essay uses the concept of a hegemonic discourse to embrace each of the various kinds of cultural chauvinism already existing in Taiwanese society, while Liao uses the term grand narrative to accomplish the same purpose. The greatest point of divergence between my own argument and his lies in the fact that Liao subsumes postcolonialism under the larger rubric of postmodernism, while I contend that this perspective is completely incompatible with the realities of postwar Taiwanese history.

First of all, there is the issue of historical explanation. Liao Xianhao declares that the postmodern spirit has already taken root in Taiwan, but he fails to come to terms with the question of how it was formed. If it is seen as an all-encompassing ideological trend, such that even Taiwan's postcolonial history could be included within it, then we should be able to identify a historical period of gestation of postmodern thought in Taiwanese society itself. If, however, this postmodernity resembles instead the modernism that was imported during the 1960s—suddenly appearing in the absence of any special historical conditions—then it must be seen as nothing more or less than a form of neocolonialism. Taiwanese society has only partially accepted the challenge presented by foreign schools of thought and is only a passive character subject to outside influence, not possessing any autonomously subjective aspirations.

Postmodernism was introduced into Taiwanese society following the relaxing of martial law in the 1980s. Even if it is true that, during this period, Taiwan began to be influenced by postindustrial society or late capitalism, that is not sufficient to demonstrate that postmodern thought had any historical ground prior to this. What I want to stress here is that the postmodern spirit did not arise naturally out of Taiwanese society itself and, as a result, has absolutely no connection with Taiwan's postwar history. Therefore, I remain highly dubious about any attempt to take the counterhegemonic tendencies of the current generation of Taiwanese writers and uniformly group them under the rubric of postmodern thought.

Furthermore, there is also the issue of the structure of power. The dominance of postwar neocolonialism resulted in the colonial presence in society becoming more invisible. In other words, because the postwar martial law regime was exceedingly vast, its power permeated every corner of Taiwanese society. All the members of each class were forced to believe in a single value system. The hegemonic discourse that originated in China irrationally suppressed the already existing and solidly entrenched power regimes that had developed historically. For instance, the oppression of women under feudal patriarchy, the prejudice toward indigenous peoples on the part of Han Chinese immigrants, the rejection of homosexuals by heterosexuals — all these became forbidden topics during the height of the period of martial law.

Therefore, after martial law was abolished, the biased power structure existing within Taiwanese society finally began to manifest itself. The feminist, queer, juancun, and aboriginal issues, which had previously been obscured by historical amnesia, all reappeared during this period of remembrance. These "marginal" social groups all arrived simultaneously at the interrelated issues of recognition, identity, and subjectivity. Reallocation's demand for power and multiculturalism's demand for value both came to characterize the post–martial law atmosphere. This kind of thinking is not just decentered but decolonized. These groups' aspirations for liberation did not have to wait until the introduction of postmodern thought into Taiwan; rather, it was precisely the end of martial law that enabled previously suppressed desires to be unbound. The strategies used by each subaltern group might, perhaps, bear some resemblance to a postmodern spirit, but their ultimate goal was, certainly, not the *de*construction but the *re*construction of subjectivity. To be more precise, the pursuit of a pluralistic system actually has developed out of the internal currents of Taiwan's own history and, certainly, is not the result of influence by the root of the postmodern spirit.

Liao Ping-hui once observed: "The discourses that developed out of the experience of postmodernism's specific history are not necessarily applicable to other societies."[38] This is understandable in that various colonial experiences need not necessarily have points of overlap or mutual resonance. The development of Taiwan's postwar literature can be examined only in the context of Taiwanese society's own unique historical trajectory. A postmodern sensibility truly exists only in Western late capitalist societies and has no direct applicability to Taiwanese society. The pluralistic development of Taiwan literature has undoubtedly been influenced by the demands of Taiwan's historical development, and, therefore, its postcolonial character vastly exceeds its imported postmodern character. There are some postcolonial theories that derive from the historical experience of other Third World nations, and these need not necessarily be truly applicable to Taiwanese society either. Therefore, the question of how to interpret Taiwan's history and literary evolution, while at the same time constructing a comprehensive explanation to account for the entire literary history, represents a challenge with which any contemporary literary critic must come to terms.

The lifting of martial law did not necessarily signal the complete disappearance of Taiwan's colonial culture. Taiwanese authors gave more attention to the process of beginning to reconstruct their historical memory, and also began a deeper examination of the past political injury; thereby, a postcolonial character gradually began to manifest itself in Taiwanese society. Vigilant scholars have also very diligently used postcolonial discourses to reflect on and reevaluate Taiwan literature.[39] If this kind of attention continues, postcolonial theory will come to have a special position in the study and critique of Taiwan literature. Postcolonial literature can accept textual pluralism. Therefore, during Taiwan's postcolonial period of maturation, the appearance of literary works bearing characteristics reminiscent of postmodernism can certainly find a place.

NOTES

This essay was translated by Carlos Rojas. Unless otherwise indicated, all translations from non-English-language sources are his.

1   These quotations are taken from the version of Shimada Kinji's "Taiwan no bungakuteki kagenmatsu" [Taiwan's literary modernism] that appeared in Ozaki Hideki's *Kyūshokuminchi bungakuo no kenkyū* [A study of old colonial literature] (Tokyo: Keisō Yobō, 1971), 156–57, where there is also a discussion of Shimada's perspective on literary history. The original version of "Taiwan no bungakuteki kagenmatsu" appeared as "Taiwan de wenxue guome" [Taiwan's literary modernism] in *Wenyi Taiwan* 2.2 (1941).

    This facet of the periodization of Taiwan literature is most representative of the colonial attitudes during the period of Japanese occupation. While Shimada Kinji was serving as a lecturer at the Taipei Imperial University, he folded Taiwan literature into a politicized understanding of Japanese literature following the occupation of Taiwan. See also Ye Jimin, "Riju shidai de 'waidi wenxue' cankao" [Reference material on the "literature of the outlying regions" during the period of Japanese occupation], *Si yu yan* 32.2 (June 1995): 307.

2   This attitude is manifested particularly clearly in Liu Denghan, Zhuang Mingxuan, Huang Zhongtian, Lin Chenghuang, et al., eds., *Taiwan wenxue shi* [Tai-

wanese literary history], 2 vols. (Fuzhou: Haixia wenyi chubanshe, 1991-93), esp. 1:3-13.
3   For the literary debates over the issue of unification or secession, see Shi Minhui, ed., *Taiwan yishi lunzhan xuanji* [Selected essays from the debate on Taiwanese consciousness] (Taipei: Qianhui, 1989). For an introductory summary of these literary debates, see Xie Chunxin, "Bashi niandai chuqi Taiwan wenxue lunzhan zhi tantao" [A discussion of the Taiwanese literary debates from the early 1980s], *Taiwan wenxue guancha zazhi* [Journal for the observation of Taiwan literature] 9 (1994): 51-63.
4   Chen Fangming, *Dianfan de zhuiqiu* [Pursuit of models] (Taipei: Lianhe wenxue, 1994), 235.
5   For further discussion of this issue of literary periodization, see Yue Mengfan and Lin Yaode, eds., "Yi dangdai shiye shuxie bashi niandai Taiwan wenxue shi" [Writing 1980s Taiwanese literary history from the perspective of the present], in *Shijimo pianhang* [Fin de siècle deviations] (Taipei: Shibao wenxue, 1990), 7-12.
6   For the conventional usages of the terms *anti-Communist literature, modernist literature*, and *nativist literature*, see Ye Shitao, *Taiwan wenxueshi gang* [An outline of Taiwanese literary history] (Kaohsiung: Wenxue jie, 1987); and Peng Ruijin, *Taiwan xin wenxue yundong 40 nian* [Forty years of Taiwan's new literature movement] (Taipei: Zili baoxi, 1991).
7   A recent, representative piece using the perspective of Han chauvinism to explain Taiwanese historical development is Chen Shaoying, "Lun Taiwan de bentuhua yundong: Yi ge wenhuashi de kaocha" [Discussing Taiwan's nativist movement: A cultural-historical investigation], *Zhongwai wenxue* 23.9 (February 1995): 5-43.
8   Two discussions of the development of Taiwan literature during the war are particularly useful: Wang Shaowen, "Rizhi moqi Taiwan de zhishe shequn (1940-1945): *Wenxue Taiwan, Taiwan wenxue*, ji *Minsu Taiwan* san zazhi de lishi yanjiu" [Taiwanese intellectual organizations at the end of the period of Japanese rule (1940-1945): A historical investigation of the journals *Literary Taiwan, Taiwan Literature*, and *Taiwan Folk Customs*] (MA thesis, Qinghua University, 1991); and Liu Shuqin, "Zhanzheng yu wentan: Riju moqi Taiwan de wenxue huodong" [War and literary circles: Taiwanese literary movements during the final years of Japanese occupation] (MA thesis, Academica Sinica, 1994).
9   On the Dutch period in Taiwan's colonial history, see Leonard Blusse, "Retribution and Remorse: The Interaction between the Administration and the Protestant Mission in Early Colonial Formosa," in Gyan Prakast, ed., *After Colonialism: Imperial Histories and Postcolonial Displacement* (Princeton: Princeton University Press, 1995), 153-82.
10 For an introduction to the reception of Lu Xun's works in Taiwan during the early postwar period, see Huang Yingzhi, "Lu Xun sixiang zai Taiwan de

chuanbo, 1945–1949: Shilun zhanhou chuqi Taiwan de wenhua chongjian yu guojia rentong" [The dissemination of Lu Xun's thought in Taiwan, 1945–1949: An inquiry into cultural reconstruction and national recognition during the early postwar period], in *Rentong yu guojia: Jindai zhongxi lishi de bijiao xueshu taolunhui* [Recognition and nation: Proceedings from a conference on the comparison of Chinese and Western modern historical issues] (Taipei: Institute of Historical Studies, Zhongyang yanjiuyuan, June 1994). For the official campaign to proscribe Lu Xun's works over the past forty years, see Chen Fangming, "Lu Xun zai Taiwan" [Lu Xun in Taiwan], in *Dianfan de zhuiqiu*, 305–39.

11 Ozaki Hideki, "Kessenka no Taiwan bungaku" [Taiwan literature during the decisive battle], in *Kyūshokuminchi bungakuo no kenkyū*, 54–220.

12 For a comprehensive study of the resistance and submission of Taiwanese authors during the War of the Pacific, see Lin Ruiming, "Yundong de linghun: Juezhan shiqi Taiwan zuojia yu huangmin wenxue" [The spirit of a movement: Taiwanese authors during the war period and kōminka literature], in *Riju shiqi Taiwan shi guoji xueshu yantaohui lunwenji* [Taiwanese history during the period of Japanese occupation: A compendium of papers from an international conference] (Taipei: History Department, Academica Sinica, 1993), 443–61.

13 Wu Zhuoliu and Zhong Lihe are discussed in detail in Ping-hui Liao, "Travel in Early-Twentieth-Century Asia: On Wu Zhuoliu's 'Nanking Journals' and His Notion of Taiwan's Alternative Modernity" (chapter 12 in this volume); and Fenghuang Ying, "The Literary Development of Zhong Lihe and Postcolonial Discourse in Taiwan" (chapter 6 in this volume).

14 Zhang Henghao, "Qi ling'er de canmeng: Zhu Dianren ji qi xiaoshuo" [Vestigial dreams of a unicorn: Zhu Dianren and his fiction], in *Juexing de daoguo* [Awakened island] (Tainan: Tainan Shili wenhua zhongxin, 1995), 142. ("Qi ling'er de canmeng" originally appeared in *Taiwan wenxue* 105 [May 1987].)

15 Cited from Ozaki, "Kessenka no Taiwan bungaku," 214.

16 Sun Yat-sen's emphasis on nationalism, democracy, and people's livelihood, which became one of the underlying principles of the Nationalist government.

17 Cited from Hu Yannan, "Zhanhou Taiwan wenxueshi shang diyi ci heng de yizhi: Xin de wenxueshi fenqifa zhi shiyan" [The first lateral transplant in postwar Taiwanese literary history: An experiment with a new periodization method for literary history], *Taiwan wenxue guancha zazhi* 6 (September 1992): 32.

18 Ye, *Taiwan wenxueshi gang*, 116–17.

19 Bai Xianyong, "Liulang de Zhongguoren: Taiwan xiaoshuo de fangzhu zhuti" [Roaming Chinese: The theme of exile in Taiwan fiction], trans. Zhou Zhaoxiang, *Mingbao yuekan* [Mingbao monthly] (Hong Kong), January 1976.

20 Lü Zhenhui, "Ping Ye Shitao *Taiwan wenxueshi gang*" [A critique of Ye Shitao's *An Outline of Taiwanese Literary History*], *Taiwan shehui yanjiuqikan* [Taiwanese journal of social studies] 1.1 (1988): 225.

21 There has already been considerable scholarly attention paid to the wide influ-

ence of the journal *Xiandai wenxue* [Modern literature], including Shen Jinglan, "Dang xifeng zouguo: Liuling niandai *Xiandai wenxue* pai de lunshu yu kaocha" [When the Western wind blows over: Discussion and investigation of the 1960s Modern Literature school] (MA thesis, Guoli chenggong University, 1994); and Lin Weishu, "*Xiandai wenxue* xiaoshuo chuangzuo ji yijie de wenxue lilun de yanjiu" [A study of *Modern Literature*'s literary creation and translated literary theory] (MA thesis, Guoli zhongshan University, 1995).

22 Peng, *Taiwan xin wenxue yundong 40 nian*, 110.
23 Guan Jieming, "Zhongguo xiandai shi de kunjing" [The predicament of modern Chinese poetry], in Zhao Zhiti, ed., *Xiandai wenxue de kaocha* [Investigations of modern literature] (Taipei: Yuanhang, 1976), 142.
24 Guan Jieming, "Zai tan Zhongguo xiandai shi" [Discussing modern Chinese poetry once again], in ibid., 236–37.
25 Wang Tuo, "Yongbao jiankang dadi" [Embracing the healthy earth], in Wei Tiancong, ed., *Xiangtu wenxue taolun ji* [An anthology of discussions of nativist literature] (Taipei: privately published, 1976), 362.
26 Peng Ge, "Dui pianxiang de jingjue" [A sudden awakening regarding erroneous tendencies], in ibid., 236–37.
27 For a chronological survey of the entire span of the nativist literature debates, see Chen Zhengxing, "Taiwan de xiangtu wenxue lunzhan" [The Taiwanese nativist literature debates], ed. Lu Ren, *Ailiu* 2.2 (August 1982): 22–33; 2.3 (September 1982): 60–71. See also Zhou Yongfang, "Qishi niandai Taiwan xiangtu wenxue lunzhang yanjiu" [A study of the Taiwanese nativist literature debates of the 1970s] (MA thesis, Wenhua University, 1991).
28 Wang Tuo, "'Zhimindi yiyuan' haishi 'zizhu yiyuan'?" [Aspirations for colonialism or for autonomy?], in Wei, ed., *Xiangtu wenxue taolun ji*, 578–79.
29 Ye Shitao, "Taiwan xiangtu wenxue shi daolun" [An introduction to Taiwan nativist literature], in ibid., 69–92; Xu Nancun [Chen Yingzhen], "Xiangtu wenxue de mangdian" [Blind spot of nativist literature], in ibid., 93–99.
30 See Song Dongyang [Chen Fangming], "Xian jieduan Taiwan wenxue bentuhua de wenti" [The issue of the current stage of Taiwan's literary nativism process], *Taiwan wenyi* [Taiwanese literary arts] 86 (1984); reprinted in *Fangdan wenzhang pinming jiu* [Boldly writing articles and desperately drinking] (Taipei: Linbai, 1988).
31 Luo Qing, "Taiwan diqu de houxiandai zhuankuang" [The postmodern condition of the region of Taiwan], in *Shenme shi houxiandaizhuyi* [What is postmodernism?] (Taipei: Wusi shudian, 1989), 315.
32 Meng Fan, "Taiwan houxiandai shi de lilun yu shiji" [The theory and reality of postmodern poetry in Taiwan], in *Dangdai Taiwan xinshi lilun* [Theories of new poetry in contemporary Taiwan] (Taipei: Yangzhi, 1995), 223.
33 Andreas Huyssen, "Mapping the Postmodern," in Charles Jencks, ed., *The Post-Modern Reader* (London: Academy, 1992), 40–72.
34 Chen Guangxing, "Chaozuo houxiandai? Ping Meng Fan, Luo Qing, Zhong

Mingde de houdiandai guan" ["Fried postmodernity": A critique of the postmodern perspective of Meng Fan, Luo Qing, and Zhong Mingde], *Zili zaobao*, February 23, 1990, *Zili fukan* [Zili supplement].

35 Of the Western scholars who have studied postcolonialism, the one who has done the most useful work on the rejection of the center and cultures of resistance has undoubtedly been Edward Said. See his *Orientalism* (London: Penguin, 1978); and *Culture and Imperialism* (New York: Vintage, 1993).

36 Kwame Anthony Appiah, "The Postcolonial and the Postmodern," in Bill Ashcroft, Gareth Griffeths, and Helen Tiffin, eds., *The Post-Colonial Studies Reader* (New York: Routledge, 1995), 119–24.

37 Liao Xianhao, "Fuyan guanhua, guyin gechang: Bashi si nian duanpian xiaoshuo de houxiandai fengmao" [Seeing flowers with a doubled gaze and singing songs with a doubled voice: The postmodern air of short fiction from the year 1984], in Liao Xianhao, ed., *Bashi si nian duanpian xiaoshuo xuan* [A selection of short fiction from the year 1984] (Taipei: Erya chubanshe, 1996), 6.

38 Liao Ping-hui, "Zai Taiwan tan houxiandai yu houzhimin lunshu" [A consideration of the discussions of postmodernism and postcolonialism in Taiwan], in *Huigu xiandai: Houxiandai yu hou zhimin lunwen ji* [Looking back on the modern: A collection of essays on postmodernism and postcolonialism] (Taipei: Maitian chubanshe, 1994), 69.

39 The number of scholars in Taiwan seeking to use postcolonial theory to discuss Taiwan literature has been increasing daily, and, of them, Qiu Guifen is particularly worthy of mention. See her "'Faxian Taiwan': Jiangou Taiwan houzhimin lunshu" ["Discovering Taiwan": Postcolonial discourse on the creation of Taiwan], *Zhongwai wenxue* [Chung-wai literary monthly] 242 (July 1992): 151–67; "Xiang wo (ziwo) fangzhu de xiongdi (jiejie)men: Yuedu di er dai 'waisheng' (nü)zuojia Zhu Tianxin" [Thinking of my (self-)exiled brothers (and sisters): Reading the second-generation "mainlander" (female) author Zhu Tianwen], *Zhongwai wenxue* 255 (March 1993): 94–120; "Xingbie/quanli/zhinmin lunshu: Xiangtu wenxue zhong de qushi nanren" [Gender/power/colonial discourse: Emasculated men in nativist literature], in Zheng Mingli, ed., *Dangdai Taiwan nüxing wenxue lun* [Discussions of contemporary literature by female Taiwanese writers] (Taipei: Shibao wenhua, 1993), 13–34. These articles have all been collected in Qiu Guifen, *Zhongjie: Taiwan nüren* [Secondary intermediaries: Taiwanese women] (Taipei: Yuanzun wenhua, 1997).

3

On the Concept of Taiwan Literature

Xiaobing Tang

Few debates about literary concepts, properties, and traditions in the contemporary Chinese-speaking world have generated as much passion and anxiety, and given rise to as much intellectual provocation and reflection, as the concept of Taiwan literature, which emerged in Taiwan in the early 1980s and remained a galvanizing force well into the 1990s. The number and variety of writings devoted to the debate are simply extraordinary, while the range as well as the depth of the topics examined go well beyond academic literary studies or campaigns for stylistic innovation. At issue is, apparently, the definition and positioning of Taiwan literature, but, in this sprawling debate, literary discourse largely serves as a contentious field through which a symbolic reconfiguration is carried out. Incidentally, the conventional English rendition of *Taiwan wenxue* as Taiwan literature brings to the fore the crux of the contention.[1] Should it instead be rendered as Taiwanese literature? What, then, would Taiwanese literature connote? And what would be the relation between this body of literature and Chinese literature? More specifically, what, if any, relation is there among literatures from Taiwan, Hong Kong, and mainland China? In offering their different, often emotionally charged answers to these questions, participants in the debate cannot help but address, either directly or implicitly, questions of origins, political legitimacy, hegemonic practices and institutions, and geopolitical implications on a local as well as a global scale. Sorting out Taiwan literature amounts to articulating one's own position vis-à-vis various overlapping structures of identity. Inevitably, literary discourse turns into a commentary on Taiwan's past as much as on its future, and the meaning of both is fraught with uncertainty in an age when all exclusionary claims of sovereignty over the island seem to be gravely contested.

For all these reasons, the controversy over the nature of Taiwan literature may have no less far-reaching an impact than the calls for a literary revolution that, announcing the arrival of the May Fourth enlightenment in the late 1910s, formally ushered in a new literature [xin wenxue] that would help establish the paradigm of modern Chinese literature. At stake may be precisely the nation-centered conception and legitimation of a literary tradition in modern Chinese. Whereas the emancipatory vision shared by the proponents and practitioners of the May Fourth new literature revolved around a radically modernized Chinese nation and civilization, its underlying assumption of an integrative national identity is now actively interrogated in the discourse on Taiwan literature. The nationalist imaginary that enabled the self-assertion of new literature is both embraced and rejected, often simultaneously, by advocates of a native literary tradition. For their vision affirms the native literary tradition as of both regional and national significance, and the aspiration of Taiwan literature, at least for some polemicists, is to distinguish itself as the consciousness of a nation in formation. An increasingly diverse body of literature is, thus, given the mythopoetic task of creating and naming a new national culture and polity. Consequently, the nativist pursuit of a "new and independent literature" raises a host of intricate historical and theoretical issues and compels critical reflection on the configuration of modern Chinese literature.[2] In short, the effort to institute a "new national literature" of Taiwan at once duplicates and calls into question the ideological underpinnings of the May Fourth new literature.[3] In the nativist independence drive, there is even a distant echo of the anti-Manchu ethnic discourse that served as a double-edged emotional incitement during the last years of the Qing dynasty. From this perspective of historical continuity and repetition, the heated contention over Taiwan literature is all the more rich and resonant and demands careful attention from students of modern Chinese history and literature.

In what follows, I try to trace the development of the idea of Taiwan literature since the early 1980s. Given the enormous amount of available material and the irrepressible energy and talent that have gone into the debate, my main objective is to reconstruct and appreciate the complexity of the discourse rather than come up with yet another definition or solution. Nor is it my intention to provide a supposedly objective but not at all integrated survey of well-known publications, even though such a project is definitely desirable and ought to be undertaken at some point. Rather, my intervention takes the form of semantic tracing and discourse analysis, a strategy best suited, I believe, for gauging the intricacy and multifacetedness of the issues at hand.[4] By examining a series of key concepts and their various applications, I wish to lay bare what is invested in this extensive debate and what its implications may be. In other words, my goal is to take stock of the issue of and possibilities inherent in the concept of Taiwan literature. My reading and narrative are, no doubt, interpretive and indicative of my own position, but I take this as a necessary first step toward engaging the debate meaningfully. My "conclusions" at the end are general and, in fact, inconclusive, but I argue for the advantages that come with the designation of Taiwan literature.

TOWARD TAIWAN LITERATURE:
ZIZHU XING IN THE 1980S

In January 1981, two years after the Kaohsiung (Gaoxiong) Incident, which brought to a final, violent conclusion the nativist literary movement of the 1970s, the Taipei-based literary critic Zhan Hongzhi published a brief review in which he expressed concern that, in the distant future, the bustling literary scene in contemporary Taiwan might well be crudely discounted and relegated to the category of periphery or margin in a comprehensive history of Chinese literature [Zhongguo wenxue]. He wondered whether all the efforts by writers living in Taiwan in the past thirty years might not have been a bitter "exercise in futility."[5] Such a defeatist view caused an immediate uproar in Taiwanese literary circles, prompting some to argue earnestly that there is no need to inscribe Taiwan literature in a grand narrative of Chinese literature.[6] In an eloquent retort, the native-born critic Gao Tiansheng rejected such "unnecessary self-ingratiation" and observed that such despair about a future Chinese literary history was a symptom of a "historical disorientation" suffered by the critic: "We believe that contemporary works will accurately reveal their significance and be appropriately defined only when reviewed in the history of Taiwan literature."[7] Another commentator, Peng Ruijin, who in 1980 published a controversial essay calling for a new native-soil Taiwan literature beyond the social-realist tradition, cast Chinese literature and Taiwan literature as two reified and binary opposites: "It makes absolutely no sense for a person living on Taiwan to create Chinese culture.

By the same token, it is positively absurd to ask a Taiwanese writer to produce Chinese literature."[8] Also in response to Zhan's article, the influential journal *Taiwan wenyi* [Taiwan literature] held a symposium to discuss the definition and characteristics of Taiwan literature. A moderate opinion was voiced by the writer and critic Li Qiao, who emphasized that, as a result of reflecting and recording the historical experience of Taiwan's people, "'Taiwan literature' has achieved a unique position, significance, and value, with a literary substance that is full of potential." At the same time, Li insisted, "'Taiwan literature' is ultimately part of Chinese literature, in the same way that 'Chinese literature' is part of the literature of humanity."[9]

By all accounts, the publication of the quarterly *Wenxue jie* in January 1982 (its English title given as *Literary Taiwan* starting with the third issue) marked the beginning of a self-conscious effort to define and promote Taiwan literature as an independent entity and tradition. Based in the southern port city of Kaohsiung, the journal offered a much-cherished forum for mostly native-born writers and critics and pointedly maintained a different profile than mainstream literary journals published in Taipei, the political and cultural capital to the north. A major and lasting achievement of *Wenxue jie* was Ye Shitao's *Taiwan wenxueshi gang* [An outline of the history of Taiwan literature], which it nurtured and eventually published in 1987. Over its seven-year existence, the journal organized issue after special issue to discuss and republish works by eighteen native Taiwanese poets or writers, such as Zheng Jiongming, Yang Kui, and Zhong Lihe. By highlighting these works as part of the native literary canon, the editors of *Wenxue jie* gave substance to their claim of a modern Taiwan literature that is self-conscious and separable from other literary developments. As Peng Ruijin, the editor of a revamped *Wenxue jie* in the 1990s, would write in retrospect: From the beginning, one of the emphases of *Wenxue jie* was the rediscovery and organization of historical documents, but its main and real objective was writing a history of Taiwan literature."[10]

In addition to conscientiously fostering studies of the native literary tradition, *Wenxue jie* promoted a clearly delineated Taiwan literature. The two guiding principles that it endorsed were "originality" [*zizhu xing*] and "nativization" [*bentu hua*]. In an editorial that he wrote for the inaugural issue of the journal, Ye Shitao put forward "originality" as a pivotal value while projecting the development of Taiwan fiction. This originality, according to the veteran writer, should derive from synthesizing multiple cultural systems, traditional, native, and foreign. It distinguishes Taiwan literature from the literature produced across the Taiwan Strait, but it does not deny that Taiwan literature is part of the larger Chinese literature: "One must understand that the totality of Chinese culture is the sum of different regional cultures. If Taiwan literature continues to promote its originality, then one day when the Chinese on both sides of the strait bring about a unified and democratic nation, the experience and achievement of Taiwan literature will contribute to the growth of a future Chinese literature [*Zhongguo wenxue*]."[11] This statement reflected a stage in Ye's thinking where he still approached Taiwan literature as a part of or a link in the Chinese literary tradition. He would, therefore, mention in the editorial Shen Yanbing [Mao Dun], Ba Jin, Lin Yutang, Zhang Ailing, and Bai Xianyong as belonging to the May Fourth realist tradition of modern Chinese literature. In another essay from the same period, Ye periodized Taiwan new literature, as opposed to traditional literature, as spanning the period 1910–45 and defined its central features as anti-imperialism, antifeudalism, anticolonialism, and antisuperstitiousness. Closely following the course of a national resistance movement against Japanese occupation and colonization, twentieth-century Taiwan literature derives its originality from welding together traditional Chinese culture and Taiwanese regional culture.[12]

The key term embedded in the statements quoted above is *zizhu xing*, for which Ye Shitao offered originality as the English equivalent. He apparently arrived at this notion through a realist conception of literature as truthfully reflecting its historical condition and specificity. The growing complexity of Taiwanese society, on the threshold of the highly developed and industrialized 1980s, would impart a *uniqueness* to Taiwan literature as long as writers were capable of depicting what they witnessed. However, the Chinese phrase that Ye used, both in his *Wenxue jie* editorial and in other contexts, can have a different connotation altogether. More than "originality" or "uniqueness," *zizhu xing* in its literal meaning describes "self-determination" or "autonomy," and it was, indeed, its literal meaning, rather than an idiosyncratic translation of originality, that would gain the phrase much currency in the nativist movement. (As we will see below, by the mid-1990s Ye would feel compelled to clarify what he meant by the term and its English equivalent.)

The conceptual ambiguity of *zizhu xing* may have been accidental, but the phrase certainly acquired an active life of its own and was immediately elaborated on, for instance, by the critic Lü Li, who, in July 1982, wrote a long article on the topic. Hoping to establish a "foundation of tradition" for the 1980s, Lü offered an impassioned historical account of Taiwan literature from the early 1920s. While emphasizing the unique experience of colonial Taiwan, he located in modern Chinese literature a meaningful point of reference and announced that the mission of Taiwan literature in the contemporary "age of division" was to bring together the two currents of separate development. He was particularly pleased to see that overseas scholars were finally beginning to introduce May Fourth literature, in its truthful diversity, to Taiwanese readers.[13] For Lü Li, just as for Ye Shitao, *zizhu xing* was intensely ambiguous because it could mean either the particularity of Taiwan literature vis-à-vis Chinese literature in general or an independent course of development that thrived in spite of various suppressions, the latest being the crude cultural chauvinism instituted through the Guomindang government policies. Yet both Lü and Ye still expressed an interest in representative May Fourth writers, most of whom the government had banned on Taiwan simply because of their affiliation with the Communist regime across the strait. In the 1990s, such an intellectual affinity with the modern Chinese literary heritage would become less obvious or acknowledged, and the assumed discontinuity between the May Fourth new literature and Taiwan literature, a direct product of the Guomindang cultural policies, added ideological fuel to the discourse on literary originality or self-determination. The historical irony, as the critic Lü Zhenghui points out, lies in the fact that official suppression of the May Fourth literary tradition on Taiwan finally succeeded in reducing all mainland literature to an "alien" and incoherent entity.[14]

Another good example of how ambiguous the notion of *zizhu xing* could be comes from the editor's afterword to the inaugural issue of *Wenxue jie*. Echoing Ye Shitao's plea that true Taiwanese writers should write about the native land of Taiwan, the afterword complained that "Taiwan literature is still far from the road of self-determination [*zizhu hua*]." To stress the need of changing a quality [*zizhu xing*] into an action [*zizhu hua*], it promised that, since Ye Shitao had touched on this in his editorial, more commentators would be invited to discuss "the self-determination of Taiwan literature." The way to achieve such an objective, according to the afterword, was to practice realism and reflect the diverse reality of Taiwan in literature. A passage recapturing a crucial sentiment underlying the late 1970s debate on "native-soil literature" [*xiangtu wenxue*] stated: "We hope that works by Taiwanese writers will firmly represent the true image of the beautiful land of Taiwan, rather than be obsessed with ghosts of the past and look ungratefully down on the land and people that nurture you and supply you with milk and honey. The officious and pompous literature that relies on an empty mythology is nothing but a toxin harmful to the minds of hardworking people, a dreadful public hazard."[15] The "officious and pompous literature" denounced here refers elliptically to both the official "combat literature" [*zhandou wenxue*] that the Guomindang regime had tirelessly promoted and the "literature of nostalgia" [*xiangchou wenxue*] that had long been the hackneyed subject matter for most of the mainland writers who landed on Taiwan with the Guomindang in the late 1940s. The afterword made clear that neither could be regarded as an authentic literature of Taiwan since writers absorbed in these modes of writing never seriously identified with Taiwan's land or people. The willingness and desire to identify with and represent Taiwan would emerge as a crucial value differentiating advocates of Taiwan literature, who invariably claim to belong to the tradition of native-soil literature.

This strategy of defining authentic Taiwan literature in terms of a genuine concern and identification with the native soil had already been articulated—and articulated most systematically—by Ye Shitao in 1977. It was, therefore, no surprise when Zheng Jiongming disclosed over a decade later that Ye himself had penned the agitational afterword.[16] Ye's earlier essay briefly deals with Taiwan literature of the past several hundred years and describes a "Taiwanese consciousness" [*Taiwan yishi*] that is the product of a prolonged colonial and anticolonial history. At a time when native-soil literature was attacked mostly for its realist, left-wing, and antiestablishment tendencies, Ye's discussion of "Taiwan-centered works" that reflect "a Taiwanese position from which to view the whole world" interjected an unexpected nativist voice.[17]

Ye Shitao's 1977 intervention drew an immediate response from Chen Yingzhen, a leading socialist writer, polemicist, and defender of native-soil literature as realist and socially engaged. For Chen, the true historical value of the movement to return to the native land lay in its resistance against the imperialist culture and economic colonialism of the United States and Japan. More specifically, contemporary native-soil literature continued the May Fourth tradition of critical realism, thrived during the international and domestic crises of the 1970s, and reacted against a Western-style modernism that had prevailed on Taiwan during the 1960s.[18] Chen acknowledged that the new literature on Taiwan had a unique spiritual profile but always emphasized that, "in expressing the spirit of pursuing independence of the country and national freedom, the new literature on Taiwan has been undeniably part of the new literature in modern China."[19]

Enabled by such a totalizing view of continuity, one that accords Taiwan literature its historical significance, Chen Yingzhen was quick to detect a "blind spot" in the native-soil literature that Ye Shitao seemed to champion. The first question that Chen raised, after underscoring Ye's general statement about Taiwanese culture being a particular expression of Chinese culture, goes directly to the implications of equating the entire tradition of Taiwan literature with that of native-soil literature. His worry was that such a narrow approach would fail to reveal a more fundamental characteristic that transcends the native soil: the fact that "the new literature on Taiwan was influenced by the movement for a vernacular literature that was an intimate part of the May Fourth enlightenment movement; it has also been closely related, throughout its development, to the anti-imperialist, antifeudal literary movements in China. It serves as a link in the political, cultural, and social movements that take China as the ultimate destiny of the nation" (95–96).[20] Against this Marxian theorizing of an inclusive political identity, the notion of Taiwanese consciousness appeared vague and deliberately ambivalent; to Chen, it even hinted at an insidious form of "cultural nationalism" that would lead only to separatism (97). To overcome this blind spot, he suggested the term *Chinese new literature on Taiwan* as a more comprehensive and accurate designation for literary works produced on Taiwan (99).

The intriguing development following this extremely sensitive exchange was that there was no further dialogue, at least not until five years later, when *Wenxue jie* began advocating the "self-determination" and "nativization" of Taiwan literature. Yet in the 1980s and 1990s many polemicists revisited this initial skirmish and drew their own conclusions. Part of the reason that this exchange did not continue in the late 1970s was that the extensive debate about native-soil literature had more to do with political ideology than with regional, ethnic, or cultural differentiation. Establishment writers and conservative humanists, such as Peng Ge and Yu Guangzhong, were first alarmed more by traits of what they believed to be socialist realism in native-soil literature than by nativist consciousness. Their suspicion and anti-Communist rhetoric compelled the defenders of native-soil literature to assume a political position and address the present situation through a language that was directly concerned with the social nature and function of literary practices. Wang Tuo, for instance, in one of the most insightful and important essays on the subject, argued that the term *native-soil literature* might cause both conceptual and emotional confusion because it would seem to exclude the urban landscape and its reality, encourage narrow-minded regionalism, and induce self-indulgent nostalgia. For him, literary representations should extend to the totality of society, so native-soil literature is a misnomer and ought to be replaced by realist literature.[21] Refusing to be pigeonholed, several native-soil writers, such as Zhong Zhaozheng, claimed that native-soil literature is an empty concept since all literature is, in the final analysis, about the land and the people.[22] The fiction writer Zhang Xiguo participated in the debate from Chicago and echoed Chen Yingzhen's thesis by proposing a broadened "national literature" [*minzu wenxue*].[23] One critic even went so far as to announce that native-soil literature was dead, that feeble stream having merged into a greater, all-embracing current, namely, "a new realist literature that takes the Chinese nation as its starting point and is full of idealism and critical spirit."[24] Either advocating or opposing native-soil literature would, for this critic, amount to behaving like an anachronistic Don Quixote.

The pronouncement that native-soil literature is dead turned out to be both right and wrong. It was accurate insofar as it acknowledged the fact that a shared political commitment and sense of historical urgency allowed an independent group of writers to view their native land as an integral part of the national as well as the global landscape. These writers would subordinate a nativist consciousness to an anti-imperialist and antiestablishment cause that called for national solidarity and universal mobilization. A more radical voice would specifically demand a "social literature" based on class consciousness and confrontation.[25] Yet native-soil literature would also survive political sublimation and would reemerge fully in the discourse on Taiwan literature, the political thrust of which was aimed no longer at Western cultural imperialism or economic colonialism but, instead, at newly discovered Chinese chauvinism and domination.[26] It bespoke a redirected geopolitical configuration and posited a nativist identity constructed not so much through political ideology as through renewed ethnic and regional differentiations.[27] A new identity perception now pitted the native "Taiwanese" against an oppressive Chinese "other" and propelled the debate over Taiwan literature in a new direction, resulting in what, in Liao Xianhao's succinct narrative, constitutes the most extensive of the five major debates in modern Taiwanese literary history.[28]

One of the earliest essays to herald the new movement to rectify Taiwan literature, and to explicitly endorse literature as a symbol of cultural self-sufficiency and independence, appeared in 1982, featured prominently in the second issue of *Wenxue jie*. Arguing that "the priority of Taiwan literature should be its nativization [*bentu hua*]," the critic Peng Ruijin proposed a "screening criterion" by which to examine and define what constitutes Taiwan literature proper. In Peng's view, Taiwan literature had always followed its own course of development, but the sudden debate about native-soil literature made it imperative to critically reconsider what had been taken for granted. It became increasingly clear, to Peng at least, that a "misalignment of historical causes and effects has made Taiwan literature play contradictory roles."[29] Neither the narrowing term native-soil literature nor the willful national literature would do justice to the peculiar nature of Taiwan literature, which, like the history of Taiwan, is admittedly a complex record of breaks, shifts, and upheavals. Yet, according to Peng, the conflicting and multiple claims on Taiwan literature preclude crystallizing the unique quality of literature produced in this land. The urgent issue is whether to adhere to or abandon this unique "native essence." The "screening criterion" that he proposes will, therefore, establish the legitimacy of Taiwan literature and throw into relief its historical outline:

> As long as it is a work that truthfully reflects the history and reality of people living in the region of Taiwan and is rooted in this land, we can name it Taiwan literature. Therefore, although some writers may not have been born in this land or may have left it for various reasons, we can still accept them as belonging to the rank and file of Taiwan literature as long as they establish a codependent relation with the land in their works and their emotions are intimately bound to the tremors and vibrations of this land.

Conversely, when someone refuses to identify with Taiwan and insulates himself from the people, he will not be embraced "even if Taiwan literature had the widest open arms." Such an approach to identifying Taiwan literature is, according to Peng, "nativization" and should be taken as the foundation for reconstructing the native literary tradition, its earliest expressions included. The screening process will help "filter all heterogeneous elements and demonstrate that Taiwan literature proper is a product rooted in the native land" (3).

Yet, in the end, this "most discriminating screen" aims not so much at taking stock of what there is or has been as at stipulating what there must or ought to be. It presents a positive notion of Taiwan literature and endows the concept with a sacred content and value. This heavily invested concept, abstracted from the phenomenological experience of encountering literary works, is called on to help assert a collective identity and embody an authentic tradition. It becomes a sign laden with mythological aspirations. As Peng Ruijin concludes: "The inheritance of 'Taiwan literature' affirms that we are a nation with its own poetry and songs; in it we may find the self-confidence that we are a nation with its own literature" (3). At this moment, as one commentator later observed, a clearly nativist construction of Taiwan literature was introduced in literary discourse, one that pointed to a specific agenda and orientation. The geographic name *Taiwan* is charged with definite political or ideological meanings.[30] Peng Ruijin himself acknowledged as much in the different context of his *Wenxue jie* essay, writing that the Taiwan in Taiwan literature is far more than a passive geographic designation. On the contrary, it signifies a native literary tradition that transcends its natural environment (3).

The specific agenda articulated through an idealized notion of Taiwan literature is to invent a distinct and usable cultural tradition to serve the cause of Taiwan's independence. Such a reclaiming of an obscured tradition or unique spiritual heritage has been a common and potent strategy in modern nationalism and anticolonialism worldwide. The objective is to institute and fortify a new sense of collective identity, often through instilling a victim consciousness, so as to lend cultural and moral legitimacy to the pursuit of political self-determination. At the heart of modern Chinese nationalist discourse, for instance, was the same agitational evocation of both national pride and humiliation seen in Peng Ruijin's brief and adroit essay. Yet the nativization program that Peng proposed there does not directly engage the issue of Chinese nationalism or its ineluctable relevance to the current Taiwanese independence movement. This was a task that Chen Fangming undertook in a lengthy 1984 essay, through which he addressed "issues concerning the nativization of Taiwan literature at the present stage."[31]

What prompted Chen, a prominent pro-independence critic and activist, to participate in the debate was an incipient division among writers and commentators with regard to the positioning of Taiwan literature.[32] The so-called southern school, associated with *Wenxue jie* in Kaohsiung, was behind the nativization program that Peng Ruijin outlined. The much looser northern school, represented mainly by Chen Yingzhen, also a native-born Taiwanese, had its forum in *Xiachao pinglun* [China tide review] and argued that Taiwan literature should be viewed as part of a political Third World literature. The geopolitical implication of this theory was that Taiwan literature belongs to an anticolonial and nationalist tradition, one that also includes modern Chinese literature. One of Chen Yingzhen's concerns was that the realist native-soil literature was being hijacked by the rising separatist movement. More specifically, he saw the implication of an emphasis on the "originality" [*zizhu xing*] of Taiwan literature vis-à-vis Chinese literature.[33] Nativist critics, such as Xu Shuilü, quickly rejected such theorization as "Han Chinese chauvinism" and incompatible with native Taiwanese identity. The future of Taiwan literature, Xu stated succinctly, lay in "self-determination" and "nativization." To fend off possible charges of parochialism, he also offered a broadened definition of *Taiwan literature* as "a literature that embraces native Taiwan, keeps in perspective the Third World, and promotes self-deter-mination and Taiwanese consciousness."[34] Obviously, the clash between the northern and the southern schools was yet another extension of the earlier exchanges between Chen Yingzhen and Ye Shitao on the status of native-soil literature, which, in turn, can be traced even further back to different arguments during the Japanese colonial period.[35] A review of that short-circuited debate about the difference between Taiwan native-soil literature and Chinese new literature on Taiwan also serves as the entry point for Chen Fangming's essay, although Chen Fangming overlooked the fact that Ye Shitao did not use the term Taiwan literature in 1977.

In summarizing the debate over native-soil literature, Chen Fangming puts much emphasis on the coming-of-age of a Taiwanese consciousness, which is, he believes, a popular awakening against the manipulation and repression by the Guomindang since World War II. Native Taiwan literature, too, is presented as separated from the officially sanctioned literary discourse and production. This tension between grassroots resistance and the state ideological apparatus becomes a central axis around which Chen unfolds his historical review of Taiwan literature. His main target, however, is the chauvinistic "Chinese consciousness" that he detects in Chen Yingzhen and against which he portrays a nativist "Taiwanese consciousness." The fault of Chen Yingzhen's antiseparatist vision, according to Chen, is that it subjects Taiwanese consciousness to a larger Chinese consciousness and reduces Taiwan literature to a branch of Chinese literature [*Zhongguo wenxue*]. Such "fanciful thinking," furthermore, stems from a misunderstanding of Taiwanese history: "Whereas Ye Shitao's literary analysis views Taiwan in the past three-hundred-odd years as a separate, victimized colonial society, Chen Yingzhen limits his historical perspective to China in the last century and conveniently places Taiwan in the context of Chinese history" (158).

As another blatant example of such Sinocentrism, Chen Fangming refers to Zhan Hongzhi's 1981 review and laments that, like the shortsighted Chen Yingzhen, Zhan fails to understand that Taiwan and China have been separated for almost four hundred years. As an immigrant society, the Taiwanese have, according to Chen Fangming, shed their historical baggage and view the land under their feet as the center of their world: "The so-called China-centered tendencies are nothing but an emotional complex with which intellectuals are infatuated" (164). To further prove the cultural and historical separation between Taiwan and China, Chen shifts from a long-term historical review to focus on the two radically disparate societies of the present. Citing approvingly Chen Yingzhen's observation that a "consumer society" has developed on Taiwan,[36] he concludes that writers in China are still confronted with a political situation where "Chinese are oppressing Chinese." The persecution of writers and intellectuals during the Cultural Revolution was a bitter consequence not of imperialism but of "Chinese nationalism" (171–72). The more local problems on Taiwan, such as the tension among people with different "provincial origins," foreign capital investments, environmental pollution, and the polarization between rich and poor, "can be acutely felt only by writers born on Taiwan, living in Taiwan, and concerned about Taiwan" (172). Taiwan literature should, therefore, be based on Taiwanese experience, and, insofar as it pursues a "self-determining national culture" (175), Taiwan literature is also a part of Third World literature. Between nativization and a Third World perspective, Chen Fangming agrees with Xu Shuilü, there should be no contradiction.

Together with Peng Ruijin's call for nativization, Chen Fangming's systematic elaboration of an independent native tradition outlines the basic structure and content of a nativist concept of Taiwan literature. First of all, both emphasize that Taiwan literature should be rooted in the land of Taiwan and be concerned with its social condition. A continually trumpeted but abstract theme, "the land and the people," serves as both the ultimate cause for and the justification of a native literature. Literary discourse increasingly emerges as an articulation and even an embodiment of a new ethnic, or ethnonationalist, consciousness and identity. Second, in endorsing the political cause of democracy, literary nativism draws on a populist imagination to put pressure on the Guomindang government and depict China as a monolithic, intransigent totalitarian regime. Cold War ideology and rhetoric persists and offers a ready solution to complex issues. An inevitable, if also willful, blurring between political division and cultural heritage helps reduce the concept of *China* to the People's Republic and then goes on to etch the latter as an ominous threat. Thereby, the very idea of unification is demonized, and the pursuit of Taiwan literature is unequivocally equated with the defense of liberty and democracy. Third, self-determination and nativization demand that a revision of the history of Taiwan center on the native subject and reconstruct his self-consciousness. A native subjectivity, or *zhuti xing*, is what Chen, a historian by training, points to as something to be enthusiastically followed. That by the mid-1990s popular discourse was saturated by the concept of *zhuti xing* reveals the empowering force of a nativist consciousness. As a result, Taiwanese studies, especially research in Taiwanese literary and social histories, has become the hottest field, although the contemporary scene often gets glossed over.[37] Fourth, in their conception of a native Taiwan literature, both Peng and Chen subscribe to a moralizing view that acknowledges only serious and committed literature. Beginning, as Ye Shitao does,[38] with the premise that native-soil literature is a record of the painful history of the oppression of the Taiwanese people means that its authors can hardly escape an entrenched victim consciousness. In addition, they are compelled to continue valorizing the rural landscape over the urban, the imagined idyllic village life over the polluted and nihilistic city.[39] Literature becomes a sacred enterprise because it is called on to buttress an overdetermined myth of origin and destiny. As David Wang comments, between the mission of nation building and the actual form of native-soil literature, much ideological suturing is now needed to make literary practices cohere and conform.[40]

The immediate consequence of Chen Fangming's article may be his description of a China complex afflicting the unificationists, which brings into the open its combative counterpart, namely, a Taiwan complex sustaining the separatist efforts to dissociate Taiwan from China culturally and historiographically. The extensive debate centered on these two terms in the mid-1980s testifies to the explosiveness and intricacy of the "identity crisis" embroiling people on Taiwan, especially the young and educated population of the postwar era. It was also during this period that the independence movement gathered new momentum and began influencing public opinion and Guomindang control of the political process slipped. In a long 1984 essay directly engaging Chen's revision of history, the historian Yin Zhangyi examined the question of "Taiwanese consciousness" through the concept of Taiwan literature and suggested that the former is a product of the colonial rule by the Japanese. He further pointed out that, contrary to what some pro-Japanese historians have claimed, the people of Taiwan actively resisted colonial assimilation and retained a deep emotional identification with Chinese culture. The few writers who could by the 1930s compose in Japanese, such as Yang Kui, were much more concerned with the human condition in colonized Taiwan than with trying to achieve literary excellence in a colonial language.[41]

In response to the escalating tension between the unificationists and the nativists, who accused each other of distorting history, an extraordinary symposium organized by *Zhongguo luntan* [China tribune] in August 1987, shortly before the lifting of martial law, brought together noted historians, scholars, and literary critics, including Chen Yingzhen and Ye Shitao, to discuss the different dimensions of the China and Taiwan complexes. Yet, as Yang Guoshu observed in his concluding remarks, no consensus was achieved on how to resolve the conflict.[42] To a large extent, intellectual and emotional life on Taiwan since the mid-1980s has been consumed by the growing antagonism between different visions for Taiwan's future that are contingent on these two claims of identity. At the same time, it has also become increasingly clear that native-soil literature has disavowed its realist impetus and let itself become embroiled in the unification-independence debate.[43] Taiwan literature has come to serve as an effective alibi for betraying the social commitment of native-soil literature. Amid widespread uncertainty about the future, commercial culture and popular literature attracted ever larger numbers of urban, middle-class readers. Near the end of the 1980s, the critic Lü Zhenghui described the decade as a landscape of "divided native-soil and shallow culture." As the latest intellectual fashion of postmodernism swept across Taipei in the early 1990s, its uncritical celebration of particularism [*parole*] over universalism [*langue*] would add further momentum to the nativist political agenda and lead the discourse on Taiwan literature into an increasingly exclusionary discursive space.[44]

SUBJECTIVITY AND THE RIGHT OF INTERPRETATION: ZHUTI XING IN THE 1990S

At the 1987 *Zhongguo luntan* symposium, the historian Yin Zhangyi observed: "In recent years, with a tendency to identify with the native land and to abandon a 'realist Taiwanese consciousness,' the effort to create a new Taiwanese culture and develop a sovereign 'Taiwanese consciousness' has become increasingly apparent."[45] The term *zhuti xing*, which is rendered as "sovereign" here, is usually understood to mean "subjectivity." Through its wide use in the discourse on Taiwan literature, however, it has gained a strong connotation of "sovereignty." The subjectivity or self-sufficiency of Taiwan literature, which the journal *Wenxue jie* strove to affirm, is often promoted as the symbolic sovereignty of a native consciousness and, by extension, of an independent nation-state. Indeed, this close relation between a literary concept and a political movement was never something that proponents of Taiwan literature were shy about. Thus, the acknowledgment by Chen Fangming [Shi Minhui] in 1988: "Since the 1970s, the development of Taiwanese consciousness has had its concrete expressions in a political movement for democracy and a literary movement for nativization. The political movement takes Taiwanese consciousness as its guiding principle and seeks to determine the future of the island; the literary movement emphasizes a Taiwanese consciousness in literary representations of the historical experience and contemporary reality of Taiwan."[46] The pursuit of literary subjectivity would have a more radical expression in the revamped and better-financed *Wenxue jie*, renamed *Wenxue Taiwan* in 1991.[47] As the discussion unfolding in the journal grew ever more explicit in its separatist and anti-Chinese rhetoric, critical responses to a narrowing and exclusionary conception of Taiwan literature also gained force. During this stage of development, the loaded concept of subjectivity [*zhuti xing*] served a pivotal function. "What we are witnessing in the 1990s," commented Sung-sheng Yvonne Chang, "may very well be a 'reconstitution' of Taiwan's dominant culture, in which formerly alternative or oppositional formations are actively incorporated."[48]

Since the late 1980s, the assertion of a new literary subjectivity has taken the form of experimental writing in the main Taiwanese dialect, primarily

Hokkien (Fujianese). A similar effort was first made by Taiwanese writers in the 1930s and renewed half a century later when an awakened Taiwanese consciousness came to regard Mandarin Chinese as an imposed foreign medium. As Liao Xianhao perceptively points out, this desire to create a written form for a local dialect and, thereby, unify writing and speech both continues the May Fourth ideology of affirming the social value of vernacular literature and undercuts the national language that grew out of the new literature movement. It may signal the "awakening of a southern culture" that challenges a homogeneous understanding of China, but it also betrays a phonocentrism that is all too conducive to a hegemonic mentality and practice.[49] Indeed, for Lin Ruiming, another respected scholar of modern Taiwan literature, the "linguistic determinism" that underpins much of the contemporary drive toward an authentic literature in Taiwanese may risk establishing a new cultural and linguistic domination. The negation of previous literary forms could force Taiwan literature down a narrow alley.[50]

While the dialect-based writing experiment has the potential to affect any concept of Taiwan literature—most especially that of Taiwan literature as Chinese literature (because of the diverse dialects encompassed by the latter)—its implied challenge to an imagined uniform language does not make the increasingly combative nativist discourse any more aware of its own hegemonic tendencies. Instead of mounting the critique of the nationalist myth of origin and uniformity that Liao Xianhao called for in the 1988 essay "Jiegou 'Zhongguo wenhua,'"[51] the nativist advocacy of Taiwan literature remained deeply entrenched in binary thinking. In his introductory remarks for the inaugural issue of revived *Wenxue Taiwan*, the poet Zheng Jiongming announced that the journal resumed publication because it had "the ambition and determination to herald a literary movement" that would counteract misguided government policies that for too long encouraged people to ignore their own native land and place their hope in a "distant and dictatorial empire."[52]

The same impatience with the official Guomindang insistence on ultimate unification with China underlies Chen Fangming's schematic narrative dividing the history of Taiwan literature into two opposing camps, the official and the grassroots, an approach that he reiterates in a second editorial in the inaugural issue of *Wenxue Taiwan*. Calling on the journal to "raise the banner of the 1990s," Chen describes the character of Taiwan literature as "resistant, antagonistic, and rebellious."[53] The tension between such a defensive native literature, which is a constant, and an official, evolving, but nevertheless foreign literature, which includes both the *kōminka* [cultivation of imperial subjects] literature during the Japanese occupation and the anti-Communist literature supported by the Guomindang government, constitutes "the dialectical development of the history of Taiwan literature" (8). The resilient spirit of native Taiwanese writers that Chen Fangming celebrates is, nonetheless, carefully divorced from its complex history. Through a conceptual sleight of hand, Taiwan literature is at once separated from and superseded by a literature by Taiwanese, which consists only of works by native-born writers with a nativist consciousness. For the official (and alien) components of Taiwan literature are acknowledged only to be excluded from a literature by Taiwanese proper. The history of Taiwan literature is, therefore, reconstructed as the search for a native subjectivity, for a sovereign literature by and for the Taiwanese. The return to the "sovereign subject of Taiwan," in Chen Fangming's abbreviated account, was initiated in the 1960s, formally announced in the 1970s, and accomplished in the 1980s, when "a new understanding of the national identity of literature" came into existence. According to Chen: "With the rectification of Taiwan literature as such, it became possible to establish Taiwanese society as a sovereign subject" (10–11).

The goal of *Wenxue Taiwan* in the 1990s is, for Chen Fangming, to move the nation forward by means of literature, to "make Taiwan literary." He reminds native-born writers that, in an age of transformation, when the old is disintegrating and the new has yet to be created, they will face problems far more complicated than those of the past forty years. They must seriously consider "how to position themselves, literature, and Taiwan" (12). The question of positioning indeed became central for the journal, which continues to provide nativist writers and critics a privileged forum. Adopting the same layout as its predecessor, it often prominently publishes op-ed and position pieces. It forms a lively discursive space for the contested ambiguity of the concept of Taiwan literature.

The two brief op-ed pieces in the second issue of *Wenxue Taiwan*, for instance, come to different conclusions while endorsing the project of extending literary subjectivity into national sovereignty introduced in the first issue. For Chen Wanyi, a professor of Chinese at Tsing-hua University, the prospect of Taiwan literature in the 1990s is one of unprecedented vitality and diversity. While emphasizing the importance of legitimizing its sovereign subjectivity, Chen opens up Taiwan literature to include what nativists such as Chen Fangming would have a hard time embracing. The thriving literary scene draws, in Chen's view, on a variety of schools and subject matters, including "literature written in the Taiwanese dialect," "Hakka literature," "literature of the indigenous people," and "military-compound literature." Chen finds additional causes for optimism in the expanding research into the tradition of Taiwan literature and newly available materials, including mainland Chinese texts.[54] In marked contrast to Chen Wanyi's positive assessment of the new era, a more militant Li Minyong gravely deplores the "oppression and devastation" visited on Taiwan literature by the Guomindang government since the end of World War II. Li also takes further a complaint that Chen Fangming and some other nativist writers harbor against the language policy implemented by the Guomindang government in 1945, soon after it reclaimed sovereignty over Taiwan from the Japanese. By disallowing Japanese as a literary language, the government achieved, according to Li, its goal of "suppressing and destroying" Taiwan literature, whose modern form had been developed primarily in Japanese.[55] But Li downplays the fact that the colonial Japanese government had not prohibited Chinese publications until 1937, when it actively started the *kōminka* colonization campaign.[56] This allows him to claim a Japanese origin for modern Taiwan literature and, at the same time, to regard the Guomindang regime as no different in nature from the Japanese colonial rule. Against these two alien forces, he echoes Chen Fangming in identifying a "literature by Taiwanese" (or "Taiwanese literature"—*Taiwan ren wenxue*) that is characterized by "a spirit of resistance and critique" (5–6).

Although sharing a concern that rampant commercialism posed a serious threat to literary development, Chen Wanyi and Li Minyong had divergent views of what constitutes Taiwan literature and what its history and consequences are. Their two pieces reflect the different politics within the discourse on Taiwan literature and indicate the different pursuits and ideological stances that the nativization drive has brought forth since the 1980s. While dedicated scholarly research, such as Lin Ruiming's study of Lai He, the founding father of modern Taiwan literature,[57] helps reconstruct a fuller picture of the native tradition, the purist approach recognizes only a small group of Taiwanese writers as authentic. The much-acclaimed contemporary writer Lin Shuangbu, for instance, delivered a lecture on native fiction at a 1987 Democratic Progressive Party seminar in which he presented a condensed history highlighting nine representative writers and glaringly omitting the native-born Chen Yingzhen (most likely owing to his unificationist politics) and any native women writers.[58] Radicalized nativist discourse has, thanks to its exclusionary implications and revisions of history, generated much criticism and contention. Among its many steady and intelligent critics is Lü Zhenghui, a native-born scholar of Chinese literature who in 1992 warned against "a narrow-minded, self-secluded mentality of the Boxer type." The pursuit of self-determination for Taiwan literature had, he observed, an element more of conservative self-protection than of creation.[59]

Alerted by the growing opposition to a militant nativist rhetoric and practice, Peng Ruijin, now the editor of *Wenxue Taiwan*, adopted a conciliatory tone and called for critical self-reflection. "The redefinition and rearticulation of Taiwan literature," he wrote, should be based on the literary experience alone; any extraliterary imposition, mandated by political or ideological considerations, will lead only to domination. "Is it possible that, in the effort to redefine Taiwan literature, impatience led to an exclusionary self-centeredness? In our eagerness to establish Taiwan literature as an authentic tradition, did we forget our own experience of being in the 'minority' and, ignoring the existence of other 'minorities,' reveal a lack of respect and tolerance?" Another minority discourse is "the literature of indigenous people," which, if taken as a starting point for a reconsideration of Taiwan literature, would, Peng believes, lead to a new horizon. Arguing for the necessity of continually redefining the content of Taiwan literature, Peng emphasizes: "We do not have the right to restage a historical tragedy, to manufacture the authenticity of Taiwan literature and monopolize the right of interpretation. We would rather believe that Taiwan literature will demonstrate its abundant creativity through new articulations and in an atmosphere of tolerance."[60]

Shortly after offering these remarks on open-mindedness, Peng Ruijin authored a lengthy review of the controversy over the nativization program.[61] However, in dealing with opposing approaches, he appeared agitated, and his prose was laden with emotional outbursts and insufficiently considered statements. In rapid-fire succession, he took issue with a series of critics and put out a broad defense reiterating a crude version of the nativist doctrine. The first and most serious target of his indignation was a group of mainland Chinese scholars who had written about Taiwan literature and the current nativization drive from across the Taiwan Strait. Their joining in the debate amplified an interpretive voice that was believed to be associated with a real and threatening geopolitical power. As a result, Peng and other nativists quickly assumed a defensive position, resorting to their habitual victim consciousness, and vowed to keep the right of interpretation [*jieshi quan*] to the Taiwanese. The right or power of interpretation within nativist discourse is nothing but a logical extension of the sovereign subjectivity [*zhuti xing*] that Taiwan literature has secured for itself through efforts of self-determination [*zizhu xing*] and nativization [*bentu hua*]. By this point, we see how these key concepts are interlocked yet mobile. They lead to and build on one another and form a persuasive, self-reinforcing rhetorical system. Before we have a closer look at Peng's essay and examine how he employs these concepts, a brief word on the impact of mainland Chinese scholarship is in order.

As Jeffrey Kinkley points out, by the mid-1990s, "PRC scholarship on Taiwan literature is sufficiently well organized, interactive with Taiwan and international opinion, and self-reflective as to have already produced self-assessments."[62] Since the initial stage of haphazard exposure to Taiwan literature in the late 1970s, mainland scholars have rapidly built up institutional bases, published an astonishing number of general studies, and continually updated or modified their conceptual frameworks. The sheer energy and productivity of this budding field has impressed even scholars from Taiwan. Lü Zhenghui, for one, expressed envy of the collective mode of scholarly work, which he found lacking in his own environment.[63] Yet only the pioneering group of publications came from collaborative work; the more refined and more innovative studies were usually undertaken by individual scholars.[64] This initial series of mainland publications on Taiwan literature provoked the most intense response from Taiwanese writers and critics, if only because the studies often assumed an official posture and uncontested viewpoint. As Li Ruiteng observed in the early 1990s, if throughout the 1980s the debate on Taiwan literature revolved around its definition, the introduction of a jarring distant voice from the other side of the Taiwan Strait interjected new energy and significantly expanded the scope of the discussion. One direct consequence would be further radicalization of the nativist cause.[65]

The first comprehensive history of modern Taiwan literature, for instance, was published in 1987, the result of more than twenty scholars' and teachers' collective effort.[66] It appeared, coincidentally, the same year as did Ye Shitao's long-awaited history of Taiwan literature,[67] although the two otherwise have little in common. Ye's volume grew out of an involved writer's determination to document the originality of modern Taiwan literature, whereas its massive mainland counterpart, more than four times as long, was produced primarily to serve as a college textbook. In a 1990 review of the mainland volume, one of the first, Lü Zhenghui affirmed its usefulness and acknowledged that it included fundamental work for which even Taiwanese readers would have to be grateful. The greater part of Lü's review, however, was devoted to detailing the volume's abundant errors, misunderstandings, and platitudes. What Lü found most awkward, however, were those places where, unable to shed their biases and convictions, the mainland scholars lavished praise on nativist writers simply for their "realist works" while having no clue about their pursuit of independence, which, had they recognized it, would, presumably, have been alarming.[68] Here is yet another example of political ideology taking precedence over cultural identity or heritage.

A more critical, but no less constructive, review of the same volume appeared in a special section of *Zhongguo luntan* that appeared in June 1992.[69] The special section, announced on the journal's cover and offering reviews of five different works on Taiwan literature by mainland scholars between 1987 and 1991, was put together by the late Lin Yaode, a prolific and much-respected writer and poet of the younger generation. In his introductory remarks, Lin observed that, after paying lip service to government policies, the field of Taiwanese literary studies in mainland China had already gained a limited degree of autonomy [*zizhu xing*]. The entrenched "all-embracing nationalist view"—by which he meant a motherland mentality that would not accept Taiwan's independence—is understandable because, according to Lin, "a certain cultural centrism is not unique to the mainland." He further pointed out that "a fictitious self-determination of Taiwanese culture is not much different in nature from a bloated Chinese chauvinism." The real issue, therefore, is to escape a constraining regionalism and seek the common ground. Hence his prediction: "The contention over and competition for interpretive authority over each other's literature may be the most pressing topic between the two sides of the Taiwan Strait at the end of the century."[70]

The five reviewers whom Lin Yaode invited to comment on the mainland publications included scholars, writers, and critics. There was the rare concession that mainland scholars may be blessed with an objective standpoint because of their insulation from Taiwanese literary circles,[71] but, although their approaches and evaluation criteria might have varied, nearly all the reviewers complained of more than scholarly sloppiness and methodological incompetence. The most frequent criticism was about a condescending Sinocentrism, or a "central-plains mentality," that insists on incorporating Taiwan literature into Chinese literature as a branch or regional component. For example, the narrative strategy of the first volume of *Taiwan wenxue shi* [History of Taiwan literature] relies, in Wu Qiancheng's reading, on promoting unification as its starting point and, therefore, cannot but present its object of study as a subordinate other.[72] Moreover, Zhang Qijiang found that the author of *Tai Gang wenxue daolun* [Introduction to Taiwan and Hong Kong literature] often equates China and the motherland with the Chinese Communist regime, thereby turning China into "a special name for a monolithic system."[73] Meng Fan, too, resolutely rejected the view that Taiwan poetry is peripheral to the mainstream of Chinese poetry. The most qualified people to reconstruct a history of new poetry on Taiwan, he argued, are "ourselves": "After all, the right to interpret history should be in our own hands."[74]

Indeed, from this moment on, the question of who is entitled to position and define Taiwan literature gained an added urgency in nativist discourse.[75] A spontaneous response, which Peng Ruijin would expound vociferously, was that only the Taiwanese should have the right to interpret Taiwan literature.[76] However, the more cautious Lin Ruiming would acknowledge the achievements of mainland scholars and situate their production in the larger context of different national allegiances. The impoverished state of Taiwan literature studies on Taiwan reflected, according to Lin, the Guomindang government's traditional suspicion and suppression of a nativist consciousness. His hope was that, with the arrival of a democratic age, a more rigorous and more comprehensive history of Taiwan literature would become possible.[77]

A different complaint against the almost uniform presupposition found in mainland-produced histories of Taiwan literature came from Ma Sen, an established professor of literature and drama. In 1992 and 1993, Ma published two carefully argued, albeit somewhat overlapping, essays investigating the complex issues underlying the idea of Taiwan literature and exploring its "position." Citing a wide range of literary examples from the modern world, such as Joseph Conrad's importance to English literature,

Samuel Beckett's insistence on writing in French, and Vladimir Nobokov's indisputable position in American literature, he suggests that the literary language used ought to be the primary factor involved in classifying a given writer. Another criterion is the writer's nationality and citizenship. On these grounds, Taiwan literature is part of Chinese literature since most of it is written in Chinese; moreover, insofar as both the Chinese and the Taiwanese governments agree that there is only one China, Taiwan literature and mainland literature both belong to Chinese literature [*Zhongguo wenxue*].[78] As might be expected, Ma Sen's take on the position of Taiwan literature did not enjoy a friendly reception from the nativists. His frustration with histories written by mainland scholars, however, was that writers are indiscriminately labeled as Taiwanese writers simply because they reside, not in mainland China, but in Taiwan. Their political identity causes them to be viewed as a separate category.[79] Thus, according to Ma, those Taiwan-based writers who are not native-born Taiwanese find themselves in an absurd situation: they are considered Taiwanese writers by mainland scholars but not by nativists in Taiwan.[80] Although none of the mainland scholars indicated support for Taiwan's independence, in Ma's opinion they unwittingly strengthened the nativist cause by bypassing a common cultural heritage to forge an ideological solidarity with the realist writers in the tradition of native-soil literature. In other words, political ideology and literary doctrines undercut the claims and reach of an inclusive literary tradition wrought in modern Chinese.

Ma Sen's position was quickly rejected by Zheng Jiongming as anachronistic and showing no respect for a seventy-year-old native tradition. Alleging that the ghost of Han chauvinism was lurking, Zheng called attention to the struggle over "the interpretation of Taiwan literature."[81] Peng Ruijin also appeared in print reinforcing this warning.[82] Yet the situation was deemed so serious that, soon after Peng's programmatic article appeared in *Wenxue Taiwan*, the journal held a roundtable discussion to press the need to "regain the literary sovereignty of the Taiwanese people."[83]

A sense of urgency again seized nativist writers such as Ye Shitao, Zheng Jiongming, and Peng Ruijin, who participated in the roundtable discussion, and who were greatly concerned that the subjectivity of Taiwan literature would be compromised by various hostile forces, in particular mainland scholars with their own agendas. On this extraordinary occasion, Ye Shitao had a chance to explain how, drawing on the Japanese usage, he had arrived at translating originality as *zizhu xing*, which seemed to him to combine the primary qualities of creativity and particularity. It was his deliberate decision, in the early 1980s, to give originality a fresh rendering and introduce a new concept and value.[84] Thus, Ye's explanation allowed the participants in the discussion to weave into a semantic chain several key concepts that are highly mobile: originality (read: self-determination); particularity (authenticity); and subjectivity (sovereignty).[85] To safeguard the purity of this literary subjectivity, which, again, becomes a semantic surrogate for national sovereignty, Peng Ruijin at one point suggested that "an internal investigation" would be necessary to expose subversive elements.[86] Literary discourse was ever closer to the disciplinary mechanism of a vanguard political campaign, embracing paranoia. Most of the discussion, however, repeated what was already summarized in Peng's essay, which begins with a review of the nativization movement since the early 1980s and then engages its various detractors, Ma Sen and Lü Zhenghui included. To this essay we now return.

As mentioned above, the critics whom Peng confronts first and most vehemently are mainland scholars, who had by then published a number of essays to gauge "the position of Taiwan literature in Chinese literature."[87] Some of them had written specifically to engage Ye Shitao's increasingly aggressive advocacy of an independent Taiwan literature and "Taiwanese nationalism."[88] Their general view is that, considered historically, geographically, and genealogically, Taiwan literature is part of Chinese literature, just like Taiwan is part of China. Obviously, these mainland scholars echo the Chinese government's policy on the status of Taiwan, but their reasoning and intellectual language are firmly rooted in nationalist discourse and historical argument. In their invocation of a common heritage, their intervention is more emotionally and culturally charged than geopolitically motivated. Put simplistically, the direct appeal of the unification drive is that cultural identity (in the sense of sameness) ought to override ideological, political, institutional, and, finally, regional differences.

Yet Peng Ruijin's agitated response is based on a refusal to regard mainland scholars as anything other than government spokesmen or to distinguish carefully the conceptual boundaries between the Communist government and the Chinese nation, between political legitimacy and cultural resources, between Chinese literature as a modern institution that has been subjected to political service and abuse and Chinese literature as a rich and multifarious tradition. A facile resort to the ideological doctrines of the Cold

War years enables him to dismiss serious contentions by caricaturing them. At one point, he goes so far as to read the mainland critics' essays as an advance media blitz for a military invasion by the Communist army. After insisting that "Taiwan literature and Chinese literature have no common origin or understanding, backed by what one may say are completely different literary conceptions," he poses a rhetorical question: "Would it help hide the nature of Chinese literature as an abetting mouthpiece when [those scholars] distort facts and subject Taiwan literature to the realm of Chinese literature?"[89] Even if the assertions made by the mainland scholars also fail to untangle intricately enmeshed issues, Peng does not elevate the discussion to a more rigorous plane. On the contrary, he further collapses different issues and brings things to a deadlock.

The same aversion to complexity also permeates Peng's indignant rebuttal of Ma Sen's deliberation on the identity of Taiwan literature, a rebuttal fueled by Peng's belief that Ma Sen often echoes, albeit hesitantly, the opinions of mainland Chinese scholars. Once Peng determines that Ma is a clever unificationist, he shows little readiness to examine Ma's points about literature and language, about a possible discrepancy between cultural and political formations. Instead, he charges that a conspiracy is at work (namely, one designed to subjugate Taiwan literature to Chinese literature) and goes on to reiterate his nativist position. Since the greatest threat that he perceives is the "ambiguation of the demarcation of Taiwan literature," Peng finds himself compelled to condemn a variety of critics. Ma Sen, for example, represents the subversive strategy of opening up or contaminating Taiwan literature, whereas Li Ruiteng is accused of fragmenting Taiwan literature by proposing a subfield of "Taipei literature." Lü Zhenghui is exposed as having merely a native-born scholar's skin and not his bones, thanks to his "theory of cultural dependence on China." Gong Pengcheng, who argues that an inclusive literary history ought not to ignore or simplify literary works from another era, is summarily dismissed as being "too removed from the land."[90]

In the course of taking issue with such commentators, Peng makes broad statements about the objective and content of the nativization movement. While most of his claims are supported by other nativists, he pushes some arguments further and more systematically. His essay therefore offers a programmatic description of the many aspects of the nativist concept of

Taiwan literature in recent years. Besides those so far introduced, two other statements are worth noting because of their directness and their impact on nativist discourse. One expresses an ethnically charged anti-Chinese sentiment that views Guomindang rule as a period of recolonization in the wake of Japanese rule, a theory later systematized by Chen Fangming.[91] The official anti-Communist literature that the Guomindang government encouraged on Taiwan after World War II is, Peng contends, "in essence a colonial literature that moves in the opposite direction to native literature" (96). His other significant point suggests a pro-Japanese attitude that glorifies Japanese colonization from 1895 to 1945. Peng rejects the contention that Taiwan literature is a branch of Chinese literature, arguing that it is more logical to treat Japanese, Western, and Chinese literatures as separate branches or components of an all-embracing Taiwan literature.[92] Moreover, in order to deny that modern Chinese literature had a profound influence on Taiwan literature, a claim that the more historically sensitive Ye Shitao has never completely retracted,[93] Peng takes dubious pride in "the twenty-five long years of formal education in Japanese literature that people on Taiwan received before the onset of new literature on Taiwan."[94] If such an ahistorical claim of heterogeneity constitutes a postcolonial imagination or politics, it also calls into question the validity of any effort to demarcate an identifiable Taiwan literature in opposition to Chinese literature because it is precisely the national boundary that it blurs and undoes. To fully dismantle the nationalist legacy, one first must acquire a postnationalist vision and free oneself of nationalist passion and logic, which, to sum up, does not seem to be the motivation behind the advocacy of an independent Taiwan literature in general and Peng's positioning of Taiwan literature in particular.

Finally, in an ironic turn, Peng warns that, if mainland Chinese scholars, local unificationists, and leftists fail to have a good understanding of Taiwanese literary history, "they will only tie themselves up in a political doctrine that postulates a maternal body or an umbilical cord."[95] The implied message is that such a primal connection either is fictional or ought to be severed once and for all. Yet the metaphor of "reconnecting to the umbilical cord of the motherland" was most noticeably used by Ye Shitao in a 1987 essay in which he retraced the tortuous path of Taiwan literature during the transitional period of the late 1940s. According to Ye, "a strong Chinese consciousness" brought together intellectuals from Taiwan and the mainland in the immediate postwar years to rebuild a postcolonial Taiwanese culture: "This Chinese consciousness served as a vital 'umbilical cord' bringing new life to writers now gathered in Taiwan."[96] For Peng Ruijin in 1994, however, the umbilical cord is, more accurately, an alien and constricting chain.

AN INCONCLUSIVE CONCLUSION

Peng Ruijin has clearly outlined the nativist program: "Taiwan literature is nothing but an independent, self-determining national literature of Taiwan that the Taiwanese nation wishes to establish. . . . To establish Taiwan literature is to establish Taiwanese culture; without the support of Taiwanese culture, our idea of the Taiwanese nation will be no more than empty talk."[97] Invested with such a nation-building mission, the discourse on Taiwan literature is bound to become embroiled in ever larger and more complicated issues. While it thrives on the basic principles of modern nationalist ideology, a separatist conception of literature as an embodiment of a yet-to-be-acknowledged national culture will also have to confront in nationalism its ineluctable challenge, even its fatal nemesis. This is not merely a question of disproportionate distribution of resources or raw political or military might. Rather, the nativist emphasis on self-determination and on a new national identity conforms to the fundamental nationalist mandates of territorial integrity and political sovereignty that underpin the modern Chinese nation-state. In addition, the nativist claim of a different regional history does not contradict the nationalist principle of deriving legitimacy from a particular heritage or mythical origin. Until it articulates a genuinely postnationalist orientation, nativist discourse on Taiwan literature will not engage questions of origins and positions productively, other than to repeatedly assert its unique nature or a native tradition of resistance. Gong Pengcheng is only one critic among many to have pointed out that "the myth [*misi*] of nativization" will necessarily lead to a suspension of critical reflection and foster the creation of structures that similarly exclude newly created minority groups and voices.[98] The search for a clear-cut and unambiguous definition of Taiwan literature will only backfire because, in reducing historical complexity and complicity, visionaries of a pure Taiwan literature will undercut their very commitment to retrieving historical memory. Foreseeing the pitfalls and dangers of nativist discourse, Liao Xianhao, who first called for a deconstruction of Chinese culture in 1988,[99] made a compelling case in 1993 that Taiwan as an absolute signifier needed just as much deconstructing and that a postnationalist reorientation was the only viable means for creating a multiethnic and multicultural "new Taiwanese."[100]

Nanfang Shuo [Wang Xingqing] once remarked, regarding a mainland Chinese scholar's ineptitude in penetrating the discussion of Taiwan literature, that a deep-rooted factionalism among Taiwanese literary circles leads to a constant "competition of discourses." As a result, each of the several contingently formed and realigned discursive regiments "tries to seek legitimacy for itself, to delegitimate the other and deny the reason for its very existence. Caught in such discursive competition, the evolution and dialectical development of literature is often disregarded, and literary discourse becomes a parapolitical discourse. The truth disappears in discourse, and only a power struggle over literature persists."[101] This situation often leaves inadequately informed mainland scholars with one choice: to pick materials and opinions as needed for their own purposes.

Nanfang Shuo's caution reminds us of the need to first conduct a patient survey of any given discursive field. To a large extent, the present study is an effort in this direction. I am humbled by the amount of energy and creativity so far devoted to the debate on the concept of Taiwan literature and would like to offer two rather inconclusive points as a way of (temporarily) closing my discussion.

First, on the level of metacommentary, the discourse developed on Taiwan literature should be viewed and studied as an important component, both negative and positive, of the continuing Chinese project of modernity. So many fundamental questions have been raised about the composition of the Chinese nation, its modern history, and its political and cultural legitimacy that nativist discourse on Taiwan will ultimately enrich rather than enfeeble the prospect of a renewed and transformed (if not transcended) nation. Of course, renewal and transformation were central aims of China's earliest modernizers. This discourse can only expose the unfinished condition of Chinese modernity. The gradual disappearance, from the politicized native-soil literature controversy in the 1970s to the drive for Taiwan literature in the 1990s, of references to the May Fourth heritage and to its framing function reveals a historical blind spot that builds on the critical insights of nativist discourse. Despite their denunciation of Chinese chauvinism and their pursuit of an independent nation, nativists on Taiwan are still bound to confront the question of what to expect from Chinese modernity, in historical as much as contemporary terms. This invested engagement may allow different visions of the nation to emerge and even facilitate a more fluid conceptualization that will help energize and release the diverse regional and multiethnic resources embedded in Chinese civilization.

Second, the ambiguity inherent in the concept of Taiwan literature is the reason for its intellectual potency and viability. No doubt this ambiguity reflects the geopolitical instability that defines Taiwan in the contemporary world, and its loss would most likely entail undesirable consequences on many fronts. The term Taiwan literature highlights this ambiguity because it can mean several things that are not yet borne out by the body of literature in question: a literature by native-born Taiwanese (*Taiwanren wenxue*, as opposed to literature produced on Taiwan), a literature in Taiwanese (*Taiyu wenxue*, which has yet to be created), or a literature narrowly defined by its makers' citizenship (*Taiwan [guo] wenxue*, an equal of Irish, Japanese, or American literature). The real potential of Taiwan literature may ultimately lie in the enrichment and revelation that it can introduce into such notions as Hong Kong literature, Shanghai literature, or Hunan literature, all of which are accepted categories in the broad field of modern literature in Chinese. Efforts to make Taiwan literature pure, singular, and definite would only impose limits on its legitimate possibilities and reaches. Its irrepressible vitality already makes an ever more compelling case that by Chinese literature we understand not narrowly a nation-state institution (as in the modern Japanese tradition of *kokubungaku*), not just one standardized literary production, but rather a vast literature written in Chinese and interacting with long and uneven literary and cultural traditions. The concept of *Zhongguo wenxue* [literature of the Chinese nation] ought, in other words, to be broadened and replaced by that of *Zhongwen wenxue* [literature in Chinese].[102] Whether the cause of self-determination on Taiwan is successful or not, Taiwan literature will help shore up a much richer, more interactive, and more in-depth cultural geography than has ever been possible, as far as modern Chinese history or literary thought is concerned. In the final analysis, therefore, this essay could be titled "For the Concept of *Taiwan Literature*."

NOTES

I thank Sung-sheng Yvonne Chang, Gan Yang, Jason McGrath, and the two anonymous reviewers for their constructive comments. I also gratefully acknowledge a summer stipend from the National Endowment for the Humanities that facilitated research on the project.

Unless otherwise indicated, all translations from non-English-language sources are my own.

1. Scholars writing in English have three terms available to describe this body of literature: literature from Taiwan, Taiwan literature, and Taiwanese literature. Sometimes these are used interchangeably. For instance, in her foreword to "Contemporary Chinese Literature: Crossing the Boundaries" (ed. Sung-Sheng Yvonne Chang and Michelle Yeh, *Literature East and West*, special issue, 28 [1995]), Sung-Sheng Yvonne Chang uses all three phrases.
2. See Lin Shuangbu, *Dasheng shuochu ai Taiwan* [Speak loudly our love for Taiwan] (Taipei: Qianwei, 1989), 141–55.
3. See Lin Yangmin, *Taiwan ren de lianhua zaisheng* [The lotus rebirth of the Taiwanese] (Taipei: Qianwei, 1988), 175–92.
4. Some scholars have explicitly employed discourse analysis in their approach to the topic. See, e.g., Zhou Qinghua, *Taiwan wenxue yu "Taiwan wenxue"* [Taiwan literature and "Taiwan literature"] (Taipei: Shengzhi 1997).
5. Zhan Hongzhi, "Liangzhong wenxue xinling" [Two types of literary mind] (1981), in *Liangzhong wenxue xinling* (Taipei: Huangguan, 1986), 44–45.
6. As Liao Xianhao comments, Zhan Hongzhi's point has less to do with the evaluation of Taiwan literature itself than with "the mutability and historical situatedness of literary and aesthetic standards." Liao Xianhao, "From Central Kingdom to Orphan of Asia: The Transformation of Identity in Modern Taiwanese Literature in the Five Major Literary Debates," in Chang and Yeh, eds., "Contemporary Chinese Literature," 121. The same sense of finiteness and insignificance may overwhelm anyone who comes to realize the infinite future possibilities of the human condition.
7. Gao Tiansheng, "Lishi beiyun de wankang: Suixiang Taiwan wenxue de qiantu ji zhanwang" [Resisting the tragic historical destiny: Thoughts on the future prospects of Taiwan literature], *Taiwan wenyi* [Taiwan literature] 19 (May 1981): 275–83, 282.
8. Peng Ruijin, *Taiwan xin wenxue yundong sishinian* [Forty years of the new literature movement on Taiwan] (Taipei: Zili wanbaoshe wenhua, 1991), 200.
9. Li Qiao [Yi Chanti], "Wo kan 'Taiwan wenxue'" [My view on Taiwan literature], *Taiwan wenyi* 20 (July 1981): 213. For an informative account of Li's considered response and the controversy, see Gao Tiansheng, "Taiwan wenxue de qilu" [The forked road in front of Taiwan literature] (1982), in *Taiwan xiaoshuo yu xiaoshuojia* [Taiwan fiction and the novelists] (Taipei: Qianwei, 1985), 215–22.

10 Peng Ruijin, "Cong *Taiwan wenyi, Wenxue jie, Wenxue Taiwan* kan zhanhou Taiwan wenxue lilun de zai jiangou" [An overview of the reconstruction of Taiwan literary theory in postwar years by examining *Taiwan wenyi* (Taiwan literature), *Wenxue jie* (Literary Taiwan), and *Wenxue Taiwan* (Literary Taiwan)], in Feng Deping, ed., *Taiwan wenxue fazhan xianxiang* [The phenomenon of Taiwan's literary development] (Taipei: Xingzhengyuan wenhua jianshe weiyuanhui, 1996), 199–200.

11 Ye Shitao, "Taiwan xiaoshuo de yuanjing" [The future of Taiwan fiction], *Wenxue jie* 1 (1982): 2. For an English-language version, see Linda G. Wang, trans., "The Future of Taiwan Fiction," *Taiwan Literature: English Translation Series*, no. 4 (1999): 99–102.

12 "Meiyou tudi, nayou wenxue" [Without land, where is literature?] (1983), in *Meiyou tudi, nayou wenxue* (Taipei: Yuanjing, 1985), 2.

13 Lü Li, *Zai fenlie de niandai li* [In the age of division] (Taipei: Lanting shudian, 1984), 32–89.

14 Lü Zhenghui, *Zhanhou Taiwan wenxue jingyan* [The historical experience of Taiwan literature since World War II] (Taipei: Xindi wenxue chubanshe, 1992), 185–95.

15 Ye Shitao, "Bianhouji" [Editorial afterword], *Wenxue jie* 1 (spring 1982): 221.

16 Zheng Jiongming, "Taiwan wenxue de quanshi" [The interpretation of Taiwan literature], *Wenxue Taiwan* [Literary Taiwan] 9 (1994): 17.

17 Ye Shitao, "Taiwan xiangtu wenxueshi daolun" [An introduction to the history of native-soil literature on Taiwan] (1977), in Yu Tiancong, ed., *Xiangtu wenxue taolun ji* [Collection of the debate on native-soil literature], 3rd ed. (Taipei: Yuanjing, 1980), 69–92, 72. For an analysis of the different phrases of the debate over native-soil literature, see also Jing Wang, "Taiwan Hsiang-t'u Literature: Perspectives in the Evolution of a Literary Movement," in Jeannette L. Faurot, ed., *Chinese Fiction from Taiwan: Critical Perspectives* (Bloomington: Indiana University Press, 1980). "The emergence of 'Taiwanese consciousness,'" Wang writes, "was a historical necessity that could not be easily subdued by the opponents of *hsiang-t'u* [*xiangtu*] literature. Nor could it be quickly diluted into an all-embracing nationalistic sentiment, as some of the *hsiang-t'u* theoreticians predicted" (61–62). For a more recent account of the impact of native-soil literature and its rootedness in modern Taiwan history, see Zhang Wenzhi, *Dangdai wenxue de Taiwan yishi* [Taiwan consciousness in contemporary literature] (Taipei: Zili wanbao, 1993), 11–42.

18 For an informative account of the "modernist-nativist contention" and Chen Yingzhen's critique of modernism in Taiwan, see Sung-sheng Yvonne Chang, *Modernism and the Nativist Resistance: Contemporary Chinese Fiction from Taiwan* (Durham: Duke University Press, 1993), 148–76.

19 Chen Yingzhen, "Wenxue laizi shehui fanying shehui" [Literature comes from society and reflects society] (1977), in Yu, ed., *Xiangtu wenxue taolun ji*, 66.

20 Most significantly, the May Fourth tradition was carefully reclaimed by the

political left during the debate on native-soil literature. See, e.g., Li Xingzhi, "Wusi yu women tongzai" [The May Fourth movement is still with us] (1977), in ibid., 148–57.

21 Wang Tuo, "Shi xianshi zhuyi wenxue, bushi xiangtu wenxue" [It's realist literature, not native-soil literature] (1977), in ibid., 119.

22 See ibid., 118. See also Nanting, "Daochu doushi zhongsheng: 'Xiangtu wenxue' yeyi xuangao siwang" [The bells are ringing everywhere: "Native-soil literature" is pronounced dead] (1977), in Yu, ed., *Xiangtu wenxue taolun ji*, 312.

23 Zhang Xiguo, "Minzu wenxue de zai chufa" [The new departure of national literature] (1977), in *Minzu wenxue de zai chufa* (Taipei: Guxiang wenhua, 1979), 195–200. In *Minzu wenxue de zai chufa*, which anthologizes essays published in the journal *Xianrenzhang* [Cactus] during the debate over native-soil literature, we observe the effort made by a group of writers to theorize a logical development from native-soil literature to national literature, a trajectory conceivable largely in terms of the May Fourth heritage of nationalism and enlightenment.

24 Nanting, "Daochu doushi zhongsheng," 311–12.

25 See Weng Tingxun, "'Shehui wenxue' yundong yu shehui geming yundong" [The "social literature" movement and the social revolutionary movement] (1977), in Hu Minxiang, ed., *Taiwan wenxue rumen wenxuan* [Introductory essays on Taiwan literature] (Taipei: Qianwei chubanshe, 1989), 105–13.

26 For an ethnography-based analysis of how the political suppression of native-soil literature contributed to the fermenting of "Taiwan consciousness," see, e.g., Zhang, *Dangdai wenxue de Taiwan yishi*, 14–26.

27 Huang Guangguo perceptively pointed out that the native consciousness that underpinned native-soil literature had three possible new formations: a realist consciousness; a Taiwanese consciousness; and a left-wing class consciousness. See Huang Guangguo, "'Zhongguo jie' yu 'Taiwan jie': Duikang yu chulu" [The "China complex" and the "Taiwan complex": Conflict and reconciliation], *Zhongguo luntan* [China tribune] 25.1 (October 10, 1987): 11–12.

28 See Liao, "From Central Kingdom to Orphan of Asia."

29 Peng Ruijin, "Taiwan wenxue yingyi bentu hua wei shouyao keti" [Taiwan literature should take nativization as its primary agenda], *Wenxue jie* 2 (summer 1982): 1. For an English translation, see Mabel Lee, "The Primary Issue for Taiwan Literature Is Identifying with the Land," in *Taiwan Literature: English Translation Series*, no. 4 (1999): 9–11.

30 Zhou, *Taiwan wenxue yu "Taiwan wenxue,"* 12.

31 Chen Fangming [Song Dongyang], "Xian jieduan Taiwan wenxue bentuhua de wenti" [The issues concerning the nativization of Taiwan literature at the present stage] (1984), reprinted in Hu, ed., *Taiwan wenxue rumen wenxuan*, 158.

32 For further background information, see Gao Tiansheng, "Xin weiji yu xin zhanwang: Xiangtu wenxue lunzhan hou Taiwan wentan fazhan de kaocha" [New

crises and new anticipations: A survey of the development of literature in Taiwan since the native-soil literature debate] (1984), in Gao, *Taiwan xiaoshuo yu xiaoshuojia*, 223–35.

33 In the 1982 essay "Xiaofei wenhua; disan shijie; wenxue" [Consumer culture, the Third World, and literature], Chen Yingzhen wrote that, theoretically, it would be more productive to emphasize the originality of Taiwan literature, together with Third World literature (which includes Chinese literature), vis-à-vis the literature of the developed world, including Western Europe and Japan. Chen cited in Gao, *Taiwan xiaoshuo yu xiaoshuojia*, 221.

34 Xu Shuilü, "Taiwan wenxue jieshuo yu fangxiang" [The definition and orientation of Taiwan literature] (1983), in Hu, ed., *Taiwan wenxue rumen wenxuan*, 144.

35 In 1985, e.g., Song Zelai would still regard Chen and Ye as the two most important critics representing the two major schools, the origins of which, in Song's view, go back to the Japanese colonial period. See Song Zelai, preface to Gao, *Taiwan xiaoshuo yu xiaoshuojia*, 3–4.

36 See Chen, "Xiaofei wenhua; disan shijie; wenxue."

37 See Zhang Shuangying, "Tan dangdai 'Taiwan wenxue' yanjiu de qingxiang" [On the tendency of contemporary "Taiwan literature" studies], *Wenxun* 133 (November 1996): 5–7.

38 See Ye, "Taiwan xiangtu wenxueshi daolun," 73.

39 See, e.g., Chen Fangming, "Xuwu zhuyizhe de yuanxiang? Xiaoshuojia bixia de Taipeiren xingxiang" [The homeland of nihilism? Images of Taipei people from some novelists], *Taiwan pinglun* [Taiwan review] (June 1993), in Chen Fangming, *Dianfan de zhuiqiu* [The pursuit of a paradigm] (Taipei: Unitas, 1994), 242–51.

40 Wang Dewei [David Der-wei Wang], *Ruhe xiandai, zengyang wenxue? Shijiu, ershi shiji Zhongwen xiaoshuo xinlun* [How to become modern, and what to do with literature? New essays on Chinese fiction from the nineteenth and twentieth centuries] (Taipei: Maitian, 1998), 159–80.

41 Yin Zhangyi, "Taiwan yishi yu Taiwan wenxue: Jianzhi Song Dongyang, Zhang Liangze liang xiansheng" [Taiwan consciousness and Taiwan literature: Also in response to Song Dongyang and Zhang Liangze], in *Taiwan jindai shi lun* [Essays on modern Taiwan history] (Taipei: Zili, 1986), 223–27, 227–38.

42 Yang Guoshu, "Zongjie baogao" [A summary report], *Zhongguo luntan* 25.1 (October 10, 1987): 201–2.

43 In describing the three modes of tragedy in modern Taiwan fiction, Li Hanwei implies that the legacy of the "realist spirit" is the redemptive force that should help Taiwanese writers transcend various dilemmas, including the conflict between the China and the Taiwan complexes. See Li Hanwei, *Taiwan xiaoshuo de sanzhong beiqing* [Three types of pathos in Taiwan literature] (Tainan: Tainan Municipal Cultural Center, 1996), 1–42.

44 Lü, *Zhanhou Taiwan wenxue jingyan*, 129–35, 147–50.

45 Yin, "Taiwan yishi yu Taiwan wenxue," 110.
46 Chen Fangming [Shi Minhui], "Xuyan" [Preface] (1988), in *Taiwan yishi lunzhan xuanji* [Selected essays from the debate on Taiwan consciousness] (Taipei: Qianwei, 1988), 6.
47 An intriguing question is what intertextual and intellectual connections, if any, there may have been between the widespread interest in a discourse of "subjectivity" [*zhuti xing*] in Taiwan and the mainland critic Liu Zaifu's advocacy of a literary subjectivity in the mid-1980s. With the same terminology and philosophical impulse, these two formations of subjectivity are theorized from considerably different backgrounds and with divergent purposes in mind. In closely quoting Liu Zaifu, the critic Li Hanwei sees in the mainland critic's theory of literary subjectivity nothing but "a truthful description of the path of modern vernacular Taiwan literature [*Taiwan xiandai baihua wenxue*], from several decades before to the present." Li, *Taiwan xiaoshuo de sanzhong beiqing*, 30–31. For an introduction and critique of Liu's theory of subjectivity, see Jing Wang, "Romancing the Subject: Utopian Moments in the Chinese Aesthetics of the 1980s," in *High Culture Fever: Politics, Aesthetics, and Ideology in Deng's China* (Berkeley and Los Angeles: University of California Press, 1996), 195–232.
48 Sung-sheng Yvonne Chang, "Beyond Cultural and National Identities: Current Re-Evaluation of the *Kominka* Literature from Taiwan's Japanese Period," *Journal of Modern Literature in Chinese* 1.1 (July 1997): 84.
49 Liao Xianhao, *Ai yu jiegou: Dangdai Taiwan wenxue pinglun yu wenhua guancha* [Love and deconstruction: Observations on literary criticism and culture in contemporary Taiwan] (Taipei: Unitas, 1994), 67–87; Liao, "From Central Kingdom to Orphan of Asia"; Gong Pengcheng, *Taiwan wenxue zai Taiwan* [Taiwan literature on Taiwan] (Banqiao: Luotuo chubanshe, 1997), 49.
50 Lin Ruiming, *Taiwan wenxue de lishi kaocha* [A historical survey of Taiwan literature] (Taipei: Yunchen, 1996), 51–72.
51 Liao Xianhao, "Jiegou 'Zhongguo wenhua'" [Deconstruct *Chinese culture*] (1988), in *Ai yu jiegou*, 19–21.
52 Zheng Jiongming, "Yidai jiankuan zhong buhui: Wenxue Taiwan fakan ganyan" [No regret at persevering: Thoughts at the issuing of *Wenxue Taiwan*], *Wenxue Taiwan* 1 (1991): 4–5.
53 Chen Fangming, "Chengqi jiuling niandai de qizhi: *Wenxue Taiwan* fakanci" [Raise the banner of the 1990s: An inaugural essay for *Wenxue Taiwan*], *Wenxue Taiwan* 1 (1991): 9.
54 Chen Wanyi, "Zhanwan jiushi niandai Taiwan wenxue" [An overview of Taiwan literature in the 1990s], *Wenxue Taiwan* 2 (1992): 2–4.
55 Li Minyong, "Zai yazhi yu pohuai xia ranliang Taiwan wenxue xianghuo" [Light the torch of Taiwan literature under suppression and destruction], *Wenxue Taiwan* 2 (1992): 5.
56 For a critical review of recent Taiwanese scholarship on this topic and an

analysis of the complex relation of the kōminka regime to colonial kōminka literature, see Chang, "Beyond Cultural and National Identities."

57 Lin Ruiming, *Lai He de wenxue yu shehui yundong zhi yanjiu* [A study of Lai He's literature and social movements] (Tainan: Jiuyang chubanshe, 1989).
58 See Lin, *Dasheng shuochu ai Taiwan*, 107–40.
59 See Lü, *Zhanhou Taiwan wenxue jingyan*, 238.
60 Peng Ruijin, "Taiwan wenxue de zai dingyi he zai lianzu" [The redefinition and rearticulation of Taiwan literature], *Wenxue Taiwan* 8 (1993): 319–20, 321.
61 Peng Ruijin, "Taiwan wenxue dingwei de guoqu he jianglai" [The past and future of positioning Taiwan literature], *Wenxue Taiwan* 9 (1994): 93–117.
62 Jeffrey Kinkley, "Mainland Chinese Scholars' Image of Contemporary Taiwan Literature," in Chang and Yeh, eds., "Contemporary Chinese Literature," 28. See also Zhou Lin, "Dalu de Taiwan wenxue yanjiu huigu ji zhanwan" [A review of and prospects for research on Taiwan literature on the mainland], *Taiwan yanjiu jikan* [Taiwan research quarterly] 22 (winter 1988): 76–80.
63 Lü, *Zhanhou Taiwan wenxue jingyan*, 331.
64 See Kinkley, "Mainland Chinese Scholars' Image of Contemporary Taiwan Literature," 41.
65 Li Ruiteng, *Wenxue de chulu* [An outlet of literature] (Taipei: Jiuge, 1994), 129.
66 Bai Shaofan et al., *Xiandai Taiwan wenxue shi* [History of modern Taiwan literature] (Shenyang: Liaoning University Press, 1987).
67 Ye Shitao, *Taiwan wenxueshi gang* [Outline of the history of Taiwan literature] (Gaoxiong: Wenxuejie zazhishe, 1987).
68 Lü, *Zhanhou Taiwan wenxue jingyan*, 332, 334.
69 Zheng Mengli [Cheng Mingli], "Ping Liaoning daxue ban *Xiandai Taiwan wenxue shi*" [On the Liaoning University edition of *Xiandai Taiwan wenxue shi*], *Zhongguo luntan* 32.9 (June 1992): 52–56.
70 Lin Yaode, "Yuhou: Kuahai canhong" [After the rain: A broken rainbow across the sea], *Zhongguo luntan* 32.9 (June 1992): 49.
71 Wang Youhua, "Lun Lujiang ban *Taiwan xin wenxue gaiguan*" [On the Lujiang edition of *Survey of Taiwan New Literature*], *Zhongguo luntan* 32.9 (June 1992): 62.
72 Wu Qiancheng, "Tangshanren ruhe xie daoyu de wenxueshi: Ping *Taiwan wenxue shi* shangjuan de bi'an guandian" [How a mainlander writes the literary history of an island: On the other-shore viewpoint of the first volume of *Taiwan wenxue shi*], *Zhongguo luntan* 32.9 (June 1992): 69–70. Vol. 1 of *Taiwan wenxue shi* was published in 1991 by Haixia wenyi chubanshe of Fuzhou.
73 Zhang Qijiang, "'Zhongguo wenxue' shoubian shi: Qianxi *Tai Gang wenxue daolun*" [Incorporated into the history of "Chinese literature": A preliminary essay on *Tai Gang wenxue daolun*], *Zhongguo luntan* 32.9 (June 1992): 65. *Tai Gang wenxue daolun* was published in 1990 by Geodeng kexue jiaoyu chubanshe of Beijing and edited by Pan Yatun.

74 Meng Fan, "Shuxie Taiwan shishi de wenti: Jianping Gu Jitang de *Taiwan xinshi fazhanshi*" [Problems of writing a history of Taiwan poetry: A preliminary essay on Gu Jitang's *Taiwan xinshi fazhanshi*], *Zhongguo luntan* 32.9 (June 1992): 76. Gu Jitang's *Taiwan xinshi fazhanshi* [The history of Taiwan new poetry] was published in 1989 by Wenshizhe chubanshe of Taipei.

75 See Li Fengmao, "Taiwan xuejie ruhe zhengshi Taiwan wenxue yanjiu" [How academe in Taiwan should approach the study of Taiwan literature], *Wenxue Taiwan* 9 (1994): 7–9.

76 See Peng, "Taiwan wenxue dingwei de guoqu he jianglai."

77 Lin, *Taiwan wenxue de lishi kaocha*, 77–82.

78 Ma Sen, "Taiwan wenxue de diwei" [The position of Taiwan literature], *Dangdai* [Contemporary] 89 (1993): 60–64.

79 Ma Sen, "'Taiwan wenxue' de 'Zhongguo jie' yu 'Taiwan jie': Yi xiaoshuo wei li" [The "China complex" and "Taiwan complex" in "Taiwan literature": The example of fiction], *Lianhe wenxue* [Unitas] 8.5 (1992): 182–83.

80 Ma, "Taiwan wenxue de diwei," 60.

81 Zheng Jiongming, "Taiwan wenxue de quanshi" [The interpretation of Taiwan literature], *Wenxue Taiwan* 9 (1994): 4–6.

82 See Peng, "Taiwan wenxue dingwei de guoqu he jianglai."

83 See "Ba Taiwanren de wenxue zhuquan zhao huilai" [Seek to regain the literary sovereignty of the Taiwanese people], *Wenxue Taiwan* 11 (1994): 93–136.

84 Ibid., 103.

85 Gong Pengcheng, a serious critic of the nativist conception of Taiwan literature, also affirms a literary autonomy [*wenxue zizhu xing*], by which, however, he means the liberal ideal of separating literature and immediate political or social concerns. See Gong, *Taiwan wenxue zai Taiwan*, 70–73.

86 "Ba Taiwanren de wenxue zhuquan zhao huilai," 119.

87 See, e.g., Lin Chenghuang, "'Taiwan wenxue' yu 'Taiwan yishi' chuyi" [A modest discussion of "Taiwan literature" and "Taiwan consciousness"], *Taiwan yanjiu jikan* 26 (fall 1989): 69–73; and Sifan, "Shilun 'Taiwan wenxue' yu 'Taiwan yishi'" [A preliminary essay on "Taiwan literature" and "Taiwan consciousness"], *Zhongguo luntan* 32.1 (October 1991): 65–73.

88 See Zhuang Mingxuan, "Ping Ye Shitao dui Taiwan wenxue jicheng yu fanzhan chuantong wenti de jianjie" [On Ye Shitao's views on the question of the continuity and development of Taiwan literature], *Taiwan yanjiu jikan* 15 (spring 1987): 61–66.

89 Peng, "Taiwan wenxue dingwei de guoqu he jianglai," 99, 102 (quotes).

90 Ibid., 108, 110, 114. For Gong's arguments, see his *Taiwan wenxue zai Taiwan*, esp. 39–92.

91 See Chen Fangming, "Zhimin lishi yu Taiwan wenxue yangjiu: Du Chen Zhaoying 'Lun Taiwan de bentuhua yundong'" [Colonial history and Taiwanese literary studies: Reading Chen Zhaoying's essay "On the Nativization Movement on Taiwan"], *Zhongguo wenxue* 23.12 (May 1995): 110–19. See also Lin Minyong,

"Zai yazhi yu pohuai xia ranliang Taiwan wenxue xianghuo" [Light the torch of Taiwan literature under suppression and destruction], *Wenxue Taiwan* 2 (1992): 5–6.

92 See also Chen Changming, "Cong 'wenxue zhuti xing' tan: Zhongguo wenhua shi Taiwan wenhua de yi bufen" [From the perspective of "literary subjectivity": Chinese culture is part of Taiwan culture], *Wenxue Taiwan* 13 (1995): 6–8.

93 See Ye Shitao, "Zhongguo wenxue yu Taiwan wenxue" [Chinese literature and Taiwan literature], in *Taiwan wenxue de beiqing* [The pathos of Taiwan literature] (Gaoxiong: Baise, 1990), 113–15.

94 Peng, "Taiwan wenxue dingwei de guoqu he jianglai," 100. Since Peng apparently agrees with the conventionally set beginning of modern literature in Taiwan around 1920 (95), this statement can mean only that he believes that, from the very start in 1895, the Japanese colonial government had been giving its colonial subjects in Taiwan adequate training—and in Japanese literature no less. Even if this were true regardless of the numerous and often-violent rebellions in the early years of Japanese rule, he seems to discount too much the presence of Chinese publications that were not officially outlawed in Taiwan until 1936, not to mention the influential articles in the 1920s that echoed the ethos of the literary revolution in general and Hu Shi's call for a vernacular literature in particular. Furthermore, Peng too readily ignores an assessment made by Huang Deshi that, by the time Taiwan was returned to Chinese sovereignty in 1945, no more than a dozen writers could write competently in Japanese (see Yin, "Taiwan yishi yu Taiwan wenxue," 232).

95 Peng, "Taiwan wenxue dingwei de guoqu he jianglai," 105.

96 Ye Shitao, "Jixu zuguo qidai zhi hou: Cong siling niandai Taiwan wenxue laikan 'Zhongguo yishi' he 'Taiwan yishi' de xiaozhang" [After reconnecting with the umbilical cord of the motherland: A review of the waxing and waning of "Chinese consciousness" and "Taiwanese consciousness" from Taiwan literature in the 1940s] (1987), in *Zouxiang Taiwan wenxue* [Toward Taiwan literature] (Taipei: Zili wanbao, 1990), 37.

97 Peng, "Taiwan wenxue dingwei de guoqu he jianglai," 104.

98 Gong, *Taiwan wenxue zai Taiwan* (see generally 167–205).

99 See Liao, "Jiegou 'Zhongguo wenhua.'"

100 See Liao, *Ai yu jiegou*, 25–27, 28–30. The essay in question originally appeared as Liao Xianhao "Zai jiegou yu jieti zhijian paihuai: Taiwan xiandai xiaoshuo zhong 'Zhongguo shenfen' de zhuanbian" [Wavering between deconstruction and destruction: Shifts in the notion of "Chinese identity" in modern Taiwan literature], *Zhongwai wenxue* [Chung-wai literary monthly] 21.7 (1993): 193–206.

This plea for tolerance and multicultural cosmopolitanism was echoed in Ma Sen's portrayal of Taiwan as a "melting pot." See Ma, "'Taiwan wenxue' de 'Zhongguo jie' yu 'Taiwan jie,'" 173. It was also echoed in the sociologist Xiao Xinhuang's description of Taiwan as an "organic and complete cultural entity."

See Xiao Xinhuang, "Jiekai dangqian yishi xingtai fenzheng de 'jie'" [Untie the "knot" in contemporary ideological debates] [1987], in Li Yiyuan, ed., *Biansi yu zequ: 1986 nian Taiwan wenhua pipan* [Reflections and choices: Cultural critique on Taiwan in 1986] (Kaohsiung: Dunli, 1987), 150–56, 152. Xiao also asked polemicists discussing the China and Taiwan complexes to carefully separate questions of political legitimacy from those of cultural heritage. See ibid., 150–56.

101 Nanfang Shuo [Wang Xingqing], "Jiangping yijian" [Commentary], in Zheng Mingli, ed., *Dangdai Taiwan zhengzhi wenxue lun* [Politics and contemporary Taiwan literature] (Taipei: Shibao wenhua, 1994), 490–93.

102 Such is already the case with the *Journal of Modern Literature in Chinese* (1997–), based at Lingnan College in Hong Kong.

CULTURAL POLITICS

THE CONCERNS WITH issues of literary periodization, Taiwanese identity, and foreign influence discussed in the essays in part 1 are powerfully illustrated by the tension between the modernist movement of the 1960s and the subsequent nativist backlash of the late 1960s and 1970s. Modernist authors such as Bai Xianyong, Wang Wenxing, and Chen Yingzhen were interested both in formal experimentation and in abnormal and transgressive topics. Although the modernists were frequently criticized for being elitist and overly influenced by Western literary aesthetics, it could also be argued that they were motivated as well by "nationalistic" concerns with securing a place for Taiwan literature within an international sphere. In the late 1960s and 1970s, meanwhile, as modernism began to fall out of favor and Taiwan became more isolated in the international sphere owing to a series of diplomatic setbacks, former modernists such as Cheng Yingzhen and Liu Daren joined together with new authors such as Huang Chunming and Wang Zhenhe to promote a nativist aesthetic, which used realist description and rural subject matter to advance veiled critiques  of Nationalist politics and of a hegemonizing Western culture. Although both the modernist and the nativist movements were very specifically rooted in the historical conditions under which they arose, they nevertheless both have significant precedents in earlier periods. For instance, the nativism of the 1970s has its antecedents in the nativist literary debate of 1931, just as 1960s modernism was preceded by the 1950s modernist poetry movement as well as by modernist authors from the 1930s and 1940s.

The essays in this section each use a specific author or literary journal to draw broader conclusions about the formation and interrelation of different literary movements. Joyce C. H. Liu begins with a consideration of the 1930s Japanese-language author Yang Chichang, whom she identifies as "the first Taiwanese modernist poet and novelist." Liu argues that the Taiwanese literary field is characterized by a recurrent dialectic between "perverse" modernist writings and the normalizing forces of "social realism," and she accordingly examines the perverse elements of Yang's poetry as a way of both understanding Yang's own writing and providing a theoretical framework within which to understand his position within the broader literary field. Beyond individual authors like Yang Chichang, literary journals such as *Wenxue Taiwan* [Literary Taiwan] (1940–44) and *Wenji* [Literary quarterly] (1966–) often play a crucial role in the development of literary movements. In her essay, Michelle Yeh examines the role of one such journal, *Xiandaishi jikan* [Modern poetry quarterly] (1953–64), in the development of the 1950s modern poetry movement. In particular, Yeh considers the way in which political, social, and economic factors combined with aesthetic considerations to help shape the direction and contents of this movement. In the following essay, Fenghuang Ying considers the case of Zhong Lihe, who was relatively unknown when he passed away in 1960 but was subsequently appropriated by a range of nativist critics in the decades after his death. Through a careful reading of these subsequent discussions of Zhong's writings, Ying examines the constitution and evolution of these later literary movements themselves. Finally, Sung-sheng Yvonne Chang considers a figure who, in contrast to Zhong Lihe, was not so much an early harbinger of a later movement as a belated reminder of an earlier movement that had already fallen out of fashion. Wang Wenxing was one of the most prominent of the 1960s modernists, and he continued toiling on his most recent project long after the modernist movement itself had run its course. Chang examines the novel *Backed against the Sea* [*Beihai de ren*], which Wang finally completed in 1999 after having worked on it for nearly a quarter of a century. She argues that, while Taiwan's modernist movement has frequently been criticized for its heavy reliance on Western ideas and literary forms, this cultural borrowing can, in the hands of a skillful author like Wang, be used to advance a thoughtful and probing critique of Taiwanese society and culture.

4

The Importance of Being Perverse: China and Taiwan, 1931–1937

Joyce C. H. Liu

In a 1998 conference paper, I proposed to reexamine the two waves of modernism—one in the 1930s, one in the 1940s—in early Taiwan literature.[1] I reevaluated their relation to the Taiwanese modernist movement of the 1950s and suggested that the fact that these two early modernist movements were ignored and forgotten by later Taiwanese literary historians could be attributed to the historical background of the rise of Taiwan new literature as well as to the tradition that that literature maintained in later decades. From the very beginning, Taiwan new literature, under the influence of Chinese new literature and the May Fourth movement, had been imbued with heavy colors of social realism and endowed with the mission to reform society. Repeated debates between nationalistic social realism and the modernist movement, as well as the consequent cleansing and abjection of the avant-garde, show that the return to the social-realist norm has been the imperative in the history of Taiwan literature. I referred to this imperative as the Oedipal syndrome. When I used the Oedipal in dealing with issues in the socius, I was borrowing Deleuze and Guattari's concept of the molar formation, powerfully developed in *Anti-Oedipus*.[2] That is to say, psychoanalytically, the strong collective desire to organize and normalize all discourses so that they fit into the symbolic order of the nationalistic construction, the social phallus, is analogous to the process of socialization and normalization of an individual. Such a desire to cling to the whole, determined by the social phallus of the time, will consequently shape all literary and cultural identities.

This essay intends to further investigate the Oedipal syndrome in the Taiwanese literary field of the 1930s, with the hope that we can see better the complex interrelations between early Taiwanese modernism and its social context. The early Taiwanese literary field, being organized around a collective norm, has tended to synchronize the twin aims of the avant-garde in the modernist movement (i.e., that of reshaping literary conventions and that of rebuilding society) and redirect them into a social-realist track.[3] Within this normalized track, the act of seeking a brighter and more progressive society turned out to be the single cause for both literary activities and social movements. The dual impulses of the "abject"—to purge the unclean or to abandon oneself and become the "deject"—as discussed by Julia Kristeva in her *Powers of Horror* also emerge in this context.[4] Faced with this totalitarian discursive field, the modernist poet willingly plunges into writing about filth, waste, the violent, and the erotic. This is what Kristeva calls perverse writing, through which the poet maintains his resistance against the system and the norm.

The pervert and the schizophrenic, viewed from the perspective of the literary field, can be seen as embodying the defense mobilized by the libidinal energy to resist the force of organization and normalization and, by implication, Thanatos itself. The resistance, according to Kristeva, is caused by the fear of being "one" for an "other." In discussing Baudelaire and *Les fleurs du mal*, Kristeva writes: "Perversion . . . proposes its screen of *abject*, fragile films, neither subjects nor objects, where what is signified is fear, the horror of being *one* for an *other*." Modern writing, according to Kristeva, is closer to "wandering psychosis" than to neurosis, which "imposes on the individual the erotic problem of the socius."[5] Thus, the modern writer, the one by whom the abject exists, is an exile, a *"deject* who places (himself), *separates* (himself), situates (himself) and therefore strays instead of getting his bearings, desiring, belonging, or refusing."[6] Writing, then, is an act to exorcise the perversion and to empty out the filth inside the body. By writing about waste, decay, rot, the obscene, and the demonic, the pervert in language resists the norm and also its own death.

In this essay, I examine the perverse writing employed by the first Taiwanese modernist poet and novelist, Yang Chichang, and discusses its significance, his theories of the "new spirit" and the "new relation," and his impulsive longing for the writing of horror. In so doing, I first delineate the cultural background of the 1930s, in which I see the clear manifestations of the Oedipal syndrome, or what Deleuze and Guattari would call the Oedipal neurosis: a strongly organized collective will to strive for the group spirit and for the brighter side of society.

The span of time that I have selected begins with Japan's formal invasion of China in 1931 and ends with the outbreak of the Second Sino-Japanese War in 1937.[7] During this period, a sense of the serious danger that threatened China's subjectivity rose up across the nation. The slogans "national defense literature," "people's revolutionary proletarian literature," "unified front line," and "new life movement" also rapidly emerged.[8] These are clear expressions of the nationalist urge for the new order and the demand for a strong ethnic identity. The Chinese literary field of the 1930s was, therefore, dominated by an obvious nationalist tone from both the Left and the Right.[9] In 1932, Shi Zhecun, Mu Shiying, and Du Heng, with the help of Liu Naou, established the literary journal *Xiandai* [Modern] in Shanghai.[10] Facing the forceful organization and total mobilization of the contemporary literary field, the modernist group became the target of attacks from all sides, and a series of debates on its members' apolitical position as the "Free People" and the "Third Kind of People" appeared in various journals.[11] The modernist style of writing—the so-called *xinganjuepai*, or new perceptionist movement—was severely criticized, for example, as "the perverse and morbid urban life in the semicolonial region."[12]

In the same year that Japan invaded China, the Japanese colonial government in Taiwan strengthened its military control over the Taiwanese and arrested most of the Taiwanese Communist leaders. The leftist leaders and the ethnic movement advocates shifted their base to literary associations and magazines.[13] With the rise of Taiwanese nativist consciousness and the organization of the leftist literary associations, the Taiwan new literature movement became the tool of anticolonialism and social realism. *Taiwan xinminbao* [Taiwan new people's news], originally established in Tokyo, started its Chinese edition in Taiwan in 1931. The Taiwan Culture Association, an unofficial leftist organization, was formed in 1932 in Taipei and started two related magazines, *Fu'ermosha* [The Formosan] and *Xianfa budui* [The avant-garde]. In 1934, the Taiwan Literary and Art Union was formed, and Taiwan new literature appeared on the scene in 1935. It was in the context of this political atmosphere and nativist literary discourse that Yang Chichang in 1933 established the short-lived surrealist *Fengche shizhi*, also called *Le moulin*, the first modernist poetry magazine in Taiwanese literary history. Sharing a parallel destiny with *Xiandai*, which had been established, as we have seen, the previous year, *Fengche shizhi* was severely criticized by the social-realist camp as being decadent and perverse.

Both *Xiandai* and *Fengche shizhi* were reactions against the contemporary totalitarian organization of the nationalist as well as the nativist norm. The editors and writers of both journals were heavily influenced by contemporary Japanese and European modernism. Through reexamining the perverse writings of Yang Chichang, I seek to show that they offer a mode of negative consciousness, an analysis that could help explain similar perverse writings in the modernism of 1950s Taiwan as well as those in 1980s China.

Before I move on to the Taiwanese scene, a brief sketch and reassessment of the studies of 1930s modernism in China will help provide a starting point for discussion. The beginning of the New Era in China in the 1980s, the so-called *xin shiqi*, was accompanied by the rise of modernist literature such as "*menglong* poetry" (a movement combining symbolism with political critique and associated with the journal *Jintian* [Today]) and was followed by a powerful tendency to welcome Western cultures. The same dynamic forces also triggered a wave of rediscovery and reappraisal of the suppressed and long-forgotten modernist literature from the 1920s and 1930s. Dozens of histories of this literature were published in an attempt to correct the view that social-realist literature was the only legitimate trend in modern Chinese literary history.[14] Modernist literature, such as Shanghai's new perceptionist movement of the 1930s, was brought to the foreground in this new wave of literary historiography.

The studies of the modernist literature of the 1930s convey scholars' subtle criticism of the monolithic discourse that appeared in China in that decade. It is pointed out that the reason the modernist literature was dismissed and forgotten by Chinese literary historians was that in the 1930s China chose a different path from that of the modernism of the new perceptionist school. This choice—which was framed in terms of either what Zhou Yi termed the culture's choice or what Chen Houcheng referred to as the choice of history—was to head toward a new order, with a more organized, positive, progressive, correct, and uniform system.[15]

Concerning the mainstream discourse's intolerance of the "Westernized" or heterogeneous elements in literary works, the question is not only, Why did they resent the polymorphous and the perverse? but also, Why did they desire their own repression with so strong a will? What is required to answer these questions is, as suggested by Deleuze and Guattari, an analysis of "the specific nature of the libidinal investments in the economic and political spheres," with the hope of explaining why and how, "in the subject who desires, desire can be made to desire its own repression."[16]

The highly organized discursive norm in the Chinese literary field of the 1930s is similar to what Deleuze and Guattari refer to as the "molar formation" exercised in the "socius." They explain the major traits of a molar formation of a "form of gregariousness" (herd instinct) as follows:

> They effect a unification, a totalization of the molecular forces through a statistical accumulation obeying the laws of large numbers. This unity can be the biological unity of a species or the structural unity of a socius: an organism, social or living, is composed as a whole, as a global or complete object. It is in relation to this new order that the partial objects of a molecular order appear as a lack, at the same time that the whole itself is said to be lacked by the partial objects.

According to Deleuze and Guattari, the socius is a "body without organs," and "the races and cultures designate regions on this body—that is, zones of intensities, fields of potentials."[17] The norm of modern Chinese literary discourse follows the collective desire for the lack, or the phallus, which points to a new order, a more organized, progressive, correct, and uniform system. This highly cathected partial object, the new order, demands that all individual writers strive to serve the phallus, to subject the individual to the organization of the society, to advocate the future utopian nation, to reveal the corruption of the society, and to correct its wrongs.[18] In the powerful momentum of organization, all individuals willingly give up their personal fantasies and desire with vehemence such repression.

It is also within such a highly Oedipal collective neurosis that the fear of the perverse is intensified. Studies appearing in the 1980s show that, in spite of the attempted reappraisal of the Chinese modernism of the 1930s, the repulsion felt toward the abnormal, the decadent, and the perverse in modernist literature remained. Scholars of the 1930s and the 1980s share the same sentiments of fear and resentment. Yan Jiayan, a pioneer in the study of Chinese modernist literature, for example, fully demonstrated in his preface to the *Xinganjuepai xiaoshuo xuan* his severe objection to the "capitalistic" sadistic and perverted pleasure described in Shi Zhecun's story "Shi Xiu" [Shi Xiu].[19] Shi Jianwei also criticized modernist writers, such as

Mu Shiying, who, following Freudian theories, present their characters as entirely driven by sexual desire.[20]

Closely allied with the reservation about the abnormal and the perverse is the urge for writers to join the collective forces of national reformation. Shi Jianwei, for example, has insisted that all literature should "relate the fortune of individuals organically with the revolutionary tides of the time," "reveal the essential conflicts of the society," and "advocate the future ideal."[21] Such a critical stance echoes the typical leftist discourse of Ah Ying and others in the 1930s, who also demanded that writers should attend to the correct path and serve as the spokespeople of the proletariat.

The norm and the collective cannot tolerate the atomized self who refuses to enter the symbolic structure and who resists having his or her desires stabilized and identity fixed. This atomized self, or what Deleuze and Guattari term the *schizo*, does not belong to any given social order:

> The schizo is not revolutionary, but the schizophrenic process—in terms of which the schizo is merely the interruption or the continuation in the void—is the potential for revolution. To those who say that escaping is not courageous, we answer: what is not escape and social investment at the same time? The choice is between one of two poles, the paranoiac counter-escape that motivates all the conformist, reactionary, and fascisizing investments, and the schizophrenic escape convertible into a revolutionary investment.[22]

Choosing to be neither a conformist nor a fascist, the artist takes up the schizophrenic process and carries out deterritorialization and reterritorialization through creative work.

If we reexamine the "perverse and morbid" texts of the new perceptionist movement, we realize that it is from this point that these modernist writers actualized their resistance and demonstrated their revolutionary force. Shanghai had been in a peculiar position because, since the nineteenth century, the ownership of its land had been given, piece by piece, to the British, the French, and the Japanese governments; it has, therefore, been called the nation within a nation. In the early decades of the twentieth century, Shanghai witnessed the complex intermixing of multiple cultures, including not only English, French, and Japanese but also diasporic Russians, Jews, Romanians, etc. Leo Ou-fan Lee has pointed to the mixture of heterogeneous cultures of the Tang dynasty as the background in Shi Zhecun's fiction, observing that the combination of "the ancient exotic color" and the "modern psychological knowledge" makes it different from classical historical romance. However, such an "intermixing of heterogeneous cultures" perfectly reflects the conditions of Shanghai in the 1930s.[23] In his stories, Shi Zhecun creates the arena for boundary setting or crossing among diverse ethnic groups. The problems of blood origin, loyalty, history, heritage, and the authenticity of or confusion about cultural identity are prominently developed. Likewise, in the rapid montage of street scenes and psychic scenes in the work of Liu Naou and Mu Shiying, there is also an uneasiness of cultural identity in the semicolonial condition in Shanghai.[24] Finally, a similar tendency is evident in the perverse writings of Yang Chichang.

In the Taiwanese scene of the the 1930s, Yang Chichang was facing conditions similar to those of the modernist writers in Shanghai at the same time. Yang, who studied Japanese literature at Tokyo University from 1930 to 1931 and wrote exclusively in Japanese, has been repeatedly criticized for his interest in such topics as prostitution and sexuality as well as for what he described in his essay "The Dwindled Candle Flame" ["Zanshoku no honoo"] (1985) as his "decadent" and "demonic" style.[25]

When we examine the literary discursive trends of the 1930s, we soon realize that Yang was not welcomed by his contemporaries because the second wave [zai chufa] of the Taiwan new literature movement was already under way. This second wave was advocated by the Taiwan Culture Association. The theme of the first issue of *Xianfa budui*, the representative magazine of the association, was to investigate "the road of Taiwan new literature." In 1934, the editorial column of *Xianfa budui* expressed the editorial board's discontent with the formal experiments practiced by the writers of the time, including such examples as the journals *Nanyin* and *Xiaozhong*, which had "run into a wall" [peng bi], remarking that "they fall back into the sensational, sentimental, playful, and even low-class literary act."[26] *Xianfa budui* also clearly stated a desire to organize the dispersed elements and move toward the "authentic" [bengehua] path of construction. In this, we can see the internal censorship exercised within the Taiwanese literary field, checking individualized and diverse formal experimentation.

In the early 1920s, the rising Taiwan new literature movement, influenced by the May Fourth movement in China, clearly manifested its revolutionary and military tone. In the first issue of *Taiwan qingnian* [Taiwanese youth], published in 1920 in Tokyo, the editorial column stated that the purpose of the magazine was to wake up Taiwanese young people to face the cultural movement in the contemporary world: "My respectable young comrade! Come forward, and let's march together!"[27] Zhang Wojun, the most forceful advocate of Taiwan new literature, wrote several letters to the magazine in 1924, addressing Taiwanese young people, urging them to try their best to "reform the society" and not continue sleeping. Zhang exclaimed: "Come and fight, and march forward with no pause, and we'll meet our aim one day!"[28]

The same marching spirit and will to reform were echoed in the poems that appeared in *Xianfa budui* in 1934, for example, the *Xianfa budui* manifesto:

> March, the avant-garde!
> Let's march in this tense and bright atmosphere.
> With the will to soar up high,
> With the spirit that knows no limit,
> With the steps that follow the path,
> March!
> March!
> . . . . .
> The avant-garde moves forward to build a new world. Their blood and flesh are running and hot, awaiting the other troops to come.
> Don't hesitate.
> Don't doubt.
> Come.
> Let's assemble at this front line,
> Freeze the ocean,
> Move the mountain,
> Let's start,
> Until
> The new world of ours is actualized.[29]

We can clearly see here the strong desire for collective organization behind these lines and the severity hidden within such marching spirit. Deleuze and Guattari describe the "violence" and the "joy" associated with feeling oneself "a wheel in the machine, traversed by flows," and in a position "where one is thus traversed, broken, fucked by the socius."[30] The collective mobilization attracts all individuals' personal desires and leads them toward the national phallus, the new order, and the new world. The will to freeze the ocean, to move the mountain, with the running and the hot blood and the flesh, demonstrates a paranoid fantasy and the desire to obey and submit to the collective force. Following the double impulse within the avant-garde spirit—to change literary conventions and to change the world—*Xianfa budui* found the solution in the military forcefulness of the latter cause.

Such a paranoid fantasy on the part of the *Xianfa budui* writers stands in clear contrast to what Yang Chichang practiced in his poetry and fiction. For him, while the colonial situation was impossible to ignore, that reality nevertheless could not be observed and described directly. Therefore, he used a form of negative description to write about the traumatic experience of the colonized and, in this way, used textual production to put resistance into practice. He was neither willing nor able to pursue the goals of the masses, as was advocated in the *Xianfa budui* manifesto. Instead, he could only stroll about aimlessly like a flaneur, sometimes even closing his eyes as he did so. The poem "The Sunday Stroller" ["Nichiyooshiki no sanposha"] (1933) can stand as a statement of his poetics. He shuts his eyes in order to "see still-life images," thereby allowing the landscape to develop "through shattered memories," as if in a dream. Strolling through this dreamscape, the narrator sees:

> People laugh, seemingly cheerfully,
> Passing through the rainbow-shaped space formed by their laughter, dragging
>   along their sins. . . .
> . . . . .
> I stroll along, listening to the voices in the space,
> I press my ears onto my body and
> Listen to the demonlike voices from within.

In another poem from 1933, "Hallucination" ["Genei"], what he sees is the "gray brain," the "moronic country," the "cheerful people," and the "virulent hallucinations" in the colonized land:

> Shattering through the closely sealed windows of mine,
> The gray Mephistopheles broke in,
> The rhythm of his laughter painted musical notes in my brain.
> . . . . .

> The awful breath of the night falls.
> When will the snowstorm start under this forgotten colonized sky?
> The virulent hallucinations emerging from the sneer.

In the course of ordinary life, the poet sees the blizzards and fierce hallucinations that may rise up "under the forgotten colonial skies" as well as the masses who unwittingly but contentedly commit sins and transgressions and "dream in their gray brain matter of the open land of the moronic country."[31]

In another of Yang's poems, "The Green Bell-Tower" ["Aojiroi shooroo"] (1933), the narrator finds himself walking through the streets of Tainan, and, amid the sounds of "green reverberations of the tolling of the bell," the "purplish-green sound waves," and the "explosive retorts of coverless trucks," he glimpses "a prostitute who has frozen to death." In the more recent "Self-Portrait" ["Jigazoo"] (1979), Yang also uses figures of "destruction," a "romantic city," a "peaceful morning," a "desolate world," and "flickering life" to describe the city of Tainan, while the poet himself remains "buried in refuse."[32]

Yang realized his political position not through a direct manifesto but, rather, through resistance to the organized literary norms of his time and escape into perverse writing. He fully understood the censorship that Taiwanese writers faced during the 1930s and realized that, if he had written directly about reality and fully expressed what he saw and experienced, it would have been impossible to have published his writings. Since he was not content to follow the banal track of his contemporaries and write what other people expected of him, he chose to write in a "perverse way" [*yichangwei*] and revealed in his works the traumatic experience of the Taiwanese people under the colonial system.

Yang's atomized or schizophrenic style of writing, relying on scattered images, is best illustrated in the poem "Demi Rever," written in 1934:

> The morning absorbs from the violent snowstorms the lights of July.
> Wavelike sounds of music, painting, and poetry are like angels' footsteps.
> My musical ideal was the melody of Picasso's guitar.
> The sun sets with the dusk and seashells.
> Picasso. Painter of the cross. Thoughts of the flesh. Dreams of the flesh. Ballet of the flesh.
> Decadent white liquid.

> An idea that came after the third lighting of the cigar pipe
> Entered into a black glove.
> Northwesterly wind blows across the windowpane,
> As passion breathing out of the pipe turns toward the seashore.
> The pollen of dreams remains on the pale forehead, white ribbons of the wind,
> The solitary air is unstable.
> Sunlight's fallen dream
> Is in the music of the dried wooden angel. Green imagery starts to drift. Birds, fish. Beast, trees, water, and sand. They too become rain. . . .[33]

The anarchy of atomized images and the disaggregation of the will to control the text appear similar to what Nietzsche, following Paul Bourget's comments on the decadent style, observed with respect to Wagner: "That life no longer dwells in the whole. The word becomes sovereign and leaps out of the sentence, the sentence reaches out and obscures the meaning of the page, and the page gains life at the expense of the whole—the whole is no longer a whole. But this is the simile of every style of decadence: every time, the anarchy of atoms, disaggregation of the will."[34] The abandonment of rational control, the disintegration of form, the resistance to earnest observation of reality, all these things in Yang's writing are very alien to the Chinese and Taiwanese way of thinking. However, it is precisely through this alien form of abandonment and disintegration that Yang managed to probe the depths of reality and of the unconscious, which is so unusual in a Chinese and Taiwanese cultural context.

The depths of reality and the unconscious are also revealed through Yang's obsession with scenes of horror and images of death. Yang suggested that the technique employed by Hukui Keiichi, the artist who illustrated some of his books, constitutes a kind of "negative treatment" that reveals "the dark side of one's consciousness." He also explained that in his fictional piece "The Rosy Skin" ["Bara no hifu"] (1937) he tried to present "the joy of sex through blood": "I attempted to make the blood vomited by the man flow onto the body of the woman. The man caresses her bloody body with his hand, and the woman hides her face in his bosom, like two naked bloody beasts, both enjoying the ecstasy of love." This kind of "strange love" and "cruelty" is, according to Yang, meant to present the "weird beauty and the strange light" of sex so that his works can explore the "perverse state of modern neurosis."[35]

To be more specific, the perverse and even sadistic obsession with the image of death reveals Yang's perception of reality in the 1930s as a combination of beauty and decay, as is illustrated by the following excerpt from his poem "The Image of the Moon's Death—the Tombstone of a Lady, II" ["Tsuki no shisoo (Jyohimei dai nisyoo)"] (1939):

> The lustful roses,
> The fossil of flowers with the fragrance of the hair,
> The snow-white stone statue with the fragrance of the hair.
>
> From within the window we can see the candlesticks.
> The secrets of the night,
> Flowers, fruits, gems, reptiles. . . .
> Ah, the sound of the bugs' wings falling on the images of death.
>
> In the wind of failure,
> The ritual of the dancing corpses has just begun.

Such an irrational juxtaposition of beauty and decay betrays a sense of horror in the face of total failure and despair. In "The Butterfly's Thoughts—the Tombstone of a Lady, I" ["Choo no shikoo (Jyohimei dai issyoo)"] (1939), beauty and death are also closely linked:

> Purple fingers of the death lantern extended underneath its shades,
> The butterflies swarm and whiten the place,
> The secret of dreams.
>
> Through the deep channel of light,
> Exploring the fictive layers of the narrative,
> The butterflies crouch on.
>
> The night that is magically transformed,
> Is it the thinking of the bloody color?
> Into the inscriptions on the tombstone of the woman who betrayed the season,
> As numerous as the butterflies' powdered wings.[36]

In "Tainan qui dort" ["Kowareta machi—Tainan qui dort"] (1936), Yang presents more fully the trauma that he experienced during this period:

> Under the attack of pale shock,
> The crimson lips uttered a terrible cry.

> In the deathlike stillness of the dawn,
> The blood-smeared wounds of my body are heating with fever.[37]

Such a juxtaposition of beauty and death/corruption, or of beauty and the stillness of death, reveals the living conditions of Tainan that Yang was facing—that is, life in death or the life of the living dead.

Perhaps the irrational juxtaposition of the contrary states of life and death, and of beauty and corruption, corresponds to the "new relation" discussed by the surrealist poet Nishiwaki Junzaburo, whom Yang admired greatly. Similar to the "enigma" suggested by Mallarmé or Breton's "beauty of wonder," Nishiwaki emphasized the excitement in the discovery of the "new relation," which is close to the sensation of the "rational mind being attacked."[38] Mallarmé, Bréton, and Nishiwaki all refer to the way in which a poem can combine disparate elements to create a new relation, which is enough to present an overwhelming challenge to formerly fixed concepts. Yang's new relations are most clearly manifested when he uses an anti-idealized juxtaposition of incommensurate concepts. This process of atomizing and fracturing is a retreat from idealism, together with a loosening of the strictures of the text.

However, I must stress here that the new relation as manifested in Yang's poetry is meant not merely to shock or depict a wondrous beauty but also to lay bare, through a kind of "negative consciousness" or the "perverse" mode of beauty, the experience of trauma, failure, deception, and despair, an experience made all the more unbearable because it is silenced and imprisoned in the numb cheerfulness of the colonized land.

The most common way in which Yang's poetry uses a violent and anti-idealized method of bringing together disparate experiential elements is by conjoining themes of decadence and seductive beauty. Alternatively, we could say that the juxtaposition of calm happiness and decadent setback, of beauty and the death and decay that underlie it, and of a static life and the wound that lies beneath it are the keynotes of Yang's poetry and also constitute the plight in which he found himself as an inhabitant of colonial Tainan. Examples of some of his early poems addressing these themes include "Tainan qui dort" and "The Image of the Moon's Death."

When the colonial situation became a state of military conflict, Yang's poetry began to return to the theme of death with ever-greater frequency.

Therefore, "The Image of the Moon's Death" foregrounds a callous juxtaposition of life and death as well as of death and seductive beauty. The poem includes not only still and solitary images of death but also the "lustful roses" in the cemetery; we not only see the stone statue and the flower fossil but also smell the fragrance of hair permeating both. Similarly, we see not only the withered skeletons of twigs and leaves fluttering in the wind but also the mortal vestiges of deceased flowers, rotten fruits, tarnished gems, and reptiles.

The figure of the butterfly appears frequently in Yang's poetry and functions as a crucial link between the contrasting elements of cohesive beauty and mortal terror. As early as his 1935 "Veins and Butterflies" ["Joomyaku to choo"], butterflies perform an aerial dance over the corpse of a young woman who has committed suicide in a classical manner:

> In the dusk, the young woman raises her hand with its protruding veins,
> In the forest behind the sanitarium, there is the corpse of a hanging victim,
> The pleats and folds of a butterfly-embroidered green skirt are fluttering gently.

Butterflies also dance in the twilight in Tainan, this city that was defeated and effectively destroyed, while the survival of the populace is inscribed in the "defeated land" itself. The people in "Tainan qui dort," can only whistle silently, like a lifeless and hollow conch shell:

> The people who sign their names on the defeated land
> Whistle silently, empty conch shells
> Singing old histories, old lands, houses, and
> Trees, all love to meditate sweetly
> Autumn leaves fluttering in the dusk!
> For the prostitutes singing boat songs,
> The sighs of the old homeland are pale and colorless.

In "Pale Song" ["Aozameta uta"], from 1939, butterflies flutter within the morbid thoughts of another suicide victim:

> Terrified of the suicide victim's white eyes, they flutter in the music
>   of the sick leaves.[39]

In the poem "The Butterfly's Thoughts—the Tombstone of a Lady, I," published in the same year as "Pale Song" and cited above, we glimpse even more clearly the butterflies dancing in the shadows of the death lanterns that illuminate an open grave. They appear to have already learned the secrets of death and life's vacuous adornments: "Through the deep channel of light, / Exploring the fictive layers of the narrative, / The butterflies crouch on."

Living himself in a colonial territory, Yang had to participate in a thorough and compulsory normalization while still maintaining a superficial veneer of calm and happiness. He was similarly confronted with war but powerless to change or avert it. All that remained for him was a pervading sense of failure and desolation, the stubborn fantasies of violence and death and decay that lurk in the interstices between silence and repression, and the systematic terror hidden beneath these insistent fantasies.

In his poetry and fiction, Yang Chichang employs a perverse writing style that resists systematization and organization, making his the first work in modern Taiwan literature to use neurotic perversity as well as a cruel and repulsive beauty as constituent elements. If he had not insisted on this atomizing perversity, refused to enter the literary organizations of the new literature, and refused the assignation of a static identity, then he would not have had access to this perverse dimension that was so rare in early Taiwan literature; nor would he have been able to traverse the surface, textual appearance of cruel and repulsive beauty and probe a deeper liminal zone embedded within a larger symbolic economy.

Yang indicated in "The Dwindled Candle Flame" that the concepts of "pure love, vestigial sentiment, dispassionate purity, and seductive beauty" can come full circle and be transformed into "negligible darkness and shaded obscurity" while also being directly linked to the aforementioned "cruel and repulsive beauty." Furthermore, the transformation of this sort of "negligible darkness" is made possible through its being grounded on the fulcrum of a "ruthless and icy gaze." This is the way in which "those who feel deeply" regard life and death because, "in order to emotionlessly reveal it [life and death], it is necessary to tap into humanity's inherent icy stoicism."[40]

The pleasure that the observer feels while his flesh drips with fresh blood, while being entranced with the decay and seductiveness of death, or while listening carefully to the demonic voices within his own body—all these examples from Yang's poetry illustrate the ways in which he uses perverse scenarios to challenge traditional values. At the same time, they constitute a departure from the organization of forms of human desire under the Oedipus complex. Once the subject enters that organization, he or she can follow the path of desire and pursue a systematized absolute standard as well as a unified object. Gendered identity, national identification, political orientation, as well as abstract moral standards all become the foundation for a structured desire. Within it, the creation of a distinct "subjectivity" is made possible, together with an identification mechanism inclined toward the superego. The superego demands that the ego reject all the vestigial traces of the primal mother, just as it demands that the self forcibly expel all the impure elements within its own body, in order to complete the process of purification and systematization.

This negative, negating, and demonic style of brutal pleasure and cruel, repulsive beauty that Yang develops constitutes a rare exception in early Chinese and modernist Taiwan literature. Furthermore, the significance of Yang's works lies in how he uses a perverse attitude to extricate and distance himself from the conventional monoglossic discussions of new Taiwan literature and, thereby, to open up new ideological and literary terrain. Seen from this perspective, the figure of the prostitute, which continually reappears in his works between 1933 and 1939, is, therefore, an indirect expression of Taiwan's own prostituted consciousness as a colonized territory.

The topics of sex and prostitution appear frequently in many of Yang's other poems from the period 1933–39. Similarly, in such poems as "Tainan qui dort," "The Green Bell Tower," and "The Image of the Moon's Death," as well as in "The Rosy Skin" (1937), the vocabulary of blood, silence, and death gradually increased during the same general period. This slow process of change in Yang's writing runs parallel to the progress of the war between Japan and China as well as to that of the larger war in which countless Taiwanese young men were drafted to join the battle in Southeast Asia. This vocabulary of distorted emotion reveals the hidden violence as well as the suppressed fear that characterizes these scenes of death.

In order to lead his readers into a fantasy realm exploring the materiality of abstract signifiers and the margins of the human spirit, Yang used a literary strategy grounded, as we have seen him put it in "Demi-rever," in: "Thoughts of the flesh. Dreams of the flesh. Ballet of the flesh." He suggested that readers must transform their cultural identity and escape their ethnic positionality, while also demanding that poetry be removed from reality and be a product of processed reality, opaque language, and the manifestations of a developed subconscious. When we consider these aspects of his literary project, together with his use of surrealistic imagery and a demonic and seductive atmosphere, we can easily understand why his "demonic works" were repeatedly criticized by the realist literature organizations for, as he reported in "The Dwindled Candle Flame," their "indulgent beauty," "decadent beauty," "demonic beauty," "repulsive beauty," "cruel beauty," and why his mixture of modernist poetics and neurotically perverse writings constituted such a shock to the literary establishment.[41] Finally, we may also understand why the *Mingtan* and *Xianfa budui* publishing houses both failed to include him within the category of *Taiwan* new literature.

Sex and violence, as Georges Bataille discussed in *The Tears of Eroticism*, produce the same mode of intensified pleasure because each can serve as the outlet for a hidden inner fear. Consequently, the compulsive fantasy of extreme pain as well as those of violence and eroticism are strategies used to resist the suppressed horror in the face of death.[42] The subject of Bataille's discussion was the writings and paintings Sade and Goya produced during their respective periods of imprisonment: After witnessing the brutality and death of war, Sade was imprisoned for thirty years, while Goya was deaf for the final thirty-six years of his life. Both started their violent writing and painting during their period of imprisonment.

I suggest that whatever the form of imprisonment—be it institutional, physical, or cultural, such as that in which Yang found himself—forced silence in the presence of physical violence and death breeds violence and perversity in expression. Taiwan literature of the 1950s and 1960s, especially the writings in the surrealist mode during the first decades after the establishment of martial law in 1950 (e.g., those of Luo Fu), and Chinese literature of the 1980s (e.g., the work of Can Xue) both reveal a close affinity to the perverse writings of Yang Chichang.

NOTES

Unless otherwise indicated, all translations from non-English-language sources are my own.

1 See Joyce C. H. Liu, "The Abject of the Avant-Garde in Early Modern Taiwan Literature" (paper presented at the conference "Writing Taiwan," Columbia University, 1998). A revised version of this material, developed into two chapters, appeared in my *Guer, nüshen, fumian shuxie: Wenhua fuhao de weizhuangshi yuedu* [Orphan, Goddess, and the writing of the negative: The performance of our symptoms] (Taipei: Lixu, 2000), 152–89, 224–59. The Chinese version of the present essay is also included in this book (see ibid., 190–223).

2   See Gilles Deleuze and Félix Guattari, *Anti-Oedipus: Capitalism and Schizophrenia* (Minneapolis: University of Minnesota Press, 1983).
3   On the paradoxical nature of the avant-garde, see the discussion in Matei Calinescu, "The Idea of the Avant-Garde," in *Five Faces of Modernity: Modernism, Avant-Garde, Decadence, Kitsch, Postmodernism* (Durham: Duke University Press, 1996), 95–148.
4   See Julia Kristeva, *Powers of Horror: An Essay on Abjection*, trans. Leon S. Roudiez (New York: Columbia University Press, 1982).
5   Julia Kristeva, *Tales of Love*, trans. Leon S. Roudiez (New York: Columbia University Press, 1987), 340, 339.
6   Kristeva, *Powers of Horror*, 8.
7   Most literary historians' periodization of the 1930s begins with 1927 and ends with 1930. But Li Helin points out that 1931 is a significant year because of the September Eighteenth Incident (in which the Japanese army blew up a portion of the South Manchuria Railway in Shenyang, blaming the explosion on the Chinese army, and using it as a pretext to invade northeastern China). See Li Helin, *Jinershinian Zhongguo wenyi sichao lun* [Chinese literary trends from the past twenty years] (Shanghai: Shanghai Books, 1995), 261. In his "Wenxue de Shanghai: Yijiusanyi" [Literary Shanghai: 1931], in *Ruhe xiandai, zenyang wenxue* [How modern, what literature] (Taipei: Ryefield, 1998), 269, 278, David Der-wei Wang also suggests that this is the moment at which the focus of the literary movement shifted from the north to the south, from Beijing to Shanghai.
8   Compare Li, *Jinershinian Zhongguo wenyi sichao lun*, 261–71.
9   The nationalist movement started in 1930 by the rightist literati, such as Wang Ping-ling, Huang Zhenxia, Fan Zhengpo, Yie Qiuyuan, and Zhu Yingpeng, triggered the wave of nationalist literature in the 1930s. The leftists' slogans, such as Zhou Yang's "national defense literature" and Lu Xun's "nationalist revolutionary war literature of the people," shared the same nationalistic spirit. Compare Li Mu, *Sanshi niandai wenyi lun* [On the literary debates of the 1930s] (Taipei: Li Ming, 1972), 61–63.
10 Yan Jiayan points out that the novels of the new perceptionist movement (see below) were heavily influenced by contemporary Japanese literature. The new perceptionist movement started in 1928, with the journal *Wuguilieche*, established by Liu Naou. The writers for this journal included Dai Wangshu, Xu Xiachun, Shi Zhichun, Du Heng, Lin Weiyin, and Liu Naou. *Xiandai*, begun in 1932, was supported by the same group of people. See Yan Jiayan, *Zhonguo xiandai xiaoshuo liupaishi* [A history of six schools of modern Chinese fiction] (Beijing: Renmin wenxue, 1989), 125–31.
11 The debates on the "Third Kind of People" lasted from 1931 to 1933 and involved Hu Qiuyuan, Su Wen, Qu Qiubai, Zhou Yang, Lu Xun, Feng Xuefeng, Hu Feng, and Chen Wangdao, among others.
12 Yan, *Zhonguo xiandai xiaoshuo liupaishi*, 16.

13 Shi Shu's articles—e.g., Shi Shu, "Ganjue shijie—sanling niandai Taiwan linglei xiaoshuo" [Ganjue shijie: The alternative Taiwanese novels in the 1930s], in *Liangan wenxue lunji* [Collected papers on literatures from China and Taiwan] (Taipei: Xindi, 1997), 86–101, and "Riju shidai Taiwan xiaoshuo zhong tuifei yishi de qiyuan" [The decadent consciousness in Taiwanese novels in the Japanese period], in ibid., 102–120—are helpful in understanding the situation that the leftist writers of the 1930s were facing. Chen Fangming's *Zuoyi Taiwan* [The leftist Taiwan] (Taipei: Rhyfield, 1998) and *Zhimindi Taiwan: Zuoyi zhengzhi yundong shilun* [Colonial Taiwan: The history of the leftist political movements] (Taipei: Rhyfield, 1998) also provide useful information concerning the Taiwanese leftist movement in the 1920s and 1930s.
14 After Yan Jiayan's *Xinganjuepai xiaoshuo xuan* [Anthology of xinganjue fiction] (Beijing: Tenmin wenxue chubanshe, 1985), there emerged dozens of literary histories of modernist literature.
15 See Zhou Yi, "Fuguang lüeyingxiao," in *Zhongguo xiandai wenxue yanjiu zongkan* [Collection of modern Chinese literary studies] 3 (1989): 140–49, 148; and Tang Zhengxu and Chen Houcheng, eds., *Ershi shiji Zhongguo wenxue yu xifang xiandai zhuyi sichao* [1920s Chinese literature and Western modernist thought] (Chengdu: Zichuan renmin chubanshe, 1992), 357.
16 Deleuze and Guattari, *Anti-Oedipus*, 105.
17 Ibid., 342, 85.
18 On the romantic and individualistic elements in modern Chinese literature, see Leo Ou-fan Lee, "Xiandai Zhongguo wenxue zhongde langman geren zhuyi" [Romantic individualism in modern Chinese literature], in *Xiandaixing de zhuiqiu* [In search of modernity] (Taipei: Rhyfield, 1996), 92.
19 "He [Shi] has almost become a completely modernized pervert of the capitalist class. . . . Such theories would lead the literary creation to a very pathetic stage" (Yan, *Xinganjuepai xiaoshuo xuan*, 32–33).
20 Shi Jianwei, "Xianshi zhuyi haishi xiandai zhuyi: Shilun xinli fenxi xiaoshuopai de chuangzuo qingxiang ji qi lishi jiaoshun" [Realism or modernism: An examination of the creative directions in psychoanalytic fiction together with their historical lessons], *Zhonguo xiandai wenxue yanjiu congkan* [Journal of Chinese modern literature studies] 2 (1985): 51.
21 Ibid., 56. Leo Ou-fan Lee also points out that the individual is filled with heated determination to strive for collective goals and to unite with the people and with history. See Lee, "Xiandai Zhongguo wenxue zhongde langman geren zhuyi," 92.
22 Deleuze and Guattari, *Anti-Oedipus*, 341.
23 Lee, "Xiandai Zhongguo wenxue zhongde langman geren zhuyi," 166.
24 Compare Peng Xiaoyan, "Langdang tianya: Liu Na'ou yijiuerqi nian riji" [Wandering to the ends of the earth: The Diary of Liu Naou of 1927], *Zhongguo wenzhe yanjiu jikan* 12.3 (1998): 1–39.

25 Liu Xingchang, ed., Ye Di et al., trans., *Collected Works of Shuiyingping* (Tainan: Tainan Culture Center, 1995), 240–42.
26 Li Nanheng, ed., *Wenxian ziliao xuanji* [Collected documents], Rujuxia Taiwan xin wenxue [Taiwanese new literature of the Japanese period], vol. 5 (Taipei: Mingtan, 1979), 150–51; cf. Shi, "Ganjue shijie," and "Riju shidai Taiwan xiaoshuo zhong tuifei yishi de qiyuan."
27 Li, ed., *Wenxian ziliao xuanji*, 1–2.
28 Zhang Wojun, "A Letter to Taiwanese Young People," in ibid., 57, 56.
29 Li, ed., *Wenxian ziliao xuanji*, 146–47.
30 Deleuze and Guattari, *Anti-Oedipus*, 346–47.
31 Liu, ed., *Collected Works*, 81–83, 76–77.
32 Ibid., 71.
33 Ibid., 97–99.
34 Friedrich Nietzsche, *The Birth of Tragedy and the Case of Wagner*, trans. Walter Kaufman (New York: Vintage, 1967), 170.
35 Liu, ed., *Collected Works*, 241–42.
36 Ibid., 111–12, 108–10.
37 Ibid., 50–52.
38 Nishiwaki Junzaburo, *Poetics* (1929), in Du Guoqing, ed. and trans., *Nishiwaki Junzaburo's Poetry and Poetics* (Gaoxung: Chunhui, 1980), 7.
39 Liu, ed., *Collected Works of Shuiyingping*, 22, 51–52, 45.
40 Ibid., 139, 242.
41 Ibid., 242.
42 See Georges Bataille, *The Tears of Eros* (San Francisco: City Lights, 1989), 132–33.

5

"On Our Destitute Dinner Table": *Modern Poetry Quarterly* in the 1950s

Michelle Yeh

As for poetry, this silly thing, it's just like that, besides
You have seen its true form;
On our destitute dinner table
We eagerly suck a cleaned bone
—That most exquisite phrase?

Ya Xian, "Burned and Sent to T.H."

The modern poetry debate [*xiandaishi lunzhan*] in the early 1970s marks a watershed in modern Taiwan literature. Its criticism of modern poetry's overt Westernization and self-imposed alienation from society made it a harbinger of the native literature movement [*xiangtu wenxue yundong*] in 1977–79, a movement that championed local identity and social consciousness. The replacement of modernism by nativist realism in Taiwan literature in the 1980s is, thus, related directly to the native literature movement and indirectly to the earlier modern poetry debate. In terms of both its profound ramifications and its highly controversial nature, this debate is one of the most significant events in the history of modern Chinese poetry.

Literary history since the 1980s, however, has tended to accept the triumph of nativist realism over modernism at face value. Such a teleological approach overlooks the problematic assumptions underscoring the nativist position in the debate, specifically, its rigid binary oppositions between tradition and modernity and between China (this was before Taiwan was a legitimate subject) and the West, and its unexamined equations among literary style, subject matter, and the value and function of literature. The other side of the coin is the elision of the complexity of the modernist movement in Taiwan in the 1950s and 1960s. The critical thrust of some of the best modernist poetry from that period tends to be overlooked or undervalued. In short, a more balanced assessment of the debate in particular and of Taiwan's modernist poetry in general has yet to be made.

That subject, however, lies beyond the scope of the present discussion. Rather, in what follows, I will trace the origin of the debate to the rise of modernism in Taiwan poetry in the 1950s and address such questions as why modernism appealed to the poets of the postwar generation and how it became the dominant trend in the 1950s and 1960s. Specifically, my analysis will focus on the publication of the *Modern Poetry Quarterly* (hereafter *MPQ*), which played a seminal role in ushering in a new poetic movement in the postwar period.[1] The profound influence of the journal on contemporary and later poets also made it a salient target during the modern poetry debate, in which modernism was singled out for criticism.

MPQ was founded by Ji Xian, the pen name of Lu Yu (b. 1913), in Taipei on February 1, 1953. Trained as a painter in Suzhou, Ji Xian had started writing poetry, under the pseudonym Luyishi, in mainland China in the 1930s and was closely associated with the modernist journal *Xiandai*, also known as *Les contemporains*, founded by Dai Wangshu (1905–50) and Shi Zhecun (b. 1905) in Shanghai in 1932–35. By the 1940s, Ji Xian had established himself as a reputable poet and had founded a few poetry journals of his own before moving to Taiwan in 1949. In the thirteenth issue of *MPQ*, published on February 1, 1956, he announced the founding of the modernist school [*xiandaipai*]. On the cover of the journal were listed the "six principles":

1. We are a group of modernists who selectively promote the spirit of all new poetic schools since Baudelaire.
2. We believe that New Poetry is a horizontal transplant, not a vertical inheritance. This is a general assumption, a fundamental starting point, whether in theory or in practice.
3. Explore new continents of poetry, develop virgin lands of poetry, express new contents, create new forms, discover new tools, invent new techniques.
4. Emphasis on intellect.
5. Pursuit of pure poetry.
6. Patriotism. Anticommunism. Support of freedom and democracy.

The modernist school claimed a large number of members, ranging from eighty to over a hundred. It was a loose organization, however; the driving force behind it was the charismatic and energetic Ji Xian, who single-handedly ran *MPQ* and wrote the editorials. Of the school's six principles, the second was the most controversial, first in the 1950s and 1960s, and later during the modern poetry debate. *MPQ* showed signs of decline by the late 1950s and in February 1964 finally folded, after forty-five issues. After he retired from his teaching post at the Chenggong High School, Ji Xian emigrated to the United States in 1972, where he has been living in northern California. *MPQ* was revived in 1982 under the directorship of the poet Mei Xin (1935–97) and lasted another decade or so, but the reincarnation was only remotely related to the original journal and falls outside the scope of this study.

To understand the importance and contributions of *MPQ*, we must first understand the dynamics that underlay the historical context in which the journal emerged and flourished. My analysis draws on Pierre Bourdieu's theory of cultural production and, specifically, his theoretical model of the literary field, conceived as a social space in which agents, groups, or institutions utilize existing resources strategically to accumulate various types of capital (economic, social, cultural, symbolic, etc.) for the purpose of position taking. With its emphasis on the literary field as a system of relations, which offers a finite number of possibilities and imposes certain structural constraints, Bourdieu's theory is particularly useful for studying the modernist poetry movement of the 1950s.

CONTENTION BETWEEN MODERN AND TRADITIONAL POETRY

What kind of literary field did *MPQ* face in the postwar period of generally bleak social and economic conditions? Or, to put it another way, what were the existing forces with which modernist poetry had to compete and negotiate? In my view, modernist poetry ran up against two formidable forces: classical Chinese poetry and the official discourse of anticommunism.

By the time the modern poetry debate took place in the early 1970s, modern poetry had established itself as indisputably mainstream. However, in 1953, modern poetry (then better known as New Poetry or vernacular poetry) was still marginalized on the literary scene. The editorial in the second issue of *MPQ* opens with this self-deprecating remark: "Today, it is evident that New Poetry is looked down on by common people" (May 1953, front cover). The editorial in the third issue similarly notes: "It is plain for everyone to see that the existence and development of New Poetry receives little attention and runs into obstacles frequently" (August 1953, front cover).

"Obstacles" mainly refers to resistance from those who wrote classical poetry and considered it the only respectable form. Who were the advocates of the classical genre? In the editorial in the fifteenth issue, Ji Xian said: "Old Poetry exists only among a few powerful officials and eminent people, who promote it and exchange poems with one another" (October 1956, 80). Such exchanges among members of the elite have a long tradition in China and continued well into the twentieth century, in both Taiwan and mainland China.² In postwar Taiwan, the social prestige of Old Poetry was still firmly rooted; intellectuals who wrote in the classical style far outnumbered those who wrote New Poetry. When Ji Xian said that Old Poetry was written only by "a few," he most likely intended to downplay its influence and to encourage aspiring poets to pursue New Poetry. Judging from his other statements in *MPQ*, we can be certain that, in terms of both social status and cultural resources, modern poetry could hardly compete with the classical genre at the time. The editorial in the fifteenth issue, for instance, also mentions the large gathering of the traditional camp on the Poet's Day, also known as the Dragon Boat Festival, on the fifth day of the fifth lunar month: "Some [fellow modern poets] became nervous, worrying that ... New Poetry might be trampled on and die an early death. Actually, this concern is unnecessary.... Old Poetry is in the court, New Poetry is in the wild. Those of us who write modern poetry have neither power nor connections. Further, we are hard-pressed financially; we use our own money to publish poetry journals and can barely afford it" (October 1956, 80). Similarly, in the eighteenth issue, in response to Qin Zihao's (1912–63) criticism of the modernist school, Ji Xian was clearly agitated: "I have not heard [him] mock or taunt Old Poetry; he only picks on New Poetry with flippant words. Could it be that those who write Old Poetry are powerful officials, so he dares not call them names? Those who write New Poetry are mostly soldiers and students, who can be bullied?" (August 1957, 3).

These comments reveal the wide disparity in sociocultural and -economic status between Old and New Poetry. As Bourdieu points out, in the literary or artistic field, the avant-garde positions are "defined mainly negatively, by their opposition to the dominant positions."[3] An important motivation for *MPQ* was the emphasis on the power hierarchy between Old and New Poetry; it would form the basis for a new position, which will be elaborated on later.

Another piece of evidence of Old Poetry's popularity in the 1950s and 1960s comes from college campuses:

> The inaugural issue of the students' magazine at the Gaoxiong Medical School was published [in October 1955].... In it were classical *shi* poems and *ci* lyrics written by Dr. Du [Congming, the dean], faculty and staff, and students. At that time, under the promotion of Dean Du, Chinese literature professor Xu Chengzhang, and others, it was popular among students to chant poetry on campus. Dean Du had also established a Huanli Poetics Scholarship to encourage the composition of classical verse. It was not until May 1963 that the first vernacular poetry could be found in the newly published campus journal, and the Gao Med Poetry Club [the first vernacular poetry club] was founded in 1964."[4]

The presence of modern poetry clubs on university campuses notwithstanding, modern poetry was for a long time excluded from the education system. Anecdotes recounted by modern poets tell how professors of Chinese literature openly disparaged and mocked New Poetry. This did not change until September 1968, when the government instituted mandatory nine-year education. For the first time in history, two modern poems were included in the standardized curriculum for junior high schools; they were "Xiaye" [Summer night] by Yang Huan (1930–54) and "Eluanbi" [Eluanbi] by Yu Guangzhong (b. 1928).[5] By the early 1990s, the number had increased somewhat, but it was still limited to about two poems in each textbook.[6]

The denigration of New Poetry is also reflected in publishing in the postwar years. According to the statistics provided by the poet Zhang Mo (b. 1931), the four-year span from 1949 to 1952 produced twenty-six individual collections, the largest number since the May Fourth period. In 1953 alone, twenty-four poetry books were published.[7] Although the quantity had increased, political lyrics accounted for a vast proportion, while belletristic poetry remained scanty. Similarly, the newspapers published either anti-Communist poetry promoted by the government or modern poems in regular forms. The adverse situation lasted throughout the 1950s and 1960s, of which the following example is indicative.

In 1957, the unexpectedly popular *Zhongguo shixuan* [Anthology of Chinese poetry], edited by Mo Ren (b. 1920) and Peng Bangzhen (b. 1919), was published by Daye Bookstore, run by Chen Hui in Gaoxiong. In his review in *MPQ*, Ji Xian wrote: "I'd like to first pay respect to Mr. Chen Hui, the owner of Daye Bookstore, because, in this publishing industry dominated by pornography, no other man was willing to invest in printing large quantities of pure literature" (March 1957, 26). Qin Zihao was elated too: "Daye was willing to publish this 'unpopular' book. But, after it appeared, sales were fantastic, surpassing any other book published by the bookstore."⁸ Clearly, there was cause for rejoicing. Yet, as late as June 1964, in the editorial in the inaugural issue of *Li shikan* [Bamboo hat poetry journal], the poet Lin Hengtai (b. 1924) still lamented the indifference of bookstores to poetry books and journals and the neglect of poetry on the part of editors, who thought modern poetry deserved only to be "sneaked into [their newspapers]."⁹

The power hierarchy of Old and New Poetry manifested itself in a variety of ways. The long tradition of consecration of classical poetry resulted in an uneven distribution of cultural resources; equally important, the prestige of classical poetry had much to do with the perception of knowledge. Whereas the classical genre was associated with erudition and cultural refinement, modern poetry was considered unsophisticated and easy to write. This explains why it was often belittled, especially by intellectuals, a problem that had existed from the very beginning of New Poetry. Ji Xian clearly recognized this problem, as indicated in the editorial in the third issue of *MPQ*: "Some of the ideas people have about New Poetry are absurd and mistaken. ... The most serious and deadly one is that ... they think New Poetry is the easiest to write and the New Poet is the easiest to be. Its damage is more serious and more deadly than the opposition from the opponents and the attacks from the attackers" (August 1953, front cover). One of the challenges for *MPQ* was to educate the public about why modern poetry was harder to write precisely because of its seemingly unlimited freedom in language and form.

Ji Xian also held literary critics responsible for this attitude about modern poetry, which he considered to be largely a "misunderstanding perpetuated by those who think they know how to write poetry and those veteran writers who tell the public ignorant things for the sake of earning honoraria or socializing." From the introduction and discussion of theories to creative experiments, *MPQ* harshly criticized the amateur attitude prevalent on the literary scene at the time. Ji Xian pointed out that, just because an author knew how to write in the vernacular, it did not necessarily mean that he knew how to write poetry. As for poetic criticism, Ji Xian was especially harsh: "The so-called scholars and professors, the so-called theorists and critics, are all stumbling blocks for New Poetry, executioners of New Poetry!" (February 1954, 5).

MODERN POETRY AND THE OFFICIAL DISCOURSE OF ANTICOMMUNISM

The difficulty facing New Poetry was more than the resistance from classical poetry and the lack of professionalism on the poetry scene. Most, if not all, of the cultural resources in postwar Taiwan were controlled by the Nationalist regime (which comprised the three arms of the party, the government, and the military). Cultural policies were instituted shortly after the government moved to Taiwan. While censorship provided an effective preemptive deterrent to dissenting voices, literary and art awards, workshops and correspondence courses, and publications offered various incentives for writers and artists who supported the official ideology. Some of the most important measures related to poetry are the following:

> On May 20, 1949, martial law was announced (to be lifted only in 1987); in October, the literary supplement to the *New Life Daily* [Xinshengbao] *Xinshengbao* [New life daily] initiated discussions on the topic "Zhandou wenyi" [Combat literature and art].

> On March 1, 1950, Chiang Kai-shek assumed the presidency; in April, the Committee on Chinese Literature and Art Prizes was formed, followed by the Chinese Literature and Art Association [Zhonghua wenyi jiangjin weiyuanhui] (CLAA), the Youth Writing Association [Qingnian xiezuo xiehui], and the Women's Writing Association [Funü xiezuo xiehui]. In December, the CLAA advanced the slogan "Literature and Art into the Military" [*Wenyi dao junzhong qu*] and began to cultivate writers among military personnel; each branch of the military had its literary journals (e.g., *Zhongguo kongjun* [Chinese air force], *Zhongguo haijun* [Chinese navy], *Xianbing zazhi* [Military police magazine], *Zhandou qingnian* [Combat youth], and *Geming wenyi* [Revolutionary literature and art]).

On March 27, 1951 (Youth Day), literary and art circles published "Kangyi gongfei baoxing xuanyan" [Manifesto against Communist bandits' atrocities]; the Free China Poetry Recitation Team [Ziyou Zhongguo shige langsong dui] was formed, consisting of more than forty members from the CLAA, the Chinese Youth Anti-Communist and Counter-Soviet League–United Artists' Team [Zhongguo qingnian fangong kang'e lianhehui yishu gongzuodui], and the Taiwan Broadcasting Company, under the leadership of Song Ying.

In 1952, the National Taiwan University poetry recitation team performed at the law school of the university for three days; the recited poems were written by Ji Xian, Qin Zihao, Mo Ren, Zhong Lei, Zhong Dingwen, Li Sha, Peng Bangzhen, Rongzi, Deng Yuping, Yu Guangzhong, Xia Jing, and Shangguan Yu.

In 1953, Chiang Kai-shek published *Minsheng zhuyi yule liang pian bushu* [Two chapters on education and entertainment in supplement to the principle of people's livelihood], which formed the official basis for cultural policy.

In 1954, a movement was launched to "cleanse culture" and to get rid of the "three vices" [sanhai], referring to "the Red Poison," "the Yellow Menace," and "the Black Guilt."

In spring 1955, Chiang Kai-shek reiterated the cultural policy of anti-Communist art and literature.[10]

As we can see from the above outline, anticommunism, whether aimed at the People's Republic or at the Soviet Union, was a major component of postwar cultural policy. Two important incentives for writers to conform were publication and prizes. The Committee on Chinese Literature and Art Prizes, under the directorship of Zhang Daofan, then minister of the legislative yuan, announced two sets of guidelines, one to "call for literary creations" and the other to "encourage literature and art." The first category referred to the regular selection of works for publication and the second to the semiannual competitions, usually held on May 4 and November 12 (Dr. Sun Yat-sen's birthday). The criteria stipulated that the selected work should "utilize various literary techniques to promote national consciousness and contain anti-Communist and counter-Soviet meaning"; those selected were each given an honorarium of NT$100–NT$200. In the long poem competition, the first prize fetched NT$1,000, the second prize NT$800, and the third prize NT$600.[11] Considering that the average income of a state employee was a couple hundred dollars a month, those rewards would have been extremely attractive.

It is no wonder that the winning entries in the poetry competitions may be generally described as political lyrics that aptly represented the mainstream in the postwar era. An example is Zhong Lei's "Huanghe lian" [Love for the Yellow River], which won the first prize for the long poem in May 1952. Lyrical in tone, and written in ballad form, the poem of approximately three hundred lines adopts the first-person perspective of a young male soldier who addresses the female "you": "Ah Yellow River! / Forever you flow endlessly day and night / So diligent and busy." The long apostrophe expresses homesickness and love for the lost motherland, here represented by the Yellow River, the cradle of Chinese civilization. The mother-child metaphor runs through the poem. For example, the poet reminisces about his childhood: "In my golden childhood years, / Every day I leaned on / Your golden bosom; / I drank your golden / Sandy milk / And grew fast and stout."[12]

Although we should not dismiss all political lyrics of the period as propagandistic, the cultural policy nevertheless imposed severe limitations on literary creation. Like most political poetry, "Huanghe lian" is pseudolyrical in that it hides predetermined ideas and sentiments behind the facade of the personal and the spontaneous. The poem is full of formulaic language and trite imagery, such as "the galloping, surging Yellow River," "the ancient and trouble-ridden Yellow River," "the red devil," "suffering compatriots," and so on. Without exception, the political lyrics that won the prizes were odes to the lost mainland, to its majestic landscapes and ancient culture; typically, they expressed heart-wrenching homesickness, bemoaned the suffering of the people through wars and political upheavals, condemned the evil Chinese Communist Party, and vowed to recover the mainland and achieve eventual victory. "Huanghe lian" was not only published in *Wenyi chuangzuo* [Literary creations], edited by Zhang Daofan, but also broadcast by all the major radio stations in Taipei.[13]

It is somewhat ironic (although not surprising) that the anti-Communist poems in postwar Taiwan were not unlike poems of an earlier time, such as the "street-corner poems" [*jietou shi*], "poems for recitation" [*langsong shi*], and "slogan poems" [*kouhao shi*] produced during the Second Sino-Japanese War (1937–45), for which such leftist writers as Tian Jian (1916–85) and Zang Kejia (b. 1905) were well known. They have in common accessible, sentimental language; oratory form; and patriotic themes. Moreover, "Huanghe lian" begins and ends with these memorable lines from "Jiang jin jiu" [Bring the wine!] by Li Bai (701–62):

> Have you never seen
> the Yellow River waters descending from the sky,
> racing restless toward the ocean, never to return?[14]

The use of a familiar canonical poem to frame a new "canon" must have won approval from the authorities. The combination of the classical and the political-lyrical symbolically corresponds to the combination of conservatism and nationalism that prevailed in postwar Taiwan.[15] This sociocultural climate was suspicious of and hostile toward any alien idea, as suggested by Qin Zihao, who, along with Ji Xian, played a major role in the new poetic movement of the 1950s and 1960s: "On the poetry scene of Free Chinese today, no matter which [Western] school you introduce, it is unacceptable to reality; further, it is bound to be mocked by reality, whether it be romanticism, symbolism, or imagism."[16]

In addition to Old Poetry and political lyrics, which constituted the dominant forces in the postwar literary field, *MPQ* had to distinguish itself from the "new regulated verse" [*xin gelüshi*] commonly seen in the mass media. Modeled after the Crescent school [*Xinyue pai*], led by Xu Zhimo (1896–1931) and Wen Yiduo (1899–1946) in the 1920s, the new regulated verse was known for its formal regularity, with the same number of characters in each line and the same number of lines in each stanza, often in regular meters and rhymes. Because of its perfectly rectangular or square shape, the new regulated verse was mockingly referred to as "tofu cake style" [*doufugan ti*]. Ji Xian warned the readers of *MPQ*: "Whoever thinks that anything published in the literary supplements to major newspapers must be good is totally wrong. For the editor of a literary supplement does not necessarily know good poems from bad ones; besides, his tastes are inherently subjective. It is only editorial techniques that require that he use a neat square of a tofu cake to fill a blank space. What's so great about that?" (October 1955, 89).

In the 1950s, the new regulated verse was typically associated with sentimentality and shallow lyricism. Its existence was tolerated precisely because it did not constitute any threat to the official ideology. Comparable to popular love songs or popular romances in this way, it was not different from the political lyrics either, in its formulaic language and predictable content.

Given the social climate of the time, it is not surprising that the early issues of *MPQ* did, in fact, publish political lyrics, such as Li Sha's "Piaoxiang de qi" [The whistling flag] and "Songge" [Ode] and Shangguan Yu's "Nian guxiang" [Thinking of the homeland]. Ming Qiushui's "Chunfeng song" [Ode to the spring wind], for example, ends with these uplifting images: "Colorful pictures cover Free China! / Victorious songs fill the free world!" This type of poetry gradually disappeared from the journal as the New Poetry movement gathered momentum in the mid-1950s.

MPQ responded to the dominance of traditional poetry and the official discourse of anticommunism in very different ways. As discussed earlier, the journal openly opposed and challenged traditional poetry, but individual poets, including Ji Xian himself, participated in the official discourse. There are several reasons for these different tactics. First, confrontation or explicit defiance of the official discourse would carry serious political risks during the era of White Terror. Besides, it would do little to help advance the cause of modern poetry anyway.

For instance, in 1952, Ji Xian won the *MPQ* poetry competition with the poem "Xiangchou" [Homesickness]. His "Geming geming" [Revolution revolution] won the following year. In November 1953, at the poetry reading sponsored by the Ministry of Education, he recited his "symphonic poem," "Zuguo wansui shi wansui" [Long live my motherland, long live poetry]. The book of poetry that Ji Xian published in 1953, under the title *Zai feiyang de shidai* [In the soaring age], was advertised as a collection of political lyrics. According to the cover of the second issue of *MPQ*, the book contains Ji Xian's "anti-Communist and counter-Soviet poems" written from 1950 to 1953. Ya Xian also won the *MPQ* poetry competition repeatedly. His "Dongtian de fennu" [Winter's fury] won the second prize in the long poem competition in May 1954, and another long poem, "Zuguo wansui" [Long live the fatherland], won a special award in a military-sponsored contest the same year.

It is significant that these prizewinning poems are excluded from the authors' published oeuvres and are, indeed, hard to find today. Apparently, the poets did not regard their political lyrics as representative or worthy of preservation for posterity. This further supports my contention that the poets participated in the official discourse mainly to obtain the cultural resources that would have been otherwise unavailable to them. Given the fact that all such resources were in the hands of the establishment, they chose to participate in, rather than withdraw from, "combat literature and art." The result was that they were able to use the economic capital they thus obtained to sustain the private poetry journals. Further, winning contests might also give them some symbolic capital in the eyes of the establishment, which could protect and help them in their private endeavors. What happened, in essence, was a transfer of cultural resources from the official sphere to the private sphere: with the handsome rewards, the poets were able to fund privately run journals devoted to a kind of poetry that could not be more different from that endorsed by the state. In so doing, they were able to carve out a new space and gradually transform the general "ecology" of the literary field.

Cultural resources are not limited to literary prizes, of course. Many young poets were soldiers. Even if they did not participate in the official competitions, the large number of official journals provided the necessary forum for publishing their earliest works. Yet another resource was to be found in the state-sponsored writing workshops, which helped nurture a new generation of poets.

Finally, whether in the political establishment or in the modernist poetry circles, as a group recent émigrés from the mainland possessed more cultural capital than did native Taiwanese. Owing to Japanese colonization (1895–1945), native Taiwanese writers who grew up in the 1930s and 1940s were formally educated in Japanese only and typically spoke Hokkien or Hakka, two southern Chinese dialects, at home. When Taiwan was returned to China at the end of World War II, these writers were caught between two languages yet could not identify with either: Japanese, the colonizer's language that they were no longer allowed to speak, and Chinese, the language that was rightfully their mother tongue but that they hardly knew. With very few exceptions, native Taiwanese writers were faced with the unique quandary of having no language of their own. This condition of "cultural aphasia" had a far-reaching impact on the development of modern Chinese poetry in Taiwan. Some of the native writers simply gave up writing, a few continued to write in Japanese (but could not publish in Taiwan), while most of those who persisted would need fully ten years to acquire enough proficiency in Chinese to write and publish in that language. While the last group constitutes what Lin Hengtai called "the translingual generation" [*kuayue yuyan de yidai*],[17] the first and second groups may well be called "the silenced generation."

Because of the linguistic barrier and the political turmoil of the postwar years, the literary scene in the 1950s was dominated by émigré writers. The burgeoning field of modernist poetry consisted of journals and societies all founded by émigrés, including *MPQ* and the modernist school, *Lanxing* [Blue stars] (1954–), and *Chuangshiji* [Epoch poetry quarterly] (1954–). Although the journals and societies never excluded native poets and a few were frequent contributors, the émigrés' linguistic skills clearly provided a valuable form of cultural capital, which put them in an advantageous position. The fact that this inequality was never mentioned only reaffirms the workings of the literary field, in which language was not an issue of contention.

Drawing on Bourdieu's theory, I have analyzed the relation between the new modernist poetry movement, spearheaded by *MPQ*, and the literary field in postwar Taiwan. To carve out a niche, *MPQ* had to define itself against the dominant forces in the literary field, primarily Old Poetry and anti-Communist poetry, and secondarily the popular new regulated verse. Vis-à-vis Old Poetry, Ji Xian and his fellow poets emphasized the modernity and epochal spirit of modern poetry. In the editorial in the fourth issue, Ji Xian gave a wholly new interpretation to "Si wuxie" [Thoughts devoid of guile], Confucius's succinct summary of *Shijing* [Book of songs]: "'Thoughts,' the essence of poetry, refer to emotion and imagination; 'devoid of guile' means expression of genuine feelings" (November 1953, front cover). Countering the charge that modern poetry was easy and shallow, Ji Xian emphasized its essential difference from classical poetry: it did not rely on rhymes and meters but used prose to convey poeticness. He went further and advocated the decoupling of "poetry" [*shi*] from "song" [*ge*]. "*Shi* is *shi*, *ge* is *ge*, we don't say *shige*"—the title of the editorial in the twelfth issue (winter 1955)—succinctly conveys his theory.

During the modern poetry debate, some critics attributed the loss of audience for modern poetry to its lack of musicality. The "campus folk song" [*xiaoyuan min'ge*] movement that began in the mid-1970s was to some extent a reaction to the allegedly unrecitable, obscure modernist poetry of the 1950s and 1960s. Such criticism ignored the historical context in which that poetry originated. The decoupling of poetry from song advanced by Ji Xian was an effort to distinguish New Poetry not only from Old Poetry but also, implicitly, from anti-Communist songs rewarded by the Committee on Chinese Literature and Art Prizes. Those songs were broadcast on the radio and taught at schools and in the armed forces. The most famous among them include "Fangong jinxingqu" [Anti-Communist march], "Youji jinxingqu" [Guerrilla march], "Renren canzhan ge" [Everybody into war], and "Shengli ge" [Song of victory] by Zhao Youpei and "Baowei wo Taiwan" [Protect my Taiwan] by Sun Ling.

As mentioned earlier, political lyrics gradually disappeared from *MPQ*, especially after the founding of the modernist school in early 1956. Throughout its existence, the journal engaged in modernist experiments while maintaining a discreet distance from political correctness. The sixth principle of the modernist school—"Patriotism. Anticommunism. Support of freedom and democracy"—was a modification of the original one, which simply read "Atheism."[18] Although there is no doubt that Ji Xian was genuinely opposed to communism because of its repression of creative freedom, the revised sixth principle suggests a degree of political precaution that was fully called for in the postwar era.

Finally, reacting against the sentimental but popular new regulated verse, *MPQ* warned its readers and writers against outpourings of emotion and advocated intellect as the tenor of modern poetry. Another of Ji Xian's catchy editorial titles proclaimed: "Put your passion in the icebox!" (summer 1954, 45). Intellectual poetry, concrete poetry, sign poems, and cine-poems were among the experiments carried out in the journal.

The position that *MPQ* created and occupied may be described as being between the underground and the official, between the forbidden zone and the establishment. In this space, it could undertake literary endeavors relatively free from political intervention. Political correctness was the strategy, radical experiments the goal. *MPQ* emphasized that it was a "specialized, pure poetry journal," that it received no government subsidies, and that it was not widely distributed to "raise the morale among military personnel" [*laojun*] (February 1954, editorial). The profound influence that it exerted on postwar poets came from its unique aesthetic position and practice. Together, they constituted what Ji Xian referred to as "the second revolution of poetry" or new modernism, a further development of the literary revolution of 1917.

To fully appreciate the historical significance of *MPQ*, however, I must go beyond the structural constraints inherent in the literary field of postwar Taiwan and how the journal coped with and overcame them. Inseparable from *MPQ*'s strategies of position taking was its creation of new symbolic capital. Although poets might win the official economic capital for private purposes, the symbolic capital that they won in the official sphere could not be so easily transferred. Part of the oppositional position by which modernist poetry defined itself was manifest in its avant-garde aesthetics, which embodied new attitudes and perceptions with regard to poetry and the poet.

MODERNIST HABITUS

The rest of this essay will, therefore, discuss the habitus subscribed to by the modernist poets of the 1950s. Bourdieu defines *habitus* as "a system of schemes of perception and appreciation of practices, cognitive and evaluative structures which are acquired through the lasting experience of a social position"; it is "both a system of schemes of production of practices and a system of perception and appreciation of practices."[19] The habitus cultivated by *MPQ* and modernist poets generally will be discussed in terms of three aspects: professionalism; poverty; and eccentricity.

Professionalism
I mentioned above that *MPQ* was critical of amateur poets and literary critics because they gave the public mistaken perceptions of modern poetry and poets. Modernist poetry differentiated itself from Old Poetry and popular poetry (e.g., the new regulated verse) by its serious, professional attitude. Ji Xian advised young poets: "First of all, adopt a serious attitude toward writing, and do some research on what constitutes New Poetry. . . . Don't pick up your pen hastily, and don't rush to publish your work!" (August 1953, front cover). *Professional* has no economic implications here; it refers, instead, to a spiritual identification of the poet with poetry that excluded all extrinsic concerns and motivations. It bespeaks a clear distinction between the spiritual and the worldly. (Ji Xian's colleagues at Chenggong High School—with the exception of his fellow poet Song Ying [b. 1917]—had no knowledge that he was a major poet. Many poets who were servicemen also published under pseudonyms.)

If classical poetry was a hobby in which the elites dabbled at leisure, modern poetry was a vocation, a calling requiring the poet's wholehearted dedication. The desire to pursue poetry for its own sake finds a simple but ingenuous expression in the poem "Xixun" [Good news] by an unknown poet writing under the name "Shi Ji" [Century]:

> The first time my manuscript turns into printed words.
> When young, reading Heine in the shade of a tree,
> I vowed to be a poet.
>
> Now, this dream
> Has finally brought good news.
>
> *(autumn 1955, 93)*

This emphasis on the nonutilitarian, spiritual nature of poetry must have appealed to many poets and readers. Many of them had experienced a forced uprooting and exodus from the mainland and had suffered injustice and hardships. Some young soldiers had been press-ganged, and some had enlisted so they would be fed. In contrast to the dogmatic, collective consciousness imposed by the military, *MPQ* and other modernist poetry journals provided a forum for creative freedom and self-expression. A soldier himself, Wang Rong depicts how an old soldier who dies of unknown causes turns into white clouds and a winged angel:

> What remains is a spinal column
> Making a gray poet reflect deeply.
>
> *(autumn 1954, 92)*

The identification with pure poetry was inseparable from the generally repressive atmosphere of the 1950s. Whether they initially knew one another or not, the young poets developed deep empathy and friendships through the journals and journal-sponsored activities. "Wuti" [Without title] by Sha Mu (1928–86) expresses this bond in plain words:

> I don't want anyone to be above me,
> Nor anyone to be below me;
> I don't want to be anyone's slave,
> Nor to step on anyone.
> . . . . .
> I don't want anything
> Except friendship and poetry.
>
> *(February 1953, 11)*

Looking back four decades later, Yu Tiancong describes the poetry scene of the 1950s this way: "Naturally the tiny *MPQ* became a garden where we conversed with one another. To ordinary people, those words were bizarre, so bizarre as to seem absurd, but, through them, your hardships and my hardships, your helplessness and my helplessness were connected." Borrowing the title of a Sha Mu poem, Yu refers to *MPQ* as a "warmth-sharing sphere" [*tong wen ceng*].[20] In the 1951 "Yedian" [Inn in the wilderness], the young Zheng Chouyu (b. 1932) likens "the poet's profession" to running an inn in a vast desert that provides a haven for lonely travelers. Poetry is compared to a "profession" that could be passed on between generations of poets. It holds up the only light in the vast desert for the weary traveler. In "Shanju de rizi" [Life in the mountains], Zheng sings of the poet's genealogy:

> Displayed above is the poet's family tree.
> Oh, the blood relation of wisdom needs extension.
> So I carve transparent names deeply in the whole sky
> And sing. Here alone and undaunted I can be high-sounding.[21]

The sky is where the poet belongs, and the stars are his brethren. The imagery evokes the dual symbolism of the star in modern Chinese poetry as the eternity of poetry and the alienation of the poet.[22] If Li Bai is the famous Banished Immortal [Zhexian] in classical poetry, the poet as exile finds numerous echoes in modern poetry.

An important function of *MPQ* and other privately funded poetry journals in the 1950s was to assert the independence of poetic art from other pursuits. In view of the disparity in social status between Old and New Poetry, modern poets emphasized that the only criteria applicable to poetry were those intrinsic and unique to the art form. Poetry was personified as Shishen, the god of poetry, for instance, in Peng Bangzhen's "Shi de dingyi" [Definition of poetry], published in the inaugural issue of *MPQ*. In the editorial in the fifth issue, Ji Xian called for "guardians" and "martyrs of New Poetry" (February 1954, 5), images foreign to the classical tradition. The elevation of poetry to divine status distinguishes modern poetry from its traditional counterpart.

Finally, the new aesthetic embodied by *MPQ* is an overt comment on social reality. While equality and justice did not always exist in society, poets upheld these ideals in their work. As Ji Xian pronounced:

> In the world of poetry, all are equal. Whoever has talent can freely enter and stay with no strings attached. All that the great God of Poetry cares about is whether a poem is good or bad. Whatever your social status is, whether you are rich and

powerful, or poor and lowly, . . . he really doesn't care. If your poetic talent is truly great, even if you are a peddler or servant, you will be treated like a guest of honor in his palace. . . . On the other hand, if your poetic talent is mediocre or poor, even if you are an important official, you cannot receive his kindness. (October 1956, 81)

Poverty

The high respect and seriousness accorded poetry as art and the space provided for free expression by *MPQ* and other journals in the 1950s nurtured a new generation of poets. Many were students and schoolteachers, quite a few were servicemen, but, with few exceptions, all were outside the cultural establishment and came from the middle or lower-middle economic strata. To give a tragic example, Yang Huan was an army clerk and could hardly afford cigarettes. On March 7, 1954, when he got a free ticket to a movie at the last minute, he rushed to the theater, only to be run down by a train on the way, at the age of twenty. Ji Xian supported a large family on the meager income of a high school teacher and could barely fund *MPQ*. He describes how he managed it: "Editing, proof printing, proofreading, running to the printing company, making board, buying paper, cutting paper, printing covers, printing frontis pages, packaging, distributing, soliciting advertisements, asking for advertising fees, and so on and so forth. . . . I have to do everything myself. Occasionally, one or two capable students help out. That's all" (February 1956, 33). Therefore, he asked his fellow poets to do him a favor: "I wish you would not disturb the editor with trivialities, long letters, unnecessary visits, chatting, etc., thus saving the editor's time and energy as much as possible. . . . That would be the best way to love our journal" (March 1956, 35). Ji Xian borrowed the political slogan "adversity-overcoming spirit" [*ke'nan jingshen*] to describe the operation of *MPQ*; it was this spirit that sustained the journal for ten years.

By the third year of publication, the circulation of *MPQ* had increased from five hundred to two thousand, and the journal could finally make ends meet. Ji Xian hoped to make it a monthly publication when the circulation increased further to three thousand, but that never happened. In the afterword to the eleventh issue, Ji Xian thanked the readers for their support: "We know most of this journal's readers are as poor as we are, maybe even poorer" (autumn 1955, 127). Therefore, he asked them only to seek out new subscribers, not to make further donations. It seems that, as time went on, the journal's financial situation deteriorated, as indicated in the twenty-first issue, where the editor wrote: "Poverty is our Achilles' heel! . . . This issue came out late for the simple reason that we did not have money to buy paper and pay for printing. This is our true difficulty. . . . As to why this issue finally came out, it was because I sold a ring of sentimental value and a big bag of valuable books and pawned some winter clothes. What's more, a friend generously donated a few hundred dollars" (March 1958, n.p.). When *MPQ* was on the brink of folding, Ji Xian uttered "a painful sos": "For more than five years, the poetry journal that I founded with my own hands, this seafaring steamer, can I let it sink? No! No way! I still have a bicycle that I can sell. I will sacrifice all to continue to struggle for the publication of the journal, till the day I starve or freeze to death" (March 1, 1958, inside front cover). He begged readers to help out and said that he would be eternally grateful for a donation of even ten dollars.

The resulting situation helps us better appreciate Ji Xian's statement that Old Poetry was in the court, New Poetry in the wild. Poverty was another bond that connected the modernist poets, so no wonder it became part of their newly established habitus. Xiu Tao's (b. 1934) "Xinyanzhe" [The newly castrated], published in *MPQ* in 1957, presents a succinct but poignant picture:

> When she told me the price for the Debussy
> I became a castrated man
> Helpless
> I walked away
> Though she still pressed me with her disdainful eyes
> And drew WM on the glass counter with her breasts.
>
> *(March 1957, 9)*

The first-person narrator cannot even afford an album—given the economic situation of Taiwan at the time, probably a pirated copy!—of classical music. When art runs up against the dollar sign, it has no choice but to surrender. As a metaphor, castration vividly captures the sense of defeat and frustration that he experiences, but it goes further. The saleslady is the perfect embodiment of society's values, which equate manhood with earning power and money with success. The last two lines drive home the point, as from behind the counter she seems to taunt the narrator with her explicit sexuality as he walks away. The English letters *WM* pictographically evoke her breasts; they are also the first letters of *woman* and *man*. Thus, the poem makes a sarcastic comment on society from the viewpoint of an economically disadvantaged poet.

Sun Jiajun's "Dianyuan" [Store clerk] depicts a similar experience and conveys the same sense of powerlessness:

> Let me stand outside the window and adore it quietly!
> This way you won't laugh at me for not knowing the names of the goods.
>
> *(autumn 1955, 93)*

The poem is from the sequence "Taibei jietou xingyin" [Poems at Taipei's street corner], which also includes "Sanlunchefu" [Rickshaw puller], "Caxietong" [Shoeshine boy], "Jiunü" [Bar girl], "Qizhe" [Beggar], and "Huangniu" [Ticket scalper]. Employing succinct language, minimalist form (the poems run from two to eight lines each), and a wide range of perspectives and tones, the poet delineates the various faces of old Taipei. The rickshaws were banned in the 1960s, shoeshine boys are a rare sight, and the term *bar girl* has long been replaced by fancy names. The poems as a whole convey sympathy for the lower classes and critique the dehumanization resulting from materialism. Behind the prosperity of urban society is the cruel reality of inequality between the rich and the poor and the survival of the fittest.

"Jiunü" addresses this theme powerfully:

> Pouring down large quantities of alcohol,
> This is an unripe, smiling plot being harvested.
>
> Be thankful to those gentlemen who hold you in respect!
> Luckily they all hear the sound and want to taste the meat.
>
> *(autumn 1955, 93)*

The poet uses three passive images—alcohol being poured, the land "being harvested," and the meat being tasted—to suggest the powerlessness of the bar girl. The juxtaposition of "unripe" and "smiling" enhances the pathos of her situation, reminding us of a young woman who is forced to sell her body even before she is fully grown. The second couplet is full of sarcasm. It gives a bitter twist to the Confucian parable of benevolence, in which the gentleman who hears the cries of an ox before it is slaughtered does not have the heart to eat its meat. Here, the customers at the bar are referred to as "gentlemen" (their disrespect for her is ironically referred to as "respect"), but they have no qualms about tasting the "meat"; the last image also evokes Lu Xun's characterization of the oppressive Chinese culture as cannibalistic. The poem reveals the unbearable humiliation to which the bar girl is subjected.

MPQ published many poems that empathize with the oppressed and the marginalized in society. They might not necessarily have come from any consciousness of social critique or aim at conveying moral messages; more likely, they derived from the personal experiences of the poets in the hard-pressed postwar period. Poverty made them identify with poetry even more single-mindedly because it symbolized a world that transcended and was better than the harsh reality, pointing to freedom and equality based on individual talents rather than wealth and status. The poor but dedicated poet evolved into an emblem of human dignity and idealism.

Whether on behalf of Ji Xian's *MPQ* or of *Chuangshiji*, founded in 1954 by Ya Xian, Zhang Mo, and Luo Fu (b. 1928), it was not uncommon for poets to go to the pawnshop to keep a journal going. By the 1970s, as Taiwan became more and more prosperous, the economic condition of most poets had improved. Poverty was no longer a mark of the vocation, and rarely did a journal fold owing to financial difficulty. By the 1990s, the poor poet of the 1950s had long since become a fantastical figure.

Eccentricity
The new modernist aesthetics also declared a radical individualism vis-à-vis the world represented by the establishment and popular culture. This explains the recurrence of the image of the poet as a solitary wanderer, a rebel, an eccentric, or even a madman. Here is Sha Mu's "Wo shi guaidan de shengwu" [I am a monstrous creature]:

> I curse things that others praise,
> I despise everything that people like,
> I love what I love,
> Hate what I hate,
> I am a monstrous creature,
> No power can change that.
> I am I.
>
> Say I am a heretic,
> Say I am insane,

> Fine,
> But I still have primitive innocence
> And the anger stirred up by all ugliness.
> Proudly, in long strides,
> I walk forward
> And, loudly,
> Sing my own song.
>
> I am a monstrous creature,
> No power can change it.
> I am I.
>
> *(August 1953, 69)*

Running through many poems from the 1950s is the opposition between the singular "I" and the plural "they" (or "people"), one based on vast differences in lifestyle and values. Sha Mu's singing "my own song" is the same as Ji Xian's "I have my own song."[23] The image of the madman also appears frequently in *MPQ*. Xin Yu (b. 1933) calls himself "madman" in the poem "Ai" [Love] (May 1954, 33). Shang Qin (b. 1930), under an earlier pen name, Luo Ma, compares himself to a hoodlum, who

> Breaks into an ancient garden that has survived in the twentieth century
> Freezes the wind
> Tramples the flowers
> Melts the snow
> Smears the moon
> Chops down fourteen foreign trees on the curvabridge
> Knocks down every Western brick in the art gallery
> Destroys all your potted plants
> I am a hoodlum
>
> *(winter 1954, 141)*

It is noteworthy that the poet wants to destroy both ancient China and the West. China is defined here by the four lines containing the images of "wind," "flowers," "snow," and "moon." These words form a phrase in Chinese (*feng hua xue yue*) that refers to trivial literature of pretty images and, by extension, frivolous love stories. This notion also harks back to the modernist objection to sentimental popular poetry discussed earlier.

The poet who disregards all conventions is laughed at and rejected by society. "Duanju" [Short verse] by Xue Guanghua depicts the poet who thinks naively that he can change the world, but the result is "humiliation and torture" and the guillotine. Yet he refuses to compromise as he faces death:

> Whack!
> Rolling down with the head is the madman's book of poetry,
> And the crowd's roaring laughter,
> And the falling sun.
>
> The wind comes to sneer at the poet too,
> Touching his blood-stained hair, clothes,
> His unclosed eyes,
> His book of poems written with blood.
>
> There it is, his book of poetry!
>
> *(spring 1955, 13)*

The modernist poets emphasized nonconformity and eccentricity, distinguishing themselves even from other writers. The second-person "you" in Chu Qing's (b. 1926) "Ni de zan'ge" [In praise of you] is ordinary writers:

> My noble "writers"!
> How I am amazed at your world
> Where the people are all the same, their hearts are equally straight,
> Their faces are equally flat,
> So no wonder I look strange and eccentric —
> I am a poet with sharp horns and a disgusting face!
>
> *(February 1954, 23)*

The intentional use of negative self-description suggests another form of defiance of popular culture, which the modernist poets saw as dominated by philistines and consisting of commercialized art. In his "Yinyue" [Music], Wu Yingtao (1916–71) associates "decadent jazz" with "city clamor" and contrasts it with Beethoven (November 1953, 72). In the same issue is Situ Wei's "Hualang suojian" [Scene at the art gallery], which critiques the hypocrisy of artists:

> Two daikons with a price tag of five thousand dollars,
> Four black hawks demanding ten taels of gold;

> On the painting *Hungry People* of cheap humanitarianism,
> Flows the famished look of gold.
> In the gallery where authors do business elegantly,
> Inflation is malign!
> What a skinny artist,
> In a graceful pose like a bamboo in the wind
> With a flattering smile
> He listens to the potbellied tycoon
> (While admiring with a squint)
> And exclaims, in a gentle falsetto,
> At the rising costs of paints, matting, and artisans.
>
> *(November 1953, 65)*

Underlying the satire against popular music, commercialized art, or popular literature is the poet's discontent with rampant materialism, his refusal to conform to mediocre but authoritative conventions, and his exposé of society's "cheap humanitarianism." It is in this context that the new modernist aesthetics advanced by *MPQ* and other journals should be understood. It is also in this context that we can appreciate the irreverence and humor of Xiu Tao's "Cheshang" [On the bus]:

> That's even stranger
> On the bus a little maggot stands up for an old maggot
> So maggots are full of contradictions
> And relatively complex.
>
> *(March 1957, 9)*

CONCLUSION

MPQ was privately funded and produced by crude printing technology. Yet, within four years, its subscription base exceeded two thousand, and it is estimated to have reached more than ten thousand readers. Even in the entire history of modern Chinese poetry, these are remarkable figures. The reasons that this journal emerged in the early 1950s and exerted enormous influence on Taiwan's poetry scene are multifarious and complex. Ji Xian and his fellow poets effectively employed their cultural capital and converted the official cultural resources to provide the necessary means for the publication of *MPQ*.

The establishment of a new position in the literary field necessarily changes the field, what I call its ecology, and creates new symbolic capital. In my view, the most important new symbolic capital is a set of mutually reinforced dispositions, tastes, and practices. It includes the notion of poetry as a vocation and as a spiritual pursuit of the individual, the disadvantaged position of the poet in the social and economic structure, and the radical individualism that sets the poet apart from popular literature and mass culture. If the rise of a new trend almost always takes an oppositional stand vis-à-vis the mainstream, the concrete forms of opposition depend on the particular historical conditions, structural constraints as well as finite potentialities. We find both continuities and discontinuities between the modernist poetry of the 1950s and the poetry of the 1990s. The two periods share the general belief in the personal and private nature of poetry and the poet's individualism but differ in terms of the poet's economic status and the attitude, at least of some, toward popular culture.

To conclude, I cite Ji Xian's prose poem "Zuihou de yigen huochai" [The last match], written in 1953. The use of the masculine personal pronoun to refer to the match suggests that it is a metaphor for the poet. Illustrating the modernist aesthetics discussed here, the poem expresses the pride of the poet in standing up to forces much greater than he is; it celebrates eccentricity and conveys a mix of tragic and optimistic sentiments. As we read the poem, we cannot but realize that the 1950s are a thing of the past:

> The last match, lying quietly, in the matchbox. No one knows his value and meaning, nor cares about his existence. His energy is very limited, his light negligible, but he is going to bring about the swift collapse and destruction of a vast empire, to make a symphonic performance end abruptly, to create the next three thousand centuries of enlightened epochs, or maybe to light up a new sky lamp when the sun, the moon, and the stars worry about being taken away. He waits quietly....
>
> Someday, I will let you see, the curtain of a tragedy rises, a miracle appears: I am a match, the very last one. (August 1953, 48)

NOTES

Unless otherwise indicated, all translations from non-English-language sources are my own.

1 *Xiandaishi jikan*, or the *Modern Poetry Quarterly*, was published in Taipei by Xiandaishi she from 1953 to 1964. I'd like to thank Shang Qin for providing a set of *MPQ*, without which this study would not have been possible. Documentation for all citations from *MPQ* will be provided in the text.
2 See Michelle Yeh, "Frontier Taiwan: An Introduction," in Michelle Yeh and N. G. D. Malmqvist, eds., *Frontier Taiwan: An Anthology of Modern Chinese Poetry* (New York: Columbia University Press, 2001).
3 Pierre Bourdieu, *The Field of Cultural Production* (New York: Columbia University Press, 1993), 66.
4 Amiba shishe [Amoeba Poetry Society], ed., *Amiba shixuan* [Amoeba poetry anthology] (Taipei: Qianwei chubanshe, 1985), 327.
5 See Xu Wangyun, "Yu shijian juezhan: Taiwan xinshikan sishinian fendou shulue" [The final battle with time: Forty years of struggle of modern poetry journals in Taiwan], *Zhongwai wenxue* [Chung-wai literary monthly] 19.5 (October 1990): 115.
6 See Xi Mi [Michelle Yeh], "Jintian weisheme yao du shi?" [Why do we read poetry today?], *Lianhebao* [United daily], literary supplement, August 26-27, 1995, reprinted in Xi Mi [Michelle Yeh], *Shi shenghuo* [Poetic life] (Guilin: Guangxi shifan daxue chubanshe, 2004), 139-51.
7 Zhang Mo, *Taiwan xiandaish bianmu (1949-1991)* [A bibliography of modern poetry in Taiwan (1949-1991)] (Taipei: Erya chubanshe, 1992), 3-7.
8 Qin Zihao, *Shi de bianxian fangfa* [Methods of expression in poetry] (Taipei: Zengwen chubanshe, 1977), 182 (Qin's review originally appeared in the *Lianhebao* literary supplement in 1957).
9 Lin Hengtai, *Jianzhe zhi yan* [Words of someone who was there] (Zhanghua: Zhanghua xianli wenhua zhongxin, 1993), 300.
10 See Ying Feng-huang, *Guangfuhou Taiwan diqu wentan dash jiyao* [Chronicle of major events on the literary scene of postwar Taiwan] (Taipei: Xingzhengyuan wenhua jianshe weiyuanhui, 1985); and Yang Bichuan, *Taiwan xiandaishi nianbiao* (1945 nian 8 yue-1994 nian 9 yue) [Chronicle of modern Taiwanese history (August 1945-September 1994)] (Taipei: Yiqiao chubanshe, 1996).
11 Ge Xianning and Shangguan Yu, *Wushinian lai de Zhongguo shi'ge* [Fifty years of Chinese poetry] (Taipei: Zhengzhong shuju, 1965), 81-82.
12 Wang Zhijian et al., eds., *Liushinian shi'ge xuan* [An anthology of sixty years of poetry] (Taipei: Zhengzhong shuju, 1973), 274-75.
13 Ibid., 284.

14 Burton Watson, trans. and ed., *The Columbia Book of Chinese Poetry: From Early Times to the Thirteenth Century* (New York: Columbia University Press, 1984), 207.
15 See Edwin A. Winckler, "Cultural Policy on Postwar Taiwan," in Stevan Harrell and Chün-chieh Huang, eds., *Cultural Changes in Postwar Taiwan* (Boulder: Westview, 1994), 22–46.
16 Qin, *Shi de bianxian fangfa*, 126–27.
17 Lin Hengtain, "Kuayue yuyan de yidai shiren men—cong Yinlinghui tanqi" [A generation of translingual poets—beginning with the Silver Bell Society], *Li* [Bamboo hat poetry bimonthly] 127 (June 1985), reprinted in *Jianzhe zhi yan*, 230–36. In this essay, Li notes that he has used the phrase previously to describe the linguistic transition for his generation.
18 According to Lin Hengtai's recollection: "A few days before the founding of the modernist school, we all received from Ji Xian 'Newsletter Number 2 of the Modernist School.' The newsletter contained a draft of 'Principles of the Modernist School.' I remember that the sixth principle was 'Atheism,' but, when the formal announcement came, it had been changed to 'Patriotism. Anticommunism. Support of freedom and democracy'" ("Xinshi de zai geming" [The second revolution of New Poetry], in *Jianzhe zhi yan*, 254).
19 Pierre Bourdieu, "Social Space and Symbolic Power," *Sociological Theory* 7.1 (spring 1989): 19.
20 Yu Tiancong, "Huainian Mei Xin" [In Memory of Mei Xin], *Chuangshiji* 112 (1997): 104.
21 Translated by Shiu-Pang Almberg in *Frontier Taiwan: An Anthology of Modern Chinese Poetry*, ed. Michelle Yeh and N. G. D. Malmqvist (New York: Columbia University Press, 2001), 218.
22 See Michelle Yeh, *Modern Chinese Poetry: Theory and Practice since 1917* (New Haven: Yale University Press, 1991).
23 Xi Mi [Michelle Yeh], "Wo you wo de ge: Ji Xian zaoqi zuopin tanxi" [I Have My Own Songs: The Early Poetry of Ji Xian], *Xiandaishi jikan*, n.s., 21 (February 1993): 4–13.

6

The Literary Development of Zhong Lihe and Postcolonial Discourse in Taiwan

Fenghuang Ying

On August 4, 1960, the writer Zhong Lihe coughed up his lifeblood and died. In the year and a half before he passed away, Zhong had published a number of excellent short stories in the literary supplement [*fukan*] of *Lianhebao* [United daily]. He had also won the acclaim of his fellow writers in the late 1950s for the polished language and authentic emotions of his realistic style. In August, just after newspapers published the news of his death from illness amid poverty and obscurity, distraught laments by the likes of Ma Ge, Wen Xin, and Lin Haiyin appeared in the *Lianhebao* literary supplement, edited at the time by Lin Haiyin. Preceding these pieces was Fang Yizhi's "Dao Zhong Lihe" [Eulogy for Zhong Lihe], which appeared in the newspaper *Zhengxin* on August 11, 1960.

But that was it. Looking back at these short pieces, it seems that the writer's sudden death may have created a few small ripples in Taiwan, but to say that it stirred "literary circles" would certainly be overstating the case. Perhaps it would be more accurate just to speak of the fiction writers' community. Simply put, the ripples stirred only those writers who published their short stories in a single literary supplement and the short story lovers who read the supplement. The writers had lost a talented colleague and felt great sympathy for one of their own who had died in such circumstances. Zhong had left behind unfinished business, in that his works had not yet been published in book form in Taiwan. Indeed, so desperate was he to finish that business that he included in his will a plea for donations from his fellow writers. Lin Haiyin took up the cause, put out the call in Taipei, and, together with a few others, established the Zhong Lihe Posthumous

Publication Committee. Lin has written that she "gathered together a few thousand dollars by collecting donations of NT$50 here and NT$100 there. The advance orders for the book were very good, and [we] were able to repay everything as soon as it was published."[1]

It was as a result of these efforts that the first of Zhong Lihe's books to be published in Taiwan, *Yu* [Rain], was printed. Its release date was rushed to coincide with the ritual commemoration on the hundredth day following the author's death, and a copy was placed on the offerings table to console his dead spirit. Even given that, in Taiwan in the late 1950s, the market for literature was not booming in the way it would in the 1970s and 1980s, how could it have been so difficult to get a book printed? Innumerable pages of "anti-Communist literature" had already been printed, and enough romance novels to fill a good-sized valley were being churned out. Publishers specializing in literary works, such as the Daye Bookstore, the Guangqi Publishing Company, and Wentan Publishing, collectively produced more than a hundred distinct genres of books. From this statistic, one can easily deduce that Zhong Lihe was on the fringes of the literary world of his day, and it is, therefore, not hard to imagine the difficulties and the loneliness that he faced.

If Taiwan's literary history had concluded at the end of the 1960s, if time had stopped and the period from the 1970s to the 1990s had never taken place, this prolific writer who returned to Taiwan from Beijing after the war and was at the peak of his powers in the 1950s would most likely have simply been buried under the subsequent mass of anti-Communist fiction and essays expressing longing for a lost homeland. Zhong Lihe would have silently disappeared from the literary history of the decade and would never have achieved his current level of fame. But, of course, history did not come to a halt. The 1970s nativist movement in Taiwan literature was followed, in the 1980s, by the Taiwanese consciousness debate. Finally, the 1990s were characterized by debates over postcolonial theory. Each of the major cultural debates that have engaged Taiwan's literary scene have pulled Zhong's work into their discussions and evaluated it. In the wake of these controversies, his person and his work have been gradually incorporated into the literary canon.

The most obvious example of this process is Taiwan's nativist movement, which began in the 1970s and peaked sometime after the middle of that decade. This movement put great stock in realism and called for the intelligentsia to focus on the ground beneath their feet and the cultural environment of the society in which they actually lived. For instance, Tang Wenbiao's long "Lai xi'ai Zhong Lihe" [Appreciating Zhong Lihe] strongly affirms Zhong's place as a model "nativist writer" (he excelled at writing about people engaged in agricultural pursuits).[2] At that time, a collection of the native writer Huang Chunming's short stories was already very popular and had been through several printings.[3] Furthermore, other excellent indigenous writers such as Wang Zhenhe and Chen Yingzhen, who had been writing for many years, were becoming more and more famous. It was probably the spirit of the age that led to the publication of Zhong's complete works in 1976, sixteen years after his death.[4] In other words, it was during the nativist movement that Zhong's work first began to be widely known; we might even say that the rising tide of the nativist debate lifted Zhong's work along with it.

As discussed in Chen Fangming's "Postmodern or Postcolonial? An Inquiry into Postwar Taiwanese Literary History" (chapter 2 in this volume), since the 1980s books on literary history from both Taiwan and mainland China have traditionally designated Taiwan literature of the 1950s, 1960s, and 1970s as being primarily anti-Communist, modernist, and nativist, respectively. Such pigeonholing in decade-long blocks makes it difficult to deal with writers, such as Zhong Lihe, whose literary career spans more than ten years. One important question addressed by this essay concerns which literary period the 1950s "nativist" writer Zhong should be placed under. A second consideration is Zhong's very particular "China experience." In the later part of the Japanese occupation of Taiwan (1937–45), when the island was being forcibly imperialized (referred to as the *kōminka* period), this writer who had grown up in colonial Taiwan was away from the island. His violation of the long-standing taboo in Chinese culture against marrying someone with the same surname (even if there is no direct blood relation involved) forced him to leave his hometown and go to China. Zhong subsequently spent eight years wandering about mainland China and by 1945 had published his first collection of short stories in Chinese, *Jiazhutao*—at a time when many other Taiwanese writers of his generation, such as Lü Heruo (b. 1914) and Zhang Wenhuan (b. 1909), were still able to write only in Japanese.[5]

In other words, Zhong got an earlier start on overcoming the language barrier than did other writers; for example, Chen Huoquan, Yang Kui, and

Zhong Zhaozheng all had to learn Chinese from scratch after the war. Furthermore, Zhong's experiences in and views on China were recorded from an early date in the form of diaries and letters, with the result that his works became both a focal point and frequently cited examples in the subsequent heated debates over the issues of "cultural identity," "ethnic consciousness," and "the Chinese complex" of the 1980s. Of course, Zhong's "China experience" has seen different interpretations and uses in these discussions. For example, when his life story was made into a movie—the 1980 *Yuanxiang ren* [The journey home], directed by Li Xing, and starring Qin Han and Lin Fengjiao—it was done by the Guomindang's Central Motion Picture Studio. In Chen Yingzhen's critique of *Jiazhutao*, however, the meaning of this image of "home" is turned completely on its head. Looking at Chen's title—"Yuanxiang de shiluo: Shiping *Jiazhutao*" [The lost home: Critiquing *Jiazhutao*]—it is hard to miss his meaning. But Chen's diligent examination of Zhong's "identity crisis" and "postcolonial character" maintained Zhong's popularity in the new wave of postcolonial debate in the 1990s.[6]

Of course, these theoretical debates did not concern Zhong alone; they have typically been referred to as "ideological disputes." But, if they led to the gradual canonization of Zhong's literary works, we must ask what the nature of their relation to Zhong's work actually is. This essay will address both Zhong Lihe and his work within the context of the major debates of the 1970s and the two following decades. It will look back at the different ideas and points of contention in critics' responses to Zhong's work, beginning with Tang Wenbiao, Lin Zaijue, Zhang Liangze, Ye Shitao, Chen Yingzhen, and Gu Tianhong. These debates also constitute the actual development of the Taiwanese literary trends—"social consciousness," "ethnic consciousness," and "postcolonialism"—that collectively represent the three most important aspects of Zhong's work. So, while we take another look at Zhong Lihe, we can also seek his place in the history of Taiwan literature. I will examine the hitherto unexplored postcolonial character of Zhong's work, drawing on postcolonial theory to attempt to "bring Zhong home" to his appropriate place in history. That is, while Zhong is obviously a nativist writer, he is even more an important writer of the 1950s, one who stood with one foot in the Japanese colonial era and the other in the period that followed.

THE 1970S: SOCIAL CONSCIOUSNESS AND ZHONG LIHE'S WORKS

It was in the early 1970s that critics began to note and discuss the social consciousness of Zhong Lihe's work. In terms of being a "literary epoch," the 1970s was, according to the critics, a very "complete decade."[7] Important sociopolitical events marked both its opening and its close: the Fishing Island Incident of 1970 (a dispute over islands not explicitly addressed in the Treaty of Shimonoseki, which escalated in 1971 following the discovery of oil fields in the area) and the Kaohsiung Incident at the end of 1979. In between, there were shocks from the international arena, including the U.S. rapprochement with mainland China and Taiwan's loss of its seat in the United Nations. Collectively, these events very clearly illustrated Taiwan's international standing and domestic situation. The social transformations caused a gradual change in the attitude of the island's intelligentsia, who began demanding that those living in Taiwan establish a footing there (as opposed to always looking back to the mainland) and begin participating in social reform. Against this background, Taiwan's literary arena was torn by two major battles, one at the beginning of the decade and the other at its end.

The first of these battles occurred in 1972, started by Guan Jieming and Tang Wenbiao in *Zhongguo shibao* [China times], *Wenji* [Literature quarterly], and *Zhong-wai wenxue* [Chung-wai literary monthly]. This polemic focused on the modern poetry of Taiwan, claiming that the so-called new poetry was escapist, empty, destructive of morality, and without social consciousness. The heart of the criticism is obviously directed at the rise of Western modernism in the 1960s. This first battle is generally known as the new poetry debate. The second was larger in scale and was known as the nativist literature debate. It began in 1977, and the number of authors and critics joining the fray—from Chen Yingzhen and Wang Tuo to Ye Shitao, Peng Ge, Yu Guangzhong, and Zhu Xining—led to the formation of several different camps. Shi Shu put it well when she observed that this was "one of the great dialogues between literature, reality, and history in the history of Taiwanese letters."[8]

A cursory glance at the new poetry debate might give the impression that it was unrelated to the nativist literature debate. But a careful look at the former shows it to have been a preliminary skirmish on the way to the full-scale war that was the latter and, therefore, the first part of the literary conflict that was to rage throughout the 1970s. For example, Guan Jieming is critical of modern poetry's imperfect understanding and awkward use of Western techniques, stating: "They [Taiwanese writers' modernist poems] are the products of literary colonialism . . . perpetually imitative, plagiarized, mere mimicries."[9] Similarly, the lengthy series of heated papers by Tang Wenbiao has a simple core argument: using the idea of social consciousness to criticize the idea of "art for art's sake."[10] For example, Tang states: "Poets are born here [in Taiwan]. They grow up here. But the literature they produce is without any social consciousness, lacks historical orientation, and fails to express the desperation and hope of the people. Each work only papers itself over in existentialist language, using a few conventional and meaningless words and expressions—the eternal human condition, snow, night, death, blood—to masturbate."[11] Further proof that the new poetry debate was only the first part of the battle of the 1970s is that, despite the drubbing that Tang administered to the modern poetry movement of Taiwan, he nevertheless found something positive to say about it—by pulling Zhong Lihe ("a southern Taiwanese country boy" according to Tang) into the debate. Tang is full of admiration for the strong points of Zhong's work, as the following passage reveals: "Because Chinese literature has always been a game for scholars/officials and talented city dwellers, it has always been extremely finicky in its tastes. For this reason, Zhong Lihe's 'rural literature' is obviously especially precious. Through Zhong, we hope to understand the life of rural Taiwan in the 1950s. His fiction most certainly has a social value in addition to its literary value."[12] This passage is almost a direct restatement of Tang's criticism of modern poetry. And, coming from this left-wing advocate of the arts and flag bearer of the entire cultural community, it was a valuable affirmation.

However, if we consider this critique from the perspective of Zhong Lihe and his lonely path in literary history, it is rough both in its style and in its theoretical underpinnings. Strictly speaking, it does not meet the standards of literary criticism, as the following two excerpts demonstrate:

> Zhong Lihe's fiction includes stories of love and running away from home. This kind of "rebellion against tradition" and "struggle for the freedom to marry as one chooses" had *relevance to the period*. However, by the 1950s it was clearly dated. (emphasis added)

> At that time [i.e., under Japanese colonial rule], when the Chinese were being bullied by the Japanese and these great people were engaged in their war of resistance against Japan, he did not take a more active stand and did not participate in more constructive activities. On the basis of this, one cannot help but state that his worldview was too parochial. In such circumstances, he wrote only of the turnings within the maze of his own romantic life. (281)

Even if we let pass the leftist cliché, we must wonder how Tang can speak in one breath of Zhong's "relevance to the period" and in the next of his being "dated."

Another troubling point is that the whole theme of the greatness, or the lack thereof, of the people engaged in the resistance against Japan has no relevance to Zhong's actual works. Given the fact that the time period to which Tang is referring is the period of Japanese colonial rule, he must have in mind the novel *Lishan nongchang* [Lishan farm] (1961), Zhong's only work set against this backdrop. We must, therefore, ask why, in writing of a farm, it is necessary to draw a connection to the "great war of resistance." It is also difficult to fathom what the failure to mention the war with Japan has to do with a "parochial worldview." If we take Tang's reasoning to its logical extreme, every work on the war with Japan should be one of the world's great books. Moreover, referring to the "greatness" of the war of resistance against the Japanese is surely taking a very Chinese perspective. Tang forgets that the Taiwan of that day was under Japanese colonial rule. To the extent that a Taiwanese would have taken part in that "holy war" (281), it would normally have been as a conscripted Japanese soldier fighting *against* the Chinese.

The social consciousness of Zhong's work is obviously one of its outstanding points, although I do not agree with Tang's view that "through Zhong" it is possible "to understand the life of rural Taiwan in the 1950s." Instead, I would state that Zhong's fiction has a social value *in addition to* its literary value. His readily recognizable social consciousness is the feature that most distinguishes his work from that of other writers. This kind of "value" is not, however, necessarily nonliterary.

We see an inclination to social consciousness in Zhong's thinking in a diary entry: "I've read Lin Yutang's *My Country and My People, Between Tears and Laughter* and am currently reading *The Importance of Living* for the second time. It strikes me very strongly that Lin Yutang is just this kind of person, the kind who often misunderstands; who, on seeing a person hanging himself, thinks that person is swinging on a swing."[13] This tendency also permeates his series of four "hometown" short stories, which describe the withered, heart-wrenching scenes he encountered on his journey from Beijing back to southern Taiwan. For example, "Zhu tou zhuang" [The bamboo-head village], the first story in the series, begins: "[Outside the train] the endless fields are all lying listless, clearly revealing the sickness of the rice. The people on the train [farmers] gaze disorientedly at the fields outside the train windows just as family members watch at a deathbed."[14]

"Shanhuo" [Mountain fire], the second story in the series, also depicts "a pathetic, startling scene." Because of an "idiotic superstition," the villagers set fires all over the mountain. As a result, what Zhong saw on his return to the home from which he had been away for so long was desolation: "The leaves and limbs were gone. The acacias, teaks, great bamboos, and other trees that used to compose the scene were gone; the scalped trunks and limbs made a wordless appeal to the heavens. At their feet, the mountains coldly displayed the burned, gray-black corpses."[15] These close observations of Taiwanese rural villages, noting their withered reality, were not in accord with government proclamations that spoke of "bountiful harvests" everywhere and whitewashed over the truth of the situation. It is this aspect of Zhong's work that fits the ideal that Tang and others advocated: the writing of literature that "walks the muddy ground, which is created out of this society."[16] Zhong wrote what the majority of farmers wished to speak.

Another participant in the debates, Zhang Liangze, was a particularly passionate advocate of Zhong's work, playing in the 1970s the role that Lin Haiyin had played in the 1960s. Zhang, who taught at Tainan's National Cheng Kung University, elevated Zhong's work from the living room to the lecture hall. During the two-year period 1973–74, he wrote four articles on Zhong.[17] And, in the summer of 1973, he presented an important lecture on him to the students and faculty of National Taiwan University's Chinese Department. That the lecture elicited the question, "What dynasty did Zhong Lihe live in?" reveals the extent of the ignorance surrounding Zhong's work in particular and Taiwan literature in general.

THE 1980S: CHINESE ETHNIC IDENTITY
AND ZHONG LIHE'S WORKS

In the new poetry debate of the first half of the 1970s, social consciousness and leftist principles were advocated. The relation of this debate to Zhong's works has been addressed above. However, in addition to the question of social consciousness, the nativist debate of the latter half of the decade raised the issue of "Chinese ethnic consciousness," which is closely linked to the debates and intellectual trends of the 1980s. This was not only the source of the subsequent "Taiwan complex" and "China complex" debates but also the starting point for all later discussions of ethnic identity.

Introductory literary history texts mark the start of the nativist debate with Yu Guangzhong's publication of the short essay "Lang lai le" [The wolf has come] in July 1977.[18] However, I would, instead, mark the start of the debate with an event that occurred three months earlier, namely, Ye Shitao's publication of "Taiwan xiangtu wenxueshi daolun" [An introduction to the history of Taiwan's nativist literature] in May 1977.[19] The next month, Chen Yingzhen responded with "'Xiangtu wenxue' de mangdian" [The blind spots of 'nativist literature'],[20] and the debate heated up. Essays by figures such as Yu Guangzhong and Peng Ge then opened up new fronts. But, with the benefit of hindsight, we can see that it was Ye and Chen who drew the primary battle lines. Not only do the theses of the following twenty years quote their works, but the major debates of the 1980s can also be seen as extensions of their debate.

Ye's introductory article is primarily a description of the long history of Taiwan nativist literature viewed from the perspective of Taiwanese consciousness. But Chen attacked that position as soon as the article appeared, arguing that the "anti-imperial, anticolonial character" of Taiwan literature makes it "a Third World literature" while at the same time placing it within the stream of Chinese literature. Chen strongly stressed "Chinese ethnic consciousness" and criticized "Taiwanese consciousness" as a "forced effort to create a separate consciousness."[21] In fact, at the same time that the Ye-Chen debate was going on, the "Chinese ethnic identity" debate was expanding to include criticism of actual literary works.[22]

Coincidentally, when the debates of the 1970s reached their most fevered pitch, the key figures behind each—Tang Wenbiao in the case of the new poetry debate and Chen Yingzhen in the case of the nativist debate—both cited Zhong Lihe's work in support of their respective social consciousness and ethnic identity positions. In other words, these two most important trends in thought can both be seen in Zhong Lihe's writings. Of course, Tang and Chen put Zhong's work to much different uses. The former cites it as a positive example, using it to advocate and support the idea of social consciousness. Chen, on the other hand, uses *Jiazhutao* as a counterexample, which is patently obvious from his title, "Yuanxiang de shiluo" [The lost home].

Zhong Lihe's *Jiazhutao* was written in 1944 and published in April 1945 under the pen name Jiang Liu. It was the only book of fiction that Zhong himself published during his lifetime. The time period in which he wrote it is critical. In 1944, the Second Sino-Japanese War was not yet over, and Beijing was under Japanese government. Although Zhong was an important postwar writer in 1950s Taiwan, this is the only work we have of his predating the end of the war. Moreover, in it he wrote of his experience of life in occupied Beijing. After the rise of a "nativist consciousness" in Taiwan, very few critics looked at *Jiazhutao*. And most literary histories (especially those written in mainland China) simply gloss over it as early and technically immature—if they mention it at all.

The longish novella *Jiazhutao* appears first in the collection. In roughly thirty-five thousand words, it describes the lives of the people in a Beijing residential compound. Although the world of the novella is the subjective world of the writer, there are socialist overtones that reflect the influence of Lu Xun. Zhong uses the main character—a coldly observant member of the intelligentsia "from the South"—to criticize the dark side of the people of Beijing, their greed, selfishness, poverty, and dirtiness, and their vain and argumentative nature. These characteristics are revealed both directly and indirectly through the plot and the dialogue.

Chen Yingzhen is one of the few postwar critics to give particular attention to this work. His review critiques and analyzes what he considers to be Zhong's mistakes. According to Chen, Zhong is "listlessly trying to separate himself from his ethnic group and its fate." Chen also feels that Zhong, who was born into the wealthy landowning class, has "completely lost confidence in his own people" and that, as a result, his ethnic identity "is in serious crisis." His conclusion is that Zhong does not recognize China's problems and its fate, that he does not see "China's true self hidden in the midst." According to Chen, China's decline is due to its being "caught in a debilitating battle, externally with imperialism and internally with feudalism"; the country is undergoing "necessary birthing pains." Chen places Zhong's work within the second of the three types of colonial literature that he identifies in the review—basically, a type of work produced by members of a colonialist intelligentsia who have "lost confidence in their own ethnic group."[23]

Chen's review is an excellent example of how, in the 1970s, the notion of a Chinese ethnic consciousness was turned into an ideology and became a tool with which to criticize literature. One cannot help but note that Zhong Lihe actually traveled to mainland China, lived in Beijing for six years, and wrote *Jiazhutao* from his own experience. By contrast, at the time Chen Yingzhen wrote his critique, he had never even visited the mainland. Chen states that Zhong fails to see China's true self, implying that he, who has never been there, can. It seems that it was not Zhong who created his ethnic consciousness out of an imagined reality.

If Zhong had not possessed tremendous confidence in the Chinese people, he would not, after the difficulties he faced in marrying a woman of the same surname, have taken his beloved bride away from his hometown to go traveling around the mainland. Zhong had had a very thorough Japanese (colonial) education and would have faced no linguistic barriers in going to Tokyo to study, as had so many others. Moreover, unless Chen subconsciously felt that Zhong was not as truly Chinese as the people of Beijing, would he have refused to grant Zhong the right to criticize the dark side of the Chinese character? In fact, for Zhong, who had made his first trip to Beijing at the age of twenty-six, to write a work so piercing in its assessment of the Chinese character after only six short years of observation is incontrovertible proof of his extraordinary talent.

It is interesting to note that the people of Beijing themselves are not critical of Zhong in the way Chen was. They do not feel that Zhong "has lost his Chinese stand."[24] Moreover, mainland scholars sum up Zhong's work by stating that what makes it remarkable is precisely its "passionate (Chinese) ethnic sensibility." This is attributed to the fact that Zhong lived, for the first half of his life, "in a region under Japanese imperialist control [and, therefore,] appreciates the ordeal of the Chinese people living under imperialist rule."[25]

If we consider *Jiazhutao*—both the collection and the novella—in the perspective of Taiwan's literary history, we see that it was a rarity, a detailed observation by a Taiwanese writer of life in Beijing prior to the end of the war. In his review, Chen also affirms its "realistic character," the picture that it paints of "drug use, selfishness, theft, pleasure at the misfortunes of others, prostitution, and indolence": "This was a typical residential compound; this was the Beijing of that day. This was China. No one should have the slightest doubt about its [the story's] realism" (98). Considered from the perspective of Tang Wenbiao's standards for social consciousness mentioned above, Zhong's work is a valuable historical and social record. As Tang says: "In his fiction, Zhong writes of lives of poverty. He tells the story of China's penury."[26]

As a realistic work of fiction, *Jiazhutao* pulls no punches. Zhong was raised in a big Taiwanese farming family and attended the private (Chinese) school in the village before entering a public (Japanese) elementary school. He therefore not only wrote Chinese with control and fluidity but also made use of his agricultural background to create colorful similes:

> They were born and raised in a hard, barren, stony land. They themselves were like weeds growing in the shadows, unlit by the sun, unnourished by the rain and dew. (11)

> They bore what they had to, were content with what they had and silent. They could, like the wild boar, live in their dirty, damp, dimly lit spaces and find them comfortable and be content. (3)

> They neither complained to the heavens nor felt bitterness toward mankind. They worked as diligently as oxen, never tiring. (17)

Interestingly, it is in such passages that Chen bases his review's other major criticism of the novella: that Zhong writes too much about "them." The use of so many third-person plural pronouns creates the impression that Zhong, "who actually lived in the residential compound," was separate from the characters he described, that he made himself a "bystander" (101). Today, when we read *Jiazhutao* afresh, it is difficult to see why Zhong would have been criticized in this way. He is very clear in his depiction of the main character, Zeng Simian, who has "come to Beijing from his hometown in the south" (1:15). Given that the main character is from elsewhere, it is only natural that he would be something of an outsider in Beijing. It is very difficult to see this portrayal as an instance of the author's "trying to separate himself from his ethnic group."

It has already been mentioned that not many people had read or were discussing *Jiazhutao* in the 1970s. Moreover, in the minds of most of his readers, Zhong was a nativist writer, someone "homeward bound" who, with his wife, had fled to the mainland. It has also already been stated that the course of thought was permeated and directed by the idea of Chinese ethnic consciousness. Therefore, most of Zhong's readers in the 1970s did not identify him on the basis of his works (such as criticizing his Beijingese characteristics) but rather according to his "homeward journey." An obvious example of this approach can be seen in the film *Yuanxiang ren*, in which the overarching symbol of Zhong's life and character is the ancestral homeland [*yuanxiang*], and the writer's giving up everything to flee to the ancestral homeland of the culture he yearns for—mainland China—is stressed.

In contrast to most people's image of Zhong as the "hometown guy," the young scholars of the 1970s had begun to involve themselves with research on nativist literature and had a new explanation. A key article from this era by Lin Zaijue voices the proposition that Zhong's work represents one of the "spirits of Taiwanese literature"—the other being Yang Kui—and begins to map out the character of nativist literature. (The article was published in 1973, so we could view it as marking the beginning of this sort of research.) It also explicitly notes the difference between Zhong and Yang, stating that Zhong "expresses [his] silent forbearance." Lin emphasizes Zhong's compassion: "He participates in the disasters and misfortunes of his compatriots and community. . . . The self and other characters of Zhong Lihe's fiction silently bear the burden of their ordeals. Their forbearance is staunch and resolute."[27]

When Lin mentions Zhong's "forbearance," he implies a contrast with Yang Gui's "spirit of resistance." Yang's resistance is naturally directed at repression under Japanese colonialism. But what colonial master required Zhong's forbearance? In the first half of his article Lin discusses "Taiwanese intelligentsia in a dual environment, [consisting of both] colonial and old society" (7), which seems to point to Japan. However, in the second half of the article, especially where she discusses Zhong, she cites only those of his works that deal primarily with rural villages in postwar Taiwan and does not even mention his *Lishan nongchang*. Obviously, Zhong's forbearance is not resistance to Japanese colonial power. In fact, during the kōminka period in Taiwan, Zhong himself was in Beijing. Furthermore, Zhong never wrote in

Japanese. It seems very clear, then, that his forbearance is unrelated to the Japanese.

In conclusion, in the 1970s Zhong received the affirmation of scholars, and a biographical film attracted still more attention to him. This attention prompted the creation of a Zhong Lihe memorial, which was completed in the 1980s. This building dedicated to Zhong, whose work encompassed the two defining characteristics of the era, nativism and Chinese ethnic consciousness, was the first of its kind to be dedicated to a Taiwanese postwar writer. It is an honor unique to Zhong among writers of the 1950s. The hubbub and glory that surrounded him during this period were in sharp contrast to the neglect and loneliness that he endured during the 1950s.

NOTES

Unless otherwise indicated, all translations from non-English-language sources are my own.

1 Lin Haiyin, "Yi xie hui yi" [Some memories], in *Zhong Lihe can ji* [A collection of Zhong Lihe fragments] (Taipei: Yuanxing, 1976), 214.
2 Tang Wenbiao [Shi Junmei], "Lai xi'ai Zhong Lihe" [Appreciating Zhong Lihe], *Wenji* [Literature quarterly] 2 (November 15, 1973): 60–76. This essay has been reprinted in *Zhong Lihe can ji*, 257–84. All subsequent quotations of it are taken from the latter edition.
3 Huang Chunming, *Luo* [The gong] (Taipei: Yuanjing chuban shiye gongse, 1974). Some of the stories appear in Howard Goldblatt, trans., *The Drowning of an Old Cat and Other Stories* (Bloomington: Indiana University Press, 1980).
4 Zhang Liangze, ed., *Zhong Lihe quanji* [The complete works of Zhong Lihe], 8 vols. (Taipei: Yuanxing chubanshe, 1976).
5 See Zhong Lihe [Jiang Liu], *Jiazhutao* [Oleander] (Beijing: De Zeng, 1945), reprinted in Zhang, ed., *Zhong Lihe quanji*, 1:1–64.
6 Chen Yingzhen, "Yuanxiang de shiluo: Shiping *Jiazhutao*" [The lost home: Critiquing *Jiazhutao*], *Xiandai wenxue* [Modern literature], literary suppl., no. 1 (July 1, 1977), reprinted in Chen Yingzhen, *Gu'er de lishi, lishi de gu'er* [Historial orphans, and orphans of history] (Taipei: Yuanjing chuban shiye gongsi, 1984), 97–109.
7 See, e.g., Chen Fangming, "Qiling niandai Taiwan wenxueshi daolun" [Introduction to the literary history of 1970s in Taiwan], in *Dianfan de zhuiqiu* [The pursuit of a paradigm] (Taipei: Lianhe wenxue chubanshe, 1994), 222.
8 Shi Shu, *Xiandai de xiantu: Liang an wenxue lunju* [Modern native place: A collection of essays from both sides of the Taiwan Strait] (Taipei: Xin Di, 1997), 308.
9 Guan Jieming, "Zhongguo xiandai shi de kunjing" [The predicament of modern

Chinese poetry], *Zhongguo shibao renjian fukan* [*China Times* human affairs supplement], no. 2 (1972): 28–29, reprinted in Zhao Zhiti, ed., *Wenxue, xiuzou* [Literature, restfully walking] (Taipei: Yuanxing chubanshe, 1976), 127–42 (quote appears on 142).

10 The series began with Tang Wenbiao's "Shi de Moluo" [The decline of poetry], originally published in *Wenji* 1.8 (1973), and reprinted in Tang Wenbiao, *Tianguo bu shi women de* [Heaven does not belong to us] (Taipei: Lianjing, 1976). It ended with his "Jiangbi de xiandai shi" [The rigor mortis of modern poetry], originally published in *Zhongwai wenxue* [Chung-wai literary monthly] 2.3 (1973): 18–23, and reprinted in Tang, *Tianguo bu shi women de*, 139–44.

11 Tang Wenbiao, *Tianguo bu shi women de*, 190.

12 Tang, "Lai Xi'ai Zhong Lihe," 260.

13 *Zhong Lihe riji* [Zhong Lihe's diary], in Zhang, ed., *Zhong Lihe quanji*, 6:177.

14 Zhong Lihe, "Zhu tou zhuang" [The bamboo-head village], *Taiwan wenyi* [Taiwan literature] 5 (1964): 25–47, 26, reprinted in Zhang, ed., *Zhong Lihe quanji*, 2:205–20, 207.

15 Zhong Lihe's "Shanhuo" [Mountain fire] originally appeared in *Taiwan wenyi* 1.5 (1964): 25–47. The quotations given in the text are taken from the reprinting of the story in Zhang, ed., *Zhong Lihe quanji*, 2:221–34, 221, 222, 224. For the third and fourth stories in the series, see Zhong Lihe, "Ah Huang shu" [Uncle Ah Huang], and "Qinjia yu shan'ge" [Relatives and folk songs], reprinted in Zhang, ed., *Zhong Lihe quanji*, 2:235–46, 247–61. All four stories were originally written ca. 1950.

16 Tang, "Lai xi'ai Zhong Lihe," 278.

17 Zhang Liangze, "Cong Zhong Lihe de yishu shuoqi: Lihe sixiang chutan" [Speaking from Zhong Lihe's posthumous papers: Initial exploration of Zhong's idea], *Zhongwai wenxue* 11 (November 1973): 100–112, "Zhong Lihe de wenxue guan" [Zhong Lihe's literary view], *Wenji* 2.11 (November 1973): 48–59, "Zhong Lihe zuopin gaishu" [General survey of Zhong Lihe's works] *Shuping shumu* [Book review and bibliography] 9.1 (1974): 107–15, 10.2 (1974): 117–25, 11.3 (1974): 64–71, and "Zhong Lihe zuopin zhong de Riben jingyan he zuguo jingyan" [The experiences of Japan and motherland in Zhong's works], *Zhongwai wenxue* 2.1 [April 1974]: 32–57.

18 Yu Guangzhong, "Lang lai le" [The wolf has come], *Lianhebao* [United daily], July 8, 1977, literary supplement.

19 Ye Shitao, "Taiwan xiangtu wenxueshi daolun" [An introduction to the history of Taiwan's nativist literature], *Xiachao* [Xia dynasty] 14 (May 1977): 68–75.

20 Chen Yingzhen [Xu Nancun], "'Xiangtu wenxue' de mangdian" [The blind spots of 'nativist literature'], *Taiwan wenyi* 5.55 (1977): 107–12, reprinted in Chen Yingzhen, *Gu'er de lishi*, 17–23.

21 Ibid., 111 (21).

22 See, e.g., Chen's "Yuanxiang de shiluo."

23 Ibid., 106–7.

24 Ibid., 100.
25 Pan Cuijing, "Taiwan sheng zuojia: Zhong Lihe" [Zhong Lihe: A writer from the province of Taiwan], *Wenxue pinglun* [Literary criticism], no. 3 (1980): 133.
26 Tang, "Lai Xi'ai Zhong Lihe," 264.
27 Lin Zaijue, "Taiwan wenxue de liang zhong jingshe: Yang Kui yu Zong Lihe zhi bijiao" [Two spirits in Taiwanese literature: A comparison of Yang Kui and Zhong Lihe], *Zhong-wai wenxue* 2.7 (December 1973): 4–20, 15.

7

Wang Wenxing's *Backed against the Sea*, Parts I and II: The Meaning of Modernism in Taiwan's Contemporary Literature

Sung-sheng Yvonne Chang

In "Critical Texts, Mass Artifacts," Marilyn Ivy analyzes the oddity of a book on poststructuralism and deconstruction—Asada Akira's *Kozo to chikara* [Structure and power]—suddenly becoming a best seller in Japan in 1983. She argues that the key to the book's phenomenal popularity lay in the unconventional image of its young author, which helped convey a provocative message: "knowledge is 'play'"; it is "a matter of style." This was a powerfully emancipatory idea for the book's targeted audience, the "young university test takers, those caught in the tightly programmed Japanese educational system, in which the exigencies of the exam system—the 'examination hell'—almost completely determine the chances of knowledge [success?]." Ivy calls this the *Asada Akira phenomenon* and uses it to illustrate a prominent aspect of contemporary Japan's "postmodern condition," in which knowledge is transformed into an "object of desire," a commodity.[1]

What is illuminating about Ivy's analysis is that she emphasizes contextual factors governing texts' reception over their actual contents and intellectual trends. The potency of imported intellectual trends, then, derives from their promise to help native intellectuals redress the "lacks" and "excesses" of the dominant culture in their own society. Although there are no guarantees, first encounters typically trigger fantasies about any new thought system's power to shake up the host society. Those less deeply implicated in the dominant culture's control mechanisms—the younger generation, minority intellectuals—are particularly susceptible to such fantasies. This is the premise on which I base my reexamination of the two major Western-inspired intellectual/cultural trends in contemporary Taiwan, the modernist (late 1950s–early 1970s) and the postmodernist (late 1980s–) movements.

MODERNIST AND POSTMODERNIST TRENDS IN TAIWAN

Modernism has become nostalgic in Taiwan—no longer "forever innovative, forever new," as it once seemed. Nowadays, the progressive, prophetic aura that once belonged to modernism drifts less certainly over the loosely defined postmodernism. However, when considered against their historical contexts in Taiwan, the two imported trends actually look much alike. Both, for instance, caught on at moments when changing conditions permitted (or even inspired) public expression of formerly suppressed discontent. The modernist trend emerged when Taiwan's first postwar generation of intellectuals came of age, coinciding with the initial signs of economic upswing and a broad relaxation of the Nationalist government's coercive cultural policies. Similarly, the burgeoning of radical cultural trends under the rubric of postmodernism was concurrent with the return of exiled and other overseas intellectuals after the lifting of martial law in 1987, at the height of Taiwan's social affluence.

Regardless of how modernism and postmodernism relate to each other in Western contexts, in Taiwan they have both offered alternative cultural visions, challenging the dominant cultural ideology. The modernists challenged martial law Taiwan's neotraditionalist moralism with iconoclastic individualism, and, against the perceived shortcomings of Taiwan's destitute cultural environment of the 1950s and 1960s, they launched a "high-culture quest," including a demand for artistic and institutional professionalism. Supported by a liberal conception of social stratification, the modernists were cultural elitists, unlike the postmodernists, who generally espouse a populist agenda. Indeed, some of the energy behind the postmodern trend derives from the sheer joy of being able to pursue what is perceived as a more truly radical intellectual line, as opposed to the modernists' merely different interpretation of an ideology, Western liberalism, that was at least rhetorically embraced all along by the martial law regime as part and parcel of its postwar relationship with the United States.

Again, however, there is a high degree of contextual resemblance between the two intellectual trends, not just in their "alternative" nature but also in their respective agents, institutional support, and general courses of development. Both came to public attention after establishing footholds on college campuses, and both were quickly assimilated by the cultural establishment, in spite of their potentially subversive content, thanks to being led by privileged-class intellectuals affiliated with prestigious institutions.

Of the two, the modernist movement has had the greater impact on literary production, surviving a period of sharp criticism, primarily by left-leaning nativist critics (especially Chen Yingzhen) who viewed the modernists as compradors to Western cultural imperialism. This began in the 1970s and stigmatized the modernists as ideological reactionaries through the 1980s.

In the 1990s, as the post–martial law cultural field became more thoroughly market oriented, a new breed of mass media–based cultural critics appeared on the stage. Some, like Yang Zhao, offered refreshing new interpretations of Taiwan's modernist phenomenon that replaced the dogmatic leftist criticism. These revisions, however, are limited by being conceived in a journalistic mode—with immediacy and the mass audience foremost in mind, they offer only comparatively facile critiques, not exactly the kind of contextual understanding hoped for in a serious literary analysis.

A proper contextual study of Taiwan's modernist literature should begin by trying to understand the enterprise as the modernists themselves conceived it. One overriding motive of the movement was, as I have argued elsewhere, its high-culture quest.[2] Part of the modernists' arduous emulation of Western literary modernism was an earnest subscription to the philosophy that underpinned modernist aesthetics. Behind formal experimentation were the notions of epistemological uncertainty and the arbitrary nature of linguistic signs as well as the avant-garde impetus to subvert social praxis. Meanwhile, the modernists' inward searching was prompted by the existentialist assertion of life's fundamental absurdity, Freudian skepticism of socially sanctioned ethical norms, and a rationalist conception of moral relativism.

Today, the Taiwanese modernists' faith in the universal validity of Western cultural concepts seems politically incorrect. These concepts are now often seen as complicit in the capitalist West's imperialist project at an earlier moment in history. This, however, should not prevent us from acknowledging the positive role that they played at times in non-Western societies' artistic renaissances during the second half of the twentieth century.

In Taiwan, the rise of the modernist movement in the 1950s and 1960s was heavily influenced by American liberal ideology. Thanks to the island's postwar diplomatic ties with the United States, a loosely defined liberalism gained popularity among Taiwanese intellectuals and was to some degree tolerated by the right-wing ruling regime. In a decidedly stagnant cultural landscape dominated by political propaganda, the imported liberal vision was perceived as emancipatory. Its rationalist notion of progress, and especially Daniel Lerner's social-scientific formula of progress from "traditional" to "modern" civilization, offered a particularly welcome alternative to the government's conservative, traditionalist cultural narrative.[3]

Unlike Lei Zhen, Li Ao, and some of the other more radical liberal intellectuals associated with the *Ziyou Zhongguo* [Free China review] and *Wenxing* [Literary star] magazines, modernist writers were more interested in aesthetic issues than in overt political dissent. While their mantra of artistic autonomy was often blamed for fostering socially disengaged literature ("art for art's sake"), it did serve as an effective antidote to the constraints that were stifling Taiwan's cultural sphere.

In the late 1960s and early 1970s, modernists who studied in the United States were further influenced by the radical expressions of humanist ideals in the American counterculture movement.[4] However much the nativists would later rail against humanism and individualism as undesirable products of Western capitalist society, at the time these too made effective tools for the modernists' critique of Taiwan's dominant culture. So it is that two pinnacles of Taiwan's modernist literature in its mature stage, Bai Xianyong's *Niezi* [Crystal boys] and Wang Wenxing's own *Jiabian* [Family catastrophe], both challenge the ethical underpinnings of the Chinese tradition where they begin, in the central father-son relationship that suppresses individual motives and desires.

The modernists also reacted against an array of particular problems and deficiencies that they found in the literature of the day, including amateurism, unexamined devotion to an overly exalted traditionalist style, the May Fourth legacy of lyrical sentimentalism, and the politically truncated notion of human nature favored in the government's anti-Communist cultural campaigning. Finally, consciously reacting to the romanticized humanitarianism of the leftist strand of the new literature tradition, modernist writers applied a rationalist realism to their own portrayals of poverty, suffering, and the human capacity for compassion, securing a unique place in modern Taiwanese literary history.[5]

In a nutshell, while the modernists acted primarily in the artistic realm, they were also reacting against a politically instituted, conservative dominant culture. The alternative visions that they offered were defined against the particular "lacks" and "excesses" of their specific historical context. The modernists' high-culture quest was an elitist vision, to be sure, but not a wholesale importation of detached foreign ideals. Instead, it was driven by, and responded to, conditions on the ground in Taiwan—and to historically significant effect. Modernist aesthetic conceptions have had a lasting impact on Taiwan's literary mainstream, especially on baby-boom-generation writers. The baby boomers, however, have tried to split the difference between "high" and "popular" culture, responding to the transformations of the 1980s and 1990s by becoming less resistant to market imperatives.[6] Meanwhile, veteran modernists like Wang Wenxing and Li Yongping have continued to pursue the modernist literary project on its original terms, in defiance of the drastically changed cultural climate.

Li Yongping published the sequel to his 941-page novel *Haidong qing* (1992) in 1998.[7] Meanwhile, the second part of Wang Wenxing's *Beihai de ren* [Backed against the sea] appeared in book form in the summer of 1999— the first part had appeared in 1981—after being serialized first in the literary monthly *Lianhe wenxue* [Unitas].[8] The two parts of Wang's *Backed against the Sea*, bookending twenty-two years of Taiwan's literary history, exemplify the modernists' high-culture quest and its close connection to the sociocultural dynamics of the society that Wang depicts. That is why I have chosen Wang's masterwork for extended discussion.

WANG WENXING'S BACKED AGAINST THE SEA, PART I

It appears indisputable that both the philosophical import and the presentation of the first part of *Backed against the Sea* are heavily indebted to the Western literary tradition. Wang apparently intends the four books the narrator takes with him into exile—Tolstoy's *Resurrection*, Nietzsche's *Thus Spake Zarathustra*, Dostoyevsky's *Notes from the Underground*, and Gide's *The Fruits of the Earth*, all modern Western classics that deal with such topics as civilization, values, rationality, alienation, and moral responsibility—to suggest to the reader the intellectual scope of the novel. Also, according to Wang himself, in this work he deliberately tries to appropriate the "seriocomic" mode as well as the techniques of parody and black humor, all of which are modeled on modern Western literature. The Western influence certainly diminishes *Backed against the Sea*'s claim to originality. As Leo Lee perceptively points out, the novel contains visible affinities with such contemporary Western literary works as Philip Roth's *Portnoy's Complaint* and Joyce's *Ulysses* and even with the Hollywood movie *Candy* (Christian Marquand, 1968).[9] Traces of Samuel Beckett's later novels, such as *Molloy*, are also obvious both in the novel's theme of existentialist absurdity and in the antihero's racy narrative style.

It may not be too far-fetched to argue that this indebtedness to, or "derivativeness" from, the Western literary tradition is a logical consequence of a basic assumption of Taiwan's modernists, one that Wang Wenxing has taken more seriously and substantiated with more solid efforts than any other writer. The modernists believed from the beginning that the Western modernist tradition could provide them with the intellectual frames and technical means unavailable in the native Chinese narrative tradition but necessary if they were to examine in depth important issues about life. *Backed against the Sea*, then, is a remarkable attempt to explore these issues and to communicate them through artistically sophisticated presentational modes deemed endemic to Western literary modernism. I will specifically call attention to two thematic aspects of the work. First, since the local sociocultural settings inevitably serve as the object of his philosophical contemplation, Wang offers some thought-provoking insights about contemporary Taiwanese society as well as about humanity. Second, as the modernists consciously take literary writing as an "intellectual project," it is natural that their philosophical inquiries are often deeply interwoven with personal preoccupations. In Wang's case, such inquiries are inseparable from his genuine subscription to Enlightenment rationality and his persistent interest in interpersonal communication and the workings of fate (in both the metaphysical and the practical senses).

The narrator of *Backed against the Sea* is a Beckett-style antihero, a middle-aged, retired military man of doubtful moral reputation who addresses himself as "*Ye*," a slang form of self-address connoting arrogance (literally, *ye* means "father" or "your father"; when used in conversation, it implies an insult to one's conversational partner). Once again, Wang adopts a setting familiar from existentialist literature. The narrator has recently fled from the center of Taiwan's modern civilization, Taipei, to an impoverished fishing village on the island's coastline, Shenkeng ao [Deep pit harbor], in order to escape the adverse consequences of his embezzling and gambling. He is a loner free of familial and social obligations, and his sole purpose in life is to fulfill two sets of basic needs: those of a physical nature (food and sex) and those springing from his exceptionally lively, although somewhat uncultured, intellect. Realizing after his arrival at the harbor that there are no fish to catch during this season, he is forced to operate a fortune-telling stand to maintain a minimal subsistence. The peculiar nature of this profession and the great amount of leisure that it provides unexpectedly lead him to an uncanny spiritual quest, unleashing contemplations about important issues that are luxuries denied modern individuals caught up in normal, civilized lives.

On the discursive level, the whole novel is made up of the antihero's extended monologue on a sleepless night, a monologue that willfully mixes insight with heresy, rational thought with pure nonsense. The first hundred pages, approximately half of the book, form a large unit consisting primarily of the narrator's pseudophilosophical reflections on things near and far, ranging from food prices in local restaurants to ideas about freedom and democracy. Even the episode in which the narrator relates his fortune-telling experience contains more speculation than action. The second half of the book, however, mainly recounts incidents that occur during the first ten days of the narrator's stay at the harbor. Although antisocial by temperament, he makes some contacts with local residents, such as the clerks in a certain Dialect Research Bureau—he boards there for cheap meals—and girls in local brothels and teahouses.

The antihero's seemingly nonsensical remarks are a disguised critique of Taiwanese society at a time when an export economy and industrialization had initiated a structural transformation. The location where the story takes place, Deep Pit Harbor, a half-deserted fishing village only miles away from Taipei, is a symbol of all the ills brought about by this process. As an exile of the modern metropolis of Taipei and a newcomer to the village, the narrator is psychologically situated halfway between the two extremes of modern civilization: a unique vantage point from which to observe and comment on both the universal condition of social progress and the particular cultural ideology that has dominated post-1949 Taiwanese society.

Unlike the socialist idealism advocated by the nativists, Wang's critique is offered not through direct thematic formulations but obliquely through the special dynamics of narrative discourse. The middle-aged veteran represents a special socio-ideological group—middle- and lower-class mainlander émigrés—and his coarse vitality, piquant wit, and childlike fascination with the signifying processes of language are crucial components of Wang's attempt to unravel the unexamined assumptions underlying popular opinions shared by the same speech community. While the narrator tries to amuse himself by thinking through words, words are also thinking through him. At the same time, he derives pleasure from distorting set phrases, twisting popular idioms, poking fun with maxims, and naming and deliberately misnaming situations; his discourse becomes a parody of the very act of conceptualizing things in language. As Bakhtin pointed out: "The ideological becoming of a human being . . . is the process of selectively assimilating the words of others."[10] In this book, many of the words that appear underlined, in parentheses, or in boldface type may be read as marks of public "myths" prevalent in post-1949 Taiwan. The narrator's conscious or unconscious distortion of them calls attention to the ideological basis of this particular culture.

The date of the story, specifically identified by the author as 1962, is significant in that the 1960s marked Taiwan's economic takeoff. While the country marched full speed toward industrialization and capitalism, discrepancies between urban and rural modes of living rapidly increased. Taipei at this time was already a modern metropolis in embryonic form, considerably more prosperous than other parts of the island, whereas Deep Pit Harbor, separated from Taipei by just a four-hour train ride, represents the island's numerous backward regions, the "blood" of which was being sucked by the unremitting process of urban expansion. Yet, unlike the nativists who have treated the city-village hostility solely from the standpoint of the often-idealized rural people, Wang sees the city and the rural regions as links in the same economic chain. Thus, the disappointed narrator complains that "everything good has been exported to Taipei"—choice fruit, meat, and even good-looking girls (15–16). Deep Pit Harbor is depicted not as a precapitalist pastoral haven—in fact, the narrator considers pastoral to be a mere euphemism for primitive poverty and a result of ordinary people's romantic imagination (and sheer ignorance) about the countryside (19) — but rather as a mirror image and a parody of the city, where everything is stripped bare or driven to its extreme so that the absurdity inherent in this civilization is bluntly exposed. For example, the prominent presence of foreign religion in Taiwan is symbolized by the Catholic church, the only specimen of modern architecture in the village, a solid brick structure standing aloof on a hill in sharp contrast with the town's shabby cottages made of wood and straw. The impoverished residents of the fishing village use the pawnshop as a local bank, one whose financial strategy is described as "cutting off the flesh of one part of the body to fill the wound in another part" (18). Sex, food, and religion are the important trades that prosper in this place despite, or as a consequence of, the general poverty — probably because the enjoyment of food and sex are the only rights that the poor and the rich share (17–18).

In the first quarter of the book, the narrator's thoughts mostly revolve around the absurdities of "civilized" life in a more universal sense. For example, in his typical aphoristic manner, the narrator contemplates the nature of the memoir as a literary genre. In order to write a memoir, one must first be a celebrity (as if only celebrities have memory). Therefore, the memoir is a literary genre the value of which comes not from the efforts involved in writing it but, rather, solely from the efforts made before one picks up the pen — somewhat like the onetime collection of life insurance benefits (2). Or, recalling the troubles he has gone through to obtain medical proof of his ulcer — which caused massive bleeding for many years — in order to be discharged from military service, the narrator jeers at the unreasonable requirement for such proof with an absurd analogy: as if a new baby must hold in its little fist a "birth certificate" to prove that it has actually been born (11). The person who helped the narrator get the certificate acts as if he has done him a great favor; in fact, he has usurped the "ownership" of the ulcer, while the narrator bled for it (11–12). Once, the narrator asks in puzzlement why all the people in society must have a "profession." Is it possible for person without a profession to show "signs of existence" (54–55)? This is one of many remarks with existentialist overtones.

The narrator's deliberation on food prices offers an interesting comment on the intriguing phenomenon of customer psychology. He first suggests that "seasonal price" ought to be added as the fifth idol to Francis Bacon's list since every customer seems to be in awe of it, intimidated by its underlying arbitrariness. Theoretically, however, a restaurant's seasonal price does not have to be expensive—it might even be relatively cheap. The narrator thus decides to order a dish offered at such a forbidding cost. It turns out, however, that not one of the dishes marked "seasonal price" is even available. In fact, many of the shabby-looking local food stands have colorful posters advertising fancy dishes for decorative purposes only. The real food they sell, all unappetizing snacks, is "one price for all," NT$2, regardless of quantity. The narrator sarcastically remarks that this is an epoch-making innovation: instead of prices being set according to the value of commodities, commodities are regulated by their prices (20–22). The parodic use of economic terms throughout the book expresses Wang's observation that contemporary Taiwanese society was going through an important transition. The abstraction of experience, the arbitrariness of value under the market system, and the phenomenon of fetishization are manifestations of the logic of capitalism.

Such intellectual reflections on "modern" experiences are not merely "ideological distraction[s]" or a way "of displacing the reader's attention from history and society to . . . experiences of the individual monad"; they undoubtedly have a realistic import, albeit in a modernist sense, as Fredric Jameson suggests.[11] The novel's references to the social setting of Taiwan in the 1960s and early 1970s probably show more originality and perceptiveness than any other literary representation of the period. For example, by frequent parodic use of urban jargon to refer to local phenomena in Deep Pit Harbor—such as saying that the local clinic has adopted the latest in "open-style" management by treating patients in front of people passing through—the narrator sarcastically measures the backward fishing village against the standards of modern civilization embodied by the city or Taipei, calling attention to an immense disparity between the two (17). The narrator's own story may be taken as the epitome of the chaotic social conditions of Taiwan in the years following the retreat from the mainland. Because he is a veteran, his only social connections in Taiwan are with people from his home province on the mainland, especially those of the same clan. He relied on one of them to help him leave the army and find a job, repaying the favor by running errands in an illegal business in which the helper was involved. However, the narrator's embezzlement from a small office fund is discovered, and his patron refuses to continue supporting him. Infuriated by this "betrayal," the narrator complains with indignation: "Treating me this way, do they possess any human feelings [*qing*] and a sense of justice [*yi*] at all?" (7–8). It is, of course, preposterous for the narrator to invoke such outdated codes of honor as qing and yi, which govern interpersonal relationships in the old social formations, while he himself follows a more utilitarian, predatory kind of rule. Yet this very self-contradiction and this confusion of values nicely offer a glimpse of the way in which both residue from the feudalist past and modern utilitarianism, or pure lawless exploitation, dominated post-1949 Taiwanese society before greater order was established.

The most intricate social critique, however, rests in the author's commentary on the dominant cultural ideology. An excellent example is the narrator's deliberation on materialism. In a didactic mood, he begins by preaching against the "American lifestyle" that he has seen in Hollywood movies. He disapproves of the Americans' excessive material comfort and their dedicating a whole lifetime to work in order to possess all kinds of machines—televisions, videotape recorders, washing machines, lawn mowers, and fancy cars. He regrets that, in their materialistic culture, no American understands the "true meaning of life." The speech is concluded with a profound-sounding dictum that turns out to be the narrator's own invention: "Life is not to be used but to be cherished, to be appreciated with leisure. ... In any case, one should try to be a person, instead of being occupied with work—as I, *Ye* himself, have always said." No sooner is this proudly pronounced than he senses something wrong with this line of thought:

> Hey, wait a second, wait a second, wait a second, to put it this way seems, it seems, a little weird. It sounds as if I am the kind of person who is "content with poverty and finds happiness in the Way" and who, "being content, is always happy"; that I all year long need only two or three sweaters and one single pair of shoes to live on, doesn't it? Of course not—of course not, of course not. *Ye* naturally wants to chase after wealth and fame and beautiful women to embrace. *Ye* thus is a person full of contradiction, knowing, *clearly* knowing that wealth and glory are not worth anything, and from the beginning there is not an iota of need to aspire for it, yet *Ye* just, in spite of everything, wants it *"badly," "cannot"* do without it.—*Contradiction!—Contradiction!—Ye* as a person is an ennn-or-mous *contradiction!—Ye is "contradiction."* (30–31)

The denunciation of Western materialism on moral grounds nicely manifests the narrator's false consciousness, conditioned by the prevailing neotraditionalist, conservative cultural discourse. The narrator belongs to a socioideological, sociolinguistic group that upholds this moralist stance, and, as a language user, he unconsciously perpetuates the mythifying function of words. The novel's greatest feat, however, is its persistent disruption of the socially constructed moral consciousness. Although unwittingly reiterating the language of his community, the narrator, being an original thinker of sorts, refuses to submit to its categories and, thus, is not constrained by its logic. The powerful weapon to which he repeatedly resorts in order to resist the tyrannous control of language is arbitrariness. Like any other language user, he cannot attain a transcendental standpoint; he can only rebel against language by bluntly declaring that he chooses to honor the logic of "contradiction" and by arbitrarily reversing his position when it suits his whim.

Thus, through exposing the logical fallacies, paradoxes, and deceptive nature of common discourse, Wang engages in a process of "ironic demythification" whereby his own critique of the society's moralistic neotraditionalism is refracted, if not directly reflected. While there has never been a shortage of cultural criticism in modern Chinese literature, this novel is a rare example of the "writerly text" that offers a forceful criticism of the dominant cultural discourse.

Many elements of the novel combine to paint a realistic picture of some peculiar phenomena in post-1949 Taiwanese society. The narrator's use of all sorts of military metaphors in his account of sexual experiences reminds readers not only of his own background as a soldier but also of the prominent military presence in Taiwanese society as a whole. The narrator's diagnosis of the problem with contemporary Taiwan literature—that it has created too many poets but little good poetry and that it is too easy to get literary fame, partly because writing is nonlucrative and, therefore, irrelevant in this materialistic society—reflects insights with which many people have come to concur. Above all, the most important matrix of themes in the book involves poverty, the poverty of the socially disadvantaged—in this case, mainlander settlers—within a thriving economy.

As material scarcity was a prevalent social phenomenon in the years following the retreat, both modernists and nativists who launched their careers in the late 1950s and early 1960s were preoccupied with the theme of poverty. There was a marked difference in their approaches, however. Whereas the nativists celebrated the human potential for dignity in the face of a humiliating environment, the modernists showed more concern with the individual's capacity for compassion in the face of other people's suffering. The nativists privileged Taiwan's rural inhabitants; the modernists dealt more with the urban underclass. The nativists showed a tendency to romanticize, while the modernists strove to attain an unsentimental realism.

Poverty in *Backed against the Sea* is first of all treated in its personal, psychological dimension. Having run out of luck, and full of resentment, the narrator is ready to blame anyone but himself—thus the outburst, the string of profanities, that opens the book. The condition of impoverishment generates not only anger and discontentment but also a struggle to survive. The narrator's resourcefulness in obtaining the basic necessities—in making everything *wanneng* [multifunctional], such as the all-purpose bathtub converted into a bed and a desk—even earns him a self-congratulatory grin. Such a robust and defiant victim of poverty evokes little sympathy, even if he is not responsible for his predicament. A mainlander veteran without valuable social connections, the narrator is, indeed, a member of one of the most disadvantaged social groups at the time.

The antihero's wretched condition not only is treated without sentimentality but also plays a significant role in the novel's special text-reader dynamic. As his external possessions are reduced to the very minimum, his apathetic contemplation of other people's problems and his disinterested, perversely witty observations about the sheer destitution of Deep Pit Harbor are freed from ordinary moral implications and work with a Brechtian alienating effect. One example is his "original" discovery about human eating habits—working-class people love sweet things because they need more calories; those who know the art of using salt have a higher degree of civilization (22). Or, noticing that, before the fish come to the harbor, the local people have nothing to do but loaf around all day, the narrator questions why God should have given brains to these people; all they do is use them to fill up parts of their lower body (57). The dehumanizing quality of poverty is expressed no place else in modern Chinese literature in such a caustic manner.

The work not only plumbs the "depth" of Taiwan's contemporary civilization where poverty resides, as symbolically conveyed by the name Deep Pit Harbor, but also tries to probe the deep recesses of individual moral capacity. Since such early short stories as "Wanju shouqiang" [The toy pistol] (1960) and "Heiyi" [Black coat] (1964), Wang Wenxing has been questioning the possibility of meaningful interpersonal relations and the innate perversity of human nature. Such questions are pressed more compellingly in the second half of the first part of this novel, in which the narrator comes into contact with members of the Dialect Research Bureau and local prostitutes.

Rather than discuss the relevant scenes in detail here,[12] I turn to a paratextual incident that not only provides additional perspective on the moral dimensions of Wang's work but also returns to the topic of the limitations of knowledge with which I opened this essay. At the same time, the biographical "incident" in question falls roughly a third of the way between the publication of the two parts of *Backed against the Sea* and, therefore, provides a convenient way of suturing consideration of the two works.

The incident involves the author's own engagement with organized religion. Wang Wenxing has indicated that, in the first part of *Backed against the Sea*, he tried to present a fundamentally atheistic view. Paradoxically, however, the highly rational search narrated in this book confirms a provisionality that anticipates a later religious quest by the author himself. When the narrator logically, if not at all scientifically, tests his hypothesis, the procedure proves so artfully devised that the very signs that suggest the improbability of the hypothesis also serve as evidence of undeniability. Since the narrator has conceived the rules for this quest in intellectual terms, his search must remain open-ended if he cannot rule out the possibility of a positive answer.

That Wang formally converted to Catholicism in 1986 may indicate acceptance of this provisionality. He had made an uncharacteristically direct statement about his religious quest in a note published in a literary journal in 1985.[13] The author of the note, watching a bird pecking at its own image reflected in a mirror, feels sorry for the creature in its futile search for self-knowledge. The knowledge that we human beings possess about its plight is, the author reasons, by definition inaccessible to the bird since it requires a perspective that only human beings can have. The apparently metaphoric situation in this note echoes the hypothesis verbalized by the narrator in *Backed against the Sea* about a higher order of intelligence, a transcendental existence with superior knowledge about human beings. The message is this: human beings should acknowledge the limitations of their perspective; any denial of the possibility of a universal hierarchy is only presumptuous. Again, most rationalistically, the author reaches a conclusion negatively, based on a rational choice to honor the hypothetical.

WANG WENXING'S *BACKED AGAINST THE SEA, PART II*

The second part of *Backed against the Sea* continues the story line from the first part with another long monologue by the antihero protagonist Ye, this time during the sleepless night of February 21, 1962, forty days after the self-addressed speeches that constitute the first part. Ye has been reduced to utter destitution in the interim, and this accounts for the changes in style, mood, and thematic presentation in the sequel.

Backed against the Sea, Part I takes place ten days after Ye arrives at the fishing village, Deep Pit Harbor, where he seeks refuge and tries to eke out an existence after every door is closed to him in Taipei. Although it is not fishing season, there is still hope; and, more important, Ye is in a jolly, exploratory mood. The monologue in the first part contains random thoughts recounted in stream-of-consciousness style, many involving people Ye has just met in the village.

A discharged air force captain with one bad eye, and a vagabond of sorts, Ye is, nonetheless, a vital character with some education and native intelligence. Amid his quasi-intellectual comments and amused juggling of words and aphorisms are sparks of insight that reveal the paradoxical relation among "truths," "half-truths," and ways of perceiving reality that are normally taken for granted. Meanwhile, the considerable delight that Ye takes in the misfortunes of his new acquaintances is presented as a sign less of his own peculiar meanness than of something common to the human condition.

Plot and external actions in the sequel are more straightforward, and there is a marked decrease in convoluted verbal exercises. The focus of the episodes has shifted largely to the narrator's own experiences, which include some misdeeds of a morally dubious nature. The general mood is considerably grimmer. The playfulness that dominates the first part of the novel is replaced by latent anxiety and foreboding that turn out to be justified. At the end of the novel, Ye's train of thought is abruptly cut off when a gang of locals break in, murder him, and throw him into the sea—ostensibly for the minor crimes that he has recently committed in the area.

Most of the major themes from the first part are revisited in the second, but often cast in a different light, as is the antiromantic theme. Nearly half the sequel is devoted to two separate but equally pathetic love affairs, the most recent with an old, hideous-looking, and extremely unfriendly local prostitute known as Red Hair. Unreasonably infatuated, Ye composes long and passionate love letters, begging for a chance to "be together in private and talk about their hearts' feelings" (202). Red Hair's utter incomprehension and relentless scorn are not enough to cool his passion, and the "affair" comes to an end only with her sudden departure owing to declining business at the whorehouse. Ye then recounts a previous romantic encounter in Taipei, when Cai Suzhen, a homely girl with a menial job, became unexplainably attached to him after a bicycle accident involving them both. This time the roles are reversed, with Ye treating the girl like dirt and even attempting to prostitute her to a gambling partner.

The antiromantic motif, parodying popular fiction, has been prominent in Taiwan's modernist literature, and the difference between pulp romance and the crude realities of romantic love is a favorite subject of Wang's. Here, he even has his narrator, Ye, explicitly mock the romantic convention of the boy and the girl crashing into each other's arms in an accident scene.

The story having shifted away from the vagaries of the narrator's inner consciousness depicted in the first part of the novel, these more naturalistically presented incidents in the second part begin to direct the reader's attention to Ye's awkward social position. Evidently, his semieducated background makes him a misfit among the real "proletariat" in the fishing village. The kind of "spiritual" relationship that he projects onto Red Hair suggests the chasm between his own psyche and those of the people around him. Justifying his distaste for Cai Suzhen, he suggests that his ideal mate would be an "elementary school teacher"—someone who would match his status as an "intellectual" (261). This "class mentality" may be characteristic of the socio-ideological group (the new mainlander settlers) that Ye belongs to and partly explains his alienation and the tragedies that befall him. The fate of maladjusted mainlanders in Taiwan is obviously a sensitive subject, but Wang's treatment largely avoids the political pitfalls by working primarily through formal devices rather than overt narrative references, an issue that will be addressed in more detail below.

Three episodes compose the middle section of the second part: a bout with the flu that inspires Ye's thoughts on bodily existence; another glimpse of the buffoonery in the madhouse of the Dialect Research Bureau; and Ye's dialogues with a Canadian Catholic priest. While recapitulating such existentialist themes as life's absurd fragility, human ignobility, and the rationalist religious quest, these episodes are somewhat lackluster and less dramatically presented than their counterparts in the first part. There, *Ye*'s flamboyant imagination and high-spirited pseudo-intellectual inquiries often bring contradictions, paradoxes, and real insights into an interesting confluence. By contrast, the second part is bogged down in pragmatism and the stark logic of reality. Depicted without the context of their sociological circumstances, the characters in the Dialect Research Bureau appear downright contemptible. Also missing is the surrealistic, carnivalesque gaiety found in the first part, where the bureau was virtually a lunatic circus. The rationalist questions about theology that *Ye* poses to the Canadian priest are stated in such plain terms—without the titillating presence of mystery found in the fortune-telling episode—that they fail to be imaginatively provocative. But this tone may well be justified as *Ye*'s questioning here is only a pretext for borrowing money from the priest.

We may, thus, regard the strain imposed on the content and style of these episodes as corresponding to "the pressure of reality," which becomes increasingly overwhelming as the story progresses. This correspondence between form and content is even more pronounced near the end of the second part, when the narrator is alarmed by a noise from the darkness outside: "Could it be that his pursuers had already found his whereabouts?" (361). Fear begins to seep in, and the rest of the novel alternates between anxiety, despair, and cruelty, climaxing with the murder of a dog in a scene that ominously foreshadows *Ye*'s own death shortly thereafter.

The last section of the novel begins with an account of *Ye*'s failed attempt to land a government job in the Dialect Research Bureau. The position is awarded instead to the relative of a staff member who brings in illegal income for the director. Infuriated by the unfair decision, *Ye* makes a scene that results in the suspension of his meal plan with the bureau. He is at the end of his rope when an unexpected visitor, Dong Yutang, comes to share his lodging that very night. Dong's background is similar to *Ye*'s, but he has become a millionaire with his rice-ball business, and his story is the occasion for a harsh commentary on Taiwan's economic explosion. More concretely than in the first part—in which *Ye* makes offhand remarks about the arbitrary nature of commodity prices and about the "blood" of rural areas being drained to nourish urban growth—the dark side of Taiwan's capitalist transformation is exposed with caustic realism. Dong's dehumanizing, military-style management of his two "grand systems" of manufacture and distribution fits perfectly the classical Marxist account of labor exploitation. The episode also reconfirms *Ye*'s unfitness for the modern city, even as his refuge in Deep Pit Harbor is about to be encroached on by people like Dong, who has come in search of new opportunities to expand his business. *Ye* continues to muse about the roles played by chance and luck in life, even after Dong gives him a no-nonsense lecture on what it takes to get rich in the modern way.

It is at this point that the reader is invited to make a moral judgment about *Ye*'s behavior over the next few days, as he stumbles through failed attempts at robbery and theft before resorting at last to "buying" his groceries and whorehouse visits on credit. However, what appears to be an ideologically charged depiction of justified desperation pulls back from the brink of moral clarity at the last moment, when we see *Ye* join members of the Cao family in the capture and killing of a stray wolfhound.

This is a superlative episode. The crude experience of violence is depicted with breathtaking vividness and a compelling sense of immediacy. The eerie atmosphere quickly becomes genuinely terrifying as the dog's pursuers, equipped with wooden sticks and kitchen knives, their faces and throats wrapped in ragged cloths, appear to be seriously risking their lives against the fierce counterattacks of the trapped animal. Ironically, it is the aged mistress and the family's youngest son (aged seventeen) who deliver the fatal blows. The ferocious animal is said to have "stood up like a man" before launching its desperate attacks, symbolically making "cannibals" of those who later eat the meat at their New Year's Eve feast. Everyone at the banquet table praises the dog's heroic performance and its "guts" (369).

The macabre incident is at once absurd, compellingly real, and intimately touching in a grotesque manner. The absurdity comes partly from the mismatch between the mundane motive for killing (greed for luxurious food) and the excessive cruelty (to the prey) and danger (to the hunters) that it calls up; it also derives from the acquiescent attitude of all the participants, none of whom question the necessity and legitimacy of the drastic action. Yet what seems to undersignify on one plane of reality often oversignifies on another. If the killing is insufficiently justified in a practical sense, it is abundantly meaningful at the symbolic level as a ritual act. The establishing facts that the Cao family speaks a little-known dialect—unintelligible to *Ye*—and worships exotic deities already hint at the killing's ritual nature. Then, in the act itself, the cohesiveness of the community (the family) is reaffirmed through the subjugation and disposal of an intruder, and bloodshed and heroism are required to complete the ceremony. The dog is then eaten at a family meal during an important festival. A better occasion to link sacrificial signification and everyday life practice could hardly be imagined.

That *Ye* is likened to the wolfhound as a prey of fate (symbolized by the vulture that suddenly reappears on the day before *Ye*'s death) seems apparent enough. But what is he sacrificed for? The Red Hair incident, in retrospect, more than anything else marks *Ye* as an intruder whose presence on the local scene invites suspicion. Meanwhile, his reckless behavior at the Dialect Research Bureau cuts him off from the mainlander connection that could have provided some protection. The actual crimes that precipitate *Ye*'s lynching are minor, but, here again, if the drastic measure taken by the local people is unjustified at a commonsense level, it might be understood as ritual, satisfying a latent motive to safeguard and reaffirm the cohesiveness of the community and, ultimately, its members' sense of identity.

CONCLUSION

This is not, however, quite the whole story. Themes contained in literary works produce results by acting on the reader's intellect. But there is another important dimension to the modernist aesthetic project: the conscious manipulation of formal cues to achieve specific psychic effects. The modernists' elaborate imagery, symbolic structures, and rhetorical devices are not there to hide meanings that might otherwise be clearly formulated. They are supposed to act on the semiconscious mechanical process of reading in a mesmerizing way. Wang Wenxing's seemingly idiosyncratic approach to this aesthetic project focuses on the fiction's narrative discourse, in particular the voice.

A common criticism of Wang's novels that paradoxically sheds light on the nature of his artistic project is that they are not written in "good Chinese." Somewhat like faulting an abstract painting for not being realistic enough, the remark nonetheless reveals the point of divergence between the received wisdom about Chinese literary language and the modernist aesthetic project. "Good" Chinese writing is saturated with time-honored conventions from a rich literati tradition, and it is judged according to the writer's ability to master, or to innovate on the basis of, these conventions, which are often very far removed from ordinary speech. In *Backed against the Sea*, however, Wang aims to reproduce speech in a heightened manner. He invents a psychoacoustic system of signifying symbols, applying systematic syntactic variations and different type styles and underscores to the written text. The system is designed to simulate the tone, modulation, and other emotive qualities of the speech of different individuals, whose speech habits are, in turn, determined by complex variables like class, gender, and ethnic and professional background. In fact, the aphorisms and other set phrases that appear in *Ye*'s monologue are often parodies of the remnants of the literati style that show up (too often, Wang would say) in modern Chinese language, a manner of speaking that arguably characterizes the mainlander community of which *Ye* is a member.

Since Wayne Booth, rhetorical devices in narrative fiction have been seen as instrumental in controlling the distance between the reader and fictional characters and, thus, in determining the reader's degree of empathy and identification. The psychoacoustic effects that Wang strives for in *Backed against the Sea* are, apparently, intended to generate an intersubjective communion between the reader and the novel's characters, an important strategy and one meant to convey the novel's central theme. Poverty, of course, is the immediate narrative cue. *Ye* is turned off in the second part by Cai Suzhen's "air of poverty" (246) and generally reacts with callous indifference to other characters whose lives are similarly afflicted. The dubious character of the narrator, most unflatteringly portrayed in the second part, puts the reader squarely to the test: should *Ye*'s abject behavior, both before and after his own circumstances become truly desperate, be summarily dismissed as moral depravity?

The moral complexity of *Ye*'s case is a classic statement of rationalist humanism, which was the core spirit of the earlier, liberally inclined modernist movement. Wang pits rationalist complexity against the romanticized visions of human relations that dominated public discourse on morality in Taiwan's martial law period—simplifications that served the interests of both the authoritarian regime and the commercial market. This kind of trenchant ideological criticism is largely absent in the market-friendly mainstream literature of the baby-boom generation. There is, moreover, a certain continuity between Wang's agenda and the postmodernist project.

The postmodernists prefer more activist approaches, but their various cultural critiques—radical feminism, queer discourse, etc.—target the same hegemonic moral conservatism with which Wang takes issue. He is arguably the more sophisticated intellectual critic, able to contemplate such hot topics as mainlander-Taiwanese conflict and identity-group politics with greater philosophical depth than the "postmodern" interventionalists, who are usually more concerned with immediate political aims.

The powerful social commentaries found in the two parts of *Backed against the Sea* make an eloquent case that modernism in Taiwan is something much more than a mere intellectual import. In the hands of writers like Wang Wenxing, it cannot be reduced to an emblem of cultural or capitalist imperialism; by and large, Taiwan's modernists are serious intellectuals who seek to identify and critique, through the lens of imported ideologies, deep-seated "lacks" and "excesses" in contemporary Taiwanese society. In fact, the comparatively narrow fixations of the proliferating postmodernist tribes seem more vulnerable to the pejorative connotations of the *import* label. Meanwhile, what finally distinguishes Wang Wenxing both as a writer and as a modernist is his intellectual elitism. Wang is presumptuous enough to go on experimenting with form in the interest of a continuing effort to modify his readers' outlook on morality, knowing full well that many of them will not take up the challenge.

NOTES

This chapter includes a revised version of my "Modernist Literature in Taiwan Revisited—with an Analysis of Wang Wenxing's *Backed against the Sea, Part II*," *Tamkang Review* 24.2 (1998): 1–19. The newly added part in the section "Wang Wenxing's *Backed against the Sea, Part I*" is selected from the second half of chapter 4 of my *Modernism and the Nativist Resistance: Contemporary Chinese Fiction from Taiwan* (Durham: Duke University Press, 1993).

Unless otherwise indicated, all translations from non-English-language sources are my own.

1   Marilyn Ivy, "Critical Texts, Mass Artifacts: The Consumption of Knowledge in Postmodern Japan," in *Postmodernism and Japan* (Durham: Duke University Press, 1989), 29. For Ivy's discussion of Asada Akira's *Kozo to chikara: Kogoron o koete* [Structure and power: Beyond semiotics] (Tokyo: Keisoshobo, 1983), see 26–33. Ivy elaborates: "The new Japanese discourse on knowledge wants to go beyond the use value, the functional role of knowledge, in order to liberate desire (in relation to knowledge) as play and constitute a new notion of knowl-

edge both beyond use value and knowledge for knowledge's sake. . . . This 'going beyond' use value is precisely 'exchange value,' which is valorized in the commodity form as the object (and mirror) of desire" (32).

2 Sung-sheng Yvonne Chang, *Modernism and the Nativist Resistance: Contemporary Chinese Fiction from Taiwan* (Durham: Duke University Press, 1993).

3 See Daniel Lerner, *The Passing of Traditional Society: Modernizing the Middle East* (New York: Free Press, 1958).

4 Evidence abounds in works by such well-known writers as Bai Xianyong, Chen Yingzhen, Wang Wenxing, and Li Ang.

5 This theme features prominently in such representative modernist works as Wang Zhenhe's "Jiazhuang yi niuche" [An oxcart for dowry], Wang Wenxing's *Beihai de ren* [Backed against the sea], and Bai's *Niezi*.

6 The best examples are Li Ang and Zhang Dachun.

7 See Li Yongping, *Haidong qing* (Taipei: Lianhe wenxue, 1992). The sequel has a different title, *Zhu Ling manyou xianjing* [Zhu Ling in wonderland] (Taipei: Lianhe wenxue, 1998). Carlos Rojas ("Li Yongping and Spectral Cartography," chapter 14 in this volume) discusses both *Haidong qing* and *Zhu Ling manyou xianjing*.

8 Wang Wenxing, *Beihai de ren*, vol. 1 [Backed against the sea, vol. I] (Taipei: Hongfan shudian, 1981), and *Beihai de ren*, vol. 2 [Backed against the sea, vol. II] (Taipei: Hongfan shudian, 1999). I would like to specially thank Mr. Wang Wenxing for allowing me to read the manuscript before the book appeared in print.

9 Leo Ou-fan Lee, "Beyond Realism: Thoughts on Modernist Experiments in Contemporary Chinese Writing," in Howard Goldblatt, ed., *Worlds Apart: Recent Chinese Writing and Its Audiences* (Armonk: M. E. Sharpe, 1990), 75–76.

10 Mikhail Bakhtin, "Discourse in the Novel," in Michael Holquist, ed., *The Dialogic Imagination* (Austin: University of Texas Press, 1981), 341.

11 Jameson has argued against Lukács's understanding of modernism as "ideological distraction," arguing: "The modernist project is more adequately understood as the intent, following Norman Holland's convenient expression, to 'manage' historical and social, deeply political impulses, that is to say, to defuse them, to prepare substitute gratifications for them, and the like. But we must add that sum impulses cannot be managed until they are aroused; this is the delicate part of the modernist project, the place at which it must be realistic in order in another moment to recontain that realism which it has awakened." Fredric Jameson, *The Political Unconscious: Narrative as a Socially Symbolic Act* (Ithaca: Cornell University Press, 1981), 266.

12 For a detailed discussion of several of them, see my *Modernism and the Nativist Resistance: Contemporary Chinese Fiction from Taiwan* (Durham: Duke University Press, 1993), 133–44.

13 Wang Wenxing, "Shouji xuchao" [Notes, continued], *Lianhe wenxue* 13 (November 1985): 98–107.

HISTORY, TRUTH, AND TEXTUAL ARTIFICE

IT MAY BE TRUE that all nations are grounded, as Ernest Renan famously observed, on a process of systematic forgetting of their own pasts, just as the discipline of historiography itself has frequently been complicit with strategies of political legitimization. Taiwan's Nationalist government, however, has, nevertheless, gone to unusual lengths in its efforts to control and whitewash its own history. The most dramatic instance of this sort of historical censorship was the Nationalists' suppression of all public discussions of the infamous February Twenty-eighth Incident of 1947, in which a rather unremarkable confrontation between a handful of Nationalist police and an illegal cigarette peddler led to a violent conflict between the police and concerned bystanders, leaving one bystander dead. Over the next couple of weeks, this initial confrontation quickly escalated into a series of mass protests throughout the island, briefly allowing the Taiwanese to regain political control from the Nationalists. The Nationalists, however, responded with a military crackdown that ultimately resulted in the execution of thousands of Taiwan's intellectual and political elite. The subsequent imposition of martial law on the island effectively suppressed not only any subsequent challenges to Nationalist rule but also all formal discussions of topics that might elicit criticism of the Nationalist government. It was not until the lifting of martial law in the late 1980s that oppositional moments such as the February Twenty-eighth Incident, which had been kept alive at the level of popular memory for the previous four decades, were finally permitted to be discussed openly.

While the essays in parts 1 and 2 of this volume were all concerned with issues of literary history, the four essays in part 3 are concerned, instead, with literary attitudes toward history. David Der-wei Wang begins by looking at Jiang Gui's anti-Communist novel *The Whirlwind* (1957), also known as *A Tale of Modern Monsters*. In his own insistently historical reading of the novel (in which he brings it into dialogue with related works from the Ming and Qing dynasties), Wang argues that, while Jiang is ostensibly motivated by the principle that we can learn from the past, his novel in fact inadvertently illustrates the precise opposite—that the act of retelling the past serves not so much to exorcise the monster of history as to resurrect and perpetuate it. In the following essay, Yomi Braester considers similar questions of history and amnesia in his reading of two 1980s novellas by Liu Daren and Chen Yingzhen, suggesting that they both use the genre of the mystery novel to critique the historical aporia of the martial law period, foregrounding the vast gulf between personal and collective memory. Gang Gary Xu then turns to the female author Su Weizhen and, in particular, her use of themes of performance in her novels *Island of Silence* (1994) and *Leaving Tongfang* (1996). Xu argues that Su remobilizes the epistemological ambiguity inherent in theatrical performance into an affirmation of embodied identity. Finally, Kim-chu Ng considers Su Weizhen's contemporary Zhang Dachun, focusing on Zhang's insistent thematization of mendacity in his works. Sharply critical of what he identifies as the cavalier and, ultimately, hermetic quality of Zhang's fiction, Ng argues that Zhang's fascination with the theme of lying is symptomatic of his reluctance to engage in a meaningful way with broader social issues in his literature. Somewhat paradoxically, however, Ng concludes that it is precisely in this refusal to "represent the Taiwanese experience" that Zhang's fiction helps illuminate the impact of commodity aesthetics on the contemporary urban Taiwanese experience.

8

The Monster That Is History: Jiang Gui's *A Tale of Modern Monsters*

David Der-wei Wang

The dream of reason produces monsters.
                            Francisco Goya

In Taiwan in the fall of 1957, the émigré mainland Chinese writer Jiang Gui [Wang Yijian] (1908–80) published a novel titled *Jin taowu zhuan* [A tale of modern monsters]. This novel chronicles Communist activities in a small town in Shandong Province from the 1920s through the 1940s, and it culminates with a macabre riot costing hundreds of lives. At the center of the novel is a pair of amateur revolutionaries, Fang Xiangqian, a Confucian literatus–turned–Marxist ideologue, and his nephew, Fang Peilan, a local militia chieftain with a dubious past as a highway bandit. Via their yearning for reform, their revolutionary action, and their downfall amid internecine Party struggles, Jiang Gui describes how the two Fangs' utopian project ends up producing a monstrous machine that engulfs its makers.

With such a plot, *A Tale of Modern Monsters* can be read as an example of anti-Communist fiction, the major literary genre in Taiwan in the 1950s. This genre comprises works that lash out at Communist evils while projecting an imminent Nationalist restoration.[1] A dedicated Nationalist Party member, Jiang Gui made it clear that he wrote *A Tale of Modern Monsters* to bear witness to Communist atrocity,[2] and he would have had no qualms seeing it serve the purposes of propaganda. However, perhaps for the reasons to be discussed shortly, the novel never drew much official attention. First titled *Xuanfeng* [The whirlwind], it was completed in January 1952, but over the next six years it was rejected by at least ten publishers. This seems odd at a time when the government tried every method—from prize contests to publicity stunts—to solicit anti-Communist works and to sponsor their publication.³ In 1957, Jiang retitled the novel *A Tale of Modern Monsters* and printed five hundred copies at his own expense. As he later reported, beyond the roughly two hundred copies given away to friends and scholars, the book made little impression on the market.⁴

Critics, nevertheless, responded warmly. Both Jiang Mengling and Hu Shi, two of the literary giants at the time, welcomed *A Tale of Modern Monsters* as a powerful testimony to the horror of the Chinese Communist revolution.⁵ Thanks to the sponsorship of the U.S. Information Service, the novel was formally published by a commercial press in 1959, with its title changed back to *The Whirlwind*. When C. T. Hsia discussed *The Whirlwind* in the revised edition of his *A History of Modern Chinese Fiction* in 1971, he was enlisting the novel in the canon of modern Chinese fiction. Hsia praised *The Whirlwind* as a work best encapsulating the modern Chinese literary tradition from the late Qing to the post–May Fourth era. By this he meant that Jiang Gui captured both the "satirical" and the "humanitarian" strains of modern Chinese fiction since the turn of the century yet never fell prey to either sentimentalism or the urge to propagandize, as did most of his contemporaries.⁶

Hsia's and other critics' readings, perceptive as they are, have focused on the linkage between the novel and ongoing national politics. But in our time, when the debate between pro- and anti-Communist literature is just another costly quarrel from the past century, such comments have limitations. The lasting power of *The Whirlwind* lies elsewhere: in the multiple developments of Chinese history and their fictional representations and in Jiang Gui's ability to *configure* history. If the novel is still compelling, it is not so much because Jiang tells a truthful anti-Communist story as because he manages to address issues that still concern us, such as: How did political calamity and personal trauma during the "great divide" of 1949 affect ways of imagining and inscribing history? How can we make sense of a modernity that is so full of irrationalities and contradictions as to preclude any coherent, rational "emplotment"? How do we negotiate the relations between historiography, ideology, and the literary representation of scars? And, above all, what drove authors to seek an ethical and intellectual heritage in a century that purported to break with tradition and to reach the end of history?

I suggest a first answer to these questions about *The Whirlwind* by re-invoking the title of its second incarnation, *Jin taowu zhuan*, or *A Tale of Modern Monsters*. Behind it lies Jiang Gui's indebtedness to a premodern Chinese fictional trope, one crucial to an understanding of his vision of modern Chinese history. He adopted *Jin taowu zhuan* as the title because the novel was inspired by a late Ming novel, *Taowu xianping* [An idle commentary on monsters] (1629). Allegedly by Li Qing (1602–83), this work deals with the rise and fall of Wei Zhongxian (1568–1627), the vicious eunuch of the Tianqi reign of the Ming (1621–27), and Madame Ke (d. 1627), the emperor's wet nurse, who together almost brought down the dynasty. Jiang Gui sees *A Tale of Modern Monsters* as taking up the moral intent of the late Ming novel: both aim at "recounting evils so as to admonish."⁷

But why *taowu*? In his preface, Jiang offers the following explanation:

> Legends have it that Zhuanxu had a wayward son named Taowu. *Taowu* also refers to broken wood, which, in my judgment, is as despicable as the *shu* [useless wood] in the *Zhuangzi*. Both references thus partake of the allegorical meaning. By association, *taowu* also indicates a monster. Moreover, the historiography of the ancient Chu kingdom is called *taowu*, meaning to "recount evils so as to admonish." In fiction, there is a work entitled *Taowu xianping*, which tells of the evildoings of Wei Zhongxian and Madame Ke, in service of the goal of moral improvement.⁸

With the clues in this passage as points of departure, one can trace *taowu*'s etymological origins, among which the following are most suggestive. The taowu appears in the *Shenyi jing* [Classic of the supernatural and the strange] as a monster of ancient times: "[The monster taowu] looks like a tiger, with hair two feet long. It has a human's face, a tiger's feet, a pig's teeth, and a tail as long as eighteen feet. It likes to fight and will never withdraw."⁹ In the *Shiji*, Sima Qian writes: "Prince Zhuanxu has a wayward son who turns his back on any moral teachings and is incorrigible. This son is called *taowu* by the world."¹⁰ Identified as Zhuanxu's son Guen, the taowu is said to be among the four major evils of ancient times, which were tamed and exiled by Prince Shun to withstand *chimei*, the ghostly mountain spirits, on the frontiers. Similar references can also be found in the classics such as the *Zuozhuan*, *Zhouli*, and *Shangshu*.¹¹

Yet equally important is the fact that *Taowu* is identified with history as a narrative account of bygone events that "records the evil deeds of the monstrous and the invincible."¹² This usage can best be illustrated in the *Mencius*:

The *Sheng* of the Chin [Jin], the *T'ao U* (*Taowu*) of Ch'u (Chu), and the *Spring and Autumn Annals* of Lu are the same kind of work. The events recorded concern Duke Huan of Ch'i (Qi) and Duke Wen of Chin (Jin), and the style is that of official historian.[13]

Moreover, the association of the taowu with history may have something to do with the divinatory power with which the monster is endowed. Anthropologists have pointed out that, in the ancient Chu region, the taowu was taken as a creature of auspicious nature because it had the capacity to foresee the future. *Xiangdong jiwen* [Accounts of the eastern Hunan region] recounts: "The taowu is an animal that can foresee the future, so it can always run away before the hunters arrive. Since history reveals both past and future, it is referred to as *taowu*." Because of its ferocious nature and mysterious visionary ability, the taowu became one of the guardian creatures of the imperial tombs.[14]

With these references in mind, we can take a look at Jiang Gui's apologia for his novel, written in a manner reminiscent of the opening chapter of Cao Xueqin's *Hongloumeng* [The dream of the red chamber]: "The author of *A Tale of Modern Monsters* is in his forties. Recollecting the way he led the first half of his life, he cannot express enough remorse over his degeneration. He wrote the novel with the honest and sincere purpose inherent in all good literature; he harbors no wish to publicize sordid deeds. The novel is based on the goal of 'recounting evils so as to admonish.'"[15] What is striking is the fact that Jiang Gui has retrieved the rhetorical *and* the ethical roots of classical historiography. *Taowu* denotes a monster from ancient times known for its bizarre appearance and ferocious nature, like a tiger with a human face (or a human with a tiger body), loving to fight, and reluctant to stop. Even when bracketed as familial black sheep or social outlaw, the taowu is humanized, and vice versa: specimens of humanity have been enlisted in the armies of bestiality. The image of the taowu is a liminal zone where the inhuman and the human confessedly mingle, a region that is legally and morally anomalous. Evil monster and evil human are seen as intersecting in looks and deeds, a view that blurs the cultural and natural boundaries that humanity would draw around itself.

More intriguingly, history, or taowu, as Jiang Gui describes it, is an inscription of the acts and consequences of evildoers; it is meant to recount the past in such a way as to caution subsequent generations against immorality and aberration. Chinese historiography, to be sure, comprises a full range of views on how history makes sense. The particular view that Jiang holds contemplates humanity as an ambiguous existence, forever subject to the test of evil; as such, it calls for either the inner awakening to or the external enforcement of the human moral constitution so as to avoid deviations. Extrapolating Jiang's logic, one can argue that, although the professed goal of history is revealing virtue in order to exclude evil, the act of historical writing is made possible ironically by the continued accumulation—inclusion—of that which is immoral and, therefore, excludable. This historiographic vision generates its own antithesis: insofar as its moral telos holds true and valid in the long run, history, as a narrated account of bygone events, performs its function negatively, as an agency revealing only vice, waste, and anomaly. In other words, history admonishes the good only by adducing elements that prolong, or even belie, the search for the good.

Therefore, when fiction is written under the name of *taowu*, it bespeaks the complicity of civilization in its own discontents. This is a pessimistic brand of historiography, and, in the case of Jiang Gui, it threatens to turn into a sinister irony as it emplots the human past. As Jiang and his predecessors would have it, each generation witnesses, withstands, and helps produce the monster of its own times. With the anomalous and polymorphous mediation of the taowu—as monster, as broken timber, as outlaw, or as records of evil—we find ourselves ever coping with the inhuman of the past in the hope of eradicating it in the future. Yet at any fold of time we may come to realize that the inhuman is all too human. A monster looms over the human struggle for self-betterment. *Because of* its cruelty and ambiguity, the taowu intensifies our motivation to remember the past.

With Jiang Gui's contemplation of history as my point of reference, I trace out in the following a preliminary fictional genealogy of the taowu from the late Ming to the modern period. I discuss how Li Qing's *Idle Commentary on Monsters* renews the fictional imaginary of history versus evil in late imperial China and inspires Jiang Gui's *Tale of Modern Monsters*, in theme as well as discursive format. In the historical space between these two works, I examine a little-known late Qing/early republican novel, *Taowu cuibian* [A compendium of monsters] (1916) by Qian Xibao. With its ambiguous laughter at clowns who turn the late Qing empire upside down and its biting sarcasm on social absurdities, *A Compendium of Monsters* no doubt belongs to the tradition of late Qing exposés, in which Jiang Gui was well versed, but evidence regarding his knowledge of it is yet to be found. By linking these three works together, my intent is not to establish verifiable relations of influence and reception but, rather, to look into how each responds to its own crisis by reawakening the ancient monster from its historical slumbers. These works all present themselves as depicting the violence and grotesquerie in and of history, but they do not necessarily establish a coherent dialogue among them. They call attention to the menacing changeability of history, in which the form of monstrosity cannot be predicted, only its persistence.

A TALE OF MODERN MONSTERS

A Tale of Modern Monsters opens with Fang Xiangqian's organizing an underground Communist cell in the city T (Tsi-nan [Jinan], the capital of Shandong). Despite his gentry background and Confucian training, Fang finds Marxist proletarian revolution the most effective remedy for China's malaise. While Fang Xiangqian's firm belief in communism leads him to support the revolution, his nephew Peilan joins the cell simply because of a chivalric bent and discontent with the family status quo.

Revolving around the two Fangs' rise to power is a cluster of subplots that include the corruption and decline of four old houses of the Fang family; the continued confrontation and collaboration among bandits, underground society, warlord forces, Nationalist armies, and Japanese aggressors; the tragicomedy of a group of "new youth" in search of revolution and romance; and the sudden prosperity of two prostitutes, Pang Yuemei and her daughter Pang Jinlian, thanks to the political chaos. These plots constitute the mosaic of an early republican Chinese community in drastic transformation.[16]

Even with such a sketchy summary, Jiang Gui's ambition to expose the complexities of traditional Chinese systems is clear. Jiang would have agreed with Lu Xun's charge that, behind Chinese society's facade of propriety and civility, "cannibalism" prevailed. This cannibalism has long infiltrated the most minute aspects of Chinese life, in such a way that its victims can end up becoming the accomplices of their victimizers. For instance, in the most prominent household of the Fang clan, the matriarch Mistress Fang turns out to be a sadist, taking nightly pleasure in abusing her late husband's concubine, while her son, Ranwu, is an indiscriminate lecher.[17] Ranwu's wife is known for her feminine virtues. Her way of edifying her husband is, nevertheless, to condone and then help plan the rape of a village girl, thereby making her a proper concubine.

Not unlike Lu Xun's Madman, Fang Xiangqian abhors the fate of the young descendants of these families because they have been brought up to become either cannibals or dishes to be served to cannibals. To "save the children," Fang concludes, the most effective way is to guide them toward the light of communism. He sends his daughter and his cousin, among other youngsters, to study in the Soviet Union.

But Jiang Gui parts with Lu Xun by describing an even darker world of violence and irrationality. Writing on the eve of the revolution, Lu could still create a figure such as the Madman, who recognized traditional institutions as cannibalism. However ambiguous, the Madman's critique contains a moral vision, one that would be adopted by the new society. Writing after the revolution, Jiang was convinced that it had compounded rather than done away with extant social and personal insanity. In the name of overthrowing the old cannibalism, a higher cannibalism had been established, uplifted by technology to a new level of perpetrated violence.

As the novel develops, Fang Xiangqian's plan is thwarted by the failure of the 1927 Communist Revolution, but the Japanese invasion of China in 1937 creates a new opportunity. While Fang Xiangqian and Fang Peilan form an anti-aggression "Whirlwind Column" from their rural bands combined with the local militia, they carry on a secret collaboration with the Japanese military that enables them to annihilate a group of guerrillas loyal to the Nationalist regime. They even establish their own county government in rivalry with the puppet one and manage to win the endorsement of both Japanese and Nationalist forces.

It is in this context that Jiang observes the most chilling interplay between the old and the new forms of cannibalism. After the new local government is established, all the men and women of the four Fang families are driven off their properties, and most die in the course of the persecution that follows. At the end of the novel, the prostitute Pang Yuemei is honored as the "Mother of the Revolution" and her daughter Pang Jinlian is appointed "Director of the Revolutionary Women's Committee." Ranwu's wife is made a maid to the Pangs and a prostitute of the cheapest class.

While he never conceals his tendentious posture, Jiang is not motivated merely by partisanship in his critique of communism, for he spares no effort in mocking the rightist figures. Above all, he harbors little confidence in Chinese humanity in general; he sees fanatics, perverts, opportunists, hypocrites, and cowards in both rightist and leftist parties, both high and low classes, and both younger and older generations.

I therefore argue that Jiang derives his power not from his attack on the Chinese Communist revolution as such but from his apprehension at seeing any system, radical or conservative, malfunction in historical practice. In the posture of a social pathologist, he looks into the morbidities in Chinese society, of which the Communist revolution is only the most recent syndrome. Central to his story is inevitable decadence despite the revolution's promise of enlightenment and progress. In contrast with the linear, cause-and-effect description that most of his peers provide of the rise of Chinese communism, Jiang offers a scenario in which political, moral, libidinous, and other forces interact and generate a monstrosity that is beyond logical figuration. He may begin his novels with a clear historical/ideological agenda, but his narrative obeys a "genealogy" of deviations, in the best Foucauldian sense.[18]

I will have more to say in the next two sections about Jiang's historiographic vision, in association with the late Ming and late Qing taowu tales. Most important here is the question that haunts *A Tale of Modern Monsters*: If a search for rationality constitutes a major part of China's modernity project, how does one come to terms with the plague of irrationalities that spread across China in the first half of the modern century? This leads us to rethink the way Jiang creates the novel's central figure, Fang Xiangqian. An eager student of the scientific formulation of communism, Fang believes that such searches are necessitated by history and concludes that the revolution that he is launching is the one "that will thoroughly destroy the old society . . . and build a new society from the beginning."[19] Meanwhile, he argues that, before the "final" revolution comes, society is destined to sink to the lowest depths and that a revolutionary is entitled to help precipitate this fall so as to hasten the rejuvenation.

This is a strange combination of the Machiavellian reasoning of "the end justifies the means" and an apocalyptic faith in humanity's ability to leap from total fall to total salvation. But Fang Xiangqian is outwitted by the contingencies of history; the revolution simply does not unfold in accordance with his formula. Despite his wish to prove the scientific truth of Communist historicism, he stumbles once theory is put into practice. He can never summon his followers to carry out his orders. Little surprise, then, that, when the local insurrection turns into chaos, he should find himself among the first group of counterrevolutionaries to be liquidated.

Here sounds Jiang's gravest note about the paradox of rationality and violence in modern Chinese revolution. Insofar as he is an enlightened intellectual ostracized by a callous society, Fang Xiangqian is a revolutionary in the vein of Lu Xun's heroic Madman. Fang may even have been among the thousands of readers once enchanted by the Madman's defiant stature and humanitarian concern. Whereas the Madman is incarcerated and can only utter the futile cry, "Save the children," Fang Xiangqian and his ilk are determined to realize the lonely hero's dream. His adventure nevertheless exemplifies that, when Lu's literary cry is taken literally, the dialectic about the Madman's sanity/insanity may lose its enigmatic power and backfire. Charged with a moral imperative and temporal urgency, Fang's commitment to communism brings to light the hidden curse of Lu's story. He and his followers replace the Madman's paranoia with political fanaticism and transform the lonely hero's anarchist impulse into a total(itarian) call to arms; thus, they become the most dangerous readers of Lu Xun.

We can now better interpret the ambiguous characterization of Fang Xianqian. Jiang never makes Fang an archvillain in accordance with anti-Communist formulas; instead, he portrays him as a mixture of shortsighted visionary and ineffective activist. Through such a peculiar characterization, Jiang examines the dilemmas and dangers hidden in revolutionary utopianism. Fang incites rebellious impulses among his followers yet fails to meld them into any coherent body. His eclectic approach collapses hitherto noninteractive elements into a grotesque conglomeration. The taowu, it will be recalled, is an anomaly.

With Fang Xiangqian as a modern embodiment of the taowu, Jiang suggests a different kind of evil and violence often overlooked by historians and literati. Fang is not a competent revolutionary, but he may cause society more harm precisely through his imperfect villainy (or heroism). Above all, modern (Communist) revolution was made possible not by selected leaders but by hundreds and thousands of supporters like Fang despite their individual limitations. With their contradictory attributes of dedication and fanaticism, vision and naïveté, and altruism and cannibalism, they constitute the enormous body of the modern monster.

In his inquiry into the terms of revolution, Jiang makes sexual politics the last site of ideological contestation. *A Tale of Modern Monsters* is impressive for its seemingly endless account of sexual deviations. Fang Xiangqian's grandfather, an honorable retired official and a landlord, is known for his bizarre lust for nuns. His gallant public image aside, Fang Peilan is a man frustrated by an arranged marriage. He can find solace only among local prostitutes, the older and uglier the better. Fang Ranwu's mother, Mistress Fang, has an addiction to opium as well as to her young servant, who in his own turn is involved with a lowly prostitute known for her large, unbound feet.

But Jiang is equally cynical about the new generation's sexual encounters. The novel opens with the decapitation of the Communist leader Shi Shenzhi, punishment for his affair with a local opera singer. Another revolutionary, Dong Yinming, is jailed for accidental patricide allegedly resulting from the incestuous affair between his father and his wife. To assert egalitarianism, the daughter of a veteran Nationalist party member, a four-time divorcée, volunteers herself to men of the lower depths; despite difference in class and upbringing, Fang Xiangqian's niece is persuaded to marry a battalion commander officer. But none of these characters can surpass Fang Ranwu, whose insatiable lust for women epitomizes the total abandon in the world of Fangzhen.

C. T. Hsia comments that, of Jiang's characters, "the sensualists, like the revolutionaries, are impatient with the human condition, and demand unlimited scope for their appetites."[20] While this observation provides an important clue to Jiang's moral scheme of sexuality, it may have limited it to a rather conventional scope. It is all too common that leftist and rightist literature both demonize their antagonists by first smearing them in their private lives, particularly in the sexual department. To say that Jiang equates revolutionaries with sex maniacs or vice versa would only reconfirm his image as a conservative ideologue. What I want to argue is that, his conservative ideology notwithstanding, Jiang adopts a radical way to articulate his agenda. To demonstrate the negative impact of revolution on Chinese mores, he portrays not a selected group but almost all his characters as overwhelmed by the power of desire.

A Tale of Modern Monsters can be taken as a showcase of the Marxian/Freudian interplay between the political unconscious and libidinous desire. From the perspective of Bakhtinian carnival, Jiang's parading of sexual absurdities may also be suggestive of the "bodily principle" that overthrows decorum in a moment of social upheaval.[21] We can quickly point out his conservative bearings, however: Jiang does not indicate enough confidence in the sublation of libido to a higher state of ideological and behavioral momentum, nor is he optimistic enough to embrace the total emancipation of the "carnivalesque" body. But behind Jiang's reservation about the revolutionary élan vital lies an unlikely fixation: the way in which he details sexual transgressions betrays as much abhorrence of as fascination with the human capacity to fall. This fixation propels Jiang to explore the boundary of eros and polis at its most treacherous points.

If one agrees with Bataille (and Freud) that "violence is what the world of work excludes with its taboos,"[22] then the modern project of revolution, as Jiang understands it, makes a disturbing attempt to reconcile the opposing poles of this binary. Revolution works through violence and violation. It provides the venue where the banishment of violence through taboo, its opposition to reason, can be subverted. In other words, violence is not opposed to reason; rather, it is the completion of revolutionary logic.

Thus, under Jiang's treatment, corporeal eroticism is no longer a salacious interlude but, rather, a violent and deleterious sacrificial theater performance. Placed at the border of discipline and desire, sexuality is the sign at once of incommensurable difference between individuals and of that difference's utter dissolubility through revolutionary appropriation. It can catalyze a mode of violation bordering on death, on murder.

As the novel unfolds, more and more characters are involved in the macabre game of sensuality as they are either aroused or disturbed by the call for revolution. Unsurprisingly, Jiang's version of "revolution and love" culminates in his portraits of the prostitutes Pang Yuemei and Pang Jinlian. Just as the two Fangs are committed to ideological force, so the Pangs exert sexual power. They contribute their bodies to the reactionaries and revolutionaries, Japanese invaders and local bandits, merchants, scholars, and gentry. In between they also run a successful opium-trafficking network. The Pangs prosper even more after the leftists take over Fangzhen. By comparing politics to prostitution, Jiang follows an old convention. But he is able to push the analogy to the extreme, thereby laying bare the destructive power of sexuality over politics, and vice versa.

The last part of *A Tale of Modern Monsters* describes scenes of collective violence and ecstasy. People in Fangzhen are organized by the new Communist regime to liquidate old, feudal forces. There arises an eerie atmosphere of carnival that at any moment can turn into the chaos of mob hysteria. The orgiastic ecstasy of revolution will not be completed without the ritual of sacrifice, and women such as Fang Ranwu's wife are among the first group of victims. In describing this ecstasy arising from revolution and the collective inflicting of pain and suffering on the chosen scapegoats, Jiang reveals the ultimate horror behind the erotics of dissolution/revolution.

AN IDLE COMMENTARY ON MONSTERS

On the publication of *A Tale of Modern Monsters* in 1957, critics were quick to point out Jiang's indebtedness to classical Chinese fiction.[23] Jiang is aware of this; he makes clear in an interview that, "before the age of twenty," he had been "interested in only three books: *The Dream of the Red Chamber; The Water Margin;* and *The Scholars.*"[24] While these three classics influenced Jiang in various ways, they do not constitute a coherent formal and thematic matrix for *A Tale of Modern Monsters.* I suggest that the missing piece lies in an obscure late Ming novel, *An Idle Commentary on Monsters.* The two "monster" novels appear at first glance to be different in terms of a wide range of aspects, but the fact that they both refer to the same archaic image of the taowu suggests that both explore the genealogy of evil within China's history.

Published in 1629, *An Idle Commentary on Monsters* was one of a series of fictional indictments of the eunuch Wei Zhongxian after his suicide in 1627. Not until recent years was its author identified as Li Qing.[25] Wei Zhongxian, the most notorious of the eunuchs of the late Ming, rose to power in the Tianqi reign thanks to his connection with the emperor's wet nurse, Madame Ke. Together, Wei and Ke manipulated the emperor, accelerating the decline of a dynasty already mired in factional struggles, barbarian invasions, local riots, bureaucratic corruption, and eunuch corruption. Wei and Ke lost their power immediately after the Tianqi emperor's death and were quickly eradicated by his successor, Emperor Chongzhen. But the dynasty had been damaged beyond repair. The Ming came to an end in less than two decades.[26]

In the wake of Wei Zhongxian's death, there appeared a series of fictional accounts exposing his evildoings and commemorating the virtuous suffering under his tyranny. *An Idle Commentary on Monsters* should be regarded as the most ambitious. The first twenty chapters of the novel concentrate on Wei Zhongxian's early life. We are told that he is the illegitimate son of a female acrobat and a female impersonator. In his search for his father, he undergoes a series of adventures—as a traveling merchant, a playboy, a eunuch's assistant, and a gambler—until he is set up by a group of hooligans and robbed and thrown into a river. When he regains consciousness on shore, he is in excruciating pain, hungry dogs having bitten off his genitalia.

The adventures of Wei Zhongxian at different social strata are reminiscent of the genre of *faji biantai*, or sagas about a nobody who becomes a hero.[27] Wei's story, however, must be read as one of the few premodern full-length narratives that highlight an antihero's life; his ascendance to power, even if bracketed by a predestined fall, serves as a powerful counterexample to the conventions of the heroic saga.[28] Compare *An Idle Commentary on Monsters* with a novel of the same time such as Yuan Yuling's *Suishi yiwen* [Forgotten tales of the Sui] (1633), which deals with Qin Shubao's heroic deeds in the founding days of the Tang, and Li Qing's subversive intention is clear.[29] Moreover, episodes concerning Wei's romantic liaisons and domestic life reflect influences of contemporary *renqing xiaoshuo*, or novels of manners, as best illustrated by the *Jinpingmei* [The golden lotus].[30] Li displays an almost naturalistic interest in describing Wei's low inclinations and the environment conducive to his degradation.

Li treats Wei's castration as the moment at which his worldly success finally begins. What follows is an account of how Wei manages to enter the palace; encounters Ke Yinyue, his old sweetheart, who happens to have become the emperor's wet nurse; and joins with her to create a clique in opposition to righteous officials. Odd as it may appear, a domestic ambience lingers even when court politics reaches its most macabre moments. Amid endless killings and schemes, Wei and Ke show consistent concern for their relatives' and allies' welfare, as if they were the benign patriarchs of a Confucian family. Meanwhile, however disfigured or deprived, Wei and Ke carry on their mutual emotional attachment, punctuated by occasional misunderstandings and squabbles, like any ordinary couple.

In this novel that deplores a dynastic decline due to devilish courtiers, it may be surprising that Wei Zhongxian and Ke Yinyue's private life should command so much attention and that such characters *do not* appear as total human demons. This brings one to rethink the tension between the novel's avowed goal of indicting the greatest villains of the time and its curiosity about the practice of daily life, even the villains.' By inserting mundane, private details into its narrative, *An Idle Commentary on Monsters* domesticates, so to speak, the epic magnanimity required of a novel with such a thematic scope.

One might conjecture that Li Qing is incapable of imagining villainy at a fuller scale. I would disagree. As mentioned above, the burgeoning interest in secular reality among authors and readers of late Ming popular fiction must have encouraged Li to consider historical figures' backgrounds, temperaments, motives, and behavior in a more comprehensive and material light.[31] He thus infiltrates the "high-mimetic" world of the traditional historical novel such as, say, *Sanguozhi yanyi* [The romance of three kingdoms] with traits drawn from the "low-mimetic" terrain.[32] History may still be presided over by figures who exert a massive impact on public lives, but these figures are shown as beings no less occupied by the trivialities that concern ordinary men and women.

More challenging is the fact that such an approach to history and reality gives rise to a different fictional concept of evil. The early life of Wei Zhongxin impresses us with his mediocrity, in both talent and judgment. Despite his inclination to pursue things low and unruly, more often than not he stumbles. His luck turns after he enters the palace, and, by the time of the Tianqi emperor's enthronement, he has become the most powerful person at court. However, Wei does not come across as a larger-than-life villain; rather, he behaves more like an entrepreneur eager to enjoy and preserve newly won power and fortune. As his ambition amplifies out of proportion to his new capacity, his flaws resurface. His lack of foresight leads him from one unexpected danger to another; his vanity demands compliments of the most superficial kind. Above all, his insatiable desire for power and blood suggests a twisted psyche corresponding to a deformed physique.

The way in which Li Qing portrays Wei Zhongxian's villainy, or lack of sufficient villainy, should not be taken lightly. Precisely because the gap between Wei's mediocre character and the great disaster he causes is so obvious, one must reconsider Li's notion of the human capacity to err. If he was not born with an extraordinary capacity for evildoing, what makes Wei Zhongxian such a monstrous being in later years?

The Wei in the middle of the novel brings to mind Ximen Qing of *The Golden Lotus*. Ximen Qing is a debauchee-cum-opportunist; thanks to good luck as well as shrewd maneuvering, he manages to gain wealth and power in a short time. Blinded by hubris, he immerses himself in sensual pleasure and, thus, rushes to his own destruction. Critics have suggested that, for all its surface sensation, Ximen Qing's is a morality tale about an Everyman who fails to curb his desires.[33] Wei Zongxian's rise and fall is similar in that he allows himself to be consumed by excessive vanities. Wei is a flawed usurper just as Ximen is a flawed sensualist. Their defects, although all too human, make them no less susceptible to superhuman temptation. Once the machine of evil is set in motion, mediocrity proves just as efficient as any full-scale villainy in inducing monstrosity.

Li Qing's depiction of Wei Zhongxian accentuates late Ming fiction writers' renewed interest in the genesis of evil. Evil does not necessarily appear as a mysterious given, nor does it have to be perpetrated by a great villain. Rather, with the right timing and agency, it can arise from ordinary creatures and circumstances. This mundane view may be symptomatic of the changing discourse of realism in late Ming fiction, which juxtaposes secular concerns, sensuous details of everyday life, conventional and unconventional wisdom, and competing narrative formats in order to bring out the "effect of the real" in its full complexity. The minute episodes of Wei's early adventures and his life at court familiarize a historical figure otherwise inaccessible to the imagination. Thus, beyond the supernatural pretext that is its frame, *An Idle Commentary on Monsters* actually demonstrates Li's endeavor to naturalize evil—as well as narrative conventions of evil—into the continuum of lived experience.

Such an approach to evil can also be understood in terms of the debate over fate versus will and natural endowment versus self-cultivation, issues that occupied elite fiction writers in the late sixteenth century and in the seventeenth.[34] I cannot delve deeply into these issues, but I do want, nevertheless, to suggest that tracing the vicissitudes of Wei Zhongxian's life shows how *An Idle Commentary on Monsters* contributes to the debate. The novel gives a decadent twist to the popular late Ming notion that even a commoner can transcend himself when enlightened by an innate call for edification. It implies that, once he is set free to mold his own subjectivity, he is just as capable of evil as he is of virtue.[35]

From a different perspective, scholars have already noted that the late Ming intellectuals' conviction of the attainability of the good by every man created an unexpected moral anxiety. That is, insofar as he is endowed with the immense capacity to achieve virtue and expected to do so, the individual is left with little room for mistakes in pursuit of his goal.[36] Between the promised sainthood and its default, he is thrown into a continued test of his moral integrity; any slight misstep risks an irredeemable fall. The apparently free-spirited call for self-betterment is ironically underlaid by a strict demand for self-rectification, so it engenders a grave tension between what one is and what one should be.[37] For a late Ming/early Qing scholar such as Chen Que (1604–77), humans are faced with an almost existential challenge of becoming "either saint or beast" [*rufei shengren, jishi qinshou*].[38]

Wei Zhongxian's story can be read as an allegory about the capricious terms through which a person negotiates his own moral character. Li Qing may not have consciously played out the tortuous dialectic of late Ming Confucian discourse; research is yet to be done regarding his intellectual heritage. But, on a more general level, his novel registers, in a form of negative dialectic, the late Ming intellectuals' concern about historical turmoil, personal responsibility, and moral transcendence. When tested by external and internal stimuli, humanity is seen as responding on its own and will be held accountable for the consequences in the most profound way. Wei's story is about a man's degradation to the level of not just beast but monster. That he can appear understanding and generous to selected people reminds us all the more of his potential for being good and his failure to realize that potential.

Above all, in Li's treatment of Wei Zhongxian, what is most impressive is not so much his conspiratorial capacity as the efficient way in which his will is carried out by his followers. The spy network and the surveillance system could neither have been invented solely by Wei nor have functioned so well merely under his aegis. The real taowu cannot be identified only with Wei, who is merely the human face on a monstrous regime; nor is the recounting of the evils of the late Ming exhausted by a litany of Wei's treachery and bloodthirstiness. My reading is that, if the Ming regime is known for its cruel, hegemonic rule and its meticulous implementation of coercive power, this sinister machine finally seems out of control—or, rather, achieves its full, monstrous potential—when Wei is put in charge. If the Ming can arguably be described as the first full manifestation of the modern state, in the sense that it was administered "rationally" by ordinary men in service to absolute power, then the proof of this modernity must lie in revealing the ordinariness of Wei, before and after his assumption of the key position in the bureaucracy of terror.

The reading offered above adds a contested dimension to the issue of good and evil in *An Idle Commentary on Monsters*. While Li Qing may be completely sincere in his search for balance between the extremes of human nature, the way in which he describes "contemporary affairs" may have guided him to a different set of questions, questions that can no longer be subsumed merely at the level of intellectual debate. The moral tension between sainthood and bestiality described above can, accordingly, be expanded. It is a tension between the conventional approach to history, underlaid by the periodic cycle of good versus evil and the articulation of orthodoxy, and the unconventional approach, marked first by a heightened anxiety about the feasibility of virtue and then by a premonition that something beyond human reason is looming large. Li could not have been fully aware of this tension. But his innovations, from the mixture of genres to the trivialization of villainy, are directed to renewing questions about history.

An impatient reader may find in *An Idle Commentary on Monsters* and *A Tale of Modern Monsters* a parallel between the late Ming days, when Wei Zhongxian and his gang almost ruined the Ming empire, and the mid-twentieth century, when the Chinese Communists turned the Republic upside down. But explaining Jiang Gui's intention should not be limited to invoking such a moralist parallel. Three hundred years apart, the two moments are, after all, marked by very different sets of challenges and crises. It is when we look into Jiang's survey of the Communist genealogy as well as the "technology" of evil that his indebtedness to the late Ming novel becomes clear.

There is, nevertheless, a more subtle relation between *An Idle Commentary on Monsters* and *A Tale of Modern Monsters* in terms of their authors' disposition of evil and moral responsibility. Jiang may have learned from *An Idle Commentary on Monsters* to furnish his world with unscrupulous opportunists and scoundrels, but, unlike his predecessor, he does not foreground any of his characters on the scale of Wei Zhongxian. Mao Zedong and other Communist leaders remain only mysterious names. Mao's wife, Jiang Qing, is introduced as a local girl kidnapped and thrown into an unlikely trajectory from an actress to a leftist cadre and Mao's woman.[39]

Instead of the centripetal structure of the late Ming novel, in which the minor evil forces are drawn to the archvillain, *A Tale of Modern Monsters* has a looser configuration. The two protagonists responsible for the Communist turmoil, Fang Xiangqian and Fang Peilan, are presented as self-deceiving idealists who fail to discern the fatal weakness of their plan; nor are they gifted with either charisma or leadership to unify various forces.

They manage to instigate the local insurrection, but they can hardly control its rampageous outcome. Worse, in the end, they become victims of their own campaigns.

I have pointed out that *An Idle Commentary on Monsters* offers a new, realistic view of evil by domesticating and humanizing it. This new form of evil is by no means less dangerous to dynastic stability; rather, its power of "petty wickedness" can circulate among social strata so efficiently as to aggregate into a force of unexpected magnitude. I have also argued that, besides this realistic approach to villainy, Li Qing already insinuates a "machine" at work in the absence of human agency. In *A Tale of Modern Monsters*, Jiang radicalizes this concept of evil by relativizing it. While in the late Ming novel corruption and conspiracy are associated in one way or another with Wei Zhongxian, evil disseminates throughout Jiang's world amorphously. Fang Xiangqian and Fang Peilan mean to do good for their community and are dedicated practitioners of communism, whatever their understanding of it. But their noble cause ends up becoming the pretext for both old and new forms of abuse. When their progressive agenda brings out the primitive baseness of people in Fangzhen or their altruist dedication results in a cannibalistic circus, Jiang calls attention to the antinomy of modern evil: the most spectacular horror can be carried out in the name of the most magnificent claims to rationality.

Jiang's vision of evil also has a dimension of anonymity. This may at first sound like a paradox because, throughout the novel, Jiang never hesitates to call the Communists the perpetrators of the chaos in modern China. But like Li Qing, he must combat a far more mysterious force beyond the conventional, human dimension. His view of Communist anonymity can be interpreted in three ways. First, the Communist revolution starts out billing itself as a proletarian revolution, by and for the "nobody" of the old society. Once the revolution is mobilized, the power structure assumes a new posture of invisibility in the name of "the Party." Second, when villains and revolutionaries proliferate in Jiang's novel, it becomes increasingly hard to pin down a central author of the chaos in the same way that tradition holds Wei Zhongxian accountable for the fall of the Ming. Third, we come to Jiang's recognition of the Communist revolution at its most vicious: it blurs one's ability to name, to make a clear judgment on its nature. In a way, Jiang has deliberately foresworn the Ming novel's technique of drawing a single human face on the monster. By not allowing readers the luxury of centralizing blame, he shows that totalitarian evil can prevail only with the energetic participation of countless ordinary human beings. The other title of *A Tale of Modern Monsters*, *The Whirlwind*, comes to mind. A whirlwind is a storm that blows violently in spiral form, drawing floating objects into the vacuum at its center.

A COMPENDIUM OF MONSTERS

For all its descriptions of irrationalities and cruelties, *A Tale of Modern Monsters* is couched in a peculiar narrative mode of laughter. Amid the corpus of literature shouting about Communist atrocities, the novel stands out for its determination to mock and ridicule. In his criticism of *A Tale of Modern Monsters*, C. T. Hsia likens it to Dostoyevsky's *The Possessed*. He comments that, as political novels, both contemplate "a humanity relentlessly selfish and relentlessly bent toward self-destruction" and both adopt "the pose of derisive laughter to drive home the lesson of anarchy and help assert the claims of sanity." Hence their shared style "drenched in buffoonery."[40]

In terms of the affective capacity of narrative, modern Chinese literature best manifests itself in two modes, tears and indignant cries. Liu E presented his theory of "weeping" in the preface to his *Lao Can youji* [The travels of Lao Can] and, thus, initiated the profusion of "tears and sniveling" in Chinese works.[41] Lu Xun, on the other hand, voiced his "call to arms" in the post–May Fourth days and foregrounded the imperative of social critique and reformist radicalism. Both are symptoms of what C. T. Hsia calls the "obsession with China."[42] However, there also exists a muffled tradition of laughter that includes at least selected works by writers from Lao She to Zhang Tianyi and from Lu Xun to Qian Zhongshu. Through laughter, these writers mock political abuses, poke fun at social manners and morals, and insinuate a deep anxiety about the nation's fate. As argued elsewhere, while they are inspired by the satirical paradigm of *Rulin waishi* [The scholars], they draw their immediate models from the corpus of late Qing exposés.[43]

A Tale of Modern Monsters carries on this tradition, with an even stronger impulse toward radical laughter. Thanks to his excessive desire to deride and mock and his seemingly endless parading of profanities and perversities, Jiang surpasses his May Fourth predecessors in emulating late Qing exposé writers. He sees villainy as not just horrible but absurd, so much so that the only possible response is laughter. More evidence has yet to be traced regarding Jiang's reception of late Qing exposés. But, as I discuss next, it is hard to imagine that Jiang would have created his circus of buffoonery without knowing works such as Li Boyuan's *Guchang xianxing ji* [Exposure of officialdom] (1905) or Wu Jianren's *Ershinian mudu zhi guaixiangzhuang* [Eyewitness report of strange things of the past twenty years] (1910). These are the major works of the exposé genre, and they have been extensively analyzed by scholars.⁴⁴ Here, for a comparative study, I focus on an obscure novel titled *A Compendium of Monsters*, by Qian Xibao.

Although Jiang Gui may never have read Qian Xibao's novel, I choose to discuss it for two reasons. Since the taowu is not a common image in the Chinese fictional vocabulary, any invocation of it calls attention to its historical legacy. That both *A Tale of Modern Monsters* and *A Compendium of Monsters* refer in their titles to the same ancient monster bespeaks a shared tropic repertoire. Like Jiang, Qian feels obliged to explain, at the end of his work, that his novel exhibits the taowu because "it depicts no single good person throughout."⁴⁵ More important, when set next to Li's *An Idle Commentary on Monsters* and Jiang's *A Tale of Modern Monsters*, Qian's novel provides a unique late Qing perspective from which to examine the fictional metamorphosis of the monster over the course of history.

A Compendium of Monsters describes the absurd ways in which a group of literati and middle-ranking bureaucrats quest for fame and fortune in late Qing society. The novel was completed in 1905 but not published until 1916, five years after the founding of the Republic. Perhaps for this reason, it has fallen between the cracks of literary history and remained unknown to readers until recent years. We know little about the author, Qian Xibao, except that he was a native of Hangzhou and that he served in various clerical posts in the late Qing and early republican eras. Judging by his references to novels such as *The Travels of Lao Can*, *Huo diyu* [Living hell], and *Exposure of Officialdom*, Qian must have been quite familiar with the exposé tradition of the early years of the first decade of the twentieth century.

A Compendium of Monsters introduces a string of stories in which characters try every possible method to advance themselves in the bureaucratic hierarchy. In one case, a junior official volunteers his wife as a "remedy" for his superior's mysterious illness; in another, an eager position seeker contributes his stepmother, his sister, and his wife to a governor's assistant so as to win himself an office. Where bribery is systemized into a routine enterprise, legal justice becomes a euphemism for marketable opinion.

Nevertheless, *A Compendium of Monsters* distinguishes itself by foregrounding two major characters, Jia Duanfu and Fan Xingpu. Jia Duanfu wins high esteem in both scholarship and moral cultivation. In his youth, he is said to have once rejected seduction by his master's concubine; his abstinence from any extramarital liaisons makes him a legend in an officialdom used to such activities. For all his neo-Confucian discipline, however, Jia cannot keep his wife, mistress, and even children from falling into laxity. As he is being promoted to higher and higher posts on account of his moral supremacy, one family scandal after another besets him. By the end of the novel, Jia has been tricked out of his entire fortune by his butler and is nothing more than a penniless, retired moral emblem.

Jia Duanfu's friend Fan Xingpu is an unscrupulous opportunist who has taken on the guise of an incorruptible judge-investigator. Wherever he is assigned, Fan launches bloody crackdowns on rioters and revolutionaries, so he soon becomes a rising star in the estimation of his conservative seniors. Meanwhile, he marries a female descendant of a rich family, then seduces his sister-in-law and his wife's maid. As the future looks more promising than ever, Fan finds himself charged with sexual misconduct, and, as a result, he loses his position, family fortune, wife, mistresses, and only son. He finally dies a pathetic, lonely death.

Qian Xibao attacks his villains most emphatically by describing their sexual transgressions. This is where his novel provides a surprising parallel to Jiang's *Tale of Modern Monsters*, also characterized by an unusual subtext of prurient sexuality. With a clear ironic intent, Qian uses Jia to usher us into a dizzying network of perversities. While he manages a saintly image in public, Jia is a sex maniac in private. He abuses his wife in bed, forcing her to perform all the sex acts he denigrates in public. After the death of his wife, his butler's daughter occupies his attentions, but he refuses to marry her, even as concubine, for he wants to maintain a reputation as a man above desire. Jia's wife has her own lover, who in his turn has raped Jia's daughter. Later on, Jia's daughter seduces her own brother and eventually causes his death.

Incest is seen among other characters too. To console his widowed daughter-in-law, an officer of the defense ministry develops an affair with her; in another case, a governor loves his daughter so much that he shares her bed. In yet another case, an assistant prefect helps out a clerk's promotion, bribed by the opportunity to sleep with the clerk's concubine, daughter, and daughter-in-law. Bisexuality, homosexuality, and transvestism constitute other important obsessions. One of the interludes describes an official's marrying his fifth concubine, who turns out to be a young man trained as a courtesan. The servant who seduces Jia Duanfu's wife and daughter is equally interested in men. When he reappears at the novel's end, he becomes the lover not of Jia Duanfu's maid/mistress but of her father.

Chen Pingyuan suggests that such abundant references to sexual deviations point to the convergence of the two genres of late Qing fiction, the exposé [*qianze xiaoshuo*] and depravity fiction [*xiaxie xiaoshuo*].[46] However, depravity fiction normally deals with sexual transactions within the pleasure quarters, where even the most licentious practice is taken for granted. What makes *A Compendium of Monsters* unique is its interest in sex scandals in regular households and among upright personalities. When the cultural constructs fall apart, desire penetrates every area of life and results in a collision of bodies and the functions supposedly regulating them. Qian Xibao thus foregrounds a society observing no boundaries, the literary boundary included.

I suggest that *An Idle Commentary on Monsters* derives its themes from the late Ming debate over the terms of virtue versus the terms of evil. On the premise that even an ordinary person is capable of achieving total good, any compromise with human weakness is seen as a dangerous slip into the domain of evil. The line between "the saint" and "the beast" is so strict yet so fine that it generates tremendous anxiety among those engaged in self-cultivation. At another level, I question whether such a rationale can fully explain Wei Zhongxian's villainy since he constitutes only part of the brutal late Ming political machine that goes haywire. The contrast between these two assumptions brings out, I conclude, the historiographic tension of *An Idle Commentary on Monsters*.

The case of Jia Duanfu contains an intricate twist. Whereas the late Ming dichotomy of sainthood and bestiality sets up a perilous test of moral constitution, the late Qing dichotomy of morality and immorality, as Qian Xibao would have it, is no more than a pragmatic transaction. Jia Duanpu strives to become a moralist only *after* he has weighed the pros and cons of his options. In turning down the seduction of his master's concubine, the event that first makes him known as a Confucian gentleman, Jia is said to have been motivated not by any concerns of decency but by a last-minute calculation. He knows what he may gain by temporarily curbing his desire; aware of a world of higher profitability, he invests a moment of frustration in the purchase of long-term political advantage.

What kind of historical view does such a plot imply? This question leads to the gist of the novel's moral scheme. Throughout, Qian Xibao distinguishes two types of evildoer, fraudulent gentlemen [*wei junzi*] and genuine petty crooks [*zhen xiaoren*]. Whereas the former hide their disingenuous motives behind benign postures, the latter entertain no qualms in pursuing their base goals. But *xiaoren* has another layer of meaning in the Confucian tradition; it refers to commoners or ordinary people with limited moral resources, those who rely on the Confucian gentleman to set standards for and edify them.[47] To Qian, while both are equally despicable, hypocrites are more dangerous because one can hardly see their true nature, as opposed to the petty crooks or commoners who lay bare their motives. Thus, in contrast to Jia and Fan is a group of characters who appear more likable, ironically owning to their visible unscrupulousness.

Involved here is a quirky system that values not virtue over evil but one kind of evil over another. If the society is already beyond any moral remedy, Qian seems to hint, one may as well settle for the less ambiguous form of evil since its threat is, at least, perceivable from the outset. When hypocrites prevail, they switch from one role to another and upset a representational system already in shambles. Characters like Jia Duanfu and Fan Xingpu do not merely fool people around them. As they perfect the art of simulation, they become more and more convinced by the images they project. They literally turn a matter of morals into one of manners.

If in Li Qing's *An Idle Commentary on Monsters* history is perceived as the continued confrontation between good and evil, in Qian's *A Compendium of Monsters* it appears as an evolution of the principles that "evils always defeat good" and "the greater evil defeats the minor one," to quote Milena Dolželová-Velingerová.[48] The debate over man's choice between sainthood and bestiality inherent in Li's novel has become gratuitous in Qian's world; the tension between human agency and the invisible political machine does not induce any poignant deliberation. True, justice seems to be done when both Jia Duanfu and Fan Xingpu suffer most horribly for their imposture. But this justice can be only a wayward one when the petty crooks are spared the consequences of, or in some cases even rewarded for, their misdeeds. By normal standards, these crooks' "honesty" about their base nature should not have exonerated them, at least not any more than the hypocrites' efforts to project honesty freed them. Above all, Qian writes as if questioning whether the conventional differentiation between gentlemen and petty crooks should not have veiled the search for the "genuine" issue, that times have changed and old institutions reveal their cracks.

Compared with Qian Xibao, who seems no longer convinced by any established value system, Jiang Gui may appear rather conservative because he does have serious beliefs. I suggest, nevertheless, that Jiang's political commitment, which should have evoked the usual tears or "call to arms," and his posture—laughter—are so incompatible that his narrative is all the more poignant. His modernity stems precisely from this mixture of traits drawn from his predecessors. He writes as if trying to merge the two images of the taowu demonstrated by the late Ming and late Qing novels discussed here. Whereas his vigilance about every man's susceptibility to evil echoes the tenor of *An Idle Commentary on Monsters*, his cynicism about the availability of evil to every man's order suggests the impact of late Qing exposés such as *A Compendium of Monsters*. That he strives to recount evils so as to admonish, à la the Ming, never keeps him from posing the late Qing question on the murky boundaries of virtue and truth. Through mixing apparently disparate discourses on the taowu, Jiang reinscribes the monstrosity of history in a modern mode.

Let us revisit the thesis of *A Tale of Modern Monsters* that, in Jiang's time, history has come to a halt and orthodoxy has been usurped. To rescue history, Jiang takes it as his obligation to recount evils so as to admonish in an unorthodox manner. While Wei Zhongxian of *An Idle Commentary on Monsters* shows how orthodoxy can easily be seized by conspirators and traitors, those clowns in *A Compendium of Monsters* demonstrate a less distant analogy, by displaying the chicanery of more recent times. In the case of Wei Zhongxian, the eunuch's presumptuous plan to take over first the court and then the empire is treated as the cause of dynastic crisis. The notion of usurpation is brought forth to explain Wei's deeds, although the novel's subtexts already point to factors that can hardly be subsumed by it. Wei would then be condemnable because he allows himself to aspire to what he is not and cannot be. His downfall is doomed, as imperial will reasserts its authenticity and again receives the mandate of heaven.

Qian's framework, such as it is, is that of a world in which the value system has already been duplicated surreptitiously. Fragile legitimacy and its fictitious representation have been reduced to an endless game of exchange; any effort to improve the status quo is bound to become a (self-)parody. In other words, Qian concentrates on not the metaphysics of usurpation but those of duplication. If usurpation in Li's world still implies sacrilege for its violation of an orthodoxy that is irreplaceable, duplication, as Qian employs it, points to a circulatory system based on the principle of exchange. Like his fellow writers, Qian mocks, reveres, and distorts his subject so as to represent it. By presenting a world in moral and axiological disorder, his novel calls into question the writer's ability to portray values coherently as well as the legitimacy of any realist mode of narrative; hence, it is an exercise in "phantom axiology."[49] Qian's vision leads us to rethink the image of the taowu that constitutes part of the novel's title, as grotesque creature in ghostly form. There is no supernatural Ming framework here; the ghosts and devils described so well are recognizable inhabitants of Qing society.

A Tale of Modern Monsters still resonates with Li's thesis in that Jiang writes to retrieve a history almost lost to usurpation. But he equally adheres to Qian's claim that orthodoxy has lost its "aura" and that we have been living in an age governed by phantom axiologies. Jiang's fear of and fascination with the politics of duplication is articulated even by the title of his second anti-Communist novel, *Chongyang* [Double suns] (1960).

This view emphasizes Jiang's ambivalent attitude toward communism. By making all Communists either imposters or self-deceivers, he hints that the revolution is an illusory action, a sham, and, thus, preempts its claim to ideological substance. But can he reconcile such a view with the facts that, after the bloody civil war, the immense mainland of China has changed hands; that thousands of lives, including his own, have been traumatically affected; and that the legitimacy of the Nationalist Party is reduced to residence in a province far from the capital, content to lob propaganda shells across the strait? When imposture inflicts real pain and masquerade turns into sacrificial theater, Jiang reveals the other side of late Qing facetious satire. But he does not stop there. He cries out that the revolution is naked, its benefits as imaginary as the clothing of the old emperor, yet bought at the cost of great bloodshed. This is Jiang at his most conservative—or most radical—regarding (Communist) revolution: conservative because he still sees and names the outcome of revolution in light of historical authenticity; radical because he associates communism with a phantom automaton, a modern simulacrum, that kills.[50]

I come to the conclusion of my survey by rethinking the Spanish painter Francisco Goya's (1746–1828) caption to one of the plates in the series *Los caprichos*: "The dream of reason produces monsters." Completed in 1799, the plate is said by José Monleón to condense the postulates of the Enlightenment: "Where reason fails, the forces of the occult prevail."[51] The caption—which I employ as the epigraph to this essay—has, nevertheless, inspired much thought on the paradox of the human capacity to reason and reason's solicitation of its opposite, monstrosity.[52] Meant to insinuate a shadowy aspect of a civilization believed to have a mastery of the unknown, Goya's caption takes on an additional dimension when interpreted in the perspective of Chinese history: that monstrosity may serve as the precondition for all civilized self-understanding.

With this in mind, I have looked into the representation of monstrosity in connection with the genesis of modernity in late imperial and modern Chinese fiction. I argue that *An Idle Commentary on Monsters* contributes a unique view of history by intimating the relations between monstrosity and commonality. Following the late Ming moral discourse on the ordinary person's potential for virtue, Li Qing nevertheless insinuates a counterargument, about his equal susceptibility to evil. The story of Wei Zhongxian indicates that, given the "right" historical environment and personal cultivation, an ordinary man can achieve as much vice as virtue. Thus, to the late Ming intellectual debate on the attainability of sainthood Li Qing adds a sarcastic, decadent dimension. More polemical is Li's inquiry into personal responsibility and the imperial structure of power, which leads him to ponder not only the moral agency but also the political technology that makes a villain such as Wei Zhongxian possible.

When Qian Xibao took up the trope of the taowu almost three hundred years later, the Chinese dynastic cycle had almost completed its second turn and was about to break for good with ancient autocracy, if not with autocrats. For Qian and his contemporary writers, monstrosity can no longer be embodied by a single villain or a single set of negative values. Instead, it has been embodied in a whole society forced to rethink its axiological system. In contrast to *An Idle Commentary on Monsters*, which still entertains a longing for good versus evil as well as for a recycling of the cosmic and moral universe, Qian's novel informs us, in the mock-authoritative manner of compendia, that, in the late Qing world, good and evil duplicate each other's traits, in celebration of a world soon to be turned upside down.

In *A Tale of Modern Monsters*, Jiang asks how it was that modern enlightenment and revolution set out to do away with historical irrationalities, only to beget irrationalities on an even larger scale. He concludes that modern revolutionaries cannot circumscribe the old evil without first imagining and living it. They are monsters of their own reasoning. Jiang shares in Qian's profane laughter, which threatens to bring down all established values, while at the same time he cherishes moral schemata traceable to Li Qing's time. Communism is, thus, described both as a new, inscrutable automaton that bulldozes the old social body and as the return of a dark curse from the most ancient lore. Above all, Jiang is not afraid of exposing and parodying either his own apprehension of the increasing anonymity of modern evil or his illusory quest to retrieve lost orthodoxy as a corrective of evil. He is, therefore, able to make his novel a testimonial to and an instance of a monstrous time called the *Chinese modern*.

Long gone are the days when monsters such as the taowu were said to roam the land and devour Chinese lives. Yet, as late as the mid-twentieth century, a melancholy author such as Jiang still wrote as if guided by a deep-seated memory of this ancient monster, associating himself with his predecessors of the Ming and Qing and earlier times. Goya's words resound—"the dream of reason produces monsters"—only by Jiang's time it had become more and more difficult to tell dream from reason and harder than ever to tell which dreams were monstrous and which reasonable. Perhaps the differences are obvious only much later, but thinking so may be just a dream of historians. If one of the functions of history is to record and, therefore, eschew irrationalities, the writers I have discussed have contributed a critique not only of monsters per se but of history itself as a form of recollection. Should we really dream of a past if we must remember reality to be motivated not to relive it?

The final irony of this study is, perhaps, that all three novels discussed, novels that teach us not to forget history, have become forgotten titles in Chinese (literary) history. Neither *An Idle Commentary on Monsters* nor *A Compendium of Monsters* was rediscovered and reassessed until recent years. And Jiang's modern effort to recount evils so as to admonish has now been sent on its way into the realm of oblivion. *A Tale of Modern Monsters* was made known to readers under its own title for two years before he let it be renamed *The Whirlwind*, which in its own turn has long since gone out of print.[53] Whither the monster? Whither the dream?

NOTES

Unless otherwise indicated, all translations from non-English-language sources are my own.

1. For a thorough discussion of the rise of anti-Communist literature in 1950s Taiwan, see my "Yizhong shiqu de wenxue? Fangong xiaoshuo xinlun" [A deceased literature? New perspectives on anti-Communist fiction], in *Ruhe xiandai, zenyang wenxue: Shijiu, ershi shiji Zhongwen xiaoshuo xinlun* [The making of the modern, the making of a literature: New perspectives on nineteenth- and twentieth-century Chinese fiction] (Taipei: Maitian chuban gongsi, 1998), 141–59.
2. See Jiang Gui, preface to *Jin taowu zhuan* [A tale of modern monsters] (Tainan: Chunyulou, 1957), 4.
3. For more details about the publication of the novel, see Timothy Ross, *Chiang Kuei* (Boston: Twayne, 1974), 76–86.
4. Jiang Gui, "Zizhuan" [Autobiography], in *Wuwei ji* [Not against my wishes] (Taipei: Youshi wenyi chubanshe, 1974), 242.
5. See Jiang Menglin's letter to Jiang Gui and Hu Shi's reference to *A Tale of Modern Monsters*, both in Jiang Gui, ed., *Huaixiu shu: Xuanfeng pinglun ji* [A book of one's own: A collection of critical articles on *The Whirlwind*] (Tainan: Chunyulou, 1960), 18–19, 20–21, respectively. Of all the contemporary reviews, the one by the historical fiction writer Gao Yang (1922–92) stands out for its perceptive analysis of the novel's rhetorical and psychological nuances. See Gao Yang, "Guanyu *Xuanfeng* de yanjiu" [A study of *The Whirlwind*], in ibid., 40–86.
6. C. T. Hsia, "The Whirlwind," in *A History of Modern Chinese Fiction* (1961), rev. ed. (New Haven: Yale University Press, 1971), 555–62.
7. Jiang, preface to *Jin taowu zhuan*, 3.
8. Ibid.
9. *Shenyi jing* [Classic of the supernatural and the strange], in *Biji xiaoshuo daguan* [A compendium of *biji* fiction], vol. 1 (Taipei: Xinxing, 1985), 226.
10. Sima Qian, "Wudi benji" [Five emperors basic annals], in *Shijihuizhu kaozheng* [An annotated version of the *Shiji*], vol. 1 (Taipei: Hongye, 1980), 31.
11. For references to *taowu* as one of the four major evils in ancient China, see, e.g., *Shangshu*, "Xiashu," 6, "yugong"; *Chunqiu zuozhuan zhengyi*, Wengong, juan 20, zhuan year 18.
12. *Chunqiu zuozhuan zhengyi*, "Xu," juan 1, Chunqiuxu.
13. *Mencius*, trans. D. C. Lau (London: Penguin, 1970), 131 ("Lilou" xiapian).
14. *Xiangdong jiwen* quoted in Zhang Jun, *Chuguo shenhua yuanxing yanjiu* [A study of the mythological archetypes of the Chu] (Taipei: Wenjin chubanshe, 1994), 71.
15. Jiang, preface to *Jin taowu zhuan*, 3.
16. See Jiang, *Wuwei ji*, 5–120. Judging by biographical accounts, many of the char-

acters and episodes in the novel may derive from Jiang Gui's personal experience. Fang Xiangian, e.g., may well be modeled after Jiang's uncle Wang Xiangqian, a self-styled reformer whose idealism brought on his hometown grave disasters. Fang Peilan may also find his counterpart in reality, a remote relative of Jiang's known for his bandit heroism and vengeful spirit.

17 Mistress Fang has the sliding weight of a steelyard hung atop her bed and swings it with her foot onto the face of Lady Ximen, who has been ordered to kneel upright before her all night long. She pricks Lady Ximen with a gold hairpin, leaving half-inch-deep wounds all over her body. In winter, she beats her with red-hot stove irons.

18 For a critical introduction to Foucault's genealogical view of history, see, e.g., Hubert L. Dreyfus and Paul Rabinow, *Michel Foucault: Beyond Structuralism and Hermeneutics* (Chicago: University of Chicago Press, 1982), pt. 2.

19 Ross, *Chiang Kuei*, 86 (with modification). For the original, see Jiang, *Jin taowu zhuan*, 104–5.

20 Hsia, "The Whirlwind," 560.

21 Mikhail Bakhtin, *Rabelais and His World*, trans. Helene Iswolsky (Cambridge: MIT Press, 1968). For more discussion of the political implication of the Bakhtinian "bodily principle," see Peter Stallybrass and Allon White, *The Politics and Poetics of Transgression* (Ithaca: Cornell University Press, 1986).

22 Georges Bataille, *Eroticism: Death and Sensuality*, trans. Mary Dalwood (San Francisco: City Lights, 1986), 42. See also Sigmund Freud, *Totem and Taboo* (London: Hogarth, 1955). Bataille distinguishes three kinds of eroticism: the corporeal; the emotional; and the sacrificial. All three forms involve a movement toward dissolution, as the ultimate state of continuity, from an initial state of separateness. The locus of such a movement can be the body, the heart (the emotions), or the spirit (sacred practice). Whereas the eroticism of the body is more cynical and sinister, the eroticism of the heart and sacred eroticism are said to be less constrained and more "intellectual." See Bataille, *Eroticism*, 19–23. See also Georges Bataille, *Tears of Eros*, trans. Peter Conner (San Francisco: City Lights, 1989), particularly the last section's discussion of corporal and sacred eroticism in light of the Chinese penal form of public mutilation [*lingchi*].

23 See, e.g., Wang Jicong, "Ping *Xuanfeng*" [A critique of *Whirlwind*], in Jiang, ed., *Huaixiu shu*, 88; Ji Wuwei, "Haoshu chutou" [Let a good book stand out], in ibid., 37–38; and Gao Yang, "*Xuanfeng*, Jiang Gui, wo" [*The Whirlwind*, Jiang Gui, and me], in ibid., 137. At the most conspicuous level, the titles of all the chapters are formed in poetic couplets modeled after those of classical Chinese vernacular fiction. These titles are taken out in the new edition of *The Whirlwind* (*Xuangeng* [Taipei: Ming hua shu ju], 1959).

24 Jiang quoted in Gao, "*Xuanfeng*, Jiang Gui, wo," 137.

25 Li Qing obtained his *jinshi* degree in 1621 and served the Chongzheng reign (1628–44) until its end. He became a recluse after the Ming fell and dedicated himself to intellectual and literary studies. In "Conclusions: Judgements on the

Ends of Times" (paper presented at the symposium "From the Late Ming to the Late Qing: Dynastic Decline and Cultural Innovation," Columbia University, November 6–7, 1998), Robert Hegel holds that Li did not write *An Idle Commentary on Monsters* until after the fall of the Ming. His argument is based on the research reported in Liu Wenzhong, ed., *Taowu xianping* [An idle commentary on monsters] (Beijing: Renmin wenxue chubanshe, 1983), 570.

26 For a more detailed account of Wei Zhongxian in English, see Frederick W. Mote and Dennis Twitchett, *The Cambridge History of China*, vol. 7, pt. 1 (Cambridge: Cambridge University Press, 1988), 596–613.

27 For a recent study of the genre, see, e.g., Kang Laixin, *Faji biantai: Songren xiaoshuo xue lungao* [The making of a hero: A study of the narratology of Song fiction] (Taipei: Da'an chubanshe, 1996).

28 See the discussion in Robert Hegel, *The Novel in Seventeenth-Century China* (New York: Columbia University Press, 1980), chap. 4.

29 Whereas Qin Shubao is described as a man who "grows from teen-aged uncertainty to mature self-assurance against a background of suffering for the masses of people, court indulgence, widespread brigandage, and foreign and civil wars" (ibid., 119), Wei Zhongxian arises from a similar background yet becomes the perpetrator of the disasters that heroes such as Qin would have striven hard to avert.

30 See Lu Xun, *A Brief History of Chinese Fiction*, trans. Hsien-yi and Gladys Yang (Beijing: Foreign Language Press, 1976), chap. 14.

31 This of course has something to do with the general social and economic ethos of the late Ming. See the discussion in Hegel, *The Novel in Seventeenth-Century China*, chap. 1.

32 I am referring to Northrop Frye's terminology. See Northrop Frye, *Anatomy of Criticism* (1957; reprint, New York: Atheneum, 1968).

33 See, e.g., the succinct analysis of Ximen Qing as an Everyman in Sun Shuyu, *Jin Pingmei de yishu* [The art of *Jinpingmei*] (Taipei: Shibao chuban gongsi, 1977), chap. 7. For an approach to the characterization from the perspective of the late Ming literati's call for self-cultivation and their ironic approach to humanity, see Andrew Plaks, *The Four Masterworks of the Ming Novel* (Princeton: Princeton University Press, 1987), chap. 3.

34 See Yue Hengjun, *Yizhi yu mingyun: Zhongguo gudian xiaoshuo shijieguan zonglun* [Fate and will: A general study of the worldview in classical Chinese fiction] (Taipei: Da'an chubanshe, 1992), 131–274. See also Plaks, *The Four Masterworks of the Ming Novel*, chap. 1; and Hegel, *The Novel in Seventeenth-Century China*, chap. 4.

35 This thought is not to be confused with Xunzi's theory that humanity is born evil, taken up by David Roy in his interpretation of the moral thesis of *The Golden Lotus*. See David Roy, introduction to *Jinpingmei: The Plume in the Golden Vase*, trans. David Roy (Princeton: Princeton University Press, 1995).

36 See, e.g., the succinct discussion in Wang Fansen, "Mingmo Qingchu de renpu

yu xingguohui" [The journal of humanity and the society of moral edification in the late Ming and the early Qing], *Zhongyang yanjiuyuan lishi yuyan yanjiusuo jikan* [Journal of the Institute of History and Philology, Academia Sinica] 63.3 (1993): 695–712.

37 See the succinct discussion of the ambivalent distinction in late Ming society between *ren*, "benevolence," and *bao*, "violence," in Zhao Yuan, *Ming Qing zhiji shidafu zhi yanjiu* [A study of the intelligentsia of the late Ming and the early Qing] (Beijing: Beijing daxue chubanshe, 1999), 3–22.

38 *Chen Que ji* [Collection of Chen Que's works] quoted in Wang, "Mingmo Qingchu de renpu yu xingguohui," 682. See also Zhang Hao, *Youan yishi yu minzhu chuantong* [Dark consciousness and democratic tradition] (Taipei: Lianjing chuban gongsi, 1989), 21–27, 69–73.

39 But most fascinating is the case of Jiang Qing. Referred to only as the "Big Daughter" of the Li family, she makes her first appearance in the beginning of the novel as a girl who returns home years after being abducted and sold to a Beijing opera company. Since Fang Xiangqian knows her grandfather well and likes her looks and talent, he arranges to take her as his goddaughter. By the end of the novel, she is said to have tried to break into film but to have made her best career move when she finally became Mrs. Mao.

40 Hsia, "The Whirlwind," 560.

41 Liu E, preface to *Lao Can youji* [The travels of Lao Can] (Taipei: Lianjing chuban gongsi, 1984), 1–2. See the discussion in my *Fin-de-Siècle Splendor: Repressed Modernities in Late Qing Fiction, 1849–1911* (Stanford: Stanford University Press, 1997), 36–42.

42 C. T. Hsia, "Obsession with China: The Moral Burden of Modern Chinese Literature," in *A History of Modern Chinese Fiction*, 2nd ed. (New Haven: Yale University Press, 1971), 533–609.

43 Wang, "Mingmo Qingchu de renpu yu xingguohui," 251.

44 See, e.g., Wang, *Fin-de-Siècle Splendor*, chap. 4; and also Milena Dolželová-Velingerová, ed., *The Chinese Novel at the Turn of the Century* (Toronto: University of Toronto Press, 1980).

45 Qian Xibao, *Taowu cuibian* [A compendium of monsters] (Tianjin: Baihua wenyi chubanshe, 1989), 397.

46 Chen Pingyuan, "Qianze xiaoshuo yu xiaxie xiaoshuo: Shuo *Taowu cuibian*" [Exposé and depravity fiction: On *A Compendium of Monsters*], in *Chen Pingyuan xiaoshuoshi lunji* [Collection of critical essays on Chinese fiction by Chen Pingyuan] (Shijiazhuang: Hebei renmin chubanshe, 1996), 1428–36.

47 The *Analects*, e.g., is full of examples that contrast the Confucian gentleman, or *junzi*, with commoners, or *xiaoren*.

48 Dolželová-Velingerová, ed., *The Chinese Novel at the Turn of the Century*, 53.

49 Wang, *Fin-de-Siècle Splendor*, 191–209. As the preface to *A Compendium of Monsters* states, the novel is at its most intriguing in its approximation of human perversities: "It is not difficult to describe a ghost in terms of a wolf's head and

a hairy face, red hair and a snake's body. But it is difficult even for a painter such as Luo Liangfeng, known for his vivid portraits of devils, to draw a man harboring a devilish mentality or someone called human but actually a ghost. ... *A Compendium of Monsters* is a novel that manages to carry out this task [of representing ghosts]." Qian Xibao, preface to *Taowu cuibian*, 1.

50 See the discussion of Maoism as a simulacrum in David Apter and Tony Saich, *Revolutionary Discourse in Mao's Republic* (Cambridge: Harvard University Press, 1994), chap. 7.

51 On February 6, 1799, Francisco Goya published a series of eighty aquatint plates titled *Los caprichos*. Plate 43 is the only one that contains a title, "El sueño de la razón produce monstruos" [The dream of reason produces monsters]. The plate is said to have been conceived as the first of the series, only to be renumbered for political reasons. According to José Monleón: "In principle, *Capricho* 43 seems to condense the postulates of the Enlightenment: where reason fails, the forces of the occult prevail." See José B. Monleón, *A Specter Is Haunting Europe: A Sociohistorical Approach to the Fantastic* (Princeton: Princeton University Press, 1990), 22 (also 40–42).

52 For more discussion of the ambiguous caption, see ibid., 41.

53 The novel was reprinted in 2000, as a result of its being recognized as a canonical work in Taiwan literary history, by Juge chuban she.

9

Taiwanese Identity and the Crisis of Memory: Post-Chiang Mystery

Yomi Braester

During the dictatorial rule of Chiang Kai-shek [Jiang Jieshi] in Taiwan, from the takeover by the Guomindang (formerly Kuomintang, KMT) in the late 1940s, a Taiwanese identity has formed around silenced testimony and repressed memories. The official narrative glorified the battles fought by the KMT on the mainland before 1949, at the expense of accounts of the former soldiers' present plight, and censored references to Chiang's policy of oppression on the island, especially the executions and arrests associated with the clashes on February 28, 1947, known as the White Terror. In both cases, neither mainlanders nor native Taiwanese were able to express their personal suffering. After Chiang's demise in 1976, the gradual democratization under his son, Chiang Ching-kuo, and the lifting of martial law in July 1987, Taiwan's collective memory emerged out of the combination of these versions of the past. Yet none of the multiple narratives could create a coherent memory explaining the present.

Taiwanese citizens in the 1980s and 1990s were struggling to present a narrative of their history. This essay examines Taiwan fiction of the 1980s in the context of the politics of memory. Since the relaxation of the Chiangs' rule, a literary corpus has emerged that is forging a Taiwanese identity by reclaiming repressed memories. In this sense, the post-Chiang era may be dated back to the early 1980s. The unsaid could, it seemed, finally be spoken. Yet curiously, at the same time that the secrets of past oppression were revealed, literature and film turned to mystery. Texts—either dealing directly with the recent past or describing more abstract parables—often end without solving the riddle around which the narrative revolves. The contrast between the political and the literary discourses raises important questions. Why are the revelations denied the status of truth? Why have the memories continued to be dislocated in unstable narratives? And what are the implications of these literary constructions for Taiwanese identities?

The mystery genre is, I argue, a sign of Taiwanese writers' recognition of their inability to redress past wrongs and rewrite history into a narrative of progress and redemption. Memories shape the past through uncertain and unfinished narratives. The past can be presented only as an absence. Like Oedipus, the model mystery detective, the narrators face a riddle to which they themselves are the only answer. No witness can provide the solution in its entirety, and the storytellers put the pieces together as best they can.

A symbolic manifestation of the breakdown of memory is to be found in the many mysteries that present multiple versions of the same narrative, in a manner reminiscent of Akira Kurosawa's 1950 *Rashōmon*, which contains four versions of an event, told by different narrators, without reconciling them. Examples are fiction like Ping Lu's "Yumi tian zhi si" [Death in a cornfield] (1983) and Yang Zhao's *Anxiang miye* [Night of riddles in a dark alley] (1994) as well as films like He Fan's *Shidai zhi feng* [L'air du temps] (1990) and Yang Dechang's *Haitan de yitian* [That day on the beach] (1991). The coexistence of alternative stories has been rightly ascribed to the postmodern demise of grand narratives. In post-Chiang Taiwan, people could pick and choose from many versions of their own past, and the diverging literary accounts leave protagonists and readers alike in a position to choose their preferred explanations. Yet the crisis does not arise simply from the proliferation of histories; it resides, rather, at the present moment of bearing testimony, when memory fails to recuperate the past and generate a coherent history. Yang Zhao's *Night of Riddles in a Dark Alley*, for example, illustrates how the multiple viewpoints originate from the witness himself. The text is composed of two narratives presented in interwoven fragments. Yet there is only one narrator, who actively participates in creating two versions of his memory as he talks to two women. Memory changes not only according to whom he listens to but also according to whom he talks to. The narrator fails as an interrogator and ends up recounting a mystery because the memories erase the history that they are supposed to reconstruct.

Post-Chiang mystery points out how silences have continued to dominate the narratives of identity, how writing memory cannot turn into a historical testimony, and how individual memory is subsumed by the collective memory. These texts are post-Chiang not simply because they counter the official version of Taiwan's past but also because they draw attention to the chronic manipulation of memory that has maimed writers' capacity to bear witness. Their testimony mystifies the reader with accounts that never tally up, with unresolved detective stories. To illustrate the unresolved plots of the post-Chiang period, I offer close readings of two well-known novellas, Chen Yingzhen's (b. 1937) *Shanlu* [Mountain path] (1983) and Liu Daren's (b.1939) *Dujuan tixie* [Azaleas cry out blood] (1984). The two cannot represent the diverse literary scene in post-Chiang Taiwan, and my focus here neglects the important trend of nativist literature, which has striven to reclaim a Taiwanese history. Yet it is precisely the idiosyncratic, arguably dated political views of Chen and Liu—the former an old-fashioned Marxist, the latter a disillusioned one—that allow them to reflect on Taiwan's crisis of identity in the 1980s. The two texts address concerns central to post-Chiang Taiwan and demonstrate how memories of past repression might be too traumatic to be recorded directly or even acknowledged later. Rather, experience and linguistic expression become mutually exclusive, and memory becomes the witness's nemesis.

THE PURPLE SMOKE OF TIME

Chen Yingzhen's short stories from the 1980s illustrate the unresolved plots of the post-Chiang period. Chen, a native of Taiwan, has been one of the more conspicuous figures on the island's literary scene since the 1960s. In 1968, he was sentenced to ten years in jail for criticizing KMT rule, but he was released seven years later. His Marxist beliefs also led him to seek inspiration from the People's Republic of China (PRC), even after June 1989, a fact that cost him the support of many intellectuals. Yet, in the 1960s, Chen explicitly fashioned his social and political activism after May Fourth writers and was, perhaps, the first in Taiwan to acknowledge the strong influence of Lu Xun, whose writings were banned in Taiwan at the time.[1] After he recovered from his imprisonment and resumed writing in 1978, Chen represented the voice of the KMT's political prisoners. Chen's voice was split in two, across a temporal and cultural abyss of the years of his incarceration. His late fiction draws prominently on his seven years in prison, yet even his implicitly autobiographical writing shows the past to be inaccessible to testimony. Chen's characters, survivors of the White Terror, cannot speak and bear witness to the years of persecution and imprisonment. His works exemplify the simultaneous turn to recovering the past and acknowledging the failure of memory to retrieve the lost voices of the victims.

Of special interest are Chen's three major works of the 1980s, "Lingdanghua" [Bellflowers] (1983), "Mountain Path," and "Zhao Nandong" (1987). An apt metaphor for temporal dislocation is found in the last story, which tells of the disintegration of a prison survivor's family. Old Zhao and his wife, who participated in the anti-Japanese demonstrations in Shanghai in 1932, are thrown into a Taiwanese jail in 1947. Old Zhao is released thanks to the "special amnesty" following Chiang Kai-shek's death in 1975, only to find that his younger son, Zhao Nandong, born in jail shortly before his mother was executed, is himself imprisoned—not for his political activism but for dealing in narcotics.[2] A friend of Old Zhao's, also a released political prisoner, likens her own "anxiety at jumping into a totally different history"—that is, the historical moment of late 1970s Taiwan—to the Japanese children's tale about Urashima Tarō, who briefly visits the Dragon King's underwater palace. On returning to his hometown, Tarō finds that centuries have passed. Like him, Chen's protagonists are dislocated Rip van Winkles who cannot adjust to the changes brought by time. The Taiwanese dissidents have become exiles in their own land.

The belated reaction to historical change, and specifically the inadequacy of writing, are addressed in "Mountain Path." The story takes place in 1983 and starts with Cai Qianhui, a woman in her early fifties, being hospitalized in critical condition, but for no apparent physical illness. The doctor diagnoses her problem as a total loss of the will to live. Li Guomu, Qianhui's brother-in-law, observes that her health started deteriorating after she read that her friend Huang Zhenbo had been released after thirty-two years in jail. Huang had been arrested in 1950 for anti-KMT activities, together with Guomu's elder brother, Guokun, who was executed soon after. Following Guokun's death, Qianhui came to stay with his family and help them, explaining that she had married Guokun without his parents' knowledge.

Another version of Qianhui's story changes Guomu's perspective. The woman dies, and, when the brother-in-law puts her belongings in order, he finds an unsent letter addressed to Huang Zhenbo. The letter reveals that Qianhui was, in fact, Huang's fiancée and knew Guokun only as Huang's comrade in arms. After the two had been betrayed by Qianhui's brother, the woman decided to atone for his deceit by helping Guokun's destitute family. She concludes her letter explaining that Huang's release from jail has awakened her from the numb comfortable life she has recently enjoyed thanks to Guomu's support. Taiwan's people, including herself, have forgotten about Huang and his comrades: "I'm afraid that facing this vast, thoroughly 'tamed' world, your fight will be even harder than in the past."[3] As the memories come back, Qianhui loses her sense of purpose and chooses to put an end to her life. Her "awakening" exemplifies how trauma is experienced as a rift in time, as a wound that reaches from the past into the present.

The story of Urashima Tarō is also an apt metaphor for Qianhui. The complete story, found in the eighth-century *Manyōshū*, tells how Tarō marries the Dragon King's daughter but, after three years, is too homesick to stay in the palace. Before he leaves, the dragon's daughter gives him a box and warns him never to open it. When he goes back to his village and finds that centuries have passed while he was in the underwater palace, he opens the box. It releases a purple smoke that envelops Tarō, who transmogrifies into a crane and flies off to reunite with his wife. The Urashima tale is relevant to Chen Yingzhen's characters because it illustrates not only the futility of longing for an often-imagined home but also the difficulty of coming to terms with the consequences of one's return. Tarō does not transform (in another version, he ages in Dorian Gray fashion) until he opens the box.[4] In "Mountain Path," the effect of time sets in only when the news about Huang's release opens Qianhui's Pandora's box of memories (incidentally, in a possible echo of the Urashima tale, Guomu finds the unsent letter in a lacquer box). The traumatic effects are unleashed long after the mental wound is inflicted, in response to a seemingly harmless stimulus.

Qianhui breaks down and succumbs to a delayed death wish, observed in many trauma survivors, because the news awakens her memories as well as her consciousness of the present.[5] Once she puts down her political arms, she also lowers her psychological defenses. Living on no longer counts as a struggle in and of itself and loses its meaning. Moreover, her survival seems immoral when compared to the fate of the long imprisoned and the dead. Qianhui's very existence in the present and her ability to look back at the past undermine her mental balance more than her past suffering has done. Her newly formed historical awareness only stresses her temporal dislocation, which she can resolve only through death. As David Wang comments, her death "is a necessary means for filling in the blanks of history."[6] Ironically, Qianhui can assert the meaning of the past only through self-annihilation. Her testimony takes the form of silencing and erasure.

A TESTIMONY UNSPOKEN

Chen Yingzhen's stories show how memory can exist only in the form of split voices. "Zhao Nandong" follows closely the *Rashōmon* structure and presents the plot through the narratives of four people. In "Mountain Path," Guomu's memories are countered by Cai Qianhui's letter to Huang Zhenbo, testimony from beyond the grave that brings to the surface repressed memories and sets the historical record straight, but too late. When Qianhui finally breaks through the long silence, her words remain displaced in the unsent letter, which could have dispelled the muteness of political oppression and psychological repression.

Throughout her life, Qianhui has forced herself to keep silent, as becomes evident when Guomu, still a child, hears his sister-in-law singing a resistance song to herself. When he asks Qianhui what she is singing, she immediately stops humming and answers: "Nothing.... You can't sing, you shouldn't sing. For now" (58). Despite the implied anticipation that the day to start singing will come, Qianhui persistently shelters Guomu and leads him away from politics. Later, she commits all her secrets to the letter but, having written down all that was left untold, continues to hide her secret. She stashes the letter away, keeping her thoughts to herself. Neither her own voice nor that of her adopted brother is allowed to convey the past.

The fact that the letter remains unsent, that Qianhui may never have intended to send it, is crucial to understanding the paradox of bearing witness to a past known only through silences. Qianhui writes that she must speak out, "for both moral and emotional reasons" (61), and attempts to negotiate her own and Huang's memories. She concludes with the request that he remember her as the young woman he knew. The memories, however, hold her back from delivering any testimony. It is not simply that she is too nostalgic to reach back into the past and shatter its beautiful image. Rather, what drives Qianhui to seal the letter and keep it is her recognition that memory itself is the source of her suffering. Either in the very process of writing the letter or soon after, Qianhui realizes that traumatic experience is contained not in past events but in present remembering. The letter turns from a testimony to Qianhui's survival into an assertion of the impossibility of surviving what she has experienced. As a witness, she cannot go on living, and, as a testimony, her letter cannot be sent.

Another of the symbols employed in "Mountain Path" to convey the written word's failure to provide a timely, accurate testimony is found in an earlier episode, when Qianhui erects a tombstone for Guokun. Ironically, it is another act of KMT repression—the Kaohsiung Incident of 1979—that breaks the taboo on mentioning political prisoners. Consequently, Qianhui orders a tombstone for Guokun. It reclaims his place in memory, but the inscription keeps displacing the events. Truth is partially restored, the engraved list of surviving family members euphemistically including Guomu's family as the descendants of the deceased but omitting mention of Qianhui as Guokun's purported wife. Yet the tombstone contains fallacious references to time and place. It dates Guokun's death to 1952, when the authorities declared his demise, rather than the actual time of his execution, almost two years before. Moreover, it is erected over a grave containing only Guokun's clothes since his body has never been returned. The inscription functions at best as a mnemonic code for the ever-unutterable facts.

The half-truths engraved over Guokun's displaced grave are emblematic of the problems in testifying to a disaster that annihilates its major witnesses and silences everyone else involved. Furthermore, every testimony must struggle against previous, adulterated depositions. A case in point is the tale that Qianhui tells Guokun's family when she first joins them. Guomu is somewhat impatient with Qianhui's fondness for reiterating her life story, which might be taken for either nostalgia or obsession. Only after the unsent letter comes to light is it clear that Qianhui has been retelling her story precisely to cover up its fallacy. Only the unsent letter eventually refutes Qianhui's earlier version.

Qianhui's letter, like her fabricated life story and the inscription on Guokun's tombstone, is a displaced testimony. While its contents may be accurate, the letter fails to reach its addressee; instead, it lands in the hands of the man from whom it was supposed to be kept secret. Qianhui has kept Guomu from meeting Huang Zhenbo and learning the truth, wishing to protect her adopted brother-in-law from the pain of her memories—or perhaps she consciously does not destroy the letter, knowing that it might resurface, thereby leaving her testimony suspended. Moreover, the letter fails in a more profound sense when Guomu reads it yet keeps its contents to himself. At the end of the story, he sobs, but, when his wife asks him what is wrong, he does not tell: "Nothing . . . I . . . miss . . . sister-in-law" (66). Qianhui taught Guomu to deny the past, to stifle the songs that she would never teach him. When the time comes to bear witness, the letter can no longer change this ingrained habit.

Guomu becomes an accomplice to Qianhui's silence, equally inept at speaking out and bearing witness. When the doctor asks him the cause of Qianhui's illness, Guomu immediately thinks of Huang's release, yet he repeatedly replies that he can give no clue. At first, his refutation comes "almost instinctively" (38). The next time, he thinks: "But how can I face these doctors and nurses and tell the events of that morning [of the roundup in 1950], speak out my brother's and Huang Zhenbo's affair?" (43). It is not only that Guomu is unwilling to divulge the family secret and reveal his pain; equally important, he cannot face others with this knowledge and put himself in the position of a witness. Insofar as Cai Qianhui's plight is emblematic of Chen Yingzhen's attempt to relocate his writing in the realities of post-Chiang Taiwan, "Mountain Path" points to how literary writing is always already belated, addressing either the mute dead or the deaf living. The author cannot recover a voice free of the doubts—his own and his readers'—that have been ingrained during years of oppression and suppression.

TESTIMONY AND EXILE

Liu Daren presents a different strain of Taiwanese dissidence. Born on the Chinese mainland and, thus, considered a potential KMT sympathizer, Liu nevertheless soon became critical of the party's policies. As a result of his political activism in the early 1970s, the KMT refused him reentry to Taiwan, and he has since lived in the United States. Liu's activism brings him close to Chen Yingzhen, yet Liu's refusal to align himself with any specific group since the early 1980s, compounded by his exile and work for the United Nations, has made him harder to classify. In 1983, he was allowed to visit Taiwan for the first time since his exclusion. This visit, as well as two eye-opening tours to the PRC in 1974 and 1977, called for readjusting his political convictions and taking a step back from activism. "Writing," he said in a 1997 interview, "was my only way out." Liu found, however, that his skills had suffered from his total immersion in politics: "My writing was no longer like literature."[7]

In the early 1980s, Liu composed a trilogy consisting of "Fengjing jiu ceng an" [Scenery once familiar] and "Guguo shenyou" [Magical journey home], both written in 1983, and "Azaleas Cry Out Blood," written the following year. All three portray protagonists who return to the mainland after more than thirty years and encounter the uncanny cognitive dissonance alluded to in the stories' titles. As Wendy Larson notes, the three works shows consistent concern not only with exile and return but also with the author's position.[8] In these stories, writing tries—and fails—to assume authority, thereby causing a rupture of identity. The protagonist in "Scenery Once Familiar" seals his fate by following his talent for calligraphy. Writing becomes his "karmic obstruction."[9] In "Magical Journey Home" a man loses his U.S. documents before going through the airport passport check in the PRC. The authorities take him for a Taiwanese spy; consequently, he goes through an identity crisis and a nervous breakdown that paralyzes him even as he is asked to sign the papers for his own release.[10] In other words, he is unable to attest to who he is. When Liu's characters try to reach beyond past traumas, they find out that their present identity is distinct from their past one. Trying to anchor their sense of historical continuity in texts and documents serves only to show that writing cannot set history right. Instead, the protagonists become dependent on earlier written texts to the extent that their present and immediate testimonies are ignored.

"Azaleas Cry Out Blood" was composed shortly after Liu was first allowed to return to Taiwan and expresses his endeavors to retrieve his voice as an author in an era of political change and accounting of memory.[11] Liu addresses the repressed experiences of the Cultural Revolution as well as issues of Taiwanese ideology, specifically the KMT's suppression of public debate. The story is set in the PRC during the early 1980s. The narrator, Professor Hu, is an overseas Chinese from Singapore now teaching in the United States. He follows a clue in a Red Guard bulletin from 1968, *The Luzhou Battle Report* [Luzhou zhanxun], and finds out that his fourth aunt, Leng Yufeng, not heard from for over forty years, is living in the PRC under the name Leng Feng. Hu visits her in a sanatorium for high-ranking cadres but fails to communicate with her. Except for a single unintelligible burst, Leng Feng is incapable of even acknowledging her nephew's presence, let alone helping him understand why she suddenly severed ties with her family in the early 1930s or how she lost her sanity during the Cultural Revolution. The little information provided by the sanatorium staff implies that she had been treated brutally in 1968, after which she lost her speech for two years, and has said little ever since. Only after Hu leaves the PRC does he find the key to his aunt's past. He discovers in Hong Kong a hitherto-missing part of *The Luzhou Battle Report* that reveals that Leng Feng gave up everything to follow her teacher and lover, Luo Cheng, a Communist leader, to the Chinese hinterland. The report further discloses that, after Luo Cheng betrayed her and possibly the Communist underground in the 1930s, Leng Feng had him executed and ate his heart.

At the center of the story lies madness—Leng Feng's mad revolutionary zeal and subsequent insanity and the "madness" of the Cultural Revolution.[12] In psychoanalytic terms, the repetitive pattern of her conduct shows how Leng Feng reenacts the same punitive behavior after each betrayal by a father figure. She shows the need for an infallible father figure when she abruptly leaves her own family and falls for her teacher, Luo Cheng. When Luo betrays her, she retaliates by turning cannibal and eating his heart. Later, she projects the emotions previously reserved for Luo Cheng onto the Party and "marries the Chinese revolution" (179). The Red Guards' physical abuse is compounded by what Leng Feng could regard as being betrayed by Mao. The Great Helmsman was portrayed as the nation's father and collective superego, to whom all agency was renounced. Party cadres, the group most protected by Mao and most inculcated with his ideology, felt betrayed when the leader shifted his allegiance from the Party apparatus to the Red Guards, who accused the cadres of being covert "careerists and schemers like Khrushchev" (188). As Wang Shaoguang observes, the Cultural Revolution left most people with a sense of having been "'blinded,' 'hoodwinked,' 'cheated,' or 'used' by Mao."[13] When Leng Feng experiences this betrayal, she turns not against Mao but against herself. She loses her sanity and regresses into aphasia. Turning away from her father, Luo Cheng, and, finally, Mao results in a growing loss of touch with social structures and norms—from severing all family ties to effacing her birth name, cannibalism, and eventually stopping all verbal communication. As each personal crisis is concurrent with a major historical disruption—the civil war of the 1940s, the Anti-Rightist Campaign of the 1950s, and the Cultural Revolution—the woman's mental regression points also to a collective psychosis linked to the expectations of and setbacks in China's political sphere.

Leng Feng's mental disorder and the story's setting in an insane asylum should, however, be understood not only in psychoanalytic terms but also as an allegory of the posttraumatic displacement of memory. As in Chen's "Mountain Path," the significance of trauma lies in its return and extension into the present.

THE NARRATOR AS DETECTIVE

The regression to ever earlier roots of madness requires the narrative to establish the original experience that led to Leng Feng's posttraumatic behavior pattern. Her lack of responsiveness produces a riddle that can be solved by reading between the lines and referring to other texts. "Azaleas Cry Out Blood" derives its force from the narrator's need to retrace Leng Feng's history by detective-like working through his aunt's past.

The narrator, Professor Hu, cannot establish a coherent version of any key event or reconstitute a narrative that would reconnect the various suppressed moments in Leng Feng's life. His only approaches to the past are through his aunt, her physician, Dr. Xu, and the text of *The Luzhou Battle Report*. Each represents a different manifestation of the crisis of memory. Leng Feng offers inner resistance to recovering the past, as is clearly illustrated when Hu tries to jolt her memory by placing by her bedside a photograph of her and her sisters, taken in the 1930s. Leng Feng ignores the picture throughout his visit and never touches it. She not only disowns her family ties but also denies the very existence of the historical moment represented by the photograph. Leng Feng's psyche disintegrated when she was forced to confront her past, her mental fault lines ruptured, and her memory broke down.

At the sanatorium, Hu is met with another version of denial, namely, the political rewriting of history, represented by the elusive Dr. Xu. Hu realizes from the beginning that he must elicit information despite the doctor's resistance: "I waited patiently for my counterpart to make the move and get to the main issue. I was convinced that they had a good idea why I was visiting them; the only thing that worried me was that I did not know how much they were willing to reveal. I could only keep cautioning myself that it was better to feign ignorance and pursue any leads my counterpart would reveal unintentionally" (154). The scene stresses the plot's similarity to a detective novel, which strives to answer the whodunit through specific strategies of interrogation. The narrator's account reads as if taken right out of a classic spy thriller: the two sides exchange pleasantries while each is aware that the other knows more than he pretends and is looking for ways to gain information without revealing anything in the process. Yet the encounter between Professor Hu and Dr. Xu brings the investigation to an impasse, illustrating the tenacious resistance to resuscitating unwelcome memories.

For his own reasons, Dr. Xu cooperates with Leng Feng's denial. He not only pretends that her insanity hides no traces of any event worth pursuing but also actively helps repress her secrets. When Leng Feng suddenly utters a few incoherent words—a stunted yet hopeful sign of a willingness to communicate—Dr. Xu immediately rushes her back to her room and expresses dismay at her "regression" (183). Freudian treatment would encourage verbal expression, but Dr. Xu refers disparagingly to "this Western idealistic nonsense about psychoanalysis" (158). Significantly, the only treatment that the sanatorium applies successfully consists of prescribing traditional medication to stop internal bleeding (181). The authorities keep the symptoms of violence under cover rather than reveal the cracks in the Communist utopia.

TEXTUAL VIOLENCE

Of the three sources of information—Leng Feng herself, Dr. Xu, and *The Luzhou Battle Report*—the most complex manifestation of the crisis of memory and public testimony is the report, in which Hu encounters a more insidious form of resistance to memory, namely, textual dynamics that turn testimony against itself. The report replicates Leng Feng's insane silences and the official line of tendentious half-truths but also in itself becomes the vehicle and victim of brutal repression. Hu can avail himself only of an incomplete copy kept in a U.S. library—such Red Guard publications, usually mimeographed pamphlets, have rarely been preserved.[14] The report contains the first part of an article that presents testimony about Leng Feng's activities in the mid-1930s. When Hu has no choice but to reveal his cards and ask the official escort for the report, he is given a copy in which the text is repeatedly interrupted and mutilated and, finally, completely excised. First it is cut short by the editors' frantic interjections; then the censors cut it out completely. Symbolically, the title, "Chop off the Evil Manipulator, the Counter-Revolutionary Revisionist Two-Faced Leng Feng! Destroy Completely the New Counterattack of the Old Provincial Committee!" (such pamphlets typically had long titles), is abbreviated by the narrator to "The

'Chop Off' Text." The foreshortened form sounds even more violent than the original, suggesting a text capable of being dismembered and cannibalized or beheaded—or of perpetrating these acts on its subject.

The report demonstrates not only how writing can fail as a carrier of memory but also how texts can violently interfere in the work of remembering. It plays a major role in driving Leng Feng mad and calls explicitly for her death: "The debt of blood has to be paid in blood!" (172). "The 'Chop Off' Text" becomes a tool of violence when the Red Guards use it to incite people against Leng Feng as well as to open the wounds of her memory and make her more vulnerable. In her deposition, reproduced in the report, Leng Feng had reportedly given her version of the events during the Anti-Rightist Campaign of 1957: "[Another party member] forced me to swallow the warm, blood-dripping heart and liver taken from [Luo's] disemboweled corpse, in front of the crowd!" (188). Leng Feng uses the graphic description to arouse revulsion against her political rival and invite pity for her own plight. The Red Guards appropriate her incendiary testimony and use it as evidence, making her eat her own blood-dripping words. The article highlights how testimony, especially when committed to print, might end up cannibalizing the writer's voice.

Finally, the narrator locates the crisis of memory even within himself. Professor Hu realizes his own complicity: "Did I so bury myself from the very start in verifying the identity of the name Leng Feng that coming closer and closer to the truth only made me more reluctant to face the tragedy my subconscious confirmed must have occurred?" (172). The question remains unanswered as it becomes clear that no single observer has a hold on the past. The whodunit structure disintegrates as the multiple and incomplete texts undermine Hu's attempts to solve the historical riddle. The various voices contained in "Azaleas" not only fail to complement but also often delimit one another. The testimonies are partial and indecisive, and the story ends with the narrator's doubts unresolved.

Far from providing the solution found in most detective novels, "Azaleas" leaves the collected evidence open to interpretation. The key evidence of Leng Feng's cannibalism is provided when she finally speaks, shouting at Hu: "Eat it up, eat it up while it's hot, hurry and eat it up, hurry and eat it up!" (183). The remainder of the article, which Hu eventually retrieves in Hong Kong, quotes the same words, as Leng Feng's exhortation to the troops to eat Luo Cheng's entrails. Yet even the correspondence between Leng Feng's words to Hu and the phrase quoted in the report may be explained in a less incriminating light, as a delirious repetition of the sentence the Red Guards accused her of uttering and made her confess to. As David Wang remarks, Liu Daren uses the detective story structure to highlight the impossibility of attaining an answer. Liu's fiction gains its force from the gap between our desire to solve the riddle and the senselessness of historical contingency. In Wang's words, for Liu "history is . . . a rupture in meaning, an enigma to rationality."[15] The incomplete sentence becomes in itself emblematic of the inadequacy of testimony and of later readers' tendency to read excessive meanings into it. The *it* in *eat it up* (the Chinese phrase does without the direct object altogether) remains a sign of absence that invites increasingly parabolic readings.

THE CRY OF BLOOD

"Azaleas" addresses in particular the difficulties faced by the author who wishes to reclaim historical memory. The story's title already alludes to the inability to bear witness to trauma. Liu Daren gives new meaning to the phrase in Bo Juyi's (772–846) *Pipa xing* [The song of the lute], "What do I hear from dawn to dusk / Cuckoos cry out blood and monkeys howl mournfully."[16] The idiom has given rise to many explanations.[17] The *Yi yuan* [Garden of oddities] is particularly relevant: "A man walked in the mountains and saw a flock [of cuckoos]. He imitated them for a while, then coughed blood and died. It is said that this bird cries ceaselessly until it emits blood, which is the reason for this case of coughing blood."[18] This interpretation underscores how the bird's call lures the listener to self-immolation. It is also an apt metaphor for the confessions extracted during the Cultural Revolution—the more one spoke, the more one would implicate oneself and others. Even to imitate Maospeak often landed the chairman's avid followers in situations that cost them their lives.

Liu's text takes advantage of the fact that the azalea flower and the cuckoo share the same name in Chinese [*dujuan*] to transfer the attributes of the bird to the plant and create a complex metaphor. Like the singing cuckoos, the azaleas await the self-destructive actions of their beholders. Hu describes the flowers watered by Leng Feng: "These glittering and moist azaleas, by their hundreds and thousands, truly looked as if each of them contained a mouthful of fresh blood, thick and rancid, that crawled out of these many throats, gushing forth slowly but uncontained" (161–62).[19] The flowers stand for the mouths of bloodthirsty cannibals, but also for the self-inflicted wounds of those who open their mouths.

The azalea becomes a metaphor for the pain involved in speaking one's memories, whether of the Cultural Revolution or of the White Terror. Liu Daren returns in this text to an image presented already in Chen Yingzhen's "Qican de wuyan de zui" [Poor poor dumb mouths] (1964), whose title borrows Shakespeare's words, "sweet Caesar's wounds, poor poor dumb mouths" (*Julius Caesar* 3.2.234), to associate bloody wounds with speechless mouths.[20] In Liu Daren's text, it is, rather, mouths that are equated with wounds, evoking not only the silence imposed by mental trauma but also the potential violence committed by speech.

EXILE FROM HISTORY

The literary allusion to Bo Juyi's poem through the title of "Azaleas Cry Out Blood" also indicates the narrator's temporal and spatial dislocation. The cuckoo is said to replicate King Du Yu's lament in exile, an association kept in *The Song of the Lute*. "Azaleas" follows the allusion, weaving together Hu's inability to solve the mystery with his abortive homecoming. Hu is a doubly exiled man, an overseas Chinese living in the United States who attempts in vain to find roots and recognition in mainland China. He and Leng Feng fashion their respective journeys to the mainland as homecomings yet end up reenacting a more profound dislocation. Leng Feng tries to leave her mark on the nation's history but repeats her exile over and over again; Hu aims at understanding the past, assuming that in China he can rely on his outsider's objectivity, only to find himself unable to keep distance from events. Although he tries to bridge the silence created by violence and madness, he cannot provide conclusive testimony. Neither Leng Feng's mad utterances nor Hu's rational inquiry can clarify the past beyond doubt. When attempting to trace their identity to a homeland or an originary traumatic moment, they give the lie to the possibility of return.

That events cannot be historically pinned down is further stressed by the location where the story takes place—Luzhou. History repeats itself as the characters keep returning to the town, the homestead of Leng Feng and Hu's family. It is to Luzhou, also Luo Cheng's ancestral home, that the latter is sent on a mission and where he is caught. In Luzhou, Leng Feng faces Luo

Cheng again and eats his heart. The incriminating evidence against her is printed in *The Luzhou Battle Report*, and presumably it is also in Luzhou that she is "struggled against" and loses her sanity. It is back in Luzhou that Hu meets his aunt. "My blood too," says Hu, "should be traced to that place" (163). Luzhou—which Liu Daren loosely associates with China[21]—is the scene of crime, trauma, and compulsive repetition. History advances only to return to the same place. Hu's journey there is an attempt, doomed from the start, to penetrate the space from where no witness can escape and, in Shoshana Felman's phrasing, "testify from inside."[22]

The place where all events are anchored is elusive and unfixed. Although Luzhou is recorded as an ancient geographic region, the name has long been out of use. Literally, it means "reed islet." Like floating, disconnected, and shifting ground, Luzhou is a spot on which no one can set foot. It is the place of ideological utopia and historical dystopia, the blank space that signals the eternal displacement of traumatic experience. Hu's origins as an overseas Chinese, the allusion to King Du's tragic exile, and the undefined place-name all point out that no one can speak from a stable point in time or space to reclaim the past or even a more abstract "Chinese identity." As a parable of Liu Daren's own position, the references to exile and displacement point to the limitations of writing as a form of communication that establishes common memories with a national community of readers.

MAY FOURTH AND TAIWANESE IDENTITY

Through reference to the Cultural Revolution, an event that shook left-wing Taiwanese intellectuals and forced them to reevaluate their relation to the Chinese mainland and to May Fourth, Liu Daren's text reflects not only on the traumas of the Mao regime but also on the crisis of memory and identity in post-Chiang Taiwan. Ultimately, not only Hu's narration but also Liu's writing itself suffers from historical dislocation. "Azaleas" may be read as the author's examination of his generation and reassessment of the relevance of May Fourth's legacy to contemporary Taiwan. The short story's focus on the fragmented and demented text pays tribute to Lu Xun's "Kuangren riji" [Diary of a madman] (1918), which could be called an "ifdunit," asking if a crime has ever taken place. Both Lu Xun's and Liu Daren's texts are structured as unsolvable riddles since the respective characters are insane and incapable of giving coherent testimony. By claiming to have eaten his own sister, Lu Xun's ranting Madman discredits his diary. Professor Hu's two sources, Leng Feng and the report, have both played an active role in the violence and are, therefore, tendentious and suspect. Witnesses and victims both turn out to be likely accomplices to the crime. As in "Diary of a Madman," the truth is hard to judge, too, because the horrifying experience around which the plot revolves implicates the main characters. Liu Daren has explained, with some unease about crass analogies, that he associates Professor Hu with the moderate May Fourth reformer Hu Shi and Leng Feng with the uncompromising Lu Xun.[23] Leng Feng's name [lit. "cold peak"] may also allude to Feng Xuefeng [lit. "snow peak"], Lu Xun's close disciple and editor, who became the target of several PRC literary purges. Lu Xun's presence is felt throughout the story, both as a source of inspiration and as an icon who needs to be taken down from the pedestal on which Mao put him. "Azaleas" satirizes this distorted reception by letting the report quote the writer crudely and out of context: "Lu Xun said there's only one way to treat an underdog—hit it! Teach it not to bite again!" (188).[24] Lu Xun's critique of modern China—and, by extension, the May Fourth project as a whole—remains highly relevant to Liu Daren.

But the position of Chinese intellectuals in the 1980s was, of course, very different from the situation to which May Fourth was a reaction. Whereas Lu Xun located himself at the point of departure into modernity and debated future courses of action, Liu Daren observes the persistence and exacerbation of the social problems that Lu described. Leng Feng's fate exemplifies the return, in increasingly horrifying forms, of the paradoxes pointed out by Lu Xun. Leng Feng could have signaled personal liberation through love and joining the revolutionary camp; her elopement avoids the destitution that Lu Xun describes in "Nala zou hou zenyang?" [And what after Nora leaves home?]. Yet she meets an even more appalling end. During the Cultural Revolution, the revolutionary generation took Lu Xun's metaphoric reference to cannibalism literally, and "counterrevolutionaries" were sometimes disemboweled and devoured.[25] In telling Professor Hu, "eat it up while it's hot," as if she were presenting her nephew with a bleeding heart, Leng Feng points to the residual cannibalism of May Fourth, which symbolically carries the unfinished Enlightenment project into the 1980s and hands over the task of bearing witness to Liu Daren's generation. Yet Chen Yingzhen, Liu Daren, and other post-Chiang Taiwanese writers can only testify to a history known through silences, madness, and disrupted writing.

Liu Daren has said that he wrote "Azaleas" believing that the time had come to reclaim historical agency and counter the demand of the May Fourth generation to sacrifice oneself for the collective. The mission in the 1980s was, in Liu's view, to differentiate oneself as an individual and to "free oneself from Big Brother."[26] As a result of liberating themselves from the grand narratives and collective memory of Mao's and Chiang's dictatorships, writers turned to creating personal memories. Against the rhetoric of speaking in the name of the masses, the nation, and the revolution, they revisited and highlighted the silences that have long remained unacknowledged. Post-Chiang writers turned to mystery precisely to free themselves from the need to retrace their ancestors' footsteps and instate the past. History would be known as many stories, enriched by the unspoken words that link them together.

NOTES

Unless otherwise indicated, all translations from non-English-language sources are my own.

1. See Sung-sheng Yvonne Chang, *Modernism and the Nativist Resistance: Contemporary Chinese Fiction from Taiwan* (Durham: Duke University Press, 1993), 164. On Chen Yingzhen's critique of modernity as permeated with absurdity and violence, see Chen Yingzhen, "Xiandai zhuyi de zai kaifa—yanchu *Dengdai Guotuo* de suixiang" [Reinitiating modernism: Random thoughts on the performance of *Waiting for Godot*], in *Chen Yingzhen zuopin ji* [Collected works of Chen Yingzhen], 15 vols. (Taipei: Renjian, 1988), 8:1–8. See also Chen Yingzhen, "Bianzi he tideng—*Zhishiren de pianzhi* zixu" [The whip and the lantern: Author's preface to *The Intellectuals' Bigotry*], in ibid., 9:15–21. Lü Zhenghui makes an interesting comparison between Chen's "Zhao Nandong" and Lu Xun's parable of the iron chamber. See Lü Zhenghui, "Lishi de mengyan—shilun Chen Yingzhen de zhengzhi xiaoshuo" [The nightmare of history: On Chen Yingzhen's political fiction], in ibid., 15:214–24.
2. Chen Yingzhen, "Zhao Nandong," in *Chen Yingzhen zuopin ji*, 5:67–149.
3. Chen Yingzhen, "Shanlu" [Mountain path], in ibid., 5:65.
4. For versions of the legend, see *Nihon koten bungaku daijiten* [Encyclopedia of classical Japanese literature], 6 vols. (Tokyo: Iwanami shoten, 1983–85), 1:317–18.
5. On survivors' "postliberation trauma" and "failure to thrive," see, e.g., Henry Krystal, "Trauma and Aging: A Thirty-Year Follow-up," in Cathy Caruth, ed., *Trauma: Explorations in Memory* (Baltimore: Johns Hopkins University Press, 1995), 76–99.
6. Wang Dewei, "Lichengbei xia de chensi—dangdai Taiwan xiaoshuo de shenhua-

xing yu lishigan" [Lost in thought under the milestone: Myth and history in contemporary Taiwanese fiction], in *Zhongsheng xuanhua: Sanshi yu bashi niandai de Zhongguo xiaoshuo* [Polyphonous clamor: Chinese fiction in the 1930s and 1980s] (Taipei: Yuanliu, 1988), 276.

7 Liu Daren, interview with the author, May 29, 1997.

8 Wendy Larson, "Writing and the Writer: Liu Daren," in Martha Sherwood-Pike and Wendy Larson, eds., *Proceedings of the Summer 1986 Intensive Workshop in Chinese and Russian* (Eugene: University of Oregon, Department of Russian/ University of Oregon Press, 1987), 62.

9 Liu Daren, "Fengjing jiu ceng an" [Scenery once familiar], *Qishi niandai* [The 1970s], April 1983, reprinted in Liu Daren, *Dujuan ti xue* [Azaleas cry out blood] (Taipei: Yuanjing chubanshe, 1984), 90.

10 See Liu Daren, "Guguo shenyou" [Magical journey home], *Qishi niandai*, November 1983, reprinted in Liu, *Dujuan ti xue*, 111–51.

11 Liu Daren's "Azaleas Cry Out Blood" was first serialized in *Zhongguo shibao* [China times], March 31–April 3, 1984; it was reprinted in Liu, *Dujuan ti xue*, 153–92.

12 See Shaoguang Wang, *Failure of Charisma: The Cultural Revolution in Wuhan* (Hong Kong: Oxford University Press, 1995), 16.

13 Ibid., 4 (see also 56, 277).

14 The fictitious article resembles existing Red Guard pamphlets; one, e.g., published an article entitled "Zhanduan Liu Shaoqi shenxiang waimao bumen de heishou!" [Chop off the evil hands sent by Liu Shaoqi to the Department of Foreign Commerce!] (*Jingji pipan* [Economical critique], May 29, 1967, 2). Incidentally, a copy of the pamphlet is preserved at the Center for Chinese Studies at the University of California, Berkeley, where Liu studied.

15 Wang Dewei, "Zhuixun 'lishi' de yuwang—ping Liu Daren de 'Dujuan ti xue' he 'Qiuyang si jiu'" [The desire for "history": Comments on Liu Daren's "Azaleas Cry Out Blood" and "Autumn Sun Like Wine"], in *Yuedu dangdai xiaoshuo* [Reading contemporary novels] (Taipei: Yuanliu, 1991), 195.

16 Bo Juyi, *Pipa xing* [The song of the lute], in *Bo Juyi ji jianjiao* [Annotated variorum edition of the collected works of Bo Juyi], 6 vols. (Shanghai: Shanghai guji chubanshe, 1988), 2:685–86 (lines 73–74).

17 The belief seems to have originated in the description of the cuckoo's cry in *Jing Chu suishi ji* [Annals of Chu-in-Jing] (sixth century): "When one first hears the cuckoo's cry, it evokes separation. Trying to imitate the sound causes one to cough blood." Quoted in Lin Yin and Gao Ming, *Zhongwen dacidian* [Encyclopaedic dictionary of the Chinese language], 10 vols. (Taipei: Zhongguo wenhua daxue, 1990), 4:1671.

18 Ibid. See also Yu Shi et al., eds., *Changyong diangu cidian* [Lexicon of common literary allusions] (Shanghai: Shanghai cishu chubanshe, 1985), 463; and Stephen L. Field, "Injustice and Insanity in Liu Ta-jen's 'The Cuckoo Cries Tears of Blood,'" *Tamkang Review* 21.3 (spring 1991): 230–31.

19 The red azalea and the violence of the Cultural Revolution were also linked in Liu Daren's mind through the life of Zhou Shoujuan (1895–1968), a writer famous for his gardening skills. In a book published posthumously, Zhou describes the azalea and tells how he planted it as bonsai. In 1968, Zhou was murdered by Red Guards. Liu Daren, interview with the author, May 29, 1997. See also Zhou Shoujuan, *Huamu congzhong* [Amid flowers and trees] (Jiangsu: Jinling shuhuashe, 1981), 29–31.
20 Chen Yingzhen, "Qican de wuyan de zui" [Poor poor dumb mouths], in *Chen Yingzhen zuopin ji*, 1:153–66.
21 Liu Daren, interview with the author, May 29, 1997.
22 Shoshana Felman, "The Return of the Voice: Claude Lanzmann's *Shoah*," in Shoshana Felman and Dori Laub, *Testimony: Crises of Witnessing in Literature, Psychoanalysis, and History* (New York: Routledge, 1992), 255.
23 Liu Daren, interview with the author, May 29, 1997. Liu's image of Lu Xun as asking for "total self-sacrifice" follows the later (mis)interpretations of the author.
24 The reference is to Lu Xun's "Lun 'feiwei bolai' yinggai huanxing" [On Having to Defer "Fair Play"], in *Lu Xun zuopin quanji* [The complete works of Lu Xun], 32 vols. (Taipei: Fengyun shidai, 1989–95), 6:309–22.
25 Liu Daren was motivated to write "Azaleas" after reading a newspaper report about a man who confessed to having eaten the heart of a "traitor" to the Communist cause. Liu Daren, interview with the author, May 29, 1997. Zheng Yi has recently shown how Party members who took part in the crime were exonerated owing to their record as revolutionary activists in the 1930s and 1940s. See Zheng Yi, *Scarlet Memorial: Tales of Cannibalism in Modern China*, trans. T. P. Sym (Boulder: Westview, 1996).
26 Liu Daren, interview with the author, May 29, 1997.

10

Doubled Configuration: Reading Su Weizhen's Theatricality

Gang Gary Xu

> Every real effigy has a shadow which is its double; and art must falter and fail from the moment the sculptor believes he has liberated the kind of shadow whose very existence will destroy his repose.
>
> *Antonin Artaud*, The Theater and Its Double

Antonin Artaud (1896–1948) could be a perfect hero in the fictional world created by Su Weizhen (b. 1954), a female Taiwanese writer who has been widely read and critically acclaimed over the past two decades. Artaud was talented but single-minded, idiosyncratic yet eccentric, traits shared by Su's protagonists. He resembles Su's characters even more in his innate insanity, his willingness to sacrifice for the cause of artistic completeness, and his lifelong struggle under the shadow of death.[1] Comparable characters in Su's fiction include Fei Min, who commits suicide after the failure of her impossible love ("Pei ta yiduan" [Accompanying him just for now]); Dianqing, who hides behind a tranquil demeanor the haunting memory of her past defiance and the fire of desire rekindled by the two men in her life ("Jiuai" [Ex-lovers]); Fang Jingxin, who elopes with her lover after her mother incarcerates her and humiliates her by stripping her naked in public (*Likai tongfang* [Leaving Tongfang]); and Danne, who repeatedly comes back to the islands of the Pacific Ocean in the hope of winning over his Asian lover (*Chenmo zhi dao* [The island of silence]).

We certainly can compare these fictional characters with Antonin Artaud, but this may lead to a confusion between reality and representation. After all, Artaud, one of the acclaimed representatives of high modernism and trailblazers of postmodernism, is a historical figure. Is the parallel between him and Su Weizhen's obsessive characters a proof of the full representability [*Darstellbarkeit*] of reality in literature? If Artaud himself could answer this question, he would vehemently repudiate such a hypothesis. It is clear from his writings, including that from which the epigraph to this essay is taken, that he fought hardest against precisely the affirmation of the possibility of representing reality in art and literature. Artaud believed that, as an artistic and linguistic representation of the real, every effigy creates a shadow when it is repeated, performed, or re-presented. Artists tend to deny the existence of such a shadow because they fully believe in the power of the symbolic, but the shadow would still exist in metaphysical forms that are untenable, unstable, voiceless, and yet powerful enough to problematize representation itself.[2]

The analogy between a real person and a fictional character is, nevertheless, relevant to understanding Su Weizhen's fiction. The overlap between Su's representation and Artaud's "real" life demonstrates the absurdity and impossibility of Artaud's very existence in a world constructed and supported by the symbolic order. Artaud struggled constantly on the brink of madness during his entire life. While he was painting an overwhelming picture of an ailing society, the society brushed him aside as a psychiatric patient. The very notion of madness, however, is a technological measure employed by the dominant ideology for more effective societal control. As Michel Foucault points out, the mechanism functions by creating a separate division for madness, one completely opposite that of reason. This division becomes one of the three procedures that control, select, organize, and redistribute the production of discourse in society. Together with exclusion/prohibition, these procedures underlie "the will to truth," which "tends to exert a sort of pressure and something like a power of constraint on other discourses." Foucault further emphasizes that the importance of Artaud and other "madmen" in history lies precisely in their challenge to the will to truth: "All those who, from time to time in our history, have tried to dodge this will to truth and to put into question against truth, at the very point where truth undertakes to justify the prohibition and to define madness, all of them, from Nietzsche to Artaud and Bataille, must now serve as the (no doubt lofty) signs for our daily work." For Artaud, the point where "truth undertakes to justify the prohibition and to define madness" is highlighted by the "reasoning" function of the classical theater, where the madman is allowed to speak, but "only symbolically." Even if the madman could step forward, disarmed and reconciled, he would still be "play[ing] the role of truth in a mask."[3] What Artaud chose to do, then, was to denounce such a function of theater by completely abandoning the symbolic in his advocacy of the "theater of cruelty" and in his own life.

We can consider Artaud's theater of cruelty the theater of the unmasked madman. This is where the parallel reading between Artaud and Su Weizhen becomes possible because the latter plays around with theatricality in her fictional writing in such a way that the very division between reason and madness, or between truth and falsity, is brought into question. Of course, there is always danger inherent in such a reading. After all, theatricality in the East and theatricality in the West have different historical trajectories, no matter how effaced these differences have become in the course of more recent cultural trafficking. Therefore, we must constantly remind ourselves of the local particularities and historical specificities of Su's theatricality. The local particularities are related to her "island" image, which, as a trope, points to how insularity is reflected in Taiwan's politics and culture and how the female body is bounded by various discursive practices. The historical specificities have to do with the epoch that witnessed the lifting of martial law in 1987 and the ever-increasing tension among various ethnic and political groups.

It is within these two contexts that I read Su Weizhen's theatricality. For Su, who majored in film and drama in college, theatricality is first and foremost a metaphor for life. It denotes not only the Chinese conventional wisdom expressed by such clichés as "life is like a play" [*rensheng ru xi*] or "a play is like life" [*xi ru rensheng*] but also the postmodern concept of "life imitating/parodying art," which inverts the mimetic theory of art representing life. Here are several examples: "Fei Min looked at his face of youthfulness and cleanness, thinking: in this world there are already too many screenplays that have been performed awfully, there is no need for another one" ("Accompanying Him Just for Now").[4] This is Fei's monologue before the end of the story, and it is followed immediately by the end of her diary as well as of her life. In this monologue, she has come to realize that the love of her life is merely a play and that she has performed the wrong role, or one she never should have chosen. She insists, however, on continuing her performance in order to give a satisfying ending to the "script," in which death becomes the only choice because nothing else is more suitable to end a tragedy: "That day, Feng Zigang was going to leave on an airplane. Dianqing walked him to the gate of the hospital. She was wearing a green-colored light coat. Although it was spring already, underneath the green coat she still wore the blue gown of the hospital. Her smiling face was like the unchangeable ending on the silver screen" ("Ex-Lovers").[5]

The style in this paragraph is reminiscent of Eileen Chang, who was adept at mixing an unusual spectrum of colors with certain moods to create a visual experience at once uncannily spectacular and aberrantly etiolated. The moods are invariably tragic, and the visual effect is created by Chang's adoption of such filmic techniques as close-ups and fade-outs. By imitating Chang's style, Su is able to twist the ostensible eternity of the tragic effect in the smiling face of death by letting that face fade away. What is signified, then, is the segmentality of the life/theater metaphor: life is just another *act* of drama: "This time Quanruyi did not choose a crucial moment in the play to suddenly appear on stage and strike a pose to the audience as she usually did. When the play started, she was already in the center of the stage. Her costume was still the same, incredibly radiant as usual. She was living only for the characters in the play" (*Leaving Tongfang*).[6] This is not just any ordinary moment. Before the play, the whole "military village/compound" [*juancun*] is stirred by the news that Uncle Li is determined to forcibly retain his wife, the "mad" Auntie Li, who mysteriously left home but suddenly returned to the village as a famous actress named Quanruyi. The villagers gather in front of the stage, waiting to see the "fantastic play"—*haoxi*, another conventional metaphor borrowed from the theater—performed by Quanruyi/Auntie Li. This heroine, both "onstage" and "offstage," completely ignores the turmoil in the audience and keeps performing her most adept stage "role." In this particular moment, the author fuses theatricality and reality, performers and audience. The tragedy is, thus, pushed toward its final climax.

These examples show that beneath the theatricality, as understood through the conventional borrowing of theatrical metaphors in fiction, is something else quite unsettling. The reader is forced to ponder these questions: Who is really mad, Quanruyi or the villagers? Which is more true, the tear-jerking romantic movies or Su Weizhen's "realistic" depiction of desperate love affairs? Su plays with the metaphor of theater so skillfully that it is almost impossible to separate madness from reason or distinguish truth from falsity. To further elaborate on this point, in the following pages

I provide close readings of two of her full-length novels, *Leaving Tongfang* and *The Island of Silence*.

Su Weizhen is generally considered one of the "juancun writers" owing to her background and her military experience. However, compared to other writers of this genre, such as Yuan Qiongqiong, Zhu Tianxin, and Zhang Dachun, Su sees the juancun from a quite different perspective. David Wang criticizes Su for "not being able to explore the historical implications of *juancun* culture" in *Leaving Tongfang* because "she puts her emphasis on either tragic or strange love stories or plays (*chuanqi*)."⁷ I agree that she focuses less on the juancun per se than on love legends, for which the juancun culture merely provides a background and an atmosphere. Nonetheless, I want to point out that her "straying" into love stories reveals as much about "the historical implications of the *juancun* culture" as do other juancun-oriented works.

Wang is correct, however, in associating Su's works with such early-twentieth-century romances as *Huayue hen* [Trace of flower and moon] and *Yuli hun* [The peach-blossom spirit], an association based on thematic similarities regarding nonreproductive sex or desexualized love that goes hand in hand with death. We might even be able to trace this theme to a much earlier date, the late Ming, which witnessed the appearance of such witty and highly theatrical stories as Li Yu's "Tan Chuyu xili chuanqing, Liu Miaogu quzhong sijie" [Tan Chuyu expresses love onstage, and Liu Miaogu dies for the sake of love at the end of the play].⁸ In Li's story, a pair of opera performers seeks to consummate their love in death, only to generate a series of tragicomic consequences. There are numerous similar examples in Chinese fiction and drama. The act of dying for love is elevated in these works as the ultimate sacrifice, although it has long been scorned and censured by orthodox literary historians, who believe that there must be a "significance" in the voluntary death, either for the ethical ideal of the Way [*Dao*] or for the abstract notion of the *nation*. Against this background, the literary practice of intertwining love with death is potentially subversive because it challenges the orthodox notion of an absolute and unquestionable cause for individual behavior.

In her earlier writings, Su presents her challenge through her seemingly innocent juxtaposition of two kinds of death. Death for one's nation is touchingly depicted in the short story "Paoze" [Army comradeship], which is but one of the many "military stories" that won her important official literary prizes. Death for the sake of love stunned almost an entire generation of young readers in such stories as "Accompanying Him Just for Now." As Wang points out, this juxtaposition forms an intriguing yet powerful dialectic in Su's fiction.⁹

However, sacrifice, whether related to nationalistic sentiments or individual pathos, is not the end of Su's writings. The love legends may not bring forth "the historical implications of the *juancun* culture," but, using the theatricality of the love stories as an epistemological tool, Su is able to force readers to rethink juancun as a cultural construct rather than a historically specific social reality, which is a reduction of the complicated discursive struggles that have occurred there. This explains why, when she returns to her beloved homestead in the novel *Leaving Tongfang*, she places at the heart of the story a dominant episode in which the military village named Tongfang is "invaded" by an obscure local opera troupe.

To illustrate how theatricality has become an epistemological tool for Su, I begin with a soliloquy in another of her books, *Mengshu* [Dream writing (or, Dream book)]: "I really want to go travel by myself. Now that I have the ability of fully controlling myself, I will not feel suffocated or voided in the atmosphere of loneliness; instead, I will feel calm and stable. At the moment of loneliness, I am not a person but an eye, a heart, that moves around in a tangible space. This is not about living a life but about the state of living (no others, no self); moreover, every single organ lives by itself, and I allow that to happen."¹⁰ Similar monologues are to be found throughout Su's writings. She has even titled one of her most recent books *Danren lüxing* [Traveling alone].¹¹ This motif entails loneliness, containment, traveling in a strange land, and heightened sensitivity when conducting dialogues with oneself. At the center of all these is a figure almost identical to the "solitary philosopher" as elucidated by the German phenomenologist Edmund Husserl. Husserl argues that the actual meaning of things can come only from contemplation in loneliness because, as Bruce Wilshire succinctly summarizes, "meaning is always objectifiable within the mind of a solitary philosopher and in advance of communications between minds."¹² Solitary contemplation requires "bracketing," which blocks the most immediate actuality of things from the mind but allows a focus on many more actualities in the original meaning-giving context. The purpose of such an endeavor is to reveal the essential, which can be found only through imagination that goes beyond the "frontality" of things.

For Su, who enjoys picturing herself as the lonely thinker traveling in the land of contemplation, what the theater offers is a viewing stance that helps bracket out daily existence. Moreover, unlike the movie houses, where everything beyond the film itself is blacked out, the theater is, in general, open to all kinds of social exchanges. When we associate the theatrical performance with actualities in various social relations beyond our immediate daily experience, the essence of things will be revealed.

This phenomenological interpretation helps clarify why theater becomes the center of the narrative in *Leaving Tongfang*. On the one hand, Su elaborates greatly on the complete disruption of the juancun life by the opera troupe. Everything is halted in order to give way to the presence of a stage in the middle of the village: grandmothers are glued to the nightly performance; mothers are no longer interested in real-life rumors; and the children all take advantage of this "vacuum" to run wild. There is a peculiar kind of aura that almost resembles the "magical realist" atmosphere of García Márquez's *One Hundred Years of Solitude*, one of the texts most widely read and imitated by writers in China and Taiwan. It is as if the theater sucks everything into the theatrically unreal. However, the unreal seems to be ultimately real because the familiar world has been bracketed out or defamiliarized so much that some previously undiscovered truths become manifest.[13]

On the other hand, Su makes the theater accessible to the villagers as it helps bracket out any unrelated happenings in the village. She reorganizes the original social relations around the theater to such a dramatic extent that new perspectives on the juancun life are continuously revealed. When Uncle Yuan is entangled in his never-ending love affairs with the actress Li Qiao, the cook Auntie Qiu, and Auntie Li/Quanruyi, the whole village is permeated by an air of madness and erotic excitement. All of a sudden, nothing remains of its former tranquility and idyllic atmosphere, which, in the official discourse of the martial law period, is projected onto a community as peaceful and unitary as Utopia. The love play acted offstage eventually catches everyone's attention and turns their heads away from the repetitive performances onstage, which must yield to the "real drama" in life. In the end, the demarcation between reality and drama is completely obliterated in Auntie Li/Quanruyi's incredible performance on- and offstage.

Since life in the juancun can be so easily dramatized by simply bringing in an opera troupe, we must wonder whether the essence of the juancun culture is from the very beginning nothing but a performance. In other words, the juancun can be very well understood as an unreal construct based on Taiwan's nationalistic myth of "fighting the Communists and repossessing the mainland" [*fangong fuguo*]. That constructedness is not usually questioned because the daily existence of real people seems to cancel or conceal it. The *real* existence of the juancun or a particular kind of juancun culture is a phantasmagoric masterpiece created by ideology, which, according to Slavoj Žižek's powerful critique, "can designate anything from a contemplative attitude that misrecognizes its dependence on social reality to an action-orientated set of beliefs, from the indispensable medium in which individuals live out their relations to a social structure to false ideas which legitimate a dominant political power."[14] Only in post–martial law Taiwan can someone like Su Weizhen call attention to the mechanism of ideology by revealing the absurdity of the reality into which the "immigrants" [*waisheng ren*] woke up, emerging from a trance only to find that they were no longer young soldiers and that the second generation was being interrogated about their fidelity to Taiwan. Ironically, the villagers in *Tongfang* do not have to wait to awake to reality because they have already set up a stage on which they and the troupe are performing a play of their own, one that dramatizes reality in order to reveal its theatrical essence. In other words, the theatricality brought by the arrival of the troupe defamiliarizes the juancun to the extent that its immediate and obvious actuality is bracketed out.

Theatricality has, thus, acquired epistemological significance for Su. But, as illuminating of surrounding things as the phenomenological idea of bracketing is, it has its own limits. For one thing, the phenomenological insistence on the existence of a stable and eternal essence/truth inherently contains the dangerous implication of racial superiority. This superiority is measured by relative approximation to truth, which is thought to be accessible only through symbolic reasoning. In order not to fall into the trap of yearning for absolute truth, we must question the notion that the juancun has a certain "essence" that is approachable through lonely contemplation.

Even Su herself has shown some suspicion in her search for the essential juancun. The narrative frame of the novel is a trip from the city to the village of Tongfang, to fulfill a juancun mother's deathbed wish to have her ashes buried in the place where she spent most of her life. But, as suggested by the title of the novel, the son really makes the trip in order to sever his last ties with the village. Leaving seems possible only after the narrator reveals the juancun's essence in his recollection of childhood memories and his vivid description of everyday life there. However, the stronger the narrator's will to leave, the more acute his feeling of being stuck. The sense of futility conveyed by the narrative voice contrasts starkly with the hermeneutical effort that is made apparent in the novel's theatricality.

The shadow of death starts to darken the blissful picture of childhood when the feeling of gratuitousness becomes increasingly stronger. A good example is the love story between Uncle Gong and Auntie Xi. Just when their love begins to show promising signs, to be on the verge of giving their lives new meaning, Gong mysteriously falls prey to an unknown illness. He keeps flirting with death, frequently going in and out of the hospital. Everyone around him is exhausted, both physically and emotionally. When Auntie Xi receives notice from the hospital of Gong's critical condition, she feels almost relieved. However, what she finds in the hospital is a tomblike silence with no one around. She waits for a full day and night before finally spotting something: "The mobile bed, surrounded by nurses and doctors, all of a sudden appeared as if from nowhere. Moving toward her in the long hospital corridor, in the middle of night, the strange team looked like a parade of death" (347). Because of repetition and prolongation, death becomes nonsignificant; it can no longer be equated with love and sacrifice. Its performativity has completely hollowed out the signified and, thus, made itself an empty signifier. We cannot help but relate this slippage of meaning to Su's questioning of her own search for the essence of the juancun through the dramatization of the dual motifs of love and sacrifice.

It is only regrettable that Su is not consistent in this kind of self-reflection. In order to travel back uninterruptedly to the site of her memory, she must arrange dramatic turns that revive life as well as meanings of life, which form the core of a stabilized individual memory. It therefore does not take long for Auntie Xi to realize that the mobile bed is not the carrier of death but, rather, an uncanny display of revived life and the tremendous effort to save Uncle Gong from the brink of death. If this plot arrangement is abrupt, the reader will certainly be more surprised when, at the end of the novel, Fang Jingxin and her lover, Uncle Yu, make a miraculous return to the village long after everyone saw their burned bodies in the sugarcane field. Even more miraculous and unbelievable is the sudden revival of four-year-old Goudan's language ability: "As soon as he heard the song from the opera, Goudan started laughing and then spoke out the very first sentence of his life: 'Your wife is not some ordinary woman but a snake immortal from

Emei Mountain.' He seemed to have been stimulated by this sentence—a monk and a snake, whose antagonism was already understood by him in a previous life. That theatrical background seemed to have pulled his memory string, which was then tied into the development of the story" (110–11). The miracle is made possible in the linguistic environment created by the power of the theater. Su wants to show that the theatrical context and language can help us retrieve a hermeneutical ability, which will help us penetrate our all-too-familiar surroundings. The original significance in the symbolic is thus "revived" after the theatrical bracketing.

Su Weizhen herself, however, was not able to "leave Tongfang" until she had finished writing her next novel, *The Island of Silence*, a masterpiece that represents her final departure from an insistence on hermeneutical certainty, made possible by her interweaving of the post–martial law body politic with a theatricality that resembles to a great extent Artaud's theater of cruelty.

For Artaud, Western or Occidental theater is dead, a theater without "shadow," because it relies too heavily on written words. By *shadow*, he means the doubled configuration, which can happen only when signs are dispersed into the mise-en-scène to address not the minds but the senses of the audience. Only after acquiring the shadow can theater become independent of literary texts and language itself—an artistic freedom that Artaud dreamed of. Dissatisfied with the dead Western theater, he turned his eyes east, where he located, with ecstasy, the true theater, or the theater with a shadow. He was especially fascinated by the Balinese theater, which displayed a panoply of pure and superior theatrical conventions: gestures; angular and abruptly abandoned attitudes; syncopated modulations formed at the back of the throat; musical phrases that break off short; flights of elytra; rustlings of branches; sounds of hollow drums; robot squeakings; dances of animated manikins; and so on. This is the theater of cruelty, a term that Artaud uses to refer specifically to the theatricality of the "extreme action" that is "pushed beyond all limits." As he puts it, the "cruelty" is "a matter of neither sadism nor bloodshed"—from "the point of view of the mind, cruelty signifies rigor, implacable intention and decision, irreversible and absolute determination."[15]

Reading Artaud some sixty years after he threw the stones of cruelty into the peaceful pond of the theater, I have reservations about some of his ideas, such as his clear-cut and overgeneralized dichotomy between the

Occident and the Orient, between the written and the physical, and between the psychological and the metaphysical. He certainly has sung the praises of the Oriental while bashing the Occidental, but his choice of the primitive Orient over the cultivated Occident is, to a certain extent, a reinforcement of the demarcation between these two and an act of "othering" the Oriental.

Artaud is not the only Western intellectual who looks to the East for alternatives that can solve the problems in the West. Julia Kristeva, for instance, finds in Chinese women's excruciating pain induced by foot binding an "equal claim to the symbolic," as pointed out by Rey Chow, who observes that Kristeva can be regarded as representative of a peculiar attitude that views the East as inherently "primitive." Chow's discussion of Kristeva is very applicable to Artaud as well:

> Anthropologically, the logic that Kristeva follows may be termed "primitive," with all the ideological underpinning of the term at work: the act of wounding another's body, instead of being given the derogative meanings attributed to it by a humanistic perspective, is invested with the kind of meaning that one associates with warfare, antagonism, or even cannibalism in tribal society; the "cruelty" involved becomes a sign of the way the opponents' worth is acknowledged and reciprocated — with awe.

Chow believes that the choice of the "primitive" over the "cultivated" is as problematic as its opposite:

> Much as this act of "othering" China is accompanied with modesty and self-deprecation, which Kristeva underscores by emphasizing the speculative, culture-bound nature of her project, perhaps it is precisely these deeply cultivated gestures of humility that are the heart of the matter here. We should ask instead whether the notion that China is absolutely "other" and unknowable is not itself problematic.[16]

In Artaud's case, we should ask whether the contrast between the Balinese and the Western theater is not itself an act of exclusion, like the division between madness and sanity. The fact that Artaud had never been to Bali and saw its theater only in Paris makes his Orientalist imagination even more suspect. But we must also remember his own confusion between madness and sanity, which destabilizes from the very outset his persistence in distinguishing the Oriental from the Occidental. After all, who would take a madman's outcry for the theater of cruelty seriously?

Su's protagonists in *The Island of Silence* happen to be walking the same fine line between madness and sanity, between primitive desire and cosmopolitan sophistication. Even if the main story of the novel revolves around the encounter between a white man and an Asian woman, the relationship—or the meaningful communication between the two sides—is doomed to fail. It is probably coincidental that Su chose Bali as one of the important places to develop the love story between Chenmian, a well-traveled and highly educated Taiwanese woman, and Danne, a German PhD student engaging in anthropological fieldwork on the cultural behaviors of Pacific island dwellers. However, it is hardly a coincidence that Su Weizhen selects this particular archipelago, which includes Bali, as the major chronotope of the novel. Both Su and Artaud pay attention to the Pacific islands because the insular and isolated environment is ideal for producing a pure and nonlinguistic theatricality.

Ironically, neither Chenmian nor Danne shows any real interest in the Balinese theater that fascinated Artaud. The first night the couple reunites in Bali after a ten-month separation, they choose to go to a local restaurant where they can eat Indonesian cuisine while enjoying the Balinese theatrical performance. Chenmian is not at all impressed: "The theatrical dance had nothing particularly striking. It was merely an earlier form of dance. The only uniquely exquisite thing was the design of the restaurant."[17] Even if we take into consideration the temporal gap that separates Artaud and Chenmian as well as the change brought to Balinese theater by Western tourism, the difference between their reactions is astonishing. After all, Chenmian is a considerably Westernized modern Chinese woman, one who can equally be surprised by the primitive. Her intuitive resistance to the Balinese theater in fact reveals her natural "mimicry" as a "sophisticated" Oriental woman whose ambivalence has everything to do with being "almost the same, but not quite"—to paraphrase Homi Bhabha.[18]

Chenmian's ambivalence nevertheless enables her to see through her relationship with Danne. She makes a calm observation about her lover during the fiery theatrical performance: "Danne drank much less than usual. He raised his glass to congratulate her: 'Happy birthday!' She realized that, from that moment on, Danne had already been trying to establish the pattern of their love. If she wanted to accept, she had to accept from that very moment. The established pattern should then continue until the happening of something that could change the whole situation. On their way back, they ran into a mourning parade. Danne remarked, slightly drunk: 'How touching!'" (109). The "pattern of . . . love" is based on the insulation of remote islands, which stimulates the animal instinct and "primitive passions"[19] of the lovers. Chenmian struggles very hard to ward off the temptation of drunken bliss. She even overcomes her fear of "large pieces of continental land" (102) and goes to Germany in order to observe how Danne lives his normal life at home. From the room across the street, she acts as a voyeur, peeping into Danne's daily existence. She constantly asks herself: Is there a position in that cozy middle-class home for me, a stranger from a remote island, a reminder of Danne's "primitive past" (123–30)? On her sad discovery of a negative answer to this question, she comes back to Asia and, eventually, seeks refuge in the crowds of metropolitan Singapore. It is there, during her promiscuous interaction with a group of elite cultural producers, that she is finally able to link her affinity for islands with her own body: the island is the body, and vice versa.

Chenmian's new understanding of her body comes from a reflection on language, one similar to Artaud's contemplation of the theater of cruelty. As mentioned above, at the core of Balinese theater or the theater of cruelty is the nonexistence of written words. Everything is physically or, in Artaud's terms, metaphysically configured in the space provided by the stage. "In the Oriental theater of metaphysical tendencies," Artaud explains, "this whole complex of gestures, signs, postures, and sonorities which constitute the language of stage performance, this language which develops all its physical and poetic effects on every level of consciousness and in all the senses, necessarily induces thought to adopt profound attitudes which could be called *metaphysics-in-action*."[20]

Su expresses a similar aesthetics of representational immediacy that can become possible only when the language is transparent. For example:

> Zu raised his voice as if he were speaking under oath: "Chenmian, there is no way for people in that period to understand because there were so few facts that were at their disposal." His naked back streamed with beads of sweat, like a crying body. Only under Chenmian's comfort did his heart of tragedy become calmed.
>
> They were putting on a show. Suddenly Chenmian wished someone could see them, learn from them, and record them. They were so aware of each other's rhythm, yes, *without the mediation of language*. (230; emphasis added)

Zu, a Chinese American with the English name of Danne, is the lover of Chenmian's imagined double. The period they are talking about is the nineteenth century, the temporal setting for one of the scripts that Zu is translating. Zu pities those lovers in nineteenth-century English romances who can love each other to death without ever having sex, but he does not realize that he is transcribing his love act with Chenmian into another play, which will become another melodramatic English romance from another age. Only by ensuring that their lovemaking bodies are *seen* or *recorded visually*, as desired by Chenmian, can they prevent their love story from degenerating into another clichéd romance.

Chenmian's wish can be fulfilled only in something similar to what Teresa de Lauretis theorizes as the narrative image, which refers to "the join of image and story, the interlocking of visual and narrative registers effected by the cinematic of the look."[21] By "introducing narrative into the understanding of filmic images," as Rey Chow correctly points out, "de Lauretis is thus able to distinguish *two* sets of identifying relations for the female spectator."[22] The first is the identification with the masculine gaze, but the second, a positive one allowing women to establish their position as subjects, is a "double identification with the figure of narrative movement, the mythical subject, and with the figure of narrative closure, the narrative image."[23] Making woman the locus of double identification avoids her reduction to the image as the object of the masculine gaze. There is one possible confusion, however, in de Lauretis's introduction of the narrative into the image. In considering who is looking, one must not overlook the question, Who narrates? The central issue here has to do with the nature of narration itself—is it not precisely the means by which the male discourse is carried on or the symbolic is constructed? The confusion can be clarified only when we complement the "identification with the figure of narrative movement" with a self-awareness or a critique of the existence of the narrative, a stance that exemplifies the spirit of Artaud's "theater of the double."

In "recording" the visual image of the body, Su also combines the narrative with the image, although in the reverse direction. In order to make the combination possible, she deliberately chooses to write about the bodies' natural "reaction" to each other. Psychological explorations are kept to a minimum; generally, no reasons are given for the characters' actions. In *The Island of Silence*, the psychological aspect has been given up for the sake of the physical configuration. It is the impossibility of exploring the psychological as suggested by Su that makes the physical configuration in language possible.

On the surface, however, the story tells us exactly the opposite: psychological explorations *are* possible. Chenmian is able to retrieve her consciousness, or even her subconsciousness, by creating a doubled self whose life and psychological activity she closely follows. Brought up in a healthy family, Chenmian B has nothing in common with Chenmian A, the original. The reader should expect that Chenmian A arranges a completely different path for Chenmian B in order to experience something different in Chenmian A's own imagination. However, Chenmian B takes a path almost identical to that of Chenmian A, one marked by the same signposts: Danne; the sterling ring; promiscuity; the islands; Duoyou; and Chen'an, the brother/sister who eventually commits suicide owing to gender uncertainty. It is as if one Chenmian is not enough to reveal to the reader her psychological activity; another must be added in order to experience the same thing all over again.

We must, nevertheless, remember the conditions under which Chenmian B appears. She comes into existence when Chenmian bids a final farewell to her mother in prison. Her mother is incarcerated for killing her father, a family tragedy that leaves Chenmian traumatized. When the burden of the traumatic memory is no longer bearable, the psychopathic splitting or the multiple personality disorder produces the second Chenmian. The psychiatrists Bessel A. Van Der Kolk and Onno Van Der Hart state that the traumatic memory is different from ordinary or narrative memory—the latter is a social act, but the former is inflexible and invariable. In other words, trauma cannot be placed within the schemes of prior knowledge and is not available for retrieval under ordinary conditions.[24] In *The Island of Silence*, Chenmian's continuing pursuit of psychological truth in her double proves exactly the impossibility of retrieving and narrating the traumatic memory in ordinary language under ordinary conditions.

A scene in the novel is especially telling. Xin, a bisexual Australian running a publishing empire in Singapore, finds himself aroused by Chenmian's narration of her desire: "He followed Chenmian's narrative order to traverse her entire body, wildly wanting to explore the virginal land that Chenmian opened up for the first time for him. It was also his own land of the pure and the new. The desire for making love and seeking comfort stemmed from so deep in her heart that she discovered the very fountain of it" (200). But, as soon as she makes this discovery, Chenmian stops narrating. Xin is immediately turned off because he cannot complete the act of intercourse without the direction of Chenmian's narration, which is of a kind that functions well in describing ordinary psychological activities but would eventually run into the dead end of language.

Another Chinese novel that deals with the subject of the traumatic memory and multiple personality disorder is Nieh Hua-ling's [Nie Hualing] once-controversial but now highly acclaimed *Sangqing yu Taohong* [Mulberry and Peach].[25] The heroine of the novel, Mulberry, in a long journey through most of the disasters in twentieth-century China, has developed another self named Peach. Peach is daring, nymphomaniac, and always unsettling, to a great extent resembling Chenmian in the yearning to drift. Unlike Su, however, Nieh suggests in the novel a strong possibility of recollecting the traumatic experience. She is able to trace Mulberry's psychopathic past in a remarkably coherent narrative flow. Although on many occasions Nieh presents a fragmentary memory in fragmentary language, the fragments can still be reunited into a meaningful whole. We are shown, for example, some of the Chinese characters randomly picked by the eight-year-old Sangwa in an isolated Taipei attic. These ideographs, *guo* [country], *sha* [kill], *zhan* [battle], *zui* [guilt], etc., when read together, clearly point to the disaster-filled outside world. For Nieh, every word is part and parcel of a meaningful entity, as is the fragmented traumatic memory. By narrating the past as a reflection of the collective catastrophe, Nieh demonstrates not only her mastery of literary language but also her belief in the author's controlling of meaning.

The kind of language found in *Mulberry and Peach* is silenced on Su's islands. Instead of inquiring into Chenmian's double personality, Su simply lets the two Chenmians leave behind forever the site of their traumatic experience and march on in reticence. This "island of silence" is, indeed, the "island of speechlessness" or the "island of unnarratability." In Chenmian's schizophrenic experience, we see the doubled figure, or the shadow, of speech, which is signified by the extreme act of love and the acting out of desire. Underneath, the signified is constantly shifting in undecidability, which, based on the impossibility of recollecting the traumatic, suggests infinite possibilities in the process of searching for the lost memory. This is why Chenmian A and Chenmian B both repeatedly hear the three mysterious yet prophetic sentences: "May I?" "Do you want this life of yours?" and "Leave with me, would you?" There are no answers to these questions; all

Chenmian wants to do and can do is ask them to be repeated again and again, to be endlessly reperformed. These questions can be interpreted as being asked by the voice of the other as the death drive—the more obsessed she is with love and desire, the more intimate with death Chenmian becomes. But death here can also be figuratively read as the death of definite meaning or of the definite mode of hermeneutics.

The island of speechlessness is also the "island of the body." More than once in the novel, Chenmian feels that "the body is an island," referring to its self-enclosure, which resists not only the intrusion of the ever-changing environment but also the control of the mind. What draws Chenmian to Danne/Zu is precisely the kind of body that is pure and free of control: "Zu's body was not controlled by his mind at all. This body could exist independently, being ultimately free. It did whatever it wanted to do" (74). On the one hand, this image can be regarded as the continuation of the idealized body from the martial law period, bearing the mark of simplicity, reticence, self-control, and straightforwardness. On the other hand, the contrast between mind and body reflects the contrast between literary representation and physical configuration.

The pure body image is particularly important to Su because it is the means by which her subjectivity experiences the objective world. Her experience is not achieved through a perfect infusion of subject and object since she refuses to be probed psychologically within a symbolic order; instead, she flaunts the body in a form of textual performance. The real significance of her theatricality lies in her gesture of writing as a performance rather than in her skillful borrowing of the theater as a trope or her epistemology based on the theater of cruelty. The textual performance nevertheless enables her to make sense of the objective world and to become introspective. Here is another revealing segment of her soliloquy:

> Sitting alone in front of the dock, drinking beer, I found companionship in the great silence of life triggered by a fabulous sense of strangeness. My vision penetrated the web of light knitted by people's shadows and stopped at the dark and silent sea, in which a small island of my own is located. Eight days later, I returned to Taipei, bringing with me an incomplete manuscript. An incomplete novel, but not without depictions of real life in the reconstruction of temporal and spatial blocks. Life made me understand incompleteness.[26]

Su won second prize in the first "Million-Dollar Novel Award" sponsored by the Taiwan newspaper publisher *Shibao* [Times] in 1994.[27] The paragraph cited above—part of her essay "Reflections after Winning the Award"— seems to be telling us about understanding the completeness and autonomy in every single segment of life, no matter how incomplete it might appear to be. However, it can also be read as a dialogue between the author and Chenmian, who, more than once, does the exact same thing in the novel: she sits in front of the dock, sipping beer, staring out into the ocean. That "small island" that no one else can see in the darkness beyond human activities refers precisely to the imagined interlocutor in this dialogue between the author and her character.

On the basis of his comprehensive readings of theater, phenomenology, and Kant's notion of experience, Bruce Wilshire proposes that "we experience our bodies only through the-world-perceived-and-manipulated-by-our-bodies." He explains: "The body is such that to look at it is to look back at it from the world; it must be reflected, in a literal and trivial sense (in a mirror), and in a nonliteral and important sense. It might be compared to a transparent instrument viewable only through the mirror of the world it has already manipulated and modified; except the body is not strictly speaking an instrument, nor is the world strictly speaking a mirror."[28] Wilshire takes the body-self completely out of its cultural and political contexts, a move with which I do not agree, but his notion here is relevant to our understanding of Su's textual performance. For Su Weizhen, it appears, writing is not merely the continuation of solitary contemplation. She makes a gesture of writing solitude for the purpose of looking at the self that is looked back at by the world. In other words, she intends to experience her body through "the-world-perceived-and-manipulated-by-[her-body]." Only in her theatricality can the elements of writing, life, completeness in the incomplete, and understanding herself be united into a whole.

NOTES

Unless otherwise indicated, all translations from non-English-language sources are my own.

1 For a brief sketch of Artaud's life, see Susan Sontag, "Artaud," in Helen Weaver, trans., *Antonin Artaud: Selected Writings* (Berkeley: University of California Press, 1976).

2   See Antonin Artaud, *The Theater and Its Double*, trans. Mary Caroline Richards (New York: Grove, 1958), 12.
3   Michel Foucault, "The Order of Discourse," in R. Young, ed., *Untying the Text* (Boston: Routledge and Kegan Paul, 1981), 56, 53.
4   Su Weizhen, "Pei ta yiduan," in Wang Dewei, ed., *Su Weizhen: Fengbi de daoyu* [Su Weizhen: Closed island] (Taipei: Maitian, 1996), 143.
5   Su Weizhen, "Jiuai," in ibid., 155.
6   Su Weizhen, *Likai Tongfang* (Taipei: Lianjing, 1996), 389.
7   Wang Dewei, "Yi aiyu xingwang wei jiren, zhi geren shengsi yu duwai—shi du Su Weizhen de xiaoshuo" [Undertaking both individual's desire and nation's fortune, and leaving aside personal fate], preface to Wang, ed., *Fengbi de daoyu*, 18.
8   Li Yu, "Tan Chuyu xili chuanqing, Liu Miaogu quzhong sijie," in Li Yu, *Wusheng xi* [Silent opera], vol. 4 of *Li Yu quanji* [Complete works of Li Yu] (Hangzhou: Zhejiang guji, 1992), 251–80.
9   Wang, "Yi aiyu xingwang wei jiren," 14.
10 Su Weizhen, *Mengshu* (Taipei: Lianhe wenxue, 1995), 34.
11 Su Weizhen, *Danren lüxing* (Taipei: Lianhe wenxue, 1999).
12 Bruce Wilshire, *Role Playing and Identity: The Limits of Theatre as Metaphor* (Bloomington: Indiana University Press, 1982), 16.
13 There certainly is a connection between the phenomenological concept of *bracketing* and the Russian formalist notion of *defamiliarization*. However, differences do exist. The latter focuses on the discovery of *literariness* by way of defamiliarization, while the former insists on revealing the essence of things in the general sense through bracketing. For the definition of *defamiliarization*, see Victor Shklovsky, "Art as Technique," in L. T. Lemon and M. J. Reis, trans. and eds., *Russian Formalist Criticism: Four Essays* (Lincoln: University of Nebraska Press, 1965).
14 Slavoj Žižek, "The Spectre of Ideology," in Elizabeth Wright and Edmond Wright, eds., *The Žižek Reader* (Oxford: Blackwell, 1999), 57.
15 Artaud, *The Theater and Its Double*, 85, 101.
16 Rey Chow, *Woman and Chinese Modernity: The Politics of Reading between West and East* (Minneapolis: University of Minnesota Press, 1991), 6, 8.
17 Su Weizhen, *Chenmo zhi dao* [The island of silence] (Taipei: Maitian, 1994), 109.
18 Homi Bhabha, "Of Mimicry and Man: The Ambivalence of Colonial Discourse," *October* 28 (spring 1983): 126.
19 The reference here is, of course, to Rey Chow, *Primitive Passions* (New York: Columbia University Press, 1995).
20 Artaud, *The Theater and Its Double*, 44.
21 Teresa de Lauretis, *Alice Doesn't: Feminism, Semiotics, Cinema* (Bloomington: Indiana University Press, 1984), 140.

22 Chow, *Woman and Chinese Modernity*, 19.
23 De Lauretis, *Alice Doesn't*, 144.
24 See Bessel A. Van Der Kolk and Onno Van Der Hart, "The Intrusive Past: The Flexibility of Memory and the Engraving of Trauma," in Cathy Caruth, ed., *Trauma: Exploration of Memory* (Baltimore: Johns Hopkins University Press, 1995), 153–60.
25 Nieh Hua-Ling, *Sangqing yu Taohong* [Mulberry and Peach] (Taipei: Hanyi seyan, 1988).
26 Su Weizhen, "Reflections after Winning the Award" (1994), in *Chenmo zhi dao*, 7.
27 The first prize winner was Zhu Tianwen's *Huangren shouji* [Notes of a desolate man], which is discussed in several essays in this volume.
28 Wilshire, *Role Playing and Identity*, 155.

11

Techniques behind Lies and the Artistry of Truth: Writing about the Writings of Zhang Dachun

Kim-chu Ng

The road leading up and the road leading down
are ultimately the same road.
Heraclitus

A favorite of the Taiwanese literary world of the 1980s, Zhang Dachun has become one of the most important authors in contemporary Taiwan owing to his writing technique, the diversity of his positions, and his technical dexterity, not to mention his sheer productivity.[1] Through his emphasis on technique and his vast oeuvre of fictional works and, to a lesser extent, critical essays, together with his effective use of the literary establishment—lecturing in schools and other public forums as well as garnering a host of major awards (especially those given by *Zhongguo shibao* [China times], *Lianhe bao* [United daily news], and *Lianhe wenxue* [Unitas])—Zhang has managed to institute sensitive reforms in his own way. Thus, he has influenced the course of contemporary Taiwanese literature, including the "discovery" of several talented female writers.

At the same time, this important author has not received as much systematic critical attention as have writers who tend to focus on more specific themes, such as feminist and queer issues. It is also significant that, as a star in the Taiwanese literary world for almost two decades during a period of rapid political and social change and a concomitant unprecedented explosion of social opinion—in short, a period of identity examination (in terms of provincial origin, politics, gender, sexual orientation, and social class)—Zhang seemed to have an *inborn* artistic license. This seems even more the case with respect to the crucial issue of provincial origin. Being a fairly typical second-generation émigré writer from mainland China, he has written several works focusing on the topic of *juancun*, or "military compounds," and many of them have passed the test of time with relative ease.

Zhang's resistance to engaging in identity politics as well as to having his own identity specified[2]—in short, his figurative immunity to issues relating to identity—is, perhaps, ultimately the real problem behind, or the real issue dealt with in, Zhang's novels. Moreover, this "immunity" itself can, perhaps, be seen as a symptom of a larger phenomenon relating to the problems that plague the contemporary Taiwanese cultural scene, and this is precisely what interests me here. This topic is related to Zhang's choice of writing stance as well as his self-designated cultural role. His ideas on language and writing, his beliefs, and his philosophy—in short, his concern with the issue of mendacity—basically require an ideological analysis of his literary style and form. Through such an analysis, we can enter the world that Zhang has, or has not, chosen to probe: that of certain types of Taiwanese intellectuals, whether their attitude reflects postcolonialism or postmodernism. I will complement my discussion of Zhang by drawing comparisons with other contemporary writers, including the prominent Shanghai novelist Wang Anyi and the influential Taiwanese writer Zhu Tianxin.[3]

My reading of Zhang Dachun's work will be oriented around the following three issues. First is Zhang's history of lies and the appropriateness of such lies, the intellectual conditions that they reflect, and their "nonthematic thematic" characteristics. Borrowing the trope of the apartment from Zhang's story "Gongyu daoyou" [Guided tour of an apartment complex], we can summarize this issue by asking, Did Zhang Dachun ultimately ever leave his "apartment"? In other words, why does he continue changing his writing position? What is he ultimately looking for? Second is the earlier, formative periods of Zhang's literary style, his persona, and his ideologies. Third is the relation between enlightenment and commodity aesthetics. In short, Zhang constitutes an important individual case that can, perhaps, shed light on the intellectual conditions and spiritual state of certain novelists during a historical period characterized by excessive mechanical reproduction.

METALIES, OR THE ARTISTRY OF TRUTH

As Zhan Hongzhi has observed, *Gongyu daoyou* [Guided tour of an apartment complex] is "probably the key work in providing a better understanding of Zhang Dachun" because almost all the stories in that collection foreshadow the directions of Zhang's later development.[4] The work's importance lies in the fact that it stands as a figurative bridge spanning the two main periods of Zhang's career—periods characterized by his belief in reality and his belief in language, respectively. Excluding "Qiang" [The wall] and "Touming Ren" [Invisible man], two pieces that are more somber in their handling of Taiwan's political reality before the lifting of martial law, the fundamental tone of his later works is already established.[5] In general terms, it is Zhang's status of being "meta" that has denied him access to certain kinds of truth effect. This quality is reflected in his use of a strong metafictional style and even his abandonment of the use of a target language, or at least his refusal to accept its existence. At the same time, he has abandoned lyricism and tried to deny language any feeling.

From the writings in the *Guided Tour of an Apartment Complex* collection, including the title story itself, as well as "Pangbaizhe" [Speaker of the aside] and "Xiezuo bai wuliao lai de fangfa" [The method of writing a hundred boredoms], to the more recent *Meiyou ren xiexin gei shangxiao* [No one wrote a letter to the colonel] and *Ye haizi* [Wild child], Zhang has inserted himself into the story in a way that raises the question, Can you believe that's me (the author)?[6] In other works, we hear his voice but do not actually see him in the story. He leaves his shadow, smell, voice, and tone, producing an accent [*yudiao*] even more pronounced than the tone [*qiangdiao*] he had previously cited as a prime criterion in his evaluation of works by other novelists.[7] In short, Zhang is present in his works precisely by being absent.

In "Tanbai congkuan" [Frank confessions], Zhang described his process of transformation from the earlier period to the later. About his mass media work at *Zhongguo shibao* from 1979 to 1983, he wrote:

> [This work] led me to gradually emerge from the chrysalis of my uncontrollable, youthful emotion. I started to consider, and later discovered, how other people "narrated." At first, I always used other people's materials in my own writings. Later, I gradually realized that there was actually no need for me to go back and polish up the spoken text of each of my interviewees because each has his or her

own style of speech, which merits being preserved for its own sake. Furthermore, it is only through mastering the unique character of these oral speaking styles that it becomes possible to make a complete and clearer presentation of the material.

Later in that same essay, he continued:

> Observation and experience have allowed me to learn to avoid being too childishly naive and emotional. For quite some time after that, this habit of cold observation and introspective questioning made me quickly develop a distaste for stylized writing. It was difficult for me to "stand by" a certain style of writing a novel or a description. In fact, I could not tolerate a piece of writing that read like a novel, especially those novels that I myself had already written in a certain tone.[8]

To paraphrase a slogan used against the rightists during China's Cultural Revolution, the preceding declaration is a "frank confession, without being too strict." Applied to the lyrical style that Zhang had already abandoned in his own writing, these words sound self-deprecatory. In the first passage, he mentions that social experience had destroyed his original naïveté. Discovering the natural form of people's speech (how they recounted things in their own tones) can be considered taking hold of the secret behind the simulation of truth, the representation of the nature of form. The second passage reveals a certain impatience, a disgust with the writing style, and an intolerance for the "real nature" of novels (i.e., novels that read like novels). Form, for Zhang, is like clothing, and, once used, it can simply be discarded like a pair of battered, worn-out shoes. This coldness and impatience with form, as well as the continued search for newer forms of expression, constitute the basic spirit of works from the later period of his writing career.

Doubts: The Way of Novels

Let us begin by looking at those early works that Zhang wrote before he became impatient with form. *Jiling tu* [Birds of a feather] deals with those times untainted by either techniques of lying or the pains and worries of youth. In certain stories—those about the student who wants to commit suicide after failing the entrance examination ("Xuandang" [Suspended]); the youth preparing for the joint university entrance examination ("Juqing" [Story plot]); the university students who are either thieves or catching thieves ("Zhuofang zei" [Capturing thieves]); the leisurely lives of an old couple ("Zanmen lia yikuai qu" [Let's go together]); and the young writer who pays a prostitute for an interview in order to write a story about the miserable lives of these women of the night ("Alang zaijian Alang" [Good-bye, Alang]) — Zhang wrote in a youthful, naively touching tone or a sorrowful one to convey the sense of being at a loss. Particularly representative examples of the latter tendency are the young thief lacking in social exposure in "Siqiang Feng" [Four strong winds], the young platoon leader in *Birds of a Feather*, and the uninitiated young writer in "Good-Bye, Alang" who indulged in art for society and who wrote for the sake of feelings."

These early pieces fit into the category of what Wang Anyi, in a different context, has described as "maiden works," characterized by an innocent passion that is lost once an author matures: "They are purely perceptual in style and unblemished. . . . They follow self-made logic that does not necessarily involve an extremely rational, blow-by-blow rendition. The author shows a certain condition of being at a loss, as though he is unable to name his very own things." These works project an indescribable distress owing to the fact "that reason has not yet arrived": "There is in [them] a certain ineffable pain — a pain that does not know what it likes or does not like and that is embedded within a very painful and embarrassing topic. . . . Although confused by this world, this pain was brimming with good-hearted intentions. It wanted to accept but encountered only obstacles."[9] The same pains and doubts that characterize the initial stages of writing are clearly visible in Zhang's own maiden works, especially the preface to *Birds of a Feather*, "Shubujinyi eryi" [Writing cannot fully express the meaning].

The preface to *Birds of a Feather* includes some important sections that can assist us in understanding the Zhang Dachun of this period, the Zhang who proposed mendacity as a way of grasping reality. These passages suggest why he said that "it doesn't know what it doesn't like nor what it likes" and why this became "an ineffable pain" as well as why he "could no longer distinguish his own role" and, thus, felt it necessary to write:

> If a novel's interpretation depends on description, then what really constitutes description in a novel? What are the degrees and limits of such description? Can truth in novels ever approach a universal and perpetual standard? Will my personal interpretation measure up to such a standard? Bothered by the strict self-blame that such an interpreter must have, I have repeatedly considered these things. I have spent four years seeking material and adding to my collection, yet

it was not enough to encompass my personal experience. Why should I deal with the many travails of society? I am, then, prompted to ask wherein lies that characteristic of novels of "being worthy of attention despite belonging to one of the 'minor arts'"? And wherein lies the significance of the trivial? . . .

Having stopped writing novels for more than six months now, I often reflect on the following issues: How can I presume that my description is "real"? And how do I prove that my interpretation is not too bold and headlong? Has the cultural imagery that I have created not been distorted? At the very least, the characters in some of my stories are reflections of real people I have encountered. Be they deliberate or not, such reflections are bound to get distorted or changed and, thus, become vague. Then can I say that I exist? Is this merely a question of writing skills? Or is it a case of the writer's rights being overlooked and, thus, magnified?

Viewed from the perspective of modern Taiwanese literary history, Zhang's attitude here is, evidently, a profound response to issues left unresolved by the nativist literature debates of the 1970s. Zhang's claims that "reforms in the literary trends have already passed by" and that "realist sentiments and language have almost become universal characteristics of a new generation of novels" further reveal the self-critical historical context of his remarks.[10]

In response to his own doubts concerning the basis of truth in novels, Zhang's answer is "description," which, for him, is merely a form of hermeneutics colored by personal attitudes. However, the universal applicability of description is itself problematic. By using formulations such as "the strict self-blame such an interpreter must have" and "have I been 'fair' enough?" Zhang touches on the moral responsibility of the interpreting writer who "presents reality through description" as well as the "moral demands" of being anchored in the "real." Expressing a novelist's self-doubt, the questions can be rephrased as: How can the interpreter do it? How can he face the limits of interpretation? How can these limits be overcome? These questions can be further extended to the issue of the nature of fiction: Wherein lies the novel's characteristic of "being noteworthy, although a minor art"? And wherein lies the significance of the trivial? Is this merely a question of writing technique? Or is it a case of the writer's rights being overlooked and, thus, magnified?[11] Or, to borrow Zhang's own recent term, we might ask, What, in the end, do we really mean by the *ontology* of novels?[12]

As a work of fiction, "Good-Bye, Alang" boldly points out that the direct "representation" of another living world is practically impossible. Even if one were to throw oneself into that world, it would lead only to a series of meaningless repetitions and aporia as well as silence and irrelevance. Interestingly, Wang Anyi once had an experience that paralleled that of Alang's lover, in that she conducted interviews in the process of researching one of her works. In "Baimaoling jishi" [Record of events at Baimaoling] Wang writes about her interviews with a number of female inmates in a *laogai* [reform through labor] concentration camp, concluding:

> The interviewees basically fell into two categories: one group underwent interviews frequently, and, because of so much repetition, their accounts were quite complete and logical, and their content was also richer. The other group, however, had less exposure to interviews and, therefore, tended to give sketchy responses. The responses of the latter group tended to be inconsistent, choppy, and off the topic, although they sometimes came up with impromptu performances.

What is more important is the way in which these two sets of data were processed:

> There were two problems in processing the accounts of the first group. One issue involved determining which accounts were real and which were fabricated. The other difficulty lay in assessing the truthfulness of the informants on the basis of their fabrications. In processing data from the second group, the problem was that an understanding of psychology and logic was required to successfully arrange the materials into a complete and reliable body of facts.[13]

Both sets of data had to be reanalyzed. The first set, already endowed with form and possibly having been partially fabricated, needed a reconversion process to bring out the real facts. The second set, after having been given its form, could be arranged "into a complete and real body of facts." Although Wang felt disheartened in "having to listen avidly to the lies told by each of the more than ten women," she was, nevertheless, confident that her sound techniques had enabled her to grasp truth and reality. Through her writing, a simple human life was able to embark on a voyage of nearly infinite "possibility" (318), expressed as a possible way of existence. What this project draws on is not just a prototypical object but rather the self and, more specifically, "an experimental self," which enables it to assume an attitude of profound skepticism.

Narrative is a technology for the production of truth. Using this point to answer Zhang's doubts regarding the role of the interpreter, we can say that the interpreter, fully aware of the limits of his or her own position, can, nevertheless, provide a plausible interpretation. He or she can make it sound perfect, without having to be arbitrary. This is one way of showing the novel's characteristic of "being noteworthy, although a minor art." Yet, because of his doubts, Zhang ultimately abandoned this method, considering it an "unchosen path."[14] In fact, from doubt he turned to negation.

Nevertheless, the pain and the doubts conveyed in "Writing Cannot Fully Express the Meaning" are quite important, in that they clearly illustrate Zhang's belief in realism, as derived from the nativist debate combined with local politics. Zhang also expresses philosophical doubts about the so-called truths pronounced by those in the know. All these factors reveal his unusual sensitivity with respect to the existing realities of present-day society. As a representative second-generation mainlander author, Zhang has written works—both in his early and in his later periods—that either were at odds with prevailing worldviews or offered a revisionist view of historical causes.

By the time Zhang wrote "Frank Confessions," which itself looked back to an earlier period in his career, these doubts had started to condense into a stand of systematic negation. Displacing "affection" [*qing*], Zhang removed the subject's feelings from the object and began to observe with a cold and satiric eye. In the recent essay "Yige ci zai shijian zhong de qiyu: Yize xiaoshuo de bentilun" [A word's felicitous encounter in time: An ontology of the novel], Zhang ventures a response to his earlier doubts about the viability of an "ontology" of novels. For him, that so-called fictional ontology is merely "a word's serendipitous encounter in time." It is "making a mere serendipitous encounter into a serendipitous encounter with one's own goal" and, furthermore, "being like a wide-eyed child encountering a whole new world."[15] In short, it is the pure act of narrating when all possible fictional premises have already been exhausted.[16] These premises serve no purpose other than to merely make the novels read like novels.

Here are faint echoes of the formalist injunction: "Let literature be literature." This demand entails a return to the most basic, as well as the purest, requirement for textual production, which is an inherently reflexive one.[17] Zhang declares that this "reflexive goal" of the novel is antiutilitarian and against "surplus value" and that it is, therefore, necessary to "abandon the idea of using a work to express certain feelings, thoughts, and concepts."[18] To negate fiction becomes an act of using narration to gain access to a more general anthropological significance contained within the actual texts derived from the broader social world. Zhang therefore dismisses as banal the utilitarian dimension of literature's claim to embrace contemporary discourse and proceeds to move in an opposite direction.[19]

In so doing, Zhang returns to his earlier emphasis on the novel's status as a "minor art," together with the "importance of the trivial," which set limits on "the inherent rights of the novelist," so much so that his ontology is relegated to yet another extreme form of utilitarianism. What he tried to revive is the most primitive entertaining function of the novel. For this reason, he is no less banal than the politicians whom he despises for treating the novel as mere cultural adornment or an accoutrement of power or the scholars who regard the novel as the vehicle of great feelings, thoughts, and concepts. Zhang's negation is a typical case of being in the same boat as those who are being refuted because, as Wang Anyi has observed: "Negation is itself bound by rules; and, in fact, one must first obey these rules before negating them."[20]

Accordingly, using Zhang's negation as starting point, I return to the collection *Guided Tour of an Apartment Complex* to discuss yet another problem in his early work: What role must a novelist play, and what was Zhang himself after? In considering these questions, I also inquire into his earlier thinking on the issue of lying.

Negation: "I Disdain"
In "Qingmie wo zhege shidai" [Disdain for my epoch], Zhang sums up his negation of the existing commercialized, banal atmosphere and values of literature in the following terms: "I disdain." He postulates: "I know, therefore I disdain"; "I disdain, therefore I have the ability to know"; "I disdain, therefore I create and I disdain."[21] All these formulations clearly echo the basic tone that characterizes all those works following *Guided Tour of an Apartment Complex*. The proclamation "I disdain" can be understood in two ways. The first reading starts from the pronoun *I*. It is the subject speaking, the novelist playing a role. The other reading focuses on the verb *disdain*, a negating stand closely related to the profound tone that Zhang adopts in his later works. By the logic of the first reading, the disdainful *I* is, to paraphrase Zhan Hongzhi, a careful interpreter who has become transformed into a cynical commentator and performer.[22] Zhang's impatience and his obses-

sion with form lead him to constantly assert his position through loquacious mockery.

In the story "Guided Tour of an Apartment Complex," Zhang appears as a tour guide leading readers through his make-believe world. Furthermore, this guide is not only the creator of an imaginary reality but also a narrator, in much the same way that the woman writer in "Speaker of the Aside" fabricates dialogues and meddles in the lives of others. But, unlike this fictional female writer, Zhang, in his capacity as commentator, has placed himself in the position of being an "external" narrator, one who does not intervene and, thus, maintains a considerable distance from reality. Real events occurring in time are separated by walls, and the tour guide is effective precisely because he can either pass through those walls or simply become invisible. He is always on the scene but cannot be perceived by the participants themselves (by contrast, the protagonist in the story "Invisible Man" uses his illusions and hallucinations to replace or cover up reality). At the end of "Guided Tour," the narrator informs the tourists that the "contents" of the apartment are simply boring and that the act of writing about something boring is itself inherently boring. Similarly, in Zhang's own figurative apartment complex, one can find only these sorts of invisible tour guides, together with their boring narration. This initial premise therefore inevitably entails a logical progression whereby the fictional *I* serves as a tour guide, then narrates, becomes invisible, comments, disdains, becomes bored, and, finally, becomes ubiquitous. *I* disdain, therefore *I* am. And, conversely, *I* am, therefore *I* disdain. Such a disdaining *I*, who comments and performs, never again leaves the apartment. In fact, he cannot leave because it is actually his only home: a home otherwise known as the prison-house of language.[23]

Stories such as "Guided Tour of an Apartment Complex," "Invisible Man," "The Method of Writing a Hundred Boredoms," and "Speaker of the Aside" not only establish the thematic position of "disdaining myself" but also are quite successful in presenting it as a rationalized, textually internalized form. Internalizing his so-called tone that "decides the significance of a work" is the very foundation of the theme of disdain. When serving on the juries for various literary awards, Zhang tends to emphasize the writers' literary tone. In fact, he uses the question of tone as the basis for determining precisely how mature a writer's skills are. He offered a comprehensive discussion of this issue in his essay "Cai yingzi zhao yingzi: Yize xiaoshuo de qiangdiao pu" [Looking for shadows while stepping on them: An emphasis manual for reading a novel], where he notes: "Indeed, a work's tone can be determined by its topic and rhetoric. However, it can also be a kind of a linguistic strategy. As a linguistic strategy, a novel's tone possesses a totally inverse function and significance: readers may be engrossed by it and be drawn into the emotional aspect of the work, or, alternatively, they may detect its satiric aspects. While both possibilities coexist in the mind of the writer, the readers can choose only one of them, effectively choosing either to laugh or to cry."[24] In general, a novel's tone is determined by its theme and, in this sense, constitutes a sort of natural language. The problem, as Zhang sees it, is that the positions of readers and the writer do not overlap and that, even where the writer uses both superficial feelings and satire, readers are free to choose only one of these as a mode of interpretation.

Can satire and superficiality ultimately be combined? Or are they naturally incommensurable? From Zhang's description, these qualities seem to be related at both a linguistic and a metalinguistic level. Believing that he can make them coexist without his readers' awareness, Zhang still underestimates his audience, even though he thinks of them as "worldly" (a position that overlaps with that of the disdaining *I*). It is not a question of readers finding out but, rather, of their superficial feelings necessarily being subverted by the satire inherent in the text. This is because the latter's raison d'être was originally to cast doubts on the rationality of the former, thus denying it. Meaning is, indeed, decided by tone and form, while, by contrast, superficial feelings are just for naive readers and have long been looked down on by the disdaining *I*.

Such a dualistic model of writing is reminiscent of Roland Barthes's definition of myth as "a peculiar system," in that "it is constructed from a semiological chain which existed before it: it *is a second-order semiological system.*" In this system, which Barthes refers to as a *metalanguage*, what is dealt with is not the object of signification but, rather, the original language or signifying system in itself. There are two ways of looking at the linguistic signified: as either "the last term in a linguistic system" or "the first term in a mythological system." The first reading is called meaning, the second form: "The signifier of myth presents itself in an ambiguous way: it is at the same time meaning and form, full on one side and empty on the other. . . . When it becomes form, the meaning leaves its contingency behind; it empties itself, it becomes impoverished, history evaporates, only the letter remains."[25] For readers of mythology, it is precisely because lies have become naturalized that myths are able to exist simultaneously as meaning and as form.[26] Viewed from this perspective, Zhang has unwittingly reproduced mendacious myths, and, in the process, has distorted reality to the point of near nothingness.

In Zhang's later works, there are instances where he perhaps deliberately inserted what he thought to be two coexisting levels of signification. As a consequence, those works' meaning is, ultimately, dominated by the second reading, or level, while the first is always being negated, doubted, and subverted so that it cannot freely represent its signifieds. In fact, the first level always deflects attention, directing it to the second: the disdain for my disdain. Here, what is "meta" is at the same time original and is actually neither post nor prior to the work. Zhang has elevated the stance of "disdain for disdaining myself" to the level of a "transcendental signified," with the result that it has come to constitute his novels' ontology—the word *ontology* perpetually seeking a felicitous encounter.

Zhang has continued to mold form, yet has never stopped negating, and every few years or so has changed genres: from historical novels, to science fiction, to martial arts novels, to detective stories, to legends, and on to reportage and diary novels. What is it that he is seeking? A sense of novelty? Perhaps he is not after anything at all, but, rather, something is pursuing *him*. What is it? Or perhaps we should ask, What is Zhang really hiding from? As he says in *Da shuohuang jia* [Great liar], in the logic of lying "the first commandment of a liar is never to believe oneself." The disdain of a disdainer has haunted him like a shadow, which explains why the act of "disdaining myself" came back to haunt him. The only solution was to continually "write about different things," figuratively looking for shadows even in the process of treading on them. But this provisional solution addressed only the symptoms of the problem because the existence of the disdaining *I* is, in the end, a bottomless aporia, implying a never-ending drift. Zhang noted: that "Lies exist in a symbiotic relation with other lies, in that they mutually feed and assist each other." Because lying is an endless process, "the liar can never look back. He must insist to the very end, until the whole world and history are awash in lies."[27] Unfortunately, Zhang has embedded a self-destructive apparatus within his lies, an apparatus that also serves as the motor for his narrative and, eventually, reveals itself as it reaches exhaustion. As Roland Barthes put it: "The function of myth is to empty reality: it is, literally, a ceaseless flowing out, a hemorrhage, or perhaps an evaporation, in short, a perceptible absence."²⁸ The ultimate result of myth is to evacuate reality and, thereby, render it hollow.

What is crucial here is that Zhang's dual use of superficial feelings and implicit satire has reduced his later novels to nothing but metalies—lies about lies—and not lies per se. After all, it is natural for novels to emphasize the metaform of lies at the expense of real lies themselves.²⁹ Conversely, neglecting the techniques of lying is the artistry of truth and constitutes an underestimation of readers' ability to distinguish this type of writing. As Mario Vargas Llosa observed:

> In effect, novels lie—they can do nothing else—but that is only part of the story. The other part is that, by lying, they express a curious truth that can only be expressed in a furtive and veiled fashion, disguised as something that it is not....
>
> In the deceptions of literature, there are no deceptions.... And there is no deception because when we open a book of fiction, we adjust ourselves to witnessing a representation in which we know very well that our tears or our yawns depend exclusively on the good or bad spell that the narrator casts to make us live his lies as truths and to rely on his capacity to reproduce lived experience faithfully.³⁰

In fact, the problem is not that Zhang has told too many lies or that he has lied at all. Instead, it is that his self-attacking negation prevents him from actually taking lying seriously and also makes him afraid of communicating with his readers at the level of his real feelings and, thereby, exposing himself. He is, thus, reluctant to share his worries and fears and avoids the lyrical mode, calling it instead merely superficial feelings. More seriously, and to take a formulation of which Zhang would certainly not approve and give it new meaning, we could say that this is a sign of his having lost the ability to love and, specifically, an object-relation mode of desire.

From this perspective, Zhang's philosophy of lying actually negates the existing truth of lies (the truth of poetry). He has rendered truth superficial, reducing it to a mere performative posture and supplementary thesis.³¹ From his own explanation of his works, we can see that *Great Liar* exposes a theme further developed in *Sahuang de xintu* [Disciple of mendacity]. The latter expresses even more clearly Zhang's "faith": namely, that he is a disciple who believes in lies. His skepticism is as thorough as that of Descartes, who contended that only doubt itself is indubitable. In Zhang's case, doubt and disdain are two sides of the same coin, and his outlook can, therefore, be summarized aphoristically as: "I disdain, therefore I am."

Like Zhu Tianxin, Zhang is also a second-generation émigré from the mainland and has experienced the spiritual injury brought about by indigenization following the lifting of martial law. Both authors stand guard to protect the dignity of literature, and both use metropolitan Taipei as the realistic ground for their fiction. Similarly, both express a disdain for certain people and things, and both have also became commentators. However, when Zhu attacks that with which she is dissatisfied, she is expressing a desire to protect her beliefs. She believes in the existence of "true feelings" and uses faith to fight despair. More important, she incorporates these attitudes into her writing by probing into and exposing the dead and forlorn corners of society. If Zhang's personal philosophy can be summarized as "I disdain, therefore I am," then Zhu's attitude can be summarized as "I remember because I believe" and "I believe what I remember." Using her personal memory, Zhu rebels against collective amnesia. For the sake of her beliefs and memories, she has dared to expose her personal limitations.[32]

By contrast, Zhang appears never to have abandoned the position that he articulated in "Zoulu ren" [People walking], where he relates: "I gradually discovered that memory, dreams, history, religion, politics, and news reporting are all the same. They all become true once you start believing in them."[33] He has transformed his doubts and negations into an ontology of the novels that draws on a combination of reality and himself. However, it is a pity that this Doubting Thomas and perfect believer of lies is, in the end, not able even to believe (in) himself. As a result, all worldly events become dismal, and nothing is worth believing. There exist two ways of relating falsities. One is technically and theoretically deconstructing the truthfulness of the false texts and even taking the relativistic position that "all books have the possibility of being false" and believing that it is, ultimately, impossible to reveal absolute truth. Even he who has that truth in hand will, nevertheless, continue to suspect that it is fake.[34] The other way is directly revealing the excavated reality itself.

In the literary form of the modern novel, which is basically a Western import, it is difficult to achieve a technical breakthrough as virtually all the techniques and forms have already been nearly exhausted. Most authors develop their own performances on the basis of existing forms. Their works' significance and value, however, depend on the novelty of their survivors' experiences, together with the re-creation of form achieved through their artistry and will. This "[writing] for the sake of feelings" has as its final goal not a display of artistry itself but, rather, the use of artistry to display feelings as well as to accept the beacon of the god the author believes in.³⁵ Instead, Zhang displays the techniques that he takes pride in at the level of an artisan. Yet, despite his eagerness, he nevertheless casts off his tools and strays from the Way, while his perspective as a subject remains limited to language. That can be explained by the fact that, for Zhang, language no longer retains any practicality.

For informed, worldly readers well versed in literary conventions, no matter how complex a writer's artistry and how many cosmetics he has applied, it is easy to detect disbelief in himself in the depths of his literary works. Viewed from this perspective, Zhang's work since his early period has not really changed very much, regardless of how rich and formally complex it may be. All his recent writings share a similar motif and convey a common message, namely, the verbose carping of an intellectual who pronounces: "I doubt, I disdain, I'm not satisfied, I fuck." Although Zhang tries to simulate the styles and forms familiar to his readers, his real purpose is actually to undermine the habits and expectations with which people approach a literary creation. Yet, as a fictional narrative and as a literary form, the novel has a rational interior order that enables it to maintain a certain distance from outside reality, a distance that is, ultimately, difficult to bridge. Unlike news reporting, novels can allude to something only indirectly, not state it outright. The reason they are a "minor art" can, thus, be clearly seen: they cannot actually negate or undermine anything other than themselves (i.e., the negation of the primary-level linguistic system by a secondary-level symbolic system). This is especially true in the case of "metalies" novels.

A performer faces a similar problem, in that, "when an actor imitates the tone of Lin Yanggang in talking about juridical reform, we cannot take his ideas seriously. Instead, we must appreciate the semblance at the level of voice and facial expressions."³⁶ As Zhang observed with respect to *Shaonian datouchun de shenghuo zhouji* [The weekly journal of young Big Head Spring]: "Novels (or journals) are good not because of the story or the opinion they express, much less because of the presentation of the characters. Rather, the quality of the work is contingent on the work's technical design, which traverses different literary forms."³⁷ This formal aesthetics of "elevating narration above all else" actually focuses on the self and suggests a form of hero worship centered on the author:³⁸ the real protagonist is the performer himself, not the language or the plot, much less the work's characters. This aesthetics anticipates a sort of negative rationality, yet a rationality and will that are too subjectivized. It never allows language to carry out its own will and, naturally, never allows the mechanism of the literary work to follow its own logic. Although the writer declares that all complex formal designs are meant to increase the piece's richness and to achieve a breakthrough in existing rules on reading, the performer's omnipresent, negating chuckles reveal the lopsided obstinacy and impetuousness of an enlightener who is fundamentally opposed to the very idea of enlightenment.[39]

From "Frank Confessions" to "Disdain for My Epoch," Zhang has used the tone of a victim in identifying the lies and the monoglossia of the martial law period, together with the post–martial law dismemberment of the value system, the barrage of counterfeit goods, etc., as factors that have contributed to his becoming a "great liar." He has suggested that, under those kinds of historical circumstances, when lies are taken for truth, then even novels that take lying as their starting point lose legitimacy. It is as though only in this way can the world finally rid itself of the pollution of lies. Therefore, even though Zhang's aesthetics and practice have generally been considered to be a reflection of the postmodern and deconstructive ethos of the post–martial law era, the scars of repression at the core of his work reveal how, in reality, he has inadvertently internalized and naturalized the mendacious logic of totalitarianism. Furthermore, he has gone on to uncritically transform this totalitarian logic of lying into a sham postmodernist myth.[40] To resist the world of lies, a self-destructive apparatus has been installed within the literary piece, causing an internal schizophrenia.[41]

IF . . . THEN WHAT?

There's No Story in the City
In Zhang's two ontologies—namely, those of pure narrative and of antinarrative—we can detect a common premise: nostalgia for the native land, manifested in the form of a call for a traditional storyteller, located in the position of the pure outsider. It is only in the presence of this traditional storyteller that the so-called story can come into being in the first place. The storyteller first narrates, then intersperses the narrative with various interferences and shifts in tone, subject matter, and other details. In his outline of these two fictional ontologies, Zhang deliberately lays out a clear position: these storyteller-based ontologies have their own grammar and logic, and,

while Zhang stresses one, he rejects the other. The former is expressed in terms of a conjectural "if," while the latter is expressed through a counterfactual "then what happened?"

A representative example of the first category of works is the story "Ruguo Lin Xiuxiong" [If Lin Xiuxiong] in *Sixi youguo* [Lucky worries about his country, 1988]. The story starts with the hypothetical premise, "If Lin Xiuxiong had never been born, then . . . ," followed by a series of counterfactual situations that explore each of the various possible scenarios in which Lin Xiuxiong might have found himself. As in "Guided Tour of an Apartment Complex," in "If Lin Xiuxiong" the use of these sorts of syntactic structures illustrates the myriad possibilities available with respect to writing technique and the fates of individual characters. The motivation of Zhang's narration actually coexists with its opposite: "If *not* . . . then so and so." A good example of this practice is the following passage from *Wild Child*: "If it had not been for that rainstorm, or even if it had only been a little drizzle, I would never have run all the way home. If I hadn't sprinted directly home, I never would have gotten that damn phone call. If I hadn't received that phone call, I naturally wouldn't have said all those nasty things over the phone. If I'd never opened my big mouth on the telephone, in all probability, my life would be very different."⁴² In the interstices between these "ifs" and "if nots," the lies are set. In other comparable works, the counterfactual "ifs/if nots" are embedded within the tone of the narrative itself, making the premise even more ubiquitous and invisible.

The question "What happened next?" which has the potential to thoroughly undermine the counterfactual premise of the entire narrative, usually appears in Zhang's work in a negative way. For instance, in a discussion of Zhu Tianxin's *Xiang wo juancun de xiongdimen* [In remembrance of my buddies from the military compound], he writes: "Trimming off a novel's plot, action, dialogues, and characters actually deprives readers of an important habit when they read a piece of fiction, that being the habit of asking 'What happened next?' which is then replaced by 'Why did it happen?'"⁴³ Here he turns the question of how to read into the question of how to think. In *Wild Child*, when the narrator listens to her companion relate her sad past, he remarks: "You feel very happy . . . because you actually have nothing to do with the great dangers or immense pain being narrated in the story. You are just sitting there, eating dried snack peas and drinking iced tea. At most, you will be concerned with the question: 'Then, what happened next? And what happened after that?'" (*Wild Kids*, 255 [*Ye haizi*, 115]). The narrative form positions the reader as one who is happy and carefree and who is also a habitual consumer of fiction.

In *Wo meimei* [My kid sister], Zhang writes: "What happened next? That's the question that every reader or writer is continually asking. The instant we ask, 'What happened next?' what we are actually concerned with is time. We express our feelings through the random acts of rescue, satisfaction, and hope that time brings us."[44] As readers, we tend to affirm the redemptive effects of this counterfactual technique. Similarly, its artistic effect is directly affirmed in "Yi qingjie zhuzai yiqie" [Using plot to dominate everything]: "A novel that is plot oriented (or that 'allows the plot to dominate and highlight everything') need not concern itself with how complex 'real human nature' or 'the reality of human nature' is. The novel does not try to create (or 'fabricate') certain 'realistic' characters within its fictional system. All it has to do is make readers return to that very primitive state of 'asking what happened next' and, thus, experience suspense, surprise, satisfaction, and the undermining of the expected plot. . . ."[45] Zhang emphasizes the last point (that of "the undermining of the expected plot") as a proviso against lapsing into banality, but this ultimately seems a weak self-justification. For, when undermining has become a mere formality, it is still possible to have certain expectations. Here, the hypothetical "if/if not" is strengthened into the more didactic "it is like this/it should be like that." Meanwhile, the counterfactual "then what happened" is given a self-contradictory mechanism to become "nothing much really happened later" or "what happened later was, in fact, not what you had expected."[46] In this way, the two ontologies find a common grammatical ground.

Regardless of which ontology is applicable, and setting aside the grammar-ruled view of the world, it is clear that Zhang has, indeed, ultimately failed to leave his linguistic apartment. Here, we must discuss the circumstances under which he produced his stories and narratives and return specifically to the question of his allegorical apartment. The apartment has undoubtedly been identified as the city. Yet, Wang Anyi, a writer from the city of Shanghai, sadly observes that, in fact,

> there is no story in the city. . . . Stories have already fallen apart, and there no longer remains any complete subject matter for the prolix among us to relate.
>
> We no longer find any complete story that we can represent as a comedy on a

rainy day. Only in our hearts do we preserve a certain process, a process that is for us complete and familiar. At times, we go to interview people, hoping to capture the internal processes taking place in the minds of others. But people keep their mouths tightly shut, or else they simply tell lies. In the end, what we understand is only our own self. Therefore, only one recourse remains open to us: namely, that of turning our gaze inward. We can have only stories of our own hearts. As for the city, it has no story to tell.[47]

The disappearance of the story amounts to the disappearance of the object of the narrative. In the capitalist age, the story degenerates into news, which retains value only as long as it is new. The timeliness of news is suppressed by temporal efficiency, and news is, therefore, pushed to the sidelines by debate and discussion. However, a real story cannot be dissipated that way; instead, it retains its original depth, even after considerable time has passed.[48] For Georg Lukács, therefore, the story's degeneration is that of "a concrete possibility" into "abstract possibility."[49] For Walter Benjamin, it is a question of experiencing the disappearance of *Efahrung*, in which all events that have occurred are processed by the mass media, into experience [*Erlebnis*] that causes no shock.[50] Finally, for Jean Baudrillard, "events" are reduced to endless "simulacra."[51]

Zhang not only tends in his later works to direct himself toward the hometown that does not necessarily exist but furthermore constructs virtually all these works by adapting and commenting on recent news stories. "Frank Confessions" gives a hint regarding the origins of his unfeeling narrative: his appetite has been destroyed by news. This helps explain why he cannot neglect the fact that the loss of experiences of a storyless city has influenced the spiritual aspects of his writing and also why he continues searching for new forms, new techniques, and new positions (in both his own works and those of others). Within an overly familiar and fatigued information world, he seeks a little of what Benjamin called shock: a sort of "then what happened" type of personal redemption.

Neither "concrete possibility" (realism) nor "abstract possibility" (modernism) is Zhang's domain. He can only blaze a trail between the two, a trail that begins with the conditional "if." Zhang refuses to enter the interior world to face its shattered pieces, so the stories in his mind lapse into ontological aporia. Unable to become a novelist, he can neither leave nor give up. Furthermore, he has no faith with which to convince himself. Here, we can better understand what Zhang is running away from and why his negation is so feeble and powerless. After all, it is not a case of Adorno's "negation of art" but, rather, more akin to Freud's "disavowal":[52] Zhang disavows his primitive deficiency and his entrenched conservative views on language, novels, and literature. In a city where both storytellers and stories have disappeared, formerly marginal intellectuals have taken their place, and they preach the untimely "minor art" of the novel in public parks, private apartments, and coffee shops.

The Juvenile Period of the Heart and Mind

In Zhang's world of language, he has emphasized two key themes: lying and youth. If we say that *Guided Tour of an Apartment Complex, Great Liar,* and *Disciple of Mendacity* represent a gradual revelation of consciousness, we can use the preface to *Disciple of Mendacity* to probe Zhang's philosophy of writing, specifically, its questions regarding the nature of lying and the nature of belief, together with the giving-receiving relationship between liars and believers. *Disciple of Mendacity* is, in a way, an inadvertent exposition of Zhang's philosophy of writing, while his callous attacks in "Bendan" [Stupid fool] expose his own ideological blind spots. In contrast, works like *Guided Tour of an Apartment Complex, The Weekly Journal of Young Big Head Spring, My Kid Sister,* and *Wild Child* reveal yet another important secret through his indulgence in shameless linguistic acts and his portrayal of the anxieties of youth: the spiritual as well as the mental maturity of the metaliar.

The critic Cai Shiping once compared Zhang's *The Weekly Journal of Young Big Head Spring* to a youthful version of *Great Liar*, noting that it "takes its starting point in a youth subculture unrecognized by adults" and proceeds to "emphasize that the world of adults is nothing but a complacent, ephemeral world," one that can, therefore, be undermined.[53] Yet Zhang still displays his literary techniques for worldly readers. His legitimacy is made plausible by its exact opposite, which, however, helps expose his position and limits. The protagonist of *Wild Child*, who struggles to show off his literary technique and abilities, is, in reality, merely a vagabond child with no experience and merely doing his "practicum." By using "conditionals and counterfactuals," the child roamed imagined city streets only to be bored to death by the grown-ups, concluding that it is better to die young than to grow up.

In *My Kid Sister*, a passage in which the narrator describes the act of making love to a "chick" can serve as an allegory for the creation of literary form, style, and technique:

> Every step, every move, even every thought was like a routine ceremony. We tried to spice things up as much as we could—we'd change rooms, turn on a different light, change our clothing, or switch positions. We would try to change everything we could, but we couldn't change our bodies. That feeling was one of terror. We were both terrified that we would too easily become sick of our partner's corporal shell, and that our partner would become sick of our own....
>
> When the time came that we couldn't actively change anything else, we had no choice but to search for new bodies to be with. (*Wild Kids*, 82 [*Wo meimei*, 112])

Lovemaking, literary forms, and commodities are all the same in that we easily tire of them and then search for novelty and emphasize aesthetics.[54] In fact, they all share a common foundation: needs or desires. The "kid sister," haunted by the fear of getting weary and pregnant, feels no hate. She is, however, afraid of giving birth to someone like herself and, therefore, has an abortion. Her pet phrase, "does it mean anything?" establishes the basic tone of this novel. The anxieties of youth and of growing up, together with the dearth of objects for affection, are illustrated in the following dialogue:

> Those chicks all have at least one intrinsic characteristic in common with my sister—none of them wanted to have a child who was like them.
> "Do you think you'll ever want a child that resembles you?" my sister went on to ask.
> "Like me?"...
> Eighteen years later, I shook my head and went on to answer my sister's question. "If he's like me, he'll never grow up." (*Wild Kids*, 83–84 [*Wo meimei*, 113–14])

The last sentence identifies the frozen time frame of the legitimate position of an eternally rebellious youth, just as the "kid sister" manages to avoid maturity by going insane. Her unborn child—the identity of whose father is unknown—is stifled even before it can come into existence. Similarly, in the novel, dreams and parapraxes give hints regarding the underlying reason for her continual running away, together with her search for both a substitute and a real and realistic untouchable object of her love: she is afraid of reproduction and the womb.

Birth and reproduction, reproduction and rejection of reproduction, all are, ultimately, unable to make the characters feel true sorrow. Zhang himself continues to wander aimlessly and negate himself through form because he refuses to return home. As he himself has remarked: "I have experienced the joy of running away from home through fortuitous encounters, tribulations, and risks—in short, by actively transgressing social prohibitions."[55] He thinks that returning home represents the termination of growth, which is why he has ignored the fact that running away from home is not necessarily a type of growth. Similarly, at the end of *Wild Child*, death is chosen as a way to reject growth, or as a way to start an endless wandering. In fact, it is a confirmation of the termination of growth. It is the fear of loving that results from an inability to love. A character who cannot really feel sorrow ends up in deep sorrow, resulting in stunted growth.

Therefore, libidinal desire is converted into a desire for commodities—and it is not coincidental that Zhang's *Shaonian* [Youth] series achieved unprecedented market success. It can, therefore, be regarded as a successful commercialization of literary techniques. At the same time, it draws attention to the ingratiating attitude embedded within Zhang's philosophy of novel writing: technical and formal innovation are not done exclusively for the sake of art. As Adorno has noted, in a capitalistic market system, artistic innovation is merely a response to the expanding capital reproduction in society, done for the purpose of prolonging competitiveness.[56] The self-destruction apparatus mentioned above is also a mechanism of commodity aesthetics—that of aesthetic innovation. It is an apparatus of artificial obsolescence, a timing device that causes commodities to self-destruct so as to generate new consumer demand.[57] Zhang uses the strength of his own "brand name" to provide his readers with superficial novelty and enjoyment, even to the point of influencing Taiwan's taste in "orthodox" literary products.

CONCLUSION: REPRESENTATIONAL STRATEGIES OF A POWERLESS REPRESENTER AND THE "TAIWANESE EXPERIENCE"

I have proposed in this essay a symptomatic reading of Zhang Dachun's fictional and nonfictional works. Not only have I emphasized his representational strategies in writing about the Taiwanese experience, but I have also stressed the unprecedented artistry of lies behind such strategies. Rather than focusing on questions such as, What writing strategy did Zhang adopt? What Taiwanese experience does Zhang represent? or, What Taiwanese experience does his writing strategy represent? I have explored the questions, Why is it that his writing strategy always presents the inability to represent the Taiwanese experience? and, What does a representational strategy grounded on this inability to represent Taiwan itself ultimately reveal about the Taiwanese experience? From this perspective, the important question is not whether Zhang's works are "postmodernist" or "postcolonial" but, rather, involves the following issues.

First is the unconscious and mythical functions of the artistry and philosophy of lies. This issue involves, first of all, a historical process, that is, a bildungsroman-type reconstruction of Zhang's history of writing. From a historical perspective, his writing career is rooted in the appropriateness of an indigenous, realist literature gradually established in the aftermath of the nativist literature debates of the 1970s as well as the stringent and violent "identification test" that mainlanders in Taiwan had to undergo during this period. This was followed by the post–martial law era, during which hegemonic myths and lies were overturned and replaced by a new, diverse set of lies and myths. In that environment, Zhang, young but sincerely eager to represent the Taiwanese experience, transformed himself—after a process of soul-searching—into a performer specializing in literary acrobatics. Experience was taken over by news. From then on, he could never deviate from a journalistic way of thinking and perceiving things around him.[58] He gradually built up and put into practice his philosophy of lies and formal logic. The diversity of his stands and the proliferation of his works can be said to manifest the phantasm of plurality and the pursuit of the new that characterize post–martial law Taiwan as well as the insatiable needs of Taiwan's people. Yet it becomes apparent that Zhang has built his own lying mythology (in Barthes's use of the term) through his adopted writing strategy. Underneath his diverse stands runs a clear, single, unitary voice: that of a subject who disdains everything. That voice is directed not inward but outward and can, thus, hardly be considered introspective. Instead, it represents the top-down rational tyranny of a dictator. The victim of lies has, thus, become its best spokesman.

Zhang, who demands strict narrative logic (in contrast to the vagueness of poetry) in his novels, has tried to assert control over every stroke of the pen.

His manipulation, satirizing, and undermining of language and form are not merely an attempt to assert his will against language and form; instead, they constitute a form of alienation silently brewing deep inside him. Zhang adopted a habit of mocking how his readers develop their tastes, and, eventually, this set the basic tone for his fiction. This enjoyment of a tyrannical strategy clearly surpasses his thoughts on the pragmatic problems of Taiwan's contemporary history. From this perspective, we can see that Zhang's bildungsromans are actually novels that did not go through an awakening period and the growth of which was, therefore, stunted. His linguistic adventures show that he not only has gradually lost his role and target; he is, in fact, on the verge of losing language itself. All his pronouncements are merely monologues expressing the will of a power wielder.

Second, Zhang always uses the conditional "if" and drops the counterfactual "then what happened" to avoid an insipid technique. This also shows a temporal consciousness distorted by the rapid pace in the city, that is, the loss of the sense of the future. In Taipei, where it seems everything can be rapidly reproduced, all future things bring with them a past tense. Similarly, everything can, apparently, be fictionally performed through the counterfactual logic of the novel; not even experience or the news can escape this fate. Zhang's strategy is to tame, never to reject, although perhaps this taming resembles rejection. This strategy internalizes his logic, whether consciously or unconsciously, and is in his fiction rationalized as a necessary technical element. Events that bear no relation whatsoever to the experiences of actual people, together with those that he has not experienced personally, are further abstracted and lose their perceptual features. This makes contemporary history lose its concreteness and experiential novelty, depriving it of the marks of time, and robbing it of depth. For this reason, even those of his works that appear most pragmatic and contemporary (such as *Disciple of Mendacity* and "No One Wrote a Letter to the Colonel") easily betray their underlying ruin-like layer of the "Great Wilderness" [*Da Huangye*].

Furthermore, Zhang's series of stories centering on rebellious youth reveals a side of him that believes firmly in himself while being still rooted in the mental age of a rebellious child. He is a youth who refuses to grow up, forever bound up in a juvenile rebelliousness. Only in this way is it possible for him to remain at ease in possessing the absolute, then manifesting it in the form of youthful fascism. By writing in this manner, Zhang was announcing that he did not belong to his generation. From the perspective of "representing Taiwanese experience," this temporal regression reflects the anxieties of the new era that has no past and no future, as depicted, for instance, in the figure of Big Head Spring. In the breadth and depths of time, it is impossible to love anything or anyone other than oneself because all others inhabit an unreal space of simulacra, the world of the hypothetical "if." The soul has aged too much, and its ultimate salvation lies in the rapid external renewal of popular commodities.

This explains how Zhang's writing strategy has internalized the mechanism of commodity aesthetics as a component of a symbolic system, which is secondary to that of myth. As the subject of the "self-disdaining" designer of myths and commodities, and with a self-destructive apparatus, Zhang adopts a strategy that is the exact replica of an advertising strategy for commodities. Through his writing, a skin-deep truth belonging to popular trends is made to represent the Taiwanese urban experience: anything new is good.

All the elements of Zhang's stable mythology of lies, eternal youth, and the continual search for new products are all finally interwoven in his method,[59] which represents the self-destructive, helpless, and vacuous sorrow of a certain contemporary Taiwanese man of letters. As for us, we have yet to receive the letters he sent from Troy or Venice. We do not know whether we must continue waiting—whether if it is, indeed, true that "no one wrote a letter to the colonel."

NOTES

This essay was translated by Carlos Rojas. Unless otherwise indicated, all translations from non-English-language sources are his.

1. Zhang himself said: "Every few years or so, I have to 'change the topic' of what I write: from historical novels, science fiction, martial arts novels, detective stories, legends, to the journalistic and diary novels I myself have invented." Zhang Dachun, *Gongyu daoyou* [Guided tour of an apartment complex] (Taipei: Shibao wenhua chuban gongsi, 1994), 363.
2. With the exception of political novels, this condition is almost always classified under a similarly vague term—*postmodernism*. In this essay, I will seek to develop these vague concepts with greater precision.
3. Zhu Tianxin is discussed in more detail in Lingchei Letty Chen, "Mapping Identity in a Postcolonial City: Intertextuality and Cultural Hybridity in Zhu Tianx-

in's *Ancient Capital*" (chapter 13 in this volume), and Zhu's sister Zhu Tianwen is discussed in Ban Wang, "Re-Enchanting the Image in Global Culture: Reification and Nostalgia in Zhu Tianwen's Fiction" (chapter 16 in this volume).

4   Zhan Hongzhi, "Zhang Dachun mianmian guan" [Face-to-Face with Zhang Dachun], in Yang Ze, ed., *Cong siling niandai dao jiuling niandai: Liang'an sanbian huawen xiaoshuo yanjiuhui lunwen ji* [From the 1940s to the 1990s: Essays from the conference on Chinese-language fiction from Greater China] (Taipei: Shibao wenhua chuban shiye, 1994), 368.

5   In "Qiang," Zhang adopted a doubtful stance in dealing with intellectuals belonging to the opposition movement. Both his tone and his deliberations were akin to those in Zhu Tianxin's *Wo jide* [I remember]. In "Touming ren," Zhang's mocking, cynical tone in dealing with the shadowy spy culture of martial law days was closer to his later style. For an English translation of "Qiang," see Zhang Dachun, "The Wall," trans. Chen I-djen, *The Chinese PEN* 58 (summer 1987): 1–21.

6   For an English translation of "Pangbaizhe," see Zhang Dachun, "Speaker of the Aside," *The Chinese PEN* 56 (winter 1986): 75–85.

7   *Tone* can mean one of the following: (1) "language dictated by the material (such as dialogues of a specific role)"; (2) "a novel's narrative tone"; or (3) "special linguistic habits of the author serving as one of the elements of style." Here, I am using the term in the third sense.

8   Zhang Dachun, "Tanbai congkuan" [Frank confessions], in Yang, ed., *Cong siling niandai dao jiuling niandai*, 361, 362.

9   Wang Anyi, "Chunüzuo de shijie" [The world of maiden works], in *Xiao shijie*, January 1997, 170, 171–72.

10 Zhang Dachun, *Jiling tu* [Birds of a feather] (Taipei: Shibao, 1980), 1–2. For an English translation of *Jiling tu*, see Zhang Dachun, *Birds of a Feather*, trans. Hsinsheng C. Kao, in Joseph S. M. Lau, ed., *The Unbroken Chain: An Anthology of Taiwan Fiction since 1926* (Bloomington: Indiana University Press, 1983), 262–75.

11 Zhang, *Jiling tu*, 5–8.

12 Zhang Dachun, "Yige ci zai shijian zhong de qiyu: Yize xiaoshuo de bentilun," *Lianhe wenxue* 13.3 (1997): 14–18.

13 Wang Anyi, "Baimaoling jishi," in *Piaobo de yuyan* [Floating language] (Beijing: Zuojia chubanshe, 1996), 318.

14 Zhang, *Jiling tu*, 6.

15 Zhang, "Yige ci zai shijian zhong de qiyu," 17.

16 This probably explains why Zhang always had a special fondness for his *Da huangye xilie* [Great liar series]. See Shi Jingwen, "Zhang Dachun chuangzuo de shengmingli" [The life force of Zhang Dachun's creations], in Zhang Dachun, *Sixi youguo* [Lucky worries about his country] (1988) (Taipei: Yuanliu, 1990), 239. For Zhang, this series of works was "pure" fiction. Speaking in a more exaggerated way, the point of his pure fiction was to negate the local nativist

literature. Yet the "native" that he alludes to is that of the other side of the strait, just like in Sima Zhongyuan's Shenzhou legends.

17 This technique-oriented tendency can be seen in several of Zhang's pieces, e.g.: "Nage xianzai jidianzhong" [What time is it now?], in *Zhang Dachun de wenxue yijian* [Zhang Dachun's views on literature] (Taipei: Yuanliu, 1992), 101–32, an essay with an emphasis on paying respects to one's forebears; in his discussion of Mo Yan's novellas in "Yi qingjie zhuzai yiqie" [Using plot to dominate everything], in *Wenxue bu an: Zhang Dachun de wenxue yijian* [Uneasy literature: Zhang Dachun's views on literature] (Taipei: Lianhe wenxue, 1995), 139–48; as well as in his interest in the maiden work of Cheng Yingzhu in "Ningshi shijian" [Gazing at time], in *Wenxue bu an*, 149–56.

18 Zhang, "Yige ci zai shijian zhong de qiyu," 15.

19 In "Qingmie wo zhege shidai" [Disdaining this age of mine] (in *Wenxue bu an*, 12), in which he quoted from the classic Qing dynasty novel *Rulin waishi* [The scholars], Zhang said that he was "impatient with writing contemporary articles," thereby showing his unwillingness to compromise with existing literary values.

20 Wang, "Chunüzuo de shijie," 171.

21 Zhang, "Qingmie wo zhege shidai," 13, 13, 15.

22 For the three sides of Zhang viewed from a historical perspective—namely, those of the presenter, the commentator, and the performer—see Zhan, "Zhang Dachun mianmian guan," 365, 369, 373. From a structural point of view, the Zhang of the later period is a cross between the commentator and the performer.

23 Zhan observes: "In the eyes of Zhang Dachun, language not only fails to communicate; it also is a surrounding wall. Everyone lives in his own prison-house of language." Zhan Hongzhi, "Ji zhong yuyan jianyu: Du Zhang Dachun de xiaoshuo jinzuo" [Different kinds of prison-houses of language: Reading Zhang Dachun's recent fiction], in Zhang, *Sixi youguo*, 8. This, in turn, speaks to the issues of grammar and of history and memory, both of which are discussed in more detail below.

24 Zhang Dachun, "Cai yingzi zhao yingzi: Yize xiaoshuo de qiangdiao pu," *Lianhe wenxue* 13.12 (1997): 15.

25 Roland Barthes, *Mythologies* (New York: Hill and Wang, 1972), 114, 117.

26 Barthes points out that there are three ways of reading myth: the method of the producer of myths (accepting its ideological effects); the method of the scholars of mythology (decoding and understanding what has been distorted); and the method of the readers of mythology. See ibid., 189–90. Each method leads to a different result. This essay follows the second method: namely, that of deconstructing and understanding functions.

27 Zhang Dachun, *Da shuohuang jia* (Taipei: Yuanliu, 1989), 70, 37, 310–11.

28 Barthes, *Mythologies*, 143.

29 In his reading of *Da shuohuang jia*, David Wang has discovered a similar problem:

"I tend to think that the lies that pervade the novel are one too many, such that the reader simply finds himself at a loss. A liar may be able to tell many tall tales, but the difficult part is to make the lies sound real in the end." David Der-wei Wang, *Xiaoshuo Zhongguo: Wan Qing dao dangdai de zhongwen xiaoshuo* [Narrating China: Modern Chinese fiction from the late Qing to the contemporary era] (Taipei: Maitian, 1993), 98.

30 Mario Vargas Llosa, "Truth in Lies," in John King, ed. and trans., *Making Waves* (New York: Farrar Straus Giroux, 1996), 320, 327.

31 Here, Jameson's description of postmodernism is relevant: "A new kind of flatness or depthlessness, a new kind of superficiality in the most literal sense." Jameson also points out that "the waning of affect" is one of the characteristic signs of postmodernism. Fredric Jameson, *Postmodernism; or, The Cultural Logic of Late Capitalism* (Durham: Duke University Press, 1998), 9, 10.

32 See Zhang Dachun, "Yize lao linghun: Zhu Tianxin xiaoshuo li de shijian jiaoli" [An old soul: The temporal angle in Zhu Tianxin's novels], in *Wenxue bu an*, 23–32; David Der-wei Wang, "Lao linghun qiansheng jinshi: Zhu Tianxin de xiaoshuo" [The past incarnations and present life of an old soul: Zhu Tianxin's novels], in Zhu Tianxin, *Gudu* [Old capital] (Taipei: Maitian, 1997); and Huang Jinshu [Kim-chu Ng], "Cong Daguanyuan dao kafeiguan: Yuedu/shuxie Zhu Tianxin" [From Grand Prospect Garden to café: Reading/writing Zhu Tianxin], in Zhu, *Gudu*.

33 Zhang Dachun, "Zoulu ren," in *Gongyu daoyou*, 56.

34 Yang Zhao also perceptively observed this basic dilemma: "If one were to tell nothing but lies, why tell? If everything were lies, why tell them? If everything were lies, does it mean that 'how it is said' is no longer worth observing and is, therefore, beyond evaluation?" Yang Zhao, *Wenxue, shehui, yu lishi xiangxiang: Zhanhou wenxueshi sanwen* [Literature, society, and historical imagination: Essay on postwar literature] (Taipei: Shibao, 1995), 211.

35 David Wang once candidly made the following comments about "Jiangjun pai" [The general's monument], one of Zhang Dachun's best-received works: "Its literary creativity is not particularly strong, and the characterization of minor characters is also quite rigid. Evidently, the author had in mind something like García Márquez's *One Hundred Years of Solitude*, but he lacked García Márquez's imagination for the bizarre, and the work was not long enough to allow him to achieve comparable depth." David Der-wei Wang, *Zhongsheng xuanhua: Sanling yu baling niandai de Zhongguo xiaoshuo* [Heteroglossia: Chinese fiction from the 1930s and 1980s] (Taipei: Maitian, 1988), 273.

36 Zhan, "Zhang Dachun mianmian guan," 372.

37 Zhang Dachun, *Zhang Dachun ji* [Zhang Dachun collection] (Taipei: Yuanliu, 1992), 181.

38 Zhang, "Nage xianzai jidianzhong," 113.

39 In the important essay "Renren aidu xiju" [Everyone loves to read comedies], Zhang made an important distinction between the author's roles as interpreted

by Wang Zhenhe and Huang Chunming: Wang tried to stand on the same spot as his target readers (the man on the street in his hometown), while Huang "stood with 'this little town' and shouted at readers who were not from 'this little town.'" From this, it can be seen that, as a writer, Zhang actually stands above his readers, a position occupied by the satirist: "the moral stand of the satirist is often above those of the mocked." However, the mocked are not just the characters and events that he has written about but include his readers. This is what best differentiates Zhang from the others. See Zhang Dachun, "Renren aidu xiju," in *Zhang Dachun de wenxue yijian*, 162 (reference to Wang), 163–64 (first quote), 156 (second quote).

40 For a discussion of the postmodernist aspects of Zhang's works, see Chen Changfang, "Houxiandaizhuyi yu dangdai Taiwan xiaoshuo chuangzuo" [Postmodernism and contemporary Taiwanese literary creation], in Zhang Baoqin, Shao Yuming, and Ya Xian, eds., *Sishi nian lai Zhongguo wenxue 1949–1993* [Chinese literature from the past 40 years, 1949-1993] (Taipei: Lianhe wenxue, 1992), 243–46.

41 *Wo meimei* [My kid sister] adopted the framework of a trial therapy session with a confession-like method.

42 Zhang Dachun, *Wild Child*, in Michael Berry, trans., *Wild Kids: Two Novels about Growing Up* (New York: Columbia University Press, 2000), 139. (Most of the translations of both *Wild Child* and *My Kid Sister* [see n. 44 below] are modified from Berry's.) For the original of the passage in question, see Zhang Dachun, *Ye haizi* [Wild child] (Taipei: Lianhe wenxue, 1996), 19.

43 Zhang, "Yize lao linghun," 131–32.

44 Zhang Dachun, *My Kid Sister*, in Berry, trans., *Wild Kids*, 72. For the original of the passage in question, see Zhang Dachun, *Wo meimei* (Taipei: Lianhe wenxue, 1993), 96.

45 Zhang, "Yi qingjie zhuzai yiqie," 142.

46 Similarly, in "Chunshui hanwa" [Spring water and winter frog], the last chapter of *Sahuang de xintu* [Disciple of mendacity] (Taipei: Lianhe wenxue, 1996), Zhang himself eventually makes a cameo appearance. In *Meiyou ren xiexin gei shangxiao* [No one wrote a letter to the colonel] (Taipei: Lianhu wenxue, 1994), he surfaces now and then as the author. In the end, the author and the colonel engage in a dialogue. In "Jiaru" [And supposing], the penultimate chapter of *Ye haizi*, Zhang writes: "And supposing that you don't say a damn thing, supposing that you could forget everything before it even happened, and supposing. . . ." *Wild Kids*, 255 (*Ye haizi*, 212).

47 Wang, *Piaobo de yuyan*, 431.

48 Walter Benjamin, "The Storyteller," in *Illuminations*, trans. Harry Zohn (New York: Schocken, 1999), 90.

49 See Georg Lukács, "The Ideology of Modernism," in *The Meaning of Contemporary Realism*, trans. John Mander and Necke Mander (London: Merlin, 1962), 17–46.

50 Walter Benjamin, *Charles Baudelaire: A Lyric Poet in the Era of High Capitalism*, trans. Harry Zohn (London: Verso, 1983), 117, 154.
51 See Jean Baudrillard, *Simulacra and Simulation* (Ann Arbor: University of Michigan Press, 1995).
52 See Theodor Adorno, *Aesthetic Theory*, trans. C. Lenhaedt (London: Routledge, 1984).
53 Cai Shiping quoted in Da Touchun [Zhang Dachun], *Shaonian Datouchun de shenghuo zhouji* [The weekly journal of young Big Head Spring] (Taipei: Lianhe wenxue, 1992), 185.
54 Qi Bangyuan writes: "The speed with which Zhang Dachun changes his writing strategy is comparable to the way we churn out new technological products today." Qi Bangyuan, "Pingjia *Shaonian Da Touchun de shenghuo* zhouji" [A critique of *The Weekly Journal of Young Big Head Spring*], in Da, *Shaonian Datouchun*, 174.
55 Zhang Dachun, "Taojia/huijia de haizi: Tonghua zhong suo yincang de jinzhi yu kewang" [Running away from/back to home: The forbidden and anticipatory elements hidden within youth], in *Wenxue bu an*, 20.
56 Adorno, *Aesthetic Theory*, 31.
57 Kim-chu Ng, "Xiaoshuojia de teji biaoyan" [Authors' special performance techniques], *Zhongguo shibao: Kaijuan zhoubao* [China times: Weekend supplement], September 19, 1996, 40.
58 With the possible exception of his *Da huangye xilie*, which is a spiritual dialogue with the novels written by first-generation émigré novelists like Sima Zhongyuan, Zhu Xining, and Gao Yang.
59 In contrast with his novels, Zhang's prologues to his various works are straightforward and sincere (forgive me for using these antiquated, premodern terms), and they can, therefore, be taken as a feedback system supplementary to his fictional narratives.

SPECTRAL TOPOGRAPHIES AND CIRCUITS OF DESIRE

PART FOUR

TAIWAN IS AN ISLAND. Between the various regime changes, the multiple languages, and the waves of immigration and emigration that have repeatedly transformed Taiwan, the geographic reality of the roughly fourteen-thousand-square-mile island located about a hundred miles off of China's southeast coast becomes one of the most compelling symbols of Taiwan's identity. At the same time, however, the transnational flows of populations, cultures, and political power across Taiwan's geographic borders underscore Taiwan's embedded position within a transnational network of culture and power. Since the late Ming, Taiwan has been governed by a variety of foreign powers, including not only the Dutch (1624–62) but also the Japanese-born, mixed-race Zheng Chenggong [the pirate Koxinga] (1662–83), China's own Qing dynasty (1683–1895), the Japanese (1895–1945), and, finally, the Nationalists (1947–87). These regime changes were frequently accompanied by dramatic population shifts (e.g., about a quarter of Taiwan's population is estimated to have returned to China following the Japanese takeover in 1895, and approximately a sixth of Taiwan's post-1949 population consisted of Nationalists who had begun to flee the mainland in the late 1940s) and concerted efforts of cultural assimilation.

Each of the final five essays in this volume foregrounds Taiwan's geographic dimension, together with its position within a broader transnational network. Ping-hui Liao begins with a consideration of Wu Zhuoliu's 1942–43 travelogue *Nanking Journals*, which describes the author's trip to China to escape the oppressive Japanese colonial regime in Taiwan and his resulting disenchantment with the contemporary China that he encounters. Liao argues that this travel account enables Wu to develop a notion of Taiwan's "alternative modernity" as distinct from Japan's and China's respective modernizing projects. Lingchei Letty Chen, in her reading of the second-generation mainlander author Zhu Tianxin's novel *Ancient Capital*, looks at the ways in which Zhu's literary rendering of Taipei is directly indebted to Kawabata Yasunari's rendering of Kyoto in his 1961 novel *The Old Capital*. Chen argues that Zhu's transnational borrowing of Yasunari's earlier novel itself mirrors *Ancient City*'s own depiction of Taipei as a hybrid intersection of multiple transnational flows. The relation between transnational movement and local concerns is developed even more acutely in the recent work of the Malaysian-Chinese author Li Yongping. Carlos Rojas considers Li's 1992 novel *Haidong qing* and its unofficial 1998 sequel *Zhu Ling's Travels in Wonderland*—specifically, the way in which Li uses the figure of the Taipei city map to interrogate the relation between Taiwan and mainland China. Focusing primarily on Li Ang's 1991 novel *The Strange Garden* and her controversial 1997 collection *All Sticks Are Welcome in the Censer of Beigang*, Chaoyang Liao argues that Li's works transpose themes of reciprocity and exchange from a social level to a psychic level. Finally, Ban Wang considers recent fictional work by Zhu Tianxin's sister, Zhu Tianwen—in particular, the way in which that work seeks to capture Taipei's current status as what Saskia Sassen would call a global city.

12

Travel in Early-Twentieth-Century Asia: On Wu Zhuoliu's "Nanking Journals" and His Notion of Taiwan's Alternative Modernity

Ping-hui Liao

While the novel *Yaxiya de gu'er* [Asia's orphan] (1945) by Wu Zhuoliu (1900–1975) is often hailed as a masterpiece about Taiwan's difficult transition from colony to postcoloniality, the same author's travelogue *Nanjing chagan* [Nanking journals (lit. "Mixed feelings toward Nanking")] (1942–43) has received relatively little attention.[1] Although brief and sketchy, *Nanking Journals* in fact prefigures the plot and theme of *Asia's Orphan*. Hu Taiming, the protagonist of the novel, spends some time in Nanking, and, except for the marriage episode, his life there comes close to what the narrator experiences in the *Journals*. In this essay, I look at this short piece of travel literature in relation to Wu's other major writings and particularly to his notion of Taiwan's alternative modernity. I also refer to such works as *Shina yūki* [Travels in China] by Akutagawa Ryunosuke (1892–1927), memoirs by Ishikawa Kinichiro (1871–1945), and others to illuminate the text and context of *Nanking Journals*. In examining the travelogue and its implications for comparative study of societies and cultures, I draw on critical remarks by Edward Said, James Clifford, and Homi Bhabha on travel and border crossing.

EXOTIC MEMORIES OF FAMILIAR AND UNFAMILIAR PLACES

To avoid confusion, I should clarify that *Nanking Journals* is also the title that the editors gave to Wu's travel writing collected after his death into one volume.[2] Made up of factual reports of journeys to other parts of the world and nostalgic accounts of places revisited, the collection *Nanking Journals* (as distinguished from the single travelogue "Nanking Journals") is a series of travelogues ranging from objective accounts to exotic memories. The narratives vary from the minutely factual to the imaginary at the most personal level. In "Yin Fei youji" [Journeys to India and Africa], for example, Wu gives practically every detail regarding his itineraries; at one point, he even calculates the exact mileage that he has flown (194–95). On the other hand, several of his memoirs about his hometown and the school at which he taught early in his life reveal how places help constitute personal identity. In most cases, Wu as the narrator is either an insider addressing his former friends and colleagues or an outsider and a tourist who comments on the exotic sights and sounds.

An essential part of the volume, "Nanking Journals" is in many ways unique, the author assuming an ambivalent role, neither insider nor outsider, in a place that is both familiar and strange (or even *unheimlich* [uncanny]) to him. He is both a participant in and an observer of the fast-changing community. But he is more often a comparativist of cultures and societies, recollecting and reflecting on people and places he encounters at different times and with different mind-sets. The style is hybrid, with the narrator appropriating the voice of a journalist and of a cultural critic. Probably like Wu himself, people have difficulty adopting a single perspective in relation to what has been said about China in the 1930s.[3] This is even more the case with regard to Chinese and Japanese narratives concerning the fate of modern China. The challenge of attaining a proper distance and perspective has to do, I argue, with Wu's notion of an alternative modern Taiwan.

Wu informs readers from the start that the journey to Nanking was partly a result of his desire to get away from Taiwan, at the time still Japan's colony. Having taken a job as a reporter for *Dalu xinbao* [Mainland news], he set out on January 12, 1941, for China and, "after staying in big Shanghai for some time, went on to visit Nanking and stayed there for a year and three months." During those fifteen months—January 1941 to March 1942—Wu's notion of an alternative modernity slowly evolved. "Before I dwell on the topic of Nanking, the capital of ancient China for over four hundred years, let me reflect on the Chinese national character, an issue seemingly so remote and indifferent. Having a long history, China appears to be permanent and unchanging," he speculates. "Much has been said about the Chinese national character. However, I don't think any of the scholars, experts, and anthropologists have so far grasped the essence of China. For they largely make far-fetched judgments or have dangerous assumptions based on historical facts. One cannot understand China without comprehending its national character. Even the Chinese people don't have a clear picture about themselves" (51).

As neither a "foreigner" nor a "Chinese," Wu nevertheless has a keen eye and often comes up with illuminating stories drawing on comparative studies of Chinese and Japanese societies, of ancient and modern cultures. While critical of Chinese bureaucrats and corruption in many arenas, he is fascinated by the Chinese art of survival and by its highly flexible, albeit pragmatic, sense of social existence. He comments: "Misfortune begins with one's birth, and the most unfortunate is to be born a Chinese. But, if one has a lot of money, one finds this country most carefree and enjoyable. Such is the Chinese reality" (61). Under this reality principle, a large number of social activities—card games (mah-jongg), dining, theater, public bathing, teahouse gathering, for example—gain profundity. The ways in which the system of social signification operates baffle as well as fascinate Wu: "These people don't aim at specific targets in life or work for certain inherent values. They simply grasp whatever opportunities come their way. Everything is up to the dictates of fate. Nowhere in the world have I seen a race like the Chinese, so leisurely waiting for opportunities to turn up" (71). One could easily fault Wu for such a stereotypical representation of the Chinese and even associate it with similar condescending comments by E. M. Forster in *A Passage to India*. For instance, the latter novel remarks at one point: "When that strange race nears the dust and is condemned as untouchable, then nature remembers the physical perfection that she accomplished elsewhere, and throws out a god—not many, but one here and there, to prove to society how little its categories impress her."[4] However, Wu here is not trashing the commoners whom he encounters in Nanking. This is more evident if we juxtapose his account with what Chinese intellectuals and Japanese scholars said about the situation at the time.

TRAVELS IN CHINA

The first few pages indicate that Wu's journey to Nanking was determined by complex factors, among them desires to escape Japan's colonial culture in Taiwan and to embrace the fatherland—China. Before he left for China, Wu read a number of Japanese books on the "backwardness" of the country.

He was familiar with the Chinese classics, particularly high Tang poetry on life in the ancient capitals. In a sense, this is a homeward-bound journey, but it is also something exotic. For Wu was considered by his countrymen to be both Chinese and Japanese-Taiwanese. Informed by Japanese accounts of China, which aimed to symbolically undermine the so-called Middle Kingdom and to give it the derogatory name *Zhina*, Wu might have read a book like Akutagawa's *Travels in China* and found himself similarly caught in China-Japan antagonisms.

As Stephen Tanaka and Shu-mei Shih have demonstrated, a great number of Meiji intellectual leaders advocated the idea of Japan "parting with Asia" or becoming the first modern Asian imperial power.[5] To attain this goal, Japan was to replace China, asserting its desire to be a worthy counterpart of the West in the Orient. Not only was *Zhina* introduced as a Japanese transliteration of the Western word *China*, but more scientific terms such as *toyoshi* [Oriental historiography] and *genbun itchi* [unifying writing and speech] were also invented to construct Japanese modernity and identity. Anti-Chinese sentiments were developed and disseminated in the form of colonial education to other parts of Asia, most notably Taiwan, Korea, Manchuria, and Shanghai. The first and most successful Japanese colony, Taiwan was for fifty years (1895–1945) considered a site for the "South Advance" Project. Japanese was designated Taiwan's national language, and it is estimated that, by 1920, more than 20 percent of Taiwanese had taken Japanese names.[6]

A book full of sneers and derision, condemning Chinese civilization in all sorts of ways, *Travels in China* was a product of Akutagawa's journey to China in 1921 under the aegis of *Osaka mainichi shinbun* [Osaka daily]. The acclaimed author of *Rashōmon* and a prominent intellectual, Akutagawa was very popular among Japanese readers. The travelogue was a big hit in Japan when it came out. Akutagawa's "China" is totally the opposite of modern Japan: dirt, urine, and prostitutes on the streets and snobbish, if not pretentious, intellectuals everywhere betray the backwardness of the Chinese national character. Another author writing in a similar vein is Yokomitsu Riichi (1898–1947), who, in his novel *Furo to ginkoo* [Shanghai, 1928–32], regards the semicolonial city as a "waste dump of Asia," embodying all the grotesque and filthy elements completely unthinkable to a Japanese. Scholars have indicated the ways in which Japanese writers during the 1930s used and abused the subject of China in a very sophisticated mode of cultural translation.[7] These writers helped disseminate unfavorable images of China among Japan's common readers, and Chinese radicals studying in Japan internalized such images. A notable example was Lu Xun, who created the prototypical figure Ah Q to parody the Chinese national character. Another representative figure was the tortured Yu Dafu, whose stories about Japan are packed with such expressions of despair and self-hate as: "The way the Japanese despise the Chinese is like the way we despise pigs and dogs." "Oh, China, China, why can't you become rich and strong," one of his protagonists laments.[8]

TRAVEL AND DIASPORIC MEDIATION/MEDITATION

In *Nanking Journals*, Wu can be said to reinforce the point about China's inferiority, but with a difference, as I argue below. In several important ways, Wu deviates from the Japanese and Chinese narratives of the gaze. Japanese intellectuals constantly drew on Japanese landscape to condemn or to avoid confronting things Chinese. Wu is both repulsed and attracted by the daily life he witnesses in Nanking. He muses on the discrepancies between what he has read about China and what he sees, between the gruesome destiny the Japanese predict for China and the unfathomable vitality of the nation in dismal reality. While nostalgic for the golden past, he never loses sight of what is actually happening in everyday life. The *Journals* entries reveal his balanced views on the conflicts of interpretation concerning the fate of China between Japanese and Chinese intellectuals. His time in Nanking therefore enabled him to better comprehend cultural differences and to conceive Taiwan's alternative modernity as separate from Japan's developing and China's undeveloped modernity projects.

Several times, Wu compares the past with the present, citing Tang poetry to comment on ruinous scenes in the dark corners of Nanking. But, more often, he compares and contrasts Taiwan and Nanking in terms of sartorial and gender differences. For example, he feels that, next to Western dress and Shanghai fashions of the time, his shirts and trousers are too narrow and shabby (54–55). Even his friend Mr. Zhong's mansion with its spectacular views causes him "to lose his usual confidence" (58). Chinese women "tend to be softer and quieter," unlike Taiwanese women, "who frequently raise their voice and are rather talkative, especially when there are more than three around" (79). But he finds Taiwanese girls to be more passionate and dynamic, with better figures (58). Generally speaking, he believes that

Chinese women have benefited from the climate and traditional Confucian teaching and, as a result, are more refined and elegant. However, several incidents suggest otherwise. For instance, on his way to Nanking, he sees a young girl with richly decorated lace shoes who doesn't bother to wipe her own shoe marks off the train seat before sitting down again after reaching for her suitcase on the overhead rack (55). At other points, he similarly remarks: "Public baths in Nanking leave a lot to be desired" (60); "As for pure water, there is not much" (70). A lot of money must be spent on services and tips, and valuables are stolen by maids. Most elementary school education is conducted in unsafe and unhealthy buildings. Despite the general poverty and depravity, the Chinese cannot afford to lose face. They indulge in gambling, bragging, feasting, and showing off. The most deplorable sights, however, are the beggars practically everywhere.

All these observations come close to what the Japanese writers say about China in the 1930s. But Wu's account is a tormented and often ambivalent narrative that tries to disclose the Chinese national character in a comparative framework. He sees not only the miserable existence on the mainland but also the inadequacy of the Japanese vision of a collapsing Middle Kingdom. He believes that, by recognizing "what China is and is not," one can really appreciate the greatness of that culture. The Japanese accounts available at the time were simply superficial and self-serving, for they emphasized China's failures and problems without really understanding them. Wu comments: "A great number of Japanese tourists have visited Hanshan's temple and felt much disillusioned. They don't know how to adopt Zhang Ji's wondering perspective, alighting from the boat by the maple bridge, in order to closely appreciate the toll of the bell." As a result, he suggests, the Japanese tend to misconstrue a "great and coherent culture" (119) as corrupt at its very core.

Wu is upset with the Japanese narratives regarding the prevalence of opium use, foot binding, and corruption. These "uncivilized" social practices admittedly do exist, but, for him, they are not to be taken as representing Chinese culture. After all, Wu points out, Japanese and Chinese share a common written script, although there are noticeable differences in the use of the characters [*tongwen yichu*]. Despite its present difficulty, China reveals an amazing totality and integrity. To negate its achievements by singling out a small portion of its social ills is not only unfair but also misleading and absurd (119). On the other hand, Wu is rather ambivalent about his own "Chinese" cultural identity. He constantly returns to the young girl's sitting on her own dirty shoe marks and the beggars on the street, and he is baffled by the dominance of favor networks and private ties. On top of this, he is not a native Chinese speaker: his Taiwaneseness turns out to be helplessly entangled with the "double and split time" of psychic and national identification, to paraphrase Homi Bhabha.[9] This can be understood in the sense that he has both a "deficit" and a "surplus" of Chinese national representation and cultural membership. After all, Taiwan had been severed from China and ceded to Japan in 1895. However, the majority of the Taiwanese population came from southern China in the late Ming, and the ties to Chinese culture were strong.

Thus, in terms of "microsociological" or "micropolitical" orientation, as defined by Etienne Balibar in his recent discussion of Franco-Algerian relations, Wu had difficulty seeing himself as a member of Chinese society.[10] Making the situation more complicated, Japanese colonialism's culture left the Taiwanese themselves in limbo—neither belonging to the universalist category of being culturally Chinese nor possessing a Taiwanese particularism that colonization was attempting to repress. To claim a Taiwanese identity in China during the 1930s was to put oneself in the dangerous position of being a spy and a traitor, a position on which Wu later elaborated in *Asia's Orphan*. With all these complexities in mind, Wu never let his nostalgic feeling for China get in the way of confronting the mainland and directing his gaze inward, to reflect on Taiwan's alternative modernity in response to Japan and China. In this respect, he differed from several Japanese travelers in early-twentieth-century Asia. To illustrate this, I briefly return to a passage by Akutagawa, that reveals his pride in and nostalgia for the Japanese landscape:

> When I went to the East Asia Common Culture Academy, walking on the second floor of the dormitory, we saw a sea of blue young barley through a window at the end of the hallway. Here and there in that barley field, we saw a cluster of ordinary rape blossoms. Far beyond them we saw a huge carp streamer over a number of connected roofs. The paper carp was blowing in the wind and animatedly fluttering into the sky. This one carp streamer changed the whole scene for me. I wasn't in China.

"I felt as though I was in Japan," he continues. "But when I approached the window, I saw Chinese farmers working in the barley field before my eyes.

I felt angered, as though they weren't supposed to be there. Coming all this way to see a Japanese carp streamer in the Shanghai sky gave me a bit of joy."[11] Akutagawa both sees and passes over Chinese farmers working in the barley field because he shifts his attention to an imaginary center and envisions something that lies elsewhere and is out of place in the present.

THE RESIDENT TRAVELER

In this regard, the travel experience of Ishikawa Kinichiro could not be more revealing. A part-time Japanese teacher at the Taipei Middle School (1907–16) and full-time instructor at Taipei Normal School (1923–33), he was instrumental in introducing watercolors to Taiwan. Self-taught and dedicated to Japanese nationalism, Ishikawa was, at first, strongly influenced by modernism, particularly English impressionistic and realistic landscape watercolors. He was not very active at home and was considered a conservative artist belonging to the rather popular school of naturalism in the Meiji period (1898–1907). In the Japanese imperial army, he was an officer and interpreter who fought bravely against the Chinese (1900) and the Russians (1904–5) in a series of battles for a Manchuria under Japanese rule. In October 1907, he was appointed interpreter for the colonial government in Taiwan. He also became a part-time art and language teacher at the Taipei Middle School. During those nine years in Taiwan, he was, in many ways, an ambivalent teacher and colonizer. In some of his watercolors, he glorified victories over the natives. He toured the island widely and depicted exotic aboriginal memories in realistic detail. At the same time, he was also involved in founding the Lan-tin Tea Klatch to promote cultural exchange and to interest other Japanese artists and officers in Chinese and Taiwanese art and literature. He even organized a public exhibition of his works in 1914, one of the first in Taiwanese art history. Despite his accomplishments as an artist who made use of his impressive local knowledge, Ishikawa was still an officer and a colonizer, as demonstrated not only by the subjects of his watercolors but also by the colonial governor-general's appearance at the exhibit.

However, the situation was different when Ishikawa made his second visit to Taiwan. In September 1923, his Tokyo home was destroyed in a major earthquake. A former colleague, then principal of the Taipei Normal School, sent a telegram informing the despairing Ishikawa that he would be welcome in Taipei with a full-time teaching post. Left with no family, Ishikawa accepted the offer and spent another nine years in Taiwan. The intellectual milieu there in 1923 was very different from that of the previous decade. Now the colonial policy was under the charge of civilians rather than admirals or generals, as Hara Kei, Den Kenjiro, and others came to power. The death of the seventh governor-general, Lieutenant-General Akashi Motojiro, in October 1919 finally gave Prime Minister Hara Kei the opportunity to make the kind of reforms in the governing structures of Taiwan and Korea that he had long favored but found difficult to implement during the reign of Goto Shimpei. Hara Kei was able to appoint Den Kenjiro (1919–23) as Taiwan's first civilian governor-general and to charge him with reforming the colony.[12] These men managed to survive political struggles, first by doing remarkably well in the colonies, particularly in Taiwan, and then by ousting domestic opponents when the latter mishandled riots in the colonies. Under the policy of integration and equal treatment, of making the colonized useful subjects of the Japanese emperor, the arts and humanities were increasingly encouraged as means to tame the Taiwanese. (Before his departure for Shanghai, Wu Zhuoliu was employed as a Japanese teacher devoted to such a cause.)

As a result, when Ishikawa returned to Taipei in 1923, the painter found himself in a different cultural atmosphere, and his approach to art education had shifted from British and Japanese modes to a more French orientation, one emphasizing direct outdoor interaction with the environment. To facilitate his teaching, he translated Japanese art textbooks into Chinese and supplied local vocabulary wherever necessary. As the Taipei Normal School was a major college for future teachers, Ishikawa's influence on local artists was understandably strong, even though his ties with Japanese politicians were undercut by his civilian and teacher status. Several students later became outstanding watercolorists, including Lan Yindin (1903–79) and Hong Ruilin (1912–97). A number of transnational factors contributed to the ambivalent and benevolent roles that Ishikawa played in these years: the unexpected earthquake that shook his house and his livelihood; his recent tour of Europe and his exposure to modern French painting; the warm welcome he received from his friends in Taiwan and his position as a civilian and an art teacher; and the emergence of Taiwanese artists and a cultural elite that was beginning to win recognition in Japan. Finally, new developments in Korea and Manchuria forced Japan to readjust its colonial policy. All in all, the material culture that Ishikawa confronted in 1923 was quite different, and several of his paintings from the period reflect this, depicting numerous local subjects, so many that he has been claimed by some scholars to be an integral part of modern Taiwanese art.

However, during these nine years (1923–33) Ishikawa also deliberately suppressed the use of rhetorical devices—metaphor, in particular—in comparing the Taiwanese and Japanese landscapes.[13] During his first visit to Taiwan, for instance, he composed lyrics on the similarities between Taiwan's coast and that of Nagasaki; and metaphoric expressions abound in his articles on Taiwanese and Japanese art, suggesting ways to see one through the other. But, when he returned to Taiwan as a full-time teacher, his perspective was dramatically changed: he deliberately tried to set Japan apart from Taiwan. If Taiwan's mountains and hills impressed him as spectacular, they were but derivative of the more sublime Fuji. To Ishikawa and many other Japanese artists and scholars, the Chinese and Taiwanese landscapes were much cruder than and, hence, inferior to those of their homeland. Every scene served to remind them of the essentially inimitable and uncontestedly beautiful or sublime Japanese scenery.

This is where Wu departed from such artists as Akutagawa, Ishikawa, and even Lu Xun. His hermeneutical codes were paradoxically supplied by two metropolitan centers—Japan and China—to which he had no relation; furthermore, it was in the rift between them that his sense of an alternative selfhood developed. When Wu left for Nanking, Japan was waging wars against China and Southeast Asia; its control of Taiwan was tightened, with military staffs regaining power. So the political situation was different from that of Ishikawa's second visit to Taiwan. The psychic structure of identification with either China or Japan was, therefore, very mixed. Unlike Lu Xun and Yu Dafu, who both readily rejected China in a desire to embrace Japanese modernity, Wu regarded his visit to Nanking as a visit home, a spiritual quest, and an eternal return. However, like those writers, he was appalled and greatly disillusioned by what he witnessed on the mainland. On the other hand, he hated to be considered a Taiwanese or a Japanese colonial subject; that was the primary reason for his trip to Nanking to begin with. Yet he expresses a sense of good luck when he contrasts China with Taiwan, for the latter seems to him more advanced as a beneficiary of Japan's modernization projects. According to Wu, ambivalent sentiments toward China and

Japan are a natural outcome of Taiwan's unfortunate, marginal geographic and cultural location between the two great nations.

Many of Wu's remarks on cultural difference indicate that he was deeply troubled by the sense of lost and split identity. About the athletics meeting at the National Central University, he wrote: "In Japan all activities of the meeting would be in order and follow the program to every detail. Even though the Central University did prepare its program, nothing matched it. One had difficulty identifying the beginning and, for that matter, the end." He continued: "Students, observers, and the athletes rushed to the sports arena in a confusing commotion. Even the judges were having problems telling them apart. . . . In spite of the tumult, however, they seemed to be able to run things according to the program one way or another. I stood in awe and in great admiration of the ways in which the Chinese always managed to come up with Chinese solutions to their problems in a most amazing manner." In great amazement, Wu found that everybody seemed relaxed and in no hurry to get things done: "If the events should fail to run smoothly, time would resolve them. There is always order in the midst of chaos" (84).

COMPARATIVE STUDY IN CULTURES

Wu comments at many points, and in rather ambivalent terms, on the "favor" and relationship networks crucial to Chinese everyday life. People often build relationships over and across all sorts of networks, to gain favors or to extend them to other network members: "Nannies, servants, wards, and waiters at teahouses are integral parts of Chinese society. They have forces behind them. Seemingly powerless, they can easily accomplish what would be tremendous tasks, once their network is put to use. We shouldn't forget that, under the shadows of social disorder, these people help get things done in vital ways" (75). Even the servants and maids have to be tipped in order to keep society running properly. Compared to the Chinese, the Japanese are extremely neat and immaculate, to the point of being mysophobic. The Chinese leave their ancient buildings and national treasures in ruins, whereas the Japanese keep the temples of Kyoto and Nara in good shape. In spite of their poverty, however, the Chinese spend a great deal of energy maintaining their looks, to preserve "face." For Wu, two features immediately distinguish a Chinese person from a Japanese: shoes and hair. The Chinese like to polish their shoes, to make them shine, and they "put so much oil on their hair that even flies would slip on the surface and fall" (85).

Nevertheless, for Wu, it is ultimately the geographic immensity and undecipherable mystical elements in their national character that differentiate the Chinese from other Asians. The Chinese inscrutability is, in part, a result of the mainland's long history of social suffering: people have gotten so used to war, famine, suppression, disease, torture, and a whole assemblage of other human problems that they have essentially become indifferent to collective catastrophe, contingent misfortune, or structural violence. "They have no expressions, and it would not be easy to hear any comments on current affairs," Wu observes (84). The lack of a public sphere, however, should not obscure the fact that the Chinese way of evasion is an art of survival and a method of improvisation developed out of a specific cultural context in which political persecution is imposed on the discovery of circumstantial evidence. "In other parts of the world, there may be laws instated to protect individual freedom and to seek happiness without fear or uncertainty. From foreign perspectives, Chinese people may seem indifferent, but things are actually more complex than that," Wu explains (85).

In his succinct comparative account of two Asian cities—Nanking and Osaka, the ancient capital of Japan—Wu finds Nanking much grander in scale and better protected with its innumerable fortresses (106). The most remarkable feature of the Chinese national character, according to him, is its ability to sustain all historical changes while still maintaining its integrity. Foreigners always find it very hard to become integrated into Japanese society, but Wu meets several Japanese girls dressed in Han Chinese clothing and readily taking up Chinese forms of life. This is, in part, the result of the Confucian ethics of harmony and the people's adaptability from witnessing so many uncertainties and casualties over the past five thousand years. China offers opportunities to all in total freedom and based on simple lifestyles (115). Opportunism in various forms has pushed people of different classes to soar, but it has also helped shape the habits of gambling and opium use, to the dismay of most radical intellectuals.

As a number of critics have pointed out, clothing or fashion is a site displaying cultural difference. On his arrival in Nanking, Wu discovers that his garb is simply too narrow and short: "Compared to the Shanghai robe of grand style, it seems so out of place and almost unpresentable" (55). He is constantly attracted by the ways in which young Chinese women—in particular, high school and college students—blend traditional (or Confucian) spirituality with modern Western cultural expressions (79). However, he also finds many of them to be artificially fashionable, swayed by the most recent trends. In contrast, Taiwanese women are healthier and more straightforward. This is a point made more explicitly in the novel *Asia's Orphan*.

Wu's most traumatic encounter is at the Cock-crow Temple [Jiming si], where he meets a great number of beggars: "From the main office all the way up to the hilltop, beggars with varying deformities line up" (91). The horrifying sight reminds Wu of pictures of torture chambers in hell that he saw as a child during a visit to a temple. An encounter with a beggar who comes after him for alms with heartbreaking sobs proves even more aggravating and embittering. Throughout the *Journals*, Wu repeatedly refers to the beggar episode and the Shanghai girl's shoe marks on the seat as traumatic scenes that showed him Taiwan's radical difference from China, together with its alternative path to modernity.

ALTERNATIVE MODERNITY AND DISCREPANT COSMOPOLITANISMS

Travel, as James Clifford suggests, tends to bring about diasporic mediations between places and cultures "inseparable from specific, often violent, histories of economic, political, and cultural interaction—histories that generate what might be called *discrepant cosmopolitanisms*."[14] That is to say, foreign sites are inevitably discomforting or unsettling, putting into question one's worldview or sense of cultural belonging. In the *Journals*, Wu reveals his "mixed feelings" [*chagan*] about his stay in Nanking. His experience in the city both binds him to and detaches him from the imaginary homeland—China. On the one hand, he realizes that Japanese intellectuals' accounts of China are misleading. A traveler and a resident, he might well have appreciated China and its modernity in a number of ways. On the other hand, he has already been influenced by his exposure to Japan's colonial and modernizing projects in Taiwan; this puts him in a different mode, if not necessarily a more progressive temporality. He cannot be coeval with the Japanese and Chinese times, for he inevitably finds himself defined by the two contesting modernity projects. The abundance of beggars in Nanking only foregrounds the more advanced socioeconomic situation in Taiwan. However, as a colonial subject and a traveler, Wu belongs neither to Japan nor to China. It is in relation to Taiwan's ambivalent role between the two and its different rate of progress—behind or ahead—that his sense of alterity developed.

In this regard, Edward Said's notion of the traveler versus the potentate and James Clifford's notion of everyday practices of dwelling and traveling should both be rethought and made more complex.[15] The travel theories advocated by these two critics tend to build on a model of center versus periphery and the West versus the rest. My examination of Wu's travel narratives suggests that narrative identities are formed and unformed in the process of debunking cosmopolitan myths about the cultural other. Regarding the economy of nonmovement or the tension between movement and fixity, Clifford adumbrates: "A focus on comparative travel raises the question of dwelling, seen not as a ground or starting place but as an artificial, constrained practice of fixation."[16] The home ground must be seen as a contested site where specific historical trajectories and forces meet and negotiate with each other. By recognizing discrepant cosmopolitanisms, one may adopt the discursive strategy of nostalgia and exotic memories, as did Ishikawa. But Wu Zhuoliu's narrative seems to suggest that he traveled in the time frame of an alternative modernity. The more he looked closely at China and Japan, the more alienated he became from both. That was the starting point of his journey into Asian orphan consciousness.

Consequently, Wu uses the analogy of a fig [*wuhuaguo*] or a Taiwanese forsythia [*lianqiao*] to describe the sociocultural situation of Taiwan in relation to its fatherland and colonizers—the Japanese and then the Guomindang as manifested in Wu's *Wuhuaguo* [Fig or fruit without blossom] (1970) and his posthumous *Taiwan Lianqiao* [Forsythia, or entangling connections] (1986). A passage in *Asia's Orphan* succinctly illustrates his nuanced observation regarding Taiwan's alternative modernity: "One day, as Taiming stands in front of the garden meditating, he suddenly discovers the fig already bearing fruit, ripe and plump, although only here and there behind the huge leaves." The protagonist reasons: "All beings have two forms of life, either as Fusan flowers, which bloom beautifully without producing seeds, or as a fig, which takes no pride in providing pretty blossoms except bearing fruit in silence, unknown to the outside world." The picture of a branch of Taiwan lianqiao cutting across the fence and freely reaching out is even more suggestive: "Those branches motioning upward or extending in all directions have been trimmed, leaving only this branch, which is lucky enough to develop according to her own will."¹⁷ The image of absolute freedom may be a bit of wishful thinking on the part of Hu Taiming (and Wu Zhuoliu), but the image of a lianqiao branch soaring, combined with that of a fig bearing fruit, is certainly illuminating and auspicious.

NOTES

Unless otherwise indicated, all translations from non-English-language sources are my own. Readers should note that I refer to Wu's travelogue itself as "Nanking Journals" and the collection of his travel writing appearing under the same title as *Nanking Journals* and also that, for the sake of consistency, I cite family names first.

1. See the introductory prefaces to *Yaxiya de gu'er* and the "Short Checklist of Wu Zhuoliu Criticism" prepared by Xu Sulan at the back of Peng Rui-ching, ed., *Wu Zhuoliu ji* [Short stories by Wu Zhuoliu] (Taipei: Chien-wei, 1991).
2. Wu Zhuoliu, *Nanjing zagan* [Journal of mixed feelings toward Nanking] (Taipei: Yuanxing chubanshe, 1977).
3. Realizing that there may be chronotopical lags between the writer and the autobiographical subject, I shall, nevertheless, refer to Wu as the author of and narrator in *Nanking Journals*. For in the *Journals* Wu seems to want to give the impression that the accounts are drawn from his own personal experiences and random observations.
4. E. M. Forster, *A Passage to India* (New York: Harcourt, 1924), 217.
5. See Stephen Tanaka, *Japan's Orient* (Berkeley and Los Angeles: University of California Press, 1993); and Shu-mei Shih, *The Lure of the Modern: Writing Modernism in Semicolonial China, 1917–1937* (Berkeley and Los Angeles: University of California Press, 2001).
6. Tse-han Lai et al., *A Tragic Beginning* (Stanford: Stanford University Press, 1991), 45.
7. See Naoki Sakai, *Translation and Subjectivity: On "Japan" and Cultural Nationalism* (Minneapolis: University of Minnesota Press, 1997); Shu-mei Shih, *The Lure of the Modern: Writing Modernism in Semicolonial China, 1917–1937* (Berkeley and Los Angeles: University of California Press, 2001); and Lydia Liu, *Translingual Practice* (Stanford: Stanford University Press, 1995).
8. Yu Dafu, *Yu Dafu xiaoshuo zhuanbien* [Complete short stories of Yu Dafu] (Hangchou: Zejiang wenyi, 1991), 46, 23.
9. Homi K. Bhabha, *The Location of Culture* (New York: Routledge, 1994), 144.
10. Etienne Balabar, "Algeria, France: One Nation, or Two?" in *Giving Ground: The Politics of Propinquity*, ed. Joan Copjec and Michael Sorkin (New York: Verso, 1999), 162–72.
11. Ryunosuke Akutagawa, "Travels in China," trans. Joshua Fogel, *Chinese Studies in History* 30.4 (1997): 37.

12   Peter Duus et al., eds., *The Japanese Wartime Empire, 1931–1945* (Princeton: Princeton University Press, 1996), 289.
13   See Chuan-ying Yen, "Ishikawa on Taiwan fengjing yu shuicai hua" [Ishikawa on Taiwan landscapes and watercolors] (paper delivered at the workshop "Asian Art in the Thirties," Institute of History and Philology, Academia Sinica, Taipei, May 14, 1999).
14   James Clifford, *Routes: Travel and Translation in the Late Twentieth Century* (Cambridge: Harvard University Press, 1997), 36.
15   See Edward Said, *Reflections on Exile and Other Essays* (Cambridge: Harvard University Press, 2000), 386–404; and Clifford, *Routes*.
16   Clifford, *Routes*, 43. The quotation is taken from a question-and-answer exchange between Homi Bhabha and James Clifford after Clifford's presentation of the paper "Traveling Cultures" (ibid., 17–39) at the conference "Cultural Studies, Now and in the Future" at the University of Illinois, Champaign-Urbana, April 6, 1990.
17   Wu Zhuoliu, *Yaxiya de gu'er* (Taipei: Caogen chuban shiye youxian gongsi, 1995), 274–75.

13

Mapping Identity in a Postcolonial City: Intertextuality and Cultural Hybridity in Zhu Tianxin's *Ancient Capital*

Lingchei Letty Chen

Making inquiries into cultural identity in Taiwan is a complicated and tricky endeavor because the culture is closely tied to many other cultures—principally Chinese, but also Japanese and American, to identify just the most significant. Naming these cultural "others" and defining a Taiwanese identity requires consideration and discussion of the historical discontinuity and cultural hybridization that resulted from both external and internal political and cultural machinations. The disconnection from native culture that is due to migration (e.g., the 1949 exodus from China to Taiwan) and the imposition of a foreign culture through the fifty-year Japanese colonial rule have created for the different groups of people in Taiwan a serious and complex problem in defining not only their own but also a collective Taiwanese cultural identity. It is a double-edged struggle to overcome cultural displacement and authenticate cultural hybridity.

GRAND CULTURAL CHINA VS. SMALL ISLAND TAIWAN

Cultural identity can rely on concepts and institutions, such as ethnicity, family tradition, religion, language, class, or marginalization. Although it is carried by the individual, cultural identity is, in essence, collective (the identity of a cultural community to which the individual belongs). Stuart Hall argues that the struggle for identity always takes the form of a struggle over cultural difference.[1] Lawrence Grossberg similarly grounds his understanding of cultural identity in cultural studies analysis: "I want to ... rearticulate the category of identity and its place in cultural studies as well as in cultural politics."[2] The close link between identity and culture is particularly meaningful to people in an immigrant and postcolonial society such as Taiwan. What does it mean to be a "Taiwanese" or to represent "Taiwan" as someone who holds a passport from there? The issues of ethnicity and cultural otherness have a predominant place with respect to the other elements of this identity. The tremendous presence of foreign cultures in Taiwan results directly from the colonization by the Japanese (1895–1945) and rapidly growing capitalism since the 1960s, which has opened the door to more foreign cultural influences, particularly from the West.[3] Internal colonization began when Chiang Kai-shek's Nationalist government imposed its policy of ethnic homogeneity after its retreat to Taiwan in 1949. The idea that all people living in Taiwan are ethnically Chinese was the subject of widespread propaganda until the 1980s. During the years of oppositional movements in the 1960s and 1970s, ethnicity was a key issue. Thus, when the government's ideological control finally loosened, one of the first changes was the government's open recognition of the existence of multiple ethnic groups in Taiwan.

The more open attitude toward ethnic diversity has precipitated a series of furious debates over issues of ethnic politics and identity, such as the China-Taiwan complex, independence versus unification, questions of provincial identity [shengji wenti] and Taiwanese [benshengren] versus Chinese mainlander [waishengren], as well as a search for an acceptable definition of what exactly it means to be "Taiwanese." Possible definitions include President Li Denghui's [Lee Teng-hui] concept of "New Taiwanese" [xin taiwanren] and the last chairman of the Democratic Progressive Party (DPP) Xu Xinliang's [Hsu Hsin-liang] notion of transcending all ethnic categories to regard everyone in Taiwan as one new "rising people" [xinxing minzu] because of their characteristic energy and ability to thrive under hardship.[4] The core issue remains the concept of ethnicity, which cannot be taken as unproblematic and is always constructed through discourse and the negotiation of power. Michael M. J. Fischer has pointed out that ethnicity is not passive and static, something immune to the changes of time and space, but, rather, is "reinvented and reinterpreted in each generation by each individual. . . . Ethnicity in its contemporary form is thus neither, as the sociological literature would have it, simply a matter of group process (support system), nor a matter of transition (assimilation), nor a matter of straightforward transmission from generation to generation (socialization)."[5] The crucial question facing the various ethnic groups in Taiwan is not which group possesses ethnic "authority" but what is the pivotal connection between ethnicity and cultural identity in the contemporary social, cultural, and political milieu?

Zhu Tianxin: A Contentious Writer

To understand the significance of Zhu Tianxin's *Gudu* [Ancient capital], a representative work of "Taiwan" literature by the daughter of transplanted mainlanders,[6] it is necessary to review her shift from using *China, my native land* in previous works to using *the West* and its imports as a way of designating a cultural-historical other against which to articulate a coherent cultural identity. The fact that Zhu takes China as the model is quite obvious in her earlier works. But her awareness of Western cultural influence is already clear in the early short story "Shiyi shiwang" [Passage of things past].[7] Her obsession with information (about fashion trends and media entertainment) and knowledge (particularly from the West in fields such as mythology, philosophy, literature, and so on) is also exhibited in *Xiang wo juancun de xiongdimen* [In remembrance of my brothers in the military compound], which begins an expansion of her narrative landscape that is even more apparent in the subsequent *Ancient Capital*. The obsession with information and the widening of horizons, closely tied to the emergence of the West as the cultural-historical other in her narrative, indicates how Zhu has repositioned herself in postcolonial Taiwan. Combining postcolonial sensitivity and postmodern practice, *Ancient Capital* directs the discourse of Taiwanese cultural identity toward a more intricate discussion.

This collection of stories gives a general impression of the author's obsession with the prevalence of foreign cultural influences in Taiwan. Zhu uses foreign elements including names of cities and countries as well as terms and images from world literature, mythology, and religion; the latest and most fashionable theoretical jargon from a variety of academic disciplines; and more popular artifacts, such as pop music, fashion, and movies. These selected materials share two characteristics: they represent high cultural or social standing, and they are held as cultural icons signifying nostalgic sentiments shared by her generation in Taiwan. Zhu freely incorporates bits and pieces of foreign cultural influences as intrinsic components of her narrative strategy. Like puzzle pieces or building blocks, foreign names and details of imported knowledge are taken apart and put together in such a way as to orient her cultural critique and direct her search for a cultural identity throughout the narrative. She refers to canonical works, appropriates aesthetic ideas, and borrows titles from renowned films to pursue her agenda of reconsidering the cultural politics of Taiwan's postmodern and postcolonial condition. Her tactics of imitation and appropriation may seem to parody the cultural domination of the West but actually evoke the dysfunctionality in Taiwan's culture, in which the individual is perceived as facing problems with identity construction, particularly at the fundamental level of articulation.

There are interesting similarities between Patrick Fuery's discussion of Australia's search for cultural identity and Zhu Tianxin's own narrative endeavor. Feury draws on the Lacanian concept of the gaze, which he defines as "the positioning of the subject in relation to the object and other subjects": "[The] subject gazes but is also gazed at, and it is this sense of being gazed at by another which determines the whole sense of being." Fuery contextualizes this theory in Australia's postcolonial culture and defines a type of gaze that synthesizes postcolonial identification and postmodern practice, "a particular way of looking at the world and the culture itself and at the same time feeling positioned in a particular way." The cultural self's awareness of its position while shifting its gaze back and forth between cultural others ("the world") and itself then produces certain readings of the dynamic relation between them. This process of shifting the cultural gaze is, Fuery argues, what "constitutes the cultural identity, rather than any extraordinary set of signs [taken as distinctly Australian]."[8]

In *Ancient Capital*, Zhu Tianxin's cultural gaze oscillates between "timeless, cultural China," as Shu-mei Shih describes it, and Japanese and American culture.[9] But what is more important and complicated is Zhu's switching from the viewpoint of the gazed at to that of the gazer, and vice versa, which demonstrates how Zhu has repositioned herself in postcolonial Taiwan. This new position allows her new ways to examine her own, and, ultimately, Taiwan's, cultural identity. However, it does not point to a site that is or can be made stable; rather, it serves as an index to what is not there or to where the lack is. A crisis of cultural identity is, thus, indicated by her anxiety over whether it is possible to fill this lack.

One of the methods that Zhu adopts to resolve the crisis is that of pastiche, a postmodern narrative tactic also used by Patrick Fuery in an attempt to make sense of the concept of cultural identity in a postcolonial context.

For Fuery, pastiche is necessarily historical because it provides the missing element in the construction of postcolonial cultural identity;[10] for Zhu, pastiche invokes not so much historical nostalgia as textual hybridity, yielding space for a kind of negotiation specific to Taiwan's unique postcolonial condition. However, like parody and appropriation, pastiche is not the ultimate solution to a crisis of cultural identity. Homi Bhabha suggests that the employment of colonial mimicry—defined as "the desire for a reformed, recognizable Other, *as a subject of a difference that is almost the same, but not quite*"—can create a space of ambivalence within which the colonized will be able to negotiate a new cultural identity.[11] But the real struggle lies not in how to achieve this ambivalence but in what to do afterward, and this is precisely what Zhu finds baffling.

To legitimize one's own cultural hybridity apparently requires more than just ambivalence. How to look back on history and how to go deep into the present hybridized culture to find continuity are the real challenges faced by the colonized. Through her narratives in *Ancient Capital,* Zhu seeks to understand what is at the core of her crisis of cultural identity and to see what lies beyond. Two crucial questions are, What will she see? and, What can she do after she learns the true nature of this crisis?

CONFRONTING CULTURAL HYBRIDITY IN "ANCIENT CAPITAL"

In the novella "Ancient Capital," Zhu turns to history to find ways of resolving the problem of constructing cultural identity in an essentially hybrid milieu. She uses textual simulation to negotiate the interplay of history (time) and nostalgia (memory of images). In this story, Zhu enters an in-between space of past and present, the historical real and the imaginary, idealism and disillusionment, to find a balance between cultural hybridity and personal identity. To lay claim to a cultural identity, one must believe that it is inherently original and authentic. In "Ancient Capital," Zhu Tianxin digs deep into the very core of what cultural identity means and what reconciliations are necessary before its construction can even begin. Outflows of emotion demonstrate her painfully sharp interrogation of history, her earnest search for ways to define identity. In her pastiche of a Japanese canonical work and a colonial map, Zhu devises ways of narrating different pasts with the hope of finding the proper position on which to begin building a coherent and independent cultural identity. The struggle in this story is, essentially, between two contradicting conditions: hybridity and authenticity.

Zhu borrowed the title for this novella from Kawabata Yasunari's canonical novel *Koto* [The old capital].[12] She appropriates the Kyoto that Kawabata captures as an ideal city where the history of a place and the memory of an individual are tied together. She then projects this ideal onto modern-day Taipei, hoping to reconnect the latter, alienating city with (its) history and (her) memory. Kawabata's novel is the silhouette of history, a shadowy outline of the meaning and representation of a coherent cultural identity. Paralleling the Kawabata supertext are three subtexts: *Taiwan tongshixu* [Preface to the general history of Taiwan], a Qing dynasty publication; a tourist map of colonial Taipei; and the story of Peach Blossom Stream [Taohuayuan]. These various applications of appropriation, pastiche, and multilevel structures entail control and calculation, but, interestingly, Zhu also overwhelms the narrative with nostalgia and desires to connect and relate to a foreign city, Kyoto. History is her foremost preoccupation in "Ancient Capital," combined with concerns for legitimizing cultural hybridity.

Memory and Map

The plot of "Ancient Capital" is linear and thematically parallels that of Kawabata's novel. Zhu's novella begins with the narrator remembering her high school years, which were spent with her best friend, "A." Gradually, as they enter adulthood, the two grow apart, until one day the narrator receives a fax from A inviting her to meet her in Kyoto. The narrator thus begins her journey to Kawabata's old capital. While she awaits A's arrival, she takes a walk through the streets and alleys of the city, remembering her residence there with her daughter some years before. After waiting a day, she realizes that A will not show up and, thus, decides to return to Taipei earlier than scheduled.

At the Taipei airport, she is approached by a cabdriver who mistakes her for a Japanese tourist; without attempting to correct him, she gets into the cab and is driven into the city. As soon as she decides to return to her home city as a foreigner, everything begins to look different. A Japanese tourist map of colonial Taipei, which she finds in her bag, inspires her to revisit the city as it existed half a century earlier. The map lays out Taipei the way it was designed by the Japanese, with the streets, government buildings, and other landmarks appearing under their original names. By moving the scene back to Taipei, Zhu shifts the perspective of her cultural gaze from Kyoto, yet it is not just the present-day city she is looking at but also the colonial city, manifested on the map. This switch of perspective is made more intriguing by her pretense as a foreigner—a Japanese tourist—under which she is able to psychologically remove herself from the immediacy of the surroundings and allow the map to become a lens through which she sees the city anew. In this section, the narrator begins a journey back to the past but realizes at the end that she no longer knows where she is.

"Ancient Capital" is also a story of remembering the history of Taipei/Taiwan through the process of its cultural hybridization. References to foreign cultures characterize the narrative's cultural background. For instance, before the narrator's trip to Kyoto, the cultural scene is sketched via references to American popular music and American culture in general. In this section, the narrator recalls the Taipei of her adolescent years. As she proceeds to Kyoto, anticipating a reunion with A, the cultural scene shifts, and Kawabata's *Old Capital* provides guidance to her revisiting of the city. In the next section, where she pretends to be a foreign tourist in her home city, there are more historical and cultural references alluding to the colonial period. With each change of cultural references, space and time are structured by different principles. Revisiting her own past as well as Taipei's is the primary theme of the first section, prior to the trip to Kyoto, where conflicts between the native and the foreign are apparent. In the second section, which describes the trip, Kawabata's novel becomes the principle for constructing space and time, and the narrative is double-coded with Kawabata's. In the third section, Zhu imposes on present-day Taipei the city drawn on the colonial map so that the city is seen as a replica of old Kyoto, thus calling attention to the contrast between the historical and the contemporary.

In "Ancient Capital," Zhu's intriguing play with time and space makes Taiwan's inherent cultural hybridity apparent. In the first section, as the narrator reminisces about her adolescent years in Taipei, American popular music characterizes her memories of the 1960s and 1970s:

> At that time, if you had a brother or a sister in college, the background music would have to be the Beatles. If it was the first year in the 1970s, you would certainly hear "Candida" everywhere, all the time. In the following year, it was "Knock Three Times" by the same group.... But, since you like Don McLean's "Vincent"

and "American Pie," then let's push back two years—allow me to double-check my reference—"Vincent" got on the chart on May 13, 1972—so it must be the summer of '72. (152)

Although the mood that Zhu portrays here relies entirely on foreign artifacts, the tone is not parodic but nostalgic, as if the hybridization of Taiwan's culture is accepted without question. The first time the narrator walks (the only type of activity in the entire story),[13] some streets already appear under their former Japanese names, evoking Taiwan's most recent colonial experience. Interestingly, the narrator seems to feel alienated from the local culture and customs and intimidated when walking through a traditional market. When she climbs the hills to look out on the ocean, she tries not to notice the nearby small huts "built in Fujian/Taiwanese style" (154). Often, she likes to imaginatively romanticize a sight by endowing it with characteristics of Spain or other Mediterranean countries (e.g., 155).

In this hybrid existence, the representation of personal/private history is dominated by foreign cultural influences, while the representation of the official/public history of the city is determined by its colonial records as illustrated in the subtext of *Preface to the General History of Taiwan*. Similar to the way American popular music is used to constitute a part of the narrator's cultural consciousness, bits of actual historical details are inserted into the narrative to shed light on the island's colonial past. Thus, Zhu protests the total erasure of Taiwan's history in order to underscore the absurdity of the pan-Chinese identity that the Guomindang (formerly Kuomintang, KMT) government has strategically imposed on the people at the expense of the local history prior to 1987. Occasionally, historical reportage is woven into the narrative to establish the identity of the city:

> Jian Tan is located two *li* from the Dairaryūsha in northern Dan Sui. The barbarians came in small boats. The waterway was wide, and there was a tall Jia Dong tree—its trunk was so thick that it took several men with stretched arms to embrace it. It stood high up on the bank of the deep pool, and it is said that the Dutch drove a sword into the tree and that the sword was later wrapped by growing bulk and became a part of the tree. This place was, thus, named Sword Pond [Jian Tan]. But of course this is not what you know about Jian Tan. When you were five, your parents dressed you up and took you to the Jian Tan Zoo and Children's Playground . . . it was the only place you wanted to go. (164)

The stark contrast between the factual history of the land and the memory of the narrator indicates the disjunction of official history and personal existence, particularly when this history is not written by the native, even though it inevitably makes up a part of the collective identity. Ban Wang in his articulation of history makes a poignant observation: "Historical narrative is allegorical, not symbolic, in the sense that there is always a jagged line between our attempts at making meaning and what is sunk forever into oblivion and death."[14] This "jagged line" is precisely what Zhu intends to straighten by looking into the distant and not-so-distant past. She utilizes spatiality as a nonlinear form of writing history to delineate traces of the people who came to this island where their descendants still live. The personal/private account of the past thus differs from the official/public history in that, as the latter often concentrates on privileging and totalizing the past in order to assure the dominant power's legitimacy in the present, the former finds it more essential to make sense of the present: the individual who collects personal memory and writes a private history is the one who also bears the colonial imprint, who lives out the colonial heritage daily. The individual inheritor of the colonial experience must be able to successfully define a legitimate postcolonial identity for the future.

The interplay between the narrator's visual language and the environment reveals the place's colonial condition. Because the narrator is influenced by foreign cultures when she describes what she sees and imagines of her home city, a foreign landscape appears: gazing toward the ocean that surrounds the island, beyond the Taipei horizon, she sees San Francisco ("although none of you have ever been there" [154]) or a gray English beach depicted in movies, such as *Ryan's Daughter* or *The French Lieutenant's Woman* (162). Picturing the beauty of autumn in Taiwan, where seasonal changes are subtle, she imagines herself in New England: "Not far from the street is the dormitory of the U.S. military counsel; the style of the house reminds you of the typical houses in 1950s Hollywood movies—white walls, big windows, chimneys, and a green lawn; because every so often when you run into some vacationing American officers on the street, who will stop and say hi to you—so gentlemanlike; because at that time everyone is hooked on the TV series *Peyton Place*" (165).

Not only does her spatial language impose a foreign landscape on the native place, but her temporal language also resonates with Western mythology as the referent for chronicling her childhood and a series of Taiwan's diplomatic setbacks:

> How you long for those years when September came and you could go to school, wearing a new uniform, meeting new classmates, having new classrooms, new teachers.
>
> ... Everything was new and so full of endless possibilities ... [but] twenty years later, some politically correct writers when writing about those years, they would always write you into the political protests against the Senkakushoto incident, the United Nations incident ... and the breakup of the Taiwan-Japan relationship.... You and most other people had no idea of these incidents. In about AD 400, people stopped believing in Zeus, and, around 1650, people no longer believed in wizards and sorcerers; in 1700, a widespread suspicion of God's revelation began. Hasn't it always been like this—glory and misery of every age belonging only to very few prophets, wizards, and sorcerers? (157–58)

To demonstrate how history and postcolonial constructions of place are mutually intertwined, Zhu uses cartography to simulate the colonial space. Only by returning to the "beginning" can the narrator start to establish a link with history. Strolling through the streets of Taipei, she sees the neighborhood both as her hometown and as a big foreign concession. Taipei in the 1960s and 1970s, as preserved in her memory, is recolonized with areas resembling exotic lands and American outposts:

> In front of the Rome Hotel are many American soldiers hailing cabs ... diagonally from the hotel is Caves Books—you never walk in there or Gold Mountain Bookstore or Lin Ko Bookstore because they sell only foreign books. To you they are in a foreign concession where Chinamen and dogs are not allowed.... Entering Qing Guang Market is like entering a labyrinth.... All this makes you feel like you are in a foreign country—Christmas pudding, bread mixed with exotic spices, abundant meat products and butter, all sorts of jam, teas.... But, strangely, none of these seem to conflict with your daily life; you continue to walk in the concession, watching white-skinned, tall-nosed foreigners holding your countrywomen as if time has moved back to the Opium War period ... however, such sights do not evoke in you any feeling of unease. (166–67)

These colonial spaces do not violate her private memory of the place because they are also part of her daily existence. By including them, the narrator seems to accept the fact that colonial experience is a part of what she and her ancestors are. Zhu thus seems to suggest that denying and rebelling against the colonial heritage is not the way to construct a meaningful postcolonial identity. One must come to terms with the past in order to find meaning in the present and the future. Therefore, Zhu's personal project of "decolonizing" Taiwan is precisely a journey back to her ancestry. She embeds her memory within that of the early settlers and the aborigines (169), making the meaning of her existence a part of the collective existence of the earliest settlers—the aborigines, the Portuguese, as well as the Dutch, the Spanish, the French, and the Japanese invaders.

This personalization of the process of decolonizing Taiwan is significant because, despite the (official) historical fact that Taiwan was more than once "liberated" from its colonizers, it remains in question whether this succeeded in mending individuals' fractured sense of cultural identity. There have been two occasions when Taiwan played an important political role in relation to mainland China, even though the island has always occupied a marginal position within Chinese territory as well as within Chinese official history. Taiwan was twice decolonized; however, on neither occasion did the local people play a significant role in determining their own destiny. The first time, in the second half of the seventeenth century, the invading Manchus overthrew the Ming dynasty and established the Qing dynasty in China. The Ming loyalist resistance led by Zheng Chenggong [Koxinga] used Taiwan as its base after retreating from Xiamen in Fujian Province in 1662. At the time, Taiwan had been occupied by the Dutch since 1624, and it was Zheng's army that finally expelled them. When the Ming loyalist resistance failed in 1683, Taiwan was placed under the control of the Qing dynasty.[15] The second time Taiwan gained political importance (because of its geographic marginality) in opposing mainland Chinese power was when Chiang Kai-shek lost the civil war to Mao Zedong in 1949 and retreated to the island to continue his Nationalist regime. However, between 1662, when Taiwan was placed under Qing control, and 1949, when it came under Chiang's rule, there was a period during which it was controlled by the Japanese, beginning in 1895. Taiwan was decolonized in 1945, at the end of World War II, when Japan unconditionally surrendered to the Allies, led by the United States. Then Taiwan was returned to mainland China, but, after only four years, this tie was severed again.

Not only was decolonization from the non-Chinese not accomplished by the local people, but, afterward, they were never allowed to take control of their own land. To them, it was simply a matter of changing hands between the non-Chinese and the Chinese. The Taiwanese have begun to establish political influence and power only since the 1980s, having fought for four decades against the brutal oppression of Chiang Kai-shek's Nationalist regime. Therefore, for the individual Taiwanese to realize an independent sense of identity, it is necessary to understand the decolonization process in personal terms. By the same token, to understand the essence of the general Taiwanese identity is to accept that it is composed in part of Taiwan's colonial experience. Thus, Zhu's narrator immerses herself in different segments of the island's history when different groups of people—the early Chinese settlers and the previous foreign invaders such as the Portuguese, the Dutch, the Spanish, the French, and the Japanese—arrive.

Reproducing Cultural Authenticity
In the second section of the story, the narrator embarks on the journey to Kyoto to meet with her long-lost high school pal. Here, Zhu creates a labyrinth of intertextuality and interculturation by weaving Kawabata's Kyoto into her depiction of Taipei and mixing the city's colonial past with its postcolonial present. Plagiarizing the original text is not Zhu's primary intention. Rather, she uses Kawabata's work to simulate history, or, as Baudrillard puts it, "to resurrect the period when at least there was history, at least there was violence. . . . All previous history is resurrected in bulk—a controlling idea no longer selects, only nostalgia endlessly accumulates."[16] Indeed, Zhu's simulation of history shows how nostalgia prevails. But it is probably closer to David Wang's "imaginary nostalgia," which "questions the ontological assumption often associated with the concept of nostalgia, and refers us to the intra- and intertextual dynamics that configures the yearning for home."[17] To understand the important role that imaginary nostalgia plays in the narrative, we need to ask what it entails and how it is realized in textual practice. Nostalgia is the desire to connect with and relate to the past, and, where there is desire, there is a lack, a need. What is lacking? And what does the narrator need? How does Zhu's appropriation of Kawabata's novel express the narrator's yearning for home? In this section and the following one, as she gradually gives in to nostalgia, the protagonist also slowly betrays the anxiety and ambivalence hidden underneath the seemingly calculated and controlled narrative strategy of pastiche.

Zhu buries her deep nostalgia for an ideal past in the imitation of Kawabata's novel, maintaining thematic parallels—the desire for a utopian history, the deteriorating relation between man and nature, and the intriguing (dis)connection between the twin sisters/friends/cities. But she also laments the rapid destruction of Taipei's natural environment by both the KMT government and native Taiwanese politicians, who often obliterate history in the name of progress. Kawabata's Kyoto, a fictionalized Japanese city, ironically becomes the source of the narrator's nostalgia as well as the symbol of history. It represents the eternal city, the Peach Blossom Stream and Shangri-la that Taipei can never be.

It is also in this ancient city that the narrator's anticipated reunion with A does not happen. Although this runs contrary to the plot of Kawabata's novel, in which the estranged twin sisters, Chieko and Naeko, do reunite (but choose to remain separated at the end), the narrator feels little regret. During the narrator's visit to Kyoto, it is actually her daughter's childhood that she wishes to recapture; because everything in the city itself has been well preserved, she is able to revisit every site and corner that she and her daughter saw previously, thus reliving every memory they share. Taipei, on the other hand, cannot provide this sense of history, even a personal one. The city changes too fast—nearly every trace of its past has been modified or erased. So, ironically, the foreign denotes familiarity and historicity, while the native symbolizes alienation and temporality.

In Kawabata's novel, there is a sense of tranquillity and stillness. To achieve a poetic atmosphere, Kawabata relies on the flow of the language and the haiku-like juxtaposition of objects. In his discussion of Kawabata's *Yukiguni* [Snow country], J. Thomas Rimer explains the influence of earlier Japanese literature, such as the noh drama and haiku, on Kawabata's aesthetics and how this influence manifests itself in his "poetry of place becom[ing] poetry of self-realization": "Here Kawabata binds together the characters . . . the plot . . . the images recurrent throughout the text . . . and the thematic concern of wasted beauty, a concept that in turn evokes those characters, images, and plot. Such linking, such reinforcement, becomes impossible to unravel."[18] In his last novel, *The Old Capital*, which was one of the three novels cited by the Nobel Prize committee, Kawabata maintains the same aesthetic principle to create a sense of Kyoto's beauty and old traditions by juxtaposing the city's natural landscape with the narrative's reminiscence of its cultural heritage and through the characters and plot. Zhu imitates and applies such aesthetics. Borrowing Kawabata's principle, she attempts to re-create the same poetry, but not for an actual geographic place, for a textual place in her narrative.

Zhu's appropriation of Kawabata's Kyoto relies on the suggestive power of absence rather than attempting to simply re-present the old capital. Zhu quotes nine passages from the Kawabata text; all are short and fragmented, and all but two carry little thematic significance (the two exceptions are the passage where Chieko first realizes that Naeko is her twin sister and the farewell of the two sisters at the end of the novel). At first glance, it may seem that these quoted passages open only a small window into the world of Kawabata's Kyoto, but, in their original context, these obscure passages are parts of what brings out the essence and ambience of the tranquil and antiquated city that Kawabata painstakingly depicts. Thus, it is the near absence of Kawabata's Kyoto that provides the similar mood and atmosphere in Zhu's narrative. In other words, Zhu relies on the reader's familiarity with Kawabata's novel to avoid a direct appropriation, quoting fragments from Kawabata to create a near absence of Kyoto. She then uses this absence to simulate the city's presence in a different narrative space for different interpretations. Her minimalistic pastiche of the Japanese master shows her resistance of unconditional imitation. Her plan is not to relive Kawabata's narrative but to use it as a convenient backdrop for her own drama. Her strategy is not a gesture of cultural-political protest but a way of reconstructing a lost history.

The fragments that Zhu quotes from Kawabata's novel are juxtaposed with the main narrative, to bring the same mood to her portrayal of Kyoto as a utopian space where the presence of history is felt everywhere, as well as to contrast Kyoto with Taipei, an entirely different space where nothing lasts. In Taipei, not only are concrete public records of history, such as monuments and historical buildings, constantly in danger of demolition; the private memory of the individual is also threatened by the possibility of total erasure. Zhu describes the resulting horror:

> All of a sudden you can't even recall what the street looks like; you feel as if you were a witness to a crime who went to report it to the police, but when you led the police back to the crime scene, not only was the dead body gone, there was not even a trace of blood. Choked with tears, you tell your future husband that

this is not how the street used to be. It should look like this and that and . . . aimlessly you point your finger here and there, trying desperately to describe how the street used to be, but, deep down, you know you have completely lost your sense of direction. (201)

In the narrator's perception of Kyoto, where many institutions have been preserved over thirteen hundred years—including temples and shrines, trees and gardens, religious ceremonies and festivals—this means, on the contrary, a guarantee of continuity and preservation of personal memory. For Kawabata, traditional Japan may have slowly disappeared at the end of World War II, but, for Zhu, on the eve of the twenty-first century, Kawabata's Kyoto nevertheless remains a symbol of history and antiquity. Zhu's celebration of its historical status seems to transcend any ambivalence about Japan's previous colonial control over Taiwan. Ironically, a Japanese city's well-preserved history allows this second-generation Chinese mainlander in Taiwan to find meaning in an individual's bond to a place, which, in turn, helps provide her with an unambiguous cultural identity.

While Zhu's cultural association with Kyoto may be warranted, there arises the problem of how to reconcile this "unambiguous" cultural identity with her highly problematic ethnic identity. The bad blood between China and Japan has not dissipated since the end of World War II, and, for Zhu to claim a Chinese identity while identifying culturally and spiritually with Japan seems rather callous, if not altogether naive. But, even if she chooses to lean toward her Taiwanese identity while embracing the island's previous colonizer and Japan's historical capital as her solace, she still runs the risk of being politically insensitive. However, considering her personal background, Japanese culture is a very familiar source of inspiration. Her mother is a translator of modern Japanese literature; her (and her sister Zhu Tianwen's) mentor Hu Lancheng, who resided in Japan after the war, came to Taiwan in 1985 to teach, but, because he had been accused of being a traitor to China [hanjian], he had to return to Japan.[19] Undeniably, Zhu's choice of Japan, and Kyoto in particular, has a personal element in it, an impulse to allow herself to find comfort and safety in the metaphor of Kawabata's fiction and Kyoto's stature. But, in the end (or at least at the end of this section of the story), Zhu realizes that the historical and political burden forced on her by the choice of "Japan" is far too great to be offset by a mere "personal inclination."

The primary language in the second section is a spatial one. As the narrator walks through the space of modern Kyoto, through its parks and streets, her memories of the Taipei of her youth and of Kyoto during the time of her residence there with her daughter are constantly evoked to contrast with her immediate location. Embedded in her memory of Taipei is the imagined space of the colonial Taipei, which parallels the fictional space of Kawabata's Kyoto projected through the quoted passages. These spaces are actually simulacra at best because they are based on images, not rooted in any concrete reality. The projection of Kawabata's Kyoto and the two Taipeis conjured up by the narrator are not the "real" itself but, rather, the "fictional real," created by nostalgia for an ideal space, and lost in time.

In this way, nostalgia underlies Zhu's writing of history, but her narrator's sense of history is replaced by either another history (Kyoto's) or the media version (as in what she perceives through American movies). It is interesting, as well as baffling, to see how Zhu writes about Kyoto and how she uses it to bring out her contempt for contemporary Taipei; yet, in this contempt, there is a distinct feeling of nostalgia for the past (and better) Taipei. Is this self-denial? Does it represent a deep anxiety about how to situate herself culturally, socially, and historically? Before the narrator leaves for Kyoto, Zhu strives to rediscover and embrace Taiwan's colonial past, and she convinces us (and possibly herself as well) that she has found reconciliation with it. But as the narrative turns to another locale—and not just any other place, but Japan—her efforts to reconcile with her native land's hybrid past become a total identification with the colonizer's culture and history. Perhaps Zhu's real predicament is not where and how to find her own history but what facts she is willing to accept as her history. Her ambiguous and wavering attitude toward Taiwan's past reveals a dilemma concerning how to "write" history: Does the model of Kawabata's historical Kyoto represent the ideal? Can Taiwan's colonial/hybrid past measure up to it?

Jean Baudrillard uses the theme of neofiguration in painting to describe what history is to us today.[20] In Zhu's attempt to rediscover Taiwan's past, she has only the possibility of drawing a neofiguration that may resemble her imagination of that past. She turns to the historical and cultural Japan because, ironically, its colonization of Taiwan has created an undeniable affinity between the two cultures. Her narrator's experience in Kyoto becomes a testimony to Taipei's rapidly disappearing history. The narrator's feeling of being "at home" in Kyoto is immediately contrasted with her fear of walking in her own city. In Kyoto, she knows where to go for her favorite cup of coffee; she enjoys being part of the crowd of professional women during rush hour on the busy streets; to this city and its people, she finds herself saying, "*Tadaima*, I am back" (183). But, in Taipei, she feels alienated by the constant construction and reconstruction of streets and buildings because once familiar sights are now entirely lost to her (184). It is no wonder that, in the narrator's imaginary rediscovery of the old city accomplished by her reference to the colonial map, she is happy to recognize that Taipei occupied a similar geographic significance as Kyoto once did in Japan and, thus, can easily be a replica, or a twin city, of Kyoto (223).

This desire to see similarity between the two cities is itself a symptom reflecting the very issue that Zhu wants to explore in her narrative, namely, the discontinuity in Taiwan's historical record and the disruption of the collective memory of its people. To the generations of Taiwanese, native and mainland origins alike, who were born after 1949 (including Zhu), colonial history has not been taught, and colonial memory has not been allowed to be passed down from their parents and grandparents. There is a gap, a disruption, in the local history and the people's collective memory because the KMT government forcefully imposed another history and another memory, those of China. It is, therefore, questionable how concrete the notion of Japan as "the colonizer" would actually be for these baby boomers. The era of Japanese colonization can be both alluring and mystifying to people who have not lived through it or heard firsthand recollections of it. Japanese cultural imprints are still vivid in Taiwan's culture, yet they belong to the untaught and unexperienced past. On the one hand, these colonial imprints can be used as clues to retrace history; on the other hand, they can be a source of nostalgia and inspiration for imagining the past.

Zhu's recuperation of Kawabata's old capital is not a sign of her naïveté about history or mere romanticism for an ancient city; rather, it reveals her sense of the lack of a coherent and continuous historical and cultural heritage shared by her generation and those that follow. The historicity that Kyoto represents is authentic; the previous colonial connection between Japan and Taiwan provides a reference with which to retrace the city of Taipei as it was built during that period. A fragment of Taiwan's history can be found only in the map of the colonizer. Ironically, in Zhu's neofiguration of

Taipei, there seems to be a superimposed image of Kyoto—as if linking the two cities would ensure that, so long as Kyoto's history is well preserved, Taipei's history will somehow also be protected.

Authenticity versus Hybridity: Who Am I? Where Am I?
In the third section of the novella, the narrator returns to Taipei pretending to be a Japanese tourist and revisits the city by following a colonial map. Zhu juxtaposes the colonial version of Taipei, which exists only on the map, and the contemporary version, which, in the eyes of the narrator, is stranger. In this portion of the narrative, Zhu attempts to match the Japanese names of streets and districts in Taipei with their current Chinese names. In between rounds of this game, she uses images of Western (mainly American) landscapes or landmarks to highlight the actual collage and pastiche of Taipei's architecture and landscape—sites that for her clearly bear no indication of Taiwan's specific cultural and historical identities. As the narrator walks on, the Taipei recorded on the colonial map slowly emerges. She checks off every name as she visits the corresponding contemporary site. The "mismatch of language and landscape" emphasizes the differences among the narrator's imagination of the city drawn on the colonial map, her personal memory of the city, and her impressions of the city at present.[21] Here, the map acts as an agent to disconnect the narrator's visual image of history from the place where this image should be rooted, and, as a result, it ruptures the cohesion of history, memory, and place.

The colonial map stands as an allegory of the author's project to rewrite the present with an imagined past; it connotes order (arrangement) and meaning (representation). The layout of different zones and city landmarks with their old names structures the visual space, and the legend for each name/symbol specifies the location and nature of the structure. In his analysis of the world atlas, José Rabasa specifically points out the correlation between the legends on the map and the historicity that the map embodies in its simulated space: "The written solidifies locations while supplying meaning to the visual. . . . Inscriptions precede and determine the visibility of the contour, but they also flesh out the abstract frame. The possibility and the significance of the map thus depend on history. The inscription of the map gives place to its silhouette, but its silhouette is historical and meaningful only when it evokes a . . . history."[22] In Zhu's use of the map, the legends are expanded by the narrator's personal memory. With her added "writing," the original colonial map creates a paradoxical alliance between colonialism (denoted by the map itself) and the desire to reterritorialize the increasingly alienating city. Thus, the Taiwan Bank built in 1903, which the map records as having been designed by Nomura Ichirō in the mansard style, is regarded by the narrator as a perfect model for a Tiffany store (214). Seimonjō, the Japanese pleasure street as indicated on the map (218), is portrayed as a decayed district filled with filth and desperation. The Red Chamber Theater, designed by Kondō Sūrō and built in 1908, has a supernatural flair that is combined with the Peach Blossom Stream story as the narrator dreams up the city as an embodiment of such a paradise (220). It is to the period of Japanese colonization that Zhu appeals. Her underlying impulse is to remake the map and, thereby, evoke the coherent sense of history of which she has been deprived.

Maintaining cohesion among history, memory, and place is, for Zhu, the only way to establish an independent cultural identity. To drive home this conviction, she uses negation as her main strategy to articulate the meaning of that identity and to write about the process of bringing home the self to the native land. The colonial map becomes the narrator's guide through this process. But to use it is contradictory to her purpose: as the map can only further widen the gap between the narrator's image of Taipei (in both history and her memory) and the city in the present, the process of identification becomes the process of disidentification. "Ancient Capital" is about not cultural identity but the lack of it. Zhu establishes not what the Taiwanese individual's cultural identity should be but what it no longer can be—through the colonial map and the pastiche of Kawabata's novel, she points out a dissemination of Taiwan's history, her memory, and the place from which the two originated.

This idealization of the past contrasts with the present as a dystopia, manifested in the subtext of the Peach Blossom Stream story. The inserted text maintains its original symbolism of the Peach Blossom Stream as a utopian place that exists outside the mundane world until the end of the narrator's journey, when she loses the map and the symbolism takes on a twisted meaning.[23] Merging this subtext with the figure of modern-day Taipei, Zhu turns the story of utopia into a reality of dystopia. The moment of this change appears soon after the narrator loses her map. As she wanders into an obscure section of the city, she finds men and women sitting under trees or on broken chairs in complete idleness, the music of the Beijing

Opera playing in the background. This passage is filled with images of death and desolation—floating corpses in the nearby river, burning wild grass, indifferent dogs, and funeral music playing in the far distance. The Peach Blossom Stream she searches for is darkly reflected by this obscure village:

> Helicopters are circling in the sky, perhaps they are searching for floating dead bodies in the river; an *obasan*[24] passes by you on a motorcycle that is emitting black smoke. She probably has received a notice to identify a dead body. Under a tree is a gang of dogs who are looking at you with blank faces. . . . Across the river on the other bank a high-pitched funeral music is playing faintly; there is grass burning somewhere . . . near the highway are tall gray walls blocking the way like prison walls, so clean there is not a single graffiti on them, not even one stroke. Where is this place? . . . You burst out crying. (233)

From fiction to cartography, the dialectics of reconstructing the past via Kawabata's novel and deconstructing the present by superimposition of the colonial map suggest the ontological anxiety arising from Zhu's frustrated attempts to define a coherent cultural identity. The strategy of doubling Kawabata's *Old Capital* (with a map included) allows her to indulge in nostalgia; by hiding behind the superstructure of the Japanese canon, Zhu can claim immunity from history and, thus, escape the burden of colonialism. In her selective historical memory, the perceptions of Kyoto and old Taipei are ideal, as though the cities were set in an eternal past, beyond real historical time. Her approach to the present and the past, by way of simulacra and pastiche, produces a depressing sense of loss of a personal cultural identity. In fact, nostalgia, the desire to connect with history and to privilege the past over the present, has restructured her appropriation of the Kawabata text so that the attempt to reclaim a missing past is now refracted through simulacra.

Investigating history in "Ancient Capital," Zhu Tianxin seems to be trapped between two poles: cultural hybridity and historical authenticity. In her project of constructing a coherent cultural identity, she needs a rationale to reconcile these two essentially conflicting values. It is interesting that she should use appropriation and imitation as the main strategies to achieve this goal. Zhu recognizes that the essence of Taiwan's culture is heterogeneous and that, although it is based on Chinese culture, it has also absorbed tremendous Japanese and Western (mainly American) cultural influences—a mixed result of colonialism and capitalism. But this recognition alone is not sufficient for defining cultural identity because identity must also be situated within history. It is, therefore, necessary to map Taiwan's cultural hybridity in history; the question becomes, therefore, does history necessarily guarantee authenticity? If cultural identity is, as Stuart Hall says, a constant (re)construction, is it not also true that authenticity is a construct, not a given?[25] What remains to be seen is how Zhu will continue to carry out her project of identity construction.

NOTES

Unless otherwise indicated, all translations from non-English-language sources are my own.

1 See Stuart Hall, "Cultural Identity and Diaspora," in Jonathan Rutherford, ed., *Identity: Community, Culture, Difference* (London: Lawrence and Wishart, 1990), 222–37, and "Who Needs 'Identity'?" in Stuart Hall and Paul du Gray, eds., *Questions of Cultural Identity* (London: Sage, 1996), 1–17.
2 Lawrence Grossberg, "Identity and Cultural Studies: Is That All There Is?" in Hall and du Gray, eds., *Questions of Cultural Identity*, 88.
3 I date the beginning of the period of Japanese colonization to 1895 and the Treaty of Shimonoseki between the Qing dynasty and the Japanese government. The separation of Taiwan from Chinese rule has, thus, been established for 105 years and not the commonly believed 50 years.
4 "New Taiwanese" was a campaign slogan for the Guomindang candidate Ma Yingjiu in the Taipei city mayoral election in December 1998.

 The Rising People was used by Xu Xinliang as the title of a book—*Xinxing minzu* (Taipei: Yuanliu, 1995)—promoting a new way to historicize and conceptualize ethnicity in Taiwan. Xu seeks to transcend old ethnic categories by redefining ethnicity in terms of particular group characteristics exhibited by the people living in Taiwan—the desire to not only survive but do well, characteristics shared by all immigrant societies in the world. This is, of course, an effort motivated by the DPP's political agenda to legitimize the call for Taiwan's independence. But, nonetheless, this new concept indicates a less confrontational strategy than the party's earlier approach to separate native "Taiwanese" [*benshengren*] from Chinese mainlanders [*waishengren*].
5 Michael M. J. Fischer, "Ethnicity and the Post-Modern Arts of Memory," in James Clifford and George E. Marcus, eds., *Writing Culture: The Poetics and Politics of Ethnography* (Berkeley and Los Angeles: University of California Press, 1986), 195, 197.
6 Zhu Tianxin, *Gudu* [Ancient capital] (Taipei: Maitian, 1997).
7 Zhu Tianxin's first collection of short stories was *Fangzhou shang de rizi* [Days on the boat] (Taipei: Xinxin chubanshe, 1977). This was followed by *Zuori dang*

wo nianqingshi [Yesterday when I was young] (Taipei: San san shufang, 1981), *Weiliao* [Unfinished affairs] (Taipei: Lianhe bao she, 1982), and *Shiyi shiwang* [Passages of things past] (Taipei: San san shufang, 1989), in which the story "Shiyi shiwang" appeared.

8 Patrick Fuery, "Prisoners and Spiders Surrounded by Signs: Postmodernism and the Postcolonial Gaze in Contemporary Australian Culture," in Jonathan White, ed., *Recasting the World: Writing after Colonialism* (Baltimore: Johns Hopkins University Press, 1993), 191, 192, 205 (see also 195).

9 Shu-mei Shih, "The Trope of 'Mainland China' in Taiwan's Media," *positions* 3.1 (spring 1995): 157.

10 See Fuery, "Prisoners and Spiders," 197–201.

11 Homi Bhabha, "Of Mimicry and Man," in *The Location of Culture* (London: Routledge, 1994), 86.

12 For a translation, see Kawabata Yasunari, *The Old Capital* (1961), trans. J. Martin Holman (San Francisco: North Point, 1987).

13 David Der-wei Wang has commented that walking is Zhu's favorite activity for her characters. See David Der-wei Wang, foreword to Zhu, *Gudu*, 27.

14 Ban Wang, *The Sublime Figure of History: Aesthetics and Politics in Twentieth-Century China* (Stanford: Stanford University Press, 1997), 4.

15 Conrad Schirokauer, *A Brief History of Chinese and Japanese Civilizations*, 2nd ed. (Fort Worth: Harcourt Brace Jovanovich College, 1989), 332.

16 Jean Baudrillard, *Simulacra and Simulation*, trans. Sheila Faria Glaser (Ann Arbor: University of Michigan Press, 1994), 44.

17 David Der-wei Wang, *Fictional Realism in 20th-Century China: Mao Dun, Lao She, Shen Congwen* (New York: Columbia University Press, 1992), 253.

18 J. Thomas Rimer, *Modern Japanese Fiction and Its Traditions: An Introduction* (Princeton: Princeton University Press, 1978), 180.

19 Accounts of Hu Lancheng's connection with the Zhu family and his tremendous influence on the two Zhu sisters' literary endeavor can be found in Yang Zhao, "Man miejue de zhuanzhe: Ping Zhu tianxin xiaoshuoji wo jide" [A romantic and annihilating twist: Critique of Zhu Tianxin's collection *I Remember*], *Zili fukan* [Zili literary supplement] 7.8 (February 1991); and Yang Zhao, "Liangwei qunxun huiyou de yu: Wo suo zhidao de Zhu tianxin" [Two swimming fish: The Zhu Tianxin I know], *Zhongguo shibao renjian fukan* [China times renjian weekly magazine] 20.21 (January 20–21, 1994). For a more comprehensive view of Hu's influence on the Zhu sisters, see Zhu Tianwen, "Huayi qianshen: Ji Hu Lanchang ba shu" [A flower recalls its previous lives: Remembering eight books by Hu Lancheng], in David Der-wei Wang, ed., *Huayi qianshen* (Taipei: Maitian, 1996), 32–106; and Ng Kim-chu, "Shenji zhi wu—hou sishi hui? (Hou)xiandai qishilu?" [Dances of the goddess—the post 40 chapters? (Post)modern apocalypse?], in ibid., 265–312.

Hu Lancheng has recorded this period and his controversial involvement with Wang Jingwei. See Hu Lancheng, *Jinsheng jinshi* [This life, this world] (Taipei: San-san Bookstore, 1990). He is best known for being the former husband of Eileen Chang and a collaborator with Japan and Wang's bogus government in occupied Shanghai during the Second Sino-Japanese War. It is because of this connection with Wang that Hu has been accused by the Nationalist (KMT) government of being a traitor to China.

20 Baudrillard argues: "The history that is 'given back' to us (precisely because it was taken from us) has no more of a relation to a 'historical real' than neofiguration in painting does to the classical figuration of the real. Neofiguration is an invocation of resemblance . . . [in which objects] no longer resemble anything, except the empty figure of resemblance, the empty form of representation." Baudrillard, *Simulacra and Simulation*, 45.

21 On the "mismatch of language and landscape," see Bill Ashcroft, Gareth Griffiths, and Helen Tiffin, *The Empire Writes Back: Theory and Practice in Post-Colonial Literatures* (New York: Routledge, 1989), 140.

22 José Rabasa, "Allegories of Atlas," in Bill Ashcroft, Gareth Griffiths, and Helen Tiffin, eds., *The Post-Colonial Studies Reader* (New York: Routledge, 1995), 361.

23 The Peach Blossom Stream story is told in the preface of the poem *Taohuayuan ji* [The peach blossom stream], written by Tao Yuanming (AD 365–427), one of the most prominent poets in Chinese history, who lived during the Six Dynasties, a time of China's disunity.

24 A Japanese term for a middle-aged married woman that is very much ingrained in Taiwan's two spoken languages, Mandarin Chinese and local Taiwanese.

25 Hall, "Cultural Identity and Diaspora," 222–37.

14

Li Yongping and Spectral Cartography

Carlos Rojas

> In that Empire, the Art of Cartography attained such Perfection [in time] the Cartographers Guilds struck a Map of the Empire whose size was that of the Empire, and which coincided point for point with it.
>
> Jorge Luis Borges, "On Exactitude in Science"

Near the end of the fourth chapter, or "wandering" [*manyou*], of Li Yongping's 1998 novel *Zhu Ling manyou xianjing* [Zhuling's wanderings in Wonderland], the suggestively named vice principal Tang Baoguo [lit. Tang "protect the nation"] lectures a group of girls from the National Middle School on the question of "when should pubescent girls wear their first brassiere?" After citing some pseudoscientific Japanese research on sexual maturation, Tang points to the sagging breasts of older women to illustrate the dangers of not providing maturing breasts with adequate support. He then launches into an impassioned diatribe about the general importance of breasts and buttocks:

> Breast peaks and buttock mounds, the former protruding in the front and the latter uplifted behind: these are, after all, two prominent landmarks of the female body. At the same time, they also constitute an allusion to the two towering beacons that can lead voyagers astray on their way home! I am sure that you must have all heard of the Greek epic poem *The Odyssey*, whose protagonist Odysseus sails off course in the Mediterranean, leading him to drift for ten years, after which—

Tang breaks off his lecture at this point to entertain a question from Zhu Ling, the novel's young protagonist. When she asks what he means by the term *landmark* [*dibiao*], he replies: "A landmark is the most representative and the most striking symbol [*biaozhi*] of a city."[1]

Insofar as women's breasts can be seen, in Tang Baoguo's miniature allegory, as metaphoric landmarks, they have the paradoxical role of both orienting people and potentially leading them astray (like the legendary breasts of the Homeric Sirens). Furthermore, Tang appears to equivocate on whether he intends these metaphoric landmarks to be taken topographically (mis/orienting the viewer with regard to the spatial layout of the female body) or temporally (mis/orienting the viewer with respect to the chronological course of the female body's sexual maturation). Finally, the explicitly nationalist connotations of Tang's name and that of the middle school, combined with Tang's own reference to the city in his explication of the meaning of the term *landmark*, raise the question of whether these breasts and buttocks, figurative landmarks of the female body, might also be seen as symbolic landmarks with respect to the Taipei/Taiwan body politic.[2]

Tang Baoguo's discourse on women's breasts can itself be a heuristic landmark to help orient our reading and exegesis of *Zhu Ling's Wanderings in Wonderland*. To begin with, Tang's discussion points to the way in which the novel as a whole overlays temporal teleologies on metaphoric spatial topographies. More specifically, the passage evocatively points to how the novel thematizes female sexual maturation as both a literal subject and an ambiguous metaphorics for historical development. The issues of political schism and geographic dislocation have a distinctly personal relevance for Li Yongping, given his decidedly diasporic background: he was born in Malaysia, educated in Taiwan, received a postgraduate degree in the United States, and currently resides in Taiwan. Having begun his literary career in the mid-1980s (roughly around the time that martial law was lifted in Taiwan [1987]), he can be compared with other modernist writers active during this period, including Wang Wenxing, Wang Zhenhe, and Bai Xianyong. Their literary modernism can be seen as a partial return to the literary modernism of the 1960s, which was itself a reaction against both the highly politicized anti-Communist literature of the early post-1949 era and the highly commercialized "newspaper supplement" literature. The 1980s modernists were also writing against the nativist literature that had grown increasingly prominent in Taiwan in the 1970s. By the 1990s, the esoteric and highly aestheticized modernist literature of the previous decade had, by and large, run its course. Li, however, was one of the few authors who continued working on elaborate modernist literary projects long after modernism had become passé.[3]

In this essay, I explore the interrelated themes of spatial and temporal dislocation as they are developed in Li Yongping's two most recent novels, *Zhu Ling's Wanderings in Wonderland* and its predecessor, *Haidong qing* (1992).[4] Both are vast enterprises, essentially plotless in the high-modernist tradition, and boasting a veritably Joycean linguistic and symbolic complexity.[5] Indeed, this complexity has probably contributed to the comparative lack of scholarly work on either novel.[6] A central trope of both concerns the figurative status of the Taipei road map and specifically the manner in which—given the number of streets named after mainland Chinese cities, provinces, etc.—a map of contemporary Taipei can be seen as a "miniature spectral reflection" of a historical map of the Chinese mainland.

This problem of overdetermination at the level of spatial topography is paralleled by a similar overdetermination at the level of temporal development. Both novels take as protagonist the prepubescent girl Zhu Ling and explicitly thematize issues of pedophilia and pederasty. The themes of women's maturation and violence are developed against the backdrop of a Taipei/Taiwan that lies precariously balanced at a similar historical interstice—standing as the figurative child of the Chinese mainland while precociously representing the mainland's potential "future."

MOTHERLANDS AND MATERNITIES

By way of orienting the entry into *Haidong qing*, I turn first to another, at first sight unrelated text. In *The Sexual Life of Savages*, the renowned anthropologist Bronislaw Malinowski reports that the Trobriand Islanders in British New Guinea vehemently deny the existence of any physiological or corporal link between fathers and their children; the father is viewed as a supplemental interloper into the dyadic relationship between mother and child. This collective assertion of deadbeat fatherhood has, however, a curious correlate: the Trobrianders apparently deny with equal vehemence any suggestion that there might be an actual *resemblance* between *the mothers* and their children. This apparent paradox is explained by the simple postulate that, while the mother supplies the material matrix out of which the child is formed, it is the social bond with the father that directly determines the child's image or likeness.[7]

In a discussion of the gendered connotations of tropes of visual reproduction in different cultures, the contemporary French philosopher Jean-Joseph Goux notes that, while extreme, the perspective of the Trobriand Islanders is actually representative of several other, perhaps more familiar approaches to the relation between procreation and filiation. Aristotle, for example, suggests in his writings on animal reproduction that it is the female of the species that contributes the "matter" out of which the embryo develops and the male the "form."[8] The trope of immaculate conception seems to occupy a similar position in the Christian tradition. All three of these examples illustrate fairly obvious ways in which progenitive tropes can be mobilized to assert and perpetuate binary oppositions between matter and form, structure and content. Although these sorts of stark oppositions often appear most dramatically in the sorts of paradigms cited above, they frequently also exert a considerable degree of influence on other domains of social and intellectual consciousness. For example, I argue that Li Yongping's *Haidong qing* draws on comparable metaphoric oppositions in its fictional reflections on contemporary Taiwan's collective cultural and political identity, particularly with respect to its relation to mainland China.

The novel begins with the protagonist Jin Wu's return to Taiwan after eight years teaching literature in the United States. Li uses an elaborate linguistic and symbolic structure to portray Jin Wu's and the other characters' "aimless wanderings" through the city of Taipei, with special attention given to the seamier sides of the city—particularly the burgeoning industry of child prostitution. Occupying equal or even greater centrality in the work than Jin Wu himself is his young companion, the seven-year-old girl Zhu Ling. Zhu Ling generally represents a state of idealized purity that serves as a powerful counterpoint to the degenerate social practices of the adult world surrounding her, even as she stands at the figurative threshold of that world.

In the tradition of high literary modernism, *Haidong qing* abandons the conveniences of a traditional, linear plotline and develops as a patchwork of interrelated themes and concerns, pieced together around the directionless meanderings of the protagonists. Replete with streets and avenues named after cities and provinces from the Chinese mainland, the urban landscape of Taipei is explicitly described as a "miniature reflection of Great China" [*da zhongguo de suoying*] (iv). A recurrent theme in the novel concerns the different contributions to contemporary Taiwanese society and identity made by the founding "father" figure Sun Yat-sen (known conventionally in Taiwan as "*Guofu*" [National Father]) and by "Great China" [*da Zhongguo*]—the historical Chinese "motherland" itself. The implication is that Taiwan has inherited the bulk of the raw "material" of its cultural identity from the Chinese "mother" while deriving its specific political and social "form" from its founding father, Sun Yat-sen.

The final chapter of the novel presents this opposition in a symbolically stark manner that borrows from the sorts of figurative progenitive dichotomies discussed above. While outside the Lanling Girl's Middle School as it is letting out for the day, Jin Wu and Zhu Ling suddenly hear some students singing a song commemorating the revolutionary contributions of the "National Father," Sun Yat-sen. Jin Wu's first thought is that "today must be the anniversary of some important event in the life of the *Guofu* [Sun Yat-sen], which would explain why [the schoolchildren] are singing the song." Zhu Ling, however, corrects his misapprehension, pointing out that the date, May 11, is, in fact, a holiday of sorts, but one entirely unrelated to Taiwanese nationalist politics. That is to say, it has nothing to do with the "National Father" but is, rather, the eve of "Mother's Day" (931–32).

Even as *Haidong qing* contrasts a "maternal" cultural continuity between Taiwan and the mainland and a "paternal" rupture at the level of political, social, and national consciousness, it simultaneously contests and complicates this dichotomy. While borrowing familial and progenitive tropes to comment metaphorically on the political/national relation between Taiwan and the mainland, the novel uses these same tropes in a much more literal and direct way—but one that ultimately turns their apparent linearity on its figurative head.

One of the recurrent themes of *Haidong qing* concerns the relationship, frequently severed, between mothers and their children. This theme is best exemplified by the figure of An Lexin, who, throughout the novel, is portrayed as ostensibly searching for his mother while continually singing a popular Taiwanese ditty about longing/looking for one's mother:

Oh! Mama,
You are truly heartless,
Mama, ah,

> I searched the entire courtyard without finding you.
> Oh! Mama,
> For what other ambition was it,
> That you abandoned your children?⁹

This search, however, risks losing sight of its original object and becoming an end in itself, as suggested by one of the last An Lexin passages. Jin Wu hears Lexin singing and asks him, laughing, if he misses his mother. Lexin laughs as well and replies, no, he is "merely singing the song!" (794–95).¹⁰ Shortly thereafter, Zhu Ling repeats the same question, then asks Lexin if he has a mother at all, to which Lexin replies that he "grew up in the countryside in the South and as a result never had a chance to see her" (796).

In another of the An Lexin passages, a Taipei taxi driver remarks to Jin Wu: "Everyone in Haidong [lit. "East of the Sea"; i.e., Taiwan] is looking for their mother." This is immediately preceded by another episode in which Jin Wu is described as gazing out the window of the taxi and seeing that the clock on the wall of the national parliament building reads five past four. Jin Wu immediately looks at the wristwatch of his young female friend, Ya Xing, and, seeing that it reads four o'clock, comments to her that the parliament building clock appears to be five minutes fast. Ya Xing replies that the clock is not fast; rather, it has been stopped at five past four for many years (486). The fact that this particular scene falls in the middle of a discussion of searching for missing mothers suggests that this phenomenon may be compared to a sort of arrested temporality symbolized by the parliament clock. Furthermore, the frozen time happens to coincide almost precisely with the time on the watch worn by the young Ya Xing, pointing to a possible equation of transtemporal transferences between missing mothers and young girls.¹¹ Admittedly, if grounded merely on this single passage, these conjectures are far too speculative to be useful. However, the novel itself develops, in a fairly explicit manner, precisely these sorts of issues.

To begin with, *Haidong qing* both explicitly and implicitly thematizes the taboo topic of older men's pedophilic attraction to young girls. The basic plot of the novel concerns the protagonist, Jin Wu, a middle-aged male literature professor, and his intimate relationship with a small group of young, grade school–age girls.¹² Although at no point does the novel suggest that there is an overtly sexual dimension to their interaction, it repeatedly demonstrates its awareness of how these relationships might be misperceived by others.

In chapter 12, for example, there is an ambiguous moment when Jin Wu squeezes Zhu Ling's shoulders. She immediately jumps back and asks him what he is doing. He replies, "Nothing, I just wanted to stroke you a little," whereupon Zhu Ling's face "flushed bright red as she stared up at him with a strange expression on her face, not knowing whether to laugh or not" (819). In another scene, Jin Wu attempts to take Ya Xing out of school in the middle of the day. The female instructor who greets him obviously suspects his intentions, and he immediately has to justify himself by explaining defensively that he is a professor in the Foreign Language Department at Hai-tung University (i.e., a respected member of the community) and that he needs to tell his neighbor's child, Ya Xing, that there is a "family emergency"—a conventional excuse that at the same time ironically points to the novel's own theme of the deterritorialization of nuclear family kinship structures (481–82).

If the theme of pedophilia implicates the novel's protagonists only through a series of innuendos and misprisions, the same taboo topic is an explicit and dominant concern throughout much of the work. At the very beginning, for instance, Jin Wu remarks to the taxi driver who picks him up at the airport that there appear to be a lot of young girls out in the street for that time of night (it is three in the morning). The taxi driver replies that "as of late, when it comes to playing with women, men's tastes have changed" (29), obviously referring to the fact that Taiwanese men are taking a sexual interest in ever-younger girls.

This theme of pedophilia is elaborated most explicitly in chapter 11, when several professors discuss, among other things, the increasing prevalence of underage prostitution in Taiwan and Hong Kong. A certain Professor He Jiayu proffers the following observations:

> Today I read a report from the Republic of China Women's Rescue Fund Organization [*zhonghua minguo funü jiuyuan jijinhui*] reporting that surveys reveal that there are a hundred thousand prostitutes in the city and that the average age at which the girls enter prostitution is between twelve and fourteen.... Furthermore, the Republic of China Women's Rescue Fund Organization also reports that, as the availability increases, and as men's tastes continue to change, the age of prostitutes in the city will continue to drop precipitously. Right now, what is deemed most desirable are those girls who are still in the first or second year of middle school or even the fifth or sixth grade of primary school. (695)

The professors move on to an extended discussion of pedophilia in Japanese culture and society. At one point, for example, Professor Chen Bule remarks that the theme of "older men sexually obsessed with youth" in Japanese movies and literature has already become a motif, or literally "mother topic" [*muti*], in Japanese culture (727).

Professor Chen uses the term *motif* in a strictly academic sense, even apologizing at one point for his use of overly technical terminology. Nevertheless, this specific phrase (with its allusion to the figure of motherhood to describe the cultural phenomenon of pedophilia) points to one of the more intriguing dimensions of the theme of pedophilia in Li's novel—a potential link between it and the equally prominent theme, discussed above, of missing motherhood. Specifically, these two chains of misdirected identifications and projections (children straying from their mothers and men's libidinal impulses straying from women of their own generation onto their figurative daughters) come full circle with the novel's reflections on the phenomenon whereby part of a young girl's sexual attractiveness allegedly, and paradoxically, lies in her own embodiment of a certain "motherly quality."

This paradoxical generational conflation is presented most explicitly in the novel's portrayal of contemporary Japanese culture and society. For example, following their discussion of pedophilia, the professors in chapter 11 eventually turn to a consideration of popular Japanese cinema. Of particular interest to them is the prominent Japanese teenage actress Miyashino Yuko. Although she is actually already sixteen or seventeen, she looks as though she is only twelve; at the same time, she is described as embodying "that sort of motherly love that men are always searching for." At one point, Professor He Jiayu follows up on his earlier remarks, cited above, by observing:

> Professor Chen, what are you saying? That old Japanese men have a proclivity for young girls [*you liannütong zhi pi*]? Oh, it generally seems that way. When I was studying in the United States, I had a chance to see the documentary on the Rape of Nanjing, which the American missionary "John Ma" filmed himself. In it, there was one scene in which a group of Japanese soldiers raped a seven-year-old Chinese girl. I think that this represents the most specific, most bare-boned, and most horrid manifestation of this Japanese proclivity for young girls. Returning to our earlier topic of discussion—although Miyashino Yuko is actually sixteen or seventeen years old, she looks as if she is only twelve or thirteen. Yet, at the same time, she possesses the sort of motherly love that men are perpetually seeking.

... This sort of motherly girl actress is something Japanese male audiences have always loved the most. (741)

From these specific comments about the Second Sino-Japanese War and Japanese cinema, it is clear that young women in *Haidong qing* occupy a curious libidinal and temporal interstice. They are eroticized precisely for their (comparative) sexual immaturity; however, they are also frequently the objects of a sort of "future perfect" eroticization, whereby they embody certain maternal qualities that presumably pertain to the other end of the same incest taboo. This is seen perhaps most clearly in the novel's theme of young Taiwanese girls taking estrogen supplements to hasten their sexual development, which leaves them with "a baby's face and the body of a woman" (927).[13] Not only do the hormones facilitate the pedophilic ideal of simultaneous sexual maturity and immaturity, but, furthermore, they point to a process of reification of both maturation and femininity, enabling both qualities to be artificially separated from the individual and to become objects of investment in their own right.

The last allusion to female hormones in the novel is juxtaposed with another, closely related discussion: that of the consumption of turkey testicles. Throughout much of the novel, there are fairly regular references to the practice of eating what are literally called "turkey kidneys" [*huoji yaozi*].[14] It is not, however, until the final chapter that it occurs to Zhu Ling to ask Jin Wu what exactly these "kidneys" are. When informed that they are avian gonads, she not only is horrified but also develops an even greater sympathy for the live rooster she happens to be holding in her lap (901). This rooster had been one of a large group deliberately freed to protest America's practice of dumping unwanted turkey testicles on the Taiwanese market, where they are considered an expensive delicacy. Initially having taken the rooster out of an abstract sympathy for its predicament, Zhu Ling becomes even more attached to the bird when she realizes that she may be protecting it from emasculation. With the female hormones and the turkey kidneys, then, we have a parallel, symbolic separation of the essence of femininity and masculinity from the actual bodies they help bring to maturity.

In his second discourse on pedophilia, cited above, Professor He Jiayu moves from a remark about the Japanese soldiers raping Chinese girls during the Second Sino-Japanese War to a more extended discussion of the theme of pedophilia in contemporary Japanese culture. Although, in this specific context, the precise relation between the two themes may be ambiguous, the Rape of Nanjing, together with the issues of its significance and how it should be remembered, is a central theme in the novel as a whole. For example, in chapter 6 there is an account of an interview with a member of the Japanese national parliament, published in none other than that paragon of pedophilic fantasies the American edition of *Playboy* (known in China as *Huahua gongzi*). In this interview, the Japanese assemblyman calmly denies that the incident ever occurred at all, claiming that it was actually just a hoax staged by local Chinese to tarnish the reputations of the Japanese invaders (313). If his historical blindness can be seen as an example of Freudian displacement, then its precise inverse can, perhaps, be seen in another amusing Rape of Nanjing scene in chapter 11, grounded on a similarly Freudian logic of overdetermined condensation. Here, the group of college professors gives the fourteen-year-old girl Zhang Tong a series of dates and asks her to identify which important event in modern Chinese history is associated with them. To each date, Zhang Tong advances the same guess: the Rape of Nanjing (699).[15]

These various allusions to the Rape of Nanjing can be related to two distinct themes in *Haidong qing*. They are all explicitly bound up with the issue of historical commemoration. How are historical events to be remembered? What is their status when viewed in retrospect? As I suggested above, the novel forsakes the structuring conveniences of a conventional teleological plot. Just as the story line does not really go anywhere, the act of wandering is a major theme of the work. Amid all this aimless wandering, official and traditional holidays come to substitute, in large part, for absent topographic landmarks. The Rape of Nanjing is an example of this sort of "temporal landmark," providing a concrete, if overdetermined, historical marker in relation to which the novel's characters can orient themselves.

At the same time, these allusions to the Rape of Nanjing can also be viewed from the perspective of the theme of temporal discontinuity. Throughout the novel, the seven-year-old protagonist, Zhu Ling, repeatedly shocks her interlocutors by voicing thoughts and observations (typically dealing with either sex or politics) that suggest a much more mature consciousness: her reflections on the Rape of Nanjing itself, on accelerated maturation through the use of female hormone supplements (see, e.g., 927), on the Japanese practice of taking "sex vacations" (e.g., 791), and on the use of the term *biqin* [fleeing from Qin; i.e., from Qinshi Huang, the notoriously autocratic emperor of the Qin dynasty] to describe mainlanders who retreated to Taiwan when fleeing the Communist regime on the mainland (e.g., 292). One of the most striking instances of this double-voicing can be found near the end of the novel, when Zhu Ling recounts to Jin Wu a mysterious recent dream of hers, one in which all the bronze Sun Yat-sen statues in front of Taiwanese elementary schools suddenly come to life and proceed to search out those officials who have vandalized Sun's banners and carried off his placards. The living statues also make a point of hunting down and beheading all adults who have (sexually) taken advantage of young girls. Jin Wu is stunned that the young, supposedly innocent Zhu Ling could have such a dream: "Girl, how old are you? 'Vandalizing the banners of the National Father' [*dazhe Guofu de qihao*], 'bringing calamity to the nation and its people' [*huoguo yangmin*], 'violating young girls' [*zaojian xiao nühai*], this kind of talk doesn't sound like something a seven-year-old little girl would say." Jin Wu appears reassured when she informs him that this is actually only a story her father told her. She nevertheless hastens to add that she dreamed the same dream herself (924).

Just as the perverse, hormone-laden girls with a "baby's face and the body of a woman" are portrayed as holding a distinct appeal for at least a portion of the Taipei population of adult males, we might speculate that it is Zhu Ling's (and, to a lesser extent, her friends Ya Xing's and Zhang Tong's) diaglossic combination of childlike innocence with parodic adultlike precocity that partially accounts for Jin Wu's emotional attachment to them. The resulting Janus-like approach to temporality can, moreover, be observed in one of Jin Wu's bizarre behavioral quirks: his habitual, almost obsessive practice of checking the watches on the wrists of his young female friends to determine the time.[16] So egregious is this habit that, at one point, his female student Gong Qing asks him in exasperation: "Don't *you* yourself *ever* wear a watch?" (471). This seemingly innocent gesture of telling time from young girls' watches metonymically endows the girls with precisely the same temporal continuity that their intellectual precocity and potentially sexualized bodies appear to threaten.

I suggested above that one of the recurrent themes of the novel concerns the temporal disjunction between Taiwan and its figurative mother, the Chinese mainland, with Taipei constituting a spectral reflection of mainland topography and serving as a prophetic anticipation of the mainland's possible future. This theme of maternity "out of joint" is echoed by a series of isolated references to the Chinese custom of having postpartum mothers undergo a month of symbolic quarantine after giving birth. Known as *zuo yuezi*, or "sitting out the month," this practice generally dictates that new mothers remain indoors and away from open air and running water. Interspersed regularly throughout *Haidong qing* are numerous references to a certain "Mixin zuo yuezi center."[17] Typically short and highly repetitive, these passages focus on the spectral figures of new mothers standing silently at their windows, peering down at the street below. For example, the following account is fairly typical and is repeated virtually verbatim many times: "Across from the hot-pot restaurant there is the Mixin yuezi center. Upstairs, there is a secluded red shrine, and behind the virtually silent curtained windows there stand twenty or thirty postpartum mothers, both large and small, all nursing their infants and with their hair combed flat against their heads. Wearing nightgowns, they peer down with bright eyes at the street below" (782). This temporal interregnum between the moment of birth and the mother's reentry into normal society reproduces in miniature the historical aporia in which the novel implicitly locates the Chinese mainland. Holding their newborn babies, the mothers perpetually stand at the windows of the Mixin center, enjoying a bird's-eye view of the city streets stretching out below them. This maze of roads and alleys, together with its implicit cartographic representation, is, in turn, one of the central tropes of the novel.

Haidong qing contains several explicit discussions of the phenomenon whereby Taipei's urban cartography is a spectral reflection of mainland China's historical geography. At one point, for example, the new, aboriginal female parliamentary representative, Jianxu Yugui, comments:

> "Japan and China kill each other; Japan is defeated and China wins, so the Chinese come over here to loot and plunder! The KMT [Kuomintang, now Guomindang] and the Communists kill each other; the Nationalists are defeated and the Communists win, so the Nationalists come over here to build a presidential mansion! They haphazardly change all our street names without any justification. Really hilarious! Huayin Road, Hanyang Road, Lishan Road, Tianshui Road, Nanjing Road, Guilin Road, Emei Road. Really hilarious! They pretend that this little island of ours represents all China! Sham immortal, sham immortal!" (495)

Earlier in the same chapter, Zhu Ling's father elaborates more concisely the precise relation among Taiwan, Japan, and China as well as how "this little island of ours represents all China." He explains to Jin Wu that, when the Japanese invaded Taiwan, they renamed all the streets and other landmarks using Japanese terms. Later,

> when the Japanese surrendered, the Seventieth Regiment of the Nationalist army crossed the strait to accept the surrender, and the commanding officer of the [provincial] administrative office had some lower-level clerks from the vanguard commanding post take some large maps of China and lay them down on the table next to some Taipei maps the Japanese had printed up. Putting them together and comparing, and then a wave of the pen, and, Hah! they renamed every street and road in the entire city with Chinese names, [as if they had] returned to their own homeland. (460)

Just as the story of the Rape of Nanjing persistently haunts the narrative of the novel, this account points to how, hidden between the cartographic image and its own spectral reflection, there lie embedded traces of Japanese military aggression.

Finally, in the preface to the novel, Li Yongping himself makes yet another reference to Haidong's spectral topography, in the context of his suggestion that the novel's self-consciously "allegorical" structure might be read as having a "prophetic" significance, in that the allegorical observations about Haidong might, in the future, come to be applicable to the mainland as well. Because of its centrality to both Li's novel and my own argument here, I quote the relevant passage at length:

> Look, the novel describes that great city, located in the dynamic waves of the bright and magnificent Eastern Sea—an impregnable fortress and a base for the renaissance of the "Three People's Principles." But notice that all the street names and road names of that city *are nothing more than miniature reflections of the Great China [da Zhongguo de suoying]*: Xuzhou Zhengzhou Zhangzhou Jingzhou Gangzhou Liangzhou, Luoyang Nanyang Hengyang, Huayin Hanyin Huaiyin, Kunlun Hami Xichang Andong. Each of these roads crosses toward the Republic of China's presidential palace in the center of the city. North and south of the Yangze, above and below the Great River, the thousand-year-old imperial palace, the city of the five ethnicities, they are like a myriad of stars that shine resplendently on the road map of the temporary capital of the Republic of China—*but doesn't it bear an uncanny resemblance to a map of the Chinese mainland, quiet and at peace, eternally young through the ages? For this reason, "Haidong qing," in addition to being*

an allegory, is also a prophecy. The city described in this novel, with its countless local conditions and customs, multitudinous bustling atmosphere, all brought together in this miraculous place that is the immortal Isle of Penglai; in another ten, twenty, or maybe even fifty years, might it not also appear, under the banner of the Three People's Principles, in every city and every corner of that ancient Chinese mainland, resting place of the one billion descendants of [the two legendary Chinese emperors] Yan and Huang?

Zhu Ling, I hope that you will grow up well. (iv–v; emphasis added)

I agree with Li that this cartographic figure has a temporal valence in addition to the obvious spatial one. However, I suggest that, pace Li himself, this chronological cartography is more melancholic than prophetic. To borrow from the terms of the preceding discussion, we might say that "Donghai's" (i.e., Taipei's) maps resemble the assortment of young women who populate the novel and that the spectral and specular resemblance that they bear to the mainland parallels the young girls' resemblance to the mothers from whom they have been separated much more than it suggests what these figurative absent mothers will develop into.

At a relatively early point in the novel, Jin Wu casually quizzes An Lexin on his cartogeographic knowledge, asking him to identify the actual historical referents of the various names on a Taiwanese road map (122–24). In a similar scene in chapter 12, the roles are reversed as Zhu Ling playfully tests Jin Wu's own knowledge of historical geography by similarly asking him to identify the historical origins of Taipei landmarks (806–7). Although it occurs only once in the novel, Zhu Ling's quizzing Jin Wu can be seen as a precise inverse of Jin Wu's compulsive habit of checking the time on Zhu Ling's (and Ya Xing's and Zhang Tong's) wristwatches. In both cases, Jin Wu and Zhu Ling take figures that best represent (for them) nodes of temporal instability (namely, the city maps and the precocious, prepubescent girls) and "neurotically" redirect them into symbols of the same (unstable) temporal continuity itself.

We could take this reading a step further and suggest that Li's own systematic pattern of cartographic allusion lends the preface—and, by implication, the entire novel—a similar quality of neurotic temporal denial. Just as Jin Wu's habit of checking the young girls' watches can be read as an effort to deny and repress the temporal challenge that they themselves represent, Li's cartographic allusion can be seen as a figurative act of watch checking—

whereby he attempts to see the novel in terms of general types of teleological historical trajectories, although it is arguably most concerned with emphatically questioning the rationality and tenability of those trajectories.

In chapter 7, the young Zhang Tong tells Jin Wu: "The most unbenevolent aspect of this model 'Three People's Principles' precious island of ours is that it doesn't let young girls grow up properly" (431). A slightly different version of this statement is repeated in chapter 11: "The most inhuman aspect of this society of ours is that it doesn't let young girls grow up properly" (744). Similarly, the final line of the entire novel is Jin Wu's exhortation to Zhu Ling, "Girl, don't grow up so quickly," whereupon "Zhu Ling broke into tears" (941).[18] In view of my argument regarding the intimate imbrication and mutual transference of national and sexual developmental trajectories in the novel, we might even be tempted to conclude by inverting these claims and exhortations about girls growing up in Taiwan. That is, we might claim that it is precisely the novel's focus on Taipei's spectral cartography that can be read as a form of transference, forestalling the "proper development" of the novel's own deconstructive implications regarding Taiwanese society's historical-maturational status.

PATERNITIES AND EXPATRIATISMS

As a point of entry into Li Yongping's most recent novel, *Zhu Ling's Wanderings in Wonderland*, I turn first to an evocative passage from *Zhuangzi*:

> The emperor of the South Sea was called Shu, the emperor of the North Sea was called Hu, and the emperor of the central region was called Hundun. Shu and Hu from time to time came together for a meeting in the territory of Hundun, and Hundun treated them very generously. Shu and Hu discussed how they could repay his kindness. "All men," they said, "have seven openings so they can see, hear, eat, and breathe. But Hundun doesn't have any. Let's trying boring him some!"
>
> Every day they bored another hole, and on the seventh day Hundun died.[19]

Here is a miniature creation myth of the role of bodily penetration in Hundun's symbolic entry into the mortal world, suggesting a useful approach to the themes of maturation and transition in Li's novel.[20] That is to say, *Zhu Ling* explicitly and emphatically thematizes the role of corporal perforation as a sort of symbolic rite of passage into maturity/mortality. Specifically,

I have in mind the use of ear piercing as a symbol for a girl's maturation into womanhood. This theme is initially introduced in *Haidong qing* (374), but it is developed more systematically in *Zhu Ling*. Near the beginning of the latter novel there is a detailed discussion of how piercing a young girl's ears symbolizes the breaking of the hymen, which conventionally represents her own loss of innocence. As An Lexin explains to Zhu Ling's friend Lian Mingxin: "If a young girl wants to grow up, then she must first be shot by a man with a gun, be pierced with a hole, and bleed a drop of red, red blood" (74).[21]

When Zhu Ling herself has her ears pierced, the instrument used is referred to in Chinese (as in English) as an ear-piercing "gun" [*qiang*] (83). Furthermore, it is actually a "Japanese gun" (e.g., 73, 94, 159, etc.). The novel's repeated emphasis on this "gun" creates an uncanny juxtaposition of the trajectories of individual sexual maturation and collective national development. Zhu Ling's use of this particular term inspires such surprise and shock in her interlocutors because it evokes memories of Japanese aggression against both Taiwan and the Chinese mainland. At the same time, however, the confusion that this terminology elicits in the novel's own characters is emblematic of one of the dominant levels of symbolic significance of both *Haidong qing* and *Zhu Ling*—namely, the symbolic coupling of individual and collective maturation as projected onto the bodies of the young female protagonists and China's own body politic. The details of this coupling are multifarious and often contradictory, but, in this case, their general direction is fairly obvious: the symbolic violence imposed on the girls' bodies by means of the (Japanese) ear-piercing gun is mirrored by the violence historically imposed on the Chinese body politic by actual acts of Japanese aggression. The implication is that the latter acts of military aggression contributed to Taiwan's symbolic development and maturation in much the same way that the former practice of ear/hymen piercing contributes symbolically to the girls' own personal and physical maturation.

Further reinforcing this association is the fact that the discussion of Zhu Ling's ear piercing is roughly paralleled in the novel by references to one of the most famous historical acts of Japanese aggression against China, the so-called Rape of Nanjing. Although *Nanjing da tusha* [the great Nanjing massacre], the original Chinese term for this incident, is not as explicitly evocative of sexual transgression as the conventional English translation, the context of the incident's treatment in Li's two novels stresses the prevalence of actual rapes of Chinese women by Japanese soldiers. Furthermore, the references to ear piercing in both novels frequently occur in close proximity to evocative discussions of sexual violence during the Rape of Nanjing. In *Haidong qing*, for instance, Jin Wu discusses with Zhu Ling and Ya Xing the prospect of having their ears pierced (373–74); not long thereafter, Zhu Ling and Ya Xing, while riding on a train, read a newspaper report about gang rapes during the Rape of Nanjing (401–2). Similarly, the account of Zhu Ling's own ear piercing in *Zhu Ling* (159) is immediately preceded by a scene in which she recollects having watched a television documentary commemorating that same historical event (152–53). This parallel between sexual and national transgression is drawn even more clearly a few lines later, when Zhu Ling's friend He Lishuang adds that, while selling flowers at the bars on Zhongshan Lu [Zhongshan Road], she would occasionally have as customers old Japanese men who would grope under her skirt while reminiscing about the World War II-era competitions they used to hold, involving the piercing of young girls' "private parts" [*michu* in Chinese] with bayonets. This moment, therefore, marks a striking conflation of narratives of sexual and military transgression, with the old men's present groping marking a stark displacement of their earlier sexual violence.

He Lishuang's bars are located in the alleys adjoining Zhongshan Lu, named after Sun Yat-sen [Sun Zhongshan in Mandarin]. This allusion to Taiwan's *Guofu* follows directly on the heels of Zhu Ling's own account of her dream after having watched the Rape of Nanjing television documentary discussed above, a dream in which "the *Guofu* [Sun Yat-sen] was pointing angrily at Chiang Kai-shek's nose and cursing him" (153).[22] I argue that Sun Yat-sen and Chiang Kai-shek represent two opposing ways in which a figurative "word of the father" or "touch of the father" is juxtaposed with an allegorical understanding of female maturation. Schematically, they represent, respectively, a form of superficial, cosmetic continuity and a more violent, penetrative rupture.

First, however, I return briefly to the theme of female "maturation" as it is developed in *Zhu Ling*. In the discussion of child prostitution, the colloquial equivalent of the symbolic ear piercing is the expression "opening the jug" [*kaiguan*]. However, at one point near the end of the novel, a character mentions that he prefers "dressing one's hair" [*shulong*] as a more elliptical and euphemistic term for the process of losing one's virginity (379). This word resonates not only with the tradition of courtesanship in Chinese history but also with the sociocultural happenstance that, in contemporary Taiwan, hairdressing salons [*lifating*] are prominent sites of prostitution.²³ Furthermore, insofar as *shulong* connotes a more cosmetic, continuous view of female "maturation" and *kaiguan* connotes its more abrupt, violent side, then the *shulong/kaiguan* dichotomy can be seen as representing the individual, maturational equivalent of the Sun Yat-sen/Chiang Kai-shek dichotomy alluded to above.

These two euphemisms for the loss of virginity and (implicit) sexual maturation come together in a passing comment made by Zhu Ling in *Haidong qing*. One day (coincidentally, it happens to be "Daughter's Day" in Japan), Jin Wu notices that Zhu Ling's braid has been cut off. He asks her about it, and she explains that her mother cut it because she "is not a little girl anymore" (773–74). Here, the surface, cosmetic alterations connoted by the term *shulong* intersect with the violently transgressive connotations of *kaiguan*. Moreover, the act of cutting the braid is evocative of the practice of cutting men's queues—one of the more potent symbols of China's own "maturation" from an antiquated, imperial system into a "modern" republic. When ear piercing as a symbol of young girls' sexual maturation is discussed in *Haidong qing* and *Zhu Ling*, a question that comes up in both novels is what the equivalent rite of passage would be for young boys. In each case, the obvious parallel is drawn between female ear piercing and male circumcision (see, e.g., *Haidong qing*, 374; and *Zhu Ling*, 77). However, the relation between ear piercing and hairdressing/cutting explored in the preceding section suggests another point of entry into this question of the masculine equivalent.

Near the beginning of the sixth chapter of *Zhu Ling* is a short passage that bears some relevance to this question. Zhu Ling and her friend Lian Mingxin are using a small telescope to watch the comings and goings of the president. They discover that, after work, the president and his motorcade do not go home but, rather, proceed to Changchun [Everlasting Spring] Road—a district that the novel repeatedly describes as being renowned for its abundance of hairdressing salons–cum–sex shops. Zhu Ling asks in surprise: "How could the president go to that kind of salon [*lifating*] to have his hair done? In those kinds of hairdressing salons, it is so dark inside that he could very easily accidentally have something else snipped off while having his hair cut." Lian Mingxin finds this prospect amusing and suggests: "If things were to go wrong, the hairdressing lady might even cut off his two balls [*liang li dandan*]." Zhu Ling agrees and further notes that the newspapers once reported precisely such an incident (317). Given that the salons (operating as fronts for underage brothels) mark a topographic site of girls' early developmental transition into sexual maturity, the joke about accidental presidential emasculation may be related to the theme of female sexual maturation—and both, in turn, may be related to the novel's larger political symbolics.

We might begin to explore this possibility by positioning Lian Mingxin's salacious joke within a larger discussion of severed male gonads in both *Haidong qing* and *Zhu Ling*. For example, as discussed above, the last chapter of *Haidong qing* features the peculiar image of Zhu Ling running around disconsolate, with a live rooster grasped closely to her bosom. Similarly, the first chapter of *Zhu Ling* begins with a discussion of young girls' culinary interest in turkey testicles (35). In both novels, this delicacy is referred to discreetly as *yaozi* [kidneys], but, when Zhu Ling's friend Lin Xiangjin asks her what they are, she explains that they are *gaowan* [testicles]. When Xiangjin still fails to understand, Zhu reverts to the terminology that she and Lian Mingxin used, in the passage cited above, to refer to the presidential "balls" [*dandan*]. As the *Zhu Ling* passage makes clear, it is believed that eating turkey testicles (and rooster buttocks) will help young girls "grow up quickly" (35).

These (avian) gonads, isolated from the actual male bodies that are their point of origin, can also be related to the theme of political paternity in both novels. In the preceding discussion of *Haidong qing*, I addressed the novel's explicit thematization of the "National Father," Sun Yat-sen, and particularly the degree to which it draws on prevalent progenitive metaphors to describe how the "maternal" Chinese homeland (the mainland) is perceived as having granted Taiwan its basic cultural "matrix" while the "paternal" Sun Yat-sen is perceived as having contributed its distinguishing sociopolitical "form." Here, I expand on that earlier discussion by pointing out how both of Li's novels elaborate on metaphoric political paternity by devoting comparable attention not only to Sun Yat-sen but also to Chiang Kai-shek. Both historical figures are regarded as having played paradigmatic roles in the shaping of modern Taiwan, although there were several salient differences between them.

To begin with, both novels explicitly compare Chiang Kai-shek's role in the founding of Taiwan to Moses's leading the Israelites out of Egypt and across the Red Sea into Israel. This biblical symbolism is very prominently and explicitly foregrounded in the preface to *Haidong qing* (i–iii). If Chiang Kai-shek's role in the establishment of present-day Taiwan is grounded in his role as a military leader during the civil war and the Japanese aggression, then Sun Yat-sen's political paternity occupies a more abstract and idealized plane. That is, his thought and writings from the 1911 Revolution and early republican period are retrospectively held up as one of the cornerstones of the political identity of the Republic of China. Although the historical grounds for this are questionable, the political and ideological ones are unmistakable—turning to 1911 and republican-era political rhetoric makes it possible to elaborate a political ideology that, in theory, embraces the mainland in a way that merely looking to a military figure like Chiang Kai-shek would not.

The continuity between the themes of paternity and reproduction in the two novels' discussions of poultry gonads and founding fathers is further strengthened by the fact that the vast majority of the references in *Zhu Ling* to Sun and Chiang are actually not to the historical individuals themselves but to the assortment of plaques, statues, portraits, inscriptions, and other assorted physical and symbolic memorials that commemorate their existence and achievements. Just as Zhu Ling and Lian Mingxin joke about separating the president from the symbolic seat of his phallic authority (his "balls"), the "paternal" national-political authority of both Sun Yat-sen and Chiang Kai-shek is, in effect, disassociated from those original historical individuals and attached to a series of symbolic substitutes.

Moreover, in both novels, these themes resonate ironically with explicit thematizations of pedophilia. As discussed above, in *Haidong qing*, part of the allure of having sex with young girls is associated with the way in which their immature figures are sometimes perceived by adult men as paradoxically embodying "that motherly sort of love that men are always searching for" (741). Therefore, their sexual attraction is partially derived from their location in a peculiar temporal interstice, straddling the doubly incestuous prohibition against sleeping with one's daughter and with one's mother.[24] *Zhu Ling* offers its own, related analysis: the pedophilic allure is portrayed as being related to the urban myth that, by having intercourse with a young virgin, a man infected with an STD can "pass" the disease on to the girl (392). Not only will the girl acquire the disease, but the adult man will be able to rid himself of it and, thus, symbolically regain a sort of prelapsarian innocence. This pedophilia phenomenon has ambivalent and paradoxical implications for the significance of "paternity"—having sex with one's own figurative daughter is imagined as propelling her into symbolic, if not actual, sexual maturity while at the same time enabling the adult man to erase the ravages of his own history of sexual conquests and return to a state of symbolic purity. This exchange of sexual contamination and innocence is comparable to the temporal inversion previously observed in *Haidong qing*, whereby the prepubescent girl is refigured as the adult pedophile's symbolic mother.

The temporal paradoxes played out in the arenas of sexual politics and pedophilic transgression have an evocative parallel in the way in which both *Haidong qing* and *Zhu Ling* elaborate the symbolic relation between Taiwan and the Chinese mainland. Both novels juxtapose discussions of girls' sexual maturation with reflections on Taiwan's political and historical "maturation," suggesting that the island constitutes a symbolic embodiment of mainland China's own (potential) future (see, e.g., *Zhu Ling*, 333). Both novels, furthermore, make the almost identically phrased claim that "Taiwan's today is the mainland's tomorrow" (see *Haidong qing*, iv–v; *Zhu Ling*, 333). In this respect, *Zhu Ling* picks up on one of the dominant images of *Haidong qing*—that of mainland China staring out across the Taiwan Strait and seeing a spectral image of its own future self, an uncanny mirroring reinforced by the observation that Taiwan's (and, in particular, Taipei's) urban cartography is merely a "miniature reflection" of the political topography of the Chinese mainland: "Da Zhongguo de suoying" (*Haidong qing*, iv).

I began this section with a discussion of the themes of diaspora and expatriatism and their relation to Li's oeuvre. The sense of topographic rootlessness is reflected nicely by a concept central to Li's two most recent novels: *titou*, a Taiwanese term meaning roughly "to roam, wander, or stroll." This term, together with its various synonyms (including *piaobo, liulang, youguang, liuda*, etc.), is explicitly and repeatedly used in the novels to describe the various protagonists' characteristic means of moving through space. Like the figurative expatriate, most of the characters are never in a place where they can feel truly at home and are constantly on the move with no real topographic telos in mind.

Beyond its actual meaning of "wandering" or "roaming," the Taiwanese term *titou* is also a homonym of another binome that in Mandarin has an almost identical pronunciation (*titou*) and has a range of potential meanings, including "to cut one's hair," "to shave one's head," and even "to decapitate." There is one passage in each novel in which the characters hear the Taiwanese term and mistake it for its Mandarin homonym (*Haidong qing*, 124; and *Zhu Ling*, 322). This fortuitous pun brings together many of the various themes discussed in this essay: the literal meaning of the term suggests the bodily dislocation from a topographic point of origin, the "motherland," that is characteristic of the expatriate condition.

The potential meanings of the Mandarin homonym traverse the array of connotations suggested by the *shulong/kaiguan* dichotomy discussed above. For example, understood in the sense of "hair cutting," *titou* shares the surface, cosmetic connotations of *shulong*. At the other extreme, understood in the sense of "decapitation," the term approximates the violently transgressive connotations of *kaiguan*. Furthermore, the pun on *titou*, in the sense of "decapitation," is reinforced by a series of references throughout *Haidong qing* to the biblical story of Salome and the beheading of John the Baptist. A popular Hong Kong song on this subject is one of the first sounds that Jin Wu hears at the beginning of the novel (10), and it is followed by suggestions that Jin Wu's young female friends stand as miniature Salomes. Finally, these two mutually opposed connotations of the Mandarin *titou* ("hairdressing" and "decapitation") are juxtaposed in the presidential hairdressing anecdote, which uses the same expression first to denote conventional, cosmetic haircutting and then, in Zhu Ling's elliptical formulation, to suggest a symbolic "beheading" or emasculation.

Therefore, the various different meanings of *titou* come together to express what is, I argue, one of the implications of *Zhu Ling* as a whole for the question of the relation between symbolic paternity and expatriatism. The original Taiwanese meaning of *titou*—"to roam or wander"—suggests a certain rootless diasporic or expatriate condition. Meanwhile, the two opposed meanings of the Mandarin *titou*—"hairdressing" and "decapitation"—suggest the same cosmetic continuity/violent rupture dichotomy shared by the *shulong/kaiguan* and Sun Yat-sen/Chiang Kai-shek dyads. Moreover, Zhu Ling's salacious innuendo (which Lian Mingxin makes explicit) draws on the castrative dimension of *titou*, which can be linked to the process of positing an idealized model of individual or collective development located outside oneself.

I have argued that a central theme in Li Yongping's recent novels concerns the way in which fantasies of femininity are used in imagining a postnational Taiwanese identity. Maternity provides a model for the progenitive continuity between the Chinese mainland and Taiwan, even as girls' early sexual maturation implicitly functions as a model for a site of radical rupture between origins and current identity.

NOTES

Unless otherwise indicated, all translations from non-English-language sources are my own.

1. Li Yongping, *Zhu Ling manyou xianjing* [Zhu Ling's wanderings in Wonderland] (Taipei: Lianhe wenxue, 1998), 242.
2. In this respect, Li Yongping is drawing on a long tradition in Taoism, dating back at least as far as the fourth-century-BCE text *Zhuangzi*, of seeing "the human body [as] the image of a country." For a discussion of the genealogy of this trope, see, e.g., Kristofer Schipper, *The Taoist Body*, trans. Karen Duval (Berkeley and Los Angeles: University of California Press, 1992), 100–112.
3. Another prominent example is Wang Wenxing, discussed in Sung-sheng Yvonne Chang's "Wang Wenxing's *Backed against the Sea, Parts I and II*" (chapter 7 in this volume).
4. Li Yongping, *Haidong qing* (Taipei: Lianhe wenxue, 1992).
5. Together, the two novels total more than fourteen hundred pages, with *Haidong qing* alone running to nearly a thousand.
6. Although there have been several reviews of and short newspaper articles on the novels (including several interesting pieces in Chinese by David Der-wei Wang and Yvonne Sung-sheng Chang), I am not aware of any full-length studies of either, in either Chinese or English, other than my own. One article that came to my attention after I had completed this essay is Ng Kim-chu, "Liuli de poluozhou zhi zi he ta de muqin, fuqin" [A rambling Brahmin's son and his mother and father], in *Mahua wenxue de Zhongguoxing* [The Chineseness of Sino-Malay literature] (Taipei: Yuandao, 1998), 299–350. Although Ng devotes relatively little attention to *Zhu Ling* and *Haidong qing*, his discussion of the status of maternity and paternity in Li's oeuvre as a whole is, in some respects, consistent with my own.
7. See Bronislaw Malinowski, *The Sexual Life of Savages* (Boston: Beacon, 1987), 140–79, discussed in Jean-Joseph Goux, *Symbolic Economies: After Marx and Freud*, trans. Jennifer Curtiss Gage (Ithaca: Cornell University Press, 1978), 218–19.
8. Aristotle, *Physics* 1.9.192a23, cited and discussed in Goux, *Symbolic Economies*, 213.
9. For passages either citing or alluding to this song, see, e.g., *Haidong qing*, 130, 214, 485, 537, 553, 795.
10. For a similar exchange, see ibid., 537.
11. Compare, e.g., the most famous work about pedophilia in twentieth-century "Western" literature: Nabokov's *Lolita*. In that novel, Humbert's attraction to

young girls is explicitly explained in terms of arrested temporalities, in that his "first love" was killed suddenly while they were both still children, leaving his libido stranded at an earlier developmental stage.

12 The girls range in age from seven, in the case of Zhu Ling and Ya Xing, to fourteen, in the case of Zhang Tong.
13 For two other references to this practice, see *Haidong qing*, 665, 669.
14 See, e.g., ibid., 290, 598, 605, 795, 885. In the novel, the delicacy is invariably prepared with sesame oil and ginger threads.
15 For other prominent discussions of this historical event, see ibid., 296, 765.
16 For examples of Jin Wu's looking at Zhu Ling's watch, see ibid., 87, 782, 786, 792, 806, 811, 895, 903, 914, 936. For examples of his looking at Ya Xing's watch, see ibid., 315, 358, 746, 842, 857, 864, 869. And, for examples of his looking at Zhang Tong's watch, see ibid., 421, 423, 424, 445, 696, 712.
17 The term *mixin*, a proper name with no clear semantic value, is also a nearly precise homophone for the Chinese term *mixin*, meaning "superstition." For other references to the practice of sitting out the month, see ibid., 291, 308, 323, 550, 554, 661, 668, 682, 691, 696, 699, 707, 712, 713, 733, 744, 782, 786, 792, 922.
18 For other passages to this effect, see ibid., 391, 598, 780, 885.
19 Burton Watson, trans., *Chuang Tzu: Basic Writings* (New York: Columbia University Press, 1996), 97.
20 For similar discussions of this passage, see Norman Girardot, *Myth and Meaning in Early Taoism: The Theme of Chaos (Hundun)* (Berkeley and Los Angeles: University of California Press, 1988), 77–12; and Angela Zito, *Of Body and Brush: Grand Sacrifice as Text/Performance in Eighteenth-Century China* (Chicago: University of Chicago Press, 1997), 208.
21 In an uncanny echo of the "seven holes" of the *Zhuangzi* allegory, An Lexin speaks specifically of giving Zhu Ling and her six friends a group discount for all "seven shots" (82).
22 This dream is reminiscent of Zhu Ling's dream in *Haidong qing* (discussed above) in which the Sun Yat-sen statues come to life.
23 See *Zhu Ling*, 54, just one of many passages discussing this phenomenon.
24 For a more detailed discussion, see the preceding section.

15

History, Exchange, and the Object Voice: Reading Li Ang's *The Strange Garden* and *All Sticks Are Welcome in the Censer of Beigang*

Chaoyang Liao

Not "It happened to me," or "They did this to me," or "Fate had it in store for me," but "I was," "I did," "I saw," "I cried out."

Bruce Fink, The Lacanian Subject

It is the lowest form of bad luck to be poor. Santa Claus, who rarely comes, does not relieve it, but puts it at least into proper perspective.

Ernst Bloch, "From Spuren"

Li Ang's 1991 novel *Miyuan* [The strange garden] presents the story of Zhu Yinghong, a cultured woman whose obedience turns into creative rebellion in the course of a life inextricably bound up with the postwar history of Taiwan. As a child, Yinghong witnesses how her politically progressive father, stigmatized by the newly instated Chinese authorities as seditious and subjected to heavy surveillance, turns into a social invalid whiling life away in virtual confinement in the family garden. This life does allow him to develop interests in hobbies and cultural pursuits as well as stay close to his daughter. Years later, when her father dies, Yinghong, now a young woman, returns from abroad; only then does she learn that her mother had had to sell nearly all the family property to allow her father to indulge in his expensive hobbies. The garden itself has been sold to an in-law with the understanding that it can be bought back anytime within the next twenty years. Soon the mother also dies. Left alone, Yinghong begins to assume an instrumental role in restoring place and pride to the family tradition. But first she must endure several ordeals. Driven by a vague sense of insecurity, she falls in love with Lin Xigen, a successful land developer and a parvenu whose power somehow reminds her of her father. A protracted battle of love follows, in which the woman pursues sensual pleasures, engages in half-masochistic feminine scheming to remain desirable, helps out in the man's business, and has an abortion, haunted all the time by the memories of life in her father's garden. Eventually, she secures marriage with the man, who provides the money to reclaim and rebuild the now-dilapidated family garden so that she can donate it to a trust and open it to the public as a historic site.

Even this crude outline of the story conveys a sense of the "strangeness" of the novel: it is preoccupied with the decadent lifestyle of late-twentieth-century Taipei but, at the same time, is built on the affirmative reconstitution of communal, if not national, memory. This double thematic threading is a scheme tantalizingly resembling allegorical signification but vexed by the unequivocal mixing of contraries. What are we to make of this marriage of pedagogy and sensuality, culture and capital? Decadence, as the author herself indicates in an interview, should be free from moral implications: it is a state of extreme abandonment similar to death and eros, not one of "fallenness."[1] Death and eros are forms of encounter and fascination with otherness as matter and libido, from which the narrative must return to achieve closure. Therefore, understanding the novel means working through the implications of decadence and exploring, beyond the semblance of "abandonment," the tensions between *jouissance* and sublimation, the body and symbolic ordering.

To begin with, the intricate connections between the father and the lover as his pale, vulgarized double point to the paradoxical possibilities of decadence and its transformation: the father squanders time and money not only on the maintenance and revamping of his garden but also on cameras, audio equipment, and expensive cars; the land speculator, the master of exploitative exchange and pure capitalist conservation, takes pleasure in constantly switching sex partners as a form of symbolic accumulation, of "usage that is exchanged."[2] Eventually, with a shifting of symbolic ground not unlike that of the film *Schindler's List*, the father is vindicated by unintentionally, posthumously becoming a major cultural conservationist who preserves the historic garden.[3] The lover too is, in a sense, saved by being drawn into the role of a giver in the rehabilitation and donation of the garden.

Thus, behind the textual plunge into decadence lies a profounder negativity: a kinship between the father as benign dandy and the lover as dull exchange apparatus; the two men, as if following Georges Bataille's theorization of gift giving, complement each other in an almost Hegelian master/slave dialectic, the transcending of which becomes a major undertaking of the novel.[4] Inevitably, such an investment in negativity causes many interpretative difficulties, especially when the heroine provides no "brighter side" but, for the better part of the novel, freely indulges in sex and egotistic conservation. The attempt to articulate a logic of decadence and to explore the dark economies of exploitative exchange, at odds with the literalizing mentality of most contemporary readers, is often misread as simple lack of positive uplift and questionable indulgence in moral depravity. Early negative responses to the novel seized on Li Ang's interest in what is taken to be morbid negativity and depicted it as grossly incompatible with the more serious sides of the work, being either steeped in the "incorrect ideology" of shameless capitalism or symptomatic of a reprehensible bad taste that has produced an impoverished narrative incapable of rising above its pathologically incoherent characterization.[5] In fact, the author seems to have foreseen this harsh initial reception: the novel's introductory section presents a scene in which people respond with apathy, incomprehension, and even demands for "punishment" when asked to contribute money to help an AIDS patient (4ff.).

But the complexities of the text have not escaped more attentive eyes. A series of defenses by predominantly feminist readers have provided plausible accounts of the basic thematic project of the novel. The erotic adventures of the heroine, for example, are read as exorcising rites undertaken to bring hope to a diseased order of gender relations, as a necessary detour allowing women to be healed of wounds left by the hardships of a patriarchal world, or as part of the maturing process that women must undergo to outgrow the disciplinary norms of dominant patriarchy and achieve full sexuality or higher consciousness.[6] Beyond gender issues, however, even sympathizers might still be troubled by gaps, or, rather, uncanny links, that mystify the divided thematics of the work: justifications still seem hard to come by when lowly erotic adventures are not only undertaken in exchange for financial power but also thereby connected, against the norms of realist narration (and, implicitly, political correctness), to the rebuilding of family pride and national heritage. Echoing one of the harsh early critics, for example, Huang Yuxiu questions the "political thread" because it is asserted only in flashbacks and is insufficiently connected with the main sections dealing with the daughter's present life.[7] In a similar vein, David Der-wei Wang praises the "patience and introspective vision" of Li Ang's treatment of sexuality but expresses misgivings when she seems to be measuring the complexities of politics and history by a reductive "logic of binary oppositions" taken from simplistic feminist resistance strategies.[8]

As if responding to readers who continue to be disturbed by the marriage between culture and capital, liberation and authority, and expenditure and conservation, Li Ang presents a breakdown of the thematics of this novel in her 1997 collection of short stories *Beigang xianglu ren ren cha* [All sticks are welcome in the censer of Beigang]. The question of the unscrupulous exchange of sexual favors for political power, elaborated in the third and title story, is kept strictly separate from the higher discourse of dignified chastity and paradigmatic perseverance animating the fourth and concluding story, "Caizhuang xueji" [Rouged Sacrifice]. Lin Lizi, the principal character of "All Sticks," lives as a libertine and recapitulates Yinghong's licentious life; unprotected by a refined upbringing, however, she soon gains the reputation of a public paramour, a "censer" who welcomes "all sticks." As a result, she not only fails to obtain a satisfactory relationship but is also defenseless against the public belief that she sleeps her way into the position of a high-profile legislator. The gossipy men who moralize and fantasize about Lizi's nighttime activities are like Lin Xigen, Yinghong's lover in *The Strange Garden*, but their constant deferring of real expenditure is hopelessly bound up with verbal voyeurism and imaginary gratification. As a result, no transformation into public conservation is to be expected from either the woman's body politics or theirs. The same infertility is mirrored with inversion in "Rouged Sacrifice," where Mother Wang, the saintly widow whose husband is taken away from her marriage bed by security police and later executed, survives the trauma by ceasing to desire and by devoting herself to distracting activities (dressmaking, bridal makeup, and, later, political activism). These "third-person" pursuits recall the aesthetic fixations of the father of the earlier novel, but Mother Wang's selfless giving proceeds under the stringent logic of obligations and deadening virtue traditionally demanded of a widow and, therefore, never breaks with the centralized superego to envisage the openness of public expenditure.

Together, these two stories demonstrate what happens when the two thematic threads of the novel are *really* divorced from each other: the positioning of a woman (Lin Lizi) at the place of the obscene, licentious father is countered by the excessive privatization of public discourse (the ubiquitous whispering of the voyeuristic crowd); the elevation of a saintly woman to the height of public conscience and communal memory deprives her and others of productive vitality, eventually bringing about a series of tragic deaths, including that of Mother Wang herself.[9] Both these patterns point to necessary moments of a civilized community, but, when separated, each leads to a dangerous breakdown in either personal or communal psychic equilibrium. To borrow terms from Renaissance Neoplatonism, the protagonists of "All Sticks" and "Rouged Sacrifice" can be said to "unfold," to make more explicit through infelicitous disunion, aspects of Zhu Yinghong of *The Strange Garden*, in the same way—although with an inverting twist—as the three Graces are said to "unfold" Venus into less "complicated" states. Conversely, the interpretative difficulties of the earlier novel may be said to derive from the fact that Zhu Yinghong signifies in the way of a hybrid, an "infolded" image of esoteric meaning.[10]

The notoriety of the new collection of stories in the Taiwanese media thrives on the obvious resemblance of some of the characters to real personalities and is compounded by the author's typical disregard of propriety, familiar to readers of her earlier works and here expressed in self-indulgently lengthy presentations of terms and associations referring to genital organs.[11] Interestingly, even such epiphenomena of publication highlight forms of exchange (the author getting even with her enemies with a roman à clef) and expenditure (scandalous disclosure of, and appetite for, the private and the improper) and are, therefore, inseparable from the problematic connecting the short story collection to the earlier novel. At the same time, the swerve toward nonliterary gossip in the publicity accompanying the stories calls to mind Lizi's proposal in "All Sticks" for women to use the body "as a strategy to overthrow men and take over their power": repeated at least three times but each time cut short by the reporting text at the end of her first sentence (149, 152, 158–59), this idea never develops into any discursive complexity; likewise, the author's attempt to build a pedagogical project out of that proposal (or the cutting short of it) tends to be silenced by scandalmongering. It would be a mistake to attribute this shortchanging of symbolic meaning to lack of literary sophistication or to simple authorial complicity with patriarchal mastery (as Tuohong charges) or pathological penis envy (as Wang Haowei proclaims).[12] Since the pattern is duplicated both inside and outside the text, it has exceeded diegetic or authorial boundaries and become a symptom of the real world. In fact, the very antagonism and lack of exchange between story (with its mutilated quotations of Lizi) and high discourse points to an underlying psychic investment in public voyeurism and its interference with personal pedagogy.

In the following discussion, the Lacanian elaboration of the psychoanalytic theory of "partial drives," specifically, of gaze and voice as two objects of such drives (the scopic and the invocatory), demonstrates the referential substance and critical cogency of these works. I begin by examining the textually articulated and, therefore, more accessible themes and patterns of object economy structuring these works, which tie in with *The Strange Garden* and the issues of exchange and gift giving. Briefly, "All Sticks" is read as a story about the invasion of public signifiers by the voice and "Rouged Sacrifice" as a tale dominated by the gaze of the past. Both are partitive representations of a sphere of reciprocity where, as intimated by the earlier novel, gaze and voice engage in free exchange. The first two stories of the collection are not discussed here, but it should be possible to read them as dealing with the same (contrasting) themes as the last two, but more temperately, as if they are preparatory sketches leading up to full elaborations.

In Lacanian theory, the gaze, being an object, refers not to an act of looking with the eyes but to a "blind spot" that gives a vague sense of "returning the gaze"; the object voice, likewise, is an empty point in the other that seems to be addressing one from a level beyond any words actually heard. These are instances of the *objet petit a*, the reappearance of reflexive perception of the self in the field of the other, and as such must be excluded from consciousness, repressed, for the individual to maintain a sense of reality.[13] Without bringing in religious overtones, we may say that these objects mark an "infolding" of subjectivity because they occupy an esoteric space lying outside symbolic normativity but vested with desire and meaning, bringing together the two contradictory aspects of expenditure and conservation, of displacement into the othered and othering realm of the *objet petit a* and the reiteration of objectal sameness in perceptual performance. At the same time, the textual objectification of this infolded space in the diegetic world adds a dimension of second-order liminality to its esoteric duality, testifying to its potential reversibility into the readable and its openness to symbolic dialectization.

Early on in *The Strange Garden*, for example, there is an episode that indicates plainly that the voice will be an important element of the narrative:

writing a composition as a third grader, Zhu Yinghong begins with the sentence: "I was born in the late years of the Sino-Japanese War" (15). As this time frame is at least half a century too early, Yinghong is laughed at by the teacher and the class, and she remembers the incident ever after. But why did she write the sentence if not because something in it sounded right to her, some voice behind the actual meaning of the words, the mere conventions of the symbolic? Years later, her father rationalizes that anachronism as "in a certain sense" connecting her to a turning point in the history of Taiwan (23-24), but his words embody the dissociated presence of a "partial" voice of history that rises to sublimity without ceasing to borrow from and hide behind the hackneyed style of history textbooks imposed by the Chinese government.

Throughout the novel, the thematic thread of politics and history is articulated repeatedly. Estranging voices animate the various quoted letters of the father (presumably remembered by the daughter), folding the past into the present. Similar voices give meaning to the cultural signifiers and literary allusions inscribed all over the garden, orchestrating them into an imported but paradoxically ancestral classicism that gives Yinghong a mesmerizing aura when she first meets Lin Xigen. The ancient matriarch's curse forbidding the patriarch who deserted her to have any position in the family history holds sway over the family from generation to generation. Again, voices from elsewhere sentimentalize the songs and noises of "wine saloons," layering them with apparitions of the real. Or the voices become internalized in the "autoaffective" musings of the heroine, which "cover" the spectacles of capitalist decadence with meaning but at the same time point to the need to shield her from their uncanny emptiness. The importance of these instances of objectal intrusiveness is not their pedagogical content; indeed, the invocatory effectiveness of the ideological project of the novel has been rightfully questioned. But the underlying patterns of organization must be considered if the thematic structure of the narrative is to become intelligible. It is clear, for example, that the accentuated thread of sexuality in the novel produces a series of textual spectacles that tend to "freeze the flow of action" as their counterparts in film do,[14] and the unfailing return of the invocatory always counters and undoes the passivity of such spectacles. Here, dialectization and the mobilization of meaning (the floating of a partial voice) are what counts, not thematic determination (whether, e.g., the voice constitutes pedagogy or a traumatic encounter), testifying to the fact that partial objects represent gaps in the real, being formally delimited but devoid of content. This lack of determination allows us to flesh out the larger themes of exchange and the gift.

"All Sticks" continues and "explicates" the objectal openness informing the earlier novel. Lin Lizi's insatiable desire for sexual gratification is *heard* both in feigned utterances of pleasure (which most of her male partners enjoy) and in involuntary moans usually emitted during autoerotic acts, which "surprise" the woman herself as strikingly similar (134–35). This objectal metonymy points to a reversal of the familiar and the unfamiliar, the real and the unreal, when differing versions of the voice are linked, but the reversibility does not stop there. Beyond the exchange of sex for political favors, a more meaningful kind of exchange, again based on the indeterminacy of the object voice, is involved. On the one hand, Lizi herself is an eloquent legislator; even the representatives of women's groups who despise her must invite her to important meetings because of "her outstanding achievement and the power she wields" (152). Obviously, Lizi has a way of turning her feminine voice of ecstasy and pain into facility in symbolic transactions. The readiness with which she switches from flirtatious charm to verbal dexterity (152) signifies more than her qualifications for politics: it reveals that the symbolic ordering of public law and discursive reason is supported by, and in constant exchange with, an underside filled with the *jouissance* of the body, a superegoic imperative to enjoy, in comparison with which phallic enjoyment, the "*jouissance* of the organ," is only a pale displacement into impossibility.[15]

On the other hand, threatened by this embarrassing presence of a feminine voice, the (male) public discourse is compelled to maintain a sense of reality: it produces an endless flow of repetitious, empty gossip consisting both of metaphors linking the body to public or political language (the vagina as a censer that everyone can use, the shape of the labia as that of the island of Taiwan, and so on) and of hyperbolic fantasies and grotesque, pseudoscientific itemizations of physical features, all hinting at the woman's sexual activities. Thus, parallel to Lizi's sublimation into the political symbolic, there is a degradation of public discourse into the language of body parts. The text deflates this language of gossip gone wild (presented in passages enclosed in parentheses) by subjecting it to inconsistencies and deviations from the third-person narration. For example, after repeatedly speaking of the "forty or fifty penises" that have entered Lizi's body in her entire "career" with men of the opposition movement, the narrative becomes vague when, at one point, a rumor indicates that the figure, counted in multiples of ten because each table in a banquet seats ten people, should be "five or six, if not more than ten" times ten (139). To be precise, since Lizi sleeps only with "one man at a time," trying to do "everything a wife should have done" for the men until they lose interest (141), and since at least some of the relationships last for "a few months" (134) (and the last one much longer, until the man's marriage to someone else), it is unlikely that she could have enlisted "forty or fifty" men in the "three or four years" following her initial association with the movement (130). In fact, the exact figure becomes unimportant when, at another point, hyperbolic equivocation takes over and it is said that "at least forty or fifty different penises take turns in entering her *every day*" (140; emphasis added). Since this discourse seems to take some pride in the precision of its arithmetic (see esp. 151), such shaky counting throws other, even less verifiable, details into doubt.

The literalizing fantasies of the gossipy crowd have, of course, less to do with conforming to facts than with hiding the object voice under the comforting flow of signifiers. And what could this troubling voice say except what the gossips deplore and despise most but nonetheless wish to do, the licentious father's command: enjoy the woman? Who willingly become the "victims" (158) of this femme fatale if not the same people who confirm their positions in the symbolic by circulating the scandal and condemning her as a whore? The very moral complacency of the crowd provokes a general assault on the body. Conversely, through the conflation of the physical and the symbolic, of private and public discourses, the body, having been "overwritten" by language, refuses to remain dead but instead "writes back" by literalizing the symbolic.[16] What begins as a conflict between two extremities turns out to be an autoaffective battle of "the voice against the voice." As Mladen Dolar puts it: "If the Law, the word, the logos, had to constantly fight the voice as the other, the senseless bearer of *jouissance*, feminine decadence, it could do so only by implicitly relying on that other voice, the voice of the Father accompanying the Law." As mentioned above, Lizi proposes that women should use their bodies to reclaim power from men. But, if such a strategy works, it must be because this "voice of the Father," rendered visible in the gossip, is a mere variation of the other voice, a reminder of the forgotten underside of the transparent world of the symbolic that associates all norms of conservation with secret expenditure: "Is the voice of the Father an altogether different species from the feminine voice? Does the voice of the persecutor differ from the persecuted voice? The secret is maybe that they are both the same; that there are not two voices, but only one object voice, which cleaves and bars the Other in an ineradicable 'extimacy.'"[17]

Toward the end of the story, the feminine voice returns from the past in a more positive form. Lizi remembers her grandmother, who not only heard her coming home after school but used to "hear" the voice of the guardian spirit of the house. Now she tells the little girl: "Listen. Someone is digging, digging a well in the earth. If the digging goes too deep, one may dig through someone's roof. Then there would be big trouble" (161). This is a point of stillness that not only lacks obvious connection with the diegetic context (Lizi has been recalling early memories of "male gods") but also, refusing to develop the obvious connotations of digging, cuts short the flow of carnal metaphoricity, which elsewhere in the story has created a plethora of phantasmagoric signifiers and textualized body parts. This is the wisdom provided by the return of the object voice: the object supports the symbolic as its underside, and one should respect it by listening to it, not by digging a hole through its roof. In the first part of the story, Lizi has been trying in her own way to be a "good" woman, but the public discourse cannot and will not relinquish the pleasure of being a watchdog over the morality and the enjoyment of her body; this is what prevents her from developing any "normal" relationship with a man. Eventually, the woman has her revenge, but public discourse, and even the reporting text, pays the price by degenerating into idiotic babble, incapable of reporting or hearing Lizi's argument about women's strategy beyond the first sentence.

The dominance of the voice in "All Sticks" differs from the situation in *The Strange Garden*, where its hegemony is always countered by other forces, specifically those of the scopic drive. The "postmodern" image of the garden seen on a video wall in the introductory section of the novel is transformed into more objectal versions at various points in the text: the old photographs of the garden that "smell of death"; the mechanical vision of the camera, which reverses left and right, hiding the approaching fire from Yinghong and allowing her to take the best pictures; the family collection of hundreds of retired cameras that become defamiliarized when seen together (190, 202ff., 262). But the locus classicus of objectal vision appears at the end of the massage episode. The lovers reach new heights of thrilling pleasure by playing with each other's body while taking care not to be heard by the blind woman who is massaging the man (245ff.). This episode can easily be read as a good example of the lengths to which Li Ang will go to indulge the sensuous, but any reading that ignores how vision works in this scene is bound to remain incomplete. At one point, Yinghong becomes aware that the blind woman keeps her vacant eyes open, her shrunk irises making aimless, jerky glances in various directions, in keeping with the movement of her hands. Yinghong becomes disturbed and stops what she is doing, prompting the man to dismiss the blind woman. Then the couple proceed to have intercourse. Yinghong is "terrified and disheartened, somehow captivated by a sense of the tangibility of death but responding to the man ever more shamelessly, ever more abandoned to desire" (247). Here, sex, death, and the gaze are fused together. The blind woman's gaze points to what Walter Benjamin describes as the disintegration of the aura under modernity: "In eyes that look at us with a mirrorlike blankness the remoteness remains complete. It is precisely for this reason that such eyes know nothing of distance."[18] It is paradoxical that complete remoteness abolishes distance, but this is exactly what happens. Yinghong's reaction to this gaze is presented as if she had had a meeting with Medusa's head, which Lacan describes as "the abyss of the feminine organ," an apparition of the "ultimate real, of the essential object which isn't an object any longer, but this something faced with which all words cease and all categories fail, the object of anxiety *par excellence*."[19] But this uncanny remoteness is accompanied by the disappearance of distance from associated objects: the deathly anxiety must be allayed by the comforting presence of an imaginary other, and the process enhances Yinghong's desire for her sex partner: "Object *a* is covered over by the other's image and that is necessary if my *semblable* is to arouse my desire."[20]

This veiling of the real is necessary if the subject is not to be "blinded by the gaze or touched by the real."[21] This blocking of sight, the turning away from the blind woman's gaze, does not incapacitate the subject but, on the contrary, produces a reduced gaze that not only enables imaginary identification but also becomes the precondition for the development of symbolic complexity: "In so far as the gaze, *qua objet a*, may come to symbolize this central lack expressed in the phenomenon of castration, and in so far as it is an *objet a* reduced, of its nature, to a punctiform, evanescent function, it leaves the subject in ignorance as to what there is beyond the appearance, an ignorance so characteristic of all progress in thought that occurs in the way constituted by philosophical research."²² Appropriately, Yinghong returns to symbolic deliberations the next morning, considering how she will act in the future, telling herself that "she would never stand losing him again" (247–48). When scopic defamiliarization reaches its limits, an inner voice takes over.

This is, of course, an instance of the return of the invocatory. To generalize, if voice and gaze "relate to each other as life and death," and if "voice vivifies while the gaze mortifies,"²³ then their "infolding" in *The Strange Garden* may be said to precipitate dialectization into exchange: when the gaze is covered up (by waking up from, or to, the defamiliarizing real—e.g., by dismissing the blind woman and returning to comfortable privacy or by encountering the woman's vacant gaze), the invisible is subsumed by and reappears as the voice (the inner deliberations of the subject). Thematically, such a structural pattern subsumes death within life without obviating its relevance. In other words, the return of the invocatory remains inconclusive, always subject to further exchange with scopic objects. At the end of the novel, for example, the text seems to indicate plainly that the man will become impotent and that the couple will be unable to bear children, partly fulfilling the matriarch's curse. This would seem to amount to a negation of the vivifying voice. The dialectization of objectal economy in the narrative, however, maintains a strict reciprocity to prevent the straightforward reading from becoming conclusive. When the ghostly voice of the garden becomes uncanny and the superegoic, vengeful symbolic is going to take over, the gaze returns to save the subject. Thus, although the author herself has upheld the common reading that Yinghong will become barren (147), we have counterevidence that the curse will not come true after all. When Yinghong realizes that "she *may* never be able to give birth to his children" (emphasis added), she feels "distressed," indicating that such an outcome would not be what she intended. Then, inexplicably, the text describes her as "wanting even more eagerly to have one more look at the garden right away, lest it should turn out to have vanished, lest everything should turn out to have, as it were, never happened, to have never existed." The narrative returns to reality in the concluding paragraph of the novel, which gives the last instance of the gaze that virtually, and visually, saves Yinghong from the "distress": she regains a sense of the existence of "everything" by taking an overview of the garden from where she is sitting, and she sees it as brightly lit, "burning in prosperity" (312). If the garden has not vanished as Yinghong has imagined, why should her thoughts about possible barrenness be accepted as a trustworthy forecast?

This is how narrative reciprocity works in the objectal economy of *The Strange Garden*. To recapitulate, it is the function of the return of the invocatory to prevent the passivity of textual spectacles from becoming absolute. Conversely, when the voice of the past becomes rigid and stifling, the gaze of bodily excitation (materialist "decadence") tends to reemerge. Such a recurring pattern may have started as a structural device, a convenient way to organize the narrative, but the interlocking of objectal systems proves particularly germane to the circulation and exchange of signifiers in the narrative, which works closely with the reciprocal transformations of voice and gaze to facilitate the coexistence of disparate domains of meaning. This is the formal feature that cements the novel and, eventually, saves its general thematics from breaking into two parts.

I have read "All Sticks" as a story about what happens when the circuit of exchange is broken and the power of the voice is given over to unlimited escalation. "Rouged Sacrifice," the last story in *All Sticks*, shows the other side of the coin: when the gaze is given absolute ascendancy, the world is frozen under a vindictive public code, and the body is subjected to mortification. This story is dominated by images, most prominently the "photographs of death" of the tortured and butchered body of a victim of the February Twenty-eighth Incident, photographs taken by the victim's wife. Rumored as about to be made public on the anniversary of the massacre some fifty years later, the images are never actually seen on that day. Associated with them are photographs of other victims, common early portraits not as gory but no less disconcerting, held by family members in the memorial procession; there are also dramatizations of events of the fateful day that started off the massacre and the application of makeup, first to the "woman writer" who is to speak to the crowd and then to another dead body, that of the son of Mother Wang, also a victim's wife and a renowned makeup artist, known for chastity, integrity, and political commitment in the opposition movement. Again, these instances of the gaze of the past are all associated with death: even the writer feels estranged from the image of herself wearing makeup: she feels that she looks "definitely like herself, but also like a different person"; she gets so uncomfortable that she has to wipe some lipstick from her lips, which then look "as if they had sucked blood" (174, 184). Later in the story, she learns from the evening TV news that a fire in another part of the city has claimed the lives of more than sixty people, including the young woman who did her makeup earlier in the day. The writer's face becomes contorted with terror; she feels that "the seal of death" has been left on her face (210–11). Toward the end of the story, Mother Wang throws herself into the water and dies, presumably out of grief over her son's death, which becomes unbearable because she contributed to his suffering by not accepting his transvestism.

Why this persistent foregrounding of death? A nameless woman attributes the tragedies to the "resentment of the dead" who have been left unavenged and unconsoled for nearly fifty years (211). Even now, when a reformed government allows public memorials, the voices of the dead are not being heard. Early on, the story points to the cavalier attitude toward the meaning of history on the part of the young people who are to participate in the memorial. The young makeup woman makes it very clear that she is taking the "case" as a favor to a friend, not because she has any real interest in the "photographs of death" or the memorial activities themselves (168); similarly, the massacre "obviously means nothing" to one of the young actors to perform in the street theater on the anniversary (166). The dramatizations of the day are described in detail and intercut with comments from a floating narrative voice revealing their lack of historical credibility. Although the historical events mean a lot to a certain group of people (including the politically progressive woman writer), the general public, obviously, remains pragmatic and aloof. As language overwrites the body in "All Sticks," here material inertia freezes the discourse of historical justice into empty ideologies, mere fixations with an unrecoverable past. As the body "writes back" in the earlier story, here the silent voice of the dead returns the freezing gaze, indeed, the "stain beyond the gaze" depriving events of causality and continuity, throwing the entire society into private catastrophe (Mother Wang's drowning) and fateful randomness (the fire).[24] The gaze has become unbearable, but no signification seems possible.

A certain sense of expiation is achieved at the end of the story, which presents not a point of stillness but a fully symbolic image reintroducing time and opening out into movement: the small lotus lamp, released into the water when Mother Wang throws herself into it, moves forward in mysterious silence; the video director, on the scene to shoot the memorial activities, wishes to capture the scene but discovers that "the flickering light of the lotus lamp will be recorded by the lens only as a place of darkness" (220). The simple but moving beauty of the description of this scene must have come from the momentary revelation that there is still hope in this disintegrating social imaginary, that it is still possible to envision the movement of signifiers and the return of the voice as speaking silence. In the earlier story, Lin Lizi resists symbolic regimentation by trumping phallic power with the eloquence of the body. Here, Mother Wang makes peace with a forgetful society by disappearing into darkness so that, in the frozen scopic field of the final scene, signifiers may be known to have started moving again in the watery beyond. Read together, the two stories form a circuit of complementarity.

Intimations of hope, however, do not release Mother Wang's story from negativity. For upholders of public discourse, hagiography is a more "palatable" genre than pornographic parody, but, without the invocatory dimension of the earlier story, the hope left by the saintly woman is mute and fragile. Mother Wang's suicide adumbrates the masochistic victimhood of an entire generation of Taiwanese political dissenters, which brings our discussion back to the masochism of Zhu Yinghong (as definitively analyzed by Huang Yuxiu) and its connection with postcoloniality.[25] Masochistic sexuality is usually read as signifying submission to and collaboration with dominant powers, but Zhu brings to mind another controversially masochistic woman, Ada of Jane Campion's film *The Piano* (1993). In the film, Ada falls in love with Baines, the man who forces her into objectifying exchange (parts of the body for piano keys). This unromantic twist is nothing more than a scaled-down variant of Yinghong's masochism, but it has caused heated debates. At the same time, there is no doubt that it gives life, not death: "Ada, indeed, 'opts out' of suicide: 'What a death! What a chance! What a surprise! My will has chosen life!' The scene of Ada's death in effect *refuses death even as it stages it*, thereby making a 'taboo identification' with masochism, rendering speakable that taboo, and soliciting a possession of that masochistic voice—'it is a weird lullaby, and so it is; it is mine.'"[26]

To *possess* the masochistic voice here means to subjectify the object. When the subject comes to terms with the object voice, the lullaby becomes the place of objectal reflection, materially figured in *The Piano* by the first-person voice-over that constantly calls on the spectator to enter identification. But voice is the leftover produced by the signifying chain;[27] without the ability to produce signifiers, therefore, one would not be in a position to "possess" the voice. Ada's choice of life and "possession" of the lullaby as her own is, then, ultimately based on her earlier experience with symbolic exchange, which allows her to reshape her subjectivity. Her "contractual" relationship with Baines cannot, therefore, be read as merely a way to perpetuate the fetishization of the female body or the exploitative practices of colonial economy; in fact, it may point to a "sublime love," a love that gives up full possession of its impossible object but is content to "circle around" it, to constitute itself "against the background of an external, contractual, symbolic exchange mediated by the institution."[28]

In *All Sticks*, Lizi and Mother Wang represent two ways to miss an encounter with such objectal love. Lin Lizi's early years are full of pain and suffering because she still believes in romantic love, in playing the good wife in full possession of her lover and without any need of contractual negotiation. By contrast, Mother Wang, herself a makeup artist of some reputation, is expert in visual signification, but this mastery of the symbolic is seriously curtailed by the symbolic role of a blameless, saintly victim imposed on her by public discourse, which bars her from applying the movement of signifiers to more "vulgar," more contractual forms of subjectivity. Her voice, therefore, remains confined to an obscure place in the symbolic zoning system, potentially capable of calling forth great thunders and fires, but for the time being frozen in the "flickering light" of something most people would regard, with awe, as *not* "mine."

In retrospect, the divided thematics of *The Strange Garden*, somewhat like the split voice of *The Piano*, may be said to point to a way to negotiate the double danger as presented in "All Sticks" and "Rouged Sacrifice" and to instance complementarity within one character and to positivize and highlight the circularity of exchange as a viable way to survive and transcend psychic and historical trauma. Eventually, one must explain such necessary dialectization by referring it not to the free play of heterogeneity and "postmodern nothingness" (as Lin Fangmei indicates) but to the "traversing of fantasy" that enables the subject to position itself at the place of the object, to "subjectify" its own cause and, according to Fink, make it "one's own."[29] This object may appear as a point of stillness, as an opening out into space and movement, or as a composite of the two, like the enigmatic garden of the novel; the place occupied by such an object forms a critical beyond "in which the subject is able to act (as cause, as desirousness), and is at least momentarily out of discourse, split off from discourse: free from the weight of the Other."[30] Thus, Yinghong's reaction to the blind woman's gaze serves not only to cover up the uncanny real but also to register the afterimage of a momentary view of this critical beyond, which will, henceforth, be open to "traversing" and productive of subjectified symbolic complexity. The presence of a political thematics facilitates the drive toward open subjectivity by providing an ever-expanding network of symbolic connections, a field for the free circulation of meanings.

Circulation is, of course, based on exchange. The concept of exchange here refers to the general principle of the dialectization and mobilization of signifiers that preserves an older layer of the meaning of the concept based on "the ideal of free and just barter."[31] As indicated above, *The Strange Garden* presents many forms of exchange: between sex and capital (Yinghong's love affair); between past and present (the anachronistic reference to the "late years" of the Sino-Japanese War); between decadence and high culture (the aura of the classical garden translating into sex appeal when the couple first meet); and between the invocatory and the scopic (gaze and voice yielding to each other). The fundamental principle of these forms of exchange is the presence of a historical or historically represented sensibility responsive to voices that eroticize the past, the distant, the different. Even the ancient pirate patriarch engaged in the exchange of settled family life for adventure in faraway places. The main point is not what is exchanged or fetishized but the very form of exchange, which implies a mimetic ability to divest and reinvest subjectivity, which is not very different from the ability to traverse fantasy and reach the object. Michael Taussig refers to the natives of Tierra del Fuego as examples of this ability to mime: "What enhances the mimetic faculty is a protean self with multiple images (read 'souls') of itself set in a natural environment whose animals, plants, and elements are spiritualized to the point that nature 'speaks back' to humans, every material entity paired with an occasionally visible spirit-double—a mimetic double—of itself."[32]

There is danger, admittedly, in such *partial* subjectivity: it is always possible that the act of miming, being intimately linked to what Marcel Mauss calls "the spirit of the gift," could turn into the exploitative exchange of nothing for something.[33] This would account for the pleasure drawn by the gossipy crowds of "All Sticks" from their empty fantasies. If one refuses to confront such obscene exchange as intrusion from the real, however, one also disavows the existence of more general forms of oppression underwriting it, thus forfeiting any possibility of countering its social effectivity. A better approach is to subject such problematic forms of exchange to further exchange so that the hidden and frozen signifiers in them may start moving again and become available to public discourse.

This point is brought out in the novel most clearly by the floating voice of the father, which teaches Yinghong that the unabashedly fetishized gift of the past (the unofficial but naively totalizing representation of the history of Taiwan) can transcend its surplus pleasure by entering exchange with private justice (the ancient matriarch's curse prohibiting the symbolic return of her man) and personal remembrance and loss (the voice of the victimized father). As content, for example, the matriarch's curse has no positive meaning except as a personal expression of and demand for poetic justice. But it is lifted at the end of the novel, as explained above, not by becoming forgotten or repressed as historical debris but by entering genuine reconciliation whereby the heiress of the family, settling accounts with an enterprising man not unlike the patriarch himself, traverses mythical time to assume the matriarch's place, reactivating the subjectivity behind the curse, but making a decision *on her own*, as an individual, to end its effectivity (either by bearing children and breaking it or by becoming barren and ending the very family line transmitting it), fully confident that the injustice of the past will not be repeated in the present. It is the reintroduction of individual, subjective voices from the past (be they those of liars or sages, pirates or chaste widows) into monumental history that ensures that the latter will be interrupted constantly by the free flow of signifiers exchanging places.

Voices from the victims of the past are, therefore, heard with that form of historical memory that Walter Benjamin, combining Proustian *mèmoire involontaire* with a sense of active recollection, calls *Eingedenken*,

> a remembering that does not just repeat or reiterate the past, but which illuminates what could have been. Perhaps only momentarily, this form of remembering redeems the potential for change buried in the past. . . . [Ingeborg Bachmann and Walter Benjamin] consider the process of remembrance as a constant disrupting of the imposed continuum [of monumental history] and construct a conscious literary forum and place for the words and memories of the victims of history. The remembrance of the victims does not perpetuate suffering or reactivate it, but rather breaks down the continuity of a history that petrifies diverse experiences of pain into anonymous masses.[34]

In this light, it may be said that the two thematic threads of *The Strange Garden* are linked not by unitary coherence but by relations of exchange forming constellations of legibility out of the subjective voices of history and enabling them to disrupt the historical continuity of the present (whether that comes from the colonizer or the colonized). Continually transformed by the movement of signifiers, even the voice of the normative history of Taiwan takes on a flexibility bordering on animistic self-adjustment: Japanese, the language of the old colonizers, is used to betoken rejection of the culture of the new oppressors; connections with government officials are sought for business needs, but, when the garden is to be given away, the old grudges of the father must be honored. This is still the pragmatic historicizing of the colonized, characterized by masochistic mimicry and a healthy unwillingness to be congealed into the love of the gaze. As Yinghong becomes sure of the nature of her love only when she is taking the last view of the garden, love of the land tends to remain an abstract pedagogical command, constantly deferred into love at last sight, but therefore all the more palpable.

While it is always possible that historical memory may be distorted by public historicizing and monumentalized, the traversing of fantasy is meant to minimize that possibility by subjectifying the object, by constantly reminding the child to listen carefully but to refrain from digging holes on somebody else's roof. The strange insight of this form of remembrance points to what Michael Taussig discusses as the postcapitalist persistence of fetishism: "*Post-*capitalist animism means that although the socioeconomic exploitative function of fetishism, as Marx used that term in *Capital*, will supposedly disappear with the overcoming of capitalism, fetishism as an active social force inherent in objects will remain. Indeed it must not disappear, for it is the animate quality of things in post-capitalist society without the 'banking' mode of perception that ensures what the young Marx envisaged as the humanization of the world."[35] Under the dominant social and political discourses of contemporary Taiwan, however, Li Ang's futuristic practices, riddled with interpretative difficulties, amount to a form of textual masochism. Most readers would accept the fact that chastity is not upheld in *The Strange Garden* and "All Sticks." Some would go along with, and even celebrate, the author's undoing of traditional feminine virtue. The attempt to come to terms with the thorny problems of political identification, on the other hand, would most often be attributed to either aesthetic error or ideological blindness. Li Ang's texts retain an esoteric side even after the negative thematic unfolding of the stories; in exchange for this readerly infoldedness, one gets an innovative contemplation of a new historical sensibility that is based on political commitment and loyalty to historical memory and that may yet have profound implications for the evolving history of Taiwan.

NOTES

Unless otherwise indicated, all translations from non-English-language sources are my own.

1. Interview with Li Ang in Qiu Guifen, *(Bu) tongguo nüren guazao: Fangtan dangdai Taiwan nüzuojia* [Dissonant voices: Interviews with contemporary women writers in Taiwan] (Taipei: Yuanzun wenhua, 1998), 105.
2. See Luce Irigaray, "Women on the Market," in *This Sex Which Is Not One*, trans. Catherine Porter (Ithaca: Cornell University Press, 1985), 186.
3. See Li Ang, *Miyuan* (Taipei: Maitian, 1991), 301ff.
4. See Allan Stoekl, "Bataille, Gift Giving, and the Cold War," in Alan D. Schrift, ed., *The Logic of the Gift: Toward an Ethic of Generosity* (London: Routledge, 1997), 245–55.
5. On *The Secret Garden*'s incorrect ideology, see Lü Zhenghue, "*Miyuan* de Liangxing guanxi yu Taiwan qiye zhu de zhenmao" [Gender relations in *The strange garden* and the real face of Taiwan's entrepreneurs], *Lianhe wenxue* 83 (1991): 161–65. On its reprehensible bad taste, see Jin Hengjie, "Huangjin xin guizu: Baozhuang yu shangpin zhi jian (zai ping *Miyuan*)" [The glorious new nobility: Between display and commodity (another look at *The strange garden*)], *Dangdai* 71 (1992): 130–47; and Jin Hengjie, "Youguan Li Ang nushi 'huixiang' de jidian shuoming" [Remarks on Li Ang's "Response"], *Dangdai* 73 (1992): 132–38.
6. On eroticism as exorcism, see Huang Yuxiu, "*Miyuan* zhong de xing yu zhengzhi" [Sex and politics in *The strange garden*], in Zheng Mingli, ed., *Dangdai Taiwan nüxing wenxue lun* [Women and contemporary Taiwan literature] (Taipei: Shibao wenhua, 1993), 69–107. On the healing of patriarchal wounds, see Peng Xiaoyan, "Nüzuojia de qingyu shuxie yu zhengzhi lunshu: Jiedu *Miyuan*" [Eroticism and political discourse from a woman writer: Reading *The strange garden*], in Li Ang, *Beigang xianglu ren ren cha* [All sticks are welcome in the censer of Beigang] (Taipei: Maitian, 1997), 273–301. On the maturing process, see Jiang Baocai, "Xushi shiyan, shiluogan yu suminggan: Lun Li Ang de Miyuan," [Narrative experimentation, deprevation, and fatalism: On Li Ang's *The strange garden*], in Gong Pengcheng, ed., *Taiwan de shehui yu wenxue* [Taiwanese society and Taiwan literature] (Taipei: Dongda, 1995), 284ff.; Chen Shuchun, "*Shafu*, *Anye*, yü *Miyuan* zhong de nüxing shenti lunshu" [The discourse of the female body in *The butcher's wife*, *The dark night*, and *The strange garden*], *Wenxue Taiwan* 19 (1996): 139ff.; and Lin Fangmei, "*Miyuan* jiexi: Xingbie rentong yu guozu ren-

tong de diaogui" [Analyzing *The strange garden*: The paradox of gender identity and national identity], in Zhong Huiling, ed., *Nüxing zhuyi yu Zhongguo wenxue* [Feminism and Chinese literature] (Taipei: Liren, 1997), 271–96.

7   Huang, "*Miyuan* zhong de xing yu zhengzhi," 97ff.
8   David Der-wei Wang, "Huali de shijimo: Taiwan, nüzuojia, bianyuan shixue" [Fin de siècle splendor: Taiwan, women writers, and the poetics of marginality], in *Xiaoshuo Zhongguo: Wan Qing dao dangdai de Zhongwen xiaoshuo* [Narrating China: Modern Chinese fiction from the late Qing to the contemporary era] (Taipei: Maitian, 1993), 185ff.
9   The positioning of the woman in the place of the obscene, licentious father is theorized in Slavoj Žižek, *Enjoy Your Symptom! Jacques Lacan in Hollywood and Out* (London: Routledge, 1992), 158ff.
10 See, e.g., Edgar Wind, *Pagan Mysteries in the Renaissance*, rev. ed. (Harmondsworth: Penguin, 1967), 204–8.
11 See Lin Yupei, "Xinshu shangshi, Li Ang, Chen Wenqian tongshi luolei: Daodi shei xiang shei? Quanban xianglu jielou Lin Lizi zhen mianmu" [The new book debuts: Tears from both Li Ang and Chen Wenqian], *Jin zhoukan* 44 (September 21, 1997); and David Der-wei Wang, "Xulun: Xing, chouwen, yu meixue zhengzhi (Li Ang de qingyu xiaoshuo)" [Introduction: Sex, scandal, and the politics of aesthetics (Li Ang's fiction of sensuality)], in Li, *Beigang xianglu ren ren cha*, 9–46.
12 Tuohong, "Dang Mary yu Sally xiang yu" [When Mary met Sally], *Formosa* 5 (1997), http://www.taip.org/document/formosa/v5t5.htm; Wang Haowei, "Gai lai kankan Li Ang de wenxue chengji: Jiepou *Beigang xianglu ren ren cha*," [A timely look at Li Ang's literary achievement: Examining *All sticks are welcome in the censer of Beigang*], *Zhongguo shibao*, September 25, 1997, 41.
13 Slavoj Žižek, "'I Hear You with My Eyes'; or, The Invisible Master," in Renata Salecl and Slavoj Žižek, eds., *Gaze and Voice as Love Objects* (Durham: Duke University Press, 1996), 90ff.
14 Laura Mulvey, "Visual Pleasure and Narrative Cinema" (1975), in *Screen* Editorial Collective, eds., *The Sexual Subject: A "Screen" Reader in Sexuality* (London: Routledge, 1992), 27.
15 Jacques Lacan, *On Feminine Sexuality: The Limits of Love and Knowledge: The Seminar of Jacques Lacan, Book XX, Encore, 1972–1973*, ed. Jacques-Alain Miller, trans. Bruce Fink (New York: Norton, 1998), 6ff.; and Žižek, *Enjoy Your Symptom!* 124–28.
16 On being overwritten by language, see Bruce Fink, *The Lacanian Subject: Between Language and Jouissance* (Princeton: Princeton University Press, 1995), 12.
17 Mladen Dolar, "The Object Voice," in Salecl and Žižek, eds., *Gaze and Voice as Love Objects*, 27.
18 Walter Benjamin, "On Some Motifs in Baudelaire," in *Illuminations: Essays and*

Reflections, ed. Hannah Arendt, trans. Harry Zohn (New York: Schocken, 1969), 190.
19 Jacques Lacan, *The Ego in Freud's Theory and in the Techniques of Psychoanalysis, 1954–1955: The Seminar of Jacques Lacan, Book II*, ed. Jacques-Alain Miller, trans. Sylvana Tomaselli (New York: Norton, 1988), 164.
20 Antonio Quinet, "The Gaze as an Object," in Richard Feldstein, Bruce Fink, and Maire Jaanus, eds., *Reading Seminar XI: Lacan's "Four Fundamental Concepts of Psychoanalysis"* (Albany: State University of New York Press, 1995), 140.
21 Hal Foster, *The Return of the Real: The Avant-Garde at the End of the Century* (Cambridge: MIT Press, 1996), 138ff.
22 Jacques Lacan, *The Four Fundamental Concepts of Psychoanalysis*, ed. Jacques-Alain Miller, trans. Alan Sheridan (New York: Norton, 1977), 77.
23 Žižek, "'I Hear You with My Eyes,'" 94.
24 Ellie Ragland, "The Relation between the Voice and the Gaze," in Feldstein, Fink, and Jaanus, eds., *Reading Seminar XI*, 201.
25 See Huang, "*Miyuan* zhong de xing yu zhengzhi."
26 Suzy Gordon, "'I Clipped Your Wing, That's All': Auto-Erotism and the Female Spectator in *The Piano* Debate," *Screen* 37.2 (1996): 205.
27 Dolar, "The Object Voice," 9.
28 Renata Salecl, "I Can't Love You Unless I Give You Up," in Salecl and Žižek, eds., *Gaze and Voice as Love Objects*, 193.
29 Lin, "*Miyuan* jiexi," 293ff.; Fink, *The Lacanian Subject*, 61ff.
30 Fink, *The Lacanian Subject*, 66.
31 Theodor W. Adorno, *Negative Dialectics*, trans. E. B. Ashton (New York: Continuum, 1973), 147.
32 Michael Taussig, *Mimesis and Alterity: A Particulur History of the Senses* (London: Routledge, 1993), 97.
33 Mauss quoted in ibid., 93.
34 Karen Remmler, *Waking the Dead: Correspondences between Walter Benjamin's Concept of Remembrance and Ingeborg Bachmann's "Ways of Dying"* (Riverside: Ariadne, 1996), 32ff.
35 Taussig, *Mimesis and Alterity*, 99.

16

Reenchanting the Image in Global Culture: Reification and Nostalgia in Zhu Tianwen's Fiction

Ban Wang

The shady sides of modernization are not adequately studied by hurriedly traversing a straight line from modernity to postmodernity to globalization. The heavy toll of "progress" and "development" on many societies unprepared for rapid capitalist transformation—human, social, cultural, and psychic—renders some of modernization's accomplishments dubious and problematic. "Modernity"—the cultural, ideological, and emotive counterpart to technological and societal modernization—is a double-edged sword. Its visions of the future may promise progress, emancipation, freedom, and universal prosperity. Yet, all too often, this sanguine vision of modernization is little more than a euphemism to conceal the global standardization and unequal relations that pave the way for the penetration of capital into underdeveloped countries. Globalization, trumped up before any tangible benefits appear, may well be a new trick on the part of corporate executives and economists to revamp the earlier modernization project and to rationalize the aggressive advance of capital around the world in search of cheap labor and markets. Consider the obvious disasters in the last four to five decades: social and political upheaval; civil wars; military interventions and massacres; environmental calamity; depletion of natural resources. All resulted from worsening uneven development.[1]

The psychocultural aspect of the global condition is less obvious. The spread of global capitalist culture has had a leveling and disenchanting effect on previously "organic" communities buttressed by tradition, history, folklore, and kinship relations. In the rush to embrace economic development, consumer goods, and, above all, a uniformly standardized mass culture, such societies risk losing their cultural heritage and history. The life worlds constituted by relatively stable associations, shared collective memory and commitments, and time-honored attachments and structures of feeling are fading. If they survive at all, they tend to be packaged into one more exotic item in tour books, theme parks, or museums. The attempt to preserve the communities of imagination and memory that existed before global trade, consumptive frenzy, and stock fluctuation is becoming a bitter struggle. Some may offer consolation by arguing that local and native cultures will adopt new forms—the electronic media, for instance—to repackage and, hence, preserve their cultural identity. Arjun Appadurai speaks of "context-producing" virtual neighborhoods and "translocalities" as a flexible way to assimilate the global while re-creating the local.[2] Others place a premium on the much-touted notion of hybridity, whereby floating as a cultural chameleon or adaptable emigré is favored over place-bound rootedness. People who yearn for home away from home have, indeed, tried out these makeshift strategies. But the road to the merger between global and local, the metropolis and the village, is too treacherous for a theatrics of hybridity to handle. And the prices for changing one's identity and inventing a group's history every few minutes have not been calculated.

National literature, written in a time-honored language tied to a sedimented tradition, is both vexed and privileged in addressing the dilemma of living under the new global condition. In Taiwan, it has been scaled down to "native" literature in a global trend that weakens the sovereignty of the classic nation-state. Native literature engages both the objective and the subjective dimensions of the local in its struggle and interaction with the global. This essay discusses this dilemma and the literary response to the speed of modernization in Taiwan literature. Works by Zhu Tianwen allow us to assess the way in which native literature actively engages with the psychocultural issues of globalization in spite of its apparent aesthetic detachment. This will bring intimate expressions of literary writing to the public sphere of cultural formation. Owing to Zhu's style and critics' propensity to valorize the belles lettres, the aesthetic and the social dimensions of her writing have typically been kept apart.[3] This separation does justice neither to Zhu's work nor to the sociocultural process that occasioned it. As Adorno states: "Art perceived strictly aesthetically is art aesthetically misperceived."[4]

Zhu Tianwen's oeuvre must be placed in a context of global modernity. From the 1980s through the 1990s, Taiwan literature registered the profound social changes resulting from the island's rapid economic development and entry into the global financial and economic realm. Whether referred to as modern or postmodern, it testifies to a condition marked by a disjuncture between a traditional life world and the new global environment. Although one cannot step into the same river of modernity twice, the change in Taiwan bears analytic resemblance to the large-scale technological and social change in nineteenth-century Western Europe. Industrialization, technology, and urbanization—prime movers of modern history in the West—created a radically new environment that severed huge populations from their traditional way of life and plunged "free" laborers into the impersonal process of machine manufacturing and urban existence. Ferdinand Tönnies's classic study of the transformation from *Gemeinschaft* to *Gesellschaft* represents an exemplary attempt to grasp this change, which was nothing less than an epochal transformation from a mode of social organization based on traditional family and village communities to a modern socioeconomic structure. This structure is premised on urban existence and consumption in the anonymous market and on the rule-bound and abstract relations of civil society. With the advent of the modern age came the opposition between town and village, urban society and organic community. Critics of modernity and capitalism—including Marx, Max Weber, Lukács, Eugene Weber, Adorno, Benjamin, Marcuse, and many others—have characterized the new condition as alienating, abstracting, traumatic, or catastrophic. For them, the overriding image of technological progress and alienation is the metropolis: monstrous in its widespread, impersonal administrative structure, its regulative power, and its economic operation. The economy based strictly on the production of commodities tends to turn individuals into anonymous, random objects. Trapped in this alien setting, whose operations remain invisible to the naked eye, the individual loses the vital links to the supportive, intimate social milieu—the village, the network of kinship, the intimate and emotional setting of handicraft work and pleasure. Walter Benjamin diagnosed this as "the decline of aura" in the blinding industrial age, the "aura" being the traces of authentic experience embedded in tradition, ritualistic festivals, artworks, collective memory, and history. The fading aura also results from the loss of intimate and integrated contact with the body and creative activity.[5]

Although the classic critique of capitalist modernity often relies on a nostalgic appeal to an imagined Eden-like village, its implicit impulse to strike out alternative, livable byways beyond the uniformly boring expressway of capitalism still bears a critical edge. What looks like a withdrawal from the status quo is actually a head-on confrontation with it. Without an imagined Eden, the world ruled by the market would be too much "the way it is," rooted in the reality principle, reified in its corporate raison d'être, sanctified in the megamall bearing the logo "End of History." Thus, while the utopian impulse for the alternative is daily waning, the need for it is becoming increasingly urgent.

Alienation, abstraction, and reification are characteristic of an epochal transition from an agrarian to an industrial mode of production. They take on greater normative intensity in the face of the current changes and ruptures in China, more massive and abrupt than those in the industrial nineteenth century. What was confined to a few metropolises is now sweeping through the big cities and even rural areas in less-developed countries, so rapidly that one begins to wonder whether any green pastures still remain on the planet. Yet it is precisely the trauma of these changes outside the metropolitan centers that evokes the enduring descriptive and analytic power of the concepts reification and commodification.

Reification, as expounded by Georg Lukács, functions as a key metaphor for understanding the general condition of human beings in advanced capitalist societies. Rather than economy per se, reification refers to a cultural milieu penetrated by pervasive commodity exchange. The relation of exchange stamps the individual, body and soul, as an exchangeable item, turning a person into a faceless thing. As labor is no longer useful for personal survival and pleasure, it becomes abstract and deprived of its empirical, experiential value. Reification thus means "the progressive elimination of the qualitative, human and individual attributes of the worker."[6] For Benjamin, this would mean the degrading and withering of authentic human experience. Human experience and value, not instantly negotiable or exchangeable, are now blowing in the economic, profit-driven wind.

The ubiquitous process of commodification and reification is especially rampant and aggressive in Asian countries. Taiwanese society, with its speedy economic takeoff in the 1970s into the circuit of global capital and the world market, has virtually compressed the two hundred years of industrial modernity in the West into a few decades. Contemporary Taiwan literature has left a detailed paper trail of the damaged life amid this upheaval, and Zhu Tianwen's writing represents an acute response to and critique of the sociocultural condition of global capitalism in the late twentieth century. The emphasis on the belletristic aspect of Zhu's works may have obscured their intensely sociohistorical stratum. Zhu's fiction, for all its aesthetic detachment, illustrates the way in which Taiwan literature actively engages with the psychocultural issues of globalization. The aesthetics of literary writing needs to be considered as a response to the public arena of cultural rearticulation in a global framework. It is true that Zhu's portrayal of the situation is remarkably literary, even in the rarified context of works of art. I argue, however, that—social and political in their unconscious implications—Zhu's critiques of the global come in those unlikely places of the aesthetic-bodily: crafting of images; perception of everyday objects; and experimentation with sexuality.

Critics have discussed Zhu's exquisite literary style and carefully crafted images and texts. This style, along with a delicate sensibility, is aligned with a feminine tradition of writing marked by a penchant for freezing a stunning image as a symbol of timelessness against the chaos of history. David Wang has captured the idea well by designating this style as "a verbal alchemy," a style of writing with a magic ring.[7] We can project a historical and "global" dimension of this style by regarding it not simply as the innovation of a writer but also as a social and symbolic act carrying collective import. It is a gesture of an individual trying to articulate the deeply felt human needs being eroded by the pervasive trend of commodification and reification.

REIFICATION AND DISENCHANTMENT

Zhu Tianwen's works confront the reader with the typical global cityscape of international trade, transnational capital, and flows of media images. The city of Taipei suffocates, with high-rise office and apartment buildings competing for shrinking space and depriving the residents of breathing room. In this furnace of a metropolis, glitzy shops line the streets through which goods from all around the world flow past. Media-suffused information and communication are in the very air. The newest fashions in Paris or New York cause an overnight sensation and frenzy among Taiwanese consumers. The whimsical behavior of superstars and celebrities in the metropolitan centers in the West, through media dissemination and advertising, can quickly launch a tidal wave of imitation, instantly create a new lifestyle, and alter people's bearing, looks, and aesthetic taste. The cityscape here constitutes a complete shake-up of the traditional village. What drives this place is not national government, political movement, kinship, or morality. Rather, the engine of society, population and labor flows, and the economy is money, advertising, the insatiable desire for consumption, and, above all, the ubiquitous media.

This global scene has radically transformed the individual's relation to the immediate world of objects, perception, and imagination. This estrangement can be traced to the processes of reification and commodification. Reification strips objects of their value and meaning, which are extensions of human attributes, so that they appear to have no other value than their marketability. In transforming the object from its use value to its exchange value, from experience-enriched production to passive, experience-bleached consumption, commodification blocks and wrecks the culture's living memory and history. It erases the memory of how objects and life environments are made by humans, over a long period of time, often by hand, and how people have come to be what they are through interaction with their setting, how society has moved from then to now. As Richard Terdiman writes:

> The experience of commodification and the process of reification cut entities off from their own history. They veil the memory of their production from the consumers, as from the very people who produced them. The process, in Theodor Adorno's terms, created an unprecedented and uncanny field of "hollowed-out" objects, available for investment by any meaning whatever, but organically connected with none at all. Moreover, as Benjamin glossed Adorno's description, the rhythm—we might say the efficiency—of such "hollowing-out" of the elements of social and material life increased ceaselessly over the course of the nineteenth century.⁸

We may add that the rhythm has accelerated into a blinding speed in the last two decades in Taiwan and in the 1990s in mainland China.

In Zhu Tianwen's fiction, the experience of reification affects the individual's sensory and perceptual activity in two ways. First, sense perception is sucked into the whirlwind of media-bound and -advertised images. Since the reception of these images is mostly passive and contemplative, I call it the consumerist mode.⁹ The consumer absorbs what the media have to offer, which is mostly evanescent and sheer sensory stimuli. A second, very different kind of perception, implying discontent or even resistance, may be termed the nostalgic mode. This is a state of mind that imaginatively searches for the lost horizon among and beyond the abstracted, hollowed-out images. Active and defiant at times, it starts from a refusal to accept the present as it is. It dreams and yearns for things, feelings, relations, stories, myth—the green grass beyond the dreary and monotonous cityscape. It strives to reawaken in objects and images their magic charms and mythical aura, intensifying the utopian desire of those discontented with the current condition.

Images in the consumerist mode are fundamentally afterimages of abstracted objects in reality. Before these free-floating objects, the characters of Zhu's fiction are mere spectators eager to be hooked. Mia, the female protagonist in Zhu's "Shijimo de huali" [Fin de siècle splendor], is an insatiable image watcher in this mode: "Mia is an individual who fervently believes in the sense of smell. She lives on memories evoked by different smells."[10] Yet a specific fragrance does not bring back anything like Proustian involuntary memory that dredges up the fondly remembered past experience or emotion. It only echoes a very recent impression of a short-lived event, such as an advertising campaign, a promotion of a new product, a fashion show, a cycle of new styles, and the like. An unending stream of shades of color, brands of fabrics, textures, and stylistic variations of dress envelops Mia's perception and consciousness. She is very much "into" a hundred and one things of multicultural origins, from India, Japan, Paris, Taipei—yet their origin is precisely what is missing, flattened in her impression. The images evoke only a colored, nuanced texture, a kaleidoscope without depth, a euphoria of weightlessness, a smudge of intensity, a perpetual, dazzling present. Mia and her lover, Lao Duan, may be aesthetes of sorts, as they contemplate the multicolored palette of the skyline at sunset. But their sensibility is modeled on Monet's impressionistic painting at its most visual. The sublime outbreak of sunshine has a pure rococo effect on Mia, but this quality is emptied of its cultural memory. Instead, its extravagant glory stems from the Hollywood movie *Amadeus* (Milos Forman, 1984), which has recently boosted the sales of classical music audiocassettes in Taiwan. The lovers' emotional response to scenes of beauty seems to be shock-induced thrills. They do not possess a classic aesthetic sensibility. That they are addicted to sensation is clear from this description: "They indulge themselves too much in beautiful things. They spend their energy in long hours of admiration and contemplation or allow themselves be shocked to pieces by strange spectacles, such that they forget what they are supposed to do as lovers" (203). This self-indulgence in pure sensation, which is little more than an echo of commercialized images, is symptomatic of consumerist fetishism.

NOSTALGIA AND MOURNING

In a society of consumption and media, the individual is compelled to experience the phenomenal world at secondhand. The lived experience, involving the whole body and sensory perception, wastes away in such a heavily mediated, media-suffused setting. Thus, the search for authentic experience, for intimate contact with one's own body, with other bodies and objects, becomes critical. In Zhu's writing, the flattening of perception is countered by a nostalgic narrative of yearning.

This nostalgic mode recalls a strong tradition of Taiwan literature that expresses a longing for the lost world of the traditional village, the family, childhood, and the network of intimate friends. The "village of yearning," the *juancun* or military compound, is a constant setting in Zhu's fiction. Embodying nostalgia's rich ambivalence, *juancun* refers to a government housing project built for dependents of military personnel after the Nationalists' retreat from the mainland.[11] More than a residence, the village speaks symbolically to the hopes of returning to and recovering the lost mainland and is, thus, concomitant with a sense of loss. Yet the loss is doubled as, in time, the village becomes a venerable image, frequently articulated in literary works. In the cultural imaginary, it becomes a favorite haven that resonates with a general nostalgic desire for authentic experience, whether tied to the mainland or not. The image of the village, doubly removed from the real referent, can be attributed to an intensified loss of authenticity and innocence via accelerated socioeconomic development. This longing for a pristine village has had wide collective resonance amid the capitalist sociocultural changes in Taiwan in the decades since the 1960s.

A nostalgic seizes on traces of the past, as Susan Stewart puts it, as "the now-distanced experience, an experience which the object can only evoke and resonate to, and can never entirely recoup."[12] Out of reach, yet constantly made available, inviting yearning and caresses, the object of nostalgia works to tantalize and to appease. Aware of the impossibility of reuniting with the past, the nostalgic still yearns for and keeps on telling stories about it. The real paradise, as Marcel Proust famously observed, is the one that is lost; what is real is the narrative that is being woven around the void. The village is the lost treasure that both originates and spins off narration, encouraging the yearning for an elusive, purer past.

Zhu's story "Yidian bu zai" [Eden no more] poignantly illustrates this nostalgic mode through the short life of Zhen Sulan. Progressive alienation marks her career as a media personality, countered by her fruitless search for the lost world of home. She is known by three names, which indicate this progressive estrangement. The one most alien and hateful to her belongs to the character she plays in a hit TV drama. Significantly less hateful is the name "Zhen Li," which is given to her by her lover, the director of the drama, and signals her intimacy with him. Both are associated with her media image. "Zhen Sulan" is the name that she was given at birth and that remains on her identity card. This last name harks back to a period of her life in the juancun village that she can call her own.

Not that her childhood life in the village is an Eden-like paradise—on the contrary, it is portrayed as already lost even when she was living it. Narrated in retrospect, without sentimental halo, her childhood is one of numbing trivia, squalor, daily routines and frustrations. Her tender years bear heart-wrenching witness to the deterioration of her mother and the enduring stupidity of her father. Yet, despite its ugliness, this life is hers, offering "real" if painful experience. Sometimes she misses the "solid reassuring tit-tat sound of the sowing machine" (118). She enjoys playing the role of caring "mother" to her ailing mother. Even as a child she already cultivates a nostalgic mood, gazing with fascination at photographs of the family's happy moments in still earlier times. Toward the end of the story, before she commits suicide, the vision of the village comes back to her: "She recalls the long-gone days in the juancun village, many of them not that happy and sweet, yet all are her own. No matter how bad, how unpleasant, how sad the tears she wept, they are her own" (132).

As an actress, Zhen Sulan is a media image, packaged for mass consumption, and has little control over her own identity and body. The fate of the female character she plays on TV corresponds to her own. The character is "a rootless person in the wide world. Even if she could make decisions, things would still not be placed under control" (123). The director of the TV series, her lover, strictly dictates her bodily movement. She is instructed to watch herself, to be conscious of what she is doing in order to follow the script and the demands of the story. In one episode, she is drawing a baby face, which has eyes, a nose, and a mouth yet lacks the contours of a face. The director rightly comments that she has "no sense of the boundaries separating her from external objects." As she is being transformed into things, she also feels that "strangers often send their shadows to visit me" (133). The strangers, in their dreamy, surreal shapes, seem to come from another world, other than the present. They seem to be the shadows to which her present self is beckoning.

In a perpetually nostalgic mood, Zhen Sulan yearns for the figures of a past she knows little about. Her stellar rise in the entertainment industry represents a rupture within her already fractured life. Immersed in the nostalgic mood in an effort to fix the rupture, she does not search for a purer, better past, for the lived past was no less distressing. Rather, she turns it into a melancholy, bittersweet scene she can come back to again and again. She displays a rare ability to frame the past of her reveries within a still picture. As a nostalgic object, the family photograph, at which she never tires of gazing, proffers the memory of an age of innocence and happiness, yet it is also frozen by her gaze into a timeless tableau, purged of its lived, unpleasant reality. The danger, she muses, is that the figures in the photograph threaten to fly out of the frame (118). Zhen extends this photographic or "painterly" perception to her present life. She seeks to awaken the object for her own enjoyment. In distress, she has a way of suddenly pulling up short, on which she will begin to frame an object, a landscape, a view, into a still picture: "Looking backward at the long, dark road she has come running, she collects, reclaims, and patches up the chaotic fragments of the self" (120). A fervent nostalgic with few past resources, Zhen Sulan is more in love with nostalgia itself. Her consolation comes from an intensely contrived aesthetic relation with an imagined past. The story of her life is both a losing battle against emotional estrangement and a poignant reminder of what is missing in the media-dominated society.

SAILING TO UTOPIA

In Zhu Tianwen's fiction, we are confronted with a vast apparatus of commodity exchange, advertising, commercial spectacles, and mass media. This machinery is cultural in the sense of pertaining to an information industry. It works effectively at the bidding of the global market to make sure that everyone behaves as a functional, productive citizen. In a society saturated with media infomercials and image blitzes, individual thought and sensibility become administered and managed; yet it is extremely difficult to detect the hand that does the controlling. This authority blends invisibly into the notions of discipline, work, and pleasure. Thus, as a member of modern, rational society, the individual is required to inscribe the rules on his or her mind and body and, thereby, act as a self-disciplined person.

This consumer of "cultural goods" is less a subject, endowed with a complex internal life and rich experience, than a particle adrift with the fashions of the moment in the stream of circumstances. The inner, integrated consciousness is erased. This evaporation of subjectivity renders obsolete the classic fictional character as an emphatic, full-blooded human individual. Indeed, the idea of characterization, dependent on a notion of the whole personality endowed with a biographical past and a range of ethical attributes, is out of place. Most of Zhu's characters are flat, one-dimensional: sensualists, aesthetes, voyeurs, artist-craftsmen, and role-players constantly indulging in sensory, sensual, and sexual pleasures and thrills. They nevertheless feel helplessly trapped in the fate of being impoverished, abstract creatures, a fate that can be traced to the logic of commodities and consumable spectacles. The individual's life loses its nonnegotiable uniqueness and begins to be defined by its exchangeability and marketability. It is simply another commodity in circulation, lodged in its abstract, quantitative value relative to other things. In Zhu's fiction, even the characters' escape or defiance simulates the way in which the consumer society operates. Her celebrated novel *Huangren shouji* [Notes of a desolate man] is a case in point. The conflict between discipline and deviation is a major motif, exemplified by the testimony of the desolate man in an increasingly desolate world.

The notion of a new, subtle power structure is brought forward by the narrator's lengthy discussion of Michel Foucault and Claude Lévi-Strauss right after a description of a huge mass gathering in celebration of a national event. The gathering represents the people's ecstasy in beholding the leader and their blind confidence in the political order. Retrospectively, it also marks the happy age of innocence, when only faith prevailed, free from doubts. But that reassuring "totalitarianism" may be less passé than it seems. A new, benign control is taking over the old power of the political party. It is the administration of the mind and the body in the economically developed, global society, where not the leader but money holds sway. The previously collective, centralized authority seems obsolete and absent, yet the mind and the body are in thrall to the new control that is felt as pleasure and enjoyment.

The Bach-like harmony in the political festivities, encapsulated in the national celebration, shares an impulse that motivates Lévi-Strauss's lifetime work, the narrator goes on to say with discursive savvy. Lévi-Strauss aims at uncovering an underlying order beneath seemingly heterogeneous ethnographic data. Foucault, in contrast, is posited not so much as the opposite of Lévi-Straussian orderliness as order's fine-tuning and dressing up. Foucault detects the microtechniques employed by the repressive structure of power. For the narrator, Foucault, in his homosexuality as well as in his relentless scrutiny of the almost imperceptible disciplinary technology, offers a lesson in how not to be assimilated into the system.

The invocation of Foucault reads like a statement of purpose for the desolate, superfluous narrator in his attempt to evade and resist the subtle disciplinary power over the body. Through his analysis of disciplinary technology, Foucault reveals a form of control extending to the whole urban, postindustrial society, which appears benign and democratic yet is totalitarian and repressive. Power, in its command of sexuality as well as of consciousness, takes on a scientific, clinical, humane face: it functions in terms of rational explanation, scientific management, and therapeutic adjustment. It uses experts, doctors, and psychiatrists to smooth out its hidden constraints over the subjects. Power is so subtle and pervasive that it insinuates itself into the deepest recesses of our being, making us euphoric in happiness (false happiness, as Herbert Marcuse would have said), just like the cheering crowd on the national day. It makes us enjoy the control of our sexuality and "convinces us deeply that we are liberated in sexual openness and transparency, and gain freedom in sexual enjoyment."[13] The figure of the desolate man is a study in the difficulty of breaking out of this minuscule management of the body into a utopia of libidinal fulfillment.

It would be a mistake, however, to read *Notes of a Desolate Man* as offering license for sexual abandon. The excessive sexuality in this novel has been viewed by critics as vitally redemptive in a world where little remains but the shattered vestiges of beliefs and communal bonds. It has also been noted that the sexual pursuit in the novel is consonant with an art for art's sake tendency and with Oriental aestheticism, regarded as a principle that strains to secure value and meaning in a postindustrial world going spiritually broke.

Thus, wanton sexuality and its wistful aestheticization become almost indistinguishable, and each in its own way serves the need of redeeming lost cultural meaning.[14]

To collapse excessive sexuality into aesthetics and to credit it with redemptive potential, however, risks assigning it too much "spiritual" and emancipatory value, overlooking sexual life's bonds within a general libidinal economy, which is further embedded in the dominant political economy. The single-minded pursuit of sex is, in fact, a by-product of the reified exchange economy that separates libidinal pursuit from other, more productive but equally drive-inspired activities. Sex, here, is an afterimage of the requisite specialization of work and pleasure. The system of commodity production and advertising compartmentalizes libidinal energy and bodily pleasure in a realm sequestered from active production. In this light, the newly won freedom and autonomy of sexuality, or imaginative life for that matter, is an illusion. Sex, or libidinal life in general, is actually degraded and discounted in its splendid and useless isolation from the totality of life.

In the novel, the human body, as it is uprooted from creative, libidinally productive work and lived experience, is set adrift on a consumerist spree of "cultural and historical goods," traveling around the world as a tourist in search of exotic, outlandish sights, strange sensations, fresh thrills. Floating in the cosmopolitan ocean of unrelated passersby, it looks for an all-consuming arousal from transient and intense intimacy with other bodies. For the homosexual lovers, to cite one example, the monuments of civilization in Rome do not evoke historical consciousness and cultural memory. One does not see Rome and die; rather, one sees Rome and has sex. Cultural monuments are valued only when they are flattened into tourist postcards, to be sent to friends and made available for consumption. For the desolate man, there is hardly any distinction between the sublime beauty of Michelangelo's painting *The Creation of Adam* and his mundane enjoyment of the seductive sleeping position of his homosexual partner, which arouses in him "aesthetic" contemplation indistinguishable from sexual desire. We are told that multinational corporations are cashing in on historical sites: NHK of Japan is financing the renovation of the Sistine Chapel while making documentaries of tourist attractions. Emotionally vibrant yet street conventional, the couple will follow the designated, well-advertised route from one country to another, take photographs, and write postcards.

Their "honeymoon" travels seek new sights and sensations to serve as aphrodisiacs. Excessive sexuality, even of the kind that defies convention, does not necessarily mean "sexy" or libidinal liberation. On the contrary, pursued solely for its own sake, such excitement is desexualized rather than life enhancing. Sex orgies are pursued as ends in themselves, narrowed down and flattened out into single-minded, one-dimensional activities. In other words, sex is abstracted and, thus, impoverished, on a par with a consumable, disposable commodity.

The utopia of alleged libidinal fulfillment is, in fact, a sexual no-man's-land as the sheer intensity of sexual activity is sought to fill the emotional void. Yet a sense of utopia indeed arises when the protagonists engage in a fruitful tension between a consumerist mind-set and a consciousness informed by nostalgia, memory, and history, between an endless enjoyment of dazzling surfaces and sporadic yearnings for the depths hidden in the past. One time, after the bored repetition of sexual abandon, the desolate man thinks of marrying his lover in St. Peter's Cathedral; this indicates their search for the solemn aura of authority and authenticity offered by civilization's past. The novel devotes much attention to the indoor gatherings at which the friends are invited to appreciate a collection of their Italian friend, Mo Mo, who was an international student in China. The guests' responses suggest that nostalgia and memory can be both consumerist and utopian. The guests are invited to appreciate a disorienting array of collected items— tea, poems, music, scripts, handiwork, artworks, craft, and so forth—so miscellaneous and disparate as to seem quite incongruous, ranging from the sacred icon of the dharma to traditional embroideries from Guizhou Province in China, classical bamboo paintings and engravings, artworks from Suzhou, small donkey figurines, and even the poster for an ideological film made in the 1950s.

This array does not hark back to the specific histories and concrete contexts from which the objects originated. Such context-bound and history-ridden objects serve as souvenirs as they divert attention to the past and fuel nostalgia—a utopian desire for firsthand and authentic experience. This eclectic collection plays up the exhibition value of the ensemble, instead of serving as a strong reminder of each piece's origin or context of acquisition.[15] It functions as a form of entertainment or a showcase of exotica. This exotic display of history is precisely what strikes the narrator with a sense of incongruity and lack of appreciation. But, as the story proceeds, the social gathering around the Chinese exotica gradually gives way to a more seriously communal activity and historical consciousness. The narrator is irresistibly drawn into the appreciative circle and thrown back to concrete memories of the past. One small detail is quite significant: he looks at a photograph that captures Mo Mo's experience as foreign student in China. The faded black-and-white photograph reveals Mo Mo in a vegetable field, dressed in a Mao-style suit: 1974 at Liaoning University. Photographs in Zhu's fiction frequently authenticate the past in the service of nostalgic desire, and, in her screenplays, Zhu sometimes inserts photographs into the film's flow of images. Thus, although the eclectic collection may constitute entertainment and cater to a consumerist sensibility, the nostalgic mind reactivates the object as souvenir expressive of a yearning for the innocent and, perhaps, purer youth, for the lived experience.

Mo Mo's interest in showing his collection may serve a double purpose. He is nostalgic not so much for a specific memory of a certain place as for his pure, probably more exciting experience in China. The collection is, thus, not only retrospective but also anticipatory. Mo Mo is staging a portrait of the self for his audience and for himself through collected fragments of his past. The emphasis is on "now" rather than only on "then." The narrator senses this intimately and finally catches on to the fragility as well as the necessity of self-fashioning through nostalgia: "As I watched all this I felt as if I were witnessing the broken pieces of my own youth, strewn everywhere on the ground" (75). Mo Mo's Chinese memory serves as a source of identity. The collection reminds the desolate man of the need to collect himself and to record what is trailing behind him. The gravity of the marriage idea may be a sign of this impulse to find a stay against endless, superficial consumer items and sensual pleasures that come and go in a hurry.

REENCHANTMENT OF OBJECTS

This utopian yearning for an auratic ground also characterizes the female character Mia in "Fin de Siècle Splendor," who is portrayed as a tireless seeker of a magical aura. Walter Benjamin's concept of the aura describes Mia's project well. In a socioeconomic environment that ruptures links to the past, to unconscious memory, and to the intimate experience of one's body, she seeks the residual connection to a time when the body was more intimately and fully involved with things created by human hands. This is best dramatized in her creation of a floral shrine and homemade paper.

After a series of fashion whirlwinds, Mia becomes self-conscious about her status as a mannequin, a self-image that she cannot relate and warm up to. She realizes that, in pursuing one fashion after another, there is no authentic quality or experience to be gained and begins to play along with the ever-changing trends but keep an ironic distance. Her relationship with her lover, Lao Duan, on the other hand, suggests an occasional breach of the endless consumerist activity and reified human relations. They seem bonded by an earnest search for authentic experience absent from the ongoing world of commodities.

This search marks Mia and Lao Duan as nostalgics of a different kind. Nostalgia, here, does not designate simply a longing for the past, something poignantly portrayed in "Eden No More." Yet, as that story shows, nostalgia does not necessarily need a real object that actually existed before. The mood, in Susan Stewart's phrase, is "sadness without objects" and projects a longing for the context of origin and contact, for a realm of firsthand, lived experience, even if unreal.[16] It is simply a mood that asks more of an impoverished present. That Mia and Lao Duan are nostalgic for "the present" is evident in their shared interest in souvenirs. Lao Duan's many gifts to Mia bespeak his ability to treasure lived experience in the recent past and to preserve the intimate sense of his once being there. Mia reaches the heights of her admiration and love for him when he is able to trace her five carefully picked floor cushions to their respective stores, to the context of origin and artistic design.

All this may be dismissed as merely another instance of aping commercial fashions, à la Martha Stewart. But the utopia impulse can be channeled through commodities and "new age" fashions. The problem is how to read it. The nostalgic mode is at its most poetic when, toward the end of the story and after the repetitive cycle of fashion shows, Mia retreats from the role of model to that of what may be called a floral alchemist. Lao Duan is not at all mistaken when he feels as if he were in the company of a medieval monk, or, better, a sorceress. Mia assembles a collection of exotic plants, dry flowers and weeds, handmade, colorful oil and soap, homemade herbal tea—an overwhelming array of colors and shapes that seem an extension of her body. The collection constitutes an enchanted refuge and aura-filled space set apart from the marketplace. It is a magic circle where objects are transformed from mere short-lived items of consumption to a context of production and aesthetic appreciation. They are reenchanted—rescued from mass, commercial circulation and brought into the innermost space of privacy. What could be more privately sacred than her bathroom, a virtual shrine, continuous with intimate lived experience of the body? The room gives an authentic feel of naked, unadvertised, unfashioned, sensuous existence. The objects are also reendowed with the magic of creative efforts imbued with pleasure because they are handmade and created by Mia herself for her own enjoyment and contemplation.

But even these enchanted and enshrined objects will fade away and their authentic aura vanish. Thus, Mia's next move—more drastic—is making paper with her own hands, using fruit juice so that the paper retains fragrance. Is this another echo of the "do-it-yourself" lifestyle fashion or a creative enactment of utopian dreams? The answer turns on what purpose this activity serves. For Mia, this is a vigorous reenchantment of objects deprived of their use value for personal and aesthetic enrichment. Creating a floral shrine and making paper are two sides of the same project. Both can be seen as allegories of the immediacy of handcrafting, handwriting against vast reification. Throughout Zhu's work, this project is envisioned as writing, a kind of literary creation that snatches moments of charm and fulfillment from the disorienting flux of the consumptive culture. Parallel to Mia's pursuit, Zhu's writing rewrites and reenchants the object in an increasingly stripped-down, disenchanted world.

The flattening trends of globalization are demystifying and homogenizing native cultures, and widespread transnational capital is increasingly turning human beings into commodities. Zhu Tianwen's fiction delivers the message that this disheartening trend is not a seamless and all-consuming worldwide trap. There are endless possibilities for the individual to work through and against it. Although the magic of memory, nostalgia, and history are diminished, Zhu tries to invoke the power of these resources and reenchant objects and images with a new aura. The attempt is private, limited, and haphazard, as shown by Mia's project. It does not have collective resonance and value—not yet. But it is necessary to keep on trying. Thus, Zhu's fiction constitutes a poignant response to the loss of history and memory in the era of globalization.

NOTES

Unless otherwise indicated, all translations from non-English-language sources are my own.

1. Neil Smith, "The Satanic Geographies of Globalization: Uneven Development in the 1990s," *Public Culture* 10.1 (fall 1997): 169–89.
2. Arjun Appadurai, *Modernity at Large: Cultural Dimensions of Globalization* (Minneapolis: University of Minnesota Press, 1996), 188–99.
3. Academic criticism of Zhu Tianwen's writing often emphasizes its literary or aesthetic aspect. The social environment, the metropolis of Taipei, especially, is seen as a background to which her writing responds. I will attempt to approach contextual elements of globalization as built into the very texture of her writing. For a good example of such criticism, see Ng Kim-chu [Huang Jinshu], "Shenji zhi wu: Hou sishi hui? (Hou)xiandai qishilu" [Dances of the Goddess: Post 40 chapters? (Post)modern apocalypse?], in David Wang, ed., *Hua yi qianshen* [A flower remembers its previous lives] (Taipei: Rye Field, 1996), 265–312.
4. Theodor W. Adorno, *Aesthetic Theory*, trans., and with an introduction by, Robert Hullot-Kentor (Minneapolis: University of Minnesota Press, 1997), 6.
5. Walter Benjamin, *Illuminations: Essays and Reflections*, ed., and with an introduction by, Hannah Arendt (New York: Schocken, 1968), 180–92.
6. Georg Lukács, *History and Class Consciousness: Studies in Marxist Dialectics*, trans. Rodney Livingstone (Cambridge: MIT Press, 1971), 88.
7. David Wang, "Cong 'Kuangren riji' dao *Huangren shouji*—lun Zhu Tianwen, jianji Hu Lancheng yu Zhang Ailing" [From "Diary of a madman" to *Notes of a desolate man*—discussing Zhu Tianwen, together with Hu Lancheng and Zhang Ailing], in Wang, ed., *Hua yi qianshen*, 8.
8. Richard Terdiman, *Present Past: Modernity and the Memory Crisis* (Ithaca: Cornell University Press, 1993), 12.
9. One may say, following Michel de Certeau, that the consumer can exercise the will to choose and resist the glut of images. Like many optimistic theorists trying to defy consumer trends, de Certeau recommends the tactics of resistance, the making do, bricolage. He stakes out a space where consumption is not passive and mindless but active and self-serving. The individual consumer can construct his or her own unique sentences, to use a linguistic metaphor, with and within "an established vocabulary and syntax," i.e., the centralized, clamorous media and consumer trends. But de Certeau's consumer is very much an independent, artistic, and intellectual type of person, capable of waging a guerrilla war against all-consuming practices. Unfortunately, such a guerrilla fighter is not to be found in the shopping mall. The possibility of choice is an illusion if the mind is fed media-bound images on a daily basis. One can think of the possibility of choice and resistance if one can resort to alternative sets of images; these may be retrieved from cultural memory or tradition, which needs to be

reconsidered. See Michel de Certeau, *The Practice of Everyday Life* (Berkeley and Los Angeles: University of California Press, 1988), xi–xxiv.

10 Zhu Tianwen, "Shiji mo de huali" [Fin de siècle splendor], in Wang, ed., *Hua yi qianshen*, 201. Further references to this story, and references to "Yidian bu zai" [Eden no more], are from this edition of Zhu Tianwen's works and will be given in the text.

11 Sung-sheng Yvonne Chang, *Modernism and the Native Resistance: Contemporary Chinese Fiction from Taiwan* (Durham: Duke University Press, 1993), 207.

12 Susan Stewart, *On Longing: Narratives of the Miniature, the Gigantic, the Souvenir, the Collection* (Durham: Duke University Press, 1993), 136.

13 Zhu Tianwen, *Huangren shouji* [Notes of a desolate man] (Taipei: Shibao wenhua, 1997), 62, 63.

14 See, e.g., Ng, "Shenji zhi wu."

15 Walter Benjamin's distinction between the aura-filled cult object and the exhibition value of consumer goods derives from the Marxist distinction between use value and exchange value. This pair of ideas helps illuminate my implicit distinction here between a sensibility grounded in memory and history and a sheer consumerist hankering after depthless thrills for any object, exotic or not, that is on display, even memorabilia collected and displayed as a "feast for the eyes." We may note, in connection with the theme in Zhu's "Fin De Siècle Splendor," that the charm of commodity is double-edged: on the one hand, it delivers a minimum of "use value" disguised as seductive illusions of fulfillment; on the other hand, the commodity can have real use value by being appropriated and invested with the aura of desire and yearning by the consumer. This duality also marks Benjamin's discussion of mechanically produced commodities. See Benjamin, "The Work of Art in the Age of Mechanical Reproduction," in *Illuminations*, 224–25.

16 Stewart, *On Longing*, 14–15.

APPENDIX

Chinese Characters for Authors' Names and Titles of Works

Ah Ying　阿英
"Ai"　愛
"Alang zaijian Alang"　阿郎再見阿郎
Anxiang miye　暗巷迷夜
Ba Jin　巴金
Bai Xianyong　白先勇
"Baomaoling jishi"　白茅嶺紀事
Beigang xianglu ren ren cha　北港香爐人人插
"Bendan"　笨蛋
Bo Juyi　白居易
Cai Shiping　蔡詩萍
"Cai yingzi zhao yingzi: Yize xiaoshuo de qiangdiao pu"　踩影子找影子：一則小說的腔調譜
Can Xue　殘雪
Cao Xueqin　曹雪芹
"Caxietong"　擦鞋童
Chen Fangming　陳芳明
Chen Guangxing　陳光興
Chen Huoquan　陳火泉
Chen Pingyuan　陳平原
Chen Que　陳確
Chen Wanyi　陳萬益
Chen Yi　陳儀
Chen Yingzhen　陳映真
Chenmo zhi dao　沉默之島
"Cheshang"　車上
Chiang Chingkuo　蔣經國
Chiang Kai-chek　蔣介石
Chongyang　重陽
Chu Qing　楚卿
"Chunfeng song"　春風頌
Da Huangye　大荒野

Dai Wangshu　戴望舒
Dalu xinbao　大陸新報
Danren lüxing　單人旅行
"Dao Zong Lihe"　悼鐘理和
Dashuo huangjia　大說謊家
Deng Yuping　鄧禹平
"Dianyuan"　店員
"Dongtian de fennu"　冬天的憤怒
Du Heng　杜衡
Du Yu　杜宇
"Duanju"　短句
"Dujuan tixie"　杜鵑啼血
"Eluanbi"　鵝鑾鼻
Ershinian mudu zhi guangxiangzhuang　二十年目睹怪現象
Fang Yizhi　方以直
Fengche shizhi　風車詩誌
Fu'ermosha　福爾摩沙
"Fulan de yishu zhishang lun"　腐爛的藝術至上論
Gao Tiansheng　高天生
"Geming geming"　革命革命
Gong Pengcheng　龔鵬程
Gongyu daoyou　公寓導遊
Gu Tianhong　古添洪
Guan Jieming　關傑明
"Guguo shenyou"　故國神遊
Haidong Qing　海東青
Haitan de yitian　海灘的一天
He Fan　何凡
"Heiyi"　黑衣
Hong Ruilin　洪瑞麟
Hongloumeng　紅樓夢
Hu Lancheng　胡蘭成

Hu Shi　胡適
"Hualang suojian"　畫廊所見
Huang Chunming　黃春明
Huang Yuxiu　黃毓秀
"Huanghe lian"　黃河戀
"Huangniu"　黃牛
Huangren shouji　荒人手記
Huayue hen　花月痕
Huo diyu　活地獄
Ji Xian　紀弦
Jia zhu tao　夾竹桃
Jiabian　家變
Jiang Gui　姜貴
"Jiang jin jiu"　將進酒
Jiang Liu　江流
Jiang Mengling　蔣夢麟
"Jiangbi de xiandai shi"　僵斃的現代詩
Jiling tu ji　雞翎圖
Jin taowu zhuan　今濤杌傳
Jinpingmei　金瓶梅
"Jiuai"　舊愛
"Jiunü"　酒女
"Juqing"　劇情
"Kuangren riji"　狂人日紀
Lai He　賴和
Lai Xi'ai Zhong Lihe　來喜愛鐘理和
Lan Yinding　藍蔭鼎
"Lang lai le"　狼來了
Lao She　老舍
Lei Zhen　雷震
Li Ang　李昂
Li Ao　李敖
Li Bai　李白
Li Boyuan　李伯元
Li Denghui　李登輝
Li Minyong　李敏勇
Li Qiao　李喬
Li Qing　李清
Li Ruiteng　李瑞騰
Li Sha　李莎
Li shikan　笠詩刊
Li Xing　李行
Li Yongping　李永平

Li Yu　李漁
Liang Qichao　梁啟超
Lianhe wenxue　聯合文學
Liao Ping-hui　廖炳惠
Liao Xianhao　廖咸浩
Likai tongfang　離開同方
Lin Fengjiao　林鳳嬌
Lin Haiyin　林海音
Lin Hengtai　林亨泰
Lin Ruiming　林瑞明
Lin Shuangbu　林雙不
Lin Yaode　林燿德
Lin Yutang　林語堂
Lin Zaijue　林載爵
"Lingdanghua"　鈴鐺花
Liu Daren　劉大任
Liu Naou　劉吶鷗
Long Yingzong　龍瑛宗
Lu Xun　魯迅
Lu Yu　路渝
Lü Heruo　呂赫若
Lü Zhenghui　呂正惠
Luo Fu　洛夫
Luo Qing　羅青
Luzhou zhanxun　濾州戰訊
Ma Ge　馬各
Ma Sen　馬森
Mao Dun　茅盾
Mei Xin　梅新
Meiyou ren xiexin gei shangxiao　沒有人寫信給上校
Meng Fan　孟樊
Mengshu　夢書
Miyuan　迷園
Mo Ren　墨人
Mu Shiying　穆時英
Nanfang Shuo　南方朔
Nanjing chagan lu　南京差感錄
Nanxing　南杏
Nanyin　南音
"Ni de zan'ge"　你的讚歌
"Nian guxiang"　念故鄉
Nie Hualing　聶華苓

Niezi 孽子
"Pangbaizhe" 旁白者
"Pei ta yiduan" 陪他一段
Peng Bangzhen 彭邦楨
Peng Ge 彭歌
Peng Ruijin 彭瑞金
"Piaoxiang de qi" 飄響的旗
Ping Lu 平路
Pipa xing 琵琶行
"Qian Xibao" 錢錫寶
Qian Zhongshu 錢鍾書
"Qiang" 牆
"Qican de wuyan de zui" 淒殘的無言的嘴
Qin Han 秦漢
Qin Shubao 秦叔寶
Qin Zihao 覃子豪
"Qingmi wo zhege shidai" 輕蔑我這個時代
Qinshihuang 秦始皇
"Qizhe" 乞者
Rongzi 蓉子
"Ruguo Lin Xiuxiong" 如果林秀雄
Sahuang de xintu 撒謊的信徒
Sanguozhi yanyi 三國志演義
"Sanlunchefu" 三輪車夫
Sanqing yu taohong 桑青與桃紅
Sha Mu 沙牧
Shangguan Yu 上官予
Shangshu 尚書
Shanhuo 山火
"Shanju de rizi" 山居的日子
"Shanlu" 山路
Shaonian 少年
Shaoniann datouchun de shenghuo zhouji 少年大頭春的生活週記
Shen Yanbing 沈雁冰
Shenyi jing 神異經
"Shi de dingyi" 詩的定義
"Shi de Moluo" 詩的沒落
Shi Jianwei 施建偉
Shi Minhui 施敏輝
Shi Shu 施淑

Shi Zhecun 施蟄存
Shibao 時報
Shidai zhi feng 時代之風
Shiji 史紀
Shijing 詩經
"Shiping *Jia zhu tao*" 試評夾竹桃
"Shixiu" 石秀
"Shubujinyi eryi" 書不盡意而已
Sima Qian 司馬遷
"Siqiang feng" 四強風
Situ Wei 司徒衛
Sixi youguo 四喜憂國
Song Dongyang 宋冬陽
Song Ying 宋膺
Song Zelai 宋澤萊
"Songge" 頌歌
Su Weizhen 蘇偉貞
Suishi yiwen 隨史遺文
Sun Ling 孫陵
Sun Yatsen 孫中山
"Taibei jietou xingyin" 臺北街頭行吟
Taiwan lianjiao 臺灣連翹
Taiwan xiandaishi bianmu 臺灣現代詩編目
Taiwan xinmin bao 臺灣新民報
"Tan Chuyu xili chuanqing, Liu Miaogu guzhong sijie" 譚楚玉戲禮傳情, 劉藐姑曲終死節
"Tanbai congkuan" 坦白從寬
Tang Wenbiao 唐文標
Taowu cuibian 檮杌萃編
Tian Jian 田間
"Touming ren" 透明人
Wang Anyi 王安憶
Wang Haowei 王浩威
Wang Tuo 王拓
Wang Wenxing 王文興
Wang Xingqing 王杏慶
Wang Yijian 王意堅
Wang Zhenhe 王楨和
"Wanju shouqiang" 玩具手槍
Wei Zhongxian 魏忠賢
Wen Xin 文心

Wenji 文季
Wenxing 文星
Wenyi chuangzuo 文藝創作
"*Wo shi guaidan de shengwu*" 我是怪誕的生物
Wu Jianren 吳趼人
Wu Jinfa 吳錦發
Wu Qiangcheng 吳潛誠
Wu Xinrong 吳新榮
Wu Yingtao 吳瀛濤
Wu Zhuoliu 吳濁流
Wuhuaguo 無花果
"Wuti" 無題
Xia Jing 夏菁
Xiachao 夏潮
Xiandai 現代
Xiandaishi jikan 現代詩集刊
Xianfa budui 現法部隊
Xiang wo juancun de xiongdimen 想我眷村的兄弟們
"Xiangchou" 鄉愁
Xiaozhong 曉鐘
"Xiaye" 夏夜
"*Xiezuo bai wuliao lai de fangfa*" 解作百無聊賴的方法
Xin Shiqi 新時期
Xinshengbao 新生報
Xinyanzhe "新聞者"
Xiu Tao 秀陶
"Xixun" 喜訊
Xu Xinliang 許信良
"Xuandang" 懸盪
Xuanfeng 旋風
Ya Xian 瘂弦
Yan Jiayan 嚴家炎
Yang Chichang 楊熾昌
Yang Dechang 楊德昌
Yang Guoshu 楊國樞
Yang Han 楊喚
Yang Kui 楊逵
Yang Zhao 楊照
Yaxiya de gu'er 亞細亞的孤兒
Ye haizi 野孩子

Ye Shitao 葉石濤
"Yedian" 野店
"*Yi qingjie zhuzai yiqie*" 以情節主宰一切
Yi yuan 異苑
"Yidian bu zai" 伊甸不在
"*Yige ci zai shijian zhong de qiyu; yize xiaoshuo de bentilun*" 一個詞在時間中的奇遇：一則小說的本體論
Yin Zhangyi 尹章義
"Yinyue" 音樂
Yu Dafu 郁達夫
Yu Guanzhong 余光中
Yuan Qiongqiong 袁瓊瓊
Yuan Yuling 袁于令
"*Yuanxiang de shiluo*" 原鄉的失落
Yuanxiang ren 原鄉人
Yuli hun 玉梨魂
"Yumi tian zhi si" 玉米田之死
Zai feiyang de shidai 在飛揚的時代
Zang Kejia 臧克家
"*Zanmen lia yikuai qu*" 咱們倆一快去
Zhan Hongzhi 詹宏志
Zhang Ailing 張愛玲
Zhang Dachun 張大春
Zhang Daofan 張道藩
Zhang Henghao 張恆豪
Zhang Liangze 張良澤
Zhang Mo 張默
Zhang Qijiang 張啓疆
Zhang Tianyi 張天翼
Zhang Wenhuan 張文環
Zhang Wojun 張我軍
Zhang Xiguo 張系國
"Zhao Nandong" 趙南棟
Zhao Youpei 趙友培
Zheng Chenggong 鄭成功
Zheng Chouyu 鄭愁予
Zheng Jiongming 鄭炯明
Zhong Dingwen 鐘鼎文
Zhong Lei 鐘雷
Zhong Lihe 鍾理和
Zhong Lihe quanji 鍾理和全集

Zhong Zhaozheng　鐘肇政
Zhongguo shixuan　中國詩選
Zhongwai wenxue　中外文學
Zhouli　周禮
Zhu Dianren　朱點人
Zhu Ling manyou xianjing　朱鴒漫遊仙境
Zhu Tianwen　朱天文
Zhu Tianxin　朱天心
Zhu tou zhuang　竹頭庄
Zhu Xining　朱西甯

Zhuanxu　顓頊
"Zhuofang zei"　捉放賊
Ziyou Zhongguo　自由中國
"Zoulu ren"　走路人
"Zuguo wansui"　祖國萬隨
"Zuguo wansui shi wansui"　祖國萬歲詩萬歲
"Zuihou de yigen huochai"　最後的一根火柴
Zuozhuan　左傳

CONTRIBUTORS

YOMI BRAESTER is an associate professor of comparative literature at the University of Washington.

SUNG-SHENG YVONNE CHANG is a professor of modern Chinese literature at the University of Texas, Austin.

FANGMING CHEN is a professor of Chinese literature at Chi-nan University.

LINGCHEI LETTY CHEN is an assistant professor of modern Chinese literature at Washington University.

CHAOYANG LIAO is an associate professor of foreign literature at the University of Taiwan.

PING-HUI LIAO is a professor in the Department of Foreign Literature at Ching-Hua University.

JOYCE C. H. LIU is a professor of comparative literature at Fujen University.

KIM CHUNG is an associate professor of foreign literature at Chi-nan University.

CARLOS ROJAS is an assistant professor of modern Chinese literature and film at the University of Florida.

XIAOBING TANG is a professor of modern Chinese literature at the University of Southern California.

BAN WANG is an associate professor of modern Chinese literature at Rutgers University.

DAVID DER-WEI WANG is the Edward C. Henderson Professor of Chinese Literature at Harvard University.

GANG GARY XU is an assistant professor of modern Chinese literature at the University of Illinois, Urbana-Champaign.

MICHELLE YEH is an associate professor at the University of California, Davis.

FENGHUANG YING is an associate professor in the Department of Taiwanese Literature, National Cheng Kung University.

INDEX

abject, 94
Adorno, Theodor, 272, 274, 371–372
Ah Ying, 98
Akutagawa Ryunosuke, 11, 285, 288, 291–292, 294
"Alang zaijian Alang" (Zhang Dachun). See "Good-bye Alang"
All Sticks Are Welcome in the Censer of Beigang (Beigang xianglu ren ren cha; Li Ang), 11–12, 363; and "Rouged Sacrifice," 351–352, 360–363; voice in, 353, 355–357
alternative modernity, Taiwan's, 286–287, 289–291, 294–295, 297–299
Ancient Capital (Gudu; Zhu Tianxin), 11, 284; American popular music in, 307–308; cartographic representation in, 11, 305–307, 310, 318–320; and constructing cultural identity, 303–321; and cultural gaze, 304; and cultural hybridity, 305–308, 316; foreign elements in, 303–304; and parallels with Kawabata's The Old Capital, 306–307, 312–320; pastiche in, 304–305, 312, 314, 319. See also Zhu Tianxin
Anthology of Chinese Poetry (Zhongguo shixuan; ed. Mo Ren and Peng Bangzhen), 118
anticommunist literature, 9, 29, 33–34, 141–142, 159, 181–182, 325–326; and Jiang Gui, 205; literary prizes for, 119–121, 182; and modernist poetry, 119–127; songs, 126. See also Tale of Modern Monsters

Anxiang miye (Yang Zhao). See Night of Riddles in a Dark Alley
"Appreciating Zhong Lihe" ("Lai xi'ai Zhong Lihe"; Tang Wenbiao), 142
Artaud, Antonin, 233–235, 242–245; and Balinese theater, 242–245; and Su Weizhen, 234–235. See also theater of cruelty
Asada Akira, 156
Asia's Orphan (Yaxiya de gu'er; Wu Zhuoliu), 285, 291, 297; and alternative modernity of Taiwan, 298–299. See also Wu Zhuoliu
aura, decline of, 12, 358, 372, 384–386. See also Benjamin, Walter
Australia, 304–305
"Azaleas Cry Out Blood" ("Dujuan ti xue"; Liu Daren), 215, 221–230; and the Cultural Revolution, 221–222, 226–227; madness in, 222–223; and May Fourth, 228–230; narrator as detective in, 223–226. See also Liu Daren

Ba Jin, 55
Backed against the Sea (Beihai de ren; Wang Wenxing), 8, 92, 160–176; antiromantic theme in, 170–171; atheism in, 169; Chinese language in, 174–175; critiques of Taiwanese society in, 161–167, 172, 175–176; denunciation of Western materialism in, 166–167; influence of Western literary tradition on, 92, 160–161; Part I, 160–176; Part II, 170–175; and post-

Backed against the Sea (continued)
  modernism, 175–176; and poverty, 168, 175
Bai Xianyong, 35, 37, 55, 91, 159
Bakhtin, Mikhail, 163
Bali: as setting for *The Island of Silence*, 242–245; theater of, 242–245
Bamboo Hat Poetry Journal. See *Li shikan*
Barthes, Roland, 263–264
Bataille, Georges, 109, 191, 350
Baudelaire, Charles, 94, 114
Baudrillard, Jean, 271, 316
Beckett, Samuel, 161
Beigang xianglu ren ren cha (Li Ang). See *All Sticks are Welcome in the Censer of Beigang*
Beihai de ren (Wang Wenxing). See *Backed against the Sea*
"Bellflowers" ("Lingdanghua"; Chen Yinghzhen), 216
Benjamin, Walter, 12, 271, 358, 372–373; and *Eingedenken*, 365. See also aura, decline of
Bhabha, Homi, 291, 305
Birds of a Feather (*Jiling tu*; Zhang Dachun), 256–258
Blue Stars (*Lanxing*; journal), 125
Bo Juyi, 226–227
Borges, Jorge Luis, 324
Bourdieu, Pierre, 115–117, 125, 127
bracketing, 14, 19–22, 24; in works of Su Weizhen, 238–242
Breton, André, 105

Cai Shiping, 272
"Caizhuang xueji" (Li Ang). See "Rouged Sacrifice"
cannibalism, 186–187, 189, 222, 225, 229
capitalism. See globalization
cartographic representation, 5; in *Ancient Capital* (Zhu Tianxin), 11, 305–307, 310, 318–320; in *Haidong qing*, 327, 334–338; in *Zhu Ling's Wanderings in Wonderland*, 344. See also representation
censorship, 99, 102, 119–120; of Chinese language, 30; of Japanese language, 30; of Nationalist government, 30–31, 179
Certeau, Michel de, 13
Chang, Eileen (Zhang Ailing), 9, 55, 236
Chang, Sung-sheng Yvonne, 66, 92
Chen Fangming, 5–7, 16, 61–69, 77, 142
Chen Houcheng, 96
Chen Huoquan, 142
Chen Que, 196
Chen Wanyi, 68–69
Chen Yingzhen, 9, 37, 40, 57–59, 62–65, 70, 91, 142–143; critique of *Jiazhutao*, 143, 148–152; imprisonment of, 215; and nativist literature debate, 144, 148; short stories of, 215–220. See also "Bellflowers"; "Mountain Path"; "Zhao Nandong"
Chiang Ching-kuo [Jiang Jingguo], 213
Chiang Kai-shek [Jiang Jieshi], 15, 119, 213, 216, 312; ethnic policy of, 302; in novels of Li Yongping, 340–345
Chinese ethnic identity, 23, 302; propaganda of, 302; as tool for literary critique, 148, 150; and Zhong Lihe, 143, 148–153
Chinese language, 31, 67; in *Backed Against the Sea*, 174–175; Mandarin homonyms in, 344–345; term for Rape of Nanking (*Nanjing da tusha*), 339–340
Chinese literature, 95–99; evil in late Ming fiction, 195–197; versus literature in Chinese, 80; May Fourth Movement and, 52–59; and *menglong* poetry, 94; Modernist, 95–99; posi-

tion of Taiwan literature in, 52–80; Qing fiction, 185, 199–200, 202
Chongyang (Jiang Gui). See *Double Suns*
Chow, Rey, 243, 246
Chu Qing, 135; and *"Ni de zan'ge"* (In praise of you), 135
Chuangshiji (Epoch Poetry Quarterly; journal), 125, 133
Classics of the Supernatural and Strange (Shenyi jing), 183
Clifford, James, 297–298
colonialism: and cultural identity, 301–321; decolonization, 311–312; and development of Taiwan literature, 15–16, 26–46; economic, 39–40, 57, 59; political, 39–40. See also Guomindang government; Japanese colonial regime; KMT; martial law; Nationalist regime; postcolonial literature
colonial literature, 27–34
Committee on Chinese Literature and Art Prizes, 120, 126
Communism: and Jiang Gui, 205, 207; in *A Tale of Modern Monsters*, 181 192, 197–199
Compendium of Monsters, A (*Taowu cuibian*; Qian Xibao), 185, 200–207; historical evil in, 192–199; sexuality in, 201–202
consumerism, 375–377, 382–384. See also globalization; reification
Crystal Boys (*Niezi*; Bai Xianyong), 159
Cultural Revolution, 226–229; and "Azaleas Cry Out Blood," 221–222, 226–227

Danren lüxing (Su Weizhen). See *Traveling Alone*
Daye Bookstore, 118, 141
"Death in a Cornfield" ("Yumi tian zhi si"; Ping Lu), 214
decadence, 348–349, 354

"Definition of Poetry" ("Shi de dingyi"; Peng Bangzhen), 129
Deleuze, Gilles, 14, 93, 95, 97–98, 100
Den Kenjiro, 293
"Diary of a Madman" ("Kuangren riji"; Lu Xun), 228–229
Dolar, Mladen, 356
Dostoyevsky, Fyodor, 160, 199
Double Suns (*Chongyang*; Jiang Gui), 205
Du Heng, 95
"Dujuan ti xue" (Liu Daren). See "Azaleas Cry Out Blood"

eccentricity, and modernist poetry, 133–138
"Eden no More" ("Yidian bu zai"; Zhu Tianwen), 378–379; nostalgia in, 377–378, 385
émigré writers, 124–125
evil, 192–199; in *An Idle Commentary on Monsters*, 194–198, 202–203; in late Ming fiction, 195–197; in *A Tale of Modern Monsters*, 197–199
exile, 37–38; and testimony, 220–223, 227–228
exposé fiction. See *qianze xiaoshuo*

Fairbank, John King, 18
faji biantai (heroic sagas), 193
Family Catastrophe (*Jiabian*; Wang Wenxing), 159
Fang Yizhi, 140
February Twenty-Eight Incident, 15, 31, 179, 213, 360
feminism and feminist literature, 27, 253; reappearance of, 45–46; and *The Strange Garden*, 350–351
Fengche shizhi (Poetry Magazine), 95–96
"Fengjing jiu ceng an" (Liu Daren). See "Scenery Once Familiar"
"Fin de Siècle Splendor" ("Shijimo de

"Fin de Siècle Splendor" (continued) huali"; Zhu Tianwen), 376–377; nostalgia in, 384–386
Fink, Bruce, 348, 363
Fischer, Michael M.J, 302
Fishing Island Incident (1970), 144
Fleurs du Mal, Les (Charles Baudelaire), 94
Forgotten Tales of the Sui (*Suishi yiwen*; Yuan Yuling), 193
Formosan, The (*Fu'ermosha*; magazine), 95
Foucault, Michel, 234, 380–381
Freud, Sigmund, 272
Fu'ermosha (*The Formosan*; magazine), 95
Fuery, Patrick, 304–305
Furo to ginkoo (Yokomitsu Riichi). See *Shanghai*

Gao Tiansheng, 53
gaze, 304, 353, 357–361; in "Rouged Sacrifice," 353, 360
Gemeinschaft to Gesellschaft (Tönnies), 372
globalization, 17, 20, 366, 372–374; and aura, 358; and identity, 302, 370–386; and nostalgia, 377–379, 383–386; Taiwan literature and, 26, 254–255, 271–272, 371, 373–374; in works of Zhang Dachun, 254–255, 268, 271–274; in works of Zhu Tianwen, 371, 373–374, 379, 383–386
Golden Lotus, The (*Jinpingmei*), 194–195
Gong Pengcheng, 76, 78
"Gongyu daoyou" (Zhang Dachun). See "Guided Tour of an Apartment Complex"
"Good-Bye Alang" ("Alang zaijian Alang"; Zhang Dachun), 257–259
Goux, Jean-Joseph, 327
Goya, Francisco de, 109, 206–207
Grossberg, Lawrence, 301

Gu Tianhong, 143
Guan Jieming, 38–39; and New Poetry debate, 144–145
Guattari, Félix, 14, 93, 95, 97–98, 100
Gudu (Zhu Tianxin). See *Ancient Capital*
"Guguo shenyou" (Liu Daren). See "Magical Journey Home"
"Guided Tour of an Apartment Complex" ("Gongyu daoyou"; Zhang Dachun), 10, 254–255, 270, 272; apartment as storyless city, 270–272; disdain in, 261–262; Zhan Hongzhi on, 255. See also Zhang Dachun
Guofu (National Father, aka Sun Yatsen), 328, 334, 340, 342
Guomindang government, 213, 298, 308. See also KMT

habitus, 7; defined, 127; eccentricity and, 133–138; poverty and, 130–133; and professionalism, 127–130
Haidong qing (Li Yongping), 160, 326–346; female sexual maturation in, 325–326, 332–334, 341–346; Mandarin homonyms in, 344–345; mothers and children in, 328–329, 335, 337, 344–345; pedophilia in, 326, 329–334, 343–344; portrayal of Japanese culture in, 331–334; progenitive dichotomies in, 327–328, 341–345; Rape of Nanking in, 331–333, 336; sequel to, 160; spectral cartography in, 327, 334–338, 344; themes of Taiwan-China relationship in, 327–328, 334–346. See also Li Yongping; *Zhu Ling's Wanderings in Wonderland*
Hall, Stuart, 301, 321
Hara Kei, 293
Hasegawa Kiyoshi, 15
history and memory, 4, 8; and amnesia, 9; globalization and, 383–386; historical amnesia, 35, 38–40, 45;

historical context of Taiwan literature, 15–16, 26–46; political repression and, 213–230; in post-Chiang mysteries, 214–230; in *The Strange Garden*, 363–367; of Taipei in *Ancient Capital*, 11, 305–321; traumatic memory, 10, 213–230, 247–248; in works of Li Ang, 363–367; in *Zhu Ling's Wanderings in Wonderland*, 325–326, 338–346. See also colonialism; May Fourth; Nostalgia; Rape of Nanking; *taowu*

History of Modern Chinese Fiction, A (C. T. Hsia), 182

Hsia, C.T., 182, 190, 199

Hsu Hsin-liang, 302

Hu Lancheng, 315

Hu Shi, 182, 229

Huang Chunming, 37, 91, 142

Huang Yuxiu, 350

Huangren shouji (Zhu Tianwen). See *Notes of a Desolate Man*

Husserl, Edmund, 238

Huyssen, Andreas, 8–9

hybridity, 286, 301, 316, 371; in *Ancient Capital*, 305–308; and historical authenticity, 306, 318–320

Idle Commentary on Monsters, An (*Taowu xianping*; Li Qing), 183, 185, 191–207; evil in, 194–198, 202–203; history in, 202–203. See also *Tale of Modern Monsters*

"If Lin Xiuxiong" ("Ruguo Lin Xiuxiong"; Zhang Dachun), 269

In Remembrance of My Buddies from the Military Compound (*Xiang wo juancun de xiongdimen*; Zhu Tianxin), 269, 303

In the Soaring Age (*Zai feiyang de shidai*; Ji Xian), 123

Ishikawa Kinichiro, 285, 292–294, 298

Island of Silence, The (*Chenmo zhi dao*;

Su Weizhen), 10, 237, 242, 244–249; doubled self of Chenmian (character), 247–249; madness in, 244; theatricality in, 242–250; traumatic memory in, 247–248

Ivy, Marilyn, 156

Jameson, Fredric, 10

Japan and Japanese, 1–2, 11, 286–299; on China and Chinese, 287–291; in *Haidong qing*, 331–334; Japanese-language works, 16; and pedophilia, 331–333. See also Rape of Nanking

Japanese colonial regime, 1, 16, 27, 95, 291–295, 297–299, 301–302, 317, 319; and *kōminka*, 15, 29–33, 43; and Taiwanese literature, 27–30, 42, 65, 124, 142–143, 146, 152; and Wu Zhuoliu, 283, 286–287, 294. See also *kōminka*

Japanese language, 124; censorship of by Nationalist government, 30, 69; neglect of Taiwanese literature in, 20; renaming of streets in, 308, 336; works in, 21, 65

Ji Xian, 114–116, 119, 122, 125–127, 129–131, 133–134; defense of New Poetry, 116–119; and "Geming geming" (Revolution revolution), 123; and interpretation of "Si wuxie" (thoughts devoid of guile), 125; review of *Anthology of Chinese Poetry*, 118; and "Zuguo wansui shi wansui" (Long live the motherland, long live poetry), 123; and "Zuihou de yigen huochai" (The last match), 137–138. See also *Xiandaishi jikan*

Jiabian (Wang Wenxing). See *Family Catastrophe*

Jiang Gui, 9, 181, 183–185, 197–200, 204–207; and Communism, 205, 207. See also *Tale of Modern Monsters*

Jiang Jieshi. See Chiang Kai-shek

Jiang Jingguo. See Chiang Ching-kuo
Jiang Mengling, 182
Jiazhutao (Zhong Lihe), 142, 148–152; critique of, 143, 148–152
Jiling tu (Zhang Dachun). See *Birds of a Feather*
Jin taowu zhuan (Jiang Gui). See *Tale of Modern Monsters*
Jinpingmei. See *Golden Lotus*
Journey Home, The (*Yuanxiang ren*, Li Xing, dir.), 143, 152
juancun (military village or compound), 26–27, 69; nostalgia for, 377; *juancun* authors, 236–240, 254, 377

Kaohsiung Incident (1979), 40, 144, 219
Kawabata Yasunari, 11, 306–307, 312–320. See also *Snow country*; *Old Capital*
kōminka (imperialization), 15, 29–33, 43, 142, 152. See also Japanese colonial regime
Kinkley, Jeffrey, 71
KMT (Guomindang; aka, Kuomintang), 216, 219–221, 317. See also Guomindang government
Kurosawa Akira, 214
Koto (Kawabata Yasunari). See *Old Capital*
Kristeva, Julia, 94, 243
"Kuangren riji" (Lu Xun). See "Diary of a Madman"

Lacan, Jacques, 304, 353, 358. See also gaze
Lai He, 69
"Lai xi'ai Zhong Lihe" (Tang Wenbiao). See "Appreciating Zhong Lihe"
Lanxing (*Blue Stars*; journal), 125
Lao She, 199
laughter, 199–200, 204
Lauretis, Teresa de, 246
Leaving Tongfang (*Likai Tongfang*; Su Weizhen), 237–242; theatricality in, 239–242
Lee, Leo Ou-fan, 98, 161
Lee Teng-hui (Li Denghui), 302
Leng Feng, 229
Lerner, Daniel, 159
Lévi-Strauss, Claude, 380–381
Li Ang, 1, 11–12, 37, 348-367. See also *All Sticks Are Welcome in the Censer of Beigang*; "Rouged Sacrifice"; *Strange Garden*
Li Ao, 159
Li Bai, 122, 129
Li Minyong, 69
Li Qiao, 54
Li Qing, 183, 191, 193–198, 206. See also *Idle Commentary on Monsters*
Li Ruiteng, 71, 76
Li Sha: and "Songge" (Ode), 123; and "Piaoxiang de qi" (The whistling flag), 123
Li shikan (*Bamboo Hat Poetry Journal*), 118
Li Yongping, 2–3, 11, 160, 324–327; and cartographic representation, 11; diasporic background of, 325; as modernist author, 325–327. See also *Haidong qing*; *Zhu Ling's Wanderings in Wonderland*
Li Yu, 237
Liang Qichao, 13
Lianhebao (*United Daily*), Zhong Lihe in, 140
Liao Ping-hui, 45
Liao Xianhao, 43-44, 60, 67, 78–79
Lin Haiyin, 140; and Zhong Lei Posthumous Committee, 140–141
Lin Hengtai, 118, 124
Lin Ruiming, 67, 69, 73
Lin Shuangbu, 69
Lin Yaode, 72
Lin Yutang, 55; Zhong Lihe on, 146–147

Lin Zaijue, 143, 152
"Lingdanghua" (Chen Yinghzen). See "Bellflowers"
Linguistic determinism, 66–67
Lishan Farm (*Lishan nongchang*; Zhong Lihe), 146, 152
Lishan nongchang (Zhong Lihe). See *Lishan Farm*
Liu Daren, 2, 9, 91, 215, 220–221, 226–227; and "Magical Journey Home," 221; and May Fourth, 229–230; and "Scenery Once Familiar," 221. See also "Azaleas Cry Out Blood"
Liu E, 199
Liu Naou, 95, 99
Long Yingzong, 32
Lü Heruo, 30, 32, 142
Lü Li, 56
Lu Xun, 13, 31, 35, 149, 187, 189, 199, 228–229, 294; on Chinese national character, 289; influence of, 215
Lü Zhenghui, 35, 56, 65, 70, 75–76; on Chinese scholarship, 71–72
Lukács, Georg, 271, 373
Luo Fu, 133
Luo Ma, 134
Luo Qing, 41–42
Luyishi (pseudonym of Ji Xian). See Ji Xian
lying. See mendacity

Ma Ge, 140
Ma Sen, 73–76
madmen and madness, 187, 189; and Antonin Artaud, 234–235; in "Azaleas Cry Out blood" (Liu Daren), 222–223; in "Diary of a Madman" (Lu Xun), 228–229; in *The Island of Silence* (Su Weizhen), 244; in Modernist poetry, 134; in *A Tale of Modern Monsters*, 187, 189; and theatricality of Su Weizhen, 234–237

"Magical Journey Home" ("Guguo shenyou"; Liu Daren), 221
Malinowski, Bronislaw, 326
Mallarmé, Stéphane, 105
Mandarin. See Chinese language
Mao Dun, 35, 55
mapping. See cartographic representation
martial law, 38, 179; lifting of, 16; repression under, 32–33, 37–38, 45
Mauss, Marcel, 364
May Fourth, 17–18, 228–230; influence on Taiwan literature, 52–59, 159; and Liu Daren, 229–230; and Taiwanese identity, 228–230
media. See visual imagery and mass media
mendacity, and Zhang Dachun, 254, 257, 264–268, 272, 275, 277
Meng Fan, 41, 73
menglong poetry, 96
metalanguage, 263
military village. See *juancun*
Ming fiction, 195–197
Ming Qiushui, and "Chunfeng song" (Ode to the spring wind), 123
Miyashino Yuko, 331
Miyuan (Li Ang). See *Strange Garden*
Mo Ren, 118
modernist literature, 2–3, 6–7, 29, 34–44, 57–58, 91–92, 142; baby-boom generation authors, 160; in China, 95–99; historical detachment of, 6; and Li Yongping, 3, 325–327; and poverty, 160, 167–168; reaction against dominant culture of, 8, 157–160; relaxed cultural rules of Nationalist government and, 157; Western influence on, 157–159, 161. See also *Backed against the Sea*; globalization; postmodern literature; Wang Wenxing

modernist poetry, 7, 113–119; and anticommunism, 119–127; and the campus folk song movement, 125; contentions over New versus Old poetry, 115–119; creation of symbolic and economic capital by, 123–127, 137; debate over, 113–119, 144–145; dominance of émigré writers in, 124–125; and eccentricity, 133–138; and identity, 38–39; madmen imagery in, 134; perverse writing and, 94–109; and poverty, 130–133; and professionalism, 127–130; as Western aestheticism, 38; of Yang Chichang, 101–109. See also Ji Xian; modernist literature; *Xiandaishi jikan*

Modern Literature (Xiandai wenxue; journal), 35

Modern Poetry Quarterly. See *Xiandaishi jikan*

monster. See *taowu*

Moulin, Le. See *Fengche shizhi*

"Mountain Path" ("Shanlu"; Chen Yingzhen), 214–220, 223; testimony in, 218–220

MPQ. See *Xiandaishi jikan (Modern Poetry Quarterly)*

Mu Shiying, 95, 98–99

Mulberry and Peach (Sangqing yu taohong; Nieh Hua-ling), 248, 263; traumatic memory in, 247–248

My Kid Sister (Wo meimei; Zhang Dachun), 270, 272–273

mystery fiction, post-Chiang, 9, 214–215, 229; and "Azaleas Cry Out Blood," 223; crisis of political memory and, 213–215. See also Chen Yingzhen; Liu Daren

myth, 263–265

Nanjing chagan (Wu Zhuoliu). See *Nanking Journals*

Nanking Journals (Nanjing chagan; Wu Zhuoliu), 283, 285–291, 297. See also Wu Zhuoliu

Nanyin (journal), 99

Nationalist regime, 15–16, 18, 23, 30–33, 283, 312, 377; and censorship, 31, 179; and censorship of Japanese, 30, 69; and Chinese language, 31; ethnic policy of, 302; literary awards offered by, 119–125; and modernism, 157; and Taiwan literature, 27, 31–41

Nativist literature and authors, 7, 29, 34–42, 142, 159, 325; debate over, 36, 38–40, 52–80, 144–145, 148, 258, 260, 275; influence of May Fourth Movement on, 52–59; and poverty, 167–168; realist spirit of, 37; as resistance to colonialism, 57, 68–69; as spiritual return, 36; and Zhong Lihe, 8, 92, 141–143, 148–153

New Perceptionist movement (*xinganjuepai*), 7, 95–96, 98

New Poetry debate, 144–145, 148; and Zhong Lihe, 145. See also modernist poetry

new regulated verse (*xin gelüshi*), 122, 125–126

new Taiwanese *(xin Taiwanren)*, 302

Nieh Hua-ling, 248

Nietzsche, Friedrich, 103

Niezi (Bai Xianyong). See *Crystal Boys*

Night of Riddles in a Dark Alley (Anxiang miye; Yang Zhao), 214

Nishiwaki Junzaburo, 105

nostalgia, 306, 308, 316–317, 320; imaginary, 312; for *juancun*, 377; in works of Zhu Tiawen, 12, 363–367, 375, 377–379, 383–386. See also history and memory

Notes of a Desolate Man (Huangren shouji; Zhu Tianwen): nostalgia in, 383–384; notion of power structure in, 380–381; sexuality in, 381–383;

tourism and souvenirs in, 382–384. See also Zhu Tianwen

Oedipal syndrome, 93–95, 97
Old Capital, The (Koto; Kawabata Yasunari), 11, 306–307, 312–320; and Ancient Capital (Zhu Tianxin), 306–307, 312–320
Ozaki Hideki, 31

Pan-Taiwan Society of Artists, 33
Pan-Taiwan Society of Chinese literature, 33
"Passage of Things Past" ("Shiyi shiwang"; Zhu Tianxin), 303
pastiche, as narrative technique, 304–305, 312, 314, 319
pedophilia: in Haidong qing, 326, 329–334; in Japanese society, 331–333; in Zhu Ling's Wanderings in Wonderland, 326. See also sexuality
Peng Bangzhen, 118, 129
Peng Ge, 39, 58; and nativist literature debate, 144, 148
Peng Ruijin, 36, 53–54, 60, 62–64, 70–71, 75–78; on interpretation of Tawian literature, 73–74; and screening process, 60–61
periodization, of Taiwan literature, 29, 55, 141–142
perverse writing, 94–98; criticism of, 95–99; as resistance, 94, 96, 98, 101–103, 107–109; of Yang Chichang, 99, 102–109. See also pedophilia; sexuality
photography, in fiction of Zhu Tianwen, 379, 384
Piano, The (Jane Campion, dir.), 362–363
Ping Lu, 1, 214
political repression and resistance, 32–33, 37–38, 42–43, 45, 119–125, 145–146, 151–152, 213–230; of Chen Yingzhen, 215; of Liu Daren, 220; in "Mountain Path," 215–220; and Nativist literature, 57, 68–69; perverse writing as, 94, 96, 98, 101–109; in "Rouged Sacrifice," 360–363; in The Strange Garden, 348; in "Zhao Nandong," 216
postcolonial literature: versus postmodernism, 16, 28, 41–45; and Wu Zhuoliu, 285; and Zhong Lihe, 140–143; and Zhu Tianxin, 303–305. See also Ancient Capital; Chinese ethnic identity; colonialism; nativist literature and authors; social conciousness
post-martial law: multifaceted Taiwan literature of, 26–27, 40–41, 45–46; and postmodernism, 157. See also globalization
postmodern literature: and authors, 5, 65, 175–176, 371–372; and Backed against the Sea, 175–176; versus postcolonialism, 16, 28, 41–45; rise of post-martial law, 157; trends in, 157–160; as Western import, 27. See also globalization; modernist literature
poverty: in Backed against the Sea, 168, 175; and Modernist literature, 160, 167–168; and Modernist poetry, 130–133; and Nativist literature, 167–168
Powers of Horror (Kristeva), 94
professionalism, and modernist poetry, 127–130
prostitution, 327, 329, 340–341
Pye, Lucien, 18

Qian Xibao, 185, 200–207. See also A Compendium of Monsters
Qian Zhongshu, 199
qianze xiaoshuo (exposé fiction), 185, 199–200, 202
Qin Zihao, 116, 118, 122

Rabasa, José, 318
Rain (*Yu*; Zhong Lihe), 141
Rape of Nanking; in *Zhu Ling's Wanderings in Wonderland*, 331–333, 336, 339–340
Rashōmon (Akira Kurosawa), 9, 214, 218; and "Zhao Nandong," 218
Red Earth (*Hong tudi*; Eileen Chang), 9
reification, 273–275; defined, 373; effect on perception, 374–377; history and, 375; sexuality and, 379–383; in works of Zhang Dachun, 271–274; in works of Zhu Tianwen, 375–386. *See also* globalization
renqing xiashuo (novels of manners), 193
representation: literary strategies of, 17; of reality, 233–234. *See also* cartographic representation
resistance. *See* political repression and resistance
Rimer, J. Thomas, 313
"Rouged Sacrifice" ("Caizhuang xueji"; Li Ang), 351–352, 360–363; gaze of the past and, 353, 360. *See also All Sticks Are Welcome in the Censer of Beigang; The Strange Garden*
"Ruguo Lin Xiuxiong" (Zhang Dachun). *See* "If Lin Xiuxong"

Sade, Marquis de, 109
Said, Edward, 5, 18, 298
Sangqing yu Taohong (Nieh Hua-ling). *See Mulberry and Peach*
"Scenery Once familiar" ("Fengjing jiu ceng an"; Liu Daren), 221
schizo, 98
Searle, J.R., 10
self-determination, for Taiwan literature, 69–80
self-exile, 35, 37
Sexual Life of Savages (Malinowski), 326
sexuality: in "All Sticks," 355; and the Communist revolution, 189–192; in *A Compendium of Monsters*, 201–202; depravity fiction (*xiaxie xiashuo*), 202; effect of reification on, 379–383; in *Haidong qing*, 332–334; in *Notes of a Desolate Man*, 381–383; in *The Strange Garden*, 350–351, 354, 357–358; in *A Tale of Modern Monsters*, 189–192, 201; in *Zhu Ling's Wanderings in Wonderland*, 325–326, 338–346. *See also* pedophilia; perverse writing; prostitution
Sha Mu, 128; and "Wo shi guaidian de shengwu" (I am a monstrous creature), 133–134; and "Wuti" (Without title), 128
Shang Qin, 134
Shangguan Yu, 123
Shanghai, 97–99
Shanghai (*Furo to ginkoo*; Yokomitsu Riichi), 288
"Shanlu" (Chen Yingzhen). *See* "Mountain Path"
Shen Yanbing. *See* Mao Dun
Shenyi jing. See Classics of the Supernatural and Strange
shengji wenti (provincial identity), 302
Shi Jianwei, 97–98
Shi Shu, and nativist literature debate, 144
Shi Zhecun, 95, 97–99, 114; and "Shi Xiu," 97
Shih, Shu-mei, 288
"Shijimo de huali" (Zhu Tianwen). *See* "Fin de Siècle Splendor"
Shina yuki (Akutagawa Ryunosuke). *See Travels in China*
"Shiyi shiwang" (Zhu Tianxin). *See* "Passage of Things Past"
Situ Wei, and "Hualang suojian" (Scene of the art gallery), 136

Snow Country (Yukiguni; Kawabata Yasunari), 313
socius, 97, 100
Song Zelai, 37
Spivak, Gayatri, 3
Stewart, Susan, 377, 385
Strange Garden, The (Miyuan; Li Ang), 11–12, 363–367; decadence in, 348–349, 354; exchange and gift giving, 350, 353–355; reciprocity of voice and gaze in, 357–360; sexuality in, 350, 357–358; voice in, 353–354
strategic essentialism, 3
Structure and Power (Koza to chikara; Asada Akira), 156
Su Weizhen, 10, 233–250; as juancun writer, 236–240; and "Reflections after Winning the Award," 249–250. See also Island of Silence; Leaving Tongfang
subjectivity. See zhuti xing
Sun Jiajun, 132; and "Jiunü," 132–133; and "Dianyuan," 132
Sun Ling, and "Baowei wo Taiwan" (Protect my Taiwan), 126
Sun Yat-sen (Sun Zhongshan), 328, 334, 340, 342

Taipei, 374; and Kyoto, 11
Taiwan-China relationship, 1–2, 11, 16, 286–288, 295, 299; in Haidong qing, 327–328, 339–346; scholarship on, 15–23
Taiwan Culture Association, 95, 99
Taiwanese identity, 1–2, 12, 23; analytic models of, 17–24; in Ancient Capital (Zhu Tianxin), 303–321; and cultural identity, 291, 294–295, 301–321; and discrepant cosmopolitanisms, 297–298; and ethnicity, 301–303; and geography, 11, 283; and globalization, 302, 370–386; in Haidong qing (Li Yongping), 327–328, 344–345;

identity politics, 254; and legacy of May Fourth, 228–230; modernists and, 38–39, 157; and New Taiwanese (xin Taiwanren), 302; and provincial identity (shengji wenti), 302; "rising people" (xingxin minzu), 302; and Taiwan-China relationship, 15–23, 286–288, 295, 299, 327–328; traumatic memory and, 213–215; Wu Zhuoliu and, 286–288, 295, 299; Zhang Dachun and, 254, 273–275
Taiwanese language, 80; and cultural aphasia, 124; experiential writing in, 66–67
Taiwanese Youth (Taiwan qingnian; magazine), 99–100
Taiwan Literary and Art Union, 95
Taiwan literature and literary studies: acceptance of as term, 40; basis of on political fiction, 13; Chinese scholars on, 71–80; and colonialism, 15–16, 26–46; conceptual ambuguity of, 1–4, 7, 68, 80; debate over concept of, 52–80; geopolitical referential frames of, 21–23; globalization and, 26, 254–255, 271–272, 371–374; historical context of, 15–16, 26–46; influence of May Fourth Movement on, 52–59, 159; in Japanese, 20–21, 65; and linguistic determinism, 66–67; as a minor literature, 14; multifaceted, 26–27, 40–41, 45–46; new literature, 52–53, 95, 99–100; periodization of, 29, 55, 141–142; position in Chinese literature, 52–80; proposed screening process for, 60–61; under repression of Nationalist regime, 31–41; and strategic essentialism, 3; zhuti xing and, 64, 66–80; zizhu xing and, 55–56, 62, 71–72, 75
Taiwan qingnian (Taiwanese Youth; magazine), 99–100

Taiwan wenyi (*Taiwan Literature*; journal), 54
Taiwan xinminbao (*Taiwan New People's News*), 95
Taiwan yishi (Taiwanese consciousness), 57–67, 95, 141; criticism of, 148. See also Chinese ethnic identity; Taiwanese identity
Tale of Modern Monsters, A (*Jin taowu zhuan*; Jiang Gui), 9, 204–207; alternate title (*The Whirlwind*), 207; as anti-Communist fiction, 181–182; historical evil in, 183–186, 192–199, 204–207; influence of Ming fiction on, 183, 192, 197–198; influence of Qing exposé fiction on, 199–200; and laughter, 199–200; and origins of *taowu* (monster/history), 183–185; sexuality and revolution, 189–192, 201. See also *taowu*
Tanaka, Stephen, 288
Tang Wenbiao, 142–143; critique of Zhong Lihe by, 145–149; and New Poetry debate, 144–145, 148
taowu (monster/history), 9, 189, 196, 200, 204, 206–207; etymological origins of, 183–185. See also *Compendium of Monsters*; history and memory; *Idle Commentary on Monsters*; *Tale of Modern Monsters*
Taowu cuibian (Qian Xibao). See *Compendium of Monsters*
Taowu xianping (Li Qing). See *Idle Commentary on Monsters*
Taussig, Michael, 364, 366
Tears of Eroticism, The (Georges Bataille), 109
temporal dislocation, 343–344; in "Azaleas Cry Out Blood," 227; in *Haidong qing*, 326, 331, 333–338; in "Mountain Path," 216–217; in "Zhao Nandong," 216; in *Zhu Ling's Wanderings in Wonderland*, 325–326

Terdiman, Richard, 375
testimony: in "Azaleas Cry Out Blood," 220–228; and exile, 220–223, 227–228; failure of in post-Chiang mysteries, 213–230; in "Mountain Path," 218–220
theater of cruelty, 235, 242–245, 249. See also Artaud, Antonin
theatricality, of Su Weizhen: and Antonin Artaud, 234–235; in *Dream Writing*, 238; and Eileen Chang, 236; as epistemological tool, 238–240; in *The Island of Silence*, 10, 242–250; in *Leaving Tongfang*, 239–242; and madness, 234–237; as metaphor for life, 235–236; in *Traveling Alone*, 238
Tian Jian, 122
titou (wandering), 327, 345–346
translingual generation, 124
traumatic memory, 10, 215–230, 247–248; in "Azaleas Cry Out Blood," 220–228; identity and, 213–215; in *The Island of Silence*, 247–248; in *Mulberry and Peach*, 247–248; in post-Chiang mystery fiction, 215–230
travel and travel literature, 10–11; about China, 287–288; and discrepant cosmopolitanisms, 297–298; and tourism in *Notes of a Desolate Man*, 382–384. See also *Nanking Journals*; *Traveling Alone*; *Travels in China*
Traveling Alone (*Danren lüxing*; Su Weizhen), 238
Travels in China (*Shina yūki*; Akutagawa Ryunosuke), 11, 285, 288

Urashima Taro, 216–217

Van Der Hart, Onno, 247
Van Der Kolk, Bessel A., 247
Vargas Llosa, Mario, 265
visual imagery and mass media, 271;

consumerist mode of perception, 375–377, 382–384; nostalgic mode of perception, 375–377; and photography, 379, 384; in works of Zhu Tianwen, 374–377, 379, 383–384

Wang Anyi, 254, 257, 259, 261, 270–271
Wang, David Der-wei (Wang Dewei), 9, 64, 226, 237–238, 351, 374; and imaginary nostalgia, 312
Wang Rong, 128
Wang Shaoguang, 222
Wang Tuo, 37, 39–40, 59; and nativist literature debate, 144
Wang Wenxing, 3, 8, 91–92, 159–176; Catholicism of, 169; short stories of, 168. See also *Backed against the Sea*
Wang Zhenhe, 37, 91, 142
Wei Zhongxian, 192–198, 202, 204, 206. See also *Idle Commentary on Monsters*
Wen Xin, 140
Wen Yiduo, 122
Wenji (Literary Quarterly; journal), 92, 144
Wenxing (Literary Star; journal), 159
Wenxue jie (Literary Taiwan; journal), 54–56, 58, 60–62, 66; renaming of, 66; *Wenxue Taiwan* and, 66–68, 70, 92
Wenyi chuangzuo (Literary Creations; journal), 121
Whirlwind, The [Xuanfeng; alternate title] (Jiang Gui). See *Tale of Modern Monsters*
White Terror, 123, 213, 215, 227
Wild Child (Ye haizi; Zhang Dachun), 269
Wilshire, Bruce, 238, 250
Wo meimei (Zhang Dachun). See *My Kid Sister*
Wu Jinfa, 37

Wu Qiancheng, 73
Wu Xinrong, 32
Wu Yingtao, 135–136
Wu Zhuoliu, 11, 32; on alternative modernity of Taiwan, 285–286, 289–291, 294, 297–299; on Chinese national character, 285–287, 289–291, 296–299; and fig/forythsia analogy of Taiwan's colonization, 298–299; and Japanese colonial regime, 283, 286–287. See also *Asia's Orphan*; *Nanking Journals*

Xia Tao, and "On the Bus" ("Cheshang"), 136
Xiandaishi jikan (Modern Poetry Quarterly), 7, 123, 125–131, 133, 136–137; and anticommunism, 119–127; contentions over New versus Old poetry, 115–119; creation of symbolic and economic capital by, 123–127, 137; financial situation of, 130–131; influence of, 114–115, 128; madman imagery in, 134; and new regulated verse, 122, 125–126; and poverty, 130–133; review of *Anthology of Chinese Poetry* in, 118; six principles of, 114–115. See also Ji Xian; modernist poetry
xiandaishi lunzhan (modern poetry debate). See modernist poetry: debate over
Xianfa budui (The Avant-Garde, magazine), 95, 99–101
Xiang wo juancun de xiongdimen (Zhu Tianxin). See *In Remembrance of My Buddies from the Military Compound*
"Xiangchou" ("Homesickness"; Ji Xian), 123
xiaoyuan min'ge (campus folk song) movement, 125
xiaxie xiaoshuo (depravity fiction), 202
xin gelüshi (new regulated verse), 122, 125–126

xin shiqi (new era), 96
xin wenxue (new literature), 52–53
Xin Yu, 134
xinganjuepai (New Perceptionist movement), 7, 95–96, 98
Xiu Tao, 131, 136; and "Xinyanzhe" (The newly castrated), 131–132
Xu Shuilü, 62–63
Xu Xinliang, 302
Xu Zhimo, 122
Xuanfeng [*The Whirlwind*; alternate title]. See *Tale of Modern Monsters*
Xue Guanghua, and "Duanju" (Short verse), 135

Ya Xian, 113, 123, 133; and "Zuguo wansui" (Long live the fatherland), 123; and "Dongtian de fennu" (Winter's Fury), 123
Yan Jiayan, 97
Yang Chichang, 2, 7, 91–92, 95–96; and "Aojiroi shooroo" (The green bell-tower), 102, 108; and "Aozameta uta" (Pale song), 106–107; and "Bara no hifu" (The rosy skin), 103, 108; and "Choo no shikoo" (The butterfly's thoughts), 104, 107; "Demi Rever", 102–103; and Fengche shizhi, 95; and "Genei" (Hallucination), 101–102; and "Jigazoo" (Self-portrait), 102; and "Joomyaku to choo" (Veins and butterflies), 106; and "Tainan qui dort," 104–106, 108; and "Nichiyooshiki no sanposha" (The Sunday stroller), 101; perverse writings of, 99, 102–109; and "Tsuki no shisoo" (The image of the moon's death), 104, 106, 108; and "Zanshoku no honoo" (The dwindled candle flame), 99, 107, 109
Yang, Edward (Yang Dechang), 214
Yang Guoshu, 65

Yang Huan, 117, 130; and "Xiaye" (Summer night), 117
Yang Kui, 30, 54, 65, 142, 152; execution of, 32
Yang Zhao, 158, 214
Yaxiya de gu'er (Wu Zhuoliu). See *Asia's Orphan*
Ye haizi (Zhang Dachun). See *Wild Child*
Ye Shitao, 40, 54–58, 62–65, 71, 75, 77, 143; on interpretation of Taiwan literature, 74; on modernist literature, 34–35; and nativist literature debate, 144, 148
yichangwei (perverse way). See perverse writing
"Yidian bu zai" (Zhu Tianwen). See "Eden No More"
Yin Zhangyi, 65–66
Yokomitsu Riichi, 288
Youth, 256, 272–273
Yu Dafu, 289, 294
Yu Guangzhong, 58, 148; and "Eluanbi," 117; and nativist literature debate, 144
Yu Tiancong, 129
Yu (Zhong Lei). See *Rain*
Yuan Qiongqiong, 237
Yuan Yuling, 193
Yuanxiang ren. See *The Journey Home*
Yukiguni (Kawabata Yasunari). See *Snow Country*
"Yumi tian zhi si" (Ping Lu). See "Death in a Cornfield"

Zhan Hongzhi, 53–54, 63; on "Guided Tour of an Apartment Complex" (Zhang Dachun), 255
zhandou wenxue (combat literature), 57, 124
Zhang Dachun, 1, 10; and *Birds of a Feather*, 256–258; commodities aes-

thetics of, 273–275; counterfactual narratives of, 268–272, 275; doubts on truth in novels, 257–260; failure to engage in social issues, 266–268, 270–272; and "Good-Bye Alang," 257–259; importance of, 253; as juancun writer, 237, 254; maiden works of, 256–257; and mendacity, 254, 257, 264–268, 272, 275, 277; and *My Kid Sister*, 270, 272–273; negation and disdain of, 260–268, 272, 274; prison-house of language and, 10, 262, 270; at *Zhongguo shibao (China Times)*, 255–256; versus Zhu Tianxin, 266. *See also* "Guided Tour of an Apartment Complex"

Zhang Daofan, 120–121

Zhang Liangze, 143; on Zhong Lihe, 147

Zhang Mo, 117, 133

Zhang Qijiang, 73

Zhang Tianyi, 199

Zhang Wenhuan, 32–33, 142; imprisonment of, 32

Zhang Xiguo, 59

"Zhao Nandong" (Chen Yingzhen), 216–218; *Rashōmon* structure of, 218

Zhao Youpei, 126

Zheng Chouyu: and "Yedian" (Inn in the wilderness), 129; and "Shanju de rizi" (Life in the mountains), 129

Zheng Jiongming, 54, 57, 67, 74

Zhengxin (newspaper), 140

Zhong Lei, and "Huanghe lian" (Love for the Yellow River), 121–122

Zhong Lihe, 7–8, 32, 54, 92, 121; Chinese ethnic identity of, 142–143, 148–153; "hometown" short stories of, 147; and *Jiazhutao*, 142, 148–152; and *The journey home*, 143, 152; on Lin Yutang, 146–147; and *Lisban farm*, 146, 152; literary critiques of, 145–153; memorial building, 153; nativist literature and, 92, 141–142, 148–153; New Poetry debate and, 145, 148; obscurity and rediscovery of, 140–144; and *Rain*, 141; and social conciousness, 143–149; Zhong Lei Posthumous Committee, 140–141

Zhong Zhaozheng, 32, 59, 143

Zhongguo luntan (China Tribune), 65–66, 72

Zhongguo shibao (China Times), 144; Zhong Dachun at, 255–256

Zhongguo shixuan (Anthology of Chinese Poetry; ed. Mo Ren and Peng Bangzhen), 118

zhongwen wenxue (literature in Chinese), versus *zhongguo wenxue* (literature of the Chinese nation), 80. *See also* Chinese literature

Zhou Yi, 96

Zhu Dianren, 32

Zhu Ling manyou xianjing (Li Yongping). See *Zhu Ling's Wanderings in Wonderland*

Zhu Ling's Wanderings in Wonderland (Zhu Ling manyou xianjing; Li Yongping), 284, 324–326; cartographic representation in, 325–327; ear piercing in, 339–341; parallels of sexuality and history in, 325–326, 338–346; pedophilia in, 326, 343–344; Rape of Nanking in, 339–340; spectral cartography in, 344. *See also Haidong Qing*; Li Yongping

Zhu Tianwen, 12; and "Eden No More," 378–379; and "Fin de Siècle Splendor," 376–377; globalization and, 371, 373–374, 379, 383–386; and *juancun* settings, 377; literary style of, 374; nostalgia, 377–379; and reification, 375–376. *See also Notes of a Desolate Man*

Zhu Tianxin, 11, 254; and constructing cultural identity, 303–321; as *juancun*

Zhu Tianxin (*continued*)
writer, 237; and "Passage of Things Past," 303; versus Zhang Dachun, 266. See also *Ancient Capital; In Remembrance of My Buddies from the Military Compound*

Zhu Xining: and nativist literature debate, 144

zhuti xing (native subjectivity, sovereignty), 64, 66–80

Ziyou Zhongguo (*Free China Review*), 159

Žižek, Slavoj, 240

zizhu xing (originality, self-determination), 55–56, 62, 71–72, 75

zuo yuezi (sitting out the month), 335

A portion of chapter 1 was adapted from *Literary Culture in Taiwan: Martial Law to Market Law*, by Sung-sheng Yvonne Chang. © 2004 by Columbia University. By permission of the publisher, Columbia University Press.

Chapter 3 was adapted from an essay by Xiaobing Tang which appeared in *Modern China* (25.4, October 1999, 379–422). © 1999 by Sage Periodicals Press. By permission of the publisher, Sage Periodicals Press.

Chapter 7 includes a revised version of Sung-sheng Yvonne Chang's "Modernist Literature in Taiwan Revisited—with an Analysis of Wang Wenxing's *Backed against the Sea, Part II*," in "Literary Modernism in the Pacific Rim Revisited," special issue of *Tamkang Review* (29.2, Winter 1998, 1-19), as well as a portion of chapter 4 from Sung-sheng Yvonne Chang's *Modernism and the Nativist Resistance: Contemporary Chinese Fiction from Taiwan*, © 1993 by Duke University Press.

Chapter 8 was adapted from *The Monster That Is History: History, Violence, and Fictional Writing in Twentieth Century China*, by David Der-wei Wang. © 2004 The Regents of the University of California. By permission of the University of California Press.

Chapter 9 was adapted from *Witness Against History: Literature, Film, and Public Discourse in Twentieth Century China*, by Yomi Braester. © 2003 by the Board of Trustees of the Leland Stanford Jr. University, all rights reserved. By permission of the publisher, Stanford University Press, www.sup.org.

Chapter 13 was adapted from *Writing Chinese: Reshaping Chinese Cultural Identity*, by Lingchei Letty Chen. © 2006 by Palgrave Macmillan, all rights reserved. By permission of Palgrave Macmillan.

Chapter 14 includes a revised version of Carlos Rojas's "Paternities and Expatriatisms: Li Yongping's Zhu Ling Manyou Xianjing and the Politics of Rupture," in "Literary Modernism in the Pacific Rim Revisited," special issue of *Tamkang Review* (29.2, Winter 1998, 22-44).

Chapter 16 was adapted from *Illuminations from the Past: Trauma, Memory, and History in Modern China*, by Ban Wang. © 2004 by the Board of Trustees of the Leland Stanford Jr. University, all rights reserved. By permission of the publisher, Stanford University Press, www.sup.org.

CARLOS ROJAS is an assistant professor of modern Chinese literature and film at the University of Florida.

DAVID DER-WEI WANG is the Edward C. Henderson Professor of Chinese Literature at Harvard University.

LIBRARY OF CONGRESS CATALOGING-IN-PUBLICATION DATA

WRITING TAIWAN : A NEW LITERARY HISTORY /
EDITED BY DAVID DER-WEI WANG AND CARLOS ROJAS.
  P. CM. — (ASIA-PACIFIC)
INCLUDES BIBLIOGRAPHICAL REFERENCES AND INDEX.
ISBN-13: 978-0-8223-3851-2 (CLOTH : ALK. PAPER)
ISBN-10: 0-8223-3851-3 (CLOTH : ALK. PAPER)
ISBN-13: 978-0-8223-3867-3 (PBK. : ALK. PAPER)
ISBN-10: 0-8223-3867-X (PBK. : ALK. PAPER)
1. CHINESE LITERATURE—TAIWAN—
  20TH CENTURY—HISTORY AND CRITICISM.
I. WANG, DEWEI.
II. ROJAS, CARLOS
PL3031.T3W75 2004
895.1'509951249—DC22
2006020431

www.ingramcontent.com/pod-product-compliance
Lightning Source LLC
Chambersburg PA
CBHW020858020526
44116CB00029B/422